9/11

gale
293

D0871383

Contemporary Theatre, Film and Television

ISSN 0749-064X

Contemporary Theatre, Film and Television

A Biographical Guide Featuring Performers, Directors, Writers, Producers, Designers, Managers, Choreographers, Technicians, Composers, Executives, Dancers, and Critics in the United States, Canada, Great Britain and the World

Thomas Riggs, Editor

Volume 112

GALE
CENGAGE Learning

Detroit • New York • San Francisco • New Haven, Conn • Waterville, Maine • London

Contemporary Theatre, Film & Television, Vol. 112

Editor: Thomas Riggs

CTFT Staff: Mariko Fujinaka, Annette Petrusso, Susan Risland, Jacob Schmitt, Lisa Sherwin, Arlene True, Andrea Votava, Pam Zuber

Project Editors: Laura Avery, Tracie Ratiner

Editorial Support Services: Natasha Mikheyeva

Composition and Electronic Capture: Gary Oudersluys

Manufacturing: Rhonda A. Dover

© 2012 Gale, Cengage Learning

ALL RIGHTS RESERVED. No part of this work covered by the copyright herein may be reproduced, transmitted, stored, or used in any form or by any means graphic, electronic, or mechanical, including but not limited to photocopying, recording, scanning, digitizing, taping, Web distribution, information networks, or information storage and retrieval systems, except as permitted under Section 107 or 108 of the 1976 United States Copyright Act, without the prior written permission of the publisher.

This publication is a creative work fully protected by all applicable copyright laws, as well as by misappropriation, trade secret, unfair competition, and other applicable laws. The authors and editors of this work have added value to the underlying factual material herein through one or more of the following: unique and original selection, coordination, expression, arrangement, and classification of the information.

For product information and technology assistance, contact us at
Gale Customer Support, 1-800-877-4253.
For permission to use material from this text or product,
submit all requests online at **www.cengage.com/permissions.**
Further permissions questions can be emailed to
permissionrequest@cengage.com

While every effort has been made to ensure the reliability of the information presented in this publication, Gale, a part of Cengage Learning, does not guarantee the accuracy of the data contained herein. Gale accepts no payment for listing; and inclusion in the publication of any organization, agency, institution, publication, service, or individual does not imply endorsement of the editors or publisher. Errors brought to the attention of the publisher and verified to the satisfaction of the publisher will be corrected in future editions.

EDITORIAL DATA PRIVACY POLICY. Does this publication contain information about you as an individual? If so, for more information about our editorial data privacy policies, please see our Privacy Statement at www.gale.cengage.com.

Gale
27500 Drake Rd.
Farmington Hills, MI 48331-3535

LIBRARY OF CONGRESS CATALOG CARD NUMBER 84-649371

ISBN-13: 978-1-4144-7186-0
ISBN-10: 1-4144-7186-6

ISSN: 0749-064X

This title is also available as an e-book.
ISBN-13: 978-1-4144-7493-9
ISBN-10: 1-4144-7493-8
Contact your Gale sales representative for ordering information.

Printed in Mexico
1 2 3 4 5 6 7 15 14 13 12 11

REF
920
CON
v.112

Contents

Preface

Provides Broad, Single-Source Coverage in the Entertainment Field

Contemporary Theatre, Film and Television (*CTFT*) is a biographical reference series designed to provide students, educators, researchers, librarians, and general readers with information on a wide range of entertainment figures. Unlike single-volume reference works that focus on a limited number of artists or on a specific segment of the entertainment field, *CTFT* is an ongoing publication that includes entries on individuals active in the theatre, film, and television industries. Before the publication of *CTFT*, information-seekers had no choice but to consult several different sources in order to locate the in-depth biographical and credit data that makes *CTFT*'s one-stop coverage the most comprehensive available about the lives and work of performing arts professionals.

Scope

CTFT covers not only performers, directors, writers, and producers, but also behind-the-scenes specialists such as designers, managers, choreographers, technicians, composers, executives, dancers, and critics from the United States, Canada, Great Britain, and the world. With 222 entries in *CTFT 112*, the series now provides biographies on approximately 29,049 people involved in all aspects of theatre, film, and television.

CTFT gives primary emphasis to people who are currently active. New entries are prepared on major stars as well as those who are just beginning to win acclaim for their work. *CTFT* also includes entries on personalities who have died but whose work commands lasting interest.

Compilation Methods

CTFT editors identify candidates for inclusion in the series by consulting biographical dictionaries, industry directories, entertainment annuals, trade and general interest periodicals, newspapers, and online databases. Additionally, the editors of *CTFT* maintain regular contact with industry advisors and professionals who routinely suggest new candidates for inclusion in the series. Entries are compiled from published biographical sources which are believed to be reliable, but have not been verified for this edition by the listee or their agents.

Revised Entries

To ensure *CTFT*'s timeliness and comprehensiveness, entries from previous volumes, as well as from Gale's *Who's Who in the Theatre*, are updated for individuals who have been active enough to require revision of their earlier biographies. Such individuals will merit revised entries as often as there is substantial new information to provide. Obituary notices for deceased entertainment personalities already listed in *CTFT* are also published.

Accessible Format Makes Data Easy to Locate

CTFT entries, modeled after those in Gale's highly regarded *Contemporary Authors* series, are written in a clear, readable style designed to help users focus quickly on specific facts. The following is a summary of the information found in *CTFT* sketches:

- *ENTRY HEADING:* the form of the name by which the listee is best known.

- *PERSONAL:* full or original name; dates and places of birth and death; family data; colleges attended, degrees earned, and professional training; political and religious affiliations when known; avocational interests.

- *ADDRESSES:* home, office, agent, publicist and/or manager addresses.

- *CAREER:* tagline indicating principal areas of entertainment work; resume of career positions and other vocational achievements; military service.

- *MEMBER:* memberships and offices held in professional, union, civic, and social organizations.

- *AWARDS, HONORS:* theatre, film, and television awards and nominations; literary and civic awards; honorary degrees.

- *CREDITS:* comprehensive title-by-title listings of theatre, film, and television appearance and work credits, including roles and production data as well as debut and genre information.

- *RECORDINGS:* album, single song, video, and taped reading releases; recording labels and dates when available.

- *WRITINGS:* title-by-title listing of plays, screenplays, scripts, and musical compositions along with production information; books, including autobiographies, and other publications.

- *ADAPTATIONS:* a list of films, plays, and other media which have been adapted from the listee's work.

- *OTHER SOURCES:* books, periodicals, and internet sites where interviews or feature stories can be found.

Access Thousands of Entries Using *CTFT*'s Cumulative Index

Each volume of *CTFT* contains a cumulative index to the entire series. As an added feature, this index also includes references to all seventeen editions of *Who's Who in the Theatre* and to the four-volume compilation *Who Was Who in the Theatre.*

Available in Electronic Format

Online. Recent volumes of *CTFT* are available online as part of the Gale Biographies (GALBIO) database accessible through LEXIS-NEXIS. For more information, contact LEXIS-NEXIS, P.O. Box 933, Dayton, OH 45401-0933; phone (937) 865-6800, toll-free: 800-543-6862.

Suggestions Are Welcome

Contemporary Theatre, Film and Television is intended to serve as a useful reference tool for a wide audience, so comments about any aspect of this work are encouraged. Suggestions of entertainment professionals to include in future volumes are also welcome. Send comments and suggestions to: The Editor, *Contemporary Theatre, Film and Television,* Gale, 27500 Drake Rd., Farmington Hills, MI 48331-3535; or call toll-free at 1-800-877-GALE.

Contemporary Theatre, Film and Television

AFABLE, Sean Michael 1988–
(Sean Michael, Sean Ruegsegger)

PERSONAL

Born November 20, 1988, in CA; son of Robert and Gigi. *Religion:* Christian. *Avocational Interests:* Surfing, snowboarding, camping, playing guitar, singing.

Career: Actor. Appeared in television commercials, including Burger King and Chuck E. Cheese.

Awards, Honors: Camie Award, Character and Morality in Entertainment, 2007, for *Akellah and the Bee.*

CREDITS

Film Appearances:
(As Sean Ruegsegger) Little boy, *Delivering Milo,* Europa Films, 2001.
(As Sean Michael) Boy at well, *The Scorpion King,* Universal, 2002.
(As Sean Michael) Joel, *Little Shepherd,* Envoy Productions, 2002.
Squeaky, *Clipping Adam,* 2004.
(As Sean Michael) Tyler, *Chocolate Girls,* American Film Institute, 2004.
Dylan, *Akeelah and the Bee,* Sony, 2006.
(As Sean Michael) Son, *Channels,* Elevate Films, 2007.
Jonny Garcia, *To Save a Life,* Sony, 2009.
Stymie, *Boogie Town,* Vivendi Entertainment, 2010.

Television Appearances; Episodic:
(As Sean Michael) First boy, "The Plan," *Cold Case,* CBS, 2004.

(As Sean Michael) Stinger, "Sick Days & Spelling Bee," *Ned's Declassified School Survival Guide,* Nickelodeon, 2004.
(As Sean Michael) Stinger, "Notes & Best Friends," *Ned's Declassified School Survival Guide,* Nickelodeon, 2004.
(As Sean Michael) Anthony, "Art Breaker," *That's So Raven* (also known as *That's So Raven*), The Disney Channel, 2005.
(As Sean Michael) Lyle Snogger, "Versa Day," *Phil of the Future,* The Disney Channel, 2005.
Lucas Chen, "She Deserved It," *BlackBoxTV,* 2010.
"BlackBoxTV," *Helenna's Tinseltown Tuesdays,* 2010.

ALPAY, David 1980–

PERSONAL

Born October, 1980, in Toronto, Ontario, Canada. *Education:* Attended the University of Toronto.

Addresses: *Agent*—Agency for the Performing Arts, 405 South Beverly Dr., Beverly Hills, CA 90212; Great North Artists Management, Inc. 350 Dupont St., Toronto, Ontario M5R 1V9, Canada. *Manager*—Brian Wilkins, Kritzer Levine Wilkins Griffin Entertainment, 11872 La Grange Ave., 1st Floor, Los Angeles, CA 90025.

Career: Actor.

Awards, Honors: Genie Award nomination, best performance by an actor in a leading role, Academy of Canadian Cinema and Television, 2003, for *Ararat;* Gemini Award nomination, best ensemble performance in a comedy program or series, Academy of Canadian

Cinema and Television, 2008, for "Monopoly Man," *Billable Hours.*

CREDITS

Television Appearances; Series:
(Sometimes uncredited) Patrick, *Slings & Arrows* (also known as *Slings and Arrows*), The Movie Network, 2005.
Roderick Stelmakie, *Billable Hours,* Showcase, 2007.
Mark Smeaton, *The Tudors* (also known as *Tudors*), Showtime, BBC2, CBC, and other channels, 2008.

Television Appearances; Miniseries:
Billy Chamber, *Category 7: The End of the World,* CBS, 2005.

Television Appearances; Movies:
Dr. Carlo Scanchelli, *Whiskey Echo* (also known as *Whiskey echo*), CBC, 2005.
Douglas Faneuil, *Martha behind Bars* (also known as *Martha Stewart: Beyond Bars*), CBS, 2005.
Woody Monroe, *Unstable,* Lifetime, 2009.

Television Appearances; Specials:
(In archive footage) Raffi, *Weird Sex and Snowshoes: A Trek through the Canadian Cinematic Psyche* (documentary), 2004.
Bill, *Burnt Toast* (short operatic films), c. 2005.

Television Appearances; Episodic:
Jack, "A Felony for Melanie," *Wild Card* (also known as *Zoe Busiek: Wild Card*), Lifetime, 2004.
Donnelly, "Losing Isn't Everything," *Kevin Hill,* UPN, 2005.
Seth, "True Believer," *Dollhouse,* Fox, 2009.
Zan, "What Lies Beneath," *Miami Medical* (also known as *Miami Trauma* and *Untitled Bruckheimer/Lieber Project*), CBS, 2010.

Appeared in an episode of *Crash* (also known as *L.A. Crash*), Starz!.

Film Appearances:
Raffi, *Ararat,* Miramax, 2002.
Lonnie Dobbs, *Anniversary Present* (short film), 2005.
Mustafa, *Sabah* (also known as *Coldwater* and *Sabah: A Love Story*), Mongrel Media, 2005.
Danny, *Man of the Year,* Universal, 2006.
Paulie Stanton, *All Hat,* Odeon Films, 2007.
Chuck, *Closing the Ring* (also known as *Richard Attenborough's "Closing the Ring"*), The Works UK Distribution and other companies, 2007, The Weinstein Company, 2008.

Mark Henderson, *Inconceivable* (also known as *Art in Las Vegas*), Scion Films/Freestyle Releasing/Alliance Films/Pembridge Pictures/Prospero Pictures, 2008.
Narrator, *Ten for Grandpa* (short film), c. 2009.

Film Executive Producer:
Art Officially Favored (documentary), Atorrante Films, 2010.

ARMITAGE, Frank
See CARPENTER, John

ASPEN, Jennifer 1973–

PERSONAL

Born October 9, 1973, in Richmond, VA; married David O'Donnell (an actor), September 2, 2005. *Education:* University of California, Los Angeles, B.A.; trained at Beverly Hills Playhouse, Beverly Hills, CA. *Avocational Interests:* Photography, road trips, running, "urban dancing."

Addresses: *Agent*—Thomas Cushing, Innovative Artists, 1505 10th Street, Santa Monica, CA 90401.

Career: Actress.

CREDITS

Television Appearances; Series:
Julie, *Claude's Crib,* USA Network, 1997.
Daphne Jablonsky, *Party of Five,* Fox, 1998–2000.
Janet, *Bob Patterson,* ABC, 2001.
Karen, *Come to Papa,* NBC, 2004.
Trina Hamilton, *Rodney,* ABC, 2004–2008.

Television Appearances; Pilots:
Pam, *V.E.N.U.S. on the Hard Drive,* Fox, 1998.
Janet, *Bob Patterson,* ABC, 2001.
Trina Hamilton, *Rodney,* ABC, 2004.
Welcome to the Jungle Gym, CBS, 2006.
Meg, *Family Man,* TNT, 2008.

Television Appearances; Movies:
Toni, *The Secret She Carried,* NBC, 1996.
Shayna, *The Ranch,* Showtime, 2003.
Jeanette, *Unanswered Prayers,* 2010.

Television Appearances; Specials:

Presenter, *The 13nth Annual Genesis Awards,* Animal Planet, 1999.

Girl in church and news anchor, *Larry the Cable Guy's Star–Studded Christmas Extravaganza,* Country Music Television, 2008.

Television Appearances; Episodic:

"I've Got a Secret," *Charlie Grace,* ABC, 1995.

"Leg, Lies and Videotape," *Too Something,* Fox, 1995.

Alexis, "A Fine ROM–ance," *Hope & Gloria,* NBC, 1995.

Runaway girl, "Squash It," *Beverly Hills, 90210* (also known as *Class of Beverly Hills*), Fox, 1995.

Sharon, "Bikini Camp Slasher," *Weird Science,* USA Network, 1995.

Jamie, "Guess Who's Coming to Breakfast, Lunch and Dinner," *Married ... with Children,* Fox, 1995.

Pepper, "Lil Sister Dontcha," *Step by Step,* ABC, 1995.

Mrs. Jones, "To Die For," *In the House,* UPN, 1996.

Sharon, "Swallow 13," *Weird Science,* USA Network, 1996.

Melanie Marcos, "Other People," *Brotherly Love,* The WB, 1996.

Irene, "School's Out Forever," *Living Single,* Fox, 1996.

Tracey White, "A Day in the Life," *Chicago Hope,* CBS, 1996.

Rachel, *The Show,* Fox, 1996.

Candice, "Taillight's Last Gleaming," *NYPD Blue* (also known as *N.Y.P.D.*), ABC, 1997.

Debbie, "Again with the Sponge Cake," *Alright Already,* The WB, 1997.

Anna Roemer, "Indy Show," *The Pretender,* NBC, 1998.

Terry, "Twisted Sister," *House Rules,* NBC, 1998.

Interviewee, "Inside Scientology," *Investigative Reports,* Arts and Entertainment, 1998.

Vikki Newton, "Subject: Three Thirteen," *Freaky Links,* Fox, 2000.

Sarah, "Dyeing Is Easy, Comedy Is Hard," *Will & Grace,* NBC, 2002.

Samantha, "Flash Photography," *The King of Queens,* CBS, 2002.

Mrs. Ramsey, "Fight Night," *CSI: Crime Scene Investigation* (also known as *C.S.I.* and *CSI: Las Vegas*), CBS, 2002.

Emily, "Stay," *The Court,* 2002.

Michelle, "The One Where Monica Sings," *Friends,* NBC, 2003.

Livia, "Coventry," *The Agency* (also known as *CIA: The Agency*), CBS, 2003.

Tara Barrington, "Things She Said," *The Lyon's Den,* NBC, 2003.

Angie, "Dear Derwood," *Karen Sisco,* ABC, 2003.

Jolene Fleming, "Mockingbird," *Line of Fire,* ABC, 2003.

Elena, "Don't Stand So Close to Me," *Grey's Anatomy,* ABC, 2006.

April George, "Starlet Fever," *Shark,* CBS, 2007.

Maureen Fleming, "The Good Lawyer," *Boston Legal,* ABC, 2007.

Valerie Henry, "Til Death Do Us Part: Parts 1 & 2," *The Closer,* TNT, 2007.

Laurie Ann Morris, "A Higher Power," *Criminal Minds,* CBS, 2008.

De. Leila Maxford, "Patience," *Eli Stone,* ABC, 2008.

Kendra Giardi, "Showmance," *Glee,* Fox, 2009.

Kendra Giardi, "Preggers," *Glee,* Fox, 2009.

Kendra Giardi, "Throwdown," *Glee,* Fox, 2009.

Kendra Giardi, "Hairography," *Glee,* Fox, 2009.

Marcy Ward, "Weekend at Bobby's," *Supernatural,* The CW, 2010.

Stacy Cano, "Wild Life," *CSI: Crime Scene Investigation* (also known as *C.S.I.* and *CSI: Las Vegas*), CBS, 2010.

Mary, "Goodson Goes Deep," *$#*! My Dad Says* (also known as *Shit My Dad Says* and *Bleep My Dad Says*), 2011.

Film Appearances:

Kathy Lawrence, *A Very Brady Sequel,* Paramount, 1996.

Maria Moore, *Sometimes They Come Back ... Again* (also known as *Sometimes They Come Back 2*), Trimark Pictures, 1996.

Vicky Myers, *The Others,* Cinequanon, 1997.

Art store customer, *Changing Habits,* A–Pix Entertainment, 1997.

Susie Felton, *Screwed: A Hollywood Bedtime Story,* 1998.

Jennifer Oberon, *Some Common Things that Happen to Corpses,* 1999.

Geena, *See Jane Run,* Arrow, 2001.

(Uncredited) Nina, *Vanilla Sky,* Paramount, 2001.

Mindy, *L.A. Twister,* Indican Pictures, 2003.

Sarah, *Guy in Row Five,* Odessa/Paper Moon Films, 2005.

Cindy the realtor, *Mr. Woodcock,* New Line Cinema, 2007.

Leslie Munck, *The Frolic* (short film), Wonder Entertainment, 2008.

Struck (short film), 625 Productions/TXL Films, 2008.

Melon (short film), 2010.

Stage Appearances:

Appeared in *The Lion in Winter,* Pasadena Playhouse, Pasadena, CA; and in productions of *The Half Lives of Marie Curie, The Love of a Nightingale, A Midsummer Night's Dream, Pieta,* and *The Water Engine.*

RECORDINGS

Videos:

Herself, *Phys Ed Trauma Tales* (short documentary), New Line Home Video, 2008.

OTHER SOURCES

Periodicals:

People Weekly, September 3, 2006.

TV Guide, May 2, 1998, pp. 5–6.

Us Weekly, September 18, 2006.
Variety, July 30, 2007; September 18, 2007.

AVERS, Carlee 1985–

PERSONAL

Born January 13, 1985, in Arlington, TX. *Education:* Studied acting with Tony Gonzales, Kevin McDermott, Harriet Greenspan, Jim Gleson, Paul Weber, John Kirby, Bobbie Chance, Andrew Magarian, Michael Woolson, and the Groundlings, and at TVI.

Addresses: *Agent*—CESD, 10635 Santa Monica Blvd., Suite 130, Los Angeles, CA 90025. *Manager*—PureTalent Management, 4624 Cahuenga Blvd., #207, North Hollywood, CA 91602.

Career: Actress.

Member: Screen Actors Guild.

CREDITS

Film Appearances:
Bank teller, *Back at the Ranch* (short film), 2004.
Laura, *Over the Line* (short film), 2006.
Laura, *Are You Scared?* (also known as *Jigsaw: Game of Death*), Lions Gate Films, 2006.
(Uncredited) Nurse, *Jekyll,* Lightyear Entertainment, 2007.
Alycia Selt, *The Only Girl* (short film), 2008.
Debbie, *Off the Ledge,* Vanguard Cinema, 2009.
Ashley, *Someday We Will Get Married* (short film), 2009.
Tipsy number two, *Our Family Wedding,* Fox Searchlight, 2010.

Also appeared in *Unbridled; Persephone; Match Made.*

Television Appearances; Pilots:
Kerrie, *Danny Fricke,* Arts and Entertainment, 2008.

Television Appearances; Episodic:
Ashley, "Unfinished Business," *Commander in Chief,* ABC, 2006.
Bonnie Capistrano, "Lord of the Pi's," *Veronica Mars,* UPN, 2006.
Bonnie Capistrano, "Spit & Eggs," *Veronica Mars,* UPN, 2006.
Bonnie Capistrano, "There's Got to Be a Morning After Pill," *Veronica Mars,* UPN, 2007.

Stage Appearances:
Appeared in *Cat on a Hot Tin Roof; Anne of Green Gables; How to Succeed in Business Without Really Trying; Dangerous Liaisons; Little Women; Defying Gravity; Into the Woods.*

B

BARRETT, Michael 1970–

PERSONAL

Full name, Michael Bradley Barrett; born May 28, 1970, in Riverside, CA. *Education:* University of California, Los Angeles, B.A., 1992; Columbia University, M.F.A., 1996.

Addresses: *Agent*—United Talent Agency, 9560 Wilshire Blvd., Suite 500, Beverly Hills, CA 90212.

Career: Cinematographer.

Awards, Honors: American Society of Cinematographers Award nominations, outstanding achievement in cinematography in episodic television series, 2002 and 2003, for *CSI: Crime Scene Investigation;* American Society of Cinematographers Award, outstanding achievement in cinematography, 2003, for *CSI: Miami;* Golden Frog nomination, Camerimage, 2006, for *Bobby.*

CREDITS

Film Cinematographer:
Ticket to Ride (short film), 1996.
Cookin' (short film), 1997.
Face (short film), 1997.
Finding North, Cowboy Booking International, 1998.
Safe Men, Universal, 1998.
Changing Directions, Essential Films, 1999.
The Suburbans, Columbia TriStar, 1999.
75 Degrees in July, Vanguard Cinema, 2000.
Hide, Cataland Films, 2000.
Turn of Faith, Lightyear Entertainment, 2001.
Happy Birthday, 2001.

Skeletons in the Closet, Artisan, 2001.
The Perfect You (also known as *Crazy Little Thing*), Screen Media Films, 2002.
Lone Star State of Mind (also known as *Coyboys and Idiots* and *Texas Crime Junction*), Columbia TriStar, 2002.
Lucky 13, Metro–Goldwyn–Mayer, 2005.
Kiss Kiss Bang Bang, Warner Bros., 2005.
Goal! The Dream Begins (also known as *Goal!* and *Goal! The Impossible Dream*), Buena Vista, 2005.
Bobby, Metro–Goldwyn–Mayer, 2006.
The Mysteries of Pittsburg, Peace Arch, 2008.
You Don't Mess with the Zohan (also known as *Agent Zohan*), Sony, 2008.
Bedtime Stories, Walt Disney Studios, 2008.
Takers, Sony, 2010.
Everything Must Go, 2010.
Born to Be a Star, Columbia, 2011.

Television Cinematographer; Movies:
The Atlantis Conspiracty, HBO, 2001.
On the Edge, 2001.
Cowboys and Idiots, Starz!, 2002.

Television Cinematographer; Series:
CSI: Crime Scene Investigations (also known as *CSI: Las Vegas* and *C.S.I.*), CBS, 2001–2004.
CSI: Miami, CBS, 2004.
Close to Home, 2005–2006.
Welcome to the Captain, CBS, 2008.

Internet Cinematographer:
Prop 8: The Musical, FunnyorDie.com, 2008.

BASS, Edward 1956–
(Ed Bass)

PERSONAL

Full name, Michael Edward Bass; born 1956.

Addresses: *Contact*—Edward Bass Films, 358 Broadway, Suite 31, New York, NY 10013.

Career: Producer. Edward Bass Films, president. Also taught acting. Previously worked as a manager; founded a modeling agency in Paris. *Metropolitan* magazine, publisher.

Awards, Honors: Circle of Excellence Award, 2007.

CREDITS

Film Producer:
Slingshot, Scanbox Entertainment, 2005.
(As Ed Bass) *Come Early Morning,* Scanbox Entertainment, 2006.
Mini's First Time, Top Film, 2006.
Bobby, Metro–Goldwyn–Mayer, 2006.
As Good As Dead, Eagle, 2010.
The Hunt, Jay Goldman Films, 2010.

Film Work:
(As Ed Bass) Co–executive producer, *While She Was Out* (also known as *Alive*), Anchor Bay Films, 2008.
Executive producer, *The Killing Jar,* New Films, 2010.

Stage Producer:
Produced musicals, including *Stardust* and *Great Moments on Stage.*

WRITINGS

Screenplays:
The Hunt, Jay Goldman Films, 2010.

BEAN, Henry 1945–

PERSONAL

Born August 3, 1945, in Philadelphia, PA; son of Donald (a lawyer) and Fahny (maiden name, Schorr) Bean; married Nancy Eliason, January 3, 1968 (divorced, 1970); married Leora Barish (a writer), March 23, 1980; children: Max. *Education:* Yale University, B.A., 1967; Stanford University, M.A., 1973. *Politics:* "Left." *Religion:* Jewish.

Addresses: *Agent*—Alan Gasmer, William Morris Agency, 151 El Camino Dr., Beverly Hills, CA 90212; Creative Artists Agency, 2000 Avenue of the Stars, Los Angeles, CA 90067.

Career: Writer, producer, director, and actor. Monte Vista High School, Danville, CA, teacher of English and journalism, 1969–71.

Member: Writer's Guild of America West.

Awards, Honors: Award from PEN—Los Angeles, first book of fiction, 1983, for *False Match;* Grand Jury Prize, dramatic category, Sundance Film Festival, Screen International Award nomination, European Film Awards, Open Palm Award, Gotham Awards, Golden St. George Award and Russian Film Clubs Federation Award, both Moscow International Film Festival, nomination for Bronze Horse, Stockholm Film Festival, Humanitas Prize nomination, Sundance Film category (with Mark Jacobson), all 2001, Independent Spirit Award nominations, best first feature and best screenplay, Independent Features Project/West, 2002, and Chicago Film Critics Association Award nomination, most promising director, 2003, all for *The Believer.* Film Work: Producer (with Pierre David), *Deep Cover,* New Line Cinema, 1992. Director, *The Believer,* Fireworks Pictures, 2002. Producer and director, *Noise,* Anchor Bay Films, 2007. Film Appearances: Customer in bar, *Venus Rising,* IRS Releasing, 1995. Stein, *Un divan a New York* (also known as *A Couch in New York* and *Eine Couch in New York*), Northern Arts Entertainment, 1997. Ilio Manzetti, *The Believer,* Fireworks Pictures, 2002. Television Work; Episodic: Executive producer, *K Street,* HBO, 2003. Television Appearances; Episodic: Also appeared in "The Believer," *Anatomy of a Scene,* Sundance Channel.

RECORDINGS

Videos:
A Conversation with ... Director Henry Bean, Lions Gate Films, 2003.

WRITINGS

Screenplays:
Showboat 1988: The Remake (also known as *Showboat 1988*), 1977.
(With Shirl Hendryx) *Running Brave,* Buena Vista, 1983.
(With Pascal Bonitzer, Chantal Akerman, Jean Gruault, and Leora Barish) *Golden Eighties* (also known as *Window Shopping*), Pari/Gerick, 1986.
Internal Affairs, Paramount, 1990.
(With Michael Tolkin) *Deep Cover,* New Line Cinema, 1992.
Johnny Mnemonic, 1995.
Venus Rising, 1995.
Mulholland Falls, Metro–Goldwyn–Mayer, 1996.
Last Man Standing, New Line Cinema, 1996.

Enemy of the State, Buena Vista, 1998.
Desperate Measures, TriStar, 1998.
Armageddon, Buena Vista, 1998.
The Believer, Fireworks Pictures, 2002.
Basic Instinct 2, Twentieth Century–Fox, 2006.
Noise, Anchor Bay Films, 2007.

Also wrote (with Leora Barish) *Desire;* (with Barish) *Labyrinth Nine;* and *Who You Know.*

Television Episodes:

The Hitchhiker, HBO and USA Network, 1983.
K Street, HBO, 2003.

Novels:

False Match, Simon & Schuster, 1982.

ADAPTATIONS

The film *Venus Rising,* released by IRS Releasing in 1995, was based on a story by Bean and others.

BECK, Molly
See FERGUSON, Molly Beck

BIEHN, Michael 1956–

PERSONAL

Full name, Michael Connell Biehn; born July 31, 1956, in Anniston, AL; father, a lawyer; married Carlene Olson, July 12, 1980 (divorced); married Gina Marsh (a model), 1988 (divorced, 2008); married Jennifer Blanc (an actress), April 13, 2009; children: (first marriage) Devon and Taylor (twins); (second marriage) Caelan Michael. *Education:* Studied drama at the University of Arizona for two years; studied acting with Vincent Chase.

Addresses: *Agent*—International Creative Management, 8942 Wilshire Blvd., Beverly Hills, CA 90211; WME Entertainment, 1325 Avenue of the Americas, New York, NY 10019. *Manager*—The Hoffland Company, 9465 Wilshire Blvd., Suite 420, Beverly Hills, CA 90212. *Contact*—11220 Valley Spring Lane, North Hollywood, CA 91602.

Career: Actor. Previously worked as a credit manager and show room manager.

CREDITS

Film Appearances:
Jack Ripley, *Coach,* Crown International, 1978.
(Uncredited) Jock and basketball player, *Grease,* 1978.
Tim Warner, *Hog Wild* (also known as *Les fous de la moto*), Avco Embassy, 1980.
Douglas Breen, *The Fan,* Paramount, 1981.
Alexander, *The Lords of Discipline,* Paramount, 1983.
Kyle Reese, *The Terminator,* Orion, 1984.
Corporal Hicks, *Aliens,* Twentieth Century–Fox, 1986.
Russell Quinn, *The Seventh Sign,* TriStar, 1988.
Anthony Fraser, *Rampage,* Vestron Video, 1988.
Garnet Montrose, *In a Shallow Grave,* Skouras, 1988.
Lieutenant Hiram Coffey, *The Abyss,* Twentieth Century–Fox, 1989.
Yours to Keep, 1989.
Lieutenant James Curran, *Navy SEALS,* Orion, 1990.
Eddie Kay, *Time Bomb,* Metro–Goldwyn–Mayer/Pathe, 1991.
(Scenes deleted) Kyle Reese, *Terminator 2: Judgment Day* (also known as *T2, T2–Terminator 2–Judgment Day, T2: Extreme Edition, T2: Ultimate Edition, Terminator 2–Le jour du jugement dernier,* and *Terminator 2: Le jugement dernier*), 1991.
Taylor Brooks, *K2* (also known as *K2: The Ultimate High*), Paramount, 1992.
Anthony Fraser, *Rampage,* 1992.
Johnny Ringo, *Tombstone,* Buena Vista, 1993.
Joe Donan, *Deadfall,* Trimark Pictures, 1993.
Himself, *T2: More than Meets the Eye,* 1993.
Jackie Ryan, *In the Kingdom of the Blind, the Man with One Eye Is King* (also known as *In the Kingdom of the Blind*), 1994.
Lieutenant Bob Hargrove, *Jade,* Paramount, 1995.
Casey Woods, *Crash* (also known as *Breach of Trust, Breach of Contract,* and *Dirty Money*), 1995.
Blake, *Blood of the Hunter* (also known as *The Fiddler*), 1995.
Boyd, *Mojave Moon,* New Moon Productions, 1996.
Commander Charles Anderson, *The Rock,* Buena Vista, 1996.
Kyle Reese, *T2 3–D: Battle Across Time,* 1996.
Robert Hart, *Dead Men Can't Dance,* Imperial Entertainment, 1997.
Himself, *Directors: James Cameron* (also known as *AFI the Directors: James Cameron*), 1997.
Detective Tony Luca, *Double Edge* (also known as *American Dragons*), Orion Home Video, 1998.
Smokey Banks, *The Ride,* World Wide Pictures, 1998.
Bill, *Susan's Plan* (also known as *Dying to Get Rich* and *Dying to Get Rich! … Susan's Plan*), 1998.
John Holmes, *Wonderland,* 1999.
Sheriff Brent Marken, *Cherry Falls,* October Films, 1999.
Himself, *The Directors: William Friedkin* (also known as *AFI's the Directors: William Friedkin*), 2000.
Robert Bly, *The Art of War* (also known as *L'art de la guerre*), Warner Bros., 2000.

Craig Thornton, *Chain of Command,* 2000.
David Alexander, *Megiddo: The Omega Code 2* (also known as *Megiddo*), 8X Entertainment, 2001.
Himself, *Other Voices: Creating "The Terminator,"* MGM Home Entertainment, 2001.
Henry Gates, *Clockstoppers,* Paramount, 2002.
Macy Kobecek, *Borderline,* Columbia TriStar Home Video, 2002.
Stuart Lang, *Havoc,* New Line Home Video, 2005.
Petros Angelo, *Dragon Squad* (also known as *Mang lung* and *Dragon Heat,* Dragon Dynasty, 2005.
Strickland, *The Insatiable,* THINKFilm, 2007.
Tony Russo, *Spin* (also known as *You Are Here*), THINKFilm, 2007.
Sheriff Hague/the sheriff, *Grindhouse,* Dimension Films, 2007.
Sheriff Hague, *Planet Terror* (also known as *Grindhouse Presents: Robert Rodriguez's "Planet Terror"* and *Robert Rodriguez's "Planet Terror"*), A–Film, 2007.
Blake O'Connell, *They Wait,* Sony, 2007.
Lee, *Stiletto* (also known as *Velvet Spider*), First Look, 2008.
Landy Bretthorse, *Saving Grace B. Jones,* New Films Cinema, 2009.
FBI Agent Michael Brown, *Streets of Blood,* Anchor Bay Films, 2009.
Detective Marling, *Psych:9,* Universal, 2010.
John Tremayne, *The Blood Bond,* Birch Tree Entertainment, 2010.
Jonathan Miller, *Bereavement,* Crimson Films, 2010.

Also appeared in *The Boarder; Dead–Bang.*

Film Director:
The Blood Bond, Birch Tree Entertainment, 2010.

Television Appearances; Series:
Mark Johnson, *Operation: Runaway* (also known as *The Runaways*), NBC, 1978–79.
Chris Larrabee, *The Magnificent Seven,* CBS, 1998.
Judson Cross, *Adventure Inc.,* syndicated, 2002.
Sean Harrison, *Hawaii,* NBC, 2004.

Television Appearances; Movies:
J. D., *Zuma Beach,* NBC, 1978.
Tom Reardon, *A Fire in the Sky,* NBC, 1978.
Daniel Allen, *China Rose,* CBS, 1983.
Sebastian, *Le martyre de Saint Sebastien* (also known as *The Martyrdom of St. Sebastian*), 1984.
Eselein, *Die Nacht aus blei* (also known as *The Night of Lead*), 1985.
Bo Landry, *A Taste for Killing* (also known as *In the Company of a Killer*), USA Network, 1992.
Joe Keyes, *Deep Red,* Sci–Fi Channel, 1994.
Stash Horak, *Conundrum* (also known as *Frame by Frame*), Showtime, 1996.

Bill, *Susan's Plan* (also known as *Dying to Get Rich*), Cinemax, 1998.
Roy McLean, *Silver Wolf,* Fox Family, 1999.
Craig Thornton, *Chain of Command,* HBO, 2000.
Mike Cassidy, *The Legend of Butch & Sundance,* NBC, 2003.

Television Appearances; Miniseries:
Charles Raynor, *Deadly Intentions,* ABC, 1985.
FEMA director Jack Wallach, *Asteroid,* NBC, 1997.

Television Appearances; Pilots:
Tony, *James at 15,* NBC, 1977.
Sandman, "Logan's Run," *Logan's Run,* CBS, 1977.
Larry DeWitt, *The Paradise Connection,* CBS, 1979.
Gibby Anderson, *Steeltown,* CBS, 1979.

Television Appearances; Specials:
Seth, "The Terrible Secret," *ABC Afterschool Specials,* ABC, 1979.
The Making of "Terminator," 1984.
The Making of "Alien 3," 1992.
Arnold Schwarzenegger: Hollywood Hero, The Learning Channel, 1999.
Himself/Corporal Dwayne Hicks, *Alien Evolution,* Channel 4, 2001.
(Uncredited) Himself, *The Alien Saga,* 2002.
Himself/Kyle Reese/Corporal Dwayne Hicks, *When Muscles Ruled the World,* 2002.
Greatest Ever Disaster Movies, Channel 5, 2007.
Greatest Ever 80s Movies, Channel 5, 2007.

Television Appearances; Episodic:
Basketball player, "The Athlete," *Family,* ABC, 1979.
Officer Randall Buttman, "Bangladesh Slowly," *Hill Street Blues,* NBC, 1984.
Officer Randall Buttman, "Fowl Play," *Hill Street Blues,* NBC, 1984.
Rookie Patrolman Randall Buttman, "Rookie Nookie," *Hill Street Blues,* NBC, 1984.
The Word, 1991.
Lieutenant Matt McCrae, "Strapped," *HBO Showcase,* HBO, 1993.
Philip Thornton a.k.a. Blake, "Le sang du chasseur," *Aventures dans le Grand Nord,* 1995.
The Tonight Show with Jay Leno, NBC, 1997.
Praise the Lord, TBN, 2001.
Deputy Commissioner Leland Dockerty, "The War at Home," *Law & Order: Criminal Intent* (also known as *Law & Order: CI*), NBC, 2006.
Up Close with Carrie Keagan, two episodes, 2007.
Detective Ron Fullwood, "Cold Comfort," *Criminal Minds,* CBS, 2009.
Lieutenant Jay Frye, "O.I.S.," *Dark Blue,* TNT, 2009.

Also appeared in *Police Story,* NBC; "The Films of William Friedkin," *The Directors.*

RECORDINGS

Video Games:

Voice of Commander Michael McNeil, *Command & Conquer: Tiberian Sun* (also known as *Command & Conquer: Tiberian Sun Firestorm*), Electronic Arts, 1998.

Voice of Tech–com soldier, *The Terminator: Dawn of Fate,* Sony Computer Entertainment America, 2002.

Videos:

Under Pressure: Making "The Abyss," 1993.

Johnny Ringo, *The Making of "Tombstone,"* 2002.

The Making of "Alien 3," Twentieth Century–Fox, 2003.

Superior Firepower: The Making of "Aliens," Twentieth Century–Fox, 2003.

BLUM, Mark 1950–

PERSONAL

Born May 14, 1950, in Newark, NJ. *Education:* University of Minnesota, M.F.A.; also studied acting at the University of Pennsylvania, HB Studio, New York City, Loeb Drama Center, Cambridge, MA, and with Andre Gregory, Aaron Frankel, and Daniel Seltzer.

Addresses: *Agent*—Cornerstone Talent Agency, 37 West 20th St., Suite 1108, New York, NY 10011; Silver, Massetti, and Szatmary, 8730 West Sunset Blvd., Suite 440, West Hollywood, CA 90069.

Career: Actor and producer. National Shakespeare Company, Ulster County Community College, Stone Ridge, NY, stage manager, 1974.

Awards, Honors: Obie Award, *Village Voice,* 1989, for *Gus and Al.*

CREDITS

Stage Appearances:

Valentine, *Two Gentlemen of Verona,* National Shakespeare Company, Ulster County Community College, Stone Ridge, NY, 1974, then Rutgers University, New Brunswick, NJ, 1975.

Cleante, *The Miser,* National Shakespeare Company, Ulster County Community College, 1974, then Rutgers University, 1975.

(Off–Broadway debut) Post office clerk, *The Cherry Orchard,* Roundabout Theatre, 1976.

Villager, first angel, and man, *The World of Sholem Aleichem,* Roundabout Theatre, 1976.

Brothers, George Street Playhouse, New Brunswick, NJ, 1976.

(Broadway debut) Venetian, *The Merchant,* Plymouth Theatre, 1977.

Steve, *Say Goodnight, Gracie,* Playwrights Horizons Theatre, Manhattan Main Stage Theatre, New York City, 1978, then Actors Playhouse, New York City, 1979.

Younger son, *Table Settings,* Playwrights Horizons Theatre, then Chelsea Theatre Center, New York City, 1980.

Michael, *Key Exchange,* Orpheum Theatre, New York City, 1981–82.

Close Ties, Long Wharf Theatre, New Haven, CT, 1981.

The Cherry Orchard, Long Wharf Theatre, 1982.

Iago, *Othello,* Shakespeare Festival of Dallas, Dallas, TX, 1982.

Johnson, *Loving Reno,* New York Theatre Studio, AMDA Studio One, New York City, 1983.

Max Whitcomb, *An American Comedy,* Center Theatre Group, Mark Taper Forum, Los Angeles, 1983–84.

Lee Baum, *The American Clock,* Center Theatre Group, Mark Taper Forum, 1983–84.

Harry, *Wild Oats,* Center Theatre Group, Mark Taper Forum, 1983–84.

Peter Austin, *It's Only a Play,* Manhattan Theatre Club, New York City, 1984.

Asher, *Messiah,* Manhattan Theatre Club, 1985.

Ben, *Little Footsteps,* Playwrights Horizons Theatre, 1986.

Ben, *The Downside,* Long Wharf Theatre, 1987.

Cave of Life, Circle Repertory Theatre, New York City, 1988.

Al, *Gus and Al,* New York City, c. 1989.

Eddie, *Lost in Yonkers,* Richard Rodgers Theatre, New York City, 1991.

Tom, *Laureen's Whereabouts,* Workshop of the Players Art Theatre, New York City, 1993.

Garn, *My Thing of Love,* Martin Beck Theatre, New York City, 1995.

Alan Tolkin, *Mizlansky/Zilinsky or "Schmucks,"* Manhattan Theatre Club Stage I, New York City, 1998.

Howard Fine, *The Waverly Gallery,* Promenade Theatre, New York City, 2000.

Jensen, *Gore Vidal's "The Best Man,"* Virginia Theatre, New York City, 2000.

Leo Herman, *A Thousand Clowns,* Long Acre Theatre, New York City, 2001.

Mr. Braddock, *The Graduate,* Plymouth Theatre, New York City, 2002–2003.

Narrator and man, *The Long Christmas Ride Home,* Vineyard Theatre, New York City, 2003.

First juror, *Twelve Angry Men,* Roundabout Theatre Company, New York City, 2004–2005.

Smith, *The Music Teacher,* Minetta Lane Theatre, New York City, 2006.

Dan, *Buffalo Gal,* 59E59 Theater A, New York City, 2008.

Brigadier–General Ezra Mannon, *Mourning Becomes Electra,* Acorn Theatre, New York City, 2009.
Dr. Oliver Pfaff and Martin Rieman, *The Singing Forest,* Joseph Papp Public Theatre, Martinson Hall, New York City, 2009.

Also appeared in *Moby Dick Rehearsed,* Mark Taper Forum, Los Angeles; *Green Julia.*

Stage Work:
Assistant stage manager, *The Merchant,* Plymouth Theatre, New York City, 1977.

Film Appearances:
Intern Murphy, *Lovesick,* Warner Bros., 1983.
Gary Glass, *Desperately Seeking Susan,* Orion, 1985.
George Margolin, *Just between Friends,* Orion, 1986.
Richard Mason, *Crocodile Dundee,* Paramount, 1986.
Denny Gordon, *Blind Date* (also known as *Blake Edwards "Blind Date"*), TriStar, 1987.
Arthur Peale, *The Presidio* (also known as *The Presidio: The Scene of the Crime*), Paramount, 1988.
Ned Braudy, *Worth Winning,* 1989.
Ben Winchek, *Emma and Elvis* (also known as *The Last Resort*), 1991.
Peter, *Miami Rhapsody,* Buena Vista, 1995.
Matthew Greenberg, *The Low Life,* 1995.
Dr. Brennan, *Denise Calls Up,* 1995.
Louis, *Sudden Manhattan,* Phaedra Cinema, 1996.
Ben Marks, *Stag,* 1997.
Edward Cooperberg, *You Can Thank Me Later,* 1998.
Darrell, *Getting to Know You* (also known as *Getting to Know All about You*), 1999.
The interviewer, *Down to You,* Miramax, 2000.
Richard Baxter, *Zen and the Art of Landscaping,* 2000.
John Slyconish, *Balkanization,* 2002.
Lewis Estridge, *Shattered Glass,* Lions Gate Films, 2003.
Richardson, *The Warrior Class,* Echo Bridge Home Entertainment, 2004.
Banning, *Tiger: His Fall & Rise* (short film), 2004.
Father, *Life on the Ledge,* 2005.
New York University professor, *Step Up 3D,* Walt Disney Studios Motion Pictures, 2010.
Stuart, *The Green,* 2011.

Film Work:
Executive producer, *The Low Life,* 1995.
Associate producer, *Search and Destroy* (also known as *The Four Rules*), October Films, 1995.

Television Appearances; Series:
Ken Holden, *Sweet Surrender,* NBC, 1987.
Edison King, *Capital News* (also known as *Powerhouse*), ABC, 1990.
Ben, *Central Park West* (also known as *C.P.W.*), CBS, 1995.

Television Appearances; Miniseries:
Harry Hobbs, *The Judge* (also known as *Steve Martini's "The Judge"*), NBC, 2001.

Television Appearances; Movies:
Alan, *The Time and the Conways,* 1966.
Dr. Howard Zuckerman, *Condition Critical* (also known as *Critical Condition* and *Final Pulse*), NBC, 1992.
Wayne Satz, *Indictment: The McMartin Trial* (also known as *The Naked Movie Star Games* and *Nothing But the Truth: The McMartin Story*), HBO, 1995.
Ben Marks, *Stag,* HBO, 1996.
Jackson, *The Defenders: Payback,* Showtime, 1997.

Television Appearances; Specials:
MTV, Give Me Back My Life: A Harvard Lampoon Parody, Comedy Central, 1991.

Television Appearances; Pilots:
Ray Litertini, *Things Are Looking Up,* CBS, 1984.
Edison King, *Capital News,* ABC, 1990.
Chaos Theory, NBC, 1999.

Television Appearances; Episodic:
Dr. Vogel, "Two Balls and a Strike," *St. Elsewhere,* NBC, 1984.
Jack's son, "Contempt of Court," *Miami Vice,* NBC, 1987.
Mike Summers, "Aliens," *Roseanne,* ABC, 1992.
Brooklyn Assistant District Attorney Frank Lazar, "Jurisdiction," *Law & Order,* NBC, 1993.
Dr. Sachs, "From Hare to Eternity," *NYPD Blue* (also known as *N.Y.P.D.*), ABC, 1993.
Michael Aronson, "Seed," *Law & Order,* NBC, 1995.
FBI agent Mike Francis, "He Was Robbed," *NYPD Blue* (also known as *N.Y.P.D.*), ABC, 1995.
Larry Mohr, "What about Larry?," *Wings,* NBC, 1995.
Ben, "The History of Gil and Rachel," *Central Park West,* CBS, 1995.
Dr. Vincent, "The Highest Bidder," *New York Undercover,* Fox, 1995.
Greg Armstrong, "Face Off," *Ink,* CBS, 1996.
John, "The 1000th Show," *Frasier,* NBC, 1997.
Brooklyn Assistant District Attorney Frank Lazar, "Agony," *Law & Order,* NBC, 1998.
FBI agent Mike Francis, "Show & Tell," *NYPD Blue* (also known as *N.Y.P.D.*), ABC, 1999.
Randall Curtin, "Meadowlands," *The Sopranos,* HBO, 1999.
Representative Katzenmoyer, "Five Votes Down," *The West Wing* (also known as *The White House*), NBC, 1999.
Rabbi Jonathan Ahrenthal, "The First Commandment," *Deadline,* NBC, 2001.
Arnold Bancroft, "Goodbye Sadie," *Ed,* NBC, 2001.

State's Attorney Michael Scannel, "Evil/Doers," *The Practice,* ABC, 2002.

Dr. Philip Oliver, "Con–Text," *Law & Order: Criminal Intent* (also known as *Law & Order: CI*), NBC, 2003.

Jim Rennert, "Deadline," *CSI: Miami,* CBS, 2004.

Richard Kinrich, "Slade's Chophouse," *Judging Amy,* CBS, 2004.

Professor Larry Lewis, "Proud Flesh," *Law & Order: Criminal Intent* (also known as *Law & Order: CI*), NBC, 2006.

Dr. Macvittie, "Soldier's Heart," *New Amsterdam,* Fox, 2008.

Dr. Claus Penrose, "The Same Old Story," *Fringe,* Fox, 2008.

Expert doctor, "Dignity," *Law & Order,* NBC, 2009.

"I'm Not That Kind of Girl," *Mercy,* NBC, 2009.

Julius Kreutzer, "Unplugged," *The Good Wife,* CBS, 2010.

RECORDINGS

Taped Readings:
Found Money by James Grippando, HarperAudio, 1999.

Video Games:
Voice of Gordon Temple, *Smuggler's Run,* 2000.

Voice of Maurice Horton, Dr. Emil Hartman, and Dr. Barclay Colvin, *Alan Wake,* Microsoft, 2009.

BOCKING, Claire

PERSONAL

Education: Australian National University, B.A., European studies, 2000; studied acting at the Atwater Playhouse Method Acting School, LA Connection Improv, Rose Bruford College, IO West, and the Groundlings, and with Brian Reise, Margie Haber, and Carolyne Barry.

Addresses: *Agent*—Daily Talent Agency, 7949 Grey Teal St. North, Las Vegas, NV 89084; Nu Talent Agency, 117 North Robertson Blvd., Los Angeles, CA 90048.

Career: Actress. Provided voice of Samantha (host), Disney's Fit Forever web site.

Member: British Actors' Equity, Screen Actors Guild, Screen Actors Guild.

Awards, Honors: Canberra Area Theatre Award nomination, best actress, 1999, for *Equus;* Canberra Area Theatre Award, best supporting actress, 2000, for *Brilliant Lies;* Lillian Baylis Award, Royal Victorian Hall Foundation, 2004; Lawrence Olivier Bursary Award, Society of London Theatre, 2004.

CREDITS

Film Appearances:
Doctor, *The Abattoir* (short film), 2008.

Teacher, *Summer Homework* (short film), Short Shorts Film Festival, 2008.

Megan, *Trail of Crumbs,* 2008.

Liz, *Monday Super Fantastic,* 2009.

Christine, *Lorraine* (short film), 2010.

Tyra, *Imagine That ...,* 2010.

Jeanine, *Bocce* (short film), 2010.

Also appeared as Phoenix, *The Wind Runner;* Brenda Oliver, *Bad Medicine;* cell phone woman, *Epsilon 3.*

Television Appearances; Series:
(Sometimes uncredited) Secretary, *Mad Men,* AMC, 2007–2008.

Stage Appearances:
Appeared as Trish, *The Chalk Boy,* Company of Angels, Los Angeles; Mary, *Stuffed Grape Leaves,* Company of Angels, Los Angeles; Margaret, *My Werewolf,* Sidewalk Studio, Toluca Lake, CA; Beatrice and Joanna, *The Changeling,* Theatre Royal Haymarket, London; Lady Macbeth, *Macbeth,* Rose Bruford Theatre, London; Rona, *Home Sick,* Dafna Rubenstein, International Jewish Festival, Leeds, England; Dora, *Equus,* Canberra Theatre, Australia; Hermia, *Midsummer Night's Dream,* National Summer Shakespeare Festival, Australia; Martin and Gunilla, *Ein Reines Maedchen,* Gostenhof Theatre, Nuremberg, Germany; Katy, *Brilliant Lies,* Canberra Theatre; Rose Baum, *The American Clock,* Battersea Arts Center, London; Katherine, *Taming of the Shrew,* Rose Bruford Theatre.

OTHER SOURCES

Electronic:
Claire Bocking Official Site, http://www.clairebocking.com, October 26, 2010.

BOYD, John 1981–

PERSONAL

Full name, John H. Boyd; born October 22, 1981, in New York, NY; son of Guy Boyd (an actor); brother of

Pauline Boyd (an actress). *Education:* Graduate of Bennington College.

Addresses: *Manager*—D/F Management, 270 Lafayette St., Suite 102, New York, NY 10012.

Career: Actor. Signature Theatre Company, New York City, former intern. Nine Winds (jass record label), worked as an intern; worked as a teacher at an orphanage in Nairobi, Kenya; also worked in construction and at a preschool.

CREDITS

Film Appearances:
Colin, *Building Girl,* Magic Pad Productions, 2005.
Louis, *Stay* (short film), BrindStar Productions, 2005.
Jack, *The Notorious Bettie Page,* Picturehouse Entertainment, 2006.
Private Dooley, *Fields of Freedom,* Greystone Communications, 2006.
Grover, *Follow Me* (short film), 2006.
One–eyebrow smoker, *Lady in the Water,* Warner Bros., 2006.
Drunk guy, *Careless,* Image Entertainment, 2007.
Wyatt, *The Greatest,* Paladin, 2009.
Erik, *Mercy,* IFC Films, 2009.
Floyd Marks, *Jelly,* Cinetic Rights Management, 2010.

Television Appearances; Series:
Arlo Glass, *24,* Fox, 2010.

Television Appearances; Episodic:
Zack Burns, "Locomotion," *Law & Order,* NBC, 2005.
Kenny Ellis, "Profiteer," *Law & Order,* NBC, 2006.
(Uncredited) Ian Spencer, "In Which We Meet Mr. Jones," *Fringe,* Fox, 2008.

Stage Appearances:
The Piano Teacher, Vineyard Theatre, New York City, 2007.

Also appeared in productions of *The Crusaders, Pinwheel Freak,* and *Romania Kiss Me.*

BRENNEMAN, Amy 1964–

PERSONAL

Full name, Amy Frederica Brenneman; born June 22, 1964, in Glastonbury, CT (some sources say New London, CT); daughter of Russell L. (an environmental lawyer) and Frederica (a superior court judge) Brenneman; married Brad Silberling (a director), September 30, 1995; children: Charlotte Tucker, Bodhi Russell. *Education:* Harvard University, B.A., comparative religion, 1987; studied sacred dances in Nepal.

Addresses: *Agent*—Creative Artists Agency, 2000 Avenue of the Stars, Los Angeles, CA 90067. *Manager*—Mosaic, 9200 Sunset Blvd., 10th Floor, Los Angeles, CA 90069. *Publicist*—Slate PR, 8322 Beverly Blvd., Suite 201, Los Angeles, CA 90048.

Career: Actress and producer. Cornerstone Theatre Company (repertory group), founding member and touring company member; appeared in television commercials, including Tampax, c. 1980s.

Awards, Honors: Emmy Award nomination, outstanding supporting actress in a drama series, 1994, TV Land Award nomination, TV moment that became headline news, 2007, for *NYPD Blue;* Emmy Award nomination, outstanding guest actress in a drama series, 1995, for "For Whom the Skell Tolls," *NYPD Blue;* Q Award nomination, best actress in a quality drama series, Viewers for Quality Television; Television Producer of the Year Award in Episodic nomination (with others), PGA Golden Laurel Awards, *TV Guide* Award, favorite actress in a new series, 2000, Golden Globe Award nominations, best performance by an actress in a television series—drama, 2000, 2001, 2002, Emmy Award nominations, outstanding lead actress in a drama series, 2000, 2001, 2002, *TV Guide* Award, actress of the year in a drama series, 2001, Golden Satellite Award nomination, best performance by an actress in a series—drama, International Press Academy, 2002, Screen Actors Guild Award nomination, outstanding performance by a female actor in a drama series, 2003, all for *Judging Amy;* Gotham Award nomination (with others), best ensemble cast, Lucy Award (with Tyne Daly), Women in Film Awards, 2002; Bronze Leopard (with others), Locarno International Film Festival, 2005, both for *Nine Lives.*

CREDITS

Film Appearances:
Susan Goldman, *Bye, Bye Love,* Twentieth Century–Fox, 1995.
Amelia Harvey, *Casper,* Universal, 1995.
Eady, *Heat,* Warner Bros., 1995.
Madelyne Thompson, *Daylight,* Universal, 1996.
Laura Walker, *Fear* (also known as *No Fear* and *Obsession mortelle*), Universal, 1996.
Annie, *Lesser Prophets,* 1997.
Chrysty, *Nevada,* Storm Entertainment, 1997.
Mary, *Your Friends & Neighbors,* Gramercy, 1998.

(Uncredited) Angel in library at computers, *City of Angels,* 1998.

Herself, *The Making of "Daylight,"* 1998.

Grace, *The Suburbans,* Columbia TriStar, 1999.

Kathy, "Love Waits for Kathy," *Things You Can Tell Just By Looking at Her,* United Artists, 2000.

Adult Bo, *Off the Map,* Manhattan Pictures International, 2003.

Herself, *Love on "NYPD Blue"* (short film), Twentieth Century–Fox Home Entertainment, 2003.

Lorna, *Nine Lives,* Magnolia Pictures, 2005.

Herself, *The Making of "Heat"* (documentary), Warner Home Video, 2005.

Shelly Barnes, *88 Minutes* (also known as *88* and *88: 88 Minutes*), Columbia, 2007.

Sylvia, *The Jane Austen Book Club,* Sony Pictures Classics, 2007.

Carol, *Downloading Nancy,* Strand Releasing, 2008.

Dr. Eleanor Stone, *Mother and Child,* Sony Pictures Classics, 2009.

Change Is Gonna Come (documentary), 2009.

Film Coproducer:

Nevada, Storm Entertainment, 1997.

Television Appearances; Series:

Blanche, *Middle Ages,* CBS, 1992.

Police Officer Janice Licalsi, *NYPD Blue* (also known as *N.Y.P.D.*), ABC, 1993–94.

Judge Amy Madison Gray Cassidy, *Judging Amy,* CBS, 1999–2005.

Dr. Violet Turner, *Private Practice,* ABC, 2007—.

Television Appearances; Movies:

Blanche, *Pig in the Python,* 1992.

Television Appearances; Specials:

Title role, *Mary Cassatt: An American Impressionist,* HBO, 1999.

Presenter, *A Home for the Holidays,* CBS, 2000.

Herself, *America: A Tribute to Heroes,* 2001.

I Am My Mother's Daughter, Lifetime, 2001.

The 53rd Annual Primetime Emmy Awards, CBS, 2001.

Narrator, *"Moonlight Mile": A Journey to Screen,* 2002.

CBS at 75, CBS, 2003.

A "Dr. Phil" Primetime Special: Family First, CBS, 2004.

Television Appearances; Pilots:

Robyn O'Brien, *A.T.F.* (movie), ABC, 1998.

Television Appearances; Episodic:

Amy Wainwright, "A Christmas Secret," *Murder, She Wrote,* CBS, 1992.

Voice of Lauren Simone, "A Trophied Duck," *Duckman: Private Dick/Family Man* (animated), 1997.

Faye Moskowitz, "Merry Christmas, Mrs. Moskowitz," *Frasier,* NBC, 1998.

Faye Moskowitz, "When a Man Loves Two Women," *Frasier,* NBC, 1999.

Faye Moskowitz, "Shutout in Seattle: Parts 1 & 2," *Frasier,* NBC, 1999.

CBS Cares, CBS, 2001, 2003.

Hollywood Squares (also known as *H2* and *H2: Hollywood Squares*), syndicated, 2002.

Dr. Violet Turner, "The Other Side of This Life: Parts 1 & 2," *Grey's Anatomy,* ABC, 2007.

Entertainment Tonight (also known as *E.T.*), syndicated, 2007, 2008, 2009.

Also appeared as herself, "Amy Brenneman Revealed," *Revealed with Jules Asner,* E! Entertainment Television.

Television Talk Show Guest Appearances; Episodic:

Late Show with David Letterman, CBS, 1995, 1996, 2002, 2003.

The Daily Show with Jon Stewart (also known as *The Daily Show, A Daily Show with Jon Stewart,* and *The Daily Show with Jon Stewart Global Edition*), Comedy Central, 1998, 1999.

Late Night with Conan O'Brien, NBC, 1999.

The Tonight Show with Jay Leno, NBC, 2000.

The Late Late Show with Craig Kilborn (also known as *The Late Late Show*), CBS, 2000, 2001, 2002, 2004.

The Rosie O'Donnell Show, syndicated, 2000, 2002.

The View, ABC, 2003.

Ellen: The Ellen DeGeneres Show, syndicated, 2004, 2005, 2007, 2009.

The Late Late Show with Craig Ferguson, CBS, 2005.

Jimmy Kimmel Live!, ABC, 2005, 2007, 2009.

Up Close with Carrie Keagan, 2007.

The Bonnie Hunt Show, 2008, 2009.

Late Night with Jimmy Fallon, NBC, 2009.

Hannity, Fox News, 2010.

Television Work; Series:

Creator and co–executive producer, *Judging Amy,* CBS, 1999–2005.

Stage Appearances:

The Video Store Owner's Significant Other, Cornerstone Theatre Company, Los Angeles, 1990.

Martine, *The Learned Ladies,* Classic Stage Company, New York City, 1991.

Saint Joan of the Stockyards, Yale Repertory Theatre, New Haven, CT, 1992.

Janet, *God's Heart,* Mitzi E. Newhouse Theatre, New York City, 1997.

Top Girls, Theatre Works, Los Angeles, 2006.

A Nervous Smile, Williamstown Theatre Festival, Williamstown, MA, 2006.

Also appeared in *Sincerity Forever; Interstates,* So Grand Theatre; *Measure for Measure,* American Repertory Theatre; *Twelfth Night,* LATC; *Romeo and Juliet, Three Sisters, Peer Gynt, The Winter's Tale,* and *The Oresteria,* all Cornerstone Theatre Company, Los Angeles.

RECORDINGS

Taped Readings:

Reader of *"The Claiming of Sleeping Beauty"* by A. N. Roqulaure, Simon & Schuster.

OTHER SOURCES

Books:

Newsmakers, Issue 1, Gale Group, 2002.

Periodicals:

Interview, August, 1998, pp. 118–19.
People Weekly, January 31, 2000, p. 59.

BRENNER, David 1945–

PERSONAL

Born February 4, 1945, in Philadelphia, PA; son of Louis Yehuda (a vaudeville singer, dancer, and comedian) and Estelle Anne (maiden name, Rosenfeld) Brenner; married and divorced twice; married Elizabeth Slater, February 19, 2000; children: Cole Jay, Slade Lucas Moby, Wyatt Destry Slater. *Education:* Temple University, B.S. (with honors), mass communications. *Religion:* Jewish.

Addresses: *Agent*—Innovative Artists, 1505 10th St., Santa Monica, CA 90401.

Career: Comedian, nightclub performer, and actor. Appeared in concert halls, colleges, and nightclubs, since August, 1969; worked as producer for WBBM–TV, Chicago, IL; WRCV and KYW–TV, both Philadelphia, PA; and WNEW–TV and PBL–TV, both New York City. Also producer, director, and writer for television documentaries; appeared in television commercials. Owner of Amsterdam Billiard Clubs, New York City. *Military service:* U.S. Army, served during early 1960s, became corporal.

Awards, Honors: Artist Comedian of the Year, American Guild of Variety Actors, 1976; Las Vegas Entertainer of the Week Award, 1977; Atlantic City Comedian of the Year, 1984; College Campus Entertainer/Comedian of the Year, 1984.

CREDITS

Film Appearances:

Himself and host, *Casino Gambling,* 1983.
Catch a Rising Star's 10th Anniversary Show, Columbia/TriStar, 1983.
Young at Heart Comedians, Paramount Home Video, 1988.
Celebrity auctioneer, *Worth Winning,* Twentieth Century–Fox, 1989.
Goodnight, We Love You (documentary), 2004.
Himself, *The Aristocrats* (documentary; also known as *The @r!$t*(r@t$),* 2005.

Television Appearances; Series:

Host, *Nightlife,* syndicated, 1986–87.

Television Appearances; Movies:

Himself, *Ebony, Ivory, and Jade,* CBS, 1979.

Television Appearances; Specials:

Neil Sedaka Steppin' Out, NBC, 1976.
American Bandstand's 25th Anniversary, 1977.
Happy Birthday, Las Vegas, 1977.
Ebony, Ivory and Jade, 1979.
Catch a Rising Star's 10th Anniversary, 1982.
Steve Martin's The Winds of Whoopie, NBC, 1983.
Joan Rivers and Friends Salute Heidi Abromowitz, 1985.
Night Life with David Brenner, 1987.
The Howard Stern Show, 1987.
I Ask for Wonder: Experiencing God, ABC, 1988.
But Seriously '94, Showtime, 1995.
Freddie Prinze: The E! True Hollywood Story, E! Entertainment Television, 1998.
Andy Kaufman: The E! True Hollywood Story, E! Entertainment Television, 1998.
David Brenner: Back with a Vengeance, HBO, 2000.
Ali–Frazier: One Nation ... Indivisible, HBO, 2000.
Totally Outrageous—Love, ABC, 2001.
The Great American History Quiz, History Channel, 2001.
The 35th Annual Victor Awards, Fox Sports Network, 2001.
When Stand–Up Comics Ruled the World, VH1, 2004.
Comedy Central Presents: 100 Greatest Stand–Ups of All Time (also known as *100 Greatest Stand–Ups of All Time*), Comedy Central, 2004.
50 Hottest Vegas Moments, E! Entertainment Television, 2005.
Performer, *TMF Awards 2009,* 2009.

Also appeared as himself, *Intimate Portrait: Joan Rivers,* Lifetime.

Television Appearances; Pilots:
Balderdash, syndicated, 1993.
Ask Rita, syndicated, 2003.

Television Appearances; Episodic:
(Television debut) *The Tonight Show Starring Johnny Carson* (also known as *The Tonight Show*), NBC, 1971–84.
The Ed Sullivan Show (also known as *Toast of the Town*), 1971.
The Virginia Graham Show, 1971.
The David Frost Show, syndicated, 1971.
The Midnight Special, 1973–77.
The Dean Martin Comedy World, 1974.
Celebrity Sweepstakes, 1974.
The Merv Griffin Show, 1974.
The Mike Douglas Show, syndicated, 1975, 1977, 1979.
The Hollywood Squares, NBC and syndicated, multiple appearance, 1975–80.
Dinah!, 1978.
Just Men!, 1983.
Nightlife, syndicated, 1987.
Live! Dick Clark Presents, CBS, 1988.
Center Square, *The New Hollywood Squares,* 1988.
Esquire: About Men, for Women, 1989.
The Howard Stern Show (also known as *The Howard Stern Summer Show*), 1990.
The Late Show with David Letterman, CBS, multiple appearances, 1991–2002.
Late Night with David Letterman (also known as *The Late Show* and *Letterman*), NBC, 1993, 1994, 1996, 1997.
Late Night with Conan O'Brien, NBC, 1994, 1995, 1998, 1999.
Howard Stern, E! Entertainment Television, 1995, 1998, 2001, 2005.
The Rosie O'Donnell Show, syndicated, 1996.
The Daily Show with Jon Stewart (also known as *The Daily Show, A Daily Show with Jon Stewart,* and *The Daily Show with Jon Stewart Global Edition*), Comedy Central, 1998, 1999.
Himself, "As Others See Us," *Arli$$,* HBO, 2001.
The Howard Stern Radio Show, 2001.
Hollywood Squares (also known as *H2* and *H2: Hollywood Squares*), syndicated, 2001, 2003.
Pyramid (also known as *The $100,000 Pyramid*), 2002.
The View, ABC, 2002.
The Michael Essany Show, E! Entertainment Television, 2003.
Judge, *Pet Star,* Animal Planet, 2003.
Good Day Live, syndicated, 2005.
Extra (also known as *Extra: The Entertainment Magazine*), syndicated, 2005.
Just for Laughs (also known as *Ed Byrne's "Just for Laughs," Just for Laughs Comedy Festival,* and *Just for Laughs Montreal Comedy Festival*), 2005.
The Tonight Show with Jay Leno, NBC, 2005.

Himself, "Turn a Poker Dud into a Five Card Stud: Ed M," *Queer Eye* (also known as *Queer Eye for the Straight Guy*), 2006.
"Top 10 TV Dynamic Duos," *TV Land's Top Ten,* TV Land, 2006.
"Top 10 TV Spinoffs," *TV Land's Top Ten,* TV Land, 2006.
"Top 10 Musical Moments," *TV Land's Top Ten,* TV Land, 2006.
Comics Unleashed, 2006, 2009.
Tavis Smiley, PBS, 2009.
"My Funky Valentine," *Modern Family,* ABC, 2010.

Also appeared in *Dinah's Place,* NBC; *The Late Late Show with Tom Snyder,* CBS; *Politically Incorrect,* Comedy Central and ABC; *The Test,* FX Network; *Comics Only,* CTV and Comedy Central; *Alan King: Inside the Comedy Mind,* Comedy Central; *Ask Rita,* syndicated.

Television Producer; Specials:
David Brenner: Back with a Vengeance, HBO, 2000.

Stage Appearances:
The Laughs and Times of David Brenner (one–man show), Criterion Theatre, New York City, 1990.

Made stage debut, *Pips,* Sheepshead Bay, Brooklyn, NY.

Radio Appearances:
Hosted syndicated talk show, 1994–96.

RECORDINGS

Videos:
Host of *I Hate to Workout Workout.*

WRITINGS

Television Specials:
David Brenner: Back with a Vengeance, HBO, 2000.

Books:
Soft Pretzels with Mustard, Arbor House, 1983.
Revenge Is the Best Exercise, Arbor House, 1985.
Nobody Sees You Eat Tuna Fish, Arbor House, 1985.
If God Wanted Us to Travel ..., Pocket Books, 1990.
I Think There's a Terrorist in My Soup: How to Survive Personal and World Problems with Laughter—Seriously, 2003.

OTHER SOURCES

Books:
Broadcasting & Cable, May 13, 1996, p. 17.
Contemporary Authors, Volume 133, Gale, 1991.

Periodicals:
USA Today, February 20, 2009, p. 1D.

Electronic:
David Brenner Official Site, http://www. davidbrennersite.com, September 15, 2010.

BROWN, Arvin 1940–

PERSONAL

Full name, Arvin Bragin Brown; born May 24, 1940, in Los Angeles, CA; son of Herman S. and Annette R. (maiden name, Edelman) Brown; married Joyce Ebert (an actress), November 2, 1969 (died, 1997). *Education:* Stanford University, B.A., 1961; University of Bristol, certificate in drama (Fulbright scholar), 1962; Harvard University, M.A., 1963; postgraduate work, Yale School of Drama, Yale University, 1963–65.

Addresses: *Agent*—Paradigm, 360 North Crescent Dr., North Bldg., Beverly Hills, CA 90210. *Manager*—Andrea Simon Entertainment, 4230 Woodman Ave., Sherman Oaks, CA 91423.

Career: Director and producer. Long Wharf Theatre, New Haven, CT, supervisor of apprentice program, 1965, director of Children's Theatre, 1965–67, artistic director, 1967–97; Williamstown Theatre Festival, Williamstown, MA, associate director, 1969; Salzburg Seminar, Salzburg, Austria, lecturer on directing, 1972; International Theatre Conference, Bulgaria, Hungary, delegate, 1979; guest lecturer, New Play Center, Vancouver, British Columbia, Canada, 1980, and University of Illinois at Urbana, 1980, 1982.

Member: Theatre Communications Group (codirector, 1972–1976), National Endowment for the Arts (Theatre Advisory Panel), International Theatre Institute, Society of Stage Directors and Choreographers, Directors Guild.

Awards, Honors: Vernon Rice Award, best off–Broadway director, 1971, for *Long Day's Journey into Night; Variety* Critics' Poll Award, best off–Broadway director, 1971; Antoinette Perry Award nomination, best director of a play, 1975, for *The National Health;* Antoinette Perry Award nominations, best reproduction, 1983, for *A View from the Bridge;* Boston Theatre Critics Award, and Antoinette Perry Award nomination, best reproduction, 1984, for *American Buffalo;* Antoinette Perry Award, best reproduction, 1985, and Drama Desk Award, 1986, both for *Joe Egg;* Antoinette Perry

Award, best reproduction, 1987, for *All My Sons;* George Abbott Lifetime Achievement Award, 1992; O'Neill's People Award, 1995; honorary degrees from University of New Haven, 1976, University of Bridgeport, 1978, Fairfield University, 1985, and Albertus Magnus, 1993.

CREDITS

Stage Director:
Long Day's Journey into Night, Long Wharf Theatre, New Haven, CT, 1966.
Misalliance, Long Wharf Theatre, 1967.
The Glass Menagerie, Long Wharf Theatre, 1967.
The Rehearsal, Long Wharf Theatre, 1967.
The Indian Wants the Bronx, London, 1967.
A Whistle in the Dark, Long Wharf Theatre, 1968.
Don Juan in Hell, Long Wharf Theatre, 1968.
The Lion in Winter, Long Wharf Theatre, 1968.
A Whistle in the Dark, Mercury Theatre, New York City, 1969.
The Indian Wants the Bronx and *It's Called Sugar Plum* (double–bill), Long Wharf Theatre, 1969.
Ghosts, Long Wharf Theatre, 1969.
Tango, Long Wharf Theatre, 1969.
Hay Fever, Helen Hayes Theatre, New York City, 1970.
Country People, Long Wharf Theatre, 1970.
Spoon River Anthology, Long Wharf Theatre, 1970.
Yegor Bulichov, Long Wharf Theatre, 1970.
Long Day's Journey into Night, Promenade Theatre, New York City, 1971.
You Can't Take It with You, Long Wharf Theatre, 1971.
The Contractor, Long Wharf Theatre, 1971.
Solitaire/Double Solitaire, Long Wharf Theatre, 1971, then John Golden Theatre, New York City, 1971.
Hamlet, Long Wharf Theatre, 1972.
The Iceman Cometh, Long Wharf Theatre, 1972.
What Price Glory?, Long Wharf Theatre, 1972.
The Changing Room, Long Wharf Theatre, 1972.
"A Swan Song" in *Troika,* Long Wharf Theatre, 1972.
Juno and the Paycock, Long Wharf Theatre, 1973.
The Widowing of Mrs. Holroyd, Long Wharf Theatre, 1973.
Forget–Me–Not Lane, Long Wharf Theatre, 1973, then Center Theatre Group, Mark Taper Forum, Los Angeles, 1973.
The Seagull, Long Wharf Theatre, 1974.
The National Health, Long Wharf Theatre, 1974, then Circle in the Square, New York City, 1974.
Saint Joan, Ahmanson Theatre, Los Angeles, 1974.
Juno and the Paycock, Williamstown Theatre Festival, Williamstown, MA, 1974.
Ah, Wilderness!, Long Wharf Theatre, 1974, then Circle in the Square, 1975.
Artichoke, Long Wharf Theatre, 1975.
The Archbishop's Ceiling, Kennedy Center for the Performing Arts, Washington, DC, 1976–77.
Privates on Parade, Long Wharf Theatre, 1978.

I Sent a Letter to My Love, Long Wharf Theatre, 1978.

Mary Barnes, Long Wharf Theatre, 1979.

Who's Afraid of Virginia Woolf?, Long Wharf Theatre, 1979.

Strangers, John Golden Theatre, New York City, 1979.

Watch on the Rhine, Long Wharf Theatre, 1979, then John Golden Theatre, 1980.

American Buffalo, Long Wharf Theatre, 1980, then Circle in the Square Downtown, New York City, 1981–82, later Booth Theatre, New York City, 1983–84.

Open Admissions, Long Wharf Theatre, 1982.

The Cherry Orchard, Long Wharf Theatre, 1982.

Free and Clear, Long Wharf Theatre, 1982.

A View from the Bridge, Long Wharf Theatre, 1982, then Ambassador Theatre, New York City, 1983.

Tobacco Road, Long Wharf Theatre, 1984.

Albert Herring, Long Wharf Theatre, 1984.

Requiem for a Heavyweight, Long Wharf Theatre, 1984, then Martin Beck Theatre, New York City, 1985.

Joe Egg (also known as *A Day in the Death of Joe Egg*), Roundabout Theatre, New York City, 1984–85, then Longacre Theatre, New York City, 1985.

The Normal Heart, Long Wharf Theatre, 1985.

All My Sons, Long Wharf Theatre, 1986, then John Golden Theatre, 1987.

Self Defense, Long Wharf Theatre, 1987, then Joyce Theatre, New York City, 1987.

Our Town, Long Wharf Theatre, 1987.

Ah, Wilderness!, Yale Repertory Theatre, New Haven, CT, 1988, then Neil Simon Theatre, New York City, 1988.

The Crucible, Long Wharf Theatre, 1989.

Stage II Workshops: Established Price, Long Wharf Theatre, 1990.

The Voysey Inheritance, Long Wharf Theatre, 1990.

Picnic, Long Wharf Theatre, 1990.

Booth Is Back, Long Wharf Theatre, 1991.

A Touch of the Poet, Long Wharf Theatre, 1991.

Chinese Coffee, Circle in the Square Uptown, New York City, 1992.

Private Lives, Broadhurst Theatre, New York City, 1992.

A Month in the Country, Long Wharf Theatre, 1992.

The Twilight of the Golds, Booth Theatre, New York City, 1993.

Absurd Person Singular, Long Wharf Theatre, 1993.

Misalliance, Long Wharf Theatre, 1994.

Saturday, Sunday, Monday, Long Wharf Theatre, 1994.

The Entertainer, Long Wharf Theatre, 1995.

Denial, Long Wharf Theatre, 1995.

A Song at Twilight, Long Wharf Theatre, 1996.

Also directed *The Stronger,* University of Bristol, Bristol, England; and *A Memory of Two Mondays.*

Stage Director; Operas:

Albert Herring, Long Wharf Theatre, New Haven, CT, 1985.

Turandot, Connecticut Grand Opera, 1986.

The Tender Land, Long Wharf Theatre, 1987.

Don Giovanni, Virginia Opera, 1987.

Regina, Long Wharf Theatre, 1988.

Anna Bolena, Virginia Opera, 1989.

Cosi fan tutte, Virginia Opera, 1991.

Porgy and Bess, Metropolitan Opera, 1992.

The Crucible, Tulsa Opera, 1995.

Film Director:

Diary of the Dead, 1980.

Declaration of Independence, 2003.

Television Co–executive Producer; Series:

Hawthorne (also known as *HawthoRNe*), TNT, 2009.

Television Director; Movies:

Amahl and the Night Visitors, 1978.

A Change of Heart (also known as *Promises & Lies*), Lifetime, 1998.

Brookfield, 1999.

The Inspector General, 2000.

Just Ask My Children, Lifetime, 2001.

Open House, CBS, 2003.

Too Many Lovers, 2003.

Blessings, CBS, 2003.

Television Director; Specials:

Close Ties, E! Entertainment Television, 1983.

The Gin Game, PBS, 2003.

Television Director; Pilots:

Kevin Hill, UPN, 2004.

Television Director; Episodic:

"The Widowing of Mrs. Holroyd," *Theatre in America,* PBS, 1974.

"Forget–Me–Not Lane," *Great Performances,* PBS, 1975.

"Ah, Wilderness!," *Great Performances,* PBS, 1976.

"Changing of the Guard," *Picket Fences,* CBS, 1995.

"The Parent Rap," *Chicago Hope,* CBS, 1996.

"My Romance," *Picket Fences,* CBS, 1996.

"The Z Files," *Picket Fences,* CBS, 1996.

"Jealousy," *Relativity,* 1996.

Moloney, CBS, 1996.

Party of Five, Fox, 1997.

Nothing Sacred, ABC, 1997.

413 Hope Street, Fox, 1997.

"World's without Love," *Ally McBeal* (also known as *Ally My Love*), Fox, 1998.

"Driveway to Heaven," *To Have & to Hold,* CBS, 1998.

"Another Day," *The Practice,* ABC, 1998.

"Love and Honor," *The Practice,* ABC, 1998.

"Beauty Contest," *Dawson's Creek,* The WB, 1998.

"Free Dental," *The Practice,* ABC, 1999.

"Committed," *The Practice,* ABC, 1999.

"Music from My Life," *Any Day Now,* Lifetime, 1999.

"Higher Calling," *Snoops,* ABC, 1999.

"285 South: Part 1," *Roswell* (also known as *Roswell High*), The WB, 1999.

"Settling," *The Practice,* ABC, 2000.

"Summary Judgments," *The Practice,* ABC, 2000.

"Brothers' Keepers," *The Practice,* ABC, 2000.

"Learner's Permit," *Once and Again,* ABC, 2000.

"Ex, Lies and Videotape," *Popular,* The WB, 2000.

"In Search of Pygmies," *Ally McBeal* (also known as *Ally My Love*), Fox, 2000.

Kate Brasher, CBS, 2000.

"Vanished: Part 1," *The Practice,* ABC, 2001.

"The Claw Is Our Master," *Judging Amy,* CBS, 2001.

"Neutral Corners," *Ally McBeal* (also known as *Ally My Love*), Fox, 2001.

"Loyalties," *The Guardian* (also known as *Ochita bengoshi Nick Fallin*), CBS, 2001.

"God's Work," *The Agency* (also known as *CIA: The Agency*), CBS, 2001.

"Viva Fidel," *The Agency* (also known as *CIA: The Agency*), CBS, 2001.

"Nice Guys Finish Last," *Ed* (also known as *Stuckeyville*), NBC, 2002.

"Sleeping Dogs Lie," *The Agency* (also known as *CIA: The Agency*), CBS, 2002.

"Blood Relatives," *Crossing Jordan,* NBC, 2002.

"The Gift of Life," *Crossing Jordan,* NBC, 2002.

"Scared Straight," *Crossing Jordan,* NBC, 2002.

"Fire and Ice," *Crossing Jordan,* NBC, 2003.

"The Making of a Trial Attorney," *The Practice,* ABC, 2003.

"The Love Bandit," *Miss Match,* NBC, 2003.

The Brotherhood of Poland, New Hampshire, CBS, 2003.

"Homework," *Kevin Hill,* UPN, 2004.

"Snack Daddy," *Kevin Hill,* UPN, 2004.

"Losing Isn't Everything," *Kevin Hill,* UPN, 2004.

"Last Looks," *Everwood,* The WB, 2004.

"Complex Guilt," *Everwood,* The WB, 2005.

"A Kiss to Build a Dream On," *Everwood,* The WB, 2005.

"Free Fall," *Everwood,* The WB, 2005.

"Querida Grace," *Jack & Bobby,* The WB, 2005.

"Hang In There, Baby," *Related,* The WB, 2005.

"Batter Up," *The Closer,* TNT, 2005.

"Aftertaste," *The Closer,* TNT, 2006.

"Serving the King: Part 1," *The Closer,* TNT, 2006.

"You're a Good Man, Andy Brown," *Everwood,* The WB, 2006.

"Secrets and Lies," *Saved,* TNT, 2006.

"Fashion Police," *Shark,* CBS, 2006.

"New York Fashion: Part 1," *Men in Trees,* ABC, 2006.

"Superstar Treatment," *My Boys,* TBS, 2006.

"Wedding from Hell," *The Wedding Bells,* Fox, 2007.

"Between Here and There," *State of Mind,* Lifetime, 2007.

"Helpy Helperpants," *State of Mind,* Lifetime, 2007.

"In Which Addison Has a Very Casual Get Together," *Private Practice,* ABC, 2007.

"Grave Doubts," *The Closer,* TNT, 2007.

"Four to Eight," *The Closer,* TNT, 2007.

"Corporal Punishment," *NCIS: Naval Criminal Investigative Service* (also known as *Navy NCIS: Naval Criminal Investigative Service* and *NCIS*), CBS, 2007.

"Murder 2.0," *NCIS: Naval Criminal Investigative Service* (also known as *Navy NCIS: Naval Criminal Investigative Service* and *NCIS*), CBS, 2008.

"Speed Bump," *The Closer,* TNT, 2008.

"Dial M for Provenza," *The Closer,* TNT, 2008.

"The Miracle Job," *Leverage,* TNT, 2008.

"The Best Policy," *Lie to Me,* Fox, 2009.

"Healing Time," *Hawthorne* (also known as *HawthoRNe*), TNT, 2009.

"Bounce," *NCIS: Naval Criminal Investigative Service* (also known as *Navy NCIS: Naval Criminal Investigative Service* and *NCIS*), CBS, 2009.

"Faith," *NCIS: Naval Criminal Investigative Service* (also known as *Navy NCIS: Naval Criminal Investigative Service* and *NCIS*), CBS, 2009.

"She Works Hard for the Money," *Rizzoli & Isles,* TNT, 2010.

"The Rashomon Job," *Leverage,* TNT, 2010.

"Flesh and Blood," *NCIS: Naval Criminal Investigative Service* (also known as *Navy NCIS: Naval Criminal Investigative Service* and *NCIS*), CBS, 2010.

"Royals & Loyals," *NCIS: Naval Criminal Investigative Service* (also known as *Navy NCIS: Naval Criminal Investigative Service* and *NCIS*), CBS, 2010.

Also directed *Second Noah,* ABC.

OTHER SOURCES

Periodicals:

American Theatre, July, 2001.

BROWN, Garrett M.
(Garrett Brown)

PERSONAL

Divorced; children: one daughter.

Addresses: *Agent*—Accent Talent, 37 East 28th St., Suite 500, New York, NY 10016.

Career: Actor, writer, and director. Ensemble Studio Theatre, New York City, member of company, also artistic director of Los Angeles Project, 1998–99. Voice performer for commercials.

CREDITS

Film Appearances:

(As Garrett Brown) Actor Zelig, *Zelig,* Orion/Warner Bros., 1983.

Mr. Kaiser, *Lucas,* Twentieth Century–Fox, 1986.

Bob Russell, *Uncle Buck,* Universal, 1989.

(As Garrett Brown) Manager of LAX, *Turbulence,* Metro–Goldwyn–Mayer, 1997.

Webb Crosby, *Inventing the Abbotts,* Twentieth Century–Fox, 1997.

William McPhie, *No More Baths,* Feature Films for Families, 1998.

Mr. Williams, *The Sky Is Falling,* Showcase Entertainment, 2000.

The Priests (short film), 2000.

Henry Ramaska, *Bobby's Whore* (short film), 2000.

Father, *A.N.I. 1240* (short film), Hypnotic Films, 2003.

Ameribanx bank manager, *Fun with Dick and Jane* (also known as *Alternative Career* and *Fun with Dick & Jane*), Columbia, 2005.

Coach Finley, *Gridiron Gang,* Columbia, 2006.

Dr. Felder, *Arc,* 2006.

Gerald Golski, *Kiss the Bride,* Regent Releasing, 2007.

Apothecary, *Tocatta & Fugue,* Lavit Sef Productions, 2007.

Father, *Catalyst* (short film), 2009.

Mr. Drexler, *The Farm* (short film), 2009.

Mr. Lizewski, *Kick–Ass,* Lions Gate Films, 2010.

Television Appearances; Series:

Taylor Brown, *What a Country,* syndicated, 1986–87.

John Whitsig, *Sisters,* NBC, 1991–96.

Philip Evans, *Roswell* (also known as *Roswell High*), The WB, 2000–2001, UPN, 2001–2002.

Bishop Devery, *Big Love,* HBO, 2007–2009.

Television Appearances; Movies:

George Dooley, *The Dooley Brothers,* 1979.

Gordon, *Apology,* HBO, 1986.

Bob Shields, *Jenny's Song,* syndicated, 1988.

Roger Townsend, *The Care and Handling of Roses,* CBS, 1996.

Dana Pillsbury, *Can of Worms,* The Disney Channel, 1999.

George Walker, *Taking Back Our Town,* Lifetime, 2001.

Supernova, Hallmark Channel, 2005.

Chief Watts, *McBride: Requiem,* Hallmark Channel, 2006.

Television Appearances; Specials:

John Henderson, "The Almost Royal Family," *ABC Afterschool Special,* ABC, 1984.

Television Appearances; Episodic:

Himself, *Vicki!,* 1993.

Richard Manzak, "Caulksmanship," *NYPD Blue* (also known as *N.Y.P.D.*), ABC, 1996.

Jerry Fleiss, "Quentin Gets His Gun," *Grace under Fire,* ABC, 1997.

Jerry Fleiss, "Sam's Dad," *Grace under Fire,* ABC, 1997.

Doug Forsythe, "First Degree," *The Practice,* ABC, 1997.

Doug Forsythe, "Sex, Lies, and Monkeys," *The Practice,* ABC, 1997.

Nell, "Do Something," *7th Heaven* (also known as *7th Heaven: Beginnings*), The WB, 1997.

Inspector, "Dublin or Nothin'," *Brooklyn South,* CBS, 1997.

Officer Peter Ridley, "Hysteria," *Law & Order: Special Victims Unit* (also known as *Law & Order: SVU* and *Special Victims Unit*), NBC, 1999.

Harvey Sederberg, "Boys Will Be Girls," *Chicago Hope,* CBS, 2000.

Hyram Scott, "At Poverty Level," *Pensacola: Wings of Gold,* syndicated, 2000.

Mr. Kantor, "It's Not Just a Word," *Any Day Now,* Lifetime, 2001.

Mr. Johnson, "The Treachery of Compromise," *Judging Amy,* CBS, 2001.

Mr. Rycoff, "Chaos Theory," *CSI: Crime Scene Investigation* (also known as *C.S.I.* and *CSI: Las Vegas*), CBS, 2001.

Coach Harris, "Lies of Minelli," *Philly,* ABC, 2002.

Karl, "Heartbeat," *Strong Medicine,* Lifetime, 2002.

Father Bill Egan, "Chapter Fifty–one," *Boston Public,* Fox, 2002.

Father Bill Egan, "Chapter Fifty–two," *Boston Public,* Fox, 2002.

Nina's dad, "Bring It On Home," *That '70s Show,* 2003.

Roger, "The Boy in the Box," *Cold Case,* CBS, 2004.

Walter Shepley, "Adjourned (a.k.a. Cheers)," *The Practice,* ABC, 2004.

Frank Walker, "Hurt," *The Shield,* FX Network, 2005.

Dr. Kenneth Woodruff, "The Dearly Beloved," *The O.C.,* Fox, 2005.

Dr. Kenneth Woodruff, "The Aftermath," *The O.C.,* Fox, 2005.

Doug Melville, "Big Client," *Courting Alex,* CBS, 2006.

(As Garrett Brown) Hank Carlson, "The Places You'll Go," *Heartland,* TNT, 2007.

Dr. Frank, "The 12–Step Job," *Leverage,* TNT, 2009.

Stage Appearances:

Chester Underwood, *Whoopee!* (musical), American National Theatre and Academy Playhouse, New York City, 1979.

And Still the Dogs, Los Angeles Project, Ensemble Studio Theatre, Lillian Theatre, Los Angeles, 2002.

Robert McNamara, *Bright Boy: The Passion of Robert McNamara,* Electric Lodge, Venice, CA, 2006.

Stage Director:

"Ambulance Men," *Octoberfest 2002,* Ensemble Studio Theatre, New York City, 2002.

 SIMMS LIBRARY ALBUQUERQUE ACADEMY

WRITINGS

Stage Plays:
Home by Dusk, produced at Los Angeles Project, Ensemble Studio Theatre, Los Angeles, 2000–2001.
"Ambulance Men," *Octoberfest 2002,* produced at Ensemble Studio Theatre, New York City, 2002.

BRYANT, Joy 1976–

PERSONAL

Born October 19, 1976, in The Bronx, New York, NY; married Dave Pope (an actor), June 28, 2008. *Education:* Attended Yale University.

Addresses: *Agent*—Creative Artists Agency, 2000 Avenue of the Stars, Los Angeles, CA 90067. *Manager*—Untitled Entertainment, 1801 Century Park East, Suite 700, Los Angeles, CA 90067.

Career: Actress. Former model for Tommy Hilfiger.

Awards, Honors: Black Reel Award nomination, theatrical—best supporting actress, 2003, for *Antwone Fisher;* Young Hollywood Award, breakthrough performance—female, 2003; Black Reel Award nomination, best supporting actress, 2005, for *Gettin' the Man's Foot Outta Your Baadasssss!;* Screen Actors Guild Award (with others), ensemble of the year, 2006, Screen Actors Guild Award nomination (with others), outstanding performance by a cast in a motion picture, 2007, for *Bobby.*

CREDITS

Film Appearances:
Shane's mother, *Kite,* Execute Entertainment, 2002.
Lexi, *Showtime,* Warner Bros., 2002.
Cheryl Smolley, *Antwone Fisher,* Twentieth Century–Fox, 2002.
Priscilla, *Gettin' the Man's Foot Outta Your Baadasssss!,* Imagine Entertainment, 2003.
Gina, *Honey,* Universal, 2003.
Rita Caswell, *Three Way* (also known as *3–Way*), Columbia TriStar, 2004.
Woman at web, *Spider–Man 2* (also known as *Spider–Man 2.1* and *Spider–Man 2: The IMAX Experience*), Sony, 2004.
Sheila, *Haven,* Manga Films, 2004.
Asia, *Rhythm City Volume One: Caught Up,* BMG Distributing, 2005.
Jill, *The Skeleton Key,* Universal, 2005.
Mallory, *London,* Samuel Goldwyn, 2005.

Charlene, *Get Rich or Die Tryin',* Paramount, 2005.
Patricia, *Bobby,* Metro–Goldwyn–Mayer, 2006.
Duck's girlfriend, *The Hunting Party,* Metro–Goldwyn–Mayer, 2007.
Bianca Kittles, *Welcome Home, Roscoe Jenkins* (also known as *Meet the Jenkins*), Universal, 2008.
The Ballot or the Bullet (documentary), 2009.

Film Work:
Coproducer, *Leslie,* Global Universal Film Group, 2011.

Television Appearances; Series:
Jasmine Trussel, *Parenthood,* NBC, 2010—.

Television Appearances; Episodic:
"Antwone Fisher," *HBO First Look,* HBO, 2003.
Valeria Gallant, "Missing," *ER,* NBC, 2003.
Valeria Gallant, "Makemba," *ER,* NBC, 2003.
Valeria Gallant, "Touch & Go," *ER,* NBC, 2004.
HypaSpace (also known as *HypaSpace Daily* and *HypaSpace Weekly*), SPACE, 2005.
Late Night with Conan O'Brien, NBC, 2005.
The View, ABC, 2005.
Film '72, BBC, 2006.
Up Close with Carrie Keagan, 2008.
(Uncredited) "Preview Special," *The Rachel Zoe Project,* Bravo, 2008.
"Fashion Makes the Star Makes the Fashion," *The Rachel Zoe Project,* Bravo, 2008.
"Fashion Week to Die!," *The Rachel Zoe Project,* Bravo, 2008.
"Parenthood," *Infanity,* TV Guide, 2010.

Television Appearances; Movies:
Nikki, *Carmen: A Hip Hopera,* MTV, 2001.

Television Appearances; Specials:
The Making of "Antwone Fisher" (documentary), 2001.
Making the Movie: MTV's Hip Hop Opera: Carmen, MTV, 2001.
VH1 Hip Hop Honors 2008, VH1, 2008.
Host, *Rip the Runway,* Black Entertainment Television, 2009.

Television Appearances; Pilots:
Alice Thibadeau, *Virtuality,* Fox, 2009.

RECORDINGS

Videos:
The Story Behind Baadasssss!: The Birth of Black Cinema, Columbia TriStar, 2004.
Making of "Rhythm City Volume One: Caught Up," Ush Entertainment, 2005.

A Portrait of an Artist: The Making of "Get Rich or Die Tryin," Paramount, 2006.

"London": Behind the Scenes, Sony, 2006.

BURTON, Kate 1957–

PERSONAL

Full name, Katherine Burton; born September 10, 1957, in Geneva, Switzerland; daughter of Richard (an actor) and Sybil (a producer; maiden name, Williams) Burton; married Michael Ritchie (a stage director), 1984; children: Morgan, Charlotte. *Education:* Brown University, B.A., 1979; Yale University, M.F.A., 1982. *Politics:* Democrat.

Addresses: *Agent*—The Gersh Agency, 232 North Canon Dr., Beverly Hills, CA 90210. *Manager*—Principal Entertainment, 130 West 42nd St., New York, NY 10036.

Career: Actress. Tony Administration Committee, member.

Awards, Honors: *Theatre World* Award, 1983, for *Present Laughter, Alice in Wonderland,* and *Winners;* Daytime Emmy Award, outstanding performer in a children's special, 1996, for *Notes for My Daughter;* Joe. A. Callaway Award, Actors' Equity Foundation, 2001, Antoinette Perry Award nomination, best actress in a play, 2002, Outer Critics Circle Award nomination, all for *Hedda Gabler;* Antoinette Perry Award nomination, best featured actress in a play, 2002, for *The Elephant Man;* Emmy Award nomination, outstanding guest actress in a drama series, 2006, 2007, for *Grey's Anatomy.*

CREDITS

Film Appearances:

(Uncredited) Serving maid, *Anne of the Thousand Days* (also known as *Anne of a Thousand Days*), Universal, 1969.

Joan "J. J." Caucus, Jr., *Doonesbury: A Broadway Musical* (also known as *Doonesbury: A Musical Comedy* and *Doonesbury: A New Musical*), 1983.

Margo Litzenberger, *Big Trouble in Little China* (also known as *John Carpenter's "Big Trouble in Little China"*), Twentieth Century–Fox, 1986.

Mrs. Burns, *Life with Mikey* (also known as *Give Me a Break*), Buena Vista, 1993.

Helen Blathwaite, *August,* Samuel Goldwyn Company, 1996.

Woman in bed, *The First Wives Club,* Paramount, 1996.

Looking for Richard (documentary), Twentieth Century–Fox, 1996.

Dorothy Franklin, *The Ice Storm,* Fox Searchlight Pictures, 1997.

Cheryl, *Celebrity,* Miramax, 1998.

Rest home sister, *The Opportunists,* First Look Pictures Releasing, 2000.

Tracy, *Unfaithful* (also known as *Infidele* and *Untreu*), Twentieth Century–Fox, 2002.

Carla Cronin, *Swimfan* (also known as *Swimf@n* and *Tell Me You Love Me*), Twentieth Century–Fox, 2002.

Martha, *The Paper Mache Chase* (short film), 2003.

Sherry Baby, 2004.

Stay, Twentieth Century–Fox, 2005.

Marcia, *Some Kind of Heaven,* 2005.

Voice of Night, *The Story of a Mother,* 2006.

Helen, *Lovely by Surprise,* Filmfrgo Productions, 2007.

Doctor Randall, *What Just Happened* (also known as *What Just Happened?*), Magnolia Pictures, 2008.

Merilee, *Quid Pro Quo,* Magnolia Pictures, 2008.

Nicole Horne, *Max Payne,* Twentieth Century–Fox, 2008.

Alice Spooner, *Spooner,* Crispy Films, 2009.

Aunt Birdy, *The Kings of Appletown,* Oak Films, 2009.

Janine, *Remember Me,* Summit Entertainment, 2010.

Susan, *Consent,* Lili Pad Films, 2010.

Mrs. Ralston, *127 Hours,* Fox Searchlight, 2010.

The City of Your Final Destination, Ivory Productions, 2010.

Caris' Peace, GR Films, 2010.

Television Appearances; Series:

Anne Kramer, *Home Fires,* NBC, 1992.

Fran Richardson, *Monty,* Fox, 1994.

Dr. Renee Peters, *All My Children* (also known as *AMC*), ABC, 1994.

Assistant district attorney Susan Alexander, *The Practice,* ABC, 1997–2004.

Rose, *Rescue Me,* FX Network, 2005–2006.

Dr. Ellis Grey, a recurring role, *Grey's Anatomy,* ABC, 2005–2007.

Television Appearances; Miniseries:

Vanessa Ogden, *Ellis Island,* CBS, 1984.

Agatha Bradford, *Evergreen,* NBC, 1985.

Host, *The Hanging Gale,* Bravo, 1999.

Cindy Whiting, *Empire Falls,* HBO, 2005.

Television Appearances; Movies:

Ophelia, *Uncle Tom's Cabin,* Showtime, 1987.

Deborah, *Love Matters,* Showtime, 1993.

Katherine Donohue, *Mistrial,* HBO, 1996.

Sara Miller, *Obsessed,* Lifetime, 2002.

Connie Posey, *The Diary of Ellen Rimbauer,* ABC, 2003.

Television Appearances; Specials:

Alice, "Alice in Wonderland," *Great Performances,* PBS, 1983.

Agnes O'Neill, "Journey into Genius" (also known as "Eugene O'Neill: Journey into Genius"), *American Playhouse,* PBS, 1988.

"Richard Burton: In from the Cold," *Great Performances,* PBS, 1989.

Brenda Gardner, "Notes for My Daughter," *ABC Afterschool Specials,* ABC, 1995.

Voice, "Buckminster Fuller: Thinking Out Loud," *American Masters,* PBS, 1996.

Abigail, "Ellen Foster," *Hallmark Hall of Fame,* CBS, 1997.

Voice, *Blood Money: Switzerland's Nazi Gold* (documentary), Arts and Entertainment, 1997.

Richard Burton: Taylor–Made for Stardom (documentary), Arts and Entertainment, 2002.

Intimate Portrait: Jane Kaczmarek (documentary), Lifetime, 2002.

Narrator, *The Incredible Human Body* (documentary), PBS, 2002.

Intimate Portrait: Elizabeth Taylor (documentary), Lifetime, 2002.

Presenter, *The 56th Annual Tony Awards,* 2002.

Presenter, *The 59th Annual Tony Awards,* CBS, 2005.

Voice of novels, *Ernest Hemingway: Rivers to the Sea,* 2005.

Presenter, *The 63rd Annual Tony Awards,* CBS, 2009.

Television Appearances; Pilots:

Assistant district attorney Susan Alexander, *The Practice,* ABC, 1997.

Joy, *Washintonienne,* HBO, 2009.

Grace Graham, *The Deep End,* ABC, 2010.

Amanda Holt, *Boston's Finest,* ABC, 2010.

Television Appearances; Episodic:

Randy Lofficier, "If You Knew Sammy," *Spenser: For Hire,* ABC, 1987.

Randy Lofficier, "Play It Again, Sammy," *Spenser: For Hire,* ABC, 1988.

"Broadway's Dreamers: The Legacy of the Group Theatre," *American Masters,* 1989.

Sister Bettina, "Sisters of Mercy," *Law & Order,* NBC, 1991.

Susan Lowenberg Jones, "Keeping Up with the Joneses," *Brooklyn Bridge,* CBS, 1993.

Sheila Byrne, "My Brother's Keeper," *100 Centre Street,* Arts and Entertainment, 2001.

Attorney Erica Gardner, "Armed Forces," *Law & Order,* NBC, 2001.

Stephanie Uffland, "The Pardoner's Tale," *Law & Order: Criminal Intent,* NBC, 2001.

The Rosie O'Donnell Show, ABC, 2002.

Charlie Rose (also known as *The Charlie Rose Show*), 2002.

Attorney Erica Gardner, "Darwinian," *Law & Order,* NBC, 2004.

Sarah Brainerd, "Slow News Day," *The West Wing,* NBC, 2004.

Erica Gardner, "Cut," *Law & Order,* NBC, 2004.

Dr. Sheri Jordan, "Silent Era," *Judging Amy,* CBS, 2005.

Anthropologist, "Bones of Contention," *Numb3rs* (also known as *Num3ers*), CBS, 2005.

Sarah Miller, "Death Spiral," *Justice,* Fox, 2006.

"Anthony Hopkins," *Biography,* Arts and Entertainment, 2007.

Bonnie Barrister, "To Have and to Hold," *Medium,* NBC, 2008.

Gepetto/Miranda Cochran, "Pinocchio," *Eleventh Hour,* CBS, 2009.

Erica Gardener, "For the Defense," *Law & Order,* NBC, 2009.

Judge Victoria Adler, "Lifeguard," *The Good Wife,* CBS, 2009.

Judge Victoria Adler, "Cleaning House," *The Good Wife,* CBS, 2010.

Annette Cole, "Bully," *Law & Order: Special Victims Unit* (also known as *Law & Order: SVU*), NBC, 2011.

Stage Appearances:

(New York City debut) Daphne, *Present Laughter,* Circle in the Square, 1982.

Alice, *Alice in Wonderland,* Virginia Theatre, New York City, 1983.

May, *Winners,* Roundabout Theatre, New York City, 1983.

J. J., *Doonesbury,* Biltmore Theatre, New York City, 1983.

Eva, *The Accrington Pals,* Hudson Guild Theatre, New York City, 1984.

Pegeen, *The Playboy of the Western World,* Roundabout Theatre, 1985.

The Plough and the Stars, Roundabout Theatre, 1985.

Alexandra, *On the Verge; or, The Geography of Yearning,* Hartford Stage Company, Hartford, CT, 1985–86.

The Three Sisters, Hartman Theatre, Stamford, CT, 1985–86.

Sasha, *Wild Honey,* Virginia Theatre, 1986–87.

Isabella, *Measure for Measure,* Mitzi E. Newhouse Theatre, New York City, 1989.

Betty McNeil, *Some Americans Abroad,* Vivian Beaumont Theatre, New York City, 1990.

Alice, *Aristocrats,* Huntington Theatre Company, Boston, MA, 1990–91.

Julie, *Jake's Woman,* Neil Simon Theatre, New York City, 1992, then Center Theatre Group, James A. Doolittle Theatre, Los Angeles, 1992–93.

Lauren, Grace, and Annie, *London Suite,* Union Square Theatre, New York City, 1995.

Sarah, *Company,* Criterion Theatre, Center Stage Right, New York City, 1995.

Arcadia, Los Angeles, 1997.

Lyssa Dent Hughes, *An American Daughter,* Cort Theatre, New York City, 1997.

Mrs. Molly Burton, *The Matchmaker,* Adams Memorial Theatre Main Stage, Williamstown, MA, 1998.

Agnes, *Lake Hollywood,* Signature Theatre Company, New York City, 1999.

Daisy Connolly, *Give Me Your Answer, Do!,* Gramercy Theatre, New York City, 1999–2000.

The Beauty Queen of Lenane, Walter Kerr Theatre, New York City, 1999, then Waterford, Ireland, 2000.

Title role, *Hedda Gabler,* Huntington Theatre Company, Boston, MA, 2000–2001, then Ambassador Theatre, New York City, 2001–2002.

Pinhead/Mrs. Kendal, *The Elephant Man,* Royale Theatre, New York City, 2002.

Anna, *Boston Marriage,* Joseph Papp Public Theatre, New York City, 2002.

Three Sisters, Playhouse Theatre, London, 2003.

The Water's Edge, Nikos Stage, Williamstown Theatre Festival, Williamstown, MA, 2004.

Constance Middleton, *The Constant Wife,* American Airlines Theatre, New York City, 2005.

The Rage of Achilles, 92nd Street Y, New York City, 2005.

Kate, *The 24 Hour Plays 2005,* American Airlines Theatre, 2005.

The adult woman, *Spring Awakening,* Eugene O'Neill Theatre, New York City, 2006–2009.

Miss Moffat, *The Corn Is Green,* American Airlines Theatre, 2007.

The Grand Manner, Mitzi E. Newhouse Theatre, 2010.

Also appeared in *Romeo and Juliet,* off–Broadway production.

RECORDINGS

Taped Readings:

Loves Music, Loves to Dance, 1991.

All That Remains by Patricia Cornwell, HarperCollins, 1992.

Crooked Little Heart by Anne Lamott, Random Audio, 1997.

The Triumph of Katie Byrne by Barbara Taylor Bradford, BDD Audio, 2002.

Molly Moon's Incredible Book of Hypnotism by Georgia Byng, Harper Children's Audio, 2003.

Portrait of a Killer: Jack the Ripper by Patricia Cornwell, Putnam Berkley Audio, 2003.

Videos:

RSC Meets USA: Working Shakespeare, 2005.

OTHER SOURCES

Periodicals:

People Weekly, October 15, 2001, p. 139.

Playbill, October 31, 2001, pp. 22, 24.

BURTON, Tim 1958–

PERSONAL

Full name, Timothy William Burton; born August 25, 1958, in Burbank, CA; son of Bill (a minor league baseball player and parks department sports coordinator) and Jean (a shop manager) Burton; married Lena Gieseke (a photographer), February 24, 1989 (divorced, 1991); companion of Lisa Marie (an actress), 1992–2001; companion of Helena Bonham Carter (an actress), 2001—; children: (with Bonham Carter) Billy–Ray, Nell. *Education:* Studied animation at California Institute of the Arts, 1979–80.

Addresses: *Office*—Tim Burton Productions, 8033 Sunset Blvd., Suite 7500, West Hollywood, CA 90046. *Agent*—WME Entertainment, One William Morris Pl., Beverly Hills, CA 90212.

Career: Director, animator, producer, and writer. Walt Disney Productions, cartoon artist and apprentice animator; Tim Burton Productions, founder, 1989. Creator, writer, and director of *Stainboy* (animated Internet series), Shockwave.com, 2000. Director of television commercials, including Hollywood chewing gum, 1998, and Timex watches, 2000. Cannes Film Festival, member of jury, 1997.

Awards, Honors: Walt Disney fellow, California Institute of the Arts, 1979–80; Chicago Film Festival Award, 1982, for *Vincent;* ShoWest Award, director of the year, National Association of Theatre Owners, 1990, for *Batman;* Emmy Award (with others), outstanding animated program, 1990, for *Beetlejuice;* nomination for Golden Palm, Cannes International Film Festival, 1995, and nomination for Silver Condor, best foreign film, Argentinean Film Critics Association, 1996, both for *Ed Wood;* Golden Satellite Award nomination, best animated or mixed media picture, International Press Academy, 1997, for *Mars Attacks!;* Golden Satellite Award nomination (with others), best animated or mixed media motion picture, 1997, for *James and the Giant Peach;* Saturn Award nomination, best director, Academy of Science Fiction, Fantasy, and Horror Films, and nomination for Silver Ribbon, best director of a foreign film, Italian National Syndicate of Film Journalists, both 2000, for *Sleepy Hollow;* Video Premiere Award nomination, best internet video premiere, 2001, for *The World of Stainboy;* Leo Award (with others), best writing in a music, comedy, or variety program or series, Motion Picture Arts and Sciences Foundation of British Columbia, 2002, for *Point Blank;* Chicago Film Critics Association Award nomination, best director, Critics Choice Award nomination, best director, Broadcast Film Critics Association, David di Donatello Award nomination, best foreign film, David Lean Award for Direction nomination, British Academy of Film and Television Arts, 2004, Silver Condor nomination, best foreign film not in the Spanish language, Argentinean Film Critics Association, all for *Big Fish;* Children's Award nomination (with Richard D. Zanuck), best feature film, British Academy of Film and Television Arts, 2005, Amanda Award nomination, best foreign feature film, 2006, both for *Charlie and the Chocolate Factory;* Future Film Festival Digital Award (with Mike Johnson), Venice Film Festival, 2005, Academy Award nomination (with Mike Johnson), best animated feature film of the year, British Animation Award (with Mike Johnson), best feature, Motion Picture Producer of the Year Award nomination (with Allison Abbate), Producers Guild of America, Silver Condor nomination, best foreign film not in the Spanish language, Argentinean Film Critics Association, Silver Ribbon nomination, best director—foreign film, Italian National Syndicate of Film Journalists, 2006, all for *Corpse Bride;* Career Golden Lion, Venice Film Festival, 2007; National Board of Review Award, best director, 2007, Critics Choice Award nomination, best director, Broadcast Film Critics Association, Golden Globe Award nomination, best director—motion picture, Saturn Award nomination, best director, Academy of Science Fiction, Fantasy, and Horror Films, 2008, Empire Award nomination, best director, 2009, all for *Sweeney Todd: The Demon Barber of Fleet Street;* Career Achievement Award, Amsterdam Fantastic Film Festival, 2008; Motion Picture Producer of the Year Award nomination (with others), Producers Guild of America, 2010, all for *9;* Winsor McCay Award, Annie Awards, International Animated Film Society, 2010.

CREDITS

Film Work:
Animator, *The Island of Doctor Agor,* 1971.
Director, producer, and animator, *Stalk of the Celery* (also known as *Stalk of the Celery Monster*), 1979.
(Uncredited) Additional puppeteer, *The Muppet Movie,* 1979.
(Uncredited) Animator, *The Fox and the Hound* (animated), 1981.
Director, producer, and animator, *Luau,* 1982.
(Uncredited) Animator, *TRON,* 1982.
Director and production designer, *Vincent* (animated short film), Buena Vista, 1982.
Director and (uncredited) storyboard artist, *Frankenweenie* (animated), Buena Vista, 1984.
Director, *Pee Wee's Big Adventure,* Warner Bros., 1985.
(Uncredited) Conceptual artist, *The Black Cauldron,* 1985.
Director, *Beetlejuice* (also known as *Beetle Juice*), Warner Bros., 1988.
Director, *Batman,* Warner Bros., 1989.
Director and producer, *Edward Scissorhands,* Twentieth Century–Fox, 1990.

Director and producer, *Batman Returns,* Warner Bros., 1992.
Producer and production designer, *Tim Burton's "The Nightmare before Christmas"* (also known as *The Nightmare before Christmas*), Buena Vista, 1993.
Director and producer, *Ed Wood,* Buena Vista, 1994.
Producer, *Cabin Boy,* Buena Vista, 1994.
Producer, *Batman Forever* (also known as *Forever*), Warner Bros., 1995.
Director, *Vincent and Me,* 1995.
Director and producer, *Mars Attacks!,* Warner Bros., 1996.
Producer, *James and the Giant Peach,* Buena Vista, 1996.
Director, *Sleepy Hollow,* Paramount, 1999.
Director and producer, *The World of Stainboy* (also known as *Stainboy*), 2000.
Director, *Planet of the Apes,* Twentieth Century–Fox, 2001.
Director, *Big Fish,* Columbia, 2003.
Director, *Charlie and Charlie Factory* (also known as *Charlie and the Chocolate Factory: The IMAX Experience*), Warner Bros., 2005.
Director and producer, *Corpse Bride* (also known as *Tim Burton's "Corpse Bride"*), Warner Bros., 2005.
Director, *Sweeney Todd: The Demon Barber of Fleet Street* (also known as *Sweeney Todd*), DreamWorks, 2007.
Producer, *9* (animated), Focus Features, 2009.
Director, *Alice in Wonderland* (also known as *Alice in Wonderland: An IMAX 3D Experience*), Walt Disney Studios Motion Picture, 2010.

Film Appearances:
Mortie (the Supreme Being), *Luau,* 1982.
(Uncredited) Thug in alley, *Pee–wee's Big Adventure,* 1985.
Brian, *Singles,* Warner Bros., 1992.
(Uncredited) Corpse, *Hoffa,* 1992.
Himself, *A Century of Cinema,* 1994.
Himself, *"Sleepy Hollow": Behind the Legend,* Paramount/Mandalay Pictures, 2000.
Himself, *The Making of Tim Burton's "The Nightmare Before Christmas,"* 2000.
Himself, *De Superman a Spider–Man: L'aventure des super–heroes,* 2002.
Himself, *Beyond "Batman": Designing the Batsuit* (short documentary), Warner Home Video, 2005.
Himself, *"Batman" Heroes: Vicki Vale* (short documentary), Warner Home Video, 2005.
Himself, *"Batman" Heroes: Batman* (short documentary), Warner Home Video, 2005.
Himself, *"Batman Returns" Villains: The Penguin* (short documentary), Warner Home Video, 2005.
Himself, *"Charlie and the Chocolate Factory": Different Faces, Different Flavors* (short documentary), Warner Home Video, 2005.

Himself, *Beyond "Batman": Those Wonderful Toys— The Props & Gadgets of Batman* (short documentary), Warner Home Video, 2005.

Himself, *Beyond "Batman": Visualizing Gotham—The Production Design of Batman* (short documentary), Warner Home Video, 2005.

Himself, *Beyond "Batman": Sleek, Sexy, and Sinister— The Costumes of "Batman Returns"* (short documentary), Warner Home Video, 2005.

Himself, *Charlie and the Chocolate Factory: Designer Chocolate*, 2005.

Himself, *Beyond "Batman": Making Up the Penguin* (short documentary), Warner Home Video, 2005.

Himself, *Beyond "Batman": Building the Batmobile* (short documentary), Warner Home Video, 2005.

Himself, *Beyond "Batman": Assembling the Arctic Army* (short documentary), Warner Home Video, 2005.

Himself, *Beyond "Batman": Gotham City Revisited— The Production Design of "Batman Returns"* (short documentary), Warner Home Video, 2005.

Himself, *Beyond "Batman": From Jack to the Joker* (short documentary), Warner Home Video, 2005.

Himself, *Beyond "Batman": Nocturnal Overtures—The Music of "Batman"* (short documentary), Warner Home Video, 2005.

Himself, *"Batman Returns" Villains: Catwoman* (short documentary), Warner Home Video, 2005.

Ray Harryhausen: The Early Years Collection, Sparkhill Productions, 2005.

Himself, *Becoming Oompa–Loompa* (short documentary), Warner Bros. Entertainment, 2005.

Himself, *Shadows of the Bat: The Cinematic Saga of the Dark Knight—The Gathering Storm* (short documentary), Warner Home Video, 2005.

Himself, *Shadows of the Bat: The Cinematic Saga of the Dark Knight—The Road to Gotham City* (short documentary), Warner Home Video, 2005.

Himself, *Shadows of the Bat: The Cinematic Saga of the Dark Knight—Dark Side of the Knight* (short documentary), Warner Home Video, 2005.

Himself, *Shadows of the Bat: The Cinematic Saga of the Dark Knight—The Legend Reborn* (short documentary), Warner Home Video, 2005.

Himself, *Attack of the Squirrels!* (documentary), Warner Bros., 2005.

Himself, *Tim Burton: Dark vs. Light* (short film), 2006.

Himself, *Voices from the Underworld* (short film), 2006.

Himself, *Making Puppets Tick*, 2006.

Himself, *Inside the Two Worlds of "The Corpse Bride"* (short documentary), Warner Home Video, 2006.

Himself, *Danny Elfman Interprets "The Two Worlds"* (short documentary), Warner Home Video, 2006.

Himself, *The Animators: The Breath of Life* (short documentary), Warner Home Video, 2006.

Himself, *The Look of "9"* (short film), Universal Studios Home Entertainment, 2009.

Himself, *"9": U–Control Picture in Picture* (documentary), Universal Studios Home Entertainment, 2009.

Himself, *"9": The Long and the Short of It* (short film), Universal Studios Home Entertainment, 2009.

Himself, *Waking Sleeping Beauty*, Walt Disney Studios Motion Pictures, 2009.

Himself, *"Alice in Wonderland": Effecting Wonderland* (short film), 2010.

Himself, *"Alice in Wonderland": The Mad Hatter* (short documentary), Walt Disney Pictures, 2010.

Television Appearances; Specials:

"Premiere": Inside the Summer Blockbusters, Fox, 1989.

In the Director's Chair: The Man Who Invented "Edward Scissorhands," 1990.

Fox/MTV Guide to Summer '92, Fox, 1992.

The Bat, the Cat and the Penguin, CBS, 1992.

"Dr. Seuss' 'How the Grinch Stole Christmas'": A TNT Special Edition (also known as *How the Grinch Stole Christmas!" Special Edition*), TNT, 1994.

Masters of Illusion: The Wizards of Special Effects, 1994.

Freaks, Nerds, and Weirdos: An MTV News Special Report, MTV, 1994.

The American Film Institute Salute to Jack Nicholson, 1994.

A–Z of Horror, 1997.

Mario Bava: Maestro of the Macabre, 2000.

The Making of "Planet of the Apes," 2001.

The Inside Reel: Digital Filmmaking, PBS, 2001.

"Planet of the Apes": Rule the Planet, Fox, 2001.

The Inside Reel: Digital Filmmaking, PBS, 2001.

Super Secret Movie Rules: Superheroes, VH1, 2003.

Super Secret Movie Rules: Disaster Movies, VH1, 2004.

Mario Bava: Operazion paura, 2004.

The 100 Greatest Cartoons, Channel 4, 2005.

The Wonderful World of Roald Dahl, Channel 5, 2005.

Vernecia 2005: Cronica de Carlos Boyero, 2005.

The 3rd Irish Film and Television Awards, 2005.

The 78th Annual Academy Awards, ABC, 2006.

Summer Exhibition, 2007.

Scream 2007, Spike TV, 2007.

Scream Awards 2008, Spike TV, 2008.

Christopher Lee—Gentleman des Grauesn, 2010.

The British Academy Television Awards, BBC, 2010.

Television Appearances; Episodic:

Showbiz Today, Cable News Network, 1996.

Magacine, 1997, 2005.

"The Films of Tim Burton," *The Directors*, 1999.

Late Night with Conan O'Brien, NBC, 1999.

The Howard Stern Radio Show, 1999.

Ben, "The Quality of Mercy," *Twice in a Lifetime*, 1999.

The Martin Short Show, syndicated, 1999.

Charlie Rose (also known as *The Charlie Rose Show*), PBS, 1999, 2002, 2009.

Exposure, Sci–Fi Channel, 2000.

"The Making of *Plant of the Apes*," *HBO First Look*, HBO, 2001.

"The Battle of the Blockbusters," *Hollywood, Inc.*, 2002.

Never Before Scene, 2004.

"Big Fish," *HBO First Look*, HBO, 2004.

"Syntinen mainosmaailma," *4Pop,* 2004.

Eigo de shabera–night, 2004.

Film 2004 (also known as *The Film Programme*), BBC, 2004.

"Charlie and the Chocolate Factory," *HBO First Look,* HBO, 2005.

"Tim Burton's *Corpse Bride*," *HBO First Look,* HBO, 2005.

Silenci?, 2005.

Film 2005 (also known as *The Film Programme*), BBC, 2005.

Corazon de ..., 2005.

"Pa den rode lober med Planet Voice," *Planet Voice,* 2005.

At the Movies, 2005.

Film 2006 (also known as *The Film Programme*), BBC, 2006.

Shootout (also known as *Sunday Morning Shootout* and *Hollywood Shootout*), AMC, 2006.

The Tonight Show with Jay Leno, NBC, 2006.

"Movie Aliens," *Space Top 10 Countdown,* SPACE, 2006.

Entertainment Tonight (also known as *E.T.*), syndicated, 2007, 2009, 2010.

"*Sweeney Todd*: The Demon Barber of Fleet Street," *HBO First Look,* HBO, 2008.

"The Homecoming Opening/*Sweeney Todd* from Stage to Screen," *Broadway Beat,* 2008.

Exterieur jour, 2008.

This Morning, ITV, 2008.

La 2 noticias, 2008.

Film 2008 (also known as *The Film Programme*), BBC, 2008.

Caiga quien caiga, 2008.

Miradas 2, 2008.

Cartelera, 2008.

"Tim Burton," *The South Bank Show,* ITV, 2008.

Cinema 3, 2008, 2010.

Up Close with Carrie Keagan, 2009.

Friday Night with Jonathan Ross, BBC1 and BBC America, 2010.

Xpose, TV3, 2010.

GMTV, ITV, 2010.

Go' aften Danmark, 2010.

The 7PM Project, 2010.

Janela Indiscreta, 2010.

"2010 Academy Awards Spotlight," *Made in Hollywood,* 2010.

Le grand journal de Canal+, 2010.

"The Two Escobars," *The Fabulous Picture Show,* 2010.

The 7PM Project, 2010.

Television Appearances; Miniseries:

A–Z of Horror (also known as *Clive Barker's A–Z of Horror*), BBC, 1997.

Television Work; Series:

Creator, developer, development executive, and executive producer, *Beetlejuice* (animated), 1989–91.

Producer, *Batman: The Animated Series* (animated), Fox, 1992–93.

Creator (with Steven Spielberg), design consultant, and executive producer, *Family Dog,* CBS, 1993.

Television Work; Movies:

Director, *Hansel and Gretel,* 1982.

Television Work; Pilots:

Executive producer, *Lost in Oz* (also known as *Tim Burton's "Lost in Oz"*), syndicated, 2000.

Television Director; Episodic:

"The Jar," *Alfred Hitchcock Presents,* NBC, 1986.

"Aladdin and His Wonderful Lamp," *Faerie Tale Theatre* (also known as *Shelley Duvall's "Faerie Tale Theatre"*), Showtime, 1986.

Television Animation Designer; Episodic:

"Family Dog," *Amazing Stories* (also known as *Steven Spielberg's "Amazing Stories"*), 1987.

RECORDINGS

Videos; as Director:

Directed the music video "Bones" by The Killers, 2006.

WRITINGS

Screenplays:

(Adapter) *The Island of Doctor Agor* (animated), 1971.

Stalk of the Celery (animated; also known as *Stalk of the Celery Monster*), 1979.

Luau, 1982.

Vincent (animated short film), Buena Vista, 1982.

Mars Attacks!, Warner Bros., 1996.

The World of Stainboy (also known as *Stainboy*), 2000.

Film Stories:

(Uncredited) *Beetlejuice* (also known as *Beetle Juice*), Warner Bros., 1988.

Edward Scissorhands, Twentieth Century–Fox, 1990.

Tim Burton's "The Nightmare before Christmas" (also known as *The Nightmare before Christmas*), Buena Vista, 1993.

Television Pilots:

Lost in Oz (also known as *Tim Burton's "Lost in Oz"*), syndicated, 2000.

Television Episodes:

Alfred Hitchcock Presents, NBC, 1986.

Beetlejuice (animated), 1989.

Point Blank, 2002.

Books:
My Art and Films, HarperCollins, 1993.
The Nightmare before Christmas Pop–up Book, Mouse Works, 1993.
Burton on Burton, edited by Mark Salisbury, Faber & Faber, 1995.
The Melancholy Death of Oyster Bay and Other Stories, Morrow, 1997.

Contributor to books, including *The Art of Sleepy Hollow,* Pocket Books, 1999.

OTHER SOURCES

Books:
Authors and Artists for Young Adults, Gale, 2005.
Burton, Tim, *My Art and Films,* HarperCollins, 1993.
Contemporary Authors Online, Gale, 2010.
Gallo, Leah, *The Art of Tim Burton,* Steeles Publishing, 2009.
Henke, Ken, *Tim Burton: An Unauthorized Biography of the Filmmaker,* Renaissance Books, 1999.
Merschmann, Helmut, *Tim Burton,* Bertz Verlag, 2000.
Odell, Colin, and Michelle LeBlanc, *Tim Burton,* Pocket Essentials, 2001.
Salisbury, Mark, editor, *Burton on Burton,* Faber & Faber, 1995.
Smith, Jim, and J. Clive Matthews, eds., *Tim Burton,* Virgin Books, 2002.

Periodicals:
Empire, Issue 93, 1997, pp. 68–75.
Evening Standard (London), January 22, 2004, p. 34.
Film Review, February, 2000, pp. 62–63.
Harper's Bazaar, September, 1994.
Interview, December, 1990, pp. 110–13.
Neon, March, 1997, pp. 36–41.
Newsweek, April 9, 1999, p. 66.
Radio Times, August 17, 2002, p. 42.
Rolling Stone, July 9, 1992.
Starlog, March, 1991; July, 1992; January, 1997.
Total Film, February, 2000, pp. 50–56.
Vanity Fair, November, 1994.
Village Voice, October 4, 1994.
Washington Post, July 29, 2001, pp. G1, G6.

BURY, Karl 1971–

PERSONAL

Born March 19, 1971, in Fremont (some sources cite Toledo), OH; married Amber Gallaty, June 26, 2010.

Education: Ohio State University, B.A.; University of Washington, M.F.A.; trained at the Larry Moss Studio and with Robert Easton.

Addresses: *Agent*—Stone Manners Salners Agency, 9911 West Pico Blvd., Suite 1400, Los Angeles, CA 90035. *Manager*—Andrew Tetenbaum, ATA Management, 292 Fifth Ave., 4th Floor, New York, NY 10001.

Career: Actor. Provided voice work for commercials. Acting instructor, private coach, and founder of the Karl Bury Studio.

Member: American Federation of Television and Radio Artists, Actors' Equity Association, Screen Actors Guild.

CREDITS

Film Appearances:
Carts (short film), 1987.
Extra, *She's Having a Baby,* Paramount, 1988.
Pete, *Mutual Needs,* Magic Hour Pictures/Playboy Entertainment Group, 1997.
Flight 393 engineer, *Ground Control* (also known as *Jet*), Green Communications, 1998.
Bob Leffert, *The Majestic* (also known as *The Bijou* and *Majestic*), Warner Bros., 2001.
Tim, *Back Up, Please* (short film), Horn of the Moon Productions, 2003.
Frederick, *Starting out in the Evening,* Roadside Attractions, 2007.
Random police officer, *We Own the Night* (also known as *Undercover*), Columbia, 2007.
Patrol sergeant, *Pride and Glory* (also known as *Pride & Glory*), New Line Cinema, 2008.
Rudy Hubbard, *Sugar* (also known as *Untitled Dominican Project*), Sony Pictures Classics, 2008.
Physec, *Duplicity,* Universal, 2009.
Karl, *The Talk Man,* Neboya Films/Defendshee Productions, 2011.

Television Appearances; Series:
Alex Byrne, *Brotherhood* (also known as *Down City* and *The Hill*), Showtime, 2006–2007.

Television Appearances; Movies:
Young Emmett Davis, *Out There,* Showtime, 1995.
Jake, *Asylum,* HBO, 1996.
Kevin Cannon, *Loving Evangeline* (also known as *Harlequin Mills & Boon: Loving Evangeline* and *Harlequin's "Loving Evangeline"*), Showtime, 1998.

Television Appearances; Episodic:
First uniformed police officer, "Call Me Incontestable," *Diagnosis Murder* (also known as *Dr. Mark Sloan*), CBS, 1995.

Jeff, "Naked Again," *Rude Awakening*, Showtime, 1998.

Lawyer, "I Give Up," *Party of Five*, Fox, 1998.

"Hello, This Is Addictions Anonymous," *Rude Awakening*, Showtime, 1998.

District attorney Corelli, "Legacy," *The Practice*, ABC, 1999.

Bob Leffert, "The Majestic," *HBO First Look*, HBO, 2001.

First lawyer, "Subject: The Stone Room," *FreakyLinks* (also known as *Fearsum, Freaky Links*, and *Friik-kilinkit*), Fox, 2001.

Sam Zamero, "The Frozen Zone," *Judging Amy*, CBS, 2002.

Tom Fiske, "Sentimental Education," *The Sopranos* (also known as *Made in Jersey, Sopranos, Die Sopranos, Familia Soprano, Les Soprano, Los Soprano, Maffiozok*, and *Sopranod*), HBO, 2004.

Matt Ketchum, "The God Spot," *3 lbs.* (also known as *3 Lbs*), CBS, 2006.

Dr. Doh, "Old People Creep Me Out," *Gravity*, Starz!, 2010.

Greg Foster, "Love on Ice," *Law & Order: Criminal Intent* (also known as *Law & Order: CI*), USA Network, 2010.

Stage Appearances:

Chuck, *Invisible Friends*, Seattle Children's Theatre, Seattle, WA, 1992.

Ralph, *Awake and Sing!*, Odyssey Theatre, Los Angeles, c. 1994–95.

Billy, *The Habitation of Dragons*, Zephyr Theatre, Los Angeles, 1995.

Comet, *The Eight: Reindeer Monologues* (also known as *The Eight*), Circle X Theatre Co., Hollywood Court Theatre, Hollywood, CA, 1997.

Samuel, *Beatrice*, Circle X Theatre Co., Hudson Guild Theatre, Los Angeles, 1999.

Beowulf, *Grendel*, Circle X Theatre Co., Open Fist Theatre, Los Angeles, 2001.

Moe Axelrod, *Awake and Sing!*, Pittsburgh Public Theatre, O'Reilly Theatre, Pittsburgh, PA, 2002.

Mike, *Match*, Plymouth Theatre, New York City, 2004.

Kewpie, *Paradise Lost*, part of the America: Boom, Bust, and Baseball series, American Repertory Theatre, Loeb Drama Center, Cambridge, MA, 2010.

Appeared in other productions, including an appearance as Alvaro, *The Rose Tattoo*, Hudson Theatre; and appearances in *How to Go out on a Date in Queens* and *Man and Superman*. Circle X Theatre Co., Los Angeles, member of the company.

Stage Work:

Director, *Rosemary with Ginger*, with *The Stronger*, produced as part of an Equity showcase double-bill called *Four Women & a Waitress*, ArcLight Theatre, New York City, 2008.

WRITINGS

Writings for the Stage:
Author of *Some Day*.

BUSFIELD, Timothy 1957–
   (Tim Busfield)

PERSONAL

Born June 12, 1957, in Lansing, MI; son of Roger (a drama professor) and Jean (a secretary and college literature teacher) Busfield; married Radha Delamarter (an actress and director; divorced, 1986); married Jennifer Merwin (a fashion designer), 1988 (filed for divorce); children: (first marriage) Wilson; (second marriage) Daisy Merwin, Samuel Clark. *Education:* Graduated from East Tennessee State University; trained for the stage at the Actors Theatre of Louisville. *Avocational Interests:* Standard–bred harness horse racing.

Addresses: *Agent*—Innovative Artists, 1505 10th St., Santa Monica, CA 90401.

Career: Actor, producer, and director. Circle Repertory Co., New York City, member of company, 1981; Fantasy Theatre (a professional touring acting company), Sacramento, CA, cofounder with brother Buck, 1986; The "B" Theatre, Sacramento, cofounder and co-producer with brother Buck, 1992. Also a semi–professional baseball player for nine years.

Awards, Honors: Emmy Award nominations, outstanding supporting actor in a drama series, 1988, 1989, 1990, Emmy Award, outstanding supporting actor in a drama series, 1991, all for *thirtysomething*.

CREDITS

Film Appearances:
Soldier with mortar, *Stripes*, Columbia, 1981.

Arnold Poindexter, *Revenge of the Nerds*, Twentieth Century–Fox, 1984.

Arnold Poindexter, *Revenge of the Nerds II: Nerds in Paradise*, Twentieth Century–Fox, 1987.

Mark, *Field of Dreams*, Universal, 1989.

Dick Gordon, *Sneakers*, Universal, 1992.

Frank, *The Skateboard Kid*, Concorde/New Horizons Corp., 1993.

Tony Sacco, *Striking Distance* (also known as *Three Rivers*), Columbia, 1993.

Lou Collins, *Little Big League*, Columbia, 1994.

Fred, *Quiz Show,* Buena Vista, 1994.
Woods, *First Kid,* Buena Vista, 1996.
Robert Levin, *The Souler Opposite,* Curb Entertainment, 1997.
Brian, *Erasable You,* Dorian Productions, 1998.
Himself, *The "Field of Dreams" Scrapbook* (also known as *The "Field of Dreams" Scrapbook: The Making Of*), 1998.
Voice of heart, *Heartbeat,* 2000.
Charlie Reed, *National Security,* Columbia, 2003.
Himself, *A League of Ordinary Gentlemen,* 2004.
Himself, *"Field of Dreams": Passing Along the Pastime* (short documentary), Universal, 2004.
Himself, *The Naked Brothers Band: The Movie,* Paramount Home Video, 2005.

Television Appearances; Series:
Mark Potter, *Reggie,* ABC, 1983.
Dr. John "J. T." McIntyre, Jr., *Trapper John, M.D.,* CBS, 1984–86.
Elliot Weston, *thirtysomething,* ABC, 1987–91.
Sam Byrd, *The Byrds of Paradise,* ABC, 1994.
Tom McManus, *Champs,* ABC, 1996.
Danny Concannon, *The West Wing,* NBC, 1999–2000, 2002–2003, 2005, 2006.
Cal Shanley, *Studio 60 on the Sunset Strip* (also known as *Studio 60*), NBC, 2006–2007.

Television Appearances; Movies:
Paul Jarrett, *Strays,* USA Network, 1991.
Elfred Schultz, *Calendar Girl, Cop Killer? The Bambi Bembenek Story* (also known as *The Heart of the Lie*), ABC, 1992.
Del Calvin, *Fade to Black,* USA Network, 1993.
Assistant District Attorney John Thorn, *Murder Between Friends,* NBC, 1994.
Detective Walt Keller, *In the Shadow of Evil,* CBS, 1995.
Pete Honeycutt, *In the Line of Duty: Kidnapped* (also known as *Kidnapped: In the Line of Duty* and *In the Line of Duty: Taxman*), NBC, 1995.
Matthew Grissom, *Shadow of a Scream* (also known as *The Unspeakable* and *Roger Corman Presents "The Unspeakable"*), 1997.
Major Robert Carr, *Buffalo Soldiers,* TNT, 1997.
Ray, *Trucks,* USA Network, 1997.
Walter Ference, *When Secrets Kill,* ABC, 1997.
Connor Thornton, *Dream House,* UPN, 1998.
Henry, *Carson's Vertical Suburbia,* 1998.
Clayton Shepherd, *The Darklings,* Fox Family, 1999.
Frank Shawson, *Time at the Top,* Showtime, 1999.
Father Donnelly, *Wanted,* Cinemax, 2000.
Elliott Nesher, *Terminal Error* (also known as *Peace Virus*), PAX, 2001.
Franklin, *Dead in a Heartbeat,* TBS, 2002.

Television Appearances; Specials:
Host, "Don't Divorce the Children," *Your Family Matters,* Lifetime, 1990.

The Search for the New Ideal Man, ABC, 1992.
"Addicted to Fame," *First Person with Maria Shriver,* NBC, 1994.
The ESPY Awards, ESPN, 1996.
Walter Gordon, *What's Right with America,* CBS, 1997.
Intimate Portrait: Patricia Heaton, Lifetime, 2001.
Inside "thirtysomething," Bravo, 2001.
Intimate Portrait: Jane Kaczmarek, Lifetime, 2002.
I Love the '80s, VH1, 2002.
I Love the '80s Strikes Back, VH1, 2003.
Boomer Nation (documentary), Arts and Entertainment, 2004.
Presenter, *The 2006 Primetime Creative Arts Emmy Awards,* E! Entertainment Television, 2006.

Television Appearances; Pilots:
Matt, *Stuck in the Middle with You,* NBC, 2003.

Television Appearances; Episodic:
(As Tim Busfield) Doug, "Little Man On Campus," *Family Ties,* 1984.
(As Tim Busfield) Doug, "Best Man," *Family Ties,* 1984.
Prentiss, "C.Y.A.," *After M*A*S*H,* CBS, 1984.
Barrett, "The Advocates," *The Paper Chase,* Showtime, 1984.
Robert Bianca, "Imperfect Union," *Hotel,* ABC, 1985.
Young Matt, "My Back Pages," *Family Ties,* 1986.
Adam Gardner, "The Rat Pack," *Matlock,* 1987.
(Uncredited) *Saturday Night Live* (also known as *SNL*), NBC, 1989.
Late Night with David Letterman, NBC, 1989.
The Tonight Show Starring Johnny Carson, NBC, 1989.
The Arsenio Hall Show, 1992.
Ephraim Lipshitz, "Wall of Silence," *Screen One,* 1993.
Dr. Jon Hoffman, "Under the Bed," *The Outer Limits* (also known as *The New Outer Limits*), Showtime, 1995.
Spy Guy, "Seconds," *Lois & Clark: The New Adventures of Superman,* ABC, 1996.
Second businessman, "Food," *Tracey Takes On ...,* HBO, 1997.
"Jennifer Love Hewitt," *Celebrity Profile,* 1998.
John, "If I Could See Me Now: Part 2," *Rude Awakening,* Showtime, 2000.
All My Children, ABC, 2000.
Detective Mackowitz, "Home for the Holidays," *Cover Me: Based on the True Life of an FBI Family* (also known as *Cover Me*), USA Network, 2001.
Lloyd Stevens, "Lloyd," *Ed,* NBC, 2002.
Lloyd Stevens, "Makeovers," *Ed,* NBC, 2002.
Lloyd Stevens, "Best Wishes," *Ed,* NBC, 2002.
"Tournament 1, Game 2," *Celebrity Poker Showdown,* Bravo, 2003.
Ed Felder, "In the Dark," *Without a Trace* (also known as *W.A.T.*), CBS, 2004.
Ed Felder, "Light Years," *Without a Trace* (also known as *W.A.T.*), CBS, 2004.

Ed Felder, "Malone v. Malone," *Without a Trace* (also known as *W.A.T.*), CBS, 2004.
"Tournament 2, Game 2," *Celebrity Poker Showdown,* Bravo, 2004.
Television director/himself, "Blue Balls Lagoon," *Entourage,* HBO, 2005.
Last Call with Carson Daly, NBC, 2007.
The Naked Brothers Band, Nickelodeon, 2007.
Himself, "Running on E," *Entourage,* HBO, 2009.
Himself, "Murphy's Lie," *Entourage,* HBO, 2009.
Ray Buckland, "Brilliant Disguise," *Law & Order,* NBC, 2010.
District Attorney Mereta, "In Re: Tracy Vidalin," *Outlaw,* NBC, 2010.

Also appeared in *Love American Style,* ABC; as himself, "Field of Dreams," *Page to Screen.*

Television Work; Series:
Co–executive producer, *Ed,* NBC, 2001–2003.
Supervising producer, *Ed,* NBC, 2002.
Co–executive producer, *Without a Trace* (also known as *W.A.T.*), CBS, 2004–2006.
Consultant, *Studio 60 on the Sunset Strip* (also known as *Studio 60*), NBC, 2006–2007.
Executive producer, *Lipstick Jungle,* NBC, 2008–2009.

Television Work; Miniseries:
Co–executive producer, *Maneater,* Lifetime, 2009.
Director, "Part 1 & Part 2," *Maneater,* Lifetime, 2009.

Television Work; Pilots:
Director, *The Lyon's Den,* NBC, 2003.
Executive producer, *Damnation,* Fox, 2007.
Director, *The Ex List,* CBS, 2008.

Television Director; Episodic:
"Her Cup Runneth Over," *thirtysomething,* ABC, 1990.
"The Difference between Men and Women," *thirtysomething,* ABC, 1991.
"A Stop at Willoughby," *thirtysomething,* ABC, 1991.
"If I Could See Me Know: Part 1," *Rude Awakening,* Showtime, 2000.
"The Local Weather," *Sports Night,* ABC, 2000.
"La Forza Del Destino," *Sports Night,* ABC, 2000.
" ... And Then You Die," *First Years,* NBC, 2001.
"There's No Place Like Homo," *First Years,* NBC, 2001.
"Come Fly with Me," *Lizzie McGuire,* The Disney Channel, 2001.
Ed (also known as *Stuckeyville*), NBC, 2001–2003.
"Momento," *That's Life,* ABC, 2002.
"Another Saturday Night," *American Dreams* (also known as *Our Generation*), NBC, 2003.
"Bad Judgment," *Miss Match,* NBC, 2003.
Good Girls Don't ..., Oxygen, 2003.
Las Vegas, NBC, 2003–2007.
"Jump," *Joan of Arcadia,* CBS, 2004.

"To Thine Self Be True," *Summerland,* The WB, 2004.
Without a Trace (also known as *W.A.T.*), CBS, 2004–2006.
Studio 60 on the Sunset Strip (also known as *Studio 60*), NBC, 2006–2007.
"Sort of Like a Family," *Damages,* FX Network, 2007.
"Trade–Off," *Canterbury's Law,* Fox, 2008.
Lipstick Jungle, NBC, 2008.
"Honey," *Lie to Me,* Fox, 2009.
"Flip of the Coin," *White Collar,* USA Network, 2009.
"Where There's Smoke," *The Deep End,* ABC, 2010.
"To Have and to Hold," *The Deep End,* ABC, 2010.
"Don't Forget to Thank Mr. Zedeck," *Damages,* FX Network, 2010.
"You Were His Little Monkey," *Damages,* FX Network, 2010.
"Too Much Attitude and Not Enough Underwear," *Mercy,* NBC, 2010.
"A Perfect Storm," *The Glades,* Arts and Entertainment, 2010.
"In Re: Officer Daniel," *Outlaw,* NBC, 2010.
"In Re: Jessica Davis," *Outlaw,* NBC, 2010.
"No Ordinary Earthquake," *No Ordinary Family,* ABC, 2010.
The Defenders, CBS, 2010.

Also directed episodes of *Cover Me: Based on the True Life of an FBI Family* (also known as *Cover Me*), USA Network; *Danny.*

Stage Appearances:
Puck, *Robin Goodfellow,* Johnson City, TN, 1975.
Talley and Son, Circle Repertory Company, New York City, 1981.
A Life, Long Wharf Theatre, New Haven, CT, 1981.
Rick, "Bluffing," Norm Prescott, "Present Tense," Kirk Swell, "It's Time ...," Louie, "The Bronx Zoo," and Jennifer, "So What ...?," *Young Playwrights Festival,* Circle Repertory Company, 1982.
Henry Percy/Hotspur, *Richard II,* Circle Repertory Company, Entermedia Theatre, New York City, 1982.
Understudy for the roles of Eugene and Stanley, *Brighton Beach Memoirs,* Alvin Theatre, New York City, 1983.
(Broadway debut) Lieutenant Daniel Kaffee, *A Few Good Men,* Music Box Theatre, New York City, 1990.

Also appeared in *Richard II; A Tale Told; Mass Appeal; The Tempest; Getting Out; Founder; A Life;* as Puck, *Robin Goodfellow.*

Major Tours:
Toured in *Getting Out,* Actors Theatre of Louisville, European and Israeli cities.

OTHER SOURCES

Periodicals:
Playboy, June, 1990, pp. 57–76.

BYRD, La Monde

PERSONAL

Education: Central State University, degree in Spanish and water resource management; American Film Institute, M.F.A.

Addresses: *Manager*—Brown Leader Management Group, 3000 Olympic Blvd., Suite 1302, Santa Monica, CA 90404.

Career: Actor and producer.

CREDITS

Film Appearances:
Josh Smith, *Thomas Grey's Rainy Day* (short film), 2004.
DEA agent number one, *Totally Baked: A Pot–U–Mentary,* Vivendi Entertainment, 2007.

Film Work:
Executive producer and producer, *Privacy Policy* (short film), 2007.
Producer, *Partigiano* (short film), American Film Institute Conservatory, 2008.
Producer, *Family Jewels* (short film), 2009.
Second unit director, *The Obolus* (short film), American Film Institute Conservatory, 2009.
Unit production manager, *Through the Air to Calais or the Wonderful Cruise of Blanchard's Balloon* (short film), 2009.
Producer, *Speed–Dating,* Rockstone Releasing, 2010.

Television Appearances; Series:
Hollis, *Mad Men,* AMC, 2007–2009.

Television Appearances; Movies:
Cop, *The Governor's Wife,* Lifetime, 2008.

Television Appearances; Episodic:
Bradshaw's bodyguard, *The Late Late Show with Craig Kilborn* (also known as *The Late Late Show*), CBS, 1999.
Rick Powell, "Textbook Perfect," *For the People* (also known as *Para la gente*), Lifetime, 2002.
Marcus, "Chapter Forty–Six," *Boston Public,* Fox, 2002.
Dwayne, "The Concert," *Hidden Hills,* NBC, 2003.
Marcus, "Chapter Sixty–One," *Boston Public,* Fox, 2003.
Jason Porter, "Judas Priest," *The Shield,* FX Network, 2005.
SWAT officer, "Baby BOOM!," *Strong Medicine,* Lifetime, 2006.
M.C., "Class Dismissed," *Cuts,* UPN, 2006.
Handicapped guy, "The Serranos," *Mind of Mencia,* Comedy Central, 2006.
Robert Johnson, "Crossroad Blues," *Supernatural,* The WB, 2006.
Petty officer Wedoes, "Mr. Monk Is Underwater," *Monk,* USA Network, 2008.
Young Harry Bastille, "Young Man with a Horn," *CSI: Crime Scene Investigation* (also known as *CSI: Las Vegas* and *C.S.I.*), CBS, 2008.
Bobby Kerns, the Green Beret from 2005 until 2010, "The Good Soldier," *Cold Case,* CBS, 2010.

Stage Appearances:
Appeared as Cory Maxson, *Fences,* Dayton Playhouse, Dayton, OH.

C

CAAN, James 1940(?)–
   (Jimmy Caan)

PERSONAL

Full name, James Edmund Caan; born March 26, 1940 (some sources say 1939), in The Bronx, New York, NY; son of Arthur (a meat dealer) and Sophie Caan; brother of Ronald "Ronnie" Caan (a producer); married DeeJay Mathis (a dancer), 1960 (divorced, 1966); married Sheila Ryan (a model and actress), January 12, 1976 (divorced, 1977); married Ingrid Hajek, September 9, 1990 (divorced, 1995); married Linda Stokes, October 7, 1995 (filed for divorce, 2005); children: (first marriage) Tara; (second marriage) Scott Andrew (an actor and musician); (third marriage) Alexander James; (fourth marriage) James Arthur, Jacob Nicholas. *Education:* Attended Michigan State University; studied drama at Hofstra College (now University); trained for the stage with Sanford Meisner at the Neighborhood Playhouse and with Wynn Handman. *Religion:* Jewish. *Avocational Interests:* Tennis, basketball, skiing, martial arts (black belt in karate).

Addresses: *Office*—Openfilm.com, 12100 NE 16th Ave., North Miami, FL 33161. *Agent*—International Creative Management, 10250 Constellation Blvd., 9th Floor, Los Angeles, CA 90067; Danis Panaro Nist, 9201 West Olympic Blvd., Beverly Hills, CA 90212.

Career: Actor. Openfilm.com, North Miami, FL, member of board of directors. Worked as a rodeo rider on the professional circuit for nine years; also worked as a waiter, bouncer, lifeguard, and camp counselor.

Awards, Honors: Golden Globe Award nomination, most promising male newcomer, 1966, for *The Glory Guys;* Golden Laurel Award nomination, outstanding male new face, 1968; Emmy Award nomination, best actor in a single performance, 1972, TV Land Award (with Billy Dee Williams), blockbuster movie of the week, 2006, for both *Brian's Song;* Academy Award nomination and Golden Globe Award nomination, both best supporting actor, 1973, for *The Godfather;* Golden Globe Award nomination, best motion picture actor in a drama, 1975, for *The Gambler;* Golden Globe Award nomination, best motion picture actor in a musical or comedy, 1976, for *Funny Lady;* Golden Scroll, best actor, Academy of Science Fiction, Fantasy, and Horror Films, 1976, for *Rollerball;* Hollywood Discovery Award, outstanding achievement in acting, Hollywood Film Festival, 1999; Video Premiere Award nomination, best supporting actor, 2001, for *Luckytown;* Lifetime Achievement Award, Florida Film Festival, 2003; Daytime Emmy Award nomination, outstanding performer in a children/youth/family special, 2004, for *The Incredible Mrs. Ritchie;* Golden Boot Award nomination, Motion Picture and Television Fund, 2005; Vegas Icon Award, Las Vegas Convention and Visitors Authority, 2008; received star on Hollywood Walk of Fame.

CREDITS

Film Appearances:
(Film debut; uncredited) Soldier with radio, *Irma La Douce,* United Artists, 1963.
Randall Simpson O'Connell, *Lady in a Cage,* Paramount, 1964.
Mike Marsh, *Red Line 7000,* Paramount, 1965.
Private Anthony Dugan, *The Glory Guys,* United Artists, 1965.
Paul Montgomery, *Games,* Universal, 1967.
Alan Bourdillon "Mississippi" Traherne, *El Dorado,* Paramount, 1967.
Buck Burnett, *Journey to Shiloh,* Universal, 1968.
Lee Stegler, *Countdown,* Warner Bros., 1968.
Jimmie "Killer" Kilgannon, *The Rain People,* Warner Bros., 1969.
Lieutenant Commander John Bolton, *Submarine X–1,* United Artists, 1969.

Rabbit Angstrom, *Rabbit, Run,* Warner Bros., 1970.
Larry Moore, *T. R. Baskin* (also known as *A Date with a Lonely Girl*), Paramount, 1971.
Himself, *"The Godfather": Behind the Scenes,* 1971.
Sonny Corleone, *The Godfather* (also known as *Mario Puzo's "The Godfather"* and *Godfather*), Paramount, 1972.
Dick Kanipsia, *Slither,* Metro–Goldwyn–Mayer, 1973.
Sonny Corleone, *The Godfather, Part II* (also known as *Mario Puzo's "The Godfather, Part II"*), Paramount, 1974.
Freebie, *Freebie and the Bean,* Warner Bros., 1974.
Alex Freed, *The Gambler,* 1974.
John Baggs, Jr., *Cinderella Liberty,* Twentieth Century–Fox, 1975.
Mike Locken, *The Killer Elite,* United Artists, 1975.
Jonathan E., *Rollerball,* United Artists, 1975.
Billy Rose, *Funny Lady,* Columbia, 1975.
Jud McGraw, *Gone With the West* (also known as *Bronco Busters, Little Moon and Jud McGraw,* and *Man Without Mercy*), 1975.
Himself, *From Rome to Rollerball: The Full Circle,* 1975.
Don Rickles: Buy This Tape You Hockey Puck, 1975.
Himself, *Silent Movie,* Twentieth Century–Fox, 1976.
Harry Dighby, *Harry and Walter Go to New York,* Columbia, 1976.
Staff Sergeant Eddie Dohun, *A Bridge Too Far,* United Artists, 1977.
David Williams, *Un autre homme, une autre chance* (also known as *Another Man, Another Chance* and *Another Man, Another Woman*), United Artists, 1977.
Frank "Buck" Athearn, *Comes a Horseman,* United Artists, 1978.
George Schneider, *Chapter Two,* Columbia, 1979.
(Uncredited) Sailor in fight, *1941,* Universal, 1979.
Thomas Hacklin, Jr., *Hide in Plain Sight,* Metro–Goldwyn–Mayer/United Artists, 1980.
Frank, *Thief* (also known as *Violent Streets*), United Artists, 1981.
Jack Glenn and Jason Glenn, *Bolero* (also known as *Within Memory, Bolero: Dance of Life, Dance of Life,* and *Les uns et les autres*), Double 13, 1982.
Jolly Villano, *Kiss Me Goodbye,* Twentieth Century–Fox, 1982.
Dorothy Stratten: The Untold Story, 1985.
Clell Hazard, *Gardens of Stone,* TriStar, 1988.
Detective Sergeant Matthew Sykes, *Alien Nation,* Twentieth Century–Fox, 1988.
Paul Sheldon, *Misery,* Columbia, 1990.
Spaldoni, *Dick Tracy,* Buena Vista, 1990.
Eddie Sparks, *For the Boys,* Twentieth–Century Fox, 1991.
Dr. Scurvy, *The Dark Backward* (also known as *The Man with Three Arms*), RCA/Columbia Pictures Home Video, 1991.
Tommy Korman, *Honeymoon in Vegas,* Columbia, 1992.
Voice of reader, *Earth and the American Dream,* 1992.

Himself, *Harley–Davidson: The American Motorcycle,* 1993.
Coach Sam Winters, *The Program,* Buena Vista, 1993.
Roy Sweeney, *Flesh and Bone,* Paramount, 1993.
Jim, *A Boy Called Hate,* Dove Entertainment, 1996.
Things to Do in Denver When You're Dead, 1996.
Abe Henry, *Bottle Rocket,* Columbia, 1996.
U.S. Marshal Robert Deguerin, *Eraser,* Warner Bros., 1996.
Frank Colton, *Bulletproof,* Universal, 1996.
Sean McLennon, *North Star* (also known as *The North Star, Alaska, Duello tra I ghiacci, Grand nord,* and *Tashunga*), Goldcrest Films International, 1996.
Howard Hawks, American Artist, 1997.
Come Get Some: The Women of the WWF, Silver Vision Video, 1999.
Himself, *Playboy: Playmate Pajama Party,* 1999.
Kieran Johnson, *This Is My Father* (also known as *L'histoire de mon pere*), Sony Pictures Classics, 1999.
Frank Vitale, *Mickey Blue Eyes,* Warner Bros., 1999.
Frank Olchin, *The Yards,* Miramax, 2000.
Charlie Doyles, *Luckytown,* A Plus Entertainment, 2000.
Joe Sarno, *The Way of the Gun,* Artisan Entertainment, 2000.
Roy Baker, *Viva Las Nowhere* (also known as *Dead Simple*), Viva Las Nowhere Productions, 2001.
Himself, *Playboy Exposed: Playboy Mansion Parties Uncensored,* 2001.
Lance Huston, *In the Shadows,* Lions Gate Films, 2001.
(Uncredited) Prison warden, *Night at the Golden Eagle,* Shangri–La Entertainment, 2002.
Marvin, *City of Ghosts,* Metro–Goldwyn–Mayer, 2002.
Himself, *Misery Loves Company,* 2002.
The big man, *Dogville* (also known as *The Film "Dogville" as Told in Nine Chapters and a Prologue*), Lions Gate Entertainment, 2003.
Walter, *Dallas 362,* Dallas & Rusty/Konwiser Brothers/Sunlion Films, 2003.
Jimmy "The Con," *This Thing of Ours,* Maverick Entertainment Group, 2003.
Leonard Grey, *Jericho Mansions* (also known as *House of Jericho*), Vine International, 2003.
Walter, Buddy's biological father, *Elf,* New Line Cinema, 2003.
William Larnach, *Castle of Lies,* First Sun/Parallel Castle Pictures, 2003.
Dogville Confessions (documentary), Trust Film Sales, 2003.
Himself, *Film School for Kids* (short documentary), New Line Home Video, 2004.
Himself, *That's a Wrap* (short documentary), New Line Home Video 2004.
(Uncredited) Darren Mason, *Santa's Slay,* Lions Gate Films Home Entertainment, 2005.
Himself, *Lightfield's Home Videos,* Big Screen Entertainment Group, 2006.
Himself, *Mr. Warmth: The Don Rickles Project* (documentary), Vivendi Entertainment, 2007.

The president, *Get Smart,* Warner Bros., 2008.
Mr. Riccoli, *New York, I Love You,* Vivendi Entertainment, 2009.
Gerry Ryan, *Mercy,* IFC Films, 2009.
Jerry Haggerty, *Middle Men,* Paramount Vantage, 2009.
Voice of Tim Lockwood, *Cloudy with a Chance of Meatballs* (animated; also known as *Cloudy with a Chance of Meatballs: An IMAX Experience*), Columbia, 2009.
Himself, *Hugh Hefner: Playboy, Activist and Rebel* (documentary), Phase 4 Films, 2009.
Voice of himself, *"Family Guy" Presents: Something Something Something Dark Side* (animated), Twentieth Century–Fox Home Entertainment, 2009.
Max, *Henry's Crime,* 2010.
Himself, *A Recipe for Success: The Making of "Cloudy with a Chance of Meatballs"* (short film), Sony Pictures Home Entertainment, 2010.
Mr. Seaboldt, *Detachment,* 2011.
Agent Paul Vinsant, *Minkow,* 2011.

Film Work:
Director, *Hide in Plain Sight,* Metro–Goldwyn–Mayer, 1980.

Television Appearances; Series:
Big Ed Deline, *Las Vegas,* NBC, 2003–2007.
(Uncredited) Himself, *The Contender,* NBC, 2005.

Television Appearances; Movies:
Brian Piccolo, *Brian's Song,* ABC, 1971.
Philip Marlowe, *Poodle Springs,* HBO, 1998.
John Flinders, *Warden of Red Rock,* Showtime, 2001.
Captain Fred Moosally, *A Glimpse of Hell,* FX Network, 2001.
Dr. William Haber, *The Lathe of Heaven,* Arts and Entertainment, 2002.
Sheriff Morgan McKenna, *Blood Crime,* USA Network, 2002.
Hearts of Men, USA Network, 2002.
Harry Dewitt, *The Incredible Mrs. Ritchie,* Showtime, 2003.
Salvatore Palmeri, *Wisegal,* Lifetime, 2008.

Television Appearances; Specials:
Presenter, *The 44th Annual Academy Awards,* 1972.
Presenter, *The 46th Annual Academy Awards,* 1974.
Rickles, CBS, 1975.
Funny Girl to Funny Lady, 1975.
Celebration: The American Spirit, ABC, 1976.
Superstunt, NBC, 1977.
Playboy's 25th Anniversary Special, ABC, 1979.
Night of 100 Stars, ABC, 1982.
Kenny Rogers Classic Weekend, ABC, 1988.
All–Star Tribute to Kareem Abdul–Jabbar, NBC, 1989.
The Godfather Family: A Look Inside, HBO, 1990.
The AFI's 100 Years ... 100 Stars, CBS, 1991.

Naked Hollywood, BBC and Arts and Entertainment, 1991.
Voice, *Earth and the American Dream,* HBO, 1993.
Host, *Harley–Davidson: The American Motorcycle,* TBS, 1993.
Howard Hawks: American Artist, 1997.
AFI's 100 Years 100 Stars: America's Greatest Screen Legends, 1999.
The Making of a Mobster: "Mickey Blue Eyes," 1999.
ESPY Awards, ESPN, 2000.
Playboy: The Party Continues, 2000.
James Caan: Making a Scene, Arts and Entertainment, 2001.
Playboy: Inside the Playboy Mansion, Arts and Entertainment, 2002.
Intimate Portrait: Vanessa Marcil, Lifetime, 2003.
Nicole Kidman: An American Cinematheque Tribute, AMC, 2003.
E! Entertainer of the Year 2003, E! Entertainment Television, 2003.
Host, *Willie Nelson & Friends: Outlaws and Angels,* USA Network, 2004.
Tsunami Aid: A Concert of Hope, 2005.
The WIN Awards, 2005.
Bullets Over Hollywood, Starz!, 2005.
Presenter, *Al Pacino: An American Cinematheque Tribute,* AMC, 2006.
CMT Greatest Moments: Willie Nelson, Country Music Television, 2006.
Brando, TCM, 2007.
Mr. Warmth: The Don Rickles Project, HBO, 2007.
Chabad: To Life Telethon (also known as *Chabad Telethon, Chabad Telethon: Live,* and *The Chabad "Dancing Rabbits" Telethon*), 2008.
Hollywood Gangster, 2008.

Television Appearances; Episodic:
(As Jimmy Caan) Marty Feketi, "Bullets Cost Too Much," *Naked City,* ABC, 1961.
(As Jimmy Caan) Johnny, "And the Cat Jumped over the Moon," *Route 66,* CBS, 1961.
Arch Williams, "The Masked Marine," *Alcoa Premiere,* ABC, 1962.
Keir Brannon, "A Fist of Five," *The Untouchables,* ABC, 1962.
Buddie Simpson, "A Cry from the Mountains," *The Wide Country,* NBC, 1963.
Charley Johnson, "The Mosaic," *Dr. Kildare,* NBC, 1963.
Dr. Keith Gregory, "Justice to a Microbe," *Ben Casey,* ABC, 1963.
Jim McKinney, "Deadly Decision," *Death Valley Days* (also known as *Call of the West, The Pioneers, Trails West,* and *Western Star Theater*), syndicated, 1963.
"Shadow of Violence," *Death Valley Days* (also known as *Call of the West, The Pioneers, Trails West,* and *Western Star Theater*), syndicated, 1963.
Sergeant Beckman, "Anatomy of a Patrol," *Combat!,* ABC, 1963.

Rick Peterson, "The Hunt," *Kraft Suspense Theater* (also known as *Crisis* and *Suspense Theatre*), NBC, 1963.

"Glass Flowers Never Drop Petals," *Breaking Point,* ABC, 1964.

Jeff Brubaker, "My Son, the All American," *Channing,* ABC, 1964.

Jay Shaw/Phil Beldone, "Memo from Purgatory," *Alfred Hitchcock Presents* (also known as *Hitchcock Hour* and *The Alfred Hitchcock Hour*), NBC, 1964.

Paul, "The Echo Pass Story," *Wagon Train,* ABC, 1965.

Eugene David "Gene" Holt, "A Life in the Balance," *The F.B.I.,* ABC, 1969.

(Uncredited) Rotten Rupert of Rathskeller, "To Sire, with Love: Parts 1 & 2," *Get Smart,* 1969.

The Tonight Show Starring Johnny Carson (also known as *The Tonight Show*), NBC, 1971, 1972, 1973, 1974, 1975, 1984.

Rowan & Martin's Laugh–In, 1972.

The Merv Griffin Show, 1972.

"Tarzan/Public Enemy/Hurricane/Casablanca," *Don Adams' Screen Test,* 1975.

Donahue (also known as *The Phil Donahue Show*), 1977.

Good Morning America (also known as *G.M.A.*), ABC, 1980.

The Tonight Show with Jay Leno, NBC, 1992, 1992, 2003, 2004.

Late Show with David Letterman (also known as *Letterman* and *The Late Show*), CBS, 1994.

"Eraser," *HBO First Look,* HBO, 1996.

The Rosie O'Donnell Show, 1996.

Himself, "Movie Star," *NewsRadio,* NBC, 1996.

"Hollywood," *Unzipped,* 1999.

"The Films of Norman Jewison," *The Directors,* 1999.

The Howard Stern Radio Show, 1999.

Howard Stern, E! Entertainment Television, 1999, 2003.

Inside the Actors Studio (also known as *Inside the Actors Studio: The Craft of Theatre and Film* and *Actors Interview*), Bravo, 2000.

"Brian Piccolo," *ESPN SportsCentury,* ESPN, 2001.

Dinner for Five, Independent Film Channel, 2003.

"Filmen *Dogville,*" *Nyhetsmorgon,* 2003.

Late Night with Conan O'Brien, NBC, 2003.

"Arnold Schwarzenegger," *Biography,* Arts and Entertainment, 2003.

Jimmy Kimmel Live!, ABC, 2004.

Ed Deline, "What Happens in Vegas Dies in Boston," *Crossing Jordan,* NBC, 2004.

Voice of himself, "All's Fair in Oven War," *The Simpsons* (animated), Fox, 2004.

"Brando," *Imagine,* BBC, 2004.

"Sylvester Stallone," *Biography,* Arts and Entertainment, 2005.

Shootout (also known as *Sunday Morning Shootout* and *Hollywood Shootout*), AMC, 2005.

Magacine, 2005.

(Uncredited) Himself, "Ghostbusted," *The Girls Next Door,* E! Entertainment Television, 2005.

Ellen: The Ellen DeGeneres Show, syndicated, 2006.

"Marlon Brando," *Hollywood Greats* (also known as *The Hollywood Greats*), BBC1, 2006.

"Polar Bear Cookoff," *Rachael Ray,* syndicated, 2006.

Stage Appearances:

(Off–Broadway debut; as Jimmy Caan) The soldier, *La Ronde,* Theatre Marquee, 1960.

(Broadway debut) *Blood, Sweat, and Stanley Poole,* Morosco Theatre, 1961.

Mandingo, Lyceum Theatre, New York City, 1961.

Night of 100 Stars, Radio City Music Hall, New York City, 1982.

RECORDINGS

Video Games:

Voice of Santino "Sonny" Corleone, *The Godfather* (also known as *The Godfather: The Game*), Electronic Arts, 2006.

Voice of Santino "Sonny" Corleone, *The Godfather: Mob Wars,* Electronic Arts, 2006.

Voice of Santino "Sonny" Corleone, *The Godfather: The Don's Edition,* Electronic Arts, 2006.

Voice of Santino "Sonny" Corleone, *The Godfather: Blackhand Edition,* Electronic Arts, 2006.

OTHER SOURCES

Books:

Encyclopedia Judaica, Keter Publishing House, Ltd., 2007.

Newsmakers, Gale, 2004.

Periodicals:

Entertainment Weekly, June 28, 1996, pp. 44–46, 48, 50.

Esquire, May, 1998, p. 82.

Parade, October 12, 2003, p. 14.

People Weekly, October 4, 1993, p. 53; July 8, 1996, p. 110.

Premiere, December, 1991, p. 79; October, 2000, p. 34.

Time, May 27, 2002, p. G10.

TV Guide, July 25, 1998, pp. 27–29; September 27, 2003, pp. 55–59.

USA Today, May 12, 2010, p. 6D.

CAIRNS, Gary 1980–
(Gary James)

PERSONAL

Full name, Gary James Cairns II; born August 23, 1980, in Cleveland, OH; children: Kurt Dean. *Education:* Studied acting and nutrition.

Addresses: *Agent*—Shadz of Talent, P.O. Box 939, Casselman, Ontario K0A 1M0, Canada; Coast to Coast Talent, 3350 Barham Blvd., Los Angeles, CA 90068.

Career: Actor. Martyrstar Entertainment (production company), cofounder; GC II Productions (production company), 2004. Appeared in several advertisements. Sometimes credited as Gary James.

Member: American Federation of Television and Radio Artists, Screen Actors Guild.

CREDITS

Film Appearances:
Alex the Great (short film), c. 2002.
Bang and Whimper (short film), c. 2003.
Toby, *The Jinn,* Pathway Entertainment, 2007.
Gill, *Hero Wanted,* Sony Pictures Entertainment, 2008.
The Trip, *The Last Hurrah,* Cinema Libre Studio, 2009.
Cory, *Mad World,* 2010.
Izzy, *An American Hero,* c. 2010.
Luther, *Grown,* 2011.
Joe Thomas, *A Detour in Life,* Emiras Productions, c. 2011.

Some sources cite appearances in other films.

Television Appearances; Movies:
(As Gary Cairns) Prosper Schwee, *The Good Humor Man* (also known as *The Wrong Date*), Showtime, 2005.

Television Appearances; Episodic:
(Uncredited) Lost Kid, "Home Again," *Beverly Hills 90210* (also known as *Beverly Hills, Beverly Hills, 90210, Beverly Hills 90210 Classic, Class of Beverly Hills,* and *L.A. Beat*), Fox, 1991.
Duke, "Thanksgiving," *Once and Again* (also known as *Comecar de novo, Deuxieme chance, Noch mal mit Gefuehl, Una vez mas,* and *Vielae kerran*), ABC, 1999.
Cadet, "Flashback," *Malcolm in the Middle* (also known as *Fighting in Underpants*), Fox, 2001.
Duke, "Tough Love," *Once and Again* (also known as *Comecar de novo, Deuxieme chance, Noch mal mit Gefuehl, Una vez mas,* and *Vielae kerran*), ABC, 2001.
(Uncredited) First greeting usher, "Two Cathedrals," *The West Wing* (also known as *West Wing, The White House,* and *El ala oeste de la Casablanca*), NBC, 2001.
Bunny Higgins, "The Hammer," *Justified* (also known as *Lawman*), FX Network, 2010.

Appeared in other programs, including *NYPD Blue* (also known as *New York Blues, New York Cops—NYPD Blue, New York Police, New York Police Blues, New York Police Department, N.Y.P.D,* and *N.Y.P.D.*), ABC.

Stage Appearances:
Appeared in *Camp Fire* and *War No More,* both Modesto, CA; and in *The Salesman,* HB Playhouse.

Internet Appearances; Episodic:
Minister, "The Beginning of the End," *Poor Paul,* http://www.poorpaul.com, 2009, also broadcast on *Kold-Cast TV,* http://www.koldcast.tv, and *YouTube,* http://www.youtube.com, both c. 2009.

Appeared in other footage on the Internet.

RECORDINGS

Music Videos:
Appeared in music videos, including "Taste of Ink" by The Used, 2002; "Son's Gonna Rise" by Citizen Cope, 2005; and "Determination" by Bone Thugs–n–Harmony.

CALDERON, Paul
(Paul Calderone)

PERSONAL

Born in Puerto Rico; married Catherine (a director); children: Gabriel Alonzo, additional child. *Education:* Studied anthropology at Bernard M. Baruch College of the City University of New York.

Addresses: *Contact*—Kolstein Talent Agency, 303 N. Glenoaks Blvd., Suite L105, Burbank, CA 91502.

Career: Actor. Actors Studio, New York City, member; Intar Hispanic American Theatre, New York City, founding member of LAByrinth Theatre Company. Lee Strasberg Institute, New York City, teaching acting for film and television, 2005. *Military service:* Served in U.S. Army.

Awards, Honors: Obie Award, outstanding performance, *Village Voice,* 1995, for *Blade to the Heart.*

CREDITS

Film Appearances:
Hector, *Tenement* (also known as *Game of Survival, Tenement: Game of Survival,* and *Slaughter in the South Bronx*), Reeltime Distributing, 1985.

Tito, *Band of the Hand,* TriStar, 1986.
Speed, *Sticky Fingers,* International Spectrafilm, 1988.
Juan, *Penn & Teller Get Killed* (also known as *Dead Funny*), Warner Bros., 1989.
Serafino, *Sea of Love,* Universal, 1989.
Pizza, *The Chair* (also known as *Hot Seat*), Angelika Films, 1989.
Roger Montalvo, *Q & A,* TriStar, 1990.
Joey Dalesio, *King of New York,* Artisan Entertainment, 1990.
Blacky, *Criss Cross* (also known as *CrissCross* and *Alone Together*), Metro–Goldwyn–Mayer, 1992.
(As Paul Calderone) First cop, *Bad Lieutenant,* Creative Exposure, 1993.
Thomas Richie, *The Firm,* Paramount, 1993.
Paul, *Pulp Fiction,* Miramax, 1994.
Landwick, *Hand Gun,* Shooting Gallery, 1994.
Jesus at Hambones, *Clockers,* MCA/Universal, 1995.
Norman, "The Man from Hollywood," *Four Rooms,* Miramax, 1995.
Professor, *The Addiction,* October Films, 1995.
Angel Delgado, *Condition Red* (also known as *Condition Red—Haelytystila* and *Draussen lauert der tod*), Oak Islands Films/Overseas FilmGroup, 1995.
(Uncredited) Undercover FBI agent, *Kiss of Death,* 1995.
Reinaldo "Ricky", *Lotto Land,* Cinepix Film Properties, 1996.
Raymond, *Sweet Nothing,* Warner Bros., 1996.
Hector, the medic, *Cop Land,* Buena Vista/Miramax, 1997.
Carl, *O.K. Garage* (also known as *All Revved Up*), New City Releasing, 1998.
Raymond Cruz, *Out of Sight,* MCA/Universal, 1998.
Sergeant Diaz, *One Tough Cop,* Columbia TriStar, 1998.
Sandro Guzman, *Girlfight,* Screen Gems, 2000.
(Uncredited) Officer, *Bait* (also known as *Piege* and *Wild Chase*), Warner Bros., 2000.
Manny Rivera, *Once in the Life,* Lions Gate Films, 2000.
Dellwo, *The Last Castle,* DreamWorks, 2001.
Carlos DeJesus, *Kill the Poor,* IFC Films, 2003.
Brown, *21 Grams,* Focus Features, 2003.
Rastafarian man, *Indoumentados,* 2005.
Deputy Director Cortes, *The Sentinel,* Twentieth Century–Fox, 2006.
Blue, *Pistol Whipped* (also known as *The Marker* and *Dantotsu*), Sony Pictures Home Entertainment, 2008.
Bobby, *Grand Slammed,* 2009.
Carl, *The Hungry Ghosts,* Eastgate Pictures, 2009.
Oscar Perez, *A Kiss of Chaos,* 2009.
The old man, *Make the Whole World Kin* (short film), 2009.
Rafa, *La soga* (also known as *The Butcher's Son*), 7–57 Releasing, 2009.
Father, *Down This Road* (short film), 2010.
Carlos, *Raju* (short film), 2010.
Randall, *Two Birds* (short film), 2010.

Hughie Luke, *Burning Daylight,* 2010.
Detective Jenkins, *Gun,* 2010.

Film Work:
Executive producer, *Grand Slammed,* 2009.
Coproducer, *Dancing with the Spirits* (documentary), 2009.
Second unit director, *Burning Daylight,* 2010.

Television Appearances; Series:
Ruben Fundora, *Dream Street,* NBC, 1989.
Agent Del Delgado, *One Life to Live,* ABC, 1998.
Miami Joe, *How to Make It in America,* HBO, 2010—.

Television Appearances; Miniseries:
(As Paul Calderone) Bitong, *Doubletake,* CBS, 1985.

Television Appearances; Movies:
(As Paul Calderone) Street vendor, *Rockabye,* CBS, 1986.
Anderez, *The Old Man and the Sea* (also known as *Ernest Hemingway's "The Old Man and the Sea"*), NBC, 1990.
Garcia, *The Keys,* NBC, 1992.
Boulez, *Montana* (also known as *Nothing Personal*), HBO, 1998.
Detective Jesse, *Oxygen* (also known as *Dying to Escape*), Cinemax, 1999.
Guy, *Rock the Boat* (also known as *The Atlantis Conspiracy*), HBO, 2000.
Ralph, *3 A.M.,* Showtime, 2001.
(As Paul Calderone) Derek Basha, *Suburban Madness,* CBS, 2004.

Television Appearances; Pilots:
Lieutenant Vance Pickett, *Dark Angel,* Fox, 1996.
Detective at prison, *The Black Donnellys,* NBC, 2007.

Television Appearances; Episodic:
Nicky, "The Home Invaders," *Miami Vice,* NBC, 1985.
Gabriel, "Prodigal Son," *Miami Vice,* NBC, 1985.
Rat Heart, "Reign of Terror," *The Equalizer,* CBS, 1985.
"Dead Drop," *The Equalizer,* CBS, 1986.
Don Gallego, "Everybody's in Showbiz ...," *Miami Vice,* NBC, 1987.
Chacon, "Shadow Play," *The Equalizer,* CBS, 1987.
Lunza, "I Confess," *Spenser: For Hire,* 1987.
Father Torres, "The Secret Sharers," *Law & Order,* NBC, 1991.
Miguel Cortez, *The Hat Squad,* CBS, 1992.
Rodriguez, "Virus," *Law & Order,* NBC, 1993.
Carlos Ortiz, "To Protect and Serve," *New York Undercover,* Fox, 1994.
Detective Jimmy Badillo, "Ex–Corpus Delicti," *The Wright Verdicts,* CBS, 1995.

Detective Jimmy Badillo, "Sins of the Father," *The Wright Verdicts,* CBS, 1995.

Emilio Vasquez, "Innocent Bystanders," *New York Undercover,* Fox, 1995.

Arnell Flores, "Blue Boy," *New York Undercover,* Fox, 1996.

Jesse Castillo, "Monster," *Law & Order,* NBC, 1998.

Palmieri, "Sunday in the Park with Jorge," *Law & Order,* NBC, 2001.

Himself, "Inside the Walls of 'The Last Crusade,'" *HBO First Look,* HBO, 2001.

Mr. Caffey, "Unfinished Business," *Third Watch,* NBC, 2001.

Dan Martinez, "An Open Book," *The Education of Max Bickford,* CBS, 2002.

Jojo Rios, "Legion," *Law & Order: Criminal Intent* (also known as *Law & Order: CI*), NBC, 2003.

Kenneth Silva, "Veteran's Day," *Law & Order,* NBC, 2004.

Detective, "Truth or Consequences," *Law & Order: Trial by Jury,* NBC, 2005.

Assemblyman Eric Molina, "Fat," *Law & Order: Special Victims Unit* (also known as *Law & Order: SVU* and *Special Victims Unit*), NBC, 2006.

Manny Trillo, "Unchained," *Lie to Me,* Fox, 2009.

Marcus Feingold, "Disciple," *Law & Order: Criminal Intent* (also known as *Law & Order: CI*), NBC, 2010.

Also appeared (as Paul Calderone) as Rosario, *Dellaventura,* CBS.

Stage Appearances:

Short Eyes, Second Stage Theatre, McGinn–Cazale Theatre, New York City, 1985.

Dealer and Che, *Cuba and His Teddy Bear,* New York Shakespeare Festival, Susan Stein Shiva Theatre, Public Theatre, then Longacre Theatre, both New York City, 1986.

Mantequilla Decima, *Blade to the Heart,* New York Shakespeare Festival, Anspacher Theatre, Public Theatre, New York City, 1994.

Troilus and Cressida, Public Theatre, New York City, 1995.

Federico, *Dancing on Her Knees,* New York Shakespeare Festival, LuEsther Hall, Public Theatre, New York City, 1996.

Second militia guard and Lieutenant Portuondo, *Two Sisters and a Piano,* New York Shakespeare Festival, Susan Stein Shiva Theatre, Public Theatre, 2000.

Also appeared in *First Breeze of Summer; Richard III; The Trial of Sgt. Deluca,* all New York City.

RECORDINGS

Music Videos:

Appeared as a dealer, "Bad" by Michael Jackson, 1987.

WRITINGS

Screenplays:

Bad Lieutenant, 1992.

CAMPBELL, Neve 1973–

PERSONAL

Given name rhymes with "Bev"; full name, Neve Adrienne Campbell; born October 3, 1973, in Guelph, Ontario, Canada; immigrated to United States, 1994; daughter of Gerry (a high school drama teacher) and Marnie (a psychologist and yoga instructor; maiden name, Neve) Campbell; sister of Christian Campbell (an actor and producer) married Jeff Colt (an actor and songwriter), April 3, 1995 (divorced, 1998); married John Light (an actor), May 5, 2007. *Education:* Studied at National Ballet School of Canada, 1982–87. *Religion:* Roman Catholic. *Avocational Interests:* Dance, swimming, horseback riding, inline skating, yoga and meditation, reading, singing, listening to classical music, making jewelry.

Addresses: *Agent*—International Creative Management, 10250 Constellation Blvd., 9th Floor, Los Angeles, CA 90067; Danis Panaro Nist, 9201 West Olympic Blvd., Beverly Hills, CA 90212. *Manager*—Forster Entertainment, 12533 Woodgreen, Los Angeles, CA 90066. *Publicist*—PMK*BNC, 8687 Melrose Ave., 8th Floor, Los Angeles, CA 90069.

Career: Actress and producer. Blue Sphere Alliance (production company), Los Angeles, founding partner, c. 1998; founded a theatre company with brother Christian Campbell in Los Angeles. Appeared in television and print commercials. Tourette Syndrome Association, national spokesperson. Former ballet dancer.

Awards, Honors: Family Film Award, best television actress, 1996, for *The Canterville Ghost;* Saturn Award, best actress, Academy of Science Fiction, Horror, and Fantasy Films, and MTV Movie Award nomination, best female performance, both 1997, for *Scream;* Blockbuster Entertainment Award, favorite horror actress, and MTV Movie Award, best female performance, both 1998, for *Scream 2;* MTV Movie Award nomination (with Matt Dillon and Denise Richards), best kiss, 1999, for *Wild Things;* named one of the fifty most beautiful people of the year, *People Weekly,* 1998; MTV Award nomination, best female performance, 2000, and Blockbuster Entertainment Award, favorite horror actress, 2001, both for *Scream 3;* Prism Award, outstanding performance in a television movie or miniseries, 2003, for *Last Call.*

CREDITS

Film Appearances:

Deputy Jesse Donovan, *The Dark,* Imperial Entertainment, 1994.

Rose, *Ruskin* (also known as *The Passion of John Ruskin*), 1994.

Tristesse, *Paint Cans,* 1994.

Deidre, *Love Child,* 1995.

Bonnie, *The Craft,* Columbia, 1996.

Sidney Prescott, *Scream,* Dimension Films, 1996.

Sidney Prescott, *Scream 2,* Dimension Films, 1997.

Julie Black, *54,* Miramax, 1998.

Renee Weber, *Hairshirt* (also known as *Too Smooth*), Lions Gate Releasing, 1998.

Voice of adult Kiara, *The Lion King II: Simba's Pride* (animated), Buena Vista Home Video/Walt Disney Home Video, 1998.

Suzie Marie Toller, *Wild Things* (also known as *wildthings* and *Sex Crimes*), Columbia, 1998.

Amy Post, *Three to Tango,* Warner Bros., 1999.

Sarah, *Panic,* Artisan Entertainment, 1999.

Herself, *Predators from Beyond Neptune,* 1999.

Sidney Prescott, *Scream 3,* Miramax/Dimension Films, 2000.

Ellen Rash, *Drowning Mona,* Destination Films, 2000.

Herself, *Conjuring "The Craft,"* 2000.

Herself, *Behind the "Scream,"* 2000.

Alice, *Investigating Sex* (also known as *Intimate Affairs*), Janus Films/Kingsgate Films, 2001.

Against the Current, 2002.

Made in Canada, Volume 1: Best of the CFC, Asylum, 2002.

Missy Lofton, *Lost Junction,* Metro–Goldwyn–Mayer Home Entertainment, 2003.

Loretta "Ry" Ryan, *The Company* (musical), Sony Pictures Classics, 2003.

Vera Barrie, *When Will I Be Loved,* IFC Films, 2004.

Princess Elizabeth, *Churchill: The Hollywood Years,* 2004.

Chloe Richards, *Blind Horizon,* Lions Gate Films, 2004.

Herself, *The Outsider,* Westlake Entertainment Group, 2005.

Ellen Minnola, *Relative Strangers,* First Look International, 2006.

Herself, *O Lucky Malcolm!,* Warner Home Video, 2006.

Margaret Stilwell, *Partition,* Myriad Pictures, 2007.

Abi, *I Really Hate My Job,* Barnholtz Entertainment, 2007.

Marie, *Closing the Ring* (also known as *Richard Attenborough's "Closing the Ring"*), Weinstein Company, 2007.

Herself, *Journey of the Heart: The Making of "Partition"* (documentary), Warner Home Video, 2007.

Voice of Cassie, *Agent Crush,* Fantastic Films International, 2008.

Narrator, *Dirty Oil* (documentary), Dogwoof Pictures, 2009.

Film Producer:

Hairshirt (also known as *Too Smooth*), Lions Gate Releasing, 1998.

The Company (musical), Sony Pictures Classics, 2003.

Television Appearances; Series:

Daisy McKenzie, *Catwalk,* MTV, 1992–93.

Julia Salinger Holbrook, *Party of Five,* Fox, 1994–2000.

Olivia Maidstone, *The Philanthropist,* NBC, 2009.

Television Appearances; Miniseries:

Holly, *Burn Up,* BBC2, Global TV, and Planet Green, 2008.

Television Appearances; Movies:

Jess Foy, *The Forget–Me–Not Murders* (also known as *Janek: Forget–Me–Not Murders*), CBS, 1994.

Beth, *I Know My Son Is Alive* (also known as *Web of Deceit*), NBC, 1994.

Nepeese, *Baree* (also known as *Baree: The Wolf Dog, Bari,* and *Northern Passage*), 1994.

Virginia "Ginny" Otis, *The Canterville Ghost,* ABC, 1996.

Frances Kroll, *Last Call* (also known as *Fitzgerald*), Showtime, 2003.

Missy Lofton, *Lost Junction,* USA Network, 2003.

Miss Poppy, *Reefer Madness: The Movie Musical,* Showtime, 2005.

Television Appearances; Specials:

The Witching Hour, 1996.

Paparazzi, E! Entertainment Television, 1998.

Celebrity Profile: Jennifer Love Hewitt, E! Entertainment Television, 2000.

"Scream": The E! True Hollywood Story, E! Entertainment Television, 2001.

Kevin Bacon: Am I Me?, Arts and Entertainment, 2002.

101 Reasons the 90's Ruled, 2004.

"Scream Queens": The E! True Hollywood Story, E! Entertainment Television, 2004.

Reefer Madness: Grass Roots (short documentary), Showtime, 2005.

Live Earth (also known as *Live Earth 7.7.07, Live Earth: The Concerts for a Climate in Crisis,* and *SOS: The Movement for a Climate in Crisis*), NBC, 2007.

The Making of "I Really Hate My Job," 2008.

Television Appearances; Awards Presentations:

Presenter, *The 1997 MTV Movie Awards,* MTV, 1997.

Presenter, *The 1997 MTV Video Music Awards,* MTV, 1997.

Presenter, *The 49th Annual Primetime Emmy Awards,* CBS, 1997.

Presenter, *The 1998 MTV Movie Awards,* MTV, 1998.

Blockbuster Entertainment Awards, UPN, 1998.

Presenter, *The 70th Annual Academy Awards,* ABC, 1998.

The 2000 Blockbuster Entertainment Awards, Fox, 2000.
7th Annual Prism Awards, FX Network, 2003.
Scream Awards, 2008.

Television Appearances; Episodic:
(Uncredited) Student, "Pirate Radio," *My Secret Identity,* 1991.
Laura Capelli, *The Kids in the Hall,* CBC and HBO, 1992.
Nonnie Walker, "Tale of the Dangerous Soup," *Are You Afraid of the Dark?,* 1994.
Trish Collins, "Kundela," *Kung Fu: The Legend Continues,* 1994.
Nepeese, "Bari," *Aventures dans le Grand Nord,* 1994.
MADtv, Fox, 1995, 1996.
Late Night with Conan O'Brian, NBC, 1996.
Late Show with David Letterman, CBS, 1996, 2001.
The Rosie O'Donnell Show, syndicated, 1996, 1998, 1999, 2000, 2001.
Host, *Saturday Night Live* (also known as *SNL*), NBC, 1997.
The Tonight Show with Jay Leno, NBC, 1998, 2001, 2002.
"The Films of Wes Craven," *The Directors,* Encore, 1999.
Access Hollywood, syndicated, 1999, 2000.
Rotten TV, VH1, 2000.
Tussen de sterren, 2003.
The Early Show, CBS, 2003, 2004.
Ellen: The Ellen DeGeneres Show, syndicated, 2004.
Charlie Rose (also known as *The Charlie Rose Show*), PBS, 2004.
Last Call with Carson Daly, MTV, 2004.
Tinseltown TV, International Channel, 2004.
Live with Regis and Kelly, 2004.
Today (also known as *NBC News Today* and *The Today Show*), NBC, 2004.
Late Show with David Letterman (also known as *Letterman* and *The Late Show*), CBS, 2004.
Late Night with Conan O'Brien, NBC, 2004.
The View, ABC, 2004.
"Charities," *Open Access,* The Tennis Channel, 2004.
This Morning, ITV, 2004.
"Val Kilmer," *Biography,* Arts and Entertainment, 2004.
Dinner for Five, Independent Film Channel, 2005.
Punk'd, MTV, 2005.
The Bigger Picture (also known as *The Bigger Picture with Graham Norton*), BBC, 2006.
Richard & Judy, Channel 4, 2006.
GMTV, ITV, 2006.
Debra, "Head Games," *Medium,* NBC, 2007.
Debra, "Heads Will Roll," *Medium,* NBC, 2007.
P. D. McCall, "Everything Comes to a Head," *Medium,* NBC, 2007.
Celebrity guest, "Obama Ball," *ADHDtv: With Lew Marklin* (also known as *The LMS* and *The Lew Marklin Show*), 2008.
Xpose, TV3, 2009.

Voice of Cassandra, "Rednecks and Broomsticks," *The Simpsons* (animated), Fox, 2009.
(Uncredited) Voice of Cassandra, "O, Brother, Where Bart Thou?," *The Simpsons* (animated), Fox, 2009.
Maud Brewster, *Sea Wolf,* 2010.

Stage Appearances:
Member of ballet chorus, *The Phantom of the Opera,* Pantages Theatre, Toronto, Ontario, Canada, c. 1989–90.

Performed in *The Nutcracker* and *Sleeping Beauty,* both National Ballet of Canada.

WRITINGS

Films Stories:
The Company, Sony Pictures Classics, 2003.

OTHER SOURCES

Books:
Furman, Elina, *Neve Campbell: An Unauthorized Biography,* Renaissance Books, 2000.
Newsmakers 1998, Issue 2, Gale, 1998.
Tracy, Kathleen, *Neve Campbell,* ECW Press, 2000.

Periodicals:
Cosmopolitan, January, 1997, p. 80.
Daily Mail (London), October 7, 2005, p. 33.
Dance, February, 2003, p. 11.
Entertainment Weekly, June 21, 1996, p. 24; August 22, 2003, p. 81.
Interview, January, 1997, p. 60.
Jane, May, 1999, pp. 93–97.
Movieline, Volume 8, number 5, 1996, p. 14.
People Weekly, May 27, 1996, pp. 79–80; July 15, 1996; May 11, 1998, p. 103; May 8, 2000, p. 106.
Premiere, Volume 5, number 4, 1997, p. 27.
Rolling Stone, October 6, 1994, p. 93; September 18, 1997, pp. 56–60.
Sassy, June, 1996.
Teen, April, 2000.
Time, March 23, 1998, p. 78.
Time International, March 30, 1998, p. 44.
TV Guide, August 14, 1996; February 8, 1997, pp. 22–24, 26–28.

CANTONA, Eric 1966–

PERSONAL

Born May 24, 1966, in Marseilles, France; brother of Joel Cantona (an actor); married Isabelle Ferrer, February 28, 1987 (divorced, 2003); married Rachida Brakni (an actress), June 16, 2007; children: (first marriage) two; (second marriage) one. *Avocational Interests:* Painting.

Addresses: *Agent*—Artmedia, 20 Avenue Rapp, Paris 75007, France.

Career: Actor. Former professional soccer player for Manchester United, Marseille, and Leeds United, retiring in 1997; involved with beach soccer in France. Appeared in television commercials, including Nike athletic wear, 1996–98, 2002, and Rasoirs Bic Orange, 1999.

CREDITS

Film Appearances:

Lionel the rugby player, *Happiness Is in the Field* (also known as *Le bonheur est dans le pre*), Bac Films, 1995.

Question d'honneur (short film), 1997.

Monsieur de Foix, *Elizabeth* (also known as *Elizabeth: The Virgin Queen*), Gramercy, 1998.

Antoine Capella, *Mookie,* President Films, 1998.

Himself, *Enfoires en coeur,* 1998.

Jo Sardi, *Les enfants du Marais,* Gala Films, 1999.

Himself, *United in the 90's* (documentary), 1999.

Joueur de petanque number two, *The High Life* (also known as *La grande vie!*), Sagittaire Films, 2001.

Himself, *Manchester United: The Official History 1878–2002* (documentary), VCI Distribution, 2002.

Le commissaire Selena, *The Over–Eater* (also known as *L'outremanageur*), TFM Distribution, 2003.

Himself and un comedien qui refuse de tourner avec Laurent, *The Car Keys* (also known as *Les clefs de bagnole*), 2003.

Une belle histoire, 2005.

Pierre (L'oiseau bleu), *La vie est a nous!,* Bac Films, 2005.

Alban, *Le deuxieme souffle,* ARP Selection, 2007.

Man at bar, *Jack Says,* Your Indie Films, 2008.

Thierry Grimandi, *French Film* (also known as *French Lovers Have All the Answers*), Vertigo Films, 2008.

Eric, *Looking for Eric,* IFC Films, 2009.

Gerard, *Ensemble, c'est trop,* 2010.

Thierry, *Les mouvements du bassin* (also known as *The Pelvis Moves*), 2010.

Film Work:

Director, *Apporte–moi ton amour* (short film), 2002.

Television Appearances; Miniseries:

Corto Maltese, 2001.

Television Appearances; Specials:

(Uncredited) Player, *Eleven Men Against Eleven,* Channel 4, 1995.

Himself, *Les guignols, les dix premieres annees,* 1999.

Jack, *Papillon noir,* 2008.

Michael Lombardi, *La liste,* 2009.

Presenter, *The 2009 European Film Awards,* 2009.

(Uncredited) Himself, *Gilles Jacob: Citizen Cannes* (documentary; also known as *Gilles Jacob, l'arpenteur de la croissette*), 2010.

Television Appearances; Episodic:

Tout le monde en parle, 2001, 2005.

The Football Years, 2002.

L'hebdo cinema, 2006.

Le grand journal de Canal+, 2006, 2009, 2010.

Quelli che … il calcio, 2009.

Xpose, TV3, 2009.

Friday Night with Jonathan Ross, BBC1 and BBC America, 2009.

"Ajami," *The Fabulous Picture Show,* 2009.

Cinema 3, 2009.

OTHER SOURCES

Periodicals:

Daily Mail (London), June 4, 1996, p. 69; May 22, 1997, p. 28.

Evening Standard (London), April 23, 2009, p. 11; May 13, 2009, p. 9.

Sports Illustrated, May 26, 1997, p. 36.

CARPENTER, John 1948–

(Frank Armitage, Johnny Carpenter, John T. Chance, Rip Haight, Martin Quatermass)

PERSONAL

Full name, John Howard Carpenter; born January 16, 1948, in Carthage, NY (raised in Bowling Green, KY); son of Howard Ralph (a music professor) and Milton Jean (maiden name, Carter) Carpenter; married Adrienne Barbeau (an actress), January 1, 1979 (divorced, 1988); married Sandy King (a producer), December 1, 1990; children: (first marriage) John Cody. *Education:* Attended Western Kentucky University, c. 1968; graduate work in film at the University of Southern California, 1968–72. *Avocational Interests:* Helicopter piloting, music, Elvis, old Cadillacs, basketball.

Addresses: *Agent*—William Morris Agency, One William Morris Place, Beverly Hills, CA 90212. *Publicist*—Guttman Associates PR, 118 S. Beverly Dr., Suite 201, Beverly Hills, CA 90212. *Contact*—c/o Big Deal Productions, Inc., 5632 Van Nuys Blvd., Van Nuys, CA

91411. *Manager*—Echo Lake Entertainment, 421 S. Beverly Dr., 8th Floor, Beverly Hills, CA 90212.

Career: Director, producer, actor, screenwriter, and composer. Performer in the rock group, Coup de Villes; The Horror Hall of Fame, member of board of directors; Emerald Productions (a production company), founder; Hye Whitebread Productions (a production company), cofounder, 1979.

Member: Directors Guild of America, Writers Guild of America—West, American Society of Composers, Authors, and Publishers.

Awards, Honors: Academy Award, best short subject (live action), 1970, *The Resurrection of Bronco Billy;* Golden Scroll Award (with others), best special effects, Nebula Award nomination, best dramatic writing, Science Fiction and Fantasy Writers of America, 1976, for *Dark Star;* London Film Festival special award, 1977; Edgar Allan Poe Award, best made–for–television mystery movie, Mystery Writers of America, 1978, for *Someone's Watching Me!;* New Generation Award, Los Angeles Film Critics Association Awards, 1979; Critics' Prize, Avoriaz Film Festival, 1979, for *Halloween;* Critics' Prize, Avoriaz Film Festival, 1980, for *The Fog;* American Institute for Public Service Jefferson Award, outstanding public service benefitting local communities, 1980; Saturn Award nomination, best director, Academy of Science Fiction, Horror, and Fantasy Films, 1982, for *Escape from New York;* Grand Prize Award nomination, Avoriaz Fantastic Film Festival, 1984, for *Christine;* Saturn Award nomination, best music, 1987, for *Big Trouble in Little China;* Saturn Award nomination, best music, Critics Award, Avoriaz Fantastic Film Festival, 1988, for *Prince of Darkness;* International Fantasy Film Award nomination, best film, 1989, Saturn Award nomination (with Alan Howarth), best music, 1990, for *They Live;* CableACE Award (with Bill Phillips), writing a movie or miniseries, 1991, for *El Diablo;* International Fantasy Film Award nomination, best film, 1993, for *Memoirs of an Invisible Man;* International Fantasy Film Award nomination, best film, 1994 for *Body Bags;* Critics Award, Fantasporto, and International Fantasy Film Award nomination, best film, 1995, both for *In the Mouth of Madness;* Best Film Award nomination, Sitges Catalonian International Film Festival, 1995, for *Village of the Damned;* George Pal Memorial Award, Academy of Science Fiction, Fantasy and Horror Films, 1996; Saturn Award, best music, Bram Stoker Award nomination, other media, 1999, both for *Vampires;* Best Film Award nomination, Catalonian International Film Festival, 2001, for *Ghosts of Mars;* Best Film Award nomination and Carnet Jove Special Mention, Sitges Catalonian International Film Festival, 2006, for *Masters of Horror;* Lifetime Achievement Award, Bram Stoker Awards, 2007; Time–Machine Honorary Award, Sitges Catalonian International Film Festival, 2008.

CREDITS

Film Work:

Director, *Revenge of the Colossal Beasts* (short film), 1962.

Director, *Terror from Space* (short film), 1963.

(As Johnny Carpenter) Director, *The Warrior and the Demon* (short film), 1969.

Director, *Sorcerer from Outer Space* (short film), 1969.

Director, *Gorgo versus Godzilla* (short film), 1969.

Director, *Gorgon, the Space Monster* (short film), 1969.

Editor, *The Resurrection of Bronco Billy* (short film), Universal, 1970.

Editor, *Last Foxtrot in Burbank,* 1973.

Producer, director, and music director, *Dark Star,* Jack H. Harris, 1974.

Director and (as John T. Chance) editor, *Assault on Precinct 13* (also known as *John Carpenter's Assault on Precinct 13*), Turtle Releasing Company, 1976.

Director and (uncredited) producer, *Halloween* (also known as *John Carpenter's Halloween*), Compass, 1978.

Director, *Elvis* (also known as *Elvis the Movie*), 1979.

Director, *The Fog* (also known as *John Carpenter's "The Fog"*), Avco Embassy, 1980.

Director, *Escape from New York* (also known as *John Carpenter's "Escape from New York"*), Avco Embassy, 1981.

(With Debra Hill) Producer, director, *Halloween II* (also known as *Halloween II: The Nightmare Isn't Over!*), Universal, 1981.

(With Hill) Producer, *Halloween III: Season of the Witch* (also known as *Season of the Witch*), Universal, 1982.

Director, *The Thing* (also known as *John Carpenter's "The Thing"*), Universal, 1982.

Director, *Christine* (also known as *John Carpenter's "Christine"*), Columbia, 1983.

Executive producer, *The Philadelphia Experiment,* New World, 1984.

Director, *Starman* (also known as *John Carpenter's "Starman"*), Columbia, 1984.

Director, *Big Trouble in Little China* (also known as *John Carpenter's "Big Trouble in Little China"*), Twentieth Century–Fox, 1986.

Executive producer, *Black Moon Rising,* 1986.

(As Martin Quatermass) Director, *Prince of Darkness* (also known as *John Carpenter's "Prince of Darkness"*), Universal, 1987.

(As Frank Armitage) Director, *They Live* (also known as *John Carpenter's "They Live"* and *They Live!*), Universal, 1988.

Director, *Memoirs of an Invisible Man* (also known as *Les aventures d'un homme invisible*), Warner Bros., 1992.

Director, *In the Mouth of Madness* (also known as *John Carpenter's "In the Mouth of Madness"*), New Line Cinema, 1995.

Director, *Village of the Damned* (also known as *John Carpenter's "Village of the Damned"*), Universal, 1995.

Director, *Escape from L.A.* (also known as *John Carpenter's "Escape from L.A."*), Paramount, 1996.

Director, *John Carpenter's "Vampires"* (also known as *Vampires* and *Vampire$*), Sony Pictures, 1998.

Director, musician, and orchestrator, *Ghosts of Mars* (also known as *John Carpenter's "Ghosts of Mars"*), Screen Gems, 2001.

Director and executive producer, *Vampires: Los Muertos* (also known as *John Carpenter's "Vampires: Los Muertos"* and *John Carpenter Presents Vampires: Los Muertos*), Sony Pictures Entertainment, 2002.

Producer, *The Fog,* Sony Pictures Entertainment, 2005.

Director, *The Ward* (also known as *John Carpenter's "The Ward"*), 2010.

Film Appearances:

No Place to Land, 1958.

(Uncredited) Gang member, *Assault on Precinct 13,* 1976.

(Uncredited) Voice of Paul, Annie's boyfriend, *Halloween* (also known as *John Carpenter's "Halloween"*), Compass, 1978.

(Uncredited) Bennett, church janitor, *The Fog* (also known as *John Carpenter's "The Fog"*), Avco Embassy, 1980.

(Uncredited) Voice of second Secret Service man and helicopter pilot, *Escape from New York* (also known as *John Carpenter's "Escape from New York"*), Avco Embassy, 1981.

(Uncredited) Norwegian in video footage, *The Thing* (also known as *John Carpenter's "The Thing"*), 1982.

(Uncredited) Man in helicopter, *Starman* (also known as *John Carpenter's "Starman"*), 1984.

(With the Coupe de Villes) *The Boy Who Could Fly,* 1986.

(Uncredited) Worker in Chinatown, *Big Trouble in Little China* (also known as *John Carpenter's "Big Trouble in Little China"*), Twentieth Century–Fox, 1986.

(As Rip Haight) Helicopter pilot, *Memoirs of an Invisible Man* (also known as *Les aventures d'un homme invisible*), Warner Bros., 1992.

Trench Coat Man, *The Silence of the Hams* (also known as *Il silenzio dei prosciutti*), 1994.

(As Rip Haight) Man at phone booth, *Village of the Damned* (also known as *John Carpenter's "Village of the Damned"*), Universal, 1995.

Himself, *The American Nightmare,* 2000.

(In archive footage) Himself, *Scoring Resident Evil,* Columbia TriStar Home Video, 2002.

Do You Remember Laurie Zimmer?, 2003.

(In archive footage) Himself, *Halloween: 25 Years of Terror,* 2006.

Going to Pieces: The Rise and Fall of the Slasher Film, 2006.

Halloween: Faces of Fear, 2007.

The Secret World of Superfans, 2008.

Science of Horror, 2008.

Lovecraft: Fear of the Unknown, 2008.

Dead On: The Life and Cinema of George A. Romero, 2008.

Tales from the Script, 2009.

Nightmares in Red, White and Blue, 2009.

Television Work; Series:

Editorial assistant, *Real World/Road Rules Challenge: Fresh Meat,* MTV, 2006.

Television Work; Movies:

Director, *Someone's Watching Me!* (also known as *High Rise*), NBC, 1978.

Director, *Elvis,* ABC, 1979.

Executive producer, *El diablo,* 1990.

Executive producer and segment director, "The Gas Station," and "Hair," *John Carpenter Presents "Body Bags"* (also known as *Body Bags*), Showtime, 1993.

Television Director; Episodic:

"John Carpenter's Cigarette Burns," *Masters of Horror,* 2005.

"Pro–Life," *Masters of Horror,* 2006.

Television Appearances; Movies:

Coroner, "The Morgue," *John Carpenter Presents "Body Bags"* (also known as *Body Bags*), Showtime, 1993.

Television Appearances; Miniseries:

A–Z of Horror (also known as *Clive Barker's "A–Z of Horror"*), 1997.

The 100 Scariest Movie Moments, 2004.

Television Appearances; Specials:

Fear on Film: Inside "The Fog," 1980.

Fear in the Dark, 1991.

Masters of Illusion: The Wizards of Special Effects, 1994.

The Reality Trip, 1997.

After Sunset: The Life & Times of the Drive–In Theater, AMC, 1997.

Masters of Fantasy: John Carpenter, Sci–Fi Channel, 1998.

Faces of Evil, TNT, 2000.

The American Nightmare, Independent Film Channel, 2000.

Guns for Hire: The Making of "The Magnificent Seven," Channel 4, 2000.

Mario Bava: Maestro of the Macabre, 2000.

Dario Argento: An Eye for Horror, Independent Film Channel, 2000.

Game–Show Mania, E! Entertainment Television, 2000.

AFI's 100 Years, 100 Thrills: America's Most Heart–Pounding Movies, CBS, 2001.

(Uncredited) Himself, *Hidden Values: The Movies of the Fifties,* TCM, 2001.

Boogeymen II: Masters of Horror (also known as *Masters of Horror*), 2002.

"Halloween": A Cut Above the Rest, 2003.

The 100 Greatest Scary Moments, Channel 4, 2003.

Super Secret Movie Rules: Slashers (also known as *SSMR: Slashers*), 2004.

Tales from the Crypt: From Comic Books to Television, AMC, 2004.

05 Spaceys, 2005.

THS Investigates: Inside the Mind of a Serial Killer, 2005.

The Perfect Scary Movie, Channel 4, 2005.

Hollywood's Greatest Villains, History Channel, 2005.

Big John, 2006.

Bloodsucking Cinema, 2007.

Starz Inside: Fantastic Flesh, Starz!, 2008.

Monsterland, 2009.

Television Appearances; Episodic:

Cinema 3, 1986.

Firstworks, TMC, 1988.

"The Hero Strikes Back," *Signals,* 1990.

"Chasing the Hollywood Dream," *Carrie on Hollywood,* 1995.

"Action Effects: Ultimate Action," *Movie Magic,* 1996.

The Directors, Starz, 1998–2005.

"Scream," *E! True Hollywood Story,* E! Entertainment Television, 2001.

The Daily Show with Jon Stewart (also known as *The Daily Show, A Daily Show with Jon Stewart,* and *The Daily Show with Jon Stewart Global Edition*), 2001.

"Ghosts of Mars," *HBO First Look,* 2001.

"Franka Potente und John Carpenter," *Into the Night with …* (also known as *Durch die nacht mit …*), 2003.

"It Came from Japan," *Animal Icons,* Animal Planet, 2005.

Film '72, BBC, 2006.

RECORDINGS

Videos:

Himself, *After Sunset: The Life & Times of the Drive–In Theater,* 1995.

Himself, *100 Years of Horror: Witchcraft and Demons,* 1996.

Himself, *100 Years of Horror: Sorcerers,* 1996.

Himself, *100 Years of Horror: Maniacs,* 1996.

Himself, *100 Years of Horror: Gory Gimmicks,* 1996.

Himself, *100 Years of Horror: Aliens,* 1996.

Himself, *100 Years of Horror: Demons,* 1996.

Himself, *Unmasking the Horror,* 1998.

The Thing: Terror Takes Shape (also known as *John Carpenter's The Thing: Terror Takes Shape*), 1998.

Himself, *"Halloween" Unmasked 2000,* Anchor Bay Entertainment, 1999.

"Ghosts of Mars": Special Effects Deconstruction, 2001.

Himself, *Scoring Ghosts of Mars,* Columbia TriStar Home Video, 2001.

Himself, *Red Desert Nights: Making "Ghosts of Mars,"* Columbia TriStar Home Video, 2001.

Himself, *Tales from the Mist: Inside "The Fog,"* Metro–Goldwyn–Mayer/United Artists Home Entertainment, 2002.

Something to Do with Death, 2003.

The Wages of Sin, 2003.

An Opera of Violence, 2003.

Return to "Escape from New York," 2003.

Cinemaker, 2004.

John Carpenter: Fear Is Just the Beginning … The Man and His Movies, 2004.

Christine: Finish Line, 2004.

Christine: Fast and Furious, 2004.

Christine: Ignition, 2004.

Snake Plissken: Man of Honor, 2005.

Seeing Through "The Fog" (also known as *See Through the Fog: The Making of "The Fog"*), 2006.

Feeling the Effects of "The Fog" (also known as *Feeling the Effects of the Fog: Specials Effects Featurette*), 2006.

Whiteout Conditions: The Remaking of a Horror Classic (also known as *Whiteout Conditions: Remaking a Horror Classic*), 2006.

Born to Controversy: The Roddy Piper Story, 2006.

Celluloid Apocalypse: An Interview with John Carpenter, 2006.

Amazing! Exploring the Far Reaches of Forbidden Planet, 2006.

Final Delivery: The Making of "Pro Life," 2007.

The Fearmakers Collection, 2007.

In the Master's Shadow: Hitchcock's Legacy, 2008.

Pure Cinema: Through the Eyes of the Master, 2008.

Bernard Herrmann: Hitchcock's Maestro, 2008.

The Master's Touch: Hitchcock's Signature Style, 2009.

More Tales from the Script, 2010.

Video Games:

Voice of Dr. Faraday, *The Thing,* 2002.

WRITINGS

Film Writings:

(With Jim Rokos) Screenplay and score composer, *The Resurrection of Bronco Billy* (short film), Universal, 1970.

(With Dan O'Bannon) Screenplay and score composer, *Dark Star,* Jack H. Harris, 1974.

Screenplay and score composer, *Assault on Precinct 13* (also known as *John Carpenter's "Assault on Precinct 13"*), Turtle Releasing Company, 1976.

(With David Zelag Goodman) Screenplay, *The Eyes of Laura Mars,* Columbia, 1978.

(With Debra Hill) Screenplay and score composer, *Halloween* (also known as *John Carpenter's "Halloween"*), Compass, 1978.

(With Hill) Screenplay and score composer, *The Fog* (also known as *John Carpenter's "The Fog"*), Avco Embassy, 1980.

(With Nick Castle) Screenplay and (with Alan Howarth) score composer, *Escape from New York* (also known as *John Carpenter's "Escape from New York"*), Avco Embassy, 1981.

(With Hill) Screenplay and (with Howarth) score composer, *Halloween II* (also known as *Halloween II: The Nightmare Isn't Over!*), Universal, 1981.

(With Howarth) Composer, *Halloween III: Season of the Witch* (also known as *Season of the Witch*), Universal, 1982.

(With Howarth) Composer, *Christine* (also known as *John Carpenter's "Christine"*), Columbia, 1983.

(With Howarth) Composer, *Big Trouble in Little China* (also known as *John Carpenter's "Big Trouble in Little China"* and *Ghost Hunters*), Twentieth Century–Fox, 1986.

(With Desmond Nakano and William Gray) Screenplay, *Black Moon Rising*, New World, 1986.

(As Martin Quatermass) Screenplay and (with Howarth) score composer, *Prince of Darkness* (also known as *John Carpenter's "Prince of Darkness"*), Universal, 1987.

(As Frank Armitage) Screenplay and score composer, *They Live* (also known as *John Carpenter's "They Live"* and *They Live!*), Universal, 1988.

Composer, *Halloween 4: The Return of Michael Myers* (also known as *Halloween 4*), 1988.

(With Howarth) Composer, *Halloween 5: The Revenge of Michael Myers* (also known as *Halloween 5*), Galaxy International, 1989.

Composer, *Kickboxer from Hell*, 1992.

(With Jim Lang) Composer, *In the Mouth of Madness* (also known as *John Carpenter's "In the Mouth of Madness"*) New Line Cinema, 1995.

(With Dave Davies) Composer, *Village of the Damned* (also known as *John Carpenter's "Village of the Damned"*), Universal, 1995.

Screenplay and composer, *Halloween: The Curse of Michael Myers* (also known as *Hall6ween*), 1995.

Screenplay and (with Shirley Walker) score composer, *Escape from L.A.* (also known as *John Carpenter's "Escape from L.A."*), Paramount, 1996.

Screenplay and theme composer, "Halloween," *Halloween: H2O* (also known as *Halloween H2O: Twenty Years Later*), Miramax, 1998.

Composer, *John Carpenter's "Vampires"* (also known as *Vampires* and *Vampire$*), Sony Pictures, 1998.

Screenplay, *Meltdown*, 1999.

Composer, *"Halloween" Unmasked 2000*, Anchor Bay Entertainment, 1999.

Screenplay, composer, *Ghosts of Mars* (also known as *John Carpenter's "Ghost of Mars"*), Screen Gems, 2001.

(With Hill) Screenplay, composer, *Halloween: Resurrection 2002*, Dimension Films, 2002.

Screenplay, *Assault on Precinct 13*, 2005.

Screenplay, *The Fog*, Sony Pictures Entertainment, 2005.

Screenplay and composer, *Halloween* (also known as *Rob Zombie's "Halloween"*), 2007.

Composer, *Halloween II* (also known as *H2: Halloween II* and *Rob Zombie's "Halloween II"*), 2009.

Composer, *Judith: The Night She Stayed Home*, 2010.

Composer, *The Ward*, 2010.

Film Songs:

"Halloween Theme," *Terror in the Aisles*, Universal, 1984.

"Halloween Theme," *Haider lebt–1. April 2021*, 2002.

"Halloween Theme," *The Life of David Gale*, 2003.

"The Crazies Come Out," *Grindhouse*, 2007.

"Back To The Pod/The Crazies Come Out," *Planet Terror* (also known as *Grindhouse Presents: Robert Rodriguez's "Planet Terror"* and *Robert Rodriguez's "Planet Terror"*), 2007.

Television Movies:

(With William A. Schwartz) *Zuma Beach*, NBC, 1978.

Someone's Watching Me! (also known as *High Rise*), NBC, 1978.

(With Greg Strangis) *Better Late Than Never*, NBC, 1979.

El Diablo, 1990.

Blood River, 1991.

John Carpenter Presents "Body Bags" (also known as *Body Bags*), Showtime, 1993.

Silent Predators, TBS, 1999.

Television Movies; Scores:

(With Jim Lang), *John Carpenter Presents "Body Bags"* (also known as *Body Bags*), Showtime, 1993.

Television Series; Songs:

"Halloween Theme," *Bassie en Adriaan en de reis vol verrassingen*, 1994.

Video Game Scores:

Sentinel Returns, 1998.

OTHER SOURCES

Books:

Cumbow, Robert C., *Order in the Universe: The Films of John Carpenter*, Scarecrow, 2000.

International Dictionary of Films and Filmmakers, Volume 2: *Directors*, St. James Press, 1996.

Muir, John Kenneth, *The Films of John Carpenter*, McFarland & Company, 2000.

Periodicals:
Entertainment Weekly, November/December, 1997, pp. 98–103.
Film Comment, September/October, 1996, pp. 50–54; January, 1999, p. 26.
Hollywood Reporter, October 26, 1998, p. 13.

CASNOFF, Philip 1955–
(Phil Casnoff, Phillip Casnoff)

PERSONAL

Born August 3, 1955, in Philadelphia, PA; married Roxanne Hart (an actress), 1984; children: Alexander, Macklin McKee.

Addresses: *Agent*—Don Buchwald and Associates, 6500 Wilshire Blvd., Suite 2200, Los Angeles, CA 90048. *Manager*—Darris Hatch Management, 9538 Brighton Way, Suite 308, Beverly Hills, CA 90210.

Career: Actor, singer, and pianist.

Member: American Federation of Television and Radio Artists, Actors Equity Association, Screen Actors Guild, Directors Guild of America.

Awards, Honors: *Theatre World Award,* outstanding new performer, 1988, for *Chess;* Drama Desk Award nomination, c. 1989, for *Up Against It;* Golden Globe Award nomination, best actor in a miniseries or television movie, 1993, for *Sinatra.*

CREDITS

Film Appearances:
Aaron, *Uchu kara no messeji* (also known as *Message from Space, Return to Jelucia,* and *Message from Space: Galactic Wars*), United Artists, 1978.
Ricardo Bouma, *You Better Watch Out* (also known as *Christmas Evil* and *Terror in Toyland*), Pan American Pictures, 1980.
Bergman, *Gorp* (also known as *G.O.R.P.*), American International Pictures, 1980.
Mitchell, *Jersey Girl,* Triumph Releasing, 1992.
Michael Reddick, *Temptation,* Starlight, 1994.
Detective Battaglia, *Saints and Sinners,* MDP Worldwide, 1994.
Kennedy, *How Stella Got Her Groove Back,* Twentieth Century–Fox, 1998.
Victor Marchetta, *Material Girls,* Metro–Goldwyn–Mayer, 2006.
Mr. Johnson, *Switchback,* 2010.

Film Work:
Associate producer, *Switchback,* 2010.

Television Appearances; Series:
David Landau, *The Hamptons,* ABC, 1983.
Brian Murdock, *The Edge of Night* (also known as *Edge of Night*), 1984.
Rob Riviera, *One Life to Live,* ABC, 1990.
Detective James Vitelli, *Under Suspicion,* CBS, 1994–95.
Prisoner number 99S233 Nikolai Stanislofsky, *Oz,* HBO, 1999–2000.
Chief of Staff Dr. Robert Jackson, *Strong Medicine,* Lifetime, 2000–2005.

Television Appearances; Miniseries:
Lafayette, *George Washington,* CBS, 1984.
Elkanah Bent, *North and South* (also known as *North and South Book I*), ABC, 1985.
Elkanah Bent, *North and South, Book II* (also known as *Love and War*), ABC, 1986.
Marty Loftus, *Hands of a Stranger,* NBC, 1987.
Frank Sinatra, *Sinatra,* CBS, 1992.
Elkanah Bent, *Heaven & Hell: North & South, Book III* (also known as *John Jakes' "Heaven & Hell: North & South, Book III"* and *North and South, Book III*), ABC, 1994.
Simon Hirsch, *Zoya* (also known as *Danielle Steel's "Zoya"*), NBC, 1995.

Television Appearances; Movies:
Dancer, *The Renegades,* ABC, 1982.
Detective Patrick Shaunessy, *The Red Spider,* CBS, 1988.
Lieutenant Guilford, *Ironclads,* TNT, 1991.
Charlie Lapidus, *Red Wind,* USA Network, 1991.
Nick Van Pelt, *Special Report: Journey to Mars,* CBS, 1996.
Greg Radkin, *Little Girls in Pretty Boxes,* Lifetime, 1997.
Richard Davis, *Blood on Her Hands,* ABC, 1998.
Richard Davis, *Tempting Fate,* ABC, 1998.
Cortez, *Chameleon,* UPN, 1998.
John Walker, *The Defenders: Taking the First,* Showtime, 1998.
Mackey, Dustin's boss, *Kiss Tomorrow Goodbye,* Starz!, 2000.
Al Glasser, *For All Time,* CBS, 2000.
Jack Stanton, *The President's Man: A Line in the Sand,* CBS, 2002.
Lance Saxon, *Jane Doe: Eye of the Beholder,* Hallmark Channel, 2008.

Television Appearances; Specials:
Harvey Schmidt, "Out of Step," *ABC Afterschool Special,* ABC, 1984.
The American Television Awards, ABC, 1993.

Television Appearances; Pilots:
Suddenly Susan, NBC, 1996.

Television Appearances; Episodic:
Iannis, "King of America," *American Playhouse,* PBS, 1982.
(As Phil Casnoff) Ben Pearson, "License to Steele," *Remington Steele,* NBC, 1982.
Chris Wood, "Slippage," *Tales from the Darkside,* syndicated, 1984.
"Bum Tip," *Crazy Like a Fox,* CBS, 1985.
Det. James Vitelli, "Serial Killer: Parts 1 & 2," *Under Suspicion,* 1994.
Jack Chambers, "A Fighting Chance," *Sisters,* NBC, 1995.
Jack Chambers, "Matters of the Heart," *Sisters,* NBC, 1995.
Jack Chambers, "Enchanted May," *Sisters,* NBC, 1995.
Paul Acosta, "Christmas Truce," *Chicago Hope,* CBS, 1995.
Cantor Gary Isaac, "The Cantor Show," *The Nanny,* CBS, 1996.
Eric, "Too Beautiful for You," *Wings,* NBC, 1996.
Bill Carter, "Little Girl Lost," *Promised Land,* CBS, 1996.
William Cobb, "Necros," *The Hunger,* Showtime, 1997.
John Fellowes, "Conspiracy," *Players,* NBC, 1998.
Dr. Dan Litvak, "Masquerade," *ER,* NBC, 1998.
Jerome Slocombe, "Innocent," *Fantasy Island,* ABC, 1999.
Danny Rogers, "Of Human Bondage," *The Practice,* ABC, 1999.
Harris, "Livegirls.now," *Walker, Texas Ranger,* CBS, 1999.
Grant Connor, "Seven Deadly Sins," *Diagnosis Murder* (also known as *Dr. Mark Sloan*), CBS, 1999.
"14 Steps/Damaged Goods/Ballerina Dreams," *Chicken Soup for the Soul,* PAX, 2000.
Ilya Korska, "Pixies" (also known as "Little Women"), *Law & Order: Special Victims Unit* (also known as *Law & Order: SVU* and *Special Victims Unit*), NBC, 2001.
Dr. Bernard Gadston, "War of the Words," *Frasier,* NBC, 2002.
Bill Talbot, "Slaughter," *Law & Order,* NBC, 2002.
Assistant District Attorney Nick Forster, "The Line," *Law & Order: Trial by Jury,* NBC, 2005.
Donald Clarence, "Candy," *Without a Trace* (also known as *W.A.T.*), CBS, 2006.
Maurice Connors, "Longshot," *Numb3rs* (also known as *Num3ers*), CBS, 2006.
Dr. Sanchez, "Sleeping Beauty," *Crossing Jordan,* NBC, 2007.
Clive Ambrose, "Echoes," *Dollhouse,* Fox, 2009.
Clive Ambrose, "Meeting Jane Doe," *Dollhouse,* Fox, 2009.
Clive Ambrose, "Getting Closer," *Dollhouse,* Fox, 2009.

Television Director; Episodic:
Strong Medicine, Lifetime, 2003–2005.

(As Phillip Casnoff) "Mr. Monk Stays in Bed," *Monk,* USA Network, 2005.
(As Phillip Casnoff) "Mr. Monk and the Captain's Marriage," *Monk,* USA Network, 2005.

Stage Appearances:
Acolyte, nobleman, swordsman, and courtesan, *Rockabye Hamlet* (musical), Minskoff Theatre, New York City, 1976.
Bobbie Gotteson and the spider monkey, *The Triumph of the Spider Monkey,* Phoenix Playworks, Playhouse Theatre, 1979.
Fedya, *Chinchilla,* Phoenix Theatre, Marymount Manhattan Theatre, New York City, 1979.
David Ben Yonkel, *King of Schnorrers,* Harold Clurman Theatre, New York City, 1979.
John, *Mary Stuart,* New York Shakespeare Festival, LuEsther Hall, Public Theatre, New York City, 1981.
Constance and the Musician, American Place Theatre, New York City, 1981.
Poins, *Henry IV, Part I,* New York Shakespeare Festival, Delacorte Theatre, Public Theatre, New York City, 1981.
Freddie Trumper, *Chess* (musical), Imperial Theatre, New York City, 1988.
Richard Dudgeon, *The Devil's Disciple,* Circle in the Square, New York City, 1988–89.
Ian McTurk, *Up Against It,* New York Shakespeare Festival, LuEsther Hall, Public Theatre, 1989.
John Blackthorne, *James Clavell's "Shogun": The Musical,* Marquis Theatre, New York City, 1990–91.
Macheath, *The Threepenny Opera* (musical), American Conservatory Theatre, Geary Theatre, San Francisco, CA, 1999.
Norman's Ark, John Anson Ford Ampitheatre, Hollywood, CA, 2008.

Also appeared in *Grease;* as Billy Flynn, *Chicago,* New York City.

RECORDINGS

Albums:
Performed for the original cast recording of *Chess.*

CAUTHEN, Kal

PERSONAL

Education: Studied acting with Kristen Shaw, Terri Vaughn, Tasha Smith, Andrea Bubride, Sidra Smith, Saunde Shurin, Douglas Turner Ward, and Bill Duke.

Addresses: *Agent*—The People Store, Atlanta, GA. *Manager*—C Paper Chase Management, Atlanta, GA.

Career: Actor.

Member: American Federation of Television and Radio Artists, Screen Actors Guild.

CREDITS

Film Appearances:
Well–dressed man, *Love Goggles,* Transmission Films, 1999.
Detective Clark, *A Packing Suburbia,* Cinema Esperanca International, 1999.
Dancer, *Friday Night Fever* (short film), 2004.
Drew Madison, *King of Hearts,* York Entertainment, 2005.
Larry, *Unforgiven Sins* (also known as *Unforgiven Sins: The Case of the Faceless Murders*), 2006.
(Uncredited) Banquet guest, *Why Did I Get Married?* (also known as *Tyler Perry's "Why Did I Get Married?"*), Lions Gate Films, 2007.
(Uncredited) Restaurant ambassador, *American Gangster,* Universal, 2007.
Captain Arnold, *Gold Digger Killer,* Warner Vision Entertainment, 2007.
Pimp, *7 Days of Yellow,* 2009.
Wayne, *It's Never Too Late,* 2010.

Also appeared as Calvin, *Prodigal Son;* Lyndon, *Chameleon* (short film); Uncle Wayne, *It's Never Too Late* (short film); Vinnie Dee, *Heal House* (short film); Teddy Brooks, *Silent Cries* (short film); drug addict, *Addicted* (short film); Sheldon, *A Women's Worth* (short film).

Television Appearances; Series:
Kal, *All My Children,* ABC, 1997–2004.
Detective William Bryce, *Atlanta Homicide* (also known as *Atlanta Investigations: HD (Homicide Division)*), 2008–2009.

Television Appearances; Movies:
Detective Williams, *Partners,* 2010.

Television Appearances; Episodic:
Second rescue worker, "How to Bury a Millionaire," *Spin City,* ABC, 1999.

Television Appearances; Others:
Appeared as cohost and judge, *Who's Got That Vibe?;* Mr. Nefertari, *Nefertari.*

Television Work; Episodic:
Collaborating director, "Open Eyes," *Atlanta Homicide* (also known as *Atlanta Investigations: HD (Homicide Division)*), 2008.

Producer, "Fallen Soldier," *Atlanta Homicide* (also known as *Atlanta Investigations: HD (Homicide Division)*), 2008.

Stage Appearances:
Appeared as Elder Reed, "A Hot Mess," *Hurricane Church;* Big Daddy, drug dealer, and addict, *Tell Hell I Ain't Coming;* Guy Veona Thomas, *A Dance Between Friends.*

OTHER SOURCES

Electronic:
Kal Cauthen Official Site, http://www.kalcauthen.com, October 26, 2010.

CHANCE, John T.
   See CARPENTER, John

CHASMAN, Steve
   (Steven Chasman)

PERSONAL

Married Nadia Fares (an actress), July, 2002; children: Shana Leelee, Cylia Marti (some sources cite name as Cecilia Marti). *Education:* University of Pennsylvania, undergraduate degree; Emory University, law degree, 1991.

Addresses: *Office*—Current Entertainment/ACE Media, 9200 Sunset Blvd., 10th Floor, Los Angeles, CA 90069.

Career: Producer. Current Entertainment (production and management company), Los Angeles, founder and manager/producer; joined with Atlas Entertainment to form ACE Media, LLC, 2006. Worked as an agent at International Creative Management, 1993–99; and as a contract lawyer at Whiteford Taylor Preston in Washington, DC and Baltimore, MD.

CREDITS

Film Producer:
Kiss of the Dragon (also known as *KOD: Kiss of the Dragon*), Twentieth Century–Fox, 2001.
(As Steven Chasman) *The One* (also known as *Jet Li's "The One"*), Columbia, 2001.

The Transporter (also known as *Transporter*), Twentieth Century–Fox, 2002.

Coproducer, *Taxi* (also known as *New York Taxi, Taxi: The Maximum, Taxi NY,* and *Taxi 2004*), Twentieth Century–Fox, 2004.

(As Steven Chasman) *Transporter 2* (also known as *Transporter Extreme, Transporter: Extreme,* and *Transporter—The Mission*), Twentieth Century–Fox, 2005.

Unleashed (also known as *Danny the Dog*), Focus Features, 2005.

Executive producer, *Chaos* (also known as *Hit & Blast*), Capitol Films, 2005.

Executive producer, *DOA: Dead or Alive* (also known as *Dead or Alive, DOA,* and *D.O.A.—Dead or Alive*), Dimension Films, 2006.

(As Steven Chasman) *War* (also known as *Rogue Assassin*), Lions Gate Films, 2007.

The Bank Job (also known as *Baker Street, Bank Job,* and *D–Notice*), Lions Gate Films, 2008.

Transporter 3 (also known as *Transporter 3: Unlimited*), Lions Gate Films, 2008.

Blitz, Lions Gate Films, c. 2010.

The Killer Elite, c. 2011.

Worked on other films.

Television Work; Movies:

Producer, *Invincible* (also known as *Invincibles*), TBS, 2001.

CHESTNUT, Morris 1969–

PERSONAL

Full name, Morris L. Chestnut; born January 1, 1969, in Cerritos, CA; married Pam Byse (an actress), 1995; children: two. *Education:* Studied finance and drama at California State University at Northridge, 1991; studied acting at Crossroads Academy, Los Angeles. *Avocational Interests:* Playing Texas Hold 'Em poker.

Addresses: *Agent*—Creative Artists Agency, 2000 Avenue of the Stars, Los Angeles, CA 90067.

Career: Actor. Won Madden Bowl, 1998.

Member: Phi Beta Sigma.

Awards, Honors: Image Award nomination, outstanding actor in a motion picture, National Association for the Advancement of Colored People, 2000, for *The Best Man;* Black Reel Award nomination, network/cable—best actor, 2002, for *The Killing Yard.*

CREDITS

Film Appearances:

Ricky Baker, *Boyz N the Hood* (also known as *Boys in the Hood*), Columbia, 1991.

Locker room kid, *The Last Boy Scout,* Warner Bros., 1991.

Harold Lee, *The Inkwell* (also known as *No Ordinary Summer*), Buena Vista, 1994.

Bobby Zachs, *Under Siege 2: Dark Territory* (also known as *Under Siege 2*), Warner Bros., 1995.

McCool, *G.I. Jane,* Buena Vista, 1997.

Lance Sullivan, *The Best Man,* MCA/Universal, 1999.

Jackson Smith, *The Brothers,* Screen Gems, 2001.

Keith Fenton, *Two Can Play That Game,* Columbia TriStar, 2001.

Ray, *Scenes of the Crime,* TF1 International, 2001.

Tracey Reynolds, *Like Mike,* Twentieth Century–Fox, 2002.

Donald Robert Johnson/49er One, *Half Past Dead,* Columbia TriStar, 2002.

Travis, *Confidence,* Lions Gate Films, 2003.

Tommy Drake, *Ladder 49,* Buena Vista, 2003.

Himself, *Friendly Fire: Making an Urban Legend* (short documentary; also known as *"Boyz N the Hood": Friendly Fire—Making an Urban Legend*), Columbia TriStar Home Entertainment, 2003.

Evan Fields, *Breakin' All the Rules,* Screen Gems, 2004.

Gordon Mitchell, *Anacondas: The Hunt for the Blood Orchid* (also known as *Anacondas 2: The Hunt for the Blood Orchid*), Screen Gems, 2004.

Himself, *The N Word* (documentary; also known as *The N–Word: Divided We Stand*), Urban Works Entertainment, 2004.

Top Buchanan, *The Cave,* Screen Gems, 2005.

Presenter, *The 14th Annual Inner City Destiny Awards,* Tri Destined Studios, 2006.

Travis Sanders, *The Game Plan,* Buena Vista, 2007.

Benjamin Armstrong, *The Perfect Holiday,* Yuri Film Group Releasing, 2007.

Dave Johnson, *Not Easily Broken,* Screen Gems, 2009.

Marcelles Wynters, *Love in the Nick of Tyme,* Lions Gate Films, 2009.

Film Work:

Executive producer, *Not Easily Broken,* Screen Gems, 2009.

Producer, *Love in the Nick of Tyme,* Lions Gate Films, 2009.

Executive producer, *Takers,* Screen Gems, 2010.

Television Appearances; Series:

Jeff Carswell, *Out All Night,* NBC, 1992–93.

Mal Robinson, *C–16: FBI* (also known as *C–16*), ABC, 1997–98.

Ryan Nichols, *V,* ABC, 2009—.

Television Appearances; Movies:
Prince Franklin, *In the Line of Duty: Street War* (also known as *Urban Crossfire*), NBC, 1992.
Title role, *The Ernest Green Story,* The Disney Channel, 1993.
Andre, *Firehouse,* 1997.
Shango, *The Killing Yard,* Showtime, 2001.
Leo Moore, *The Prince of Motor City,* ABC, 2008.

Television Appearances; Specials:
Host, *Miss Collegiate African American Pageant,* syndicated, 1993.
The 26th Annual NAACP Image Awards, NBC, 1994.
The 31st Annual NAACP Image Awards, Fox, 2000.
Presenter, *The Source Hip–Hop Music Awards 2001,* UPN, 2001.
2nd Annual BET Awards, 2002.

Television Appearances; Pilots:
Ryan Nichols, *V,* ABC, 2009.

Television Appearances; Episodic:
Jason Woodman, "A Family Affair," *Freddy's Nightmares,* 1990.
Dion, *Drexell's Class,* Fox, 1991.
The Tonight Show with Jay Leno, NBC, 1992.
Ebony/Jet Showcase, 1993.
Host, *Soul Train,* 1994.
Hamilton Brown, "Love Thy Neighbor," *Living Single,* Fox, 1994.
Hamilton Brown, "Mystery Date," *Living Single,* Fox, 1994.
The Martin Short Show, syndicated, 1999.
ICU Nurse Frank "Rambo" Bacon, "Under Control," *ER,* NBC, 2000.
ICU Nurse Frank "Rambo" Bacon, "The Visit" (also known as "I Loved You, God, How I Loved You"), *ER,* NBC, 2000.
Himself, "Two Can Play That Game," *The Ananda Lewis Show,* 2001.
106 & Park Top 10 Live (also known as *106 & Park*), Black Entertainment Television, 2005.
Agent Oakes, "The Man in the Wall," *Bones,* Fox, 2005.
"Xmas in March," *In the Cutz* (also known as *In the Mix*), Urban America, 2006.
Up Close with Carrie Keagan, 2007, 2010.
"Morris Chestnut & Chadam," *The Jace Hall Show,* 2009.
The Wendy Williams Show, 2009.
The Mo'Nique Show, Black Entertainment Television, 2009.
Entertainment Tonight (also known as *E.T.*), syndicated, 2010.

Television Work; Series:
Executive producer, *Stage Black* (also known as *David E. Talbert Presents: "Stage Black"*), 2007.

RECORDINGS

Music Videos:
Appeared in "Blame It" by Jamie Foxx.

OTHER SOURCES

Books:
Contemporary Black Biography, Volume 31, Gale, 2001.

CHIRCHER, Theresa
    See **CHURCHER, Teresa**

CHRISTIAN, Shawn 1965–

PERSONAL

Full name, Shawn Patrick Christian; born December 18, 1965, in Grand Rapids, MI; married Deborah Quinn (a model), May 18, 1996; children: Kameron. *Education:* Ferris State University, degree in business, 1989.

Addresses: *Agent*—Innovative Artists, 1505 10th St., Santa Monica, CA 90401. *Manager*—Burstein Company, 15304 Sunset Blvd., Suite 208, Pacific Palisades, CA 90272.

Career: Actor. Worked as a model in Chicago, IL. Alibi Lounge, Big Rapids, MI, worked as bartender and assistant manager.

Awards, Honors: *Soap Opera Digest* Award nomination, hottest male star, 1996, for *As the World Turns;* Congressional Medal of Merit for youth leadership in his community.

CREDITS

Film Appearances:
Wink Hendricks, *Beautiful,* Destination Films, 2000.
Desert Jack Sawyer, *Tremors 3: Back to Perfection,* Universal Studios Home Video, 2001.
Rory Reisman, *50 Ways to Leave Your Lover* (also known as *How to Lose Your Lover*), New Line Cinema, 2004.
Pilgrim man, *For Your Consideration,* Warner Independent Pictures, 2006.

Lieutenant Left Arm, *Meet Dave,* Twentieth Century–Fox, 2008.

Ken, *Mating Dance,* Westlake Entertainment Group, 2008.

Alex, *Only One Can Play* (short film), A Black Number Production, 2009.

Tommy Carson, *Small Town Saturday Night,* Grindstone Entertainment Group, 2010.

Television Appearances; Series:

Mike Kasnoff, *As the World Turns,* CBS, 1994–97.

Val Poole, *Wind on Water,* NBC, 1998.

Wayne, *Beverly Hills, 90210* (also known as *Class of Beverly Hills*), Fox, 1999.

Ross Rayburn, *One Life to Live,* ABC, 2002.

Wade Brixton, *Birds of Prey* (also known as *BOP*), The WB, 2002–2003.

Johnny Durant, *Summerland,* The WB, 2004–2005.

Dr. Derek Stephenson, *Las Vegas,* NBC, 2006.

Dr. Daniel Jonas, *Days of Our Lives* (also known as *DOOL* and *Days*), NBC, 2008–10.

Brandon, *Venice the Series,* 2010.

Television Appearances; Movies:

Eugene Farrow, *CTS: Toronto,* 1999.

Jake Cunningham, *Undercover Christmas,* CBS, 2003.

Danny Pelosi, *Murder in the Hamptons,* Lifetime, 2005.

Tom Kent in 2010, *Secrets of the Mountain,* NBC, 2010.

Television Appearances; Specials:

Presenter, *The 23rd Annual Daytime Emmy Awards,* CBS, 1996.

Host, *The 12th Annual Soap Opera Awards,* NBC, 1996.

Television Appearances; Pilots:

Electra's Guy, syndicated, 2000.

Malcolm Cross, *Red Skies,* USA Network, 2002.

Johnny, *Immediate Family,* The WB, 2003.

Television Appearances; Episodic:

Star Search, 1994.

Quinn Ragowski, "Motherly Love," *Pacific Palisades,* Fox, 1997.

Quinn Ragowski, "Sweet Revenge," *Pacific Palisades,* Fox, 1997.

Quinn Ragowski, "End Game," *Pacific Palisades,* Fox, 1997.

Danny, "Gay Yellow Pages," *Ellen* (also known as *These Friends of Mine*), ABC, 1997.

Trevor Davis, "Dream Racer," *Malcolm & Eddie,* UPN, 1997.

Adam Galbreth, "Inside Traitor," *Team Knight Rider,* syndicated, 1997.

The plumber, "Special Delivery," *Men Behaving Badly* (also known as *It's a Man's World*), NBC, 1997.

Police Officer Adams, "Justice for All, and …," *Step by Step,* CBS, 1998.

Police Officer Adams, " … Justice for Some," *Step by Step,* CBS, 1998.

Nick, "Three Stages of Love," *The Love Boat: The Next Wave,* UPN, 1999.

Josh, "Is There a Woogy in the House?," *Charmed,* The WB, 1999.

Josh, "When Bad Warlocks Go Good," *Charmed,* The WB, 1999.

Josh, "Blind Sided," *Charmed,* The WB, 1999.

Josh, "Out of Sight," *Charmed,* The WB, 1999.

Dr. Lawrence Brandon, "Call to Glory," *Pensacola: Wings of Gold,* syndicated, 1999.

Dr. Brandon, "Behind Enemy Lives," *Pensacola: Wings of Gold,* syndicated, 1999.

Dr. Lawrence Brandon, "At Poverty Level," *Pensacola: Wings of Gold,* syndicated, 2000.

Randall, "The Time They Decided to Date," *Time of Your Life,* Fox, 2000.

Michael Ellins, "Run, Val, Run," *V.I.P.,* syndicated, 2000.

Patrick Haynes/Chad Matthews, "Table Stakes," *CSI: Crime Scene Investigation* (also known as *CSI: Las Vegas* and *C.S.I.*), CBS, 2001.

Adam Flynn, "Believers," *Crossing Jordan,* NBC, 2001.

Adam Flynn, "Digger: Parts 1 & 2," *Crossing Jordan,* NBC, 2001.

Santa, "An Office and a Gentleman," *Spin City,* ABC, 2001.

Dr. Schiff, "The One with Ross's Step Forward," *Friends,* NBC, 2001.

Dennis, "Hot from the Oven," *The Chronicle* (also known as *News from the Edge*), Sci–Fi Channel, 2002.

Kevin, "L.A. Woman," *Becker,* CBS, 2002.

Detective Stokes, "Nocturne," *Haunted,* UPN, 2002.

Grant, "The Dawn Patrol," *The Drew Carey Show,* ABC, 2002.

Kevin, "Nightmare on Becker Street," *Becker,* CBS, 2003.

Thad, "Nipple Effect," *Coupling,* NBC, 2003.

Stephen James, "Love Don't Love Nobody," *10–8: Officers on Duty* (also known as *10–8*), ABC, 2004.

Hair dresser, "The Shampoo Effect," *Happy Family,* NBC, 2004.

Jared Hart/FBI Special Agent Darren Merritt, "Truth or Dare: Parts 1 & 2," *1–800–MISSING* (also known as *Missing*), Lifetime, 2004.

SoapTalk, SoapNet, 2005.

Tim Bauer, "The Black Widow," *Boston Legal,* ABC, 2005.

Tim Bauer, "Schadenfreude," *Boston Legal,* ABC, 2005.

Tim Bauer, "Finding Nimmo," *Boston Legal,* ABC, 2005.

John, "Chick Stuff," *Hot Properties,* ABC, 2005.

Ryan Chisholm, "Jamalot," *CSI: NY* (also known as *CSI: New York*), CBS, 2005.

Travis, "Cowboys and Iranians," *Will & Grace,* NBC, 2006.

Carl Silvers, "Rio," *CSI: Miami,* CBS, 2006.

Dr. Fisher, "There's No Place Like Home," *Runaway,* The CW, 2006.
Dr. Fisher, "Mr. Rader Goes to Washington," *Runaway,* The CW, 2006.
Dr. Fisher, "End Game," *Runaway,* The CW, 2006.
"Father of the Bride Redux," *Las Vegas,* NBC, 2006.
Wyatt Jenkins, "The Cradle Will Rock," *Ghost Whisperer,* CBS, 2007.
Jack Sager, "Try to Remember," *A Side Order of Life,* Lifetime, 2007.
Kerry Conklin, "Every Breath You Take," *Shark,* CBS, 2007.

CHURCHER, Teresa
(Theresa Chircher)

PERSONAL

Education: Qualified life coach (MASC).

Addresses: *Agent*—Amanda Howard Associates, 21 Berwick St., London W1F 0PZ, England.

Career: Actress. Worked as a public speaker and life coach. Also known as Theresa Chircher.

Member: Screen Actors Guild.

Awards, Honors: Screen Actors Guild Award, outstanding performance by the cast of a theatrical motion picture, Critics Choice Award, best acting ensemble, Broadcast Film Critics Association, Florida Film Critics Circle Award, best ensemble cast, Online Film Critics Society Award, best ensemble, Special Achievement Award for outstanding acting ensemble, Golden Satellite awards, International Press Academy, and Phoenix Film Critics Society Award nomination, best acting ensemble, all 2002, and Chlotrudis Award, best cast, 2003, all with others, all for *Gosford Park.*

CREDITS

Film Appearances:
Anita "Dipsy" Morris, *Little England,* Boudicca Films, 1996.
Ruth Lonsdale, *Kiss Kiss Bang Bang* (also known as *The Sexy Mysterious Murders*), Boudicca Films, 2000.
Bertha, *Gosford Park,* USA Films, 2001.
Yvonne (disco girl), *Redemption Road,* Fusion International Sales, 2001.
Jane, *Little Clumps of Hair* (short film), 2003.
Cynthia, *Being Julia,* Sony Pictures Classics, 2004.

Charlotte, *Oliver Twist,* TriStar, 2005.
Television journalist, *Color Me Kubrick* (also known as *Colour Me Kubrick, Colour Me Kubrick: A True …ish Story, Me, Myself & Kubrick,* and *Me, Myself & Stanley*), Magnolia Pictures, 2005.
Bird, *Dumped* (short film), 2006.
Governess, *Angel,* IFC Films, 2007.
Nurse Anne, *Desert Flower,* National Geographic Entertainment, 2009.
Shirley Beckett, *Hell's Pavement,* Oopic Films, 2009.
Mrs. Davies, *Creation* (also known as *Annie's Box, Nature, Origin,* and *Untitled Charles Darwin Project*), Newmarket Films, 2010.

Television Appearances; Miniseries:
Jane Smith, *Bomber,* ITV, 2000.
Nurse Sarah Jenkins, *The Swap,* ITV, 2002.
(Uncredited) Woman with baby, *Colditz* (also known as *Escape from Colditz*), ITV, 2005.

Television Appearances; Movies:
Martha Brown, *In Search of the Brontes,* BBC, 2003.
Sinclair, *Belonging* (also known as *The Web of Belonging*), ITV, 2004.
Clara, *Ballet Shoes,* BBC, 2007.
Mrs. Lewis, *Affinity,* ITV, 2008.

Television Appearances; Episodic:
Student nurse, "Monday Bloody Monday," *Casualty* (also known as *Casual+y* and *Front Line*), BBC, 1997.
Fern Lambert, "Innocency of Life," *Kavanagh QC* (also known as *Kavanagh Q.C.*), Central, 1998.
Suzy Gold, "Anyone Who Had a Heart," *Holby City* (also known as *Holby*), BBC, 2000.
(As Theresa Chircher) Melanie Jankovich, "Second Class Ticket," *Doctors,* BBC, 2003.
(Uncredited) Sarah, *Spooks* (also known as *MI–5*), BBC, PBS, Arts and Entertainment, BBC Canada, and other channels, 2003.
Elsie Patterson, "The Hollow," *Agatha Christie: Poirot* (also known as *Agatha Christie's "Poirot," Hercule Poirot, Poirot,* and *Poirot: The Hollow*), ITV and Arts and Entertainment, 2004.
Louise Willis, "It's a Man Thing," *Casualty* (also known as *Casual+y* and *Front Line*), BBC, 2006.
Denise Templeton, "A Funny Thing Happened on the Way to Willesden," *The Last Detective,* ITV, 2007.
Mrs. Tarling, *Garrow's Law,* BBC, 2009.

Stage Appearances:
Suzie Silliass and Wynona, *Night Lights* (also known as *Nightlights*), The Birds Nest Theatre, London, 1995.
Jane, *Girls of Slender Means,* Stellar Quines Theatre Company, Assembly @ George Street, Edinburgh, Scotland, 2009.

Appeared as Olga, *Three Sisters,* and as Mrs. Lovett, *Womberang,* both Avondale Theatre, London; as Agnes, *Agnes of God,* Jermyn Street Theatre, London; as the girl (the title role), *The Girl with No Hands,* Bromley Pavilion, Bromley, England; as Beth, *The Grimm Telling,* The Studio, Beckenham, England; as Sue Murray, *The Truth Game,* Brixton Shaw Theatre, London; and as Melissa, *Videogames,* The Actor's Playpen, Los Angeles.

Major Tours:

Sharon, *Destination Earth,* Quantum Touring, c. 2000.

COLLETTI, Stephen 1986–

PERSONAL

Full name, Stephen August Colletti; born February 7 (some sources cite February 13), 1986, in Newport Beach, CA; some sources cite that his father is in the food industry and his mother is a flight attendant. *Education:* Attended San Francisco State University. *Avocational Interests:* Surfing.

Addresses: *Agent*—Barry McPherson, Agency for the Performing Arts, 405 South Beverly Dr., Beverly Hills, CA 90212. *Manager*—Rob Levy, Untitled Entertainment, 1801 Century Park East, Suite 700, Los Angeles, CA 90067.

Career: Actor. Worked at a surf shop in southern California.

Awards, Honors: Named one of "young Hollywood's up and coming for 2005," *Teen Vogue,* 2005; Teen Choice Award nomination, choice television reality/variety star—male, 2005, for *Laguna Beach: The Real Orange County.*

CREDITS

Television Appearances; Series:
Himself, *Laguna Beach: The Real Orange County* (also known as *Laguna Beach*), MTV, 2004–2005.
Chase Adams, *One Tree Hill* (also known as *Ravens, Filoi gia panta, Les freres Scott, Tunteet pelissae,* and *Tuti gimi*), The CW, beginning 2007.

Some sources cite an appearance in *Bug Juice* (also known as *Bug Juice: Our Summer at Camp, Bug Juice 2,* and *Bug Juice 3*), The Disney Channel.

Television Appearances; Specials:
Drummer, *Cleats of Imminent Doom* (short film), Independent Film Channel, 2005.
Himself, *MTV New Year of Music: New Year's Eve 2006,* MTV, 2006.
Host, *MTV Goes Gold: New Year's Eve 2007,* MTV, 2007.

Television Appearances; Awards Presentations:
The Fourth Annual TRL Awards (also known as *Fourth Annual MTV TRL Awards*), MTV, 2006.

Television Appearances; Episodic:
Himself, *Total Request Live* (also known as *TRL, TRL Weekend,* and *Total Request with Carson Daly*), MTV, 2004, 2005, 2007.
Himself, "Stephen and Tyson's 24 Hour Spring Breakout," *Celebrity Undercover* (also known as *MTV's "Celebrity Undercover"*), MTV, 2006.
Host, *Total Request Live* (also known as *TRL, TRL Weekend,* and *Total Request with Carson Daly*), MTV, 2006.
Himself, *Canada A.M.* (also known as *Canada AM, Canada AM Weekend,* and *Canada A.M. Weekend*), CTV, 2006.
Himself, *Punk'd* (also known as *Harassment*), MTV, 2006.
Himself, "A Date with the Past," *The Hills,* MTV, 2008.
(Uncredited; in archive footage) Himself, "All Good Things ...," *The Hills,* MTV, 2010.

Film Appearances:
Robert, *Normal Adolescent Behavior* (also known as *Fucking Teens, Havoc 2: Normal Adolescent Behavior, Normal Adolescent Behavior—A story of a teenager, A Story of a Teenager,* and *Ultimatum*), New Line Cinema, 2007.
Brandon, *Shannon's Rainbow,* Supernova Media/Summit Works, 2009.
Daniel Franklin, *What We Became* (short film), 2009.
Lou Masters, *Tinslestars,* Skelligs Productions, 2009.
Evan, *Maskerade,* Active Entertainment, 2010.
Jim, *Kill Katie Malone,* Artifact 2613/Illuminary Pictures/Scatena & Rosner Films, 2010.

Stage Appearances:
Appeared in stage productions, beginning c. 1997.

COOKE, Tricia

PERSONAL

Married Ethan Coen (a producer, director, and writer), October 2, 1993; sister–in–law of Joel Coen (a producer, director, and writer).

Addresses: *Agent*—United Talent Agency, 9560 Wilshire Blvd., Suite 500, Beverly Hills, CA 90212.

Career: Film editor, producer, director, and writer. Also worked as apprentice film editor, assistant film editor, associate film editor, and camera assistant.

Awards, Honors: Eddie Award nomination (with Ethan Coen), best edited comedy or musical feature film, American Cinema Editors, 2001, for *O Brother, Where Are Thou?*; Audience Award, outstanding narrative short film, L.A. Outfest, 2003, and Best Documentary Award, short film category, Dallas Out Takes, 2004, both (with Jennifer Arnold) for *Where the Girls Are.*

CREDITS

Film Editor:
Betty, Creative Light Worldwide/Panorama Entertainment, 1997.
Where the Air Is Cool and Dark, E.I. Independent Cinema, 1998.
The Big Lebowski, Gramercy, 1998.
Weeping Shriner (short film), Bald Guy with a Dent in His Head Productions, 1999.
O Brother, Where Art Thou? (also known as *Oh, Brother!*), Buena Vista, 2000.
The Man Who Wasn't There, USA Films, 2001.
(And producer and director) *Where the Girls Are* (short documentary), Mike Zoss Productions, 2003.
A Uniform Used to Mean Something ... (short film), 2004.
Hindsight Is 20/20 ... (short film), 2004.
The Notorious Bettie Page, Picturehouse Entertainment, 2005.
The Ex (also known as *Fast Track*), Metro–Goldwyn–Mayer, 2006.
(And producer and director) *Don't Mess with Texas* (short film), Cherry Films NYC, 2008.
(And producer) *The Thorny Rose* (short film), Cherry Films NYC, 2008.
Eve (short film), Handsomecharlie Films/Relativity Media/Verisimilitude, 2008.
"Natalie Portman" segment, *New York, I Love You,* Vivendi Entertainment, 2009.
Solitary Man, Anchor Bay Films, 2010.

Television Film Editor; Movies:
The 4th Floor, HBO, 1999.

WRITINGS

Screenplays:
Don't Mess with Texas (short film), Cherry Films NYC, 2008.

COSTER, Nicolas 1934–
(Nicholas Coster, Nick Coster)

PERSONAL

Full name, Nicolas Dwynn Coster; born December 3, 1934, in London, England; father, a New Zealand marine commander; married Candace Hilligoss (an actress and novelist; divorced, 1981); married Beth Pantel, January 17, 1982; children: (first marriage) two daughters; (second marriage) Ian. *Education:* Attended the Royal Academy of Dramatic Arts; studied acting at Sanford Meisner's Neighborhood Playhouse; studied film at New York University. *Avocational Interests:* Scuba diving.

Career: Actor. Guthrie Theatre, Minneapolis, MN, founding member. Appeared in television commercials, including Coca–Cola, 2007, and American Century Investments, 2007. Cousteau Society, founding member. Military service: U.S. Coast Guard skipper.

Awards, Honors: *Soap Opera Digest* Award nomination, outstanding actor in a supporting role on a daytime serial, 1986, Daytime Emmy Award nominations, outstanding supporting actor in a drama series, 1986, 1988, Soap Opera Digest Award, outstanding actor in a supporting role—daytime, 1988, Daytime Emmy Award nominations, outstanding lead actor in a drama series, 1991, 1992, all for *Santa Barbara.*

CREDITS

Film Appearances:
(Uncredited) Seaman, *Titanic,* Twentieth Century–Fox, 1953.
(Uncredited) Cadet Wilson, *Sea of Lost Ships,* 1953.
Asa Polsen, *The Outcast* (also known as *The Fortune Hunter*), Republic Pictures, 1954.
(Uncredited) Humphrey, Young Squire, *The Black Shield of Falworth,* 1954.
(Uncredited) Student, *The Eternal Sea,* 1955.
Roy Fellows, *City of Shadows,* Republic Pictures, 1955.
Light Fantastic, Embassy Pictures, 1964.
Harry Lindsay, *My Blood Runs Cold,* Warner Bros., 1965.
James Quinn, *The Sporting Club,* AVCO Embassy, 1971.
Markham, *All the President's Men,* Warner Bros., 1976.
Major Sidney Huff, MacArthur's aide, *MacArthur* (also known as *MacArthur, the Rebel General*), Universal, 1977.
Spitzer, *The Big Fix,* Universal, 1978.
David Fillmore, *Slow Dancing in the Big City,* United Artists, 1978.

U.S. Olympic team doctor, *Goldengirl,* AVCO Embassy, 1979.

Harris, *Just You and Me, Kid,* Columbia, 1979.

Dr. Stone, *The Concorde: Airport '79* (also known as *Airport '79, Airport '80: The Concorde, The Concorde,* and *S.O.S. Concorde*), Universal, 1979.

Fitzgerald, *The Electric Horseman,* Universal, 1979.

Mr. Whitney, *Little Darlings,* Paramount, 1980.

Warden Henry Sampson, *Stir Crazy,* Columbia, 1980.

(Uncredited) Poker player, *The Hunter,* 1980.

Walter, *Why Would I Lie?,* 1980.

Avery, *The Pursuit of D. B. Cooper* (also known as *Pursuit*), Universal, 1981.

Paul Trullinger, *Reds,* Paramount, 1981.

Hunt Shelton, *Big Business,* Buena Vista, 1988.

Dr. Phillip Jellinak, Sr., *How I Got into College,* 1989.

Harry Lovell, *Betsy's Wedding,* Buena Vista, 1990.

Admiral Torrance, *Freedom Strike,* A–Pix Entertainment, 1998.

Charles, *Love Happens,* Curb Entertainment, 1999.

Emcee, *Miss Supreme Queen,* 1999.

Bum Joe, *Blood Type,* 1999.

Harry, *A Day Out with Gordy,* 2002.

Mr. Stewart, *Plot 7,* Silver Plane Films, 2007.

Loman, *Loman's Tale* (short film), 2007.

Jack Gibson, *Race,* 2008.

Shadow on the Wall (short film), 2008.

Dr. Wallace, *Family of Four,* 2009.

Midlife (short film), 2010.

Dr. Woodley, *Dancing on a Dry Salt Lake,* 2010.

Television Appearances; Series:

Dr. Matt Steele, *Young Dr. Malone,* NBC, 1962–63.

Professor Paul Britton, *The Secret Storm,* CBS, 1964, 1967–69.

John Eldridge, *Our Private World,* CBS, 1965.

John Eldridge, *As the World Turns,* CBS, 1966.

Robert Delaney, *Somerset* (also known as *Another World: Somerset* and *Somerset: Bay City*), NBC, 1970–72.

Robert Delaney, *Another World* (also known as *Another World: Bay City*), NBC, 1970–71, 1972–76, 1980, 1989.

Chief J. C. Carson, *The Misadventures of Sheriff Lobo* (also known as *Lobo*), NBC, 1980–81.

Dr. Morris Whitford, *Ryan's Four,* ABC, 1983.

Anthony Makana, *One Life to Live,* ABC, 1983–84.

Lionel Lockridge, *Santa Barbara,* NBC, 1984–88, 1990–93.

Steve Andrews, *All My Children,* ABC, 1988–89.

Eduardo Grimaldi, *As the World Turns,* CBS, 1993–95.

Mayor Jack Madison, *The Bay* (also known as *The Bay the Series*), 2010.

Television Appearances; Miniseries:

Peter Ajemian, *The Word,* CBS, 1978.

Matty Firestone, *Princess Daisy,* NBC, 1983.

Television Appearances; Movies:

(As Nicholas Coster) Dr. Paul Jellico, *Where's Everett,* 1966.

General Philip Sheridan, "The Court–Martial of George Armstrong Custer," *Hallmark Hall of Fame,* NBC, 1977.

Governor, *A Fire in the Sky,* NBC, 1978.

Dr. Roberts, *Long Journey Back,* ABC, 1978.

Carl, *Friendly Fire,* ABC, 1979.

Bud Hensen, *The Solitary Man,* CBS, 1979.

(Uncredited) *The Women's Room,* ABC, 1980.

The Day the Bubble Burst, NBC, 1982.

Maurice Carver, *M.A.D.D.: Mothers Against Drunk Drivers,* NBC, 1983.

Uncle Edgar, *Beverly Hills Madam* (also known as *Ladies of the Night*), NBC, 1986.

Mr. Gorman, *Incident at Dark River* (also known as *Dark River—A Father's Revenge*), TNT, 1989.

General Renning—"Icarus," *By Dawn's Early Light* (also known as *Red Alert*), HBO, 1990.

Natural Selection (also known as *Dark Reflection*), Fox, 1994.

Harry Winslow, *Hearts Adrift,* USA Network, 1996.

Arthur Durning, *Full Circle* (also known as *Danielle Steel's "Full Circle"*), NBC, 1996.

Ezra Bushmaster, *The Dukes of Hazzard—Hazzard in Hollywood,* CBS, 2000.

Gavin Green, *Flower Girl,* Hallmark Channel, 2009.

Television Appearances; Specials:

Stanford McKay, *You Are the Jury,* NBC, 1986.

The 4th Annual "Soap Opera Digest" Awards, NBC, 1988.

Television Appearances; Pilots:

Charlie Perkins, *Grandpa Goes to Washington,* 1978.

Linderman, *Ebony, Ivory and Jade,* CBS, 1979.

Bert Arkins, *Bender,* CBS, 1979.

Whitford, *Ryan's Four,* ABC, 1983.

Mr. Hamilton, *Smart Guys,* NBC, 1988.

Dr. Carter Bart, *South of Sunset,* CBS, 1993.

Television Appearances; Episodic:

"No Leave for the Captain," *The United States Steel Hour* (also known as *The U.S. Steel Hour*), CBS, 1959.

(Uncredited) Civil service applicant, "The Shield," *Naked City,* ABC, 1959.

Don Simmons, "The Accident," *The Defenders,* CBS, 1961.

"Thou Art Woman," *Directions,* ABC, 1962.

"The Living End," *No Time for Sergeants,* ABC, 1964.

Binkie, "Charlie Paradise: The Tragic Flute," *Brenner,* CBS, 1964.

"The Living End," *No Time for Sergeants,* ABC, 1965.

Kenneth Layton, "Far Below," *Felony Squad,* ABC, 1966.

Rod McHew, "Peter by Moonlight," *Occasional Wife,* NBC, 1966.

Gregory, "Bad Bet on a 459–Silent," *The Green Hornet* (also known as *The Green Hornet*), ABC, 1967.

"The Witness," *N.Y.P.D.,* ABC, 1967.

"Bull's Eye," *The Blue Knight,* CBS, 1976.

Professor Croydon, "Angels on the Air," *Charlie's Angels,* ABC, 1977.

Lansford Ingalls, "I Remember, I Remember," Little House on the Prairie (also known as *L.H.O.T.P.* and *Little House: A New Beginning*), NBC, 1978.

"The Dream," *Baretta,* ABC, 1978.

Jeremy Greene, "Women Write Stories, and the Men Buy a Horse," Husbands, Wives & Lovers, CBS, 1978.

"A Matter of State," *The Amazing Spider–Man,* CBS, 1978.

Augie La Rocca, "The Dating Game" (also known as "Ann's Dating Game"), *One Day at a Time,* CBS, 1978.

Joe Morris, "Act of Love," *Dallas,* CBS, 1978.

Silas Lockhart, "The Deadly Dolphin," *Wonder Woman* (also known as *The New Adventures of Wonder Woman* and *The New Original Wonder Woman*), CBS, 1978.

Andre, "A Matter of State," *The Amazing Spider–Man,* CBS, 1978.

Al Krantz, "Starting Over," *Family,* ABC, 1978.

(As Nicholas Coster) Augie Augustine, "A Good Clean Bust with Sequel Rights," *The Rockford Files* (also known as *Jim Rockford, Private Investigator*), NBC, 1978.

August La Rocca, "The Dating Game," *One Day at a Time,* CBS, 1978.

"False Images," *The Runaways,* NBC, 1979.

"Episode 3," *The Lazarus Syndrome,* AB, 1979.

Colonel Drake, "Blind Rage," *The Incredible Hulk,* CBS, 1979.

Zev Arno, "A Chilling Surprise," *Kate Loves a Mystery* (also known as *Kate Columbo* and *Mrs. Columbo*), NBC, 1979.

"Loose Larry's List of Losers," *Tenspeed and Brown Shoe,* NBC, 1980.

"The Ghost Maker," *Paris,* CBS, 1980.

Allerick, "Olympiad," *Buck Rogers in the 25th Century,* NBC, 1980.

Lyle Sloan, "Jock's Trial: Parts 1 & 2," *Dallas,* CBS, 1980.

Rogers, "Miss Hard Hat USA," *When the Whistle Blows,* ABC, 1980.

Derek Frye, "The Least Dangerous Game," *Simon & Simon,* CBS, 1981.

(As Nicholas Coster) "Blue Collar," *Today's F.B.I.,* ABC, 1982.

Fred Brunis, "Blue and Broken–Harted," *Hart to Hart,* ABC, 1982.

Warner, "The Butler Did It (A Bird in the Hand)," *Police Squad!,* CBS, 1982.

"Favor for an Enemy," *Shannon,* CBS, 1982.

Ted Markham, "A Ghost of a Chance," *Quincy, M.E.* (also known as *Quincy*), NBC, 1982.

David Warner "Daddy's Girl," *The Facts of Life,* NBC, 1982.

Bill Spangler, "Don't Take My Wife Please," *Nine to Five* (also known as *9 to 5*), ABC, 1982.

Bill Spangler, "Three for the Money," *Nine to Five* (also known as *9 to 5*), ABC, 1983.

Bill Spangler, "The Phantom," *Nine to Five* (also known as *9 to 5*), ABC, 1983.

City Attorney David Stallings, "Pirate's Key: Parts 1 & 2," *Simon & Simon,* CBS, 1983.

Andrew "Andy" MacKenzie, "I Do?," *Magnum P.I.,* CBS, 1983.

Thomas Quinlan, "The Crystal Duck," *Hardcastle and McCormick,* ABC, 1983.

Brad Thurman, "The Shadow of Truth," *T. J. Hooker,* ABC, 1983.

(As Nicholas Coster) Ross Manley, "Return to Cadiz," *Knight Rider,* NBC, 1983.

Finch, "Beetlemania," *Teachers Only,* NBC, 1983.

David Warner "It's Lonely at the Top," *The Facts of Life,* NBC, 1985.

Phil, "Deadly Honeymoon," *Alfred Hitchcock Presents,* NBC, 1986.

David Warner, "Where's Poppa?," *The Facts of Life,* NBC, 1986.

Standford McKay, "The State of Ohio vs. James Wolsky," *You Are the Jury,* 1986.

David Warner, "Rites of Passage: Part 1," *The Facts of Life,* NBC, 1987.

Brian P. Young, "Brackman Vasektimized," *L.A. Law,* NBC, 1987.

David Warner, "The Beginning of the End," The Facts of Life, NBC, 1988.

Commissioner Farrel, "Rashomanny," *Hooperman,* ABC, 1989.

Amos Borden, "First Day/Last Day," *thirtysomething,* ABC, 1989.

Dr. Craig Zachary, "Smooth Operators," *Murder, She Wrote,* CBS, 1989.

Lowell Michaels, "Tony Does Golf," Who's the Boss?, ABC, 1989.

Gleason, "Ring of Honor," *Hunter,* NBC, 1989.

Dr. Frederick Alexander, "The Raising of Lazarus," *War of the Worlds* (also known as *War of the Worlds: The Second Invasion*), syndicated, 1989.

Wes Hofsteader, "Call of the Wild," *Life Goes On,* ABC, 1989.

Admiral Anthony Haftel, "The Offspring," *Star Trek: The Next Generation* (also known as *Star Trek: TNG*), syndicated, 1990.

Connor McCarthy, "Three for the Money," *Midnight Caller,* NBC, 1990.

Doc, "There but for the Grace," *MacGyver,* ABC, 1991.

Chester Gaddis, "The Trial: Parts 1 & 2," *Matlock,* NBC, 1991.

Andrew Blaine, "You Don't Know Me," *Jake and the Fatman,* CBS, 1991.

Mr. Azarian, "April Is the Cruelest Month," *Beverly Hills, 90210* (also known as *The Class of Beverly Hills*), Fox, 1991.

Morgan Stern, "Confession," *Law & Order,* NBC, 1991.

Black Tie Affair, NBC, 1993.

(As Nicolas Coster) "My Dinner with Nick," *Dark Justice,* CBS, 1993.

Reid Mullen, "Volunteers," *Law & Order,* NBC, 1993.

Dr. Wooodruff, "Intruders," *Nurses,* NBC, 1993.

Jinky, "Luther Get Your Gun," *Coach,* ABC, 1996.

Ellis Kodack, "The Publishing Episode," *Mr. & Mrs. Smith,* CBS, 1996.

Liam Ryan, "Pumped Up," *Silk Stalkings,* USA Network, 1997.

Senator Randall Stevens, "Politics," *Tracey Takes On ...,* HBO, 1997.

(As Nick Coster) Parker Stanley Tyler, "All the President's Women," *Gun,* ABC, 1997.

Arthur, "Paradise Found," *Women: Stories of Passion,* Showtime, 1997.

Hunter McReady, "Soldiers of Misfortune," *Pensacola: Wings of Gold,* syndicated, 1998.

(As Nicholas Coster) Judge Blaisdale, "Legend II: Vengeance," *Dr. Quinn, Medicine Woman,* CBS, 1998.

"Faith," *Michael Hayes,* CBS, 1998.

Captain Harriman, "Lost Voyage," *Timecop,* ABC, 1998.

Chancellor Stevens, "Feelin' Albright," *3rd Rock from the Sun* (also known as *3rd Rock* and *Encounters of the Personal Kind*), NBC, 1998.

Chancellor Stewart, "Paranoid Dick," *3rd Rock from the Sun* (also known as *3rd Rock* and *Encounters of the Personal Kind*), NBC, 1999.

Carl Shipman, "Ties That Bind," *L.A. Heat,* TNT, 1999.

Jed Raines, "Father Knows Best," *Gideon's Crossing,* ABC, 2000.

Mr. Oswald, "Off the Grid," *Judging Amy,* CBS, 2001.

Easton Case moderator, "The Fifth," *The Lyon's Den,* NBC, 2003.

Brogan Cooper, *Cold Case,* CBS, 2006.

"Thanks, I Needed That," *Trust Me,* TNT, 2009.

Also appeared in *Reasonable Doubts,* NBC; as Charlie, "A Loon Again, Naturally," *Crumbs,* ABC.

Television Work; Episodic:

Underwater consultant, *Santa Barbara,* NBC, 1984.

Stage Appearances:

Henry II, *Becket,* Hudson Theatre, New York City, 1961.

Admetus, *The Thracian Horses,* Orpheum Theatre, New York City, 1961.

A.D.C., *Ross,* Eugene O'Neill Theatre, New York City, 1961–62, then Hudson Theatre, New York City, 1962.

Ronnie Winterhamm, *O Say Can You See!,* Provincetown Playhouse, New York City, 1962.

Alan, *The Ninety Day Mistress,* Biltmore Theatre, New York City, 1967.

Clinton Evans Keith, *But, Seriously ...,* Henry Miller's Theatre, New York City, 1969.

Herb Shuttle, *Happy Birthday, Wanda June,* Theatre de Lys, New York City, 1970–71.

Frank, *Twigs,* Broadhurst Theatre, New York City, 1971–72, then Plymouth Theatre, New York City, 1972.

Standby for Jerry Ryan, *Seesaw,* Mark Hellinger Theatre, New York City, 1973.

Captain Amassa Delano, *The Old Glory,* American Place Theatre, New York City, 1976.

Jeff, *Otherwise Engaged,* Plymouth Theatre, New York City, 1977.

Oscar Hubbard, *The Little Foxes,* Martin Beck Theatre, New York City, 1981.

General, *Getting Married,* Circle in the Square, New York City, 1991.

Max, *Jack's Holiday,* Playwrights Horizons Theatre, New York City, 1995.

Uncle Halsey, *The Body of Bourne,* Mark Taper Forum, Los Angeles, 2001.

Krapp's Last Tape (one–man show), Seney–Stovall Chapel, Athens, GA, 2002.

Also appeared in *The Ninety–Day Mistress,* State Theatre of Pennsylvania, New Hope, PA.

D

DANIELS, Duane

PERSONAL

Addresses: *Office*—Buzzworks Theater Company, 1948 Rockford Rd., Los Angeles, CA 90039.

Career: Actor. Also a singer, performing opera for San Diego Opera and classically with the Cleveland Symphony. The Fritz Theatre, artistic director. Buzzworks Theatre, Los Angeles, CA, member of board of directors.

Awards, Honors: Outstanding Director Award, Fritz Blitz of New Plays, 2007, for *In the Wake of the Bounty.*

CREDITS

Film Appearances:
Detective Rick Sullivan, *Murder on Vine* (short film), 2007.
Hammond, *Covert* (short film), 2008.
Dr. Peter Figgstorm, *I Saved the World from Global Warning!,* 2008.
Agent, *Let Her Be* (short film), 2008.
First terrorist, *First Strike,* Camelot Entertainment Group, 2009.
Ashley's father, *The Greatest American Hero: The Fan Series* (short film), 2009.
Father, *Like Mother, Like Death* (short film), 2009.
Lou, *Fathoms Deep,* 2011.

Television Appearances; Series:
Van Clemmons, *Veronica Mars,* UPN then The CW, 2004–2007.
Detective Gerardi, *Fashion House,* MyNetworkTV, 2006.

Television Appearances; Pilots:
Van Clemmons, *Veronica Mars,* UPN, 2004.
Diner manager, *Terriers,* FX Network, 2010.

Television Appearances; Episodic:
Doctor, "The Catevari," *The Invisible Man* (also known as *I–Man*), Sci–Fi Channel, 2000.
Office assistant, "Kate," *Kate Brasher,* CBS, 2001.
Smiley, "Touched by an Alien," *The Chronicle* (also known as *News from the Edge*), Sci–Fi Channel, 2002.
Dwayne, "Water Hazard," *Tremors* (also known as *Tremors: The Series*), Sci–Fi Channel, 2003.
Edward Brennan, "The Way We Weren't," *Big Shots,* ABC, 2007.

Stage Appearances:
Appeared as Bobby, *Triple Espresso;* title role, *Sweeney Todd, the Demon Barber of Fleet Street.*

Stage Director:
Directed *In the Wake of the Bounty.*

DEEZEN, Eddie 1958–

PERSONAL

Full name, Edward Harry Deezen; born March 6, 1958, in Cumberland, MD; son of Robert and Irma Deezen; married Linda George, March 9, 1984.

Addresses: *Agent*—Danis Panaro Nist, 9201 West Olympic Blvd., Beverly Hills, CA 90212.

Career: Actor and voice performer. Appeared in television commercials as voice of Pop, Kellogg's Rice Krispies, 1997, and as voice of Nacho the cat, Taco Bell, 1997.

CREDITS

Film Appearances:

Froggy, *Laserblast,* Irwin Yablans Company, 1978.

Eugene, *Grease,* Paramount, 1978.

Richard "Ringo" Klaus, *I Wanna Hold Your Hand,* Universal, 1978.

Herbie Kazlminsky, *1941,* MCA/Universal, 1979.

Wesley the white team leader, *Midnight Madness,* Buena Vista, 1980.

Red, *Desperate Moves* (also known as *A Desperate Case, Rollerboy, Save the Last Dance for Me, Steigler and Steigler, Stiegler: A Desperate Case,* and *Stiegler: A Serious Case*), 1981.

Eugene, *Grease 2,* Paramount, 1982.

Sheldon, *Zapped!,* Embassy Pictures Corp., 1982.

Malvin, computer nerd, *WarGames,* United Artists, 1983.

Menlo, *Surf II* (also known as *Surf II: The End of the Trilogy*), Aquarius Releasing, 1984.

Sydney, *The Rosebud Beach Hotel* (also known as *Big Lobby* and *The No–Tell Hotel*), Almi Pictures, 1984.

Lane, *Delta Pi* (also known as *Mugsy's Girls*), Pegasus Films, 1985.

Voice of Donnie Dodo, *Sesame Street Presents Follow That Bird* (also known as *Follow That Bird*), Warner Bros., 1985.

Sphincter, *Polish Vampire in Burbank,* Vistar International Pictures, 1985.

Parking attendant, *The Longshot,* Orion, 1986.

Eddie Lipshultz, *The Whoopee Boys,* Paramount, 1986.

Rollie, *Million Dollar Mystery* (also known as *Money Mania*), De Laurentiis Entertainment Group, 1987.

Hancock, *Happy Hour* (also known as *Sour Grapes*), The Movie Store, 1987.

Waldo, *Dorf's Golf Bible,* 1987.

Hungry Heifer manager, *Critters 2: The Main Course* (also known as *Critter's 2*), New Line Cinema, 1988.

Dopey Deputy, *Assault of the Killer Bimbos,* Empire Pictures, 1988.

Kyle Carpenter, *Beverly Hills Vamp,* Vidmark Entertainment, 1988.

Walter, *Hollywood Boulevard II* (also known as *Back to Hollywood Boulevard*), Concorde, 1989.

Slappy the clown, *Wedding Band,* IRS Media, 1990.

Dorf Goes Auto Racing, Premiere Home Video, 1990.

Himalayan operator, *Dan Turner, Hollywood Detective* (also known as *The Raven Red Kiss–Off*), 1990.

Tony, *Mob Boss,* 1990.

Voice of Snipes, *Rock–A–Doodle* (animated), Samuel Goldwyn Company, 1991.

Pizza boy, *Teenage Exorcist,* Action International Pictures, 1991.

Voice, *We're Back! A Dinosaur's Story,* Universal, 1993.

Video cameraman, *Il silenzio dei prosciutti* (also known as *The Silence of the Hams*), October Films, 1994.

Phil the guard, *Mr. Payback: An Interactive Movie,* A.e.c., 1995.

Rancor guard who gets spit on, *Spy Hard,* Buena Vista, 1996.

Voice of Charlie, *The Brave Little Toaster to the Rescue* (animated), 1997.

Eddie, *News Traveler,* 1998.

Voice of Know–It–All, *The Polar Express* (animated; also known as *The Polar Express: An IMAX 3D Experience*), Warner Bros., 2004.

Himself, *Me and Graham: The Soundtrack of Our Lives* (documentary), 2005.

Television Appearances; Series:

Eddie Malvin, *Punky Brewster,* NBC, 1984.

Voice of Ham, *Mother Goose & Grimm* (animated; also known as *Grimmy*), CBS, 1992.

Voice of Mandark, *Dexter's Laboratory* (animated; also known as *Dexter's Lab* and *Dexter de shiyanshi*), Cartoon Network, 1996–2003.

Voice, *Life with Louie* (animated), 1996–97.

Voice of the guy boarded up in the wall, *The Weird Al Show,* CBS, 1997.

Voice, *Pigs Next Door* (also known as *Muca beal dorais*), 2000.

Voice of Larry, *Lloyd in Space* (animated; also known as *Disney's "Lloyd in Space"*), ABC, 2001.

Voice of Ned, *Kim Possible* (animated; also known as *Disney's "Kim Possible"*), The Disney Channel, 2002–2007.

Voice of Gibby Norton, *What's New, Scooby–Doo?* (animated), The WB, 2003–2005.

Television Appearances; Movies:

Eric Philpot, *Champions: A Love Story,* CBS, 1979.

Himalayan operator, *Dan Turner, Hollywood Detective* (also known as *The Raven Red Kiss–Off*), syndicated, 1990.

Don Tony, *Mob Boss,* syndicated, 1991.

Voice of Caliph, *Scooby–Doo in Arabian Nights* (animated; also known as *Scooby Doo's "Arabian Nights"* and *Arabian Nights*), syndicated, 1994.

Agent Tucker, *The Computer Wore Tennis Shoes,* ABC, 1995.

Voice of ice cream guy, *Kenny and the Chimp: Diseasy Does It! or Chimp–n–Pox,* 1998.

Voice of Mandark, *Dexter's Laboratory Ego Trip* (animated), Cartoon Network, 1999.

Voice of Ned, *Kim Possible: So the Drama* (animated; also known as *Disney's "Kim Possible Movie: So the Drama," Kim Possible: Dramatic Night,* and *Kim Possible: The Movie—Dramatic Night*), The Disney Channel, 2005.

Television Appearances; Specials:

Himself/Eugene, *VH1 Where Are They Now: "Grease,"* VH1, 1998.

Television Appearances; Pilots:
Ron Carp, *Homeroom* (also known as *Home Room*), ABC, 1981.

Television Appearances; Episodic:
Grusky, "The Big Fight," *The Facts of Life,* NBC, 1982.
Mickey Dalrumple, "Squeeze Play," *Magnum, P.I.,* CBS, 1983.
Merle Monroe, "Lady in Green," *The Fall Guy,* ABC, 1986.
Demon number two, "The Demons," *Monsters,* syndicated, 1989.
Voice of Mouth, "Darkly Dawns the Duck: Parts 1 & 2," *Darkwing Duck* (animated), ABC and syndicated, 1991.
Voice of Ringo, "Bearz 'N the Hood," *Eek! the Cat* (animated), 1992.
Voice of Road Hogs biker, "Queasy Rider," *Goof Troop* (animated; also known as *Disney's "Goof Troop"*), 1993.
Voice of Iggy Catalpa, "Joking the Chicken," *Duckman: Private Dick/Family Man* (animated), USA Network, 1994.
Voice of Melvin, "Masked Chess Boy," *Life with Louie* (animated), Fox, 1996.
Voice of Iggy Catalpa, "The Color of Naught," *Duckman: Private Dick/Family Man* (animated), USA Network, 1996.
Voice of Iggy Catalpa, "The Mallardian Candidate," *Duckman: Private Dick/Family Man* (animated), USA Network, 1996.
Voice of Bahuka, "Alcatraz–Mataz/Oahu Wahoo!," *Timon & Pumbaa* (animated), 1996.
Voice of Alivin Yasbek, "Mondo–Man," *Mighty Ducks* (animated; also known as *Mighty Ducks: The Animated Series*), 1996.
Voice of Olga/Lalalava, "Dee Dee's Rival," *Dexter's Laboratory* (animated), Cartoon Network, 1998.
Voice of Frank "Tiny" Sedgwick, "Lord of the Nerds," *Recess* (animated; also known as *Disney's "Recess: Created by Paul and Joe"*), 1999.
Voice of Oswald, "Johnny Goes to Camp," *Johnny Bravo* (animated), Cartoon Network, 1999.
Himself and Eugene, "Grease," *Behind the Music* (also known as *VH1's "Behind the Music"*), VH1, 2001.
Voice of Andy Pumpkin, "The Marshmallow," *Oswald,* CBS, 2001.
Voice of Andy Pumpkin, "Job for a Day," *Oswald,* CBS, 2001.
Voice of Mandark's computer, "Overlabbing," *Dexter's Laboratory* (animated), Cartoon Network, 2002.
Voice of ice cream guy, *Codename: Kids Next Door* (animated), Cartoon Network, 2002.
Voice of Slurpy the Bat, "A Cold Day on Fruit Salad Island/Five Nuts and a Baby," *Coconut Fred's Fruit Salad Island!* (animated), The WB, 2005.
Voice of Todd, "The Garden/Sheboodles!," *Chowder* (animated), Cartoon Network, 2009.

Also appeared as voice of Mandark, *Cartoon All–Stars to the Rescue* (animated); voice of Mandark, *Cartoon Madness* (animated); voice of Mandark, *House of Toon* (animated); voice of Mandark, *Survivor: Cartoon Cartoon vs. Nicktoons* (animated); voice of Mandark, *The Cartoon Characters Villains* (animated); voice of Mandark, "Dexter's Laboratory," *Toon Jam* (animated); voice of Mudwell the Mudbunny, *Cartoon All Stars: STOP SAMURAI JACK!* (animated).

RECORDINGS

Video Games:
Voice of Know–it–all, *The Polar Express,* THQ, 2004.
Voice of Mandark, *Cartoon Network Racing,* 2006.
Voice of Mandark, *FusionFall* (also known as *Cartoon Network Universe: FusionFall*), Majesco Entertainment, 2009.

Music Videos:
Appeared in "Party All Night" by Quiet Riot.

OTHER SOURCES

Periodicals:
Shock Cinema, fall/winter, 2000.

DeKAY, Tim 1963–
(Tim Dekay, Tim DeMay)

PERSONAL

Born June 12, 1963, in Ithaca, NY; married Elisa Taylor (an actress); children: two. *Education:* Le Moyne College, B.S., business administration; Rutgers University, M.F.A.

Addresses: *Agent*—Paradigm, 360 North Crescent Dr., North Bldg., Beverly Hills, CA 90210; TGMD Talent Agency, 6767 Forest Lawn Dr., Suite 101, Los Angeles, CA 90068. *Manager*—Lone Star Entertainment, 147 N. Poinsettia Pl., Los Angeles, CA 90036.

Career: Actor, producer, and director.

CREDITS

Film Appearances:
Stevie, *Fat Tuesday,* First Knight Productions, 1993.
New bartender, *Almost Heroes,* Warner Bros., 1998.
Pete Garrett, *The Prospector,* 1998.

(As Tim DeMay) Martin Toomey, *The Crow: Salvation* (also known as *The Crow 3: Toedliche Erloesung*), Dimension Films, 2000.

Dean Stewart, *Big Eden,* Jour de Fete Films, 2000.

Ken, *Buddy Boy,* Fine Line, 2000.

Dad, *Nice Guys Finish Last,* 2001.

Agent, *Swordfish,* Warner Bros., 2001.

Speaker, *The Third Wheel,* Miramax, 2002.

Bill, *Welcome to the Neighborhood,* 2003.

Ted, *Pauly* (short film), BuyIndies.com, 2003.

Bill Caputo, *Control,* Lions Gate Films, 2004.

Mr. Peck, *The Chumscrubber,* Newmarket Films, 2005.

Coach Garrick, *Peaceful Warrior,* DEJ Productions, 2006.

The stranger, *The Far Side of Jericho,* First Look International, 2006.

Paul, *Naked under Heaven,* 2007.

Bill, *Randy and the Mob,* Lightyear Entertainment, 2007.

Secret Service agent, *Get Smart,* Warner Bros., 2008.

Jim, *Political Disasters,* 2009.

Film Work:

Producer and director, *This Monday* (short film), 2009.

Television Appearances; Series:

Dr. Paul Thomas, *Party of Five,* Fox, 1997–99.

Jones, *Carnivale* (also known as *La feria ambulante*), HBO, 2003–2005.

David, *Tell Me You Love Me,* HBO, 2007.

Peter Burke, *White Collar,* USA Network, 2009—.

Television Appearances; Miniseries:

Max Thomas, *The Ring* (also known as *Danielle Steel's "The Ring"*), NBC, 1996.

Becky's husband, "1952," *If These Walls Could Talk,* HBO, 1996.

Professor Christopher Priest, *Night Sins,* CBS, 1997.

Mike Landry, *Invasion* (also known as *Robin Cook's "Invasion"*), NBC, 1997.

Television Appearances; Movies:

Junior officer at embassy party, *The Pentagon Wars,* HBO, 1998.

(As Tim Dekay) Robert Mercer, *Murder, She Wrote: The Last Free Man,* CBS, 2001.

Bob Kuehn, *Taking Back Our Town,* Lifetime, 2001.

Honey Vicarro, 2001.

Peter Eastman, *Chestnut Hill,* 2001.

Mr. Peck, *Walkout,* HBO, 2006.

Tim Russell, *The Russell Girl,* CBS, 2008.

Dr. Nicholas Zavaterro, *Monster Ark,* Sci–Fi Channel, 2008.

Television Appearances; Specials:

Himself, *Making "Carnivale": The Show Behind the Show* (documentary), HBO, 2003.

Richard Tregaskis, *WWII in HD,* History Channel, 2009.

Television Appearances; Pilots:

Alex, *Common Law,* 1996.

Five Houses, Fox, 1998.

True Love, ABC, 1999.

Peter Eastman, *Chestnut Hill,* NBC, 2001.

Jones, *Carnivale,* HBO, 2003.

John Miller, *Hidden Palms,* The CW, 2007.

Peter Burke, *White Collar,* USA Network, 2009.

Also appeared in *Honey Viccaro.*

Television Appearances; Episodic:

Lawrence Deon, "Destination Terminal," *SeaQuest DSV* (also known as *SeaQuest 2032*), NBC, 1995.

Lawrence Deon, "In the Company of Ice and Profit," *SeaQuest DSV* (also known as *SeaQuest 2032*), NBC, 1995.

Lawrence Deon, "Brainlock," *SeaQuest DSV* (also known as *SeaQuest 2032*), NBC, 1996.

Kevin, "The Soul Mate," *Seinfeld,* NBC, 1996.

Kevin, "The Bizarro Jerry," *Seinfeld,* NBC, 1996.

Bob, "Home Alone," *Champs,* ABC, 1996.

Reverend Tom Maxwell, "The Ghost and Mrs. Kelly," *Grace Under Fire,* ABC, 1996.

Gordon, "The Matchmaker," *The Larry Sanders Show,* HBO, 1997.

John, "We're at NBC Now," *The Naked Truth,* NBC, 1997.

J. D. Sinclair, "Smokescreen," *Touched by an Angel,* CBS, 1997.

Sonny Burnett, "A Mime Is a Terrible Thing to Waste," *Diagnosis Murder* (also known as *Dr. Mark Sloan*), CBS, 1997.

Alex, *Common Law,* ABC, 1997.

John, "Escape from L.A.," *Ellen* (also known as *These Friends of Mine*), 1998.

Brian, "Caroline and the Office," *Caroline in the City* (also known as *Caroline*), NBC, 1998.

Brian, "Caroline and the Killer Dad," *Caroline in the City* (also known as *Caroline*), NBC, 1998.

Brian, "Caroline and the Secret Bullfighter: Part 1," *Caroline in the City* (also known as *Caroline*), NBC, 1998.

Jennings Crawford, "The Linguist," *Cupid,* ABC, 1998.

Michael Kaplan, *Dogs,* ABC, 1998.

Professor Albright, "Heat," *Brimstone,* Fox, 1998.

Jerry Green, "Split Decisions," *The Practice,* ABC, 1999.

Eddie Fontenot, "Pool," *The Pretender,* NBC, 1999.

Ray Mitchel, "Cliff Gardner," *Sports Night,* ABC, 1999.

Voice, "Andy Runs Away," *God, the Devil and Bob* (animated), NBC, 2000.

Ray Mitchel, "April Is the Cruelest Month," *Sports Night,* ABC, 2000.

Owen, "The General," *Thieves,* ABC, 2001.

Kendall Willis, "A Kick in the Head," *Ally McBeal* (also known as *Ally My Love*), Fox, 2002.

Marc, "The One Where Rachel Has the Baby: Part 1," *Friends,* NBC, 2002.

Matt, "Zoo," *Malcolm in the Middle,* Fox, 2002.

Reverend Keyes, "Till Death Do Us Part," *Everwood,* The WB, 2002.

Reverend Keyes, "Snow Job," *Everwood,* The WB, 2003.

Reverend Keyes, "Blind Faith," *Everwood,* The WB, 2003.

Jim Cooper, "The Season," *Without a Trace* (also known as *W.A.T.*), CBS, 2004.

Neal Matthews, "Spark of Life," *CSI: Miami,* CBS, 2005.

Hank Lange, "Monkeys in Space," *My Name Is Earl,* NBC, 2006.

Hank Lange, "Didn't Pay Taxes," *My Name Is Earl,* NBC, 2006.

John Barnes, "Circling," *Standoff,* Fox, 2006.

Geoff Taylor from 2004 to 2006, "The War at Home," *Cold Case,* CBS, 2006.

Drew Imroth, "The Marked," *The 4400,* USA Network and Sky One, 2007.

Drew Imroth, "Ghost in the Machine," *The 4400,* USA Network and Sky One, 2007.

Pete Friscia, "Robin Hood," *Numb3rs* (also known as *Num3ers*), CBS, 2007.

Senator Patrick Kiley, "Capitol Offense," *NCIS: Naval Criminal Investigative Service* (also known as *Navy NCIS: Naval Criminal Investigative Service* and *NCIS*), CBS, 2008.

Neil Mullins, "Lie With Me," *The Cleaner,* Arts and Entertainment, 2008.

William Campbell, "Wrecking Crew," *CSI: Miami,* CBS, 2008.

Patrick Harris, "Tie Me Up, Don't Tie Me Down," *The New Adventures of Old Christine,* CBS, 2008.

Patrick Harris, "So You Think You Can Date," *The New Adventures of Old Christine,* CBS, 2008.

Patrick Harris, "Rage Against the Christine," *The New Adventures of Old Christine,* CBS, 2008.

Rich Hill, "My Nah Nah Nah," *Scrubs,* NBC, 2009.

Today (also known as *NBC News Today* and *The Today Show*), NBC, 2009.

Late Night with Jimmy Fallon, NBC, 2010.

Also appeared as patrolman, "The Penalty Phase," *Townies,* ABC; in "So What Else Happened," *L.A. Firefighters.*

Stage Appearances:

Joe Fisher, *The Show-Off,* Roundabout Theatre Company, Criterion Theatre, New York City, 1992.

Kap Clay, *Ridiculous Fraud,* McCarter Theatre, Princeton, NJ, 2006.

Also appeared in *Billy Budd,* Circle in the Square, New York City; in productions at Denver Center, Hartford Stage, Cleveland Playhouse, Cincinnati Playhouse, Pasadena Shakespeare, and others.

Major Tours:

Appeared in *Lion in Winter,* U.S. cities.

Radio Appearances:

Incident at Vichy, L.A. Theatre Works, 2002.

Also appeared in *Denial,* L.A. Theatre Works, broadcast on public radio stations.

De LANCIE, John 1948–
(John DeLancie, John deLancie)

PERSONAL

Born March 20, 1948, in Philadelphia, PA; son of John (a professional oboist) and Andrea de Lancie; married Marnie Mosiman (an actress); children: Keegan (an actor), Owen (an actor). *Education:* Attended Kent State University and Juilliard. *Avocational Interests:* Sailing.

Addresses: *Agent*—SDB Partners, Inc., 1801 Avenue of the Stars, Suite 902, Los Angeles, CA 90067; Brady, Brannon, and Rich, 5670 Wilshire Blvd., Suite 820, Los Angeles, CA 90036.

Career: Actor, producer, director, and writer. Seattle Repertory Company, member, 1980–c. 1981; L.A. Philharmonic Young Peoples Concerts, resident narrator, 1998–99; Alien Voices (production company), co–owner (with Leonard Nimoy); previously worked at L.A. Theater Works, as associate artistic director; previously member of American Shakespeare Festival at Stratford; performed with numerous orchestras in North America; hosted children's series of the Los Angeles Philharmonic, 2005. Compaq computers, spokesperson.

Awards, Honors: *Soap Opera Digest* Awards, outstanding actor in a supporting role in a daytime soap opera, 1984, 1985, *Soap Opera Digest* Award nomination, outstanding comic relief role on a daytime serial, 1986, all for *Days of Our Lives.*

CREDITS

Film Appearances:

Legacy, Arthur Productions, 1975.

Second LAPD lieutenant, *The Onion Field,* AVCO Embassy Pictures, 1979.

Alan, *Loving Couples,* Twentieth Century–Fox, 1980.

(Uncredited) *Blood Red,* Nelson, 1989.

Howard, *Bad Influence,* Triumph Releasing Corp., 1990.

Ted Bradford, Jr., vice president of High Quality Foods, *Taking Care of Business* (also known as *Filofax*), Buena Vista, 1990.

Television executive, *The Fisher King,* TriStar, 1991.

Paul/Walter Thackary, *Missing Pieces,* Orion, 1991.

Dr. Victor Mott, *The Hand That Rocks the Cradle,* Buena Vista, 1992.

Difford, *Arcade,* Paramount, 1993.

Jeff Gordon, *Fearless,* Warner Bros., 1993.

Arthur Martin, *Schemes,* Bristol Entertainment, 1994.

Himself, *Journey's End—The Saga of Star Trek: The Next Generation,* Paramount, 1995.

Russell Bennett, *Evolver,* 1995.

Ted, *Multiplicity* (also known as *Clones*), Columbia, 1996.

(Uncredited) Himself, *Trekkies* (documentary), Paramount, 1997.

Jeremiah Bedford, *The First Men in the Moon,* 1997.

(Uncredited) Voice of letter reader, *Saving Private Ryan* (also known as *Private Ryan*), DreamWorks, 1998.

Q, *Star Trek World Tour,* 1998.

Voice of Colonel John "Jack" Lynch, *Gen 13* (animated short film), Hollywood Pictures, 1998.

Various, *Roswell: The Unheard Broadcast,* 2000.

Alex Reeves, *Woman on Top,* Twentieth Century–Fox, 2000.

Himself, *Business of Acting,* 2000.

Nathan Eastman, *Quality Time* (also known as *For What It's Worth*), Film Club Productions, 2000.

Dr. Fisher, *The Catch* (short film), 2001.

(As John DeLancie) Ted, *Good Advice,* Family Room Entertainment, 2001.

Nicolas, 2001.

Dr. Gene Kramer, *Patient 14,* 2003.

Himself, *Four Fingers of the Dragon* (animated short film), 2003.

Mr. Cooper, *Burl's,* 2003.

Dr. Gene Kramer, *The Eavesdropper,* Freestyle Home Entertainment, 2004.

Principal Senseman, *Tennius,* 2007.

Nigel Pennington, *Reign Over Me,* Columbia, 2007.

(Uncredited) Barman, *The Kite Runner,* Paramount Vantage, 2007.

Host and himself, *"The Next Generation"'s Impact: 20 Years Later* (short documentary), CBS Video, 2007.

Nathan Eastman, *My Apocalypse* (also known as *Quality Time*), 2008.

Dr. Quentin Morris, *Pathology,* Metro–Goldwyn–Mayer, 2008.

Fish Halman, *Crank: High Voltage* (also known as *Crank 2, High Voltage,* and *Adrenaline: High Voltage*), Lions Gate Films, 2009.

Dick, *You,* 2009.

Chief of staff, *Gamer,* Lions Gate Films, 2009.

Dr. Frank Miller, *Recreator,* 2010.

Television Appearances; Series:

Eugene Bradford, *Days of Our Lives* (also known as *DOOL* and *Days*), NBC, 1982–86, 1989.

Q, *Star Trek: The Next Generation* (also known as *Star Trek: TNG*), syndicated, 1987–94.

Bob Adams, *Trial and Error,* CBS, 1988–89.

Professor Janos Bartok, *Legend,* UPN, 1995.

Voice of Dr. Benton C. Quest, *The Real Adventures of Jonny Quest* (animated; also known as *Jonny Quest: The Real Adventures*), Cartoon Network and syndicated, 1996–97.

Q, *Star Trek: Voyager* (also known as *Voyager*), UPN, 1996–2001.

Colonel Frank Simmons and Goa'uld, *Stargate SG–1,* Showtime and syndicated, 2001–2002.

Odin, *Charmed,* The WB, 2004–2005.

Donald Margolis, *Breaking Bad,* AMC, 2009–10.

Television Appearances; Miniseries:

Timothy Armagh, *Captains and the Kings,* NBC, 1976.

Jerome Eaton, *Testimony of Two Men,* syndicated, 1977.

Ray Chilton, *Aspen* (also known as *The Innocent and the Damned*), NBC, 1977.

Henry, *Black Beauty,* NBC, 1978.

Lieutenant Stark, *The Bastard* (also known as *The Kent Chronicles*), syndicated, 1978.

Pierre Goodman, *Scruples,* CBS, 1980.

Alastair MacQueen, *The Thorn Birds,* ABC, 1983.

Television Appearances; Movies:

Bob Connors, *SST: Death Flight* (also known as *Death Flight, Flight of the Maiden,* and *SST: Disaster in the Sky*), ABC, 1977.

(Uncredited) EKG doctor, *The Lazarus Syndrome,* 1978.

Willy Pitts, *Nightside,* ABC, 1980.

Dr. Christiansen, *The Miracle of Kathy Miller,* CBS, 1981.

John Van Fossen, *Houston: The Legend of Texas* (also known as *Gone to Texas*), CBS, 1986.

Bobby Holicker, *On Fire,* 1987.

Major Waterhouse, *Get Smart, Again!,* Fox, 1989.

Lee Drexel, *Kennonite,* ABC, 1989.

Jeffrey Howell, *Angel of Death* (also known as *Intimate Terror: Angel of Death*), CBS, 1990.

Q, *Star Trek: The Next Generation—All Good Things ...* (also known as *All Good Things ...*), syndicated, 1994.

Barry Steinbrenner, *Without Warning,* CBS, 1994.

Thomas Newmeyer, *Deep Red,* Sci–Fi Channel, 1994.

Stansfield, *Raven Hawk* (also known as *Ravenhawk*), HBO, 1996.

Russell Bennett, *Evolver,* Sci–Fi Channel, 1996.

Captain George W. Bouchard, *Final Descent,* CBS, 1997.

Lyle Windsor, *You Lucky Dog,* The Disney Channel, 1998.

Lord John Roxton, *The Lost World,* 1998.

Rolf Berger, *Border Line,* NBC, 1999.

George Bouchard, *Final Run* (also known as *Ground Panic 90 Seconds*), 1999.

Vaughn Clay, *The Big Time,* TNT, 2002.
Faith director chapel, *Darklight* (also known as *Dark Light*), Sci–Fi Channel, 2004.

Television Appearances; Specials:
The 16th Annual Daytime Emmy Awards, NBC, 1989.
"Star Trek" 25th Anniversary Special (documentary), 1991.
Journey's End: The Saga of "Star Trek—The Next Generation," 1994.
(Uncredited) Himself, *Never Say Never: The Deidre Hall Story,* 1995.
"Star Trek": 30 Years and Beyond (documentary), UPN, 1996.
The First Men in the Moon, Sci–Fi Channel, 1997.
The Lost World, Sci–Fi Channel, 1998.
Alien Voices: A Halloween Trilogy, Sci–Fi Channel, 1998.
Narrator, *Are You Being Watched?* (documentary), The Discovery Channel, 1999.
Narrator, *Return to Area 51,* 2002.
Voice, *Deadly Reptiles 2,* 2002.
Voice of Santa, *Elf Sparkle Meets Christmas the Horse* (animated), 2009.
Voice of Santa Claus, *Elf Sparkle and the Special Red Dress* (animated), 2010.

Also appeared as narrator, *Deadly Bugs,* The Discovery Channel.

Television Appearances; Pilots:
Clark, *The Man with the Power,* NBC, 1977.
Frank Vaughn, *Little Women,* NBC, 1978.
Q, *Star Trek: The Next Generation—Encounter at Farpoint* (also known as *Encounter at Farpoint*), 1987.
Bob Adams, *Trial and Error,* CBS, 1988.
Edward Stevens, "Things That Go Bump in the Night," *Christine Cromwell,* ABC, 1989.
Norman, *The Nutt House,* 1989.
Kevin, *Working,* NBC, 1997.
Captain George W. Bouchard, *Final Run,* CBS, 1999.

Television Appearances; Episodic:
Medic, "Death Probe: Parts 1 & 2," *The Six Million Dollar Man,* 1977.
(As John deLancie) Diver, "Sharks: Parts 1 & 2," *The Six Million Dollar Man,* 1977.
Policeman, "Affair of the Heart," *McMillan & Wife* (also known as *McMillan*), 1977.
"The Steel Inferno," *Emergency!* (also known as *Emergencia* and *Emergency One*), NBC, 1978.
Sargent Chapman, "Just a Matter of Time," *The Six Million Dollar Man,* ABC, 1978.
Mitchell Grady II, "Terror on a Quiet Afternoon," *Barnaby Jones,* CBS, 1978.

Dr. DeRoy, "What's a Nice Girl Like You Doing ...?," *Emergency!* (also known as *Emergencia* and *Emergency One*), NBC, 1978.
(As John deLancie) Ensign Ray Stevens, "Coronado Circle," *Switch,* 1978.
Officer, "Experiment in Terra," *Battlestar Galactica,* ABC, 1979.
John, "Garbage Man/Doctor's Wife," *Time Express,* CBS, 1979.
Dr. DeRoy, "The Convention," *Emergency!* (also known as *Emergencia* and *Emergency One*), NBC, 1979.
John Irvin, "Might As Well Be Dead," *Nero Wolfe,* NBC, 1981.
Groom, "The Wedding," *It's a Living* (also known as *Making a Living*), ABC, 1981.
Eugene Bradford, *Days of Our Lives* (also known as *Days* and *DOOL*), NBC, 1985.
The dispatcher, "Dead Run," *The Twilight Zone,* CBS, 1986.
Brian Ashford, "The Escape," *MacGyver,* ABC, 1986.
Binky Holborn, "If the Frame Fits," *Murder, She Wrote,* CBS, 1986.
Cary Deveraux, "The Perfect Man," *The New Gidget,* 1986.
Lucius Cain, "High Noon," *Hooperman,* ABC, 1988.
Matthew Drake, "The Killer," *Mission: Impossible,* ABC, 1988.
Lee Drexell, "Kennonite," *Gideon Oliver* (also known as *By the Rivers of Babylon*), 1989.
Mark Chelios, "The Beverly Hills Hangers," *L.A. Law,* NBC, 1991.
Wicks, "Good Night, Sweet Charlotte," *The Young Riders,* ABC, 1992.
"Pro Se Can You See," *Civil Wars,* ABC, 1992.
Voice of Eagleton, "The Mechanic," *Batman: The Animated Series* (animated; also known as *Batman* and *The Adventures of Batman & Robin*), Fox, 1993.
Voice of Eagleton, "Blind as a Bat," *Batman: The Animated Series* (animated; also known as *Batman* and *The Adventures of Batman & Robin*), Fox, 1993.
Q, "Q–Less," *Star Trek: Deep Space Nine* (also known as *DS9, Deep Space Nine,* and *Star Trek: DS9*), syndicated, 1993.
Gandolf Reicher, "Beautiful Songbird," *Time Trax,* syndicated, 1993.
Dr. Levinson, "The Haunted," *Matlock,* ABC, 1993.
Narrator, "Searching for Extraterrestrials," *National Geographic Explorer,* 1994.
Mitchell Garron, esquire, "Chapter Thirteen," *Murder One,* ABC, 1996.
District Attorney, "Three Weddings and a Meltdown," *Picket Fences,* CBS, 1996.
Voice of construction worker/Blaine, "Undersea Urgency," *The Real Adventures of Jonny Quest* (animated), 1996.
Voice of screaming guard, "Nemesis," *The Real Adventures of Jonny Quest* (animated), 1996.

Voice of guard, "DNA Doomsday," *The Real Adventures of Jonny Quest* (animated), 1996.

Voice of agent, "Without a Trace," *The Real Adventures of Jonny Quest* (animated), 1996.

Voice of Moffat, "Village of the Doomed," *The Real Adventures of Jonny Quest* (animated), 1996.

Voice of first guard, "Digital Doublecross," *The Real Adventures of Jonny Quest* (animated), 1997.

Mr. McFadden, "Spontaneous Combustion," *Dave's World,* CBS, 1997.

Voice of Tyler Fitzgerald, "From Brad to Worse," *Duckman: Private Dick/Family Man* (animated), USA Network, 1997.

Dr. David Lynk, "And That About Concludes Our Session," *Spy Game,* ABC, 1997.

Justinian Jones, "Jones vs. God," *Touched by an Angel,* CBS, 1997.

Mr. Lux, "Beat the Clock," *Fired Up,* NBC, 1997.

Voice of Kirilin, "Heart of Darkness," *Extreme Ghostbusters* (animated), syndicated, 1997.

Dr. Walsch, "Race with the Devil," *The Practice,* ABC, 1997.

Mr. Lux, "Mission: And A–Hopin'," *Fired Up,* NBC, 1998.

Jackson Poile, "Making Spirits Bright," *Ally McBeal* (also known as *Ally My Love*), Fox, 1998.

Donald Finley, "The Gun," *The Outer Limits* (also known as *The New Outer Limits*), Showtime and syndicated, 2000.

Al Kiefer, "20 Hours in L.A.," *The West Wing* (also known as *The White House*), NBC, 2000.

Bert Stors, "April Is the Cruelest Month," *Sports Night,* ABC, 2000.

Al Kiefer, "Mandatory Minimums," *The West Wing* (also known as *The White House*), NBC, 2000.

Marshall Gilder, "The Face," *Secret Agent Man,* UPN, 2000.

Voice of Yak in the Sack, "Canucks Amuck/Yak in the Sack," *The Angry Beavers* (animated), Nickelodeon, 2000.

Walter Bannish, "Payback," *The Practice,* ABC, 2001.

Voice, "Fun in the Sun," *Max Steel,* The WB, 2001.

Uncle Sid, "The Pearls That Were His Eyes," *Andromeda* (also known as *Gene Roddenberry's "Andromeda"*), syndicated, 2001.

King of the Links, "The Eve," *Special Unit 2* (also known as *SU2*), UPN, 2001.

Himself, "Star Trek Edition," *Weakest Link,* NBC, 2001.

Frank Newburg, "Privilege," *The Guardian* (also known as *Ochita bengoshi Nick Fallin*), CBS, 2002.

Medical examiner Thaxton, "Payback," *Crossing Jordan,* NBC, 2002.

Sid Barry, "Cui Bono," *Andromeda* (also known as *Gene Roddenberry's "Andromeda"*),syndicated, 2002.

Voice of Agent Darkbootie, "Battle of the Planets," *Invader ZIM* (animated), Nickelodeon, 2002.

Dr. Eagan, "Picture of Perfect," *Judging Amy,* CBS, 2003.

(As John DeLancie) Voice of Sinestro, "The Green Loontern," *Duck Dodgers* (animated; also known as *Duck Dodgers in the 241/2 Century*), Cartoon Network, 2003.

Tom Burke Sr., "A Death in the Family," *The Division,* NBC, 2004.

Scott Garvin, "Divorce, Detective Style," *NYPD Blue* (also known as *N.Y.P.D.*), ABC, 2004.

Dr. Dawson, "Flashpoint," *The Closer,* TNT, 2005.

Agent Darkbootie, "ZIM Eats Waffles," *Invader ZIM* (animated), Nickelodeon, 2006.

Brian Gaghan, "The Thing with Feathers," *Without a Trace* (also known as *W.A.T.*), CBS, 2006.

Warren Kovak, "Eye of the Beholder," *Shark,* CBS, 2007.

Elliott Gillum, "Dancing Lessons," *The Unit,* CBS, 2008.

Elliott Gillum, "Chaos Theory," *The Unit,* CBS, 2009.

"The Day After," *Greek,* ABC Family, 2009.

"The Dork Knight," *Greek,* ABC Family, 2009.

Television Work; Series:

Producer, *Return to Area 51,* The Discovery Channel, 2002.

Television Executive Producer; Specials:

Alien Voices: A Halloween Trilogy, Sci–Fi Channel, 1998.

The Lost World, Sci–Fi Channel, 1998.

Stage Appearances:

Marc, *Art,* South Coast Repertory Theatre, Costa Mesa, CA, 2000.

General Felix Barriaux, *Arthur Miller's "Resurrection Blues,"* Old Globe Theatre, San Diego, CA, 2004.

A Naked Girl on the Appian Way, South Coast Repertory Theatre, 2005.

Clarence Darrow, *The Great Tennessee Monkey Trial,* Rudder Theatre, College Station, TX, 2005.

Jeffrey, *A Naked Girl on Appian Way,* Segerstrom Stage, South Coast Repertory, Costa Mesa, CA, 2005.

Also appeared as Jack Tanner, *Man and Superman;* Humphrey, *The Common Pursuit.*

Radio Appearances:

Appeared as Cassius, *Julius Caesar,* BBC Radio.

Radio Director:

Directed *Fallen Angel; The Play's the Thing; The Waldorf Conference; Invasion from Mars; When Welles Collide.*

RECORDINGS

Video Games:

Voice of Q, *Star Trek: Borg,* Simon & Schuster Interactive, 1996.

Voice of Matthew "Dr. Death" Jackson, *Outlaws,* 1997.

Voice of Antonio Malochio, *Interstate '76,* 1997.
Voice of Q, *Star Trek: The Game Show,* 1998.
Voice of Antonio Malochio, *Interstate '76 Arsenal,* 1998.
Voice of Montreaux, *Gabriel Knight: Blood of the Sacred, Blood of the Damned,* Sierra OnLine, 1999.
Voice of Trias, *Planescape: Torment,* 1999.
Voice, *Star Trek: ConQuest Online,* 2000.

Taped Readings; with Others:
The Lost World, Simon & Schuster Audio, 1997.
Journey to the Center of the Earth, Simon & Schuster Audio, 1997.
Time Machine, Simon & Schuster Audio, 1997.
The Invisible Man, Simon & Schuster Audio, 1998.
The First Men in the Moon, Simon & Schuster Audio, 1998.
"Star Trek: Spock vs. Q," *Alien Voices,* Simon & Schuster Audio, 1999.
"Star Trek: Spock vs. Q—The Sequel," *Alien Voices,* Simon & Schuster Audio, 2000.

WRITINGS

Television Specials:
Alien Voices: A Halloween Trilogy, Sci–Fi Channel, 1998.
The Lost World, 1998.

Novels:
Wrote (with Peter David) *I.Q.;* (with Tom Cool) *Soldier of Light.*

Comic Books:
Wrote an issue of *Star Trek: The Next Generation,* DC Comics.

DELANEY, Padraic 1977–

PERSONAL

Born November 6, 1977, in Adamstown, County Wexford, Ireland; son of Michael and Sheelagh (an actress) Delaney. *Education:* Trinity College, Dublin, B.A., drama and theatre studies, 2001.

Addresses: *Agent*—Sarah Fargo, Paradigm, 360 Park Ave. South, 16th Floor, New York, NY 10010; Lisa Richards Agency, 108 Upper Leeson St., Dublin 4, Ireland, and 117 Waterloo Rd., London SE1 8UL, England.

Career: Actor. Cinema City (film and media festival), jury member.

Awards, Honors: Named the Irish Shooting Star, European Film Promotion, Berlin International Film Festival, 2007; Irish Film and Television Award nominations, best actor in a supporting role in a feature film and breakthrough talent, both 2007, for *The Wind That Shakes the Barley.*

CREDITS

Film Appearances:
Duncan, *An Cuainin* (short film), 2003.
Stan Curtis, *A Lonely Sky* (short film), Zanita Films, 2006.
Teddy, *The Wind That Shakes the Barley* (also known as *El viento que agita la cebada, Il vento che accarezza l'erba,* and *Le vent se leve*), IFC First Take, 2007.
Eoghan, *Eden,* Liberation Entertainment, 2008.
Shamie, *Perrier's Bounty,* Optimum Releasing, 2009, IFC Films, 2010.
Andras (Zsofi's husband), *Isztambul* (also known as *Istanbul*), Uj Budapest Filmstudio/Phanta Vision/Ripple World Pictures/Kuzey Film, 2011.
Sundance, *Blackthorn,* Aiete–Ariane Films/Arcadia Motion Pictures/Quickfire Films, 2011.

Television Appearances; Series:
Fred "Fridge" Gogan, *Legend,* Radio Telefis Eireann 2 (RTE2), 2006.
(Sometimes uncredited) George Boleyn, *The Tudors* (also known as *Tudors*), Showtime, BBC2, CBC, and other channels, 2007–2008.

Television Appearances; Movies:
Appeared in *The Cove* (short film), TG4.

Television Appearances; Awards Presentations:
Fourth Irish Film and Television Awards, Radio Telefis Eireann (RTE), 2007.

Television Appearances; Episodic:
Maurice, "Deirdre," *Pure Mule,* Radio Telefis Eireann (RTE), 2005.
Maurice, "Therese," *Pure Mule,* Radio Telefis Eireann (RTE), 2005.
Andrew McLoughlin, *The Clinic,* Radio Telefis Eireann (RTE), 2005.
Michael Casey, "The Drowning Man: Parts 1 & 2," *Single–Handed* (also known as *Single Handed, Single–Handed III,* and *Single Handed III*), Radio Telefis Eireann (RTE), 2009.

Stage Appearances:

Porter, *The Yalta Game* (one–act play), produced with the other one–act plays *White Horses* and *Come on Over* as part of *3 Plays,* Dublin Theatre Festival, Gate Theatre, Dublin, Ireland, 2001.

Walpurg, *The Madman and the Nun,* Dublin Castle, The Crypt, Dublin, 2001.

Aidan, *The Leaving,* Barnstorm Theatre Company, Watergate Theatre, Kilkenny, Ireland, 2002.

The Hollow in the Sand, Blue Raincoat Theatre Company, The Factory Performance Space, Sligo, Ireland, 2002.

Title role, *Hamlet,* Cork Opera House, Cork, Ireland, 2004.

Father Flynn, *Doubt: A Parable,* Tricycle Theatre, London, 2007–2008.

Appeared as a young priest in *Big Maggie,* Enniscorthy Theatre Group, Ireland; also appeared in *A Midsummer Night's Dream,* Civic Theatre; and *This Lime Tree Bower* (also known as *This Limetree Bower*), The Machine.

---

de MATTEO, Drea 1973–
(Drea De Matteo, Andrea de Matteo)

PERSONAL

Full name, Andrea Donna de Matteo; born January 19, 1973, in Queens, New York, NY; daughter of Albert (a furniture manufacturer) and Donna (a playwright) De Matteo; children: (with Shooter Jennings) Alabama Gypsy Rose, Waylon Albert "Blackjack". *Education:* New York University, B.F.A., film production, 1995. *Religion:* Roman Catholic.

Addresses: *Agent*—WME Entertainment, 9601 Wilshire Blvd., 3rd Floor, Beverly Hills, CA 90210. *Manager*—Untitled Entertainment, 1801 Century Park East, Suite 700, Los Angeles, CA 90067. *Publicist*—42WEST, 220 West 42nd St., 12th Floor, New York, NY 10036. *Contact*—Filth Mart, 531 E. 13th St., New York, NY 10009.

Career: Actress and playwright. Filth Mart (clothing store), New York City, co–owner; also worked as a clothing designer and furniture sales representative.

Awards, Honors: Feature Film Award, New York International Independent Film and Video Festival, 2002, for *'R Xmas;* Screen Actors Guild Award nominations (with others), outstanding performance by an ensemble in a drama series, 2001, 2002, 2003, and 2005, Emmy Award, outstanding supporting actress in a drama series, 2004, Gracie Allen Award, outstanding supporting actress in a drama series, 2005, Golden Globe Award nomination, best performance by an actress in a supporting role, 2005, all for *The Sopranos.*

CREDITS

Film Appearances:

"M" Word, 1996.

Prostitute, *Roberta,* 1999.

Hilary Harris, *Meet Prince Charming,* New City Releasing, 1999.

Henrieta, *Sleepwalk,* 2000.

Cadet Ramsey, *The Gentleman from Boston,* 2000.

The wife, *'R Xmas* (also known as *Christmas*), Pathfinder Pictures, 2001.

Melissa, *Swordfish,* Warner Bros., 2001.

(Uncredited) Club girl, *Made,* Artisan Entertainment, 2001.

Dee, *The Perfect You,* 2002.

Betsy, *Deuces Wild* (also known as *Deuces Wild—Wild en den strassen*), United Artists, 2002.

Angela, *Love Rome,* 2002.

Tracy, *Prey for Rock & Roll,* 2003.

Cadet Ramsey, *Beacon Hill,* 2003.

Hollywood Trash & Tinsel, Girl Gang Films, 2004.

Dirty Love, DEJ Productions, 2005.

Iris Ferry, *Assault on Precinct 13,* United International, 2005.

Voice of Esther, *Farce of the Penguins,* THINKFilm, 2006.

Lou Ann, *Walker Payne,* Image Entertainment, 2006.

Audrey Andrews, *Broken English,* Magnolia Pictures, 2007.

(As Drea De Matteo) Dana, *The Good Life,* Image Entertainment, 2007.

Hope, *Lake City,* Eagle Films, 2008.

Lydia, *New York, I Love You,* Palm Pictures, 2009.

Lana Gregorio, *Once More with Feeling,* Sundance Selects, 2009.

Television Appearances; Series:

Adriana La Cerva, *The Sopranos,* HBO, 1999–2004.

Gina Tribbiani, *Joey,* NBC, 2004–2006.

Wendy Teller, *Sons of Anarchy,* FX Network, 2008.

Angie Bolen, *Desperate Housewives,* ABC, 2009–10.

Television Appearances; Specials:

VH1 Divas Live: The One and Only Aretha Franklin—A Benefit Concert for VH1 Save the Music Foundation, VH1, 2001.

The 2001 MTV Movie Awards, MTV, 2001.

Host, *VH1 Big in 2002 Awards,* VH1, 2002.

A Kid Rock Christmas, VH1, 2003.

The 56th Annual Primetime Emmy Awards, ABC, 2004.

Fashion Rocks, CBS, 2005.

The 31st Annual People's Choice Awards, CBS, 2005.

The 62nd Annual Golden Globe Awards, NBC, 2005.
11th Annual Screen Actors Guild Awards, TNT, 2005.
Presenter, *The CMT Music Awards,* Country Music Television, 2005.
The 50 Greatest Television Dramas, Channel 4, 2007.
Adriana La Cerva, *Making "Cleaver,"* HBO, 2007.

Television Appearances; Pilots:
Hostess, *The Sopranos,* HBO, 1999.
The Stereo Sound Agency, MTV, 2006.

Television Appearances; Episodic:
Swift Justice, UPN, 1997.
Angela DeMarco, *Feds,* CBS, 1998.
Late Show with David Letterman (also known as *Letterman* and *The Late Show*), NBC, 2002.
Rocked with Gina Gershon, Independent Film Channel, 2004.
The Tonight Show with Jay Leno, NBC, 2004.
Ellen: The Ellen DeGeneres Show, 2004.
Jimmy Kimmel Live!, ABC, 2004, 2005.
Last Call with Carson Daly, NBC, 2004, 2005.
Live with Regis and Kelly, syndicated, 2005.
The Tony Danza Show, syndicated, 2005.
The View, ABC, 2005.
"Assault on Precinct 13: Caught in the Crosshairs," *HBO First Look,* HBO, 2005.
Al rojo vivo con Maria Celeste, 2007.
"Drea de Matteo/Laurie Simmons," *Aperture,* Gallery HD, 2007.
Entertainment Tonight (also known as *E.T.* and *This Week in Entertainment*), syndicated, 2009.
Didi, "One Step Forward," *Running Wilde,* Fox, 2010.
Sandra Roberts, "Pop," *Law & Order: Special Victims Unit* (also known as *Law & Order: SVU*), 2011.

Television Appearances; Movies:
Hilary, *Meet Prince Charming,* Cinemax, 2000.
(As Andrea de Matteo) *Callas e Onassis,* 2005.
Tanner's mother, *Fakers,* TMN, Movie Central, 2010.

WRITINGS

Stage Plays:
Wrote (with Donna de Matteo) *The Heart Transplant.*

DeMAY, Tim
    See DeKAY, Tim

DENNEHY, Elizabeth 1960–

PERSONAL

Full name, Elizabeth Hannah Dennehy; born October 1, 1960, in Jacksonville, NC; daughter of Brian Dennehy (an actor).

Addresses: *Agent*—Mitchell K. Stubbs and Associates, 8675 W. Washington Blvd., Suite 203, Culver City, CA 90232.

Career: Actress. Appeared in television commercials, including Hallmark cards, 1999.

CREDITS

Film Appearances:
Candy, *The Waterdance,* Samuel Goldwyn, 1992.
Reporter, *Clear and Present Danger,* Paramount, 1994.
Preschool teacher, *Gattaca,* Columbia, 1997.
Maria, *The Game,* Panorama, 1997.
Kathy Kimball, *The Prophecy II* (also known as *God's Army II*), Dimension, 1998.
Jimmy Pig's wife, *Soldier,* Warner Bros., 1998.
Beverly, *Red Dragon* (also known as *Roter Drache*), MCA/Universal, 2002.
Helen Brown, *Welcome to Paradise,* First Look International, 2007.
Rail crossing crowd number two, *Hancock* (also known as *Hidden from Erath*), Columbia, 2008.

Television Appearances; Series:
Christina "Blake" Bauder Lindsey Thorpe, *The Guiding Light,* CBS, 1988–89.
Sandra, a recurring role, *Charmed,* The WB, 2004–2006.

Television Appearances; Movies:
Kathy Magnuson, *A Place to Be Loved* (also known as *Shattered Family*), CBS, 1993.
Sara, *Jack Reed: A Search for Justice* (also known as *Deadly Justice*), NBC, 1994.
Shari, *Runaway Car* (also known as *Out of Control*), 1997.
(Uncredited) Miss Fogarty, *On the Edge of Innocence,* 1997.
Dr. Beverly Stokes, *The Last Man on Planet Earth,* UPN, 1999.
Jeremy's mom, *Come On, Get Happy: The Partridge Family Story,* ABC, 1999.
Mrs. Susan Sinclair, *Hard Time: Hostage Hotel* (also known as *Hostage Hotel*), TNT, 1999.
Archivist, *Murder, She Wrote: The Last Free Man,* CBS, 2001.

Television Appearances; Pilots:
Marlene, *Daisy and Chess,* Fox, 1995.

Television Appearances; Episodic:
Lieutenant Commander Elizabeth Paula Shelby, "The Best of Both Worlds: Parts 1 & 2," *Star Trek: The Next Generation* (also known as *Star Trek: TNG*), syndicated, 1990.

Beth Ryan, "Promised Land—December 22, 1971," *Quantum Leap,* NBC, 1992.

The Drakette/Allison, "The Handicap Spot," *Seinfeld,* NBC, 1993.

Dr. Anders, "The Adventures of Pat's Man and Robin," *Class of '96,* 1993.

The Drakette/Allison, "The Pilot," *Seinfeld,* NBC, 1993.

Flora, "The Date," *Brooklyn Bridge,* CBS, 1993.

Jennifer, *Sweet Justice,* NBC, 1994.

"Awakening: Parts 1 & 2," *The Lazarus Man,* TNT/ syndicated, 1996.

Dana Brown, "The Sandman," *C–16: FBI* (also known as *C–16*), ABC, 1997.

"You Shoulda Seen My Daddy," *Any Day Now,* Lifetime, 1998.

Melanie Pratt, "Everybody Plays the Mule," *NYPD Blue* (also known as *N.Y.P.D.*), ABC, 2000.

Nina Seldon, "Cold Hearts," *Chicago Hope,* CBS, 2000.

Attorney Salias, "The Undertow," *Judging Amy,* CBS, 2001.

Maura Fitzhugh, "Prodigal Dad," *Gideon's Crossing,* ABC, 2001.

Maura Fitzhugh, "The Crash," *Gideon's Crossing,* ABC, 2001.

"God's Work," *The Agency* (also known as *CIA: The Agency*), CBS, 2001.

"Deadline," *The Agency* (also known as *CIA: The Agency*), CBS, 2001.

Ms. Ford, "Sacrifice," *Numb3rs* (also known as *Num3ers*), CBS, 2005.

Victoria, "Viuda Negra," *Without a Trace* (also known as *W.A.T.*), CBS, 2005.

Sue Brantley, "The Price You Pay," *Commander in Chief,* ABC, 2006.

Samantha Taylor, "Roe vs Wade: The Musical," *Boston Legal,* ABC, 2008.

Hasting's boss, "A Cure for What Ails You," *Medium,* NBC, 2008.

Kathryn Hawkes, "Paint It Red," *The Mentalist,* CBS, 2009.

Stage Appearances:

Lady–in–Waiting, *Henry V,* Joseph Papp Public Theatre, New York Shakespeare Festival, New York City, 1984.

Donna Marsala, *Tony 'n Tina's Wedding,* St. Luke's Theatre, New York City, 1988.

Also appeared as Stella, *A Streetcar Named Desire,* South Coast Repertory Theatre, Costa Mesa, CA.

DENTON, James 1963–
   (Jamie Denton)

PERSONAL

Born January 20, 1963, in Nashville, TN; son of J. T. Denton (a dentist); married Jenna Lyn Ward, 1997 (divorced, 2000); married Erin O'Brien, December 16, 2002; children: (second marriage) Sheppard O'Brien, Malin O'Brien. *Education:* University of Tennessee, Knoxville, B.A. (with honors), broadcasting and journalism; also attended a junior college. *Religion:* Southern Baptist. *Avocational Interests:* Watching basketball and baseball, photography, and surfing the Internet.

Addresses: *Agent*—Special Artists Agency, 9465 Wilshire Blvd., Suite 470, Beverly Hills, CA 90212; Paradigm, 360 North Crescent Dr., North Bldg., Beverly Hills, CA 90210. *Publicist*—Guttman Associates PR, 118 South Beverly Dr., Beverly Hills, CA 90212.

Career: Actor. The Griffin Theatre and Strawdog Theatre Ensemble, member of company; appeared in television commercials, including Buick, 2003. Band from TV (a celebrity band), member. The Orange County Flyers (a Golden Baseball League team), co–owner. Previously worked as a radio advertising salesman and CBS television advertising salesman. Involved with animal rescue.

Awards, Honors: Science Fiction Genre Award, best actor fantasy/science fiction, ShockerFest, 2006, for *Assumption;* Screen Actors Guild Awards (with others), outstanding performance by an ensemble in a comedy series, 2005, 2006, Screen Actors Guild Award nominations (with others), outstanding performance by an ensemble in a comedy series, 2007, 2008, 2009, Prism Award, performance in a comedy series, 2008, Teen Choice Award, Television—choice actor, 2006, all for *Desperate Housewives;* After Dark Award (with others), for *Flesh and Blood;* Joseph Jefferson Award nomination, best actor, for *The Diviners.*

CREDITS

Film Appearances:

(As Jamie Denton) Ray Higgs, *Thieves Quartet,* Headliner, 1994.

The quarterback, *Basic Football,* 1994.

(As Jamie Denton) Nick, *Hunter's Moon,* 1995.

(As Jamie Denton) Keith Marks, *That Old Feeling,* Universal, 1997.

(As Jamie Denton) Buzz, *Face/Off* (also known as *Face Off*), Paramount, 1997.

(As Jamie Denton) Mitch, *Primary Colors* (also known as *Mit aller macht* and *Perfect Couple*), MCA/ Universal, 1998.

Danny, *Locked up Down Shorty's,* 2000.

Jack, *Jumbo Girl* (short film), 2004.

John, *Assumption* (short film), 2006.

Dr. Kessler, *Beautiful Dreamer,* Lantern Lane Entertainment, 2006.

Brother John, *Ascension Day,* 2007.

Elmer Winslow, *Undead or Alive: A Zombedy* (also known as *Undead or Alive*), Image Entertainment, 2007.

Agent Murphy, *Tortured,* Sony, 2008.

Band from TV: Hoggin' All the Covers, 2008.

Slim, *Karaoke Man,* 2010.

(Uncredited) Luke, *Group Sex,* 2010.

Voice of Superman/Clark Kent, *All–Star Superman* (animated), Warner Home Video, 2011.

Television Appearances; Series:

(As Jamie Denton) Mr. Lyle, *The Pretender,* NBC, 1997–2000.

(As Jamie Denton) Judge Augustus "Jack" Ripley, *Philly,* ABC, 2001–2002.

Special Agent John Kilmer, *Threat Matrix,* ABC, 2003–2004.

Mike Delfino, *Desperate Housewives,* ABC, 2004—.

Television Appearances; Movies:

(As Jamie Denton) Mr. Lyle, *The Pretender 2001* (also known as *The Pretender*), 2001.

(As Jamie Denton) Mr. Lyle, *The Pretender: Island of the Haunted* (also known as *Island of the Haunted* and *Pretender 2: Island of the Haunted*), TNT, 2001.

John Sullivan, *Custody,* Lifetime, 2007.

Television Appearances; Specials:

A Merry Mickey Celebration, ABC, 2003.

CMT: 20 Sexiest Women, Country Music Television, 2004.

VH1 Big in 04, VH1, 2004.

The 31st Annual People's Choice Awards, CBS, 2005.

ESPY Awards, ESPN, 2005.

Host, *The 2005 World Music Awards* (also known as *World Music Awards 2005*), ABC, 2005.

Miss America Pageant, 2005.

Presenter, *The 11th Annual Screen Actors Guild Awards,* TNT, 2005.

Presenter, *The 2005 American Music Awards* (also known as *The 33rd Annual American Music Awards*), ABC, 2005.

Narrator, *Primal Quest Utah,* 2006.

CMT: The Greatest—20 Sexiest Woman, Country Music Television, 2006.

CMT: The Greatest—20 Sexiest Men, Country Music Television, 2006.

Host, *Miss America 2006,* Country Music Television, 2006.

The 12th Annual Screen Actors Guild Awards, TNT, 2006.

CMT: The Greatest—Sexiest Southern Men, Country Music Television, 2006.

CMT: The Greatest—Sexiest Southern Women, Country Music Television, 2006.

Presenter, *The 40th Annual Country Music Association Awards* (also known as *40th Annual CMA Awards*), ABC, 2006.

Comic Relief 2006, TBS and HBO, 2006.

Host, *Cracker Barrel: Songs of the Year Concert,* 2007.

The 41st Annual Country Music Association Awards (also known as *41st Annual CMA Awards*), ABC, 2007.

The 12th Annual Prism Awards, Fox, 2008.

The 36th Annual People's Choice Awards, 2010.

Television Appearances; Pilots:

Dr. Adam Mitchell, *L.A. Meds,* ABC, 1997.

The Hanleys, ABC, 1998.

John Kilmer, *Threat Matrix,* ABC, 2003.

Twentysixmiles, 2008.

Television Appearances; Episodic:

(As Jamie Denton) Jack Bullock, "The Good, the Bad and The Wealthy," *Sliders,* Sci–Fi Channel, 1996.

(As Jamie Denton) Lieutenant Commander Bruce Carmichael, "Hemlock," *JAG,* NBC, 1996.

(As Jamie Denton) Rocky Talese, "Friendly Fire," *Moloney,* CBS, 1996.

(As Jamie Denton) Rob Winter, "Hostile Convergence," *Dark Skies,* NBC, 1996.

(As Jamie Denton) Dr. Howard Zaunaveld, "The Monitor Story," *Two Guys, a Girl and a Pizza Place* (also known as *Two Guys and a Girl*), ABC, 2000.

(As Jamie Denton) Jimmy Bender, "Do You Wanna Dance?," *Ally McBeal* (also known as *Ally My Love*), Fox, 2000.

(As Jamie Denton) Tom Jordan, "The Midterms," *The West Wing* (also known *The White House*), NBC, 2000.

(As Jamie Denton) Doctor, *Inside Schwartz,* NBC, 2001.

(As Jamie Denton) Daryl, "Drew Tries Hot Salsa," *The Drew Carey Show,* ABC, 2002.

(As Jamie Denton) Daryl, "The Man in the Iron Chair," *The Drew Carey Show,* ABC, 2002.

Geoffrey Roizman, "Fortunate Son," *JAG,* CBS, 2003.

Extra, syndicated, 2003.

E! News Live, E! Entertainment Television, 2003.

Cold Pizza, ESPN2, 2004.

Good Morning America (also known as *G.M.A.*), ABC, 2004, 2005.

The View, ABC, 2004, 2005, 2006, 2007, 2009.

The Tonight Show with Jay Leno, NBC, 2005.

The Oprah Winfrey Show (also known as *Oprah*), syndicated, 2005.

The Best Damn Sports Show Period, Fox Sports, 2005.

Richard & Judy, Channel 4, 2005.

"Hot to Tot," *Kathy Griffin: My Life on the D–List,* Bravo, 2005.

The Tony Danza Show, syndicated, 2005.

"Tournament 7, Game 1," *Celebrity Poker Showdown,* Bravo, 2005.

Jimmy Kimmel Live!, ABC, 2005.

"Holiday Wishes," *Extreme Makeover: Home Edition,* ABC, 2005.

Dr. Morgan, "Date of Mirth," *Reba,* The WB, 2005.

Live with Regis and Kelly, syndicated, 2005, 2007, 2008.

The Late Late Show with Craig Ferguson, CBS, 2005, 2007.

Ellen: The Ellen DeGeneres Show, syndicated, 2005, 2006, 2007.

Dr. Morgan, "The Trouble with Dr. Hunky," *Reba,* The WB, 2006.

The Megan Mullally Show, syndicated, 2006.

"2006 Celebrity Jeopardy! Game 4.," *Jeopardy!,* syndicated, 2006.

"Reba," *CMT Giants,* Country Music Television, 2006.

Entertainment Tonight (also known as *E.T.*), syndicated, 2006, 2007, 2008.

Barney Curran, "The Discarded," *Masters of Science Fiction,* ABC, 2007.

Caiga quien caiga, 2008.

(With Band from TV) Himself, "Idol Gives Back," *American Idol* (also known as *American Idol: The Search for a Superstar* and *Idol*), Fox, 2008.

(With Band from TV) Himself, "Live Results Show: One Contestant Eliminated," *American Idol* (also known as *American Idol: The Search for a Superstar* and *Idol*), Fox, 2008.

Rachael Ray, syndicated, 2008.

Last Call with Carson Daly, NBC, 2008.

"Desperate Housewives," *Infanity,* TV Guide Channel, 2008.

"El Finks," *Head Case,* Starz!, 2008.

The Bonnie Hunt Show, NBC, 2008, 2009, 2010.

"Talk to the List," *Head Case,* Starz!, 2009.

CMT Insider, Country Music Television, 2009.

The Tonight Show with Conan O'Brien, NBC, 2009.

Also appeared in *The Untouchables.*

Stage Appearances:

Steven, *In Walked Monk,* Hollywood, CA, 1999.

First inmate, *Asylum,* Court Theatre, West Hollywood, CA, 2000.

Danny, *Locked Up Down Shorty's,* Power House Theatre, Santa Monica, CA, 2001.

Also appeared as George Gibbs, *Our Town,* Nashville, TN; Stanley, *A Streetcar Named Desire,* Chicago, IL; Bebert, *Lapin Lapin,* Chicago, IL; C. C. Showers, *The Diviners,* Chicago, IL; in *Flesh and Blood; The Night Hank Williams Died; Death Trap; Thieves Quartet.*

RECORDINGS

Videos:

Himself, *Prenatal Fitness Fix,* 2006.

Himself, *Postnatal Rescue,* Acadia Films, 2007.

Music Videos:

Appeared in "Justice for All" by Dale Watson, 2007.

WRITINGS

Television Episodes:

"Talk to the List," *Head Case,* Starz!, 2009.

Stage Scores:

Wrote music for *The Night Hank Williams Died.*

OTHER SOURCES

Periodicals:

Good Housekeeping, September, 2008, p. 59.

People Weekly, April 11, 2005, p. 82.

Redbook, May, 2005, p. 48.

Electronic:

James Denton Official Site, http://www.jamesdenton. com/, October 19, 2010.

DEVICQ, Paula 1965–
(Paula DeVicq)

PERSONAL

Full name, Paula Michelle Devicq; born July 7, 1965, in Edmonton, Alberta, Canada; married Joseph Lyle Taylor (an actor), December 12, 2001 (divorced).

Addresses: *Agent*—Innovative Artists, 1505 10th St., Santa Monica, CA 90401. *Manager*—Joanne Horowitz Management, 9350 Wilshire Blvd., Suite 224, Beverly Hills, CA 90212.

Career: Actress. Began career as a model. Appeared in print ad and package for L'Oreal Excellence Ash hair color.

CREDITS

Film Appearances:

Vicki Livingston, *Kill the Man,* 1999.

Teresa, *The Breakup Artist,* Screen Media Ventures, 2004.

Holly Cooper, *The Good Student* (also known as *Mr. Gibb*), Screen Media Ventures, 2006.

Jen, *Almost Home* (short film), 2008.

Vicky Ann, *First Dog,* 2010.

Television Appearances; Series:
Kirsten Bennett, *Party of Five,* Fox, 1994–2000.
Cynthia Bennington, *100 Centre Street,* Arts and Entertainment, 2001–2002.
Sondra, *Rescue Me,* FX Network, 2004–2005.

Television Appearances; Miniseries:
Jane McCann, *The Grid,* BBC2 and TNT, 2004.

Television Appearances; Movies:
(As Paula DeVicq) Tracy Lance, *Wounded Heart,* USA Network, 1995.
Laura, *Dinner and Driving,* HBO, 2000.
Kate Moore, *The Coven,* 2004.
Vicki Shaw, *His and Her Christmas,* Lifetime, 2005.

Television Appearances; Pilots:
Kirsten Bennett, *Party of Five,* Fox, 1994.

Television Appearances; Episodic:
The Rosie O'Donnell Show, syndicated, 1998.
Miranda Shea, "Obsession," *Law & Order,* NBC, 2005.
Christine Mayfield, "Courtship," *Law & Order: Criminal Intent* (also known as *Law & Order: CI*), NBC, 2007.

Stage Appearances:
Understudy for the roles of Brenda and Collette, *Four Dogs and a Bone,* Manhattan Theatre Club Stage II, New York City, 1993.

Also appeared in *The Stumbling Tongue,* off–Broadway production; *Bob Funk,* Taramand Theatre, Los Angeles; *The Wild Goose,* Ensemble Studio Theatre, New York City.

DEVLIN, Alan

PERSONAL

Career: Actor.

Awards, Honors: Laurence Olivier Theatre Award, best actor in a supporting role, Society of London Theatre, 1984, for *A Moon for the Misbegotten.*

CREDITS

Film Appearances:
Phoelix, 1980.
Edward, *The Mouse and the Woman,* Facelift, 1980.
Priest, *The Long Good Friday,* Embassy, 1980.

Clicky, *Traveller,* 1981.
Bill, *Angel* (also known as *Danny Boy*), 1982.
Hostage, 1985.
Father Quigley, *The Lonely Passion of Judith Hearne,* Island Pictures, 1987.
Mick Barry, *The Clash of the Ash,* 1987.
"Clipper" McNabb, *Paradiso,* 1988.
Grant, *The Angry Earth,* 1989.
Lord Waterstone, *Rebecca's Daughters,* 1992.
Malone, *The Playboys,* Samuel Goldwyn, 1992.
Mr. Riley, *War of the Buttons* (also known as *La guerre des boutons, ca recommence*), Warner Bros., 1994.
Manley, *High Boot Benny,* 1994.
John Joe, *Moondance,* 1995.
Chalky White, *Resurrection Man,* PolyGram Filmed Entertainment, 1998.
Lord Mayor, *Ordinary Decent Criminal* (also known as *Ein Ganz gewoehnlicher dieb*), Miramax, 2000.
Pop Devlin, *Flick,* 2000.
Father Damian, *Song for a Raggy Boy,* ContentFilm International, 2003.
Simon Dedalus, *Bloom,* MTI Home Video, 2003.
Two Fat Ladies (short film), 2003.
Clara's father, *Waterloo Dentures* (short film), 2004.
Barney, *Tara Road,* First Look International, 2005.
Mr. O'Hickey, *The Martyr's Crown* (short film), Park Films, 2007.
Detective, *The Wednesdays* (short film), Park Films, 2007.
Joe, *Leap Year,* Universal, 2010.

Television Appearances; Series:
Joseph Macarthy, *The Crezz,* 1976.

Television Appearances; Miniseries:
Detective, *My Son, My Son,* BBC, 1979.
Eamon Duffy, *Crossfire,* 1988.

Television Appearances; Movies:
Quinn, *Honour, Profit & Pleasure,* Channel 4, 1985.
Sir Rex Ferriday, *Nineteen 96,* 1989.
Il prezzo della vita, 1993.
Doctor, *Oliver Twist,* ABC, 1997.
Father Flannery, *Sinners* (also known as *The Magdalen Laundry*), 2002.
Laurence Rush, *Omagh,* 2004.

Television Appearances; Episodic:
Tomsy Flood, "In the Curranhilty Country," *The Irish R.M.,* Channel 4 and PBS, 1985.
Detective Inspector O'Brien, "Steeled with a Kiss: Parts 1 & 2," *Remington Steele,* 1987.
Father O'Brian, "A Blind Edge," *The District Nurse,* BBC, 1987.
Sir Rex Ferriday (MI6), "Nineteen 96," *Screen One,* BBC, 1989.
Barry Madden, *The Clinic,* 2009.

Stage Appearances:
Ducking Out, Duke of York Theatre, London, 1982.
A Moon for the Misbegotten, London, c. 1984.
Sir Joseph Porter, *HMS Pinafore,* Gaiety Theatre, Dublin, Ireland, 1987.
Philadelphia Here I Come, Gaiety Theatre, 2010.

OTHER SOURCES

Periodicals:
Daily Mail (London), January 12, 2010, p. 3.

DIESEL, Vin 1967–

PERSONAL

Original name, Mark Vincent; born July 18, 1967, in New York, NY; son of Delora (an astrologer and psychiatrist) and stepson of Irving (a theatre manager and acting instructor); twin brother of Paul Vincent (a film editor). *Education:* Studied acting at the Theater for the New City, New York City; studied English at Hunter College for three years.

Addresses: *Office*—c/o One Race Productions, 2029 Century Park East, #1060, Los Angeles, CA 90067. *Agent*—Endeavor, 9701 Wilshire Blvd., 10th Floor, Beverly Hills, CA 90212. *Manager*—The Firm, 9465 Wilshire Blvd., Suite 600, Beverly Hills, CA 90212. *Publicist*—PMK/HBH, 8500 Wilshire Blvd., Suite 700, Beverly Hills, CA 90211; PMK/HBH, 650 Fifth Ave., 33rd Floor, New York, NY 10019.

Career: Actor, director, producer, and screenwriter. One Race Productions, founder; appeared in print ad for Timex watches, 1999–2000; previously worked as a bouncer at clubs in New York City and as a telemarketer.

Awards, Honors: Grand Jury Prize Award nomination, dramatic, Sundance Film Festival, 1997, for *Strays;* Screen Actors Guild Award nomination (with others), outstanding performance by a cast and Online Film Critics Society Award (with others), best ensemble cast performance, 1999, for *Saving Private Ryan;* MTV Movie Award (with Paul Walker), best on–screen team, and MTV Movie Award nomination, best male performance, 2002, for *The Fast and the Furious;* Blockbuster Entertainment Award nomination, favorite actor—horror (Internet only), 2001, for *Pitch Black;* MTV Movie Award nomination, best male performance and Teen Choice Award nomination, choice movie actor, 2003, for *XXX;* Teen Choice Award nomination, choice movie actor—comedy, 2005, for *The Pacifier;* MTV Movie Award nomination, best male performance, 2009, for *Fast & Furious;* People's Choice Award nomination, favorite action star, 2010.

CREDITS

Film Appearances:
Hospital orderly, *Awakenings,* 1990.
Mike, *Multi–Facial* (short film), 1994.
Rick, *Strays,* 1997.
Private Caparzo, *Saving Private Ryan,* DreamWorks, 1998.
Himself, *Into the Breach: "Saving Private Ryan,"* 1998.
Voice of title role, *The Iron Giant* (animated), Warner Bros., 1999.
Richard B. Riddick, *Pitch Black,* USA Films, 1999.
Chris Varick, *Boiler Room,* New Line Cinema, 1999.
Dominic Toretto, *The Fast and the Furious,* MCA/Universal, 2001.
Taylor Reese, *Knockaround Guys,* New Line Cinema, 2001.
Xander Cage, *XXX* (also known as *Triple X*), Sony Pictures Entertainment, 2002.
Sean Vetter, *A Man Apart,* New Line Cinema, 2003.
Himself, *XXX: A Filmmakers Diary,* Columbia, 2003.
Voice of Richard B. Riddick, *The Chronicles of Riddick: Dark Fury,* Universal Studios, 2004.
Riddick, *The Chronicles of Riddick* (also known as *The Chronicles of Riddick: The Director's Cut*), Universal, 2004.
Shane Wolfe, *The Pacifier* (also known as *Gnome* and *Captain Wolfe*), Buena Vista, 2005.
Jackie DiNorscio, *Find Me Guilty* (also known as *Find Me Guilty: The Jackie Dee Story*), New City Releasing, 2006.
Dominic Toretto, *The Fast and the Furious: Tokyo Drift* (also known as *Wild Speed X3: Tokyo Drift*), Universal, 2006.
Toorop, *Babylon A.D.,* Twentieth Century–Fox, 2008.
Dominic Toretto, *Los Bandoleros,* Universal, 2009.
Journey to Sundance, Hollywood Filmmakers, 2009.
Dominic Toretto, *Fast & Furious* (also known as *Fast & Furious 4* and *Wild Speed Max*), Universal Studios, 2009.
Dominic Toretto, *Fast Five,* Universal Studios, 2011.

Film Producer:
Multi–Facial (short film), 1994.
Strays, 1997.
The Chronicles of Riddick (also known as *The Chronicles of Riddick: The Director's Cut*), Universal, 2004.
Fast & Furious (also known as *Fast & Furious 4* and *Wild Speed Max*), Universal Studios, 2009.
Los Bandoleros, Universal, 2009.

Film Executive Producer:
Strays, 1997.
XXX (also known as *Triple X*), Sony Pictures Entertainment, 2002.
A Man Apart, New Line Cinema, 2003.
Hitman, 2007.

Film Director:
Multi–Facial (short film), 1994.
Strays, 1997.
Short Diversity 5, Warner Home Video, 2000.
Los Bandoleros, Universal, 2009.

Television Appearances; Specials:
Himself and host, *The Making of "The Iron Giant,"* The WB, 1999.
Riddick, *Into Pitch Black,* Sci–Fi Channel, 2000.
The Fast and the Furious Movie Special, Black Entertainment Television, 2001.
Starz on the Set: "xXx," 2002.
Riddick, *Sci–Fi Channel: The Lowdown–The Chronicles of Riddick,* Sci–Fi Channel, 2004.
MTV Movie Awards 2005 Pre–Show, MTV, 2005.
Samuel L. Jackson: An American Cinematheque Tribute, AMC, 2008.

Television Appearances; Award Presentations:
2000 Blockbuster Entertainment Awards, Fox, 2000.
Young Hollywood Awards, 2001.
Presenter, *World Stunt Awards,* ABC, 2001.
VH1 Big in 2002 Awards, VH1, 2002.
Presenter, *... MTV Movie Awards,* MTV, 2002, 2004, 2005.
Presenter, *The 3rd Annual Taurus World Stunt Awards,* USA Network, 2003.
The ... NAACP Image Awards, Fox, 2003, 2006.
Cohost, *MTV Europe Music Awards 2003,* MTV, 2003.
Video Game Awards ..., Spike TV, 2004, 2005.
The 77th Annual Academy Awards, ABC, 2005.
2006 Independent Spirit Awards, Independent Film Channel, 2006.

Television Appearances; Episodic:
"Filmen 'Saving Private Ryan'/Nyheter och vader," *Nyhetsmorgon,* 1998.
"Into the Breach: 'Saving Private Ryan'," *HBO First Look,* HBO, 1998.
The Panel, Ten Network, 2000.
The Daily Show with Jon Stewart (also known as *The Daily Show, A Daily Show with Jon Stewart,* and *The Daily Show with Jon Stewart*), Comedy Central, 2000, 2002, 2006.
The Tonight Show with Jay Leno, NBC, 2001, 2002, 2004, 2005, 2006, 2009.
The Late Late Show with Craig Kilborn, CBS, 2001, 2002.
RI:SE, 2002.

"XXx," *Player$,* 2002.
"25 Toughest Stars," *Rank,* 2002.
Tinseltown TV, International Channel, 2003.
Late Show with David Letterman, CBS, 2003, 2005, 2006.
Late Night with Conan O'Brien, NBC, 2003, 2005, 2006.
Live with Regis and Kelly, syndicated, 2003, 2005, 2006.
"Michael Jackson trial, the OC and More," *Best Week Ever with Paul F. Tompkins,* VH1, 2005.
Good Morning America (also known as *G.M.A.*), ABC, 2005.
106 & Park Top 10 Live (also known as *106 & Park*), Black Entertainment Television, 2005.
"Betrayed," *The Contender,* NBC, 2005.
Caiga quien caiga, 2005.
Ellen: The Ellen DeGeneres Show, syndicated, 2005, 2006.
"Action Heroes," *Sexiest ...,* 2006.
Private Adrian Caprazo/Taylor Reese, *Headline News,* Cable News Network, 2006.
Shootout (also known as *Sunday Morning Shootout* and *Hollywood Shootout*), AMC, 2006.
Up Close with Carrie Keagan, 2008, 2009.
Jimmy Kimmel Live!, ABC, 2009.
TV Total, 2009.
Le grand Journal de Canal+, 2009.
Friday Night With Jonathan Ross, BBC1, BBC America, 2009.
"Fast & Furious," *HBO First Look,* HBO, 2009.
Entertainment Tonight (also known as *E.T.* and *This Week in Entertainment*), syndicated, three episodes, 2009.
"Fast and Furious," *Making of ...,* 2009.
Quelli che ... il calcio, 2009.
The Movie Loft, two episodes, 2009.

Also appeared as himself, *Cribs,* MTV; himself, *The Roseanne Show;* himself, *The Martin Short Show;* himself, *Movie House.*

Television Appearances; Movies:
Richard B. Riddick, *Into Pitch Black,* 2000.

Television Appearances; Pilots:
Voice of Hannibal, *Hannibal the Conqueror,* Black Entertainment Television, 2008.

RECORDINGS

Videos:
Playboy Exposed: Playboy Mansion Parties Uncensored, 2001.
"Saving Private Ryan": Re–Creating Omaha Beach, DreamWorks, 2004.
"Saving Private Ryan": Boot Camp, DreamWorks, 2004.

"Saving Private Ryan": *Miller and His Platoon,* Dream-Works, 2004.

Video Games:
Voice of Richard B. Riddick, *The Chronicles of Riddick: Escape from Butcher Bay,* Vivendi Universal, 2004.
Voice of Milo Burik, *Wheelman* (also known as *Vin Diesel Wheelman*), Ubisoft, 2009.
Voice of Richard B. Riddick, *The Chronicles of Riddick: Assault on Dark Athena,* Atari, 2009.

Video Game Executive Producer:
Wheelman (also known as *Vin Diesel Wheelman*), Ubisoft, 2009.

WRITINGS

Screenplays:
Multi–Facial (short film), 1994.
Strays, 1997.
Los Bandoleros, Universal, 2009.

OTHER SOURCES

Books:
Contemporary Black Biography, Volume 29, Gale Group, 2001.

Periodicals:
Entertainment Weekly, August 2, 2002, p. 24.
Hollywood Reporter, June 22, 1998, p. 8; March 24, 1999, p.4.
Interview, February, 1999, p. 40.
Newsweek, July 9, 2001, p. 57.
People Weekly, August 19, 2002, p. 87.
Time, August 5, 2002, p. 61.
Variety, October 21, 2002, p. 88.

DIOL, Susan 1964–

PERSONAL

Full name, Susan Vanita Diol; born May 25, 1964, in Marquette, MI; daughter of Peter Balwant Singh and Christine Katherine Diol; married Jerry Rapp (an actor, producer, writer, and director), April 1, 1991 (divorced, 1993); married Shaun Cassidy (an actor, singer, producer, and director), May 7, 1995 (divorced, 2003); married Andy Cadiff (a director), December 6, 2003; children: (second marriage) Juliet Jones Diol Cassidy, (stepchildren) Caitlin, Jake. *Education:* Graduated from Otterbein University.

Addresses: *Manager*—Billy Miller Management, 8322 Ridpath Dr., Los Angeles, CA 90046.

Career: Actress.

CREDITS

Film Appearances:
I Love N.Y., 1987.

Television Appearances; Series:
Claudia Garrison, *Hothouse,* ABC, 1988.
Emmy Borden, *Days of Our Lives* (also known as *DOOL* and *Days*), NBC, 1990–91.
Angela Holliday, *One Life to Live,* ABC, 1993–94.
Lady Ashton, *General Hospital,* ABC, 2002.

Television Appearances; Movies:
The blonde, *Popeye Doyle,* NBC, 1986.
Lieutenant Johanson, *The Road Raiders,* CBS, 1989.
Ada Raymond, *Seduction: Three Tales from the "Inner Sanctum,"* ABC, 1992.
Ivy West, *A Perry Mason Mystery: The Case of the Jealous Jokester,* NBC, 1995.
Jean, *Her Deadly Rival,* CBS, 1995.
Marina Del Ray, *Alien Nation: Millennium,* Fox, 1996.
Connie, *Safe Harbor,* Hallmark Channel, 2009.

Television Appearances; Pilots:
Claudia, *Hothouse,* 1988.
Samantha, *Touch 'Em All McCall,* NBC, 2003.

Television Appearances; Episodic:
Cheryl, "The Shower," *The Cosby Show,* NBC, 1987.
Cheryl, "Home for the Weekend," *The Cosby Show,* NBC, 1988.
Miss Sanders, "Carol Meets the Real World," *Growing Pains,* ABC, 1989.
Lisa, "Ultimate Aphrodisiac," *FM,* 1989.
Lisa, "No Fool Like an April Fool," *FM,* 1989.
Kate Jarvis, "Old Friends," *Baywatch,* syndicated, 1990.
Beth Calavicci, "M.I.A.—April 1, 1969," *Quantum Leap,* NBC, 1990.
Donna, "Family Affair: Parts 1 & 2," *Night Court,* NBC, 1990.
Donna Montaine, "Married to the Mob," *Going Places,* 1990.
"The Valley of Death," *Paradise* (also known as *Guns of Paradise*), CBS, 1991.
Carmen Davila, "Silicon Avatar," *Star Trek: The Next Generation* (also known as *Star Trek: TNG*), syndicated, 1991.
Audrey, "The Nose Job," *Seinfeld,* NBC, 1991.
Lisa, "The Valley of Death," *Guns of Paradise,* 1991.
Valerie, "A Bundle of Trouble," *P.S. I Luv U,* 1992.

Lorraine Dalleck, "Oboe Phobia," *Civil Wars*, ABC, 1992.

Hypnotist, "Feardom of Speech," *Herman's Head*, Fox, 1992.

Miss Nicastro, *Great Scott!*, Fox, 1992.

Reasonable Doubts, NBC, 1992.

Michelle, "To Market, To Market," *Murphy Brown*, CBS, 1993.

Beth Calavicci, "Mirror Image—August 8, 1953," *Quantum Leap*, NBC, 1993.

Margaret Henderson MacNeill, "Amazing Grace," *Christy* (also known as *Catherine Marshall's "Christy"*), CBS, 1994.

Miriam, "Til Death Do Us Part," *One West Waikiki*, CBS, 1994.

Rebecca Shay, "All's Fair," *Party of Five*, Fox, 1994.

Dana Reno, "War Zone," *Walker, Texas Ranger*, CBS, 1995.

Margaret Henderson MacNeill, "The Road Home," *Christy* (also known as *Catherine Marshall's "Christy"*), CBS, 1995.

Heather, "Hooker, Line, and Sinker," *Wings*, NBC, 1995.

Helen Nichols, "The Prodigal Father," *The Client* (also known as *John Grisham's "The Client"*), CBS, 1995.

Jodie Talese, "Friendly Fire," *Moloney*, CBS, 1996.

Susan Duplain, "The One That Got Away," *Touched by an Angel*, CBS, 1996.

Dr. Danara Pel, "Lifesigns," *Star Trek: Voyager* (also known as *Voyager*), UPN, 1996.

Dr. Danara Pel, "Resolutions," *Star Trek: Voyager* (also known as *Voyager*), UPN, 1996.

"Me and Mrs. Hale," *Nick Freno: Licensed Teacher*, The WB, 1996.

Marina del Rey, "Millennium," *Alien Nation*, 1996.

Jeri Murdico, "Murder Two: Parts 1 & 2," *Diagnosis: Murder* (also known as *Dr. Mark Sloan*), CBS, 1997.

Sheila Redding, "Freebird," *Pensacola: Wings of Gold*, syndicated, 1997.

Andrea, "Weaning Isn't Everything," *Yes, Dear*, CBS, 2000.

"Where Have You Gone Sandy Koufax," *Cover Me: Based on the True Life of an FBI Family* (also known as *Cover Me*), 2000.

Jamie Lund, "Tucker's Gift," *The Fugitive*, CBS, 2001.

Debra, "The Plague Year," *The Agency* (also known as *CIA: The Agency*), CBS, 2002.

Mindy Barnes/Elise Redman, "Tall Tales," *Philly*, ABC, 2002.

Debra, "Finale," *The Agency* (also known as *CIA: The Agency*), CBS, 2002.

Alexis Davis, *General Hospital*, ABC, 2002.

Beth Dunbar, "Grissom Versus the Volcano," *CSI: Crime Scene Investigation* (also known as *CSI: Las Vegas* and *C.S.I.*), CBS, 2003.

Jennifer Harper, "Whereabouts," *Eyes*, ABC, 2005.

Carol Whitney, "More Than This," *Without a Trace* (also known as *W.A.T.*), CBS, 2006.

(Uncredited) Flight attendant, "No One Is Alone," *Desperate Housewives*, ABC, 2006.

Dr. Leslie Burke, "Witch Hunt," *NCIS: Naval Criminal Investigative Service* (also known as *Navy NCIS: Naval Criminal Investigative Service* and *NCIS*), CBS, 2006.

Kristi Duren in 2009, "Dead Heat," *Cold Case*, CBS, 2009.

Stage Appearances:

Dolly Clandon, *You Never Can Tell*, Circle in the Square, New York City, 1986–87.

OTHER SOURCES

Electronic:

Susan Diol Official Site, http://www.angelfire.com/tv2/tvgirl/bio.html, September 16, 2010.

DOWLING, Kevin

PERSONAL

Born in Australia.

Career: Director and producer. The Actor's Ensemble, founding member and artistic director.

Awards, Honors: Sydney Film Festival Award, best feature, 1994, Best Film Award (with Geoff Burton), Cleveland International Film Festival, 1995, both for *The Sum of Us*.

CREDITS

Film Work:

Co–executive producer and director, *The Sum of Us*, Samuel Goldwyn Pictures, 1994.

Executive producer and director, *Mojave Moon* (also known as *Real Blood*), Trimark Pictures, 1996.

Television Work; Series:

Field producer, *Vital Signs*, ABC, 1996.

Producer, *Close to Home*, CBS, 2006–2007.

Supervising producer, *K–Ville*, Fox, 2007–2008.

Supervising producer, *Valentine*, The CW, 2008–2009.

Television Director; Movies:

Last Rites, Starz!, 1998.

Silk Hope, CBS, 1999.

The Last Dance, CBS, 2000.

Television Work; Pilots:
Director, *Valentine,* The CW, 2008.
Director and executive producer, *Necessary Roughness,* USA Network, 2010.

Television Director; Episodic:
"Toothpick to the Heart," *Vital Signs,* ABC, 1997.
"Fear Itself," *Vital Signs,* ABC, 1997.
"The Flower King," *Dellaventura,* CBS, 1998.
(With Rob Lagomarsino) "Lives of Their Own," *Four Corners,* CBS, 1998.
"Fiesta," *Four Corners,* CBS, 1998.
"Obsession," *Magnificent 7,* CBS, 1999.
Judging Amy, CBS, 1999–2003.
"Wild Card," *Early Edition,* CBS, 1999.
"Gifted," *Early Edition,* CBS, 2000.
Ed, NBC, 2000–2002.
"The D.C. Strangler," *The District,* CBS, 2001.
"Night Moves," *The District,* CBS, 2001.
"Melt Down," *The District,* CBS, 2001.
"Netherlands," *Touched by an Angel,* CBS, 2001.
"Heebee Geebee's," *Dead Last,* The WB, 2001.
"He Who Smelt It," *Dead Last,* The WB, 2001.
"To Live and Amulet Die," *Dead Last,* The WB, 2001.
"The Princeless Bride," *Touched by an Angel,* CBS, 2002.
"A Rock and a Hard Place," *Touched by an Angel,* CBS, 2002.
"Back in the Saddle Again," *Gilmore Girls* (also known as *Gilmore Girls: Beginnings*), The WB, 2002.
"Sticks and Stones," *L.A. Dragnet* (also known as *Dragnet*), ABC, 2003.
"Acceptable Losses," *The District,* CBS, 2003.
"Coyote," *L.A. Dragnet* (also known as *Dragnet*), ABC, 2003.
Joan of Arcadia, CBS, 2003–2005.
"Killing Fields," *L.A. Dragnet* (also known as *Dragnet*), ABC, 2004.
"Silver Lining," *Law & Order: Criminal Intent* (also known as *Law & Order: CI*), NBC, 2004.
"Sex, Lies and Sonograms," *Inconceivable,* NBC, 2005.
"The Hero Dies in This One," *One Tree Hill,* The WB, 2005.
"From the Edge of the Deep Green Sea," *One Tree Hill,* The WB, 2005.
Close to Home, CBS, 2005–2007.
"The Two Princes," *E–Ring,* NBC, 2006.
"London Calling," *Related,* The WB, 2006.
"Fare Game," *CSI: NY* (also known as *CSI: New York*), CBS, 2006.
"Parent Teacher," *The Jake Effect,* Bravo, 2006.
"The Bar," *Just Legal,* The WB, 2006.
"Winter's End," *Jericho,* CBS, 2007.
"No Good Deed," *K–Ville,* Fox, 2007.
"Hail & Farewell," *Army Wives,* Lifetime, 2007.
"The Messenger," *Army Wives,* Lifetime, 2008.
"Rebellion," *Reaper,* The CW, 2008.
"Daddy's Home," *Valentine,* The CW, 2008.
"Moving Out," *Army Wives,* Lifetime, 2009.

"She's Gone," *Valentine,* The CW, 2009.
"Chapter Eleven 'The Fifth Stage,'" *Heroes,* NBC, 2009.
"The Favorite," *Reaper,* The CW, 2009.
"The Devil and Sam Oliver," *Reaper,* The CW, 2009.
"Carnelian, Inc.," *The Mentalist,* CBS, 2009.
"Be All You Can Be," *Army Wives,* Lifetime, 2010.
Past Life, Fox, 2010.
"Home Away from Home," *Drop Dead Diva,* Lifetime, 2010.
"Baby, Let's Play," *Memphis Beat,* TNT, 2010.
"The Debate Trip," *Sons of Tucson,* Fox, 2010.
"Glenn's Birthday," *Sons of Tucson,* Fox, 2010.

Also directed "A Rock and a Head Case," *That Was Then,* ABC.

Television Appearances; Episodic:
Ghost Stories, syndicated, 1997.
K–Ville, Fox, 2007.

Stage Director:
The Nerd, Helen Hayes Theatre, New York City, 1987.
Moon for the Misbegotten, Williamstown Theatre Festival, Williamstown, MA, 1990.
The Sum of Us, Cherry Lane Theatre, New York City, 1990–91.
Picnic, Williamstown Theatre Festival, 1991.
Man in His Underwear, Playwrights Horizons Theatre, New York City, 1992.
A Life in the Theatre, Jewish Repertory Theatre, New York City, 1992.

Also directed *Anna Christie; This Is the Rill Speaking; Game Plan; A Child's Piece.*

Stage Work; Other:
Producer, *True West,* New York City, 1982–84.
Producer, *The Nerd,* Helen Hayes Theatre, New York City, 1987.
General manager, *Forbidden Broadway 1988/1989,* Theatre East, 1988–89.

OTHER SOURCES

Electronic:
Kevin Dowling Official Site, http://www.directorsnet.com/dowling, June 20, 2003.

DYE, John 1963–2011

PERSONAL

Original name, John Carroll Dye; born January 31, 1963, in Amory, Mississippi; died of cardiac arrest, January 10, 2011, in San Francisco, California. Actor.

Dye is best known as Andrew, the angel of death, in the long-running television series *Touched by an Angel*. Dye studied theater at the University of Memphis, and his first role came in the 1984 comedy film *Making the Grade*. He appeared in two other comedies before transitioning to more serious roles in the 1989 short film *Mother, Mother*, about a young man with AIDS and his attempts to reconnect with his mother. Dye's later films include *The Perfect Weapon, Sioux City, Heart of the Beholder*, and *Fist of the Warrior*. Before *Touched by an Angel* began filming in 1994, Dye's notable television roles included recurring parts in *The Young and the Restless; Tour of Duty; Jack's Place; Hotel Malibu; Murder, She Wrote;* and *Promised Land*.

PERIODICALS

Boston Globe, January 15, 2011.
Los Angeles Times, January 14, 2011.

E

EJIOFOR, Chiwetel 1974(?)–
  (Chiwetal Ejiofor)

PERSONAL

Some sources cite original name as Chiwetelu Umeadi Ejiofor; born July 10, 1974 (some sources cite 1977), in London, England; son of Arinze (a doctor) and Obiajulu (a pharmacist and singer) Ejiofor. *Education:* Attended Dulwich College, London, and the London Academy of Music and Dramatic Art. *Avocational Interests:* Playing the piano, music, art.

Addresses: *Agent*—International Creative Management, 10250 Constellation Blvd., 9th Floor, Los Angeles, CA 90067; Markham, Froggatt & Irwin, 4 Windmill St., London W1P 1HF, England; Danis Panaro Nist, 9201 West Olympic Blvd., Beverly Hills, CA 90212.

Career: Actor. Blind (band), backup vocalist and performer at various venues, c. early 1990s. Conducted an acting workshop at Dulwich College, London.

Member: Screen Actors Guild Award, Academy of Motion Picture Arts and Sciences.

Awards, Honors: Jack Tinker Award, most promising newcomer, Critics' Circle Theatre awards, 2000, *Evening Standard* Theatre Award, outstanding newcomer, 2000, and Laurence Olivier Theatre Award nomination, best supporting actor, Society of West End Theatre, 2001, all for *Blue/Orange; Evening Standard* British Film Award and San Diego Film Critics Society Award, both best actor, 2002, British Independent Film Award, European Film Award nomination, and Washington, DC Area Film Critics Association Award nomination, all best actor, ALFS Award nomination, British actor of the year, London Critics Circle Film awards, and British Independent Film Award nomination, most promising newcomer, all 2003, American Black Film Festival Award, best performance by an actor, Black Reel Award, film: best actor, Chicago Film Critics Association Award nomination, most promising newcomer, and Online Film Critics Society Award nomination, best breakthrough performance, all 2004, all for *Dirty Pretty Things;* Phoenix Film Critics Society Award nomination (with others), best ensemble acting, 2004, for *Love Actually;* British Independent Film Award nomination, best actor, 2005, ALFS Award nomination, British actor of the year, London Critics Circle Film awards, 2006, Black Movie Award nomination, outstanding performance by an actor in a leading role, 2006, Golden Globe Award nomination, best performance by an actor in a motion picture—musical or comedy, 2007, and Black Reel Award nomination, best supporting actor, 2007, all for *Kinky Boots;* Black Reel Award nomination, best supporting actor, 2006, for *Serenity;* Black Reel Award nomination (with others), best ensemble, 2006, for *Four Brothers;* Rising Star Award nomination, British Academy of Film and Television Arts, 2006; Golden Globe Award nomination, best performance by an actor in a miniseries or motion picture made for television, and Image Award nomination, outstanding actor in a television movie, miniseries, or dramatic special, National Association for the Advancement of Colored People (NAACP), both 2007, for *Tsunami: The Aftermath;* Black Reel Award nomination, best supporting actor, 2007, for *Children of Men;* Gotham Award (with others), best ensemble cast, Independent Feature Project, 2007, Independent Spirit Award, best supporting male, Independent Feature Project/West, 2008, and Image Award nomination, outstanding supporting actor in a motion picture, 2008, all for *Talk to Me;* Olivier Award, best actor, 2008, for *Othello;* named an Officer of the Order of the British Empire, 2008; Black Reel Award nomination, best actor, 2008, for *Redbelt;* Screen Actors Guild Award nomination (with others), outstanding performance by a cast in a motion picture, 2008, for *American Gangster;* Golden Globe Award nomination, best performance by an actor in a miniseries or motion picture made for television, 2010, for *Endgame;* Image Award nomination, outstanding supporting actor in a motion picture, and Black Reel Award nomination, best supporting actor, both 2010, for *2012.*

CREDITS

Film Appearances:
Ensign Covey, *Amistad,* DreamWorks, 1997.
Rix, *G:MT Greenwich Mean Time* (also known as *G:mt, GMT: Greenwich Mean Time, G:MT—Greenwich Mean Time,* and *Greenwich Mean Time*), Icon Film Distribution, 1999.
Nicky Burkett, *It Was an Accident,* Pathe, 2000.
Soweto, *My Friend Soweto,* APT Films/Met Film/Skreba Films, 2001.
Okwe, *Dirty Pretty Things,* Miramax, 2002.
Mark Hayward, *3 Blind Mice* (also known as *Three Blind Mice*), Beyond Films, 2003.
Peter, *Love Actually* (also known as *Love Actually Is All Around, Untitled Richard Curtis Project, Ahava Ze Kol Ha–Sippur, Igazabol szerelem, O amor acontece, Rakkautta vain, Realmente amor, Reellement l'amour, Simplesmente amor, Tatsaechlich ... Liebe,* and *To wlasnie milosc*), Universal, 2003.
Ellis Moonsong, *Melinda and Melinda* (also known as *Melinda & Melinda* and *Untitled Woody Allen Fall Project*), Fox Searchlight, 2004.
Frank Wills, *She Hate Me,* Sony Pictures Classics, 2004.
Alex Mpondo, *Red Dust,* c. 2004.
Himself, *Why Shakespeare?* (short documentary), National Endowment for the Arts, c. 2004.
The operative, *Serenity* (also known as *Firefly* and *Firefly: The Movie*), Universal, 2005.
Simon/Lola, *Kinky Boots* (also known as *The Kinky Boot Factory*), Miramax, 2005.
Victor Sweet, *Four Brothers* (also known as *Untitled Mark Wahlberg Project*), Paramount, 2005.
Ty Trippin, *Slow Burn,* GreeneStreet Films International, 2005, Lionsgate, 2007.
Detective Bill Mitchell, *Inside Man* (also known as *Insider*), Universal, 2006.
Luke, *Children of Men,* Universal, 2006.
Dewey Hughes, *Talk to Me* (also known as *Petey Greene's Washington*), Focus Features, 2007.
Huey Lucas, *American Gangster* (also known as *The Return of Superfly* and *Tru Blu*), Universal, 2007.
Mike Terry, *Redbelt,* Sony Pictures Classics, 2008.
Dr. Adrian Helmsley, *2012* (also known as *Farewell Atlantis*), Columbia, 2009.
President Thabo Mbeki, *Endgame,* Monterey Media, 2009, also broadcast on television as part of *Masterpiece* (also known as *ExxonMobil Masterpiece Theatre, Masterpiece Classic, Masterpiece Contemporary, Masterpiece Mystery!, Masterpiece Theatre,* and *Mobil Masterpiece Theatre*), PBS, 2009.

Peabody, *Salt* (also known as *Agent Salt*), Columbia, 2010.
Lee/Evans, *Tonight at Noon,* Unison Films, c. 2010.

Some sources cite appearances in other films.

Film Work:
Director, *Slapper* (short film), Film4, 2008.

Television Appearances; Series:
Ashley Carter, *Trust,* BBC and BBC America, 2003.
Jonah Gabriel, *The Shadow Line,* BBC2, beginning 2011.

Television Appearances; Miniseries:
Ian Carter, *Tsunami: The Aftermath* (also known as *Tsunami*), BBC2 and HBO, 2006.

Television Appearances; Movies:
Ebow, *Deadly Voyage,* HBO, 1996.
Tyler Arnold, *Mind Games* (also known as *Lynda La Plante's "Mind Games"*), ITV, 2001.
President Thabo Mbeki, *Endgame,* broadcast as part of *Masterpiece* (also known as *ExxonMobil Masterpiece Theatre, Masterpiece Classic, Masterpiece Contemporary, Masterpiece Mystery!, Masterpiece Theatre,* and *Mobil Masterpiece Theatre*), PBS, 2009, also released as a feature film, Monterey Media, 2009.

Television Appearances; Specials:
Orsino, *Twelfth Night, or What You Will* (also known as *Twelfth Night*), Channel 4, 2003.
Himself, *Ceremonia de apertura del festival de cine de San Sebastian,* Canal+ Espana, 2004.
Himself, *The Ultimate Heist: Making "Inside Man,"* 2006.
Himself, *"Children of Men": Visions of the Future,* Sci–Fi Channel, 2007.
Voice of John Akii Bua, *The John Akii Bua Story: An African Tragedy* (documentary), BBC2, 2008.

Television Appearances; Awards Presentations:
The Orange British Academy Film Awards (also known as *Orange British Academy Film Awards 2003*), 2003.
Empire Movie Awards, ITV, 2008.
The 67th Annual Golden Globe Awards, NBC, 2010.

Television Appearances; Episodic:
(As Chiwetal Ejiofor) McCorkindale, "Teacher," *Murder in Mind,* BBC and BBC America, 2001.
Paul, "The Knight's Tale," *Canterbury Tales,* BBC and BBC America, 2003.

Himself, *Film '05* (also known as *Film 2005, Film of the Year,* and *The Film Programme*), BBC, 2005.

Himself, *Breakfast* (also known as *BBC Breakfast*), BBC, 2005, 2006.

Himself, *At the Movies* (also known as *Margaret & David at the Movies*), Australian Broadcasting Corporation, 2006.

Himself, *The Late Late Show with Craig Ferguson* (also known as *The Late Late Show*), CBS, 2006.

Himself, *eTalk Daily* (also known as *eTalk* and *e–Talk Daily*), CTV, 2007.

Himself, *Up Close with Carrie Keagan,* 2008.

Himself, *Cinema 3* (also known as *Cinema tres* and *Informatiu cinema*), Televisio de Catalunya (TV3), 2009.

Himself, *Tavis Smiley,* PBS, 2009.

Himself, *TMZ on TV* (also known as *TMZ*), syndicated, 2009.

Himself, *Made in Hollywood,* syndicated, 2009, 2010.

Stage Appearances:

Title role, *Othello,* multiple productions, including National Youth Theatre, England, c. 1990.

Angelo, *Measure for Measure,* Dulwich College, London, 1993.

Algernon Moncrieff, *The Importance of Being Earnest,* Dulwich College, 1994.

Never the Sinner, Dulwich College, 1994.

Agis, *The Triumph of Love,* Almeida Theatre, London, 1999.

Russell, *Sparkleshark,* National Theatre, Lyttelton Theatre, London, 1999.

Romeo, *Romeo and Juliet,* National Theatre, Olivier Theatre, London, 2000.

Young Peer, *Peer Gynt, 2000* (also known as *Peer Gynt*), National Theatre, Olivier Theatre, 2000.

Chris, *Blue/Orange,* National Theatre, Cottesloe Theatre, London, 2000, then Duchess Theatre, London, 2001.

Nicky Lancaster, *The Vortex,* Donmar Warehouse, London, 2002.

Boris Alexeyevich Trigorin, *The Seagull,* Royal Court Theatre, London, 2007.

Title role, *Othello,* Donmar Warehouse, 2007.

Member of the National Youth Theatre, England.

Major Tours:

Malcolm, *Macbeth,* British cities, 1997.

Agis, *The Triumph of Love,* British cities, 1999.

Radio Appearances:

Title role, *Othello,* BBC Radio 3, 2008.

RECORDINGS

Videos; as Himself; Documentaries:

Fallen Empire: Making "American Gangster," MCA/Universal Home Video, 2008.

Roland Emmerich: Master of the Modern Epic (short documentary), Sony Pictures Home Entertainment, 2010.

WRITINGS

Screenplays:

Slapper (short film; based on an idea by Yusuf Pirhasan), Film4, 2008.

Nonfiction:

Contributor to periodicals, including the *Guardian.*

OTHER SOURCES

Books:

Contemporary Black Biography, Volume 67, Gale, 2008.

Periodicals:

BlackBook, February, 2005, p. 96.

Chicago Tribune, May 9, 2008.

Jet, June 5, 2006, p. 48.

Los Angeles Times, April 13, 2006.

Movieline's Hollywood Life, April, 2005, p. 84.

Premiere, March, 2006, p. 30.

Total Film, August, 2005, p. 27.

USA Today, November 16, 2009, p. 2D.

Washington Post, May 9, 2008, pp. 27, 34.

ENGE, Scott 1977–

PERSONAL

Born July 9, 1977, in Knoxville, TN. *Education:* Virginia Polytechnic Institute and State University, B.Arch., 2000.

Career: Production designer and art director. Production designer for commercials for Playstation, 2005, Harrahs casino, 2005, and Easy Life furniture, 2006. Also worked as set carpenter and plasterer, construction supervisor, set builder, set dresser and set decorator, assistant property master, and assistant art director. Previously worked as a house carpenter and builder for ten years.

Member: Art Directors Guild.

CREDITS

Film Production Designer:

Guilt (short film), Flying Leap Productions, 2005.

Queen of Cactus Cove (short film), Wild Card Productions, 2005.
Curt's Brain (short film), CocaCola Company, 2006.
2 Dogs Inside (short film), Wild Card Productions, 2006.
Entry Level, PorchLight Entertainment, 2007.
Fun on Earth (short film), Lucky Eight Pictures, 2007.
(Los Angeles only) *Half–Life,* Visit Films, 2008.
The One that Got Away (short film), 2008.
Plaguers (also known as Space Hazard), Image Entertainment, 2009.
Super Capers, Roadside Attractions, 2009.
Hurt, Monterey Media, 2009.
(Los Angeles unit) *Circumstance,* Neon Productions, 2010.
(Los Angeles only) *Yohan—Barnevandrer,* Nordisk Film, 2010.

Film Art Director:
Act Like You Mean It (short film), 2005.
Exit 72 (short film), 2005.
Miss Lonelyhearts (short film), 2006.
The Red Veil (short film), Under the Fog Productions, 2006.
Fast Girl, Allumination Filmworks, 2008.
TiMER, Truckbeef, 2009.

Television Production Designer; Series:
Pushed, 2009.
I Didn't Know I Was Pregnant, Discovery Health Channel, 2009.
Heckle U, CBS, 2009.

Television Art Director; Series;:
The Resistance, Syfy, 2010.

Television Production Designer; Episodic:
"Rat Poison," *Your Kid Ate What?,* The Learning Channel, 2009.
"Michael Jackson," *Famous Crime Scenes,* VH1, 2010.
"Marvin Gaye," *Famous Crime Scenes,* VH1, 2010.
"Notorious B.I.G.," *Famous Crime Scenes,* VH1, 2010.

RECORDINGS

Videos:
Production designer for music videos by Disco Biscuits and Shawn Mullins, 2006, Leana, 2007, and Marco Antonio Solis, 2008; art director for a music video by the Starting Line, 2005.

OTHER SOURCES

Electronic:
Scott Enge Official Site, http://www.scottenge.com, October 13, 2010.

ERWIN, Bill 1914–2010
(William Erwin)

PERSONAL

Original name, William Lindsey Erwin; born December 2, 1914, in Honey Grove, Texas; died December 29, 2010, in Los Angeles, California. Actor. Character actor Erwin, whose television and film appearances spanned over 60 years, is best remembered as the cranky old man Sid Fields in a 1993 episode of *Seinfeld,* for which he received an Emmy Award nomination. He began his career with the 1941 film *You're in the Army Now,* followed by a series of small roles in action and Western movies, such as *Man from Del Rio, The Cry Baby Killer,* and *Terror at Black Falls,* throughout the 1950s and 1960s. He was cast in what many consider his most memorable film role as the bellman Arthur Biehl in *Somewhere in Time* in 1980. Erwin also had cameos in the films *Planes, Trains, and Automobiles; Home Alone; Naked Gun 33 1/3: The Final Insult;* and *Things to Do in Denver When You're Dead.* He appeared in an episode of *I Love Lucy* in 1957 and had recurring roles in a diverse list of television shows, including *Have Gun—Will Travel, The Andy Griffith Show, My Three Sons, Twilight Zone, Perry Mason, The Fugitive, Gunsmoke, Growing Pains,* and *Seinfeld.* His final television appearances included the sitcoms *King of Queens* and *My Name is Earl.*

PERIODICALS

Los Angeles Times, January 1, 2011.
New York Times, January 5, 2011.

ESCARGOT, Maurice
See OLDMAN, Gary

ESSMAN, Susie 1955–
(Sussie Essman)

PERSONAL

Full name, Susan Essman; born May 31, 1955, in Mount Vernon, NY; daughter of Leonard (a physician) and Zora (a professor of Russian) Essman; married Jim Harder (a real estate broker), September 13, 2008; stepchildren: three daughters (including Cyndi), one son. *Education:* State University of New York College at Purchase, B.A., 1977. *Religion:* Jewish.

Addresses: *Agent*—Scott Metzger, Paradigm, 360 Park Ave. S., 16th Floor, New York, NY 10010; Chris Schmidt, Paradigm, 360 North Crescent Dr. N., Beverly Hills, CA 90210; (comedy; bookings) Richard Super, Super Artists, Inc., 2910 Main St., 3rd Floor, Santa Monica, CA 90405. *Manager*—Lee Kernis, Brillstein Entertainment Partners, 9150 Wilshire Blvd., Suite 350, Beverly Hills, CA 90212.

Career: Actress and comedian. Performed for several years as a standup comedian, including appearance at Newbury Comedy Festival in England, 2007; appeared in commercials for 4C Foods, 1987–92, Aflac insurance, 2003, and other products.

Awards, Honors: Screen Actors Guild Award nominations (with others), outstanding ensemble in a comedy series, 2006, 2010, both for *Curb Your Enthusiasm.*

CREDITS

Television Appearances; Series:
Charlotte Elkman, *Baby Boom,* NBC, 1988–89.
Susie Greene, *Curb Your Enthusiasm,* HBO, 2000–2009.
Host, *Curb: The Discussion,* TV Guide Network, 2010.

Television Appearances; Movies:
Malka, *Loving Leah,* CBS, 2009.

Television Appearances; Specials:
"Women of the Night II," *On Location,* HBO, 1988.
Sally Field & Tom Hanks' Punchline Party, HBO, 1988.
The World of Jewish Humor, PBS, 1990.
Girls' Night Out, Lifetime, 1994.
Comedy Central Presents: The N.Y. Friars Club Roast of Jerry Stiller, Comedy Central, 1999.
Host, *All Access Pass: The 15th Annual American Comedy Awards,* 2001.
Host, *Comedy Central Presents Hef's Pre–Roast Party,* Comedy Central, 2001.
Comedy Central Presents: The N.Y. Friars Club Roast of Chevy Chase, Comedy Central, 2002.
Narrator, *Uncensored Comedy: That's Not Funny!,* Trio, 2003.
Comedy Central Presents: The Commies, Comedy Central, 2003.
Funny Already: A History of Jewish Comedy, Channel 4, 2004.
Paws for Style, 2006.
Legends: Rodney Dangerfield, Comedy Central, 2006.
Comic Relief, HBO and TBS, 2006.
The World's Greatest Comedy Characters, Channel 4, 2007.
Night of Too Many Stars: An Overbooked Concert for Autism Education, Comedy Central, 2008.

Comedy Central Roast of Bob Saget, Comedy Central, 2008.
T4 Movie Special: Bolt, 2009.
25 Things You Didn't Know about Curb Your Enthusiasm, TV Guide Network, 2010.

Television Appearances; Miniseries:
Heroes of Jewish Comedy, Comedy Central, 2003.
Make 'em Laugh: The Funny Business of America, PBS, 2009.

Television Appearances; Pilots:
Charlotte Elkman, *Baby Boom,* NBC, 1988.
Comics on Delivery (also known as *C.O.D.*), Comedy Central, 1997.

Television Appearances; Episodic:
(As Sussie Essman) "The Hockey Team," *Kate & Allie,* CBS, 1989.
One Night Stand, HBO, 1992.
Jewel, "Art Attack," *True Colors,* Fox, 1992.
Sports lady, *Hardcore TV,* HBO, 1994.
Aunt Ceil, "Thanksgiving Day Massacre," *Ned and Stacey,* Fox, 1995.
Ms. Shapiro, "Terminal," *Law & Order,* NBC, 1997.
"Waltz," *Dr. Katz, Professional Therapist,* Comedy Central, 1998.
Marcia, "No Orleans," *The King of Queens,* CBS, 2002.
Ron Sherwood's secretary, "Badge," *Law & Order: Criminal Intent* (also known as *Law & Order: CI*), NBC, 2002.
Helen Higgins, *Crank Yankers,* MTV, 2002, 2003.
Voice of Sadie, "Car Trouble," *Kim Possible* (animated; also known as *Disney's "Kim Possible"*), The Disney Channel, 2003.
Veronica Reynolds, "Everybody Loves Raimondo's," *Law & Order,* NBC, 2004.
The Smoking Gun TV, truTV, 2004.
Contestant, *Celebrity Poker Showdown,* Bravo, 2006.
8 Out of 10 Cats, Channel 4, 2007.
Host, "Chefs," *Better Half,* Bravo, 2007.
Million Dollar Password, CBS, 2008.
Paula's Party, 2008.
Voice, "Moon over Isla Island," *American Dad* (animated), Fox, 2009.
Herself, "Bridal Beauty," *Make My Day,* TV Land, 2009.

Also appeared in an episode of *London Underground,* Comedy Central.

Television Talk Show Guest Appearances; Episodic:
"Susie Essman," *Lauren Hutton and …,* 1995.
The Daily Show with Jon Stewart (also known as *The Daily Show* and *The Daily Show with Jon Stewart Global Edition*), Comedy Central, 1996, 2009.
The Sharon Osbourne Show (also known as *Sharon*), syndicated, 2004.

Late Night with Conan O'Brien, NBC, 2004, 2005, 2007.
Guest cohost, *The View,* ABC, 2006, 2007, 2010.
The Hour (also known as *CBC News: The Hour* and *George Stroumboulopoulos Tonight*), CBC, 2008.
The Bonnie Hunt Show, NBC, 2009.
The Tonight Show with Conan O'Brien, NBC, 2009.
Chelsea Lately, E! Entertainment Television, 2009.
Tavis Smiley, PBS, 2009.
Late Night with Jimmy Fallon, NBC, 2009, 2010.

Also guest of *Tough Crowd with Colin Quinn* and *Women Aloud,* both Comedy Central.

Film Appearances:
Tour guide, *"Crocodile" Dundee II,* Paramount, 1988.
Lilah's hairdresser, *Punchline,* Columbia, 1988.
Soho woman, *Teenage Mutant Ninja Turtles II: The Secret of the Ooze* (also known as *Mutant Ninja Turtles 2*), New Line Cinema, 1991.
Anita, *Volcano,* Twentieth Century–Fox, 1997.
Protest speaker, *The Siege* (also known as *Martial Law*), Twentieth Century–Fox, 1998.
Ellen Friedman, *Keeping the Faith,* Buena Vista, 2000.
Nurse, *The Secret Lives of Dentists,* Manhattan Pictures International, 2002.
Lieutenant Rita Carbone, *The Man,* New Line Cinema, 2005.
The Aristocrats (documentary; also known as *The @r!$t*(r@t$)*), THINKFilm, 2005.
Voice of Mittens, *Bolt* (animated), Walt Disney, 2008.
Voice of Mittens, *Super Rhino* (animated), Walt Disney Studios Home Entertainment, 2009.
Laura, *Cop Out,* Warner Bros., 2010.

Stage Appearances:
The Vagina Monologues, Westside Theatre Downstairs, New York City, 2000.

WRITINGS

Books:
What Would Susie Say: Bullshit Wisdom about Love, Life, and Comedy, Simon & Schuster, 2009.

OTHER SOURCES

Books:
Essman, Susie, *What Would Susie Say: Bullshit Wisdom about Love, Life, and Comedy,* Simon & Schuster, 2009.

Periodicals:
New York Times, October 7, 2009.

Electronic:
Susie Essman Official Site, http://www.susieessman.com, October 13, 2010.

ETIC, Stan
        See HOFFMAN, Dustin

EVANS, Evan 1975–

PERSONAL

Full name, Evan Edward Evans; born September 13, 1975, in Bergen County, NJ; son of Bill Evans (a jazz pianist); married Michele Rene (a composer), May, 1999; children: Elliot William, Miranda Sara Emily. *Education:* Attended Saddleback Junior College at age eleven; later attended University of California, Los Angeles, and Nadia Boulanger Institute, Paris. *Avocational Interests:* Poker competitions.

Addresses: *Agent*—Jeff H. Kaufman, Kaufman Agency, 12007 Laurel Terrace Dr., Studio City, CA 91604–3617.

Career: Composer, music producer, and orchestrator. E3 Records, founder, 1999; Composer Collective, president and chief executive officer; composer for radio presentations. Also worked as music supervisor and project manager, "transcriptor," music mixer and remastering engineer, sound mixer, and mixing engineer.

Awards, Honors: Disney Creativity Challenge Award, best original composition; honorable mention for Long Island International Film Expo Award (with Joseph Bauer), best original score, 2006, for *Under Surveillance.*

CREDITS

Film Work; Music Orchestrator:
Christmas in Cartoontown (animated), UAV Entertainment, 1996.
Violent Times, 1997.
Jane White Is Sick & Twisted, Artist View Entertainment/D&K Enterprises, 2002.
A Night at Sophie's, Grange Hall Productions, 2004.
Additional orchestrations, *Beethoven's Big Break,* Universal, 2008.

Film Work; Other:
Executive producer, *Under Surveillance* (also known as *Dark Chamber*), Shock–o–Rama Cinema, 2007.

Music editor, *The Kid: Chamaco* (also known as *Chamaco*), Maya Entertainment, 2009.

Associate producer, film editor, and executive score producer, *Night of the Templar,* Sampson Enterprises, 2010.

Producer and film editor, *The Message,* Clay Castle Productions, 2010.

Television Work; Movies:

Executive musical score producer, *Firsthand: Encounter,* 2009.

WRITINGS

Film Music Composer:

Joe Joe Angel & the Dead Guy, 1997.
Coyote, Mallorca Entertainment, 1997.
Killers, Leo Films, 1997.
Something Between Us (short film), American Film Institute, 1999.
Crimson Wings (short film), 1999.
NewsBreak, MTI Home Video, 2000.
TripFall, Artist View Entertainment, 2000.
Future Murder, The Asylum, 2000.
Firestorm Rising, 2001.
Crawl Space (short film), Amphion Productions/Frog Mountain Productions, 2001.
Altered Species (also known as *Rodentz*), Barnholtz Entertainment/Showcase Entertainment, 2001.
(Additional music) *Pottersville* (short film), ORT Productions, 2001.
(Additional music) *Hard Luck,* Film Kitchen, 2001.
Miss Wonton, Media Space, 2002.
The Keeper, Full–Auto Productions, 2002.
Killers 2: The Beast, The Asylum, 2002.
Revelation, Tatem Productions, 2002.
Hunting Humans, IFM World Releasing, 2002.
(Additional music) *Flophouse,* Pyramid Productions, 2002.
(Additional music) *The Source* (also known as *The Surge*), The Asylum, 2002.
Until Death, The Asylum, 2003.
Crave, Copper Hill Films, 2003.
American Almanacs: A Living History (documentary), 2003.
(Additional music) *Soul to Take* (short film), Simmons–Lathan Media Group, 2003.
Pizza: The Movie, Pinkcat Productions, 2004.
Evilution (short film), 2004.
Bollywood and Vine, Ariztical Entertainment, 2005.
Hoboken Hollow, Pumpjack Entertainment, 2006.
Under Surveillance (also known as *Dark Chamber*), Shock–o–Rama Cinema, 2007.
Blacklist: Recovering the Life of Canada Lee (documentary), Motion Factory Films, 2008.
Jack Rio, GruntWorks Entertainment/Black Hat Productions, 2008.

Skeletons in the Desert, GruntWorks Entertainment/Three Chord Productions, 2008.
MARy (also known as *Bloody Mary*), GruntWorks Entertainment, 2008.
The Poker Club, Sony Pictures Home Entertainment, 2009.
Vegan Love (short film), London Film School, 2009.
Never Surrender, Lions Gate Films, 2009.
(Additional music) *The Mercy Man,* Champawat Pictures, 2009.
Programming the Nation (documentary), Walking Shadows, 2010.
Changing Hands, Changing Hands Films, 2010.
You're Nobody 'til Somebody Kills You, Blackfoot Films/ClassCIII Productions, 2010.
Night of the Templar, Sampson Enterprises, 2010.
(Additional music) *The Devil's Gravestone,* Road Productions/Reeleyes Filmworks/Roach City Films, 2010.
(Additional music) *The Tweakers,* ZenGhetto productions, 2010.

Television Music Composer:

(Additional music) *Sworn to Secrecy* (series; also known as *Secrets of War*), 1998.
A Table for One (movie; also known as *Wicked Ways*), Cinemax, 1999.

OTHER SOURCES

Electronic:

Evan Evans Official Site, http://www.evanevans.org, October 13, 2010.

EVIGAN, Briana 1986–

PERSONAL

Some sources cite full name as Briana Barbara–Jane Evigan; born October 23, 1986, in Los Angeles, CA; daughter of Greg Evigan (an actor, singer, musician, and songwriter) and Pamela "Pam" Serpe (an actress and dancer); sister of Vanessa Lee Evigan (an actress) and Jason Evigan (a singer). *Education:* Trained with choreographer Shane Sparks.

Addresses: *Agent*—The Gersh Agency, 9465 Wilshire Blvd., 6th Floor, Beverly Hills, CA 90212; (dance) Brianna Barcus, Clear Talent Group, 10950 Ventura Blvd., Studio City, CA 91604. *Manager*—Matt Luber, Luber Roklin Entertainment, 8530 Wilshire Blvd., 5th Floor, Beverly Hills, CA 90211. *Publicist*—Samantha Hill, WKT Public Relations, 9350 Wilshire Blvd., Suite 450, Beverly Hills, CA 90212.

Career: Actress, dancer, singer, and musician. Co-founder, singer, and keyboard performer with the band Moorish Idol.

Awards, Honors: MTV Movie Award (with Robert Hoffman), best kiss, and Teen Choice Award nomination, choice movie breakout female, both 2008, for *Step Up 2: The Streets;* ShoWest Award (with others), female star of tomorrow, National Association of Theatre Owners, 2009.

CREDITS

Film Appearances:

First high school girl, *Bottoms Up* (also known as *Paris Hilton in Hollywood Scandal*), Sony Pictures Home Entertainment, 2006.

Andie West, *Step Up 2: The Streets* (also known as *Sexy Dance 2, Step up to the Streets, Step Up 2, Step Up 2: The Street,* and *Step Up 2 the Streets*), Walt Disney Studios Motion Pictures, 2008.

Cassidy Tappan, *Sorority Row* (also known as *House on Sorority Row* and *The House on Sorority Row*), Summit Entertainment, 2009.

Corey, *S. Darko* (also known as *Donnie Darko 2, S. Darko, S. Darko: A Donnie Darko Tale,* and *S. Darko: Donnie Darko 2*), Twentieth Century–Fox Home Entertainment, 2009.

Kelly Taylor, *Burning Bright* (also known as *Ravenous*), Burning Bright Productions/Launchpad Productions/Sobini Films, 2009.

Butterfly, *Subject: I Love You* (also known as *I Luv U Virus*), Radiant Studios, 2010.

Svector Orlaff, *Monster Heroes,* Tarnol Group Pictures, 2010.

Annette Langston, *Mother's Day,* Optimum Releasing/Eagle Films/Applause Entertainment, c. 2010.

Rites of Passage, Voltage Pictures, 2011.

Television Appearances; Movies:

Aubrey South, *House of the Damned* (also known as *Escape to Nowhere* and *Spectre*), Showtime, 1996.

Television Appearances; Awards Presentations:

2008 MTV Movie Awards, MTV, 2008.

The 2008 Teen Choice Awards (also known as *Teen Choice Awards 2008* and *The Teen Choice Awards 2008*), Fox, 2008.

Television Appearances; Episodic:

Herself, *Entertainment Tonight* (also known as *Entertainment This Week, E.T., ET Weekend,* and *This Week in Entertainment*), syndicated, 2007.

Helen, "New Year's Day," *Fear Itself,* NBC, 2008.

Herself, *Up Close with Carrie Keagan,* 2008, 2009.

Herself, *Xpose,* TV3 Television Network, 2009.

Appeared in other programs, including an appearance as Briana the hip hop dancer, *Next,* MTV.

RECORDINGS

Videos:

Herself, *The Making of "S. Darko"* (short documentary), Twentieth Century–Fox Home Entertainment, 2009.

Appeared in music videos, including "Numb" by Linkin Park, c. 2003; "Something Sweet" by The After Midnight Project, 2004; and "Do You Know?" c. 2007, and "Push" 2008, both by Enrique Iglesias.

WRITINGS

Film Songs; with Others:

"I'm Free," *Burning Bright* (also known as *Ravenous*), Burning Bright Productions/Launchpad Productions/Sobini Films, 2009.

"Night & Day," *S. Darko* (also known as *Donnie Darko 2, S. Darko, S. Darko: A Donnie Darko Tale,* and *S. Darko: Donnie Darko 2*), Twentieth Century–Fox Home Entertainment, 2009.

F

FEIFER, Michael 1968–

PERSONAL

Born September 11, 1968, in Brooklyn, NY; married Caia Coley, April 14, 2001; children: one.

Career: Producer, director, writer, and actor. Vista Street Entertainment, vice president for international sales. Also worked as assistant director, line producer, unit production manager, post–production supervisor, and still photographer.

Awards, Honors: Beverly Hills Film Festival Award, best producer, 2007, for *Chicago Massacre: Richard Speck;* Beverly Hills Film Festival Award, best director, 2009, for *Drifter: Henry Lee Lucas.*

CREDITS

Film Producer and Director:
Lethal Eviction (also known as *Grayson Arms*), The Asylum Home Entertainment, 2005.
The Graveyard, Lions Gate Films Home Entertainment, 2006.
A Dead Calling, North American Entertainment, 2006.
Grim Reaper (also known as *Re: Play*), MRG Entertainment, 2007.
Ed Gein: The Butcher of Plainfield, Barnholtz Entertainment, 2007.
Chicago Massacre: Richard Speck (also known as *Nurse Killer*), Barnholtz Entertainment, 2007.
Bundy: An American Icon (also known as *Bundy: A Legacy of Evil*), Barnholtz Entertainment, 2008.
B.T.K., Barnholtz Entertainment/Lions Gate Films, 2008.
Dracula's Guest, Barnholtz Entertainment/Lions Gate Films, 2008.

Boston Strangler: The Untold Story, Weinstein Company, 2008.
Drifter: Henry Lee Lucas, Barnholtz Entertainment, 2009.
Abandoned, Anchor Bay Entertainment, 2010.
Soda Springs, 2C Entertainment, 2011.

Film Producer:
Divorce Law (also known as *Illegal Affairs*), Vista Street Entertainment, 1993.
Sweet Evil, Vista Street Entertainment, 1993.
Witchcraft V: Dance with the Devil, Troma Entertainment, 1993.
Witchcraft VI (also known as *Witchcraft 666: The Devil's Mistress*), Vista Street Entertainment, 1994.
Witchcraft 7: Judgement Hour, Troma Entertainment, 1995.
Witchcraft 8: Salem's Ghost, A–Pix Entertainment, 1996.
Witchcraft IX: Bitter Flesh, Vista Street Entertainment, 1997.
Dead by Dawn, Vista Street Entertainment, 1998.
Secret Pleasures, MRG Entertainment, 1999.
The Seductress, Megastar Pictures/Prism Leisure/Third Millennium, 2000.
Choosing Matthias, Deep Step Productions, 2001.
Sensual Friends, MRG Entertainment, 2001.
The Bike Squad, Mainline Releasing, 2002.
Would I Lie to You?, Serious Dog Films, 2002.
The Silvergleam Whistle (short film), Nickel Eye Pictures, 2003.
Workout with a Knockout, Frontera Media Productions, 2004.
The Butcher (also known as *Pieces*), Lions Gate Films Home Entertainment, 2006.
Are You Scared? (also known as *Jigsaw: Game of Death*), Lions Gate Films, 2006.

Film Coproducer:
The Mesmerist, Seventh Art Releasing, 2002.
Getting Played, New Line Home Video, 2006.
(And director) *Dear Me,* Shutter Star Pictures, 2008.

Film Director:
A Nanny for Christmas, Feifer Worldwide, 2010.

Film Appearances:
Businessman and fifth cop, *Witchcraft 7: Judgement Hour,* Troma Entertainment, 1995.
Witchcraft IX: Bitter Flesh, Vista Street Entertainment, 1997.
Mr. Sullivan, *A Dead Calling,* North American Entertainment, 2006.
First Bridgewater guard, *Boston Strangler: The Untold Story,* Weinstein Company, 2008.
Admiral's carriage driver, *Dracula's Guest,* Barnholtz Entertainment/Lions Gate Films, 2008.

Television Producer and Director; Movies:
A Christmas Proposal, Lifetime, 2008.
The Dog Who Saved Christmas, ABC Family, 2009.
The Perfect Student, Starz!, 2010.
The Dog Who Saved Christmas Vacation, Starz!, 2010.

Television Producer; Movies:
Forbidden Sins, Cinemax, 2000.
One Small Hero, HBO, 2000.
Illicit Lovers, Cinemax, 2000.
The Medicine Show, The Movie Channel, 2003.

Television Appearances; Movies:
A Christmas Proposal, Lifetime, 2008.
Second police officer, *The Dog Who Saved Christmas,* ABC Family, 2009.

Television Appearances; Episodic:
Himself, *I Know My Kid's a Star* (also known as *Danny Bonaduce's Child Star*), VH1, 2008.

WRITINGS

Screenplays:
Mr. Sullivan, *A Dead Calling,* North American Entertainment, 2006.
Ed Gein: The Butcher of Plainfield, Barnholtz Entertainment, 2007.
Chicago Massacre: Richard Speck (also known as *Nurse Killer*), Barnholtz Entertainment, 2007.
Bundy: An American Icon (also known as *Bundy: A Legacy of Evil*), Barnholtz Entertainment, 2008.
B.T.K., Barnholtz Entertainment/Lions Gate Films, 2008.
Dracula's Guest, Barnholtz Entertainment/Lions Gate Films, 2008.
Boston Strangler: The Untold Story, Weinstein Company, 2008.
Drifter: Henry Lee Lucas, Barnholtz Entertainment, 2009.

Groupie, VVS Films, 2010.
Soda Springs, 2C Entertainment, 2011.

OTHER SOURCES

Electronic:
Michael Feifer Official Site, http://www.feifer.com, October 13, 2010.

FERGUSON, Colin 1972–

PERSONAL

Born July 22, 1972, in Montreal, Quebec, Canada. *Education:* Graduated from McGill University. *Avocational Interests:* Health.

Addresses: *Agent*—International Creative Management, 10250 Constellation Blvd., 9th Floor, Los Angeles, CA 90067. *Manager*—Oscars, Abrams, Zimel, and Associates, 438 Queens Street East, Toronto, Ontario M5A 1T4, Canada. *Publicist*—Wallman Public Relations, 10323 Santa Monica Blvd., Suite 109, Los Angeles, CA 90025.

Career: Actor and director. Second City (an improvisational comedy group), Detroit, MI, founding member; On the Spot (an improvisational group), Montreal, Canada, founding member, c. 1989. Previously performed stand–up routines in Canadian nightclubs.

CREDITS

Film Appearances:
Tom DeLury, *The Opposite of Sex,* Sony Pictures Classics, 1998.
Oscar, *The Surprise Party,* 2001.
Rod, *Career Suicide* (short film), 2004.
Dean, *Guy in Row Five,* 2005.
Derek, *Because I Said So,* Universal, 2007.
The Egg Factory, 2008.
The doctor, *Stan Maynard's Best Day Ever* (short film), 2008.
Happenings Around Town: The Second Season, 2008.
Pierre, *Life's a Beach,* 2010.

Film Work:
Assistant camera, *What She Really Wants* (short film), 2004.

Television Appearances; Series:
Lewis, *Then Came You,* ABC, 2000.
Patrick, *Coupling,* NBC, 2003.
A.U.S.A. David Gwynn, *Line of Fire,* ABC, 2004.

Sheriff Jack Carter, *Eureka* (also known as *A Town Called Eureka*), Sci–Fi Channel, 2006–2009, then Syfy, 2009—.

Television Appearances; Miniseries:
Todd, *Night Sins,* CBS, 1997.
Burke Christopher Andrew, *More Tales of the City* (also known as *Armistead Maupin's "More Tales of the City"*), The Movie Channel, 1998.
Andrew Chase, *Cover Me,* CBC, 1999.

Television Appearances; Movies:
Tiff Wood, *Rowing Through,* 1996.
Jimmy Flood, *A Prayer in the Dark,* USA Network, 1997.
Van Foreman, *Daydream Believers: The Monkees Story,* VH1, 2000.
Mike Curb, *Inside the Osmonds* (also known as *The Osmonds*), ABC, 2001.
Peter, *The Jenifer Estess Story* (also known as *Jenifer*), CBS, 2001.
Dr. Witt, *We Were the Mulvaneys,* Lifetime, 2002.
David, *Americana,* 2004.
Jesse Grant, *Ladies Night,* USA Network, 2005.
Charles Fitz, *Confessions of a Sociopathic Social Climber,* Oxygen, 2005.
Boby, *Mom at Sixteen,* Lifetime, 2005.
Michael Tate, *Playing House,* CTV, 2006.
Walker, *The House Next Door,* Lifetime, 2006.
Dan Casey, *Christmas in Paradise,* Lifetime, 2007.
Tom Welton, *Vinegar Hill,* CBS, 2008.
Nathan Bickerman, *Lake Placid 3,* Syfy, 2010.

Television Appearances; Specials:
I Love the '80s Strikes Back, VH1, 2003.
VH1 Big in 03, VH1, 2003.

Television Appearances; Pilots:
Texas Graces, 1996.
Coupling, NBC, 2003.

Also appeared in *The Family Business.*

Television Appearances; Episodic:
Tommy, "The Tale of C7," *Are You Afraid of the Dark?,* Nickelodeon and YTV, 1995.
Peter Garson, "Bridal Suite," *The Hunger,* Showtime, 1997.
Dr. Bennet, "The Pendulum," *Titus,* Fox, 2001.
Prince Torben of Mulravia, "The Mulravian Candidate," *Dead Last,* The WB, 2001.
David, "Free Spirit," *The Outer Limits,* 2001.
Clark Hutchinson, "Breakfast of Champions," *Becker,* CBS, 2001.
Deputy Brock, "Malcolm's Girlfriend," *Malcolm in the Middle,* Fox, 2001.

David, "Free Spirit," *The Outer Limits* (also known as *The New Outer Limits*), 2002.
Brad Ferris, "Dead Wives' Club," *Crossing Jordan,* NBC, 2003.
Himself, "A Funny Business," *Imagine,* BBC, 2003.
Eric Stone, "Trials and Errors," *Girlfriends,* UPN, 2005.
Doug Diamond, "Testing," *Teachers.* (also known as *Teachers*), NBC, 2006.
Steve, "Take One for the Team," *My Boys,* TBS, 2006.
HypaSpace (also known as *HypaSpace Daily* and *HypaSpace Weekly*), SPACE, 2006, 2007.
Dominic Whitford, "Triple Threat," *CSI: Miami,* CBS, 2007.
Entertainment Tonight (also known as *E.T.*), syndicated, 2008.
"USS Hornet," *Ghost Hunters,* Sci–Fi Channel, 2008.
Dennis Mahoney/Richard "Family Man" Brautigan, "Family Man," *Fear Itself,* NBC, 2008.

Television Director; Movies:
Director, *Triassic Attack,* 2010.

Television Director; Episodic:
"Your Face or Mine," *Eureka* (also known as *A Town Called Eureka*), Sci–Fi Channel, 2009.
"The Story of O2," *Eureka* (also known as *A Town Called Eureka*), Syfy, 2010.

Stage Appearances:
Appeared in *Julius Caesar; One Flew Over the Cuckoo's Nest.*

Internet Appearances; Web Series:
Sheriff Jack Carter, *Eureka: Hide and Seek,* 2006.

FERGUSON, Molly Beck 1972–
(Molly Beck)

PERSONAL

Original name, Molly Anne Beck; born December 17, 1972, in Foxboro, MA; married James Ferguson (a production coordinator, producer, and actor), December 31, 2001; children: Lily. *Education:* Emerson College, B.S., speech communications, 1994; graduated from the Second City Conservatory Training Program, Los Angeles, CA, 2005; studied acting with the Groundlings and at the Garage Group Acting Workshop. *Avocational Interests:* Singing.

Addresses: *Agent*—Maggie, Inc., 35 Newbury St., Boston, MA 02116; Pantheon Talent Agency, 1900 Avenue of the Stars, Suite 2840, Century City, CA 90067.

Career: Actress. Appeared in *Creep, Conventioneers,* and *Dinner Date,* all Internet releases; appeared in television commercials, including Microsoft Bing, Nexium heartburn medications, Angel Soft toilet paper, American Express, and Toyota automobiles. Previously a professional Christmas caroler with the Voices of Christmas for a decade.

Member: Actors Equity Association, Screen Actors Guild, American Federation of Television and Radio Artists, and American Society of Composers, Authors, and Publishers.

CREDITS

Film Appearances:
(As Molly Beck) Woman at station, *Lucky,* MTI Home Video, 2002.
Molly, *Cubicle the Musical* (short film), 2007.
Minta, *Happy Holidays,* Indie Rights, 2008.
Molly, *Creep* (short film), 2008.
Molly Harrison, *Slate: The Teachings of Lonnie Del Mar* (short film), 2009.
Genie, *Creative Differences,* 2010.

Also appeared in *The Town; Nuns 3; Stool Pigeon; Lucky; Settled Differences; Builders.*

Film Work:
Still photographer, *Happy Holidays,* 2008.

Television Appearances; Series:
(Uncredited) Secretary, *Mad Men,* AMC, 2008.

Television Appearances; Episodic:
Gina, "Lean on Me," *According to Jim,* ABC, 2005.
Caroler number three, "Duke Collins," *Nip/Tuck,* FX Network, 2007.
(Uncredited) Greensleever, "Undeck the Halls," *Modern Family,* ABC, 2009.

Stage Appearances:
Appeared in *What Every Woman Wants* (a cabaret), The Gardenia; *Creep,* Second City, Los Angeles; *Caucasian BBQ,* Second City, Los Angeles; *Dandelion Wine,* Colony Studio Theatre, Burbank, CA; *Louisiana Purchase,* Musical Theatre Guild, Burbank, CA; *Ragin' 'Stache,* The Ruckus, ImprovBoston, Boston, MA; as Kitty, *The Music of Denali,* Princess Cruises; understudy of five roles, *Karaoke: The Brand New Unoriginal Musical,* Nick's Comedy Shop; Edwin Drood, *Mystery of Edwin Drood,* Walpole Footlighters; Angel City 4 Alto, *City of Angels,* Orpheum Theatre; Cinderella, *Into the Woods,* Publick Theatre; Audrey, *Little Shop of Horrors,* Northern Lights Playhouse; Sally Bowles, *Cabaret,* Northern Lights Playhouse; Phyllis, *Bells Are Ringing,* Musical Theatre Guild; attendant, *Passion,* Musical Theatre Guild; Miss Krumholtz, *How to Succeed in Business Without Really Trying,* Colony Theatre; featured ensemble member, *Life's a Stitch,* Alex Theatre.

Major Tours:
Toured as Widow Piper, *Babes in Toyland,* American Family Theatre.

OTHER SOURCES

Electronic:
Molly Beck Ferguson Official Site, http://www.mollybeckferguson.com, October 30, 2010.

FOLAN, Josh 1981–

PERSONAL

Full name, Joshua Michael Folan; born August 18, 1981, in Pensacola, FL. *Education:* Ohio State University, degree in finance.

Career: Actor and producer.

CREDITS

Film Appearances:
(Uncredited) Boutique clerk, *Natale a New York,* Filmauro Distribuzione, 2006.
Charlie Quartermain, *Spiker,* Artist View Entertainment, 2007.
Billy Wagner, *4th and Forever,* 2008.
(Uncredited) Raine's dinner date, *Quid Pro Quo,* Magnolia Pictures, 2008.
Dick Laundry, *Path* (short film), 2008.
Biff, *Death on Demand,* MTI Home Video, 2008.
Jesse Swomley, *The Graduates,* Beach Movie Films, 2008.
Guy, *BS Confidential* (short film), Prime HD, 2008.
Scientist, *2k3,* 2009.
Austin, bounty hunter 1, *Bad Apples,* Nyeh Entertainment, 2009.
Danny, *Ay Lav Yu,* 2010.
Jon, *All God's Creatures,* 2011.
Jack, *Episode 50,* 2011.

Film Producer:
Bad Apples, 2009.
All God's Creatures, 2011.

Television Appearances; Series:
Josh the bartender, *All My Children,* ABC, 2006–2009.

Television Appearances; Pilots:
Himself, *Tell Me You Love Me,* HBO, 2007.

Television Appearances; Episodic:
Josh, *Stand–Up Nation with Greg Giraldo* (also known as *Friday Night Stand–Up with Greg Giraldo*), Comedy Central, 2005.
(Uncredited) Bartender, "The Window," *Love Monkey,* VH1, 2006.
(Sometimes uncredited) Himself, *Tell Me You Love Me,* HBO, 2007.
Friend number one, *As the World Turns,* CBS, 2007.
Apartment soldier, "The New King: Part One," *Kings,* NBC, 2009.
Hike leader, *As the World Turns,* CBS, 2009.

Stage Appearances:
Max, *My Life As You,* 2006.
Gabriel Utterson, *Dr. Jekyll & Mr. Hyde,* 2006.
Jack, *Boys' Life,* 2007.

Internet Appearances; Web Series:
Frat guy, "Dinner with Dax," *Viralcom,* www.joeyanddavid.com, 2008.

RECORDINGS

Music Videos:
Appeared in "Big Dreams" by Joemca & the Poets, 2008.

WRITINGS

Screenplays:
All God's Creatures, 2011.

FOX, Colin 1938–
    (Colin R. Fox)

PERSONAL

Born November 20, 1938, in Aldershot, Ontario, Canada; married Carol; children: Sarah. *Education:* Attended National Theatre School of Canada.

Career: Actor and voice artist. Worked as an announcer at CBS Montreal and as a classical music host for CJAD radio, Toronto, Ontario, Canada; affiliated with the Brandon University School of Music, Manitoba, Canada. Appeared in television commercials, including Save Our LCBO (Liquor Control Board of Ontario), 2004.

Awards, Honors: Canadian Film Award, best performance by a lead actor in a non–feature, 1971, for *Durham and the Two Nations;* Gemini Award nomination, best individual performance in a comedy program or series, Academy of Canadian Cinema and Television, 2005, for *Puppets Who Kill;* Gemini Award (with others), best individual or ensemble performance in an animated program or series, 2009, for *Atomic Betty.*

CREDITS

Film Appearances:
Ormsby, *The Reincarnate,* International Film Distributors, 1971.
Durham and the Two Nations, c. 1971.
The Discoverers, National Film Board of Canada, 1972.
Freddie, *My Pleasure Is My Business* (also known as *Die Heisseste Frau der Welt*), Brian Distributing, 1974.
American businessman, *Eclair au chocolat* (also known as *Chocolate Eclair*), Les Films Mutuals, 1979.
Dr. Alderman, *Murder by Phone* (also known as *Bells, The Calling,* and *Hell's Bells*), New World Pictures, 1980.
Spy Z, *Day of Resurrection* (also known as *Fakkutsu no hi, The End,* and *Virus*), 1980.
Arthur Herriot, *Silence of the North,* Universal, 1981.
Narrator, *Ridley: A Secret Garden,* 1981.
Ming the Merciless, *A Christmas Story,* Metro–Goldwyn–Mayer, 1983.
Maitre d', *Covergirl* (also known as *Dreamworld*), New World Pictures, 1984.
Arthur Mudgin, *Real Inside,* National Film Board of Canada, 1985.
Canada's Sweetheart: The Saga of Hal C. Banks, National Film Board of Canada, 1985.
Snyder, *My Pet Monster,* 1986.
Voice of wizard, *The Care Bears Adventure in Wonderland* (animated), Cineplex–Odeon, 1987.
(As Colin R. Fox) Clergyman, *Hello Again,* 1987.
Edmund Delhurst, *Food of the Gods II* (also known as *After Food of the Gods, Food of the Gods Part 2,* and *Gnaw: Food of the Gods II*), Concorde Pictures, 1989.
First executive, *Money,* United International, 1990.
Reverend Haines, *Beautiful Dreamers,* Hemdale, 1990.
A Star for Two, 1991.
Dr. Elton Monet, *Scanners III: The Takeover* (also known as *Scanner Force*), Republic Pictures, 1992.
Palter, *On My Own* (also known as *Il colore dei suoi occhi*), Alliance, 1992.
First trustee, *PCU* (also known as *PCU Pit Party*), Twentieth Century–Fox, 1994.

Guthrie, *Historica Minutes: Agnes Macphail,* 1994.
Ted Nelson, *Tommy Boy,* Paramount, 1995.
Rutledge, *Butterbox Babies,* Sullivan Entertainment, 1995.
Sir Thomas Beecham, *Voices from a Locked Room* (also known as *Voices*), Avenue, 1995.
Wedding guest, *Mrs. Winterbourne,* TriStar, 1996.
Jackson Carp, *Open Season,* Republic Pictures, 1996.
Scientist grandfather, *L5: First City in Space,* IMAX, 1996.
Roger Trilling, *Daylight,* 1996.
Dr. Hemingway, *In Love and War,* Warner Bros., 1996.
David Golden, *Seeds of Doubt,* 1998.
Chaim Rosenzweig, *Left Behind* (also known as *Left Behind: The Movie*), Cloud Ten Pictures, 2000.
Himself, *The Making of "Left Behind: The Movie,"* 2000.
Director, *Down to Earth* (also known as *Einmal Himmel und zuruck*), Paramount, 2001.
Pappy, *Chasing Holden,* Lions Gate, 2001.
Chaim Rosenzweig, *Left Behind II: Tribulation Force* (also known as *Tribulation Force*), Cloud Ten Pictures, 2002.
Board chairman, *Drummer Boy,* Drummerboy, 2002.
Father O'Neill, *One Week,* IFC Films, 2008.
Chairman, *Cutting for Stone,* Gallery on the Bay, 2008.

Television Appearances; Series:
Jean Paul Desmond/Jacques Eloi Des Mondes, *Strange Paradise,* CBC, 1969.
Dan Pride, *House of Pride,* CBC, 1974.
Walter Telford, *High Hopes,* CBC, 1978.
Voice of Mr. Hinkle, *My Pet Monster* (animated), ABC, 1987.
Voice of King Harkinian, *The Legend of Zelda* (animated), syndicated, 1989.
Voice of King Harkinian, *The Super Mario Bros. Super Show!,* syndicated, NBC, 1989–91.
Voice of professor, *Rupert,* CBS, 1991–97.
Voice of Large Head, *The NeverEnding Story* (also known as *Die Unendliche geschichte*), 1995.
Professor Anton Hendricks, *Psi Factor: Chronicles of the Paranormal,* syndicated, 1996–2000.
Mr. Arthur Howie, *The Adventures of Shirley Holmes,* YTV and Fox Family, 1997–98.
Fritz Brenner, *A Nero Wolfe Mystery* (also known as *Nero Wolfe*), Arts and Entertainment, 2001–2002.
Voice of Uncle Neptune/Mr. Wiggins, *Henry's World* (animated), 2002.
Newton, *Peep and the Big Wide World* (animated), Discovery Kids, 2004.
Supreme Overlord Maximus IQ, *Atomic Betty* (animated), Cartoon Network, 2004.
Doc Zombie, *The Manly Bee,* 2005.

Television Appearances; Miniseries:
Acker, *A Man Called Intrepid,* NBC, 1979.
Axel Wenner–Gren, *Passion and Paradise,* ABC, 1989.

Jim Pex, *Small Sacrifices,* ABC, 1989.
Dangerfield, *Conspiracy of Silence,* CBC and CBS, 1991.
Joe Bembenek, *Woman on the Run: The Lawrencia Bembenek Story* (also known as *Woman on Trial: The Lawrencia Bembenek Story*), NBC, 1993.
Lord Henry, *Return to Lonesome Dove,* CBS, 1993.
Samuel Langley, *The Sound and the Silence,* TNT and CTV, 1993.
Priest, *Blauvogel* (also known as *Bluehawk*), 1994.
Secretary of the Navy James Forrestal, *Hiroshima,* Showtime, 1995.
Westchester priest, *Master Spy: The Robert Hanssen Story,* CBS, 2002.
Israel Porter, *Salem Witch Trials,* CBS, 2002.

Television Appearances; Movies:
Aramis, *The Three Musketeers,* 1969.
Tom Sawyer (also known as *Adventures of Tom Sawyer*), CBS, 1973.
Leonard Zimmerman, *The War Between the Tates,* NBC, 1977.
Voice of narrator, *The Prophet from Pugwash,* 1978.
A Whale for the Killing, ABC, 1981.
Arthur Prince, *Biographies: The Enigma of Bobby Bittman,* 1988.
Theo, *Lady in the Corner,* NBC, 1989.
Brad Monroe, *In Defense of a Married Man,* ABC, 1990.
Doctor, *Descending Angel,* HBO, 1990.
Dr. Quintard, *Mark Twain and Me,* The Disney Channel, 1991.
The preacher, *A Little Piece of Heaven,* NBC, 1991.
Richard, *In the Eyes of a Stranger,* CBS, 1992.
Dr. Hatch, *Partners 'n Love,* CTV and ABC Family, 1992.
Professor Rhodes, *Deadbolt,* 1992.
Samuel Langley, *Alexander Graham Bell: The Sound and the Silence* (also known as *The Sound and the Silence*), TNT, CTV, and TVNZ, 1992.
Dr. Roche, *Bonds of Love,* CBS, 1993.
Laffin, *Dieppe,* CBC, 1993.
Professor Rhodes, *Deadbolt* (also known as *3:15 a Time for Dying*), 1993.
Judge Boland, *Sins of Silence,* CBS, 1996.
Lord Elgin, *Captive Heart: The James Mink Story,* CBS, 1996.
FBI Agent James K. Smith, *Windsor Protocol* (also known as *Jack Higgins' "Windsor Protocol"*), Showtime, 1996.
Ezra, *End of Summer,* Showtime, 1996.
Bishop McCarthy, *The Haunting of Lisa,* Lifetime, 1996.
Sir Harold, *Elvis Meets Nixon,* Showtime, 1997.
State Senator Jonathan Hoover, *Let Me Call You Sweetheart* (also known as *Mary Higgins Clark's "Let Me Call You Sweetheart"*), The Family Channel, 1997.
Fritz Brenner, *The Golden Spiders: A Nero Wolfe Mystery,* Arts and Entertainment, 2000.
The devil, *Angels in the Infield,* ABC, 2000.

John Quincy Adams, *Enslavement: The True Story of Fanny Kemble,* Showtime, 2000.

Walsh, *Dirty Pictures,* Showtime, 2000.

Doctor Lovick, *A House Divided,* Showtime, 2000.

Nedermayer, *Phantom of the Megaplex,* The Disney Channel, 2000.

Joshua L. Simonson, *The Last Debate,* Showtime, 2000.

Cal Weebs, *Laughter on the 23rd Floor* (also known as *Most Original Comedy*), Showtime, 2001.

King Leo, *Prince Charming,* TNT, 2001.

Frederick Rankin, *Drive Time Murders* (also known as *Breakfast with Dick and Dorothy*), Ion Television, 2001.

Richard Lawton, *America's Prince: The John F. Kennedy Jr. Story,* TBS, 2003.

Baron Titus Cawdor, *Deathlands* (also known as *Deathlands: Homeward Bound*), Sci–Fi Channel, 2003.

Dr. Richard Morelli, *Webs,* Sci–Fi Channel, 2003.

Professor Fitzwinkler, *A Separate Peace,* Showtime, 2004.

Bishop Stoflus, *Plain Truth,* Lifetime, 2004.

Sir Nigel, *Perfect Strangers,* CBS, 2004.

Daniel Kibbe, *Our Fathers,* Showtime, 2005.

Voice of Maximus IQ, *Atomic Betty: The No–L Nine* (animated), Cartoon Network, 2005.

Television Appearances; Specials:

Arthur Prince, *Biographies: The Enigma of Bobby Bittman* (also known as *Autobiographies: The Enigma of Bobby Bittman*), Cinemax, 1988.

Narrator, *Old Before Their Time* (documentary), The Discovery Channel, 1998.

Voice, *Quest for the Lost Tribes* (documentary), Arts and Entertainment, 2000.

Television Appearances; Pilots:

Dante Morneau, *Unnatural History,* Cartoon Network, 2010.

Television Appearances; Episodic:

John George Lambton, First Earl of Durham, "Lord Durham," *Witness to Yesterday,* CBC, 1975.

(As Colin R. Fox) Consul, "The Defector," *The Equalizer,* CBS, 1985.

(As Colin R. Fox) Bishop, "The Cup," *The Equalizer,* CBS, 1986.

Father Brandan, "Shadowsight," *Spenser: For Hire,* ABC, 1986.

Dr. Peter Marcheson, "Star Struck," *Street Legal,* CBC, 1987.

Le Croix, "Poison Pen," *Friday the 13th,* syndicated, 1987.

Victor Stouts, "If the Shoe Fits," *Alfred Hitchcock Presents,* 1987.

Dr. Herman Vandenburg, "Murder Party," *Alfred Hitchcock Presents,* 1988.

Sylvan, "Tails I Live, Heads You Die," *Friday the 13th,* syndicated, 1988.

"All Bets Off," *Diamonds,* CBS, 1988.

Mueller, "The Butcher," *Friday the 13th,* syndicated, 1989.

Voice of King Harkinian, "9001: A Mario Odyssey/On Her Majesty's Sewer Service," *Club Mario* (also known as *The Super Mario Bros. Super Show!*), 1989.

Lowell McMurrich, "Shadow Boxing," *Street Legal,* CBC, 1990.

Edward Edison, "The 10th Anniversary Special," *Maniac Mansion,* The Family Channel, 1990.

Lord Sutcliff, "Dead in the Air," *Counterstrike,* CTV, 1990.

Lord Sutcliff, "Art for Art's Sake," *Counterstrike,* CTV, 1990.

Edward Edison, "Money Dearest," *Maniac Mansion,* The Family Channel, 1991.

Edward Edison, "The New Look," *Maniac Mansion,* The Family Channel, 1991.

(As Colin R. Fox) Peter Martin, "In Memory Of," *Law & Order,* NBC, 1991.

Sandy Ferguson, "Pressure," *E.N.G.,* Lifetime and CTV, 1992.

Priest, "For I Have Sinned," *Forever Knight,* CBS, 1992.

Edward Edison, "The Prince's Broad," *Maniac Mansion,* The Family Channel, 1992.

Galeleo Dale, "Tug of War," *Road to Avonlea* (also known as *Avonlea* and *Tales from Avonlea*), The Disney Channel, 1993.

The man from the other side, "The Yellow Chamber," *Matrix,* USA Network, 1993.

Harold, "Guerrilla in My Midst," *The Mighty Jungle,* The Family Channel, 1994.

Hammersmith, "Sisters in Crime," *RoboCop,* syndicated, 1994.

Ray Lawson, "The Tale of Train Magic," *Are You Afraid of the Dark?,* Nickelodeon and YTV, 1995.

Dr. Alex Nystrom, "Near Death," *Forever Knight,* syndicated, 1995.

Tall thin man, "The Haunted Mask: Parts 1 & 2," *Goosebumps* (also known as *Ultimate Goosebumps*), Fox, 1995.

Shopkeeper, "The Haunted Mask II: Parts 1 & 2," *Goosebumps* (also known as *Ultimate Goosebumps*), Fox, 1996.

Voice of Uatu the watcher, "Learning Curve: Part 1," *The Silver Surfer* (animated), Fox, 1998.

Voice of King Cepheus, "Andromeda: The Warrior Princess," *Mythic Warriors: Guardians of the Legend,* CBS, 1998.

Voice of Menelaus, "Ulysses and the Trojan Horse," *Mythic Warriors: Guardians of the Legend,* CBS, 1999.

Senator Woodman, "New Directions," *Wind at My Back,* 1999.

Voice of professor, *Rupert,* 1999.

Christian World News, 2000.

Gelman, "Getting Out of Reverse," *La Femme Nikita* (also known as *Nikita*), USA Network, 2000.

Hans Lubeck, "Last of the Mochicas," *Relic Hunter,* syndicated, 2000.

Dr. Chaim Rosenweig, "Left Behind: The Movie," *Left Behind: The TV Series,* 2000.

Charles, "The Switch," *The Zack Files,* Fox Family and ITV, 2001.

Charles, "Dinner with Grandpa," *The Zack Files,* Fox Family and ITV, 2001.

"Old Age Pensions," *Heritage Minute,* 2003.

Fred Bradley, "Crime Dog," *Wonderfalls,* Fox, 2004.

Sir Percy Quill, "Buttons the Dresser," *Puppets Who Kill,* Comedy Central, 2005.

This Is Wonderland, CBC, 2006.

Father Brendan, "Transgressions," *Stephen King's "Dead Zone"* (also known as *The Dead Zone* and *The Dark Half*), USA Network, 2007.

Soul merchant, "Chapter Six," *Living in Your Car,* 2010.

Also appeared as Dan Pride, *House of Pride;* Hobart Hume, "Schemer's Special Club," *Shining Time Station,* PBS.

Television Additional Voices; Series:

Beetlejuice (animated), The WB, 1989.

Also provided additional voices for *WILD Cats* (animated).

Stage Appearances:

Dorland, *Soldiers,* Billy Rose Theatre, New York City, 1968.

Sir Nathaniel, *Love's Labour's Lost,* Circle Repertory Company, Circle Repertory Theatre, New York City, 1984.

Peter Kroeger, *Pack of Lies,* Royale Theatre, New York City, 1985.

Craig, *Anteroom,* Playwrights Horizons Theatre, New York City, 1985.

Tyrone Guthrie, *Guthrie on Guthrie,* Canada, 1989.

Also appeared in *Tiny Alice,* Crest Theatre, Toronto, Ontario, Canada; *Henry VI;* and narrator, *Hansel and Gretel;* narrator, *Peter and the Wolf.*

RECORDINGS

Video Games:

Voice, *Hype: The Time Quest,* 1999.

FRANCIS, Anne 1930–2011

PERSONAL

Original name, Anne Lloyd Francis; born September 16, 1930 (some sources cite 1932), in Ossining, New York; died of complications from pancreatic cancer, July 22, 2008, in Santa Barbara, California. Actress. Known primarily for playing the only female part in the 1950s Sci-Fi classic *Forbidden Planet,* Francis began her acting career at in the 1943 Broadway musical *Lady in the Dark.* Shortly thereafter, Francis signed a contract with 20th Century Fox and began appearing in supporting roles in comedies and dramas such as *Elopement, Lydia Bailey* and *Dreamboat.* After a switch to MGM in 1954, Francis was cast alongside some of the top actors of her day, including George Raft, Spencer Tracy, and Paul Newman. Her first leading role came in 1955 with *Blackboard Jungle,* in which she played the pregnant wife of a teacher (played by Glenn Ford) at a violent inner-city boy's school. Francis was cast as the female lead in *Forbidden Planet* in 1956, and roles in films such as *The Hired Gun; Girl of the Night; Funny Girl;* and *Hook, Line, and Sinker* followed, but none reached the level of popularity attained by *Forbidden Planet.* Francis starred in the television detective series *Honey West* in 1965, a role that earned her a Golden Globe award and an Emmy nomination. She had small parts in series such as *Trapper John, M.D.; Murder, She Wrote; The Golden Girls;* and *The Drew Carey Show* throughout the 1980s and 1990s. In 2004 Francis appeared in an episode of *Without a Trace.* Her memoir, *Voices from Home: An Inner Journey,* was published in 1982.

PERIODICALS

Guardian, January 3, 2011.
Los Angeles Times, January 3, 2011.
New York Times, January 3, 2011.
Telegraph, January 13, 2011.
Washington Post, January 3, 2011.

FRENCH, Kate 1985–

PERSONAL

Born 1985 in Flemington, NJ; daughter of Rob (a fashion model) and Joan (a fashion model) French; stepfather, a fashion photographer. *Education:* University of California, Santa Barbara. *Avocational Interests:* Surfing, water skiing, wake boarding, hiking, writing.

Addresses: *Agent*—Innovative Artists, 1505 10th St., Santa Monica, CA 90401. *Manager*—Energy Entertainment, 999 Doheny Dr., Suite 711, West Hollywood, CA 90069.

Career: Actress. Also worked as a model.

Member: American Federation of Television and Radio Artists, Screen Actors Guild.

CREDITS

Film Appearances:
Glen's party girl, *Accepted,* Universal, 2006.
Cute captain, *Fired Up!,* Screen Gems, 2009.
Shannon, *Sutures,* MTI Home Video, 2009.
Mindy, *K Citizen* (short film), 2009.
Emma, *Language of a Broken Heart,* 2010.
Sid, *Girltrash: All Night Long,* 2010.

Television Appearances; Series:
Brooke Crawford, *Wicked Wicked Games,* MyNetworkTV, 2006–2007.
Sasha Miller, *South of Nowhere,* The N, 2007–2008.
Niki Stevens, *The L Word,* Showtime, 2008–2009.
Riley Westlake, *Beyond the Break,* The N, 2009.
Renee, *One Tree Hill,* The CW, 2009.

Television Appearances; Episodic:
Current TV, 2008.
Elle, "Carnal Knowledge," *Gossip Girl,* The CW, 2009.
Elle, "The Age of Dissonance," *Gossip Girl,* The CW, 2009.
Rita, "Chip/Tuck," *CSI: Miami,* CBS, 2009.

FRIENDLY, David T. 1956–
(David Friendly)

PERSONAL

Born May 1, 1956; son of Fred W. and Dorothy Friendly; married Priscilla Nedd (a film editor). *Education:* Northwestern University, B.A., 1978. *Avocational Interests:* Golf, tennis, music.

Addresses: *Office*—Friendly Films, 100 North Crescent Dr., Suite 350, Beverly Hills, CA 90210.

Career: Producer. Image Entertainment, vice president of motion pictures then president of production, 1987–91; David Entertainment (a production company), president, 2004; Deep River Productions (a production company), cofounder, 2000; Friendly Films (a production company), Beverly Hills, CA, principal. Began his career as a journalist, working for *Newsweek,* 1978–84, then the *Los Angeles Times,* 1984–87.

Awards, Honors: Academy Award nomination (with others), best motion picture of the year, Film Award nomination (with others), best film, British Academy of Film and Television Arts, Independent Spirit Award (with others), best feature, Independent Features Project/West, Motion Picture Producer of the Year Award (with others), theatrical motion pictures, 2007, all for *Little Miss Sunshine.*

CREDITS

Film Executive Producer:
My Girl, Columbia, 1991.
For Love or Money (also known as *The Concierge*), Universal, 1993.
My Girl 2, Columbia, 1994.
Greedy, Universal, 1994.
(As David Friendly) *The Chamber,* Universal, 1996.
Digging to China (also known as *With You*), Legacy Releasing, 1998.

Film Producer:
Courage under Fire, Twentieth Century–Fox, 1996.
Daylight, Universal, 1996.
Out to Sea, Twentieth Century–Fox, 1997.
Doctor Doolittle (also known as *Dr. Doolittle*), Twentieth Century–Fox, 1998.
Here on Earth, Twentieth Century–Fox, 2000.
Big Momma's House, Twentieth Century–Fox, 2000.
Laws of Attraction, New Line Cinema, 2004.
Duane Hopwood, IFC Films, 2005.
The Honeymooners, Paramount, 2005.
Little Miss Sunshine, Twentieth Century–Fox, 2006.
Big Momma's House 2, Twentieth Century–Fox, 2006.
Meet Dave, Twentieth Century–Fox, 2008.
Soul Men, Metro–Goldwyn–Mayer, 2008.
Big Mommas: Like Father, Like Son, Twentieth Century–Fox, 2011.

FROST, Nick 1972–

PERSONAL

Full name, Nicholas John Frost; born March 28, 1972, in Essex, England.

Awards, Honors: British Independent Film Award nomination, most promising newcomer, 2004, for *Shaun of the Dead.*

CREDITS

Television Appearances; Series:
Mike Watts, *Spaced,* Channel 4, CBC, 1999–2001.
Voice, *Supernanny,* Channel 4, 2005.
Various, *Man Stroke Woman,* BBC, 2005–2007.

Movie Rush, Channel 4, 2006.
Commander Henderson, *Hyperdrive,* BBC, 2006–2007.

Television Appearances; Movies:
Wally, *Jim's Gift,* 1996.
Straight 8, Channel 4, 2004.

Television Appearances; Specials:
Presenter, *Celebrity Naked Ambition,* Channel 5, 2003.
Narrator, *A Very British UFO Hoax,* Channel 4, 2003.
Willy Rushton, *Comic Relief 2003: The Big Hair Do,* BBC, 2003.
Team captain, *Dude, Where's My Movie Quiz?,* MTV Europe, 2004.
The Simpsons Quiz Show, Channel 4, 2004.
Scientist, *Spider–Plant Man,* BBC, 2005.
Ed, *The 50 Greatest Comedy Films,* Channel 4, 2006.
Mike Watt, *The Big Fat Anniversary Quiz,* Channel 4, 2007.
Hot Fuzz Special, Sky Television, 2007.
Brit Awards, ITV, BBC America, 2007.
Comic Relief 2007: The Big One, BBC, 2007.
07 Spaceys, SPACE, 2007.
Suck my Geek! (documentary), 2007.
Empire Movie Awards, ITV, 2008.
The British Academy Television Awards, BBC, 2010.

Television Appearances; Episodic:
Construction worker, *Big Train,* BBC, 1998.
Engineer, *Big Train,* BBC, 1998.
Security system man, "The Big Lock–Out," *Black Books,* Channel 4, BBC America, 2000.
Narrator, "TV Sci–Fi," *Top Ten,* Channel 4, 2001.
Presenter, *Movie Mistakes Uncovered: Uncut,* Channel 5, 2002.
Danger! 50000 Volts!, four episodes, 2002.
Stone–age man, "Music," *Look Around You,* BBC, 2002.
Voice of Paul, "Moo–Ma and Moo–Pa," *Black Books,* Channel 4, BBC America, 2004.
Keith, "Txt Msg Revd," *Twisted Tales,* BBC, 2005.
Hot Jon, "Live Final," *Look Around You,* BBC, 2005.
Voice of monkey, *Dirty Tricks,* Channel 4, 2005.
Morning Glory, Channel 4, 2006.
Just a man, *Green Wing,* Channel 4, BBC America, 2006.
Film '72, BBC, 2007.
Richard & Judy, Channel 4, 2007.
Jimmy Kimmel Live!, ABC, 2007.
Last Call with Carson Daly, NBC, 2007.
Presenter, "Frost and Pegg's Perfect Night In," *Perfect Night In,* Channel 4, 2007.
Up Close with Carrie Keagan, 2007, 2009.
Friday Night with Jonathan Ross, BBC1, BBC America, 2007, 2010.
Rove Live, Ten Network, 2009.
Actor, *Breakfast,* BBC, 2010, 2011.
Top Gear, 2011.
Dias de cine, 2011.

Television Appearances; Miniseries:
John Self, *Money,* BBC2, 2010.

Film Appearances:
Sean, *The Man Who Would Be Shaun,* Universal, 2004.
Ed, *Funky Pete,* Universal, 2004.
Nick Frost, *Danger! 50000 Zombies!,* Channel 5, 2004.
Ed, *Shaun of the Dead,* Focus Features, 2004.
Don, *Kinky Boots,* Miramax, 2005.
Max, *Penelope,* Summit Entertainment, 2006.
Police constable Danny Butterman, *Hot Fuzz,* Paramount, 2007.
Baby eater, *Grindhouse,* Dimension Films, 2007.
Mr. Christopher, *Wild Child,* Universal Studios, 2008.
Doctor Dave, *Pirate Radio* (also known as *The Boat That Rocked* and *Pirates Rock*), Focus Features, 2009.
Roy, *Attack the Block,* Optimum Releasing, 2010.
Clive Gollings, *Paul,* Universal, 2010.

RECORDINGS

Videos:
Skip to the End, Channel 4, 2004.
Shaun of the Dead: EPK Featurette, Universal, 2004.
Ed, *Plot Holes: How Did Ed Get from the Cellar to the Shed?,* Universal, 2004.
Simon's Cam, Universal, 2004.
Lucy's Cam, Universal, 2004.
"Hot Fuzz": The Fuzzball Rally, Rogue Pictures, 2007.

WRITINGS

Screenplays:
Danger! 50000 Zombies!, 2004.
Simon's Cam, Universal, 2004.
Paul, Universal, 2010.

Television Specials:
Comic Relief 2007: The Big One, BBC, 2007.

Film Songs:
"Noise," *Hit and Run,* Metro–Goldwyn–Mayer, 2009.

FRYE, Soleil Moon 1976–

PERSONAL

Born August 6, 1976, in Glendora, CA (some sources say Glendale, CA); daughter of Virgil Frye (an actor) and Sondra Peluce (a talent manager and caterer); half–sister of Meeno Peluce (an actor and director) and Sean

Frye (an actor); married Jason Goldberg (a producer), October 25, 1998; children: Poet Sienna Rose, Jagger Joseph Blue. *Education:* Attended New School University for one year. *Religion:* Jewish.

Addresses: *Agent*—Danis Panaro Nist, 9201 West Olympic Blvd., Beverly Hills, CA 90212. *Manager*—Michael Goldman Management, 7471 Melrose Ave., Suites 10 and 11, Los Angeles, CA 90046.

Career: Actress, director, and screenwriter. Began acting at the age of two; appeared in magazine ad for *Showstyle*, 2001; appeared in television commercial for *One to Grow On.* The Little Seed (a baby boutique), Los Angeles, CA, co–owner, 2007—; Private Label (a baby clothing line), founder, 2009.

Awards, Honors: Young Artist Award nominations, best young actress in a television series, 1985, 1988, Young Artist Award, best young actress starring in a television series, 1986, Young Artist Award nomination (with others), best animation voice–over group, Young Artist Award nomination, best young female superstar in television, 1988, Young Artist Award, best young actress—voice–over role, 1989, all for *Punky Brewster;* Young Artist Award nomination, best young actress guest starring in a syndicated family comedy, drama, or special, 1989, for *Mickey's 60th Birthday;* Festival Award, best documentary, San Diego Film Festival, 2004, for *Sonny Boy.*

CREDITS

Film Appearances:

Gigi, *The Liar's Club,* New Horizon Picture Corp.,1993.

Julia, *The St. Tammany Miracle* (also known as *Heavenly Hoops*), 1994.

Marcie, *Pumpkinhead II: Blood Wings* (also known as *Pumpkinhead 2: The Demon Returns* and *Pumpkinhead II*), 1994.

Run a Mile …, 1995.

Sharon Stewart, *Twisted Love,* 1995.

Becky Hanson, *Mind Games,* Brimstone Productions, 1996.

Herself, *The Best of Ed's Night Party,* 1996.

Agent Kyle Rivers, *Motel Blue,* 1997.

Wild Horses (also known as *Lunch Time Special*), 1998.

Casey, *The Girls' Room* (also known as *Best of Enemies*), 1999.

Alissa, *Alex in Wonder* (also known as *Sex and a Girl*), 2001.

Herself, *Sonny Boy* (documentary), 2004.

Voice of Jade, *Bratz the Video: Starrin' & Stylin'* (animated), 2004.

For Better or for Worse, 2010.

Film Director:

(With Meeno Peluce) *Wild Horses* (also known as *Lunch Time Special*), 1998.

Sonny Boy, 2004.

Television Appearances; Series:

Penelope "Punky" Brewster (title role), *Punky Brewster,* NBC, then syndicated, 1984–88.

Voice of title role, *It's Punky Brewster* (animated; also known as *Punky Brewster*), NBC, then syndicated, 1985–89.

Tyler McKay, *Cadets,* ABC, 1988.

Herself, *Girl Talk,* 1989.

Sonya, *Where's Rodney?,* 1990.

Roxie King, *Sabrina, the Teenage Witch* (also known as *Sabrina Goes to College* and *Sabrina*), The WB, 2000–2003.

Voice of Zoey, *The Proud Family* (animated), The Disney Channel, 2001–2005.

Voice of Jade, *Bratz* (animated), 2005–2006.

Voice of Aseefa, *Planet Sheen* (animated), Nickelodeon, 2010.

Television Appearances; Movies:

Mary Elizabeth, *Missing Children: A Mother's Story,* CBS, 1982.

Linda Fray, *Who Will Love My Children?,* ABC, 1983.

Chrissie Winslow, *Invitation to Hell,* ABC, 1984.

Second Elizabeth Kovacs, *Ernie Kovacs: Between the Laughter,* ABC, 1984.

Minerva, *You Ruined My Life,* ABC, 1987.

Peggy, head cheerleader, *Summertime Switch,* ABC, 1994.

Laura, *Roger Corman Presents "Piranha"* (also known as *Piranha*), Showtime, 1995.

Emily DeCapprio, *The Secret* (also known as *The Killing Secret*), NBC, 1997.

Kyra Thompson, *I've Been Waiting for You,* NBC, 1998.

Voice of Zoey, *The Proud Family Movie* (animated), The Disney Channel, 2005.

Television Appearances; Specials:

The NBC All Star Hour, 1983.

Macy's Thanksgiving Day Parade, 1984.

Andy Williams and the NBC Kids Search for Santa, NBC, 1985.

The 37th Annual Prime Time Emmy Awards, ABC, 1985.

The NBC All–Star Hour, NBC, 1985.

The Night of 100 Stars II, ABC, 1985.

Punky Brewster, *Alvin Goes Back to School,* NBC, 1986.

NBC's 60th Anniversary Celebration, NBC, 1986.

Disney's "Golden Anniversary of Snow White and the Seven Dwarfs" (also known as *Golden Anniversary of Snow White and the Seven Dwarfs*), NBC, 1987.

Host, *Here's to You, Mickey Mouse,* The Disney Channel, 1988.

The Hollywood Christmas Parade, syndicated, 1988, 1989.

Tina, "Choose Your Own Adventure: The Case of the Silk King," *ABC Weekend Specials,* ABC, 1992.

Holidays with the Stars, E! Entertainment Television, 2000.

I Love the '80s, 2002.

Intimate Portrait: Melissa Joan Hart, Lifetime, 2003.

Tying the Knot: The Wedding of Melissa Joan Hart, ABC Family, 2003.

Voice of Jade, *Bratz Rock Angelz* (animated), Cartoon Network, 2005.

Punky Brewster: The E! True Hollywood Story, E! Entertainment Television, 2006.

Television Appearances; Pilots:

Samantha, *Little Shots,* NBC, 1983.

Tyler McKay, *Cadets,* ABC, 1988.

Sonia, *Where's Rodney?,* NBC, 1990.

Robin, *Grown Ups,* ABC, 1999.

Voice of Sally Chaffe, *Clayton,* UPN, 2001.

Voice of Aseefa, *Planet Sheen* (animated), Nickelodeon, 2009.

Television Appearances; Episodic:

Terry Harris, "Sam's New Pal," *Diff'rent Strokes,* 1985.

Princess Moon, "The Perils of Punky: Parts 1 & 2," *Punky Brewster,* 1985.

Kathy, "The Very Scary Man," *MacGruder and Loud,* 1985, "Separated in a Store," *One to Grow On,* 1986.

The New Hollywood Squares, 1987.

Fox's Fun House (also known as *Fun House*), 1988.

Charlene, "She's Not Wild about Harry," *The Law and Harry McGraw,* 1988.

Herself, "School/Day," *Girl Talk,* 1989.

Mimi Detweiler, "Growing Up," *The Wonder Years,* ABC, 1990.

Voice of Amanda Duff, "Take Elmyra Please," *Tiny Toon Adventures* (animated), 1992.

Robin, "Screech's Spaghetti Sauce," *Saved by the Bell* (also known as *Good Morning, Miss Bliss*), NBC, 1992.

Voice of Amanda Duff, "Grandma's Dead," *Tiny Toon Adventures* (animated), 1992.

Voice, "Stimpy's Fan Club," *The Ren & Stimpy Show,* 1993.

"First Comes Love," *Heaven Help Us,* 1994.

Voice of Mary, "Johnny Bravo and the Amazon Women," *The Cartoon Cartoon Show* (animated; also known as *The What a Cartoon Show*), 1996.

Voice of Mary, "Johnny Bravo/Jungle Boy in 'Mr. Monkeyman'/Johnny Bravo and the Amazon Woman," *Johnny Bravo* (animated), Cartoon Network, 1999.

Jen Miller, "The Prodigy," *Working,* NBC, 1999.

Katie, "The One with the Girl Who Hits Joey," *Friends,* NBC, 1999.

Robin, *Guys Like Us,* UPN, 1999.

Celebrity contestant, "Daytona Beach, Florida (V & VI)," *Search Party,* E! Entertainment Television, 2000.

Hollywood Squares (also known as *H2* and *H2: Hollywood Squares*), syndicated, 2000–2001.

L.A. Pool Party, 2001.

Guest host, "Bada bing, bada boom!," *Rendez–View,* 2001.

Host, *Good Day Live,* 2003.

Guest co–host, *Good Day Live,* syndicated, 2003.

Voice of Annasthesia, "License to Slumber/Three Days of the Coin Op," *The X's* (animated), 2005.

Entertainment Tonight (also known as *E.T.*), syndicated, 2007, 2009.

Voice of Punky Brewster, Lucy Van Pelt, and girl, "But Not in That Way," *Robot Chicken,* Cartoon Network, 2009.

Voice of Annie Warbucks and female turtle, "Maurice Was Caught," *Robot Chicken,* Cartoon Network, 2009.

Also appeared as guest, *Teen Win, Lose or Draw,* The Disney Channel.

Television Talk Show Guest Appearances; Episodic:

The Tonight Show Starring Johnny Carson, NBC, 1984.

The Howard Stern Show, E! Entertainment Television, 2000, 2001.

The Late Late Show with Craig Kilborn (also known as *The Late Late Show*), CBS, 2001.

The Rosie O'Donnell Show, syndicated, 2002.

Stage Appearances:

Appeared in *Orestes/I Murdered My Mother,* Los Angeles.

RECORDINGS

Video Games:

Voice of Marcie, *Bloodwings: Pumpkinhead's Revenge,* 1995.

Voice of Jade, *Bratz Rock Angelz,* 2005.

Voice of Jade, *Bratz: Forever Diamondz,* 2006.

WRITINGS

Screenplays:

Wild Horses (also known as *Lunch Time Special*), 1998.

OTHER SOURCES

Periodicals:

People Weekly, April 26, 1993, pp. 82–84; September 12, 2005, p. 95.

FUNARO, Robert 1959–
   (Bobby Funaro)

PERSONAL

Born January 23, 1959, in Brooklyn, New York, NY; has children. *Education:* Attended college; studied acting with Herbert Berghof and others.

Addresses: *Agent*—Atlas Talent Agency, 15 East 32nd St., Suite 6, New York, NY 10016.

Career: Actor. Worked as a director, producer, and play developer, led acting workshops, managed a comedy club, and worked at Madison Square Garden, New York City. Involved with events related to the television program *The Sopranos;* also involved in benefits and charitable efforts.

Member: Screen Actors Guild, Actors' Equity Association, American Federation of Television and Radio Artists.

CREDITS

Television Appearances; Series:
Eugene Pontecorvo, *The Sopranos* (also known as *Made in Jersey, Sopranos, Die Sopranos, Familia Soprano, Les Soprano, Los Soprano, Maffiozok,* and *Sopranod*), HBO, 2001–2006.

Television Appearances; Episodic:
"Bronx Cheer," *Law & Order* (also known as *Law & Order Prime*), NBC, 2001.
Police officer, "Monogamy," *Law & Order: Special Victims Unit* (also known as *Law & Order's Sex Crimes, Law & Order: SVU,* and *Special Victims Unit*), NBC, 2002.
Vinny Russo, "The Insider," *Law & Order: Criminal Intent* (also known as *Law & Order: CI*), NBC, 2002.
Philly Panzaretti, "Risk," *Law & Order: Special Victims Unit* (also known as *Law & Order's Sex Crimes, Law & Order: SVU,* and *Special Victims Unit*), NBC, 2003.
Richie Lupo, "Darwinian," *Law & Order* (also known as *Law & Order Prime*), NBC, 2004.
Uniformed police officer, "Mammon," *Law & Order* (also known as *Law & Order Prime*), NBC, 2005.
Uniformed police officer, "Sects," *Law & Order* (also known as *Law & Order Prime*), NBC, 2005.
Beat police officer, "The Apology Line," *The Unusuals,* ABC, 2009.

Beat police officer at wedding boutique, "Crime Slut," *The Unusuals,* ABC, 2009.
Detective Gibbon, "Lucky Stiff," *Law & Order* (also known as *Law & Order Prime*), NBC, 2009.
Officer Leach, "Boorland Day," *The Unusuals,* ABC, 2009.
Officer Leach, "The Circle Line," *The Unusuals,* ABC, 2009.
Sergeant Corvell, "All New," *Law & Order* (also known as *Law & Order Prime*), NBC, 2009.

Appeared in other programs, including appearances as a fire marshal, *Rescue Me* (also known as *Rescue Me: FDNY*), FX Network; and as Mosc, *Third Watch,* NBC.

Television Appearances; Pilots:
Driver, *The Unusuals,* ABC, 2009.

Stage Appearances:
Detective Bandini, *Dead! A Love Story* (also known as *Dead: A Love Story*), HB Playwrights Foundation & Theatre, New York City, c. 1985.
Alex, *Moondance Cafe* (one–act play), produced as part of *Victims of the Live Wire* (collection of one–act plays), Nuyorican Poets Cafe, New York City, 1989.
Tony, *Red Hook,* Hinton Battle Theatre Laboratory, c. 2000.
Tom Moody, *Golden Boy,* With Out Papers, The Raw Space, New York City, 2002.
Max, *Etta Jenks,* With Out Papers, Pantheon Theatre, New York City, 2003.
Mr. Skins, *Faint,* New York International Fringe Festival (also known as FringeNYC), Clemente Soto Velez Cultural Center, La Tea Theatre, New York City, 2003.
Burton, *Burn This,* With Out Papers, Shelter Studios Theatre 54, New York City, 2004.
Man, *pearls* (one–act play), produced as part of *Dread Awakening* (collection of one–act plays), 45th Street Theatre, New York City, 2006.
Charles, *fuckplays* (collection of short plays), Working Man's Clothes/The Thursday Problem, Soho Think Tank and Galapagos EVOLVE Series, Ohio Theatre, New York City, and Galapagos Art Space, Brooklyn, New York City, both 2007.
Eddie Hejazi, *The Lady Swims Today,* WBISI Productions, TADA Theatre, New York City, 2007.
Fred Santoro, *Lamppost Reunion* (staged readings), Mile Square Theatre, Hoboken Historical Museum, Hoboken, NJ, 2007.
Liam, *Love Atomic* (short play), produced as part of *New York Is Dead [5 Days to Celebrate the End]* (collection of short plays; also known as *New York Is Dead* and *New York Is Dead—A Five Night Program*), Working Man's Clothes/The Thursday Problem/Soho Think Tank, Ohio Theatre, 2008.
Tommy Bardino, *Lamppost Reunion,* ArcLight Theatre, New York City, 2008.

Eddie, *Fresh Kills,* Working Man's Clothes, 59E59, Theatre C, New York City, 2009.

Abel Znorko, *Enigma Variations,* Garage Theatre Group, Fairleigh Dickinson University, Becton Hall, Becton Theatre, Teaneck, NJ, 2010.

Donald (Bone), *The Jag* (staged readings), Premiere Stages, Kean University, Union, NJ, 2010.

Appeared in other productions, including appearances as Frankie Basta, *Birdbath* (one–play; also known as *Bird Bath*); as Mirano, *Caught,* American Place Theatre, New York City; as Tom, *Fathers Day,* The Wynn Group; and as Lieutenant Byrd, *A Soldier's Play,* No Empty Space Co. Also appeared in *Godspell* (musical) and *King of the Dogs* (staged reading).

Major Tours:
Appeared as Stanley Kowalski, *A Streetcar Named Desire,* American Players, European cities.

Stage Work:
Developer and producer, *Red Hook,* Hinton Battle Theatre Laboratory, c. 2000.

Director, *Etta Jenks,* With Out Papers, Pantheon Theater, New York City, 2003.

Affiliated with the Kill Shot Company; also worked in play selection with the Hinton Battle Theatre Laboratory.

Film Appearances:
Mile, *Are They Still Shooting?,* It Takes Two Productions, c. 1993 (some sources cite 1994).

Carmine, *I Am Woody* (short film), DTF Productions, 2003.

Trabuco, *Indocumentados,* True Cinema, 2005.

Michael Stevens, *Cutout* (short film; also known as *Cut Out* and *Cut–Out*), Cutout Pictures/Oracle Entertainment, 2006.

McCann, *American Gangster* (also known as *The Return of Superfly* and *Tru Blu*), Universal, 2007.

Phil, *I Believe in America,* I Believe in America Productions/Suzanne De Laurentiis Productions/Triplicity Entertainment, 2007.

Confessions (short film), c. 2007.

The father (Dominic), *Wish Fulfillment* (short film), Hot Pink Tux Productions, 2009.

Father Barry, *Waiting for ... Budd* (short film), Hudson Film Group, 2009.

Nino, *Mickey Donallo* (short film), 2009.

Larson, *Broadway's Finest,* 2010.

Internet Radio Appearances; Episodic:
Himself, *The Wiseguy Show* (also known as *The Wise Guy Show*), Sirius Satellite Radio, Standard Time // 75 (also known as Standard Time, Standard Time 75, Sirius 75, and Siriusly Sinatra), http://www.sirius.com, 2007.

Himself, *The IT Factor,* broadcast by CBS Radio and posted on other sites, including *Alycia Kaback,* http://www.alyciakaback.com, 2010.

RECORDINGS

Video Games:
(As Bobby Funaro) Voice of Anthony Corrado, *Grand Theft Auto IV* (also known as *GTA 4* and *GTA IV*), Rockstar Games, 2007.

FUNK, Nolan Gerard 1986–
(Nolan Funk)

PERSONAL

Born 1986 in Vancouver, British Columbia, Canada; father, a psychologist. *Avocational Interests:* Environmental issues and playing hockey.

Addresses: *Agent*—Infinite Artists, #10–206 East 6th Ave., Vancouver, British Columbia V5T 1J8, Canada; Abrams Artists Agency, 9200 Sunset Blvd., Suite 1130, Los Angeles, CA 90069. *Manager*—Untitled Entertainment, 1801 Century Park East, Suite 700, Los Angeles, CA 90067.

Career: Actor. Also a singer. Appeared in television commercials, including Playstation video gaming system. The Big Green Help, Nickelodeon, spokesperson; Champions Against Bullying, supporter. Former national gymnast and diver.

Awards, Honors: Leo Award nomination, best performance or host in a youth or children's program or series, Motion Picture Arts and Sciences Foundation of British Columbia, 2007, for *Renegadepress.com.*

CREDITS

Film Appearances:
(As Nolan Funk) Alexander, *Moon in the Afternoon* (short film), 2002.

(As Nolan Funk) Captured X–Kid, *X2* (also known as *X–Men 2,* *X–2,* *X–Men 2: X–Men United,* and *X2: X–Men United*), Twentieth Century–Fox, 2003.

(As Nolan Funk) Josh, *Hollow Man II,* Sony Pictures Home Entertainment, 2006.

Dwyer, *Deadgirl,* Dark Sky Films, 2008.

Preppy dealer, *Class Savage,* 2008.

Kevin, *18* (short film), 2009.

William, *Bereavement* (short film), 2010.
Todd, *Triple Dog,* Well Go, 2010.

Television Appearances; Series:
(As Nolan Funk) Ben Lalonde, *Renegadepress.com,* Aboriginal Peoples Television Network, 2004–2006.
Todd Palladino, *Aliens in America,* The CW, 2007.

Television Appearances; Miniseries:
(As Nolan Funk) Young Eric Crawford, "High Hopes," *Taken* (also known as *Steven Spielberg Presents "Taken"*), Sci–Fi Channel, 2002.

Television Appearances; Movies:
(As Nolan Funk) Michael Magidson, *A Girl Like Me: The Gwen Araujo Story,* Lifetime, 2006.
(As Nolan Funk) Jesse Sherman, *The Obsession,* Lifetime, 2006.
Kit Peterson, *My Name Is Sarah,* Lifetime, 2007.
Nikko Alexander, *Spectacular!,* Nickelodeon, 2009.
Derek, *Jack's Family Adventure* (also known as *Vickery's Wild Ride*), Hallmark Channel, 2010.

Television Appearances; Pilots:
(As Nolan Funk) Mitch Newton, *Sudbury,* CBS, 2004.
Dan, *Lie to Me,* Fox, 2009.

Television Appearances; Episodic:
(As Nolan Funk) Ryan, "The Brink," *Seven Days,* UPN, 2001.
(As Nolan Funk) Malcolm, "Losing It," *The L Word,* Showtime, 2004.
(As Nolan Funk) Zack Greenfield, "Krypto," *Smallville,* The CW, 2005.
(As Nolan Funk) Allan Harris, "While You Were Sleeping," *Killer Instinct,* Fox, 2006.

(As Nolan Funk) Jake Phillips, "Independence Day," *Stephen King's "Dead Zone"* (also known as *The Dead Zone* and *The Dark Half*), USA Network, 2006.
(As Nolan Funk) Jake Tanner, "Croatoan," *Supernatural,* The WB, 2006.
Brandon, "Hedge Fund Homeboys," *Castle,* ABC, 2009.
Access Hollywood, syndicated, 2009.
Today (also known as *NBC News Today* and *The Today Show*), NBC, 2009.
Ellen: The Ellen DeGeneres Show, syndicated, 2009.
Good Morning, America (also known as *G.M.A.*), ABC, 2009.
eTalk Daily (also known as *eTalk*), CTV, 2009.
Good Day New York, WYNW (New York City), 2009, 2010.
Todd, "Beyond Our Control," *Warehouse 13,* Syfy, 2010.
Todd, "Age before Beauty," *Warehouse 13,* Syfy, 2010.
Todd, "13.1," *Warehouse 13,* Syfy, 2010.
Todd, "Vendetta," *Warehouse 13,* Syfy, 2010.
Trevor Elkin, "Deja Vu/All In," *Detroit 1–8–7,* 2010.
MC Petey B, "Think Twice before You Go," *Hellcats,* 2010.

Also appeared as (as Nolan Funk) booker, "Man of the Hizzouse," *Romeo!,* Nickelodeon.

Stage Appearances:
Conrad Birdie, *Bye Bye Birdie,* Roundabout Theatre Company, 2009.

RECORDINGS

Music Videos:
Appeared in "Stay My Baby" by Miranda Cosgrove, 2008.

G

New York Times, February 11, 2011.
Telegraph, February 11, 2011.

GARRETT, Betty 1919–2011

PERSONAL

Original name, Betty Garrett; born May 23, 1919 in St. Joseph, Missouri; died of an aortic aneurysm, February 12, 2011, in Los Angeles, California. Actress. Comedic actress Garrett was considered one of Hollywood's most promising young talents in the 1940s until her career was derailed by accusations of Communist sympathies during the McCarthy era. She began as a dancer and singer in New York City nightclubs in the late 1930s and earned roles in the Broadway revues *Of V We Sing* and *Let Freedom Sing* in 1942. Garrett was understudy to Ethel Merman in the musical *Something for the Boys,* and she had roles in the musicals *Jackpot, Laffing Room Only,* and *Call Me Mister* before signing a contract with MGM studios in 1947. Several film musicals followed, including *Big City, Words and Music, Take Me Out to the Ball Game, Neptune's Daughter,* and *Out on the Town,* which starred Gene Kelly and Frank Sinatra. In 1951 Garrett's husband, actor Larry Parks, was questioned before the House Un-American Activities Committee. Both he and Garrett, who joined the Communist Party in 1941, were blacklisted from most major Hollywood productions and subsequently toured the United Kingdom as a vaudeville team. Garrett returned to Broadway in 1956 with the musical *Bells are Ringing,* followed by *Beg, Borrow, or Steal; Spoon River Anthology;* and *A Girl Could Get Lucky* in the 1960s. In 1974 she was cast as Irene Lorenzo, next door neighbor to Archie Bunker in the hit sitcom *All in the Family,* and later played the landlord Edna Babish in *Laverne and Shirley.* Garrett starred in the musicals *Meet Me in St. Louis* and *Follies* toward the end of her career and also appeared in the films *Trail of the Screaming Forehead* and *Dark and Stormy Night* in the late 2000s.

PERIODICALS

Guardian, February 13, 2011.
Los Angeles Times, February 13, 2011.

GIDDISH, Kelli 1980–

PERSONAL

Born April 13, 1980, in Cumming, GA. *Education:* University of Evansville, degree in theatre performance (with honors).

Addresses: *Agent*—Paradigm, 360 North Crescent Dr., North Bldg., Beverly Hills, CA 90210. *Manager*—One Entertainment, 12 West 57th St., Penthouse, New York, NY 10019.

Career: Actress and writer.

CREDITS

Film Appearances:
Clara, *Witches of the Caribbean,* Image Entertainment, 2005.
Sara, *Walls* (short film), 2006.
Young mother, *Death in Love,* Screen Media Films, 2008.
Simone, *The Understudy,* 2008.

Television Appearances; Series:
Diana "Di" Henry, *All My Children,* ABC, 2005–2007.
Dr. Kate McGinn, *Past Life,* Fox, 2010.
Annie Frost, *Chase,* NBC, 2010–11.

Television Appearances; Episodic:
Herself, *SoapTalk,* SoapNet, 2006.

Kara Bawson, "Outsider," *Law & Order: Special Victims Unit* (also known as *Law & Order: SVU* and *Special Victims Unit*), NBC, 2007.
Heather MacDonald, "Sort of Like a Family," *Damages,* FX Network, 2007.
Heather MacDonald, "Because I Know Patty," *Damages,* FX Network, 2007.
Dana Stipe, "Depths," *Law & Order: Criminal Intent* (also known as *Law & Order: CI*), NBC, 2007.
Ariana Murphy, "Rise and Fall," *Without a Trace* (also known as *W.A.T.*), CBS, 2008.
Carol, "Coffee, Tea or Annie," *Life on Mars,* ABC, 2009.

Stage Appearances:
Dropsy (a one–woman show), New York City, 2005.

Internet Appearances; Web Series:
Courtney, *The Burg,* www.theburg.tv, 2006–2007, 2009.
Cindy, *All's Faire,* http://allsfaire.tv, 2008.

WRITINGS

Stage Plays:
Bobbi Boland, Cort Theatre, New York City, 2003.
Dropsy (a one–woman show), New York City, 2005.

GIOVINAZZO, Vanessa Marcil
　　See MARCIL, Vanessa

GLOVER, Savion 1973–

PERSONAL

Born November 19, 1973, in Newark, NJ; son of Yvette Glover (a performer and manager). *Education:* Studied tap dancing with Michael Blevins.

Addresses: *Agent*—William Morris Agency, 151 El Camino Dr., Beverly Hills, CA 90212.

Career: Actor, dancer, and choreographer. Created his own dance company, Not Your Ordinary Tappers, 1997; has taught dance at Broadway Dance Center. Appeared in television commercials, including Chevy autos, Twix candy bars, Cingular wireless, V8 vegetable juices, and Kraft mayonnaise; choreographed a television commercial for Nike athletic shoes.

Awards, Honors: Antoinette Perry Award nomination, 1989, for *Black and Blue;* Martin Luther King, Jr., Outstanding Youth Award, 1991; Drama Desk Award nomination, best actor, c. 1993, for *Jelly's Last Jam;* Young Artist Award nomination, outstanding youth host in a television variety show, 1994, for *Sesame Street;* Drama Desk Award, Outer Critics Circle Award, two Obie awards, *Village Voice,* two Fred Astaire awards, Antoinette Perry Award nomination, best performer, and Antoinette Perry Award, best choreography, 1996, all for *Bring in da Noise, Bring in da Funk; Dance Magazine* Choreographer of the Year Award, 1996; National Endowment for the Arts grant, 1996.

CREDITS

Stage Appearances:
(Broadway debut) Title character, *The Tap Dance Kid,* 1984.
Black and Blue, Minskoff Theatre, New York City, 1989–91.
Young Jelly, *Jelly's Last Jam,* Virginia Theatre, New York City, 1992–93.
Bring in da Noise, Bring in da Funk, Ambassador Theatre, New York City, 1996–97.
Savion Glover: Downtown, Variety Arts Theatre, New York City, 1998.
Keep Bangin', Players Theatre, New York City, 1999.
Foot Notes, Wilshire Theatre, Los Angeles, 2001.
Brother Time, *Timeless: Live in Concert,* 2001.
Savion Glover with TiDii the Egg, Empire State Plaza, Albany, NY, 2002.
Classic Savion, Joyce Theatre, New York City, 2005.
Solo in Time, Joyce Theatre, 2009.
SoLE PoWER, Joyce Theatre, 2010.

Major Tours:
Bring in da Noise, Bring in da Funk, U.S. cities, 2002, later international cities.
Improvography II, U.S. cities, 2005.

Also toured in *Jelly's Last Jam,* U.S. cities.

Stage Work:
Choreographer, *Bring in da Noise, Bring in da Funk,* Ambassador Theatre, New York City, 1996–97.

Film Appearances:
Audition artist, *Driving Me Crazy,* First Run, 1988.
Louis Simms, *Tap,* TriStar, 1989.
Manray/Mantan, *Bamboozled,* New Line Cinema, 2000.
The Making of "Bamboozled," 2001.
The Wonder Kids (documentary), 2008.

Film Work:
Choreographer, *Bamboozled*, New Line Cinema, 2000.
Choreographer: Mumble, *Happy Feet* (also known as *Happy Feet: The IMAX Experience*), Warner Bros., 2006.

Television Appearances; Movies:
Bracey Mitchell, *The Wall*, Showtime, 1998.
Newcomer, *Bojangles*, Showtime, 2001.

Television Appearances; Specials:
Tap Dance in America (also known as *Gregory Hines' "Tap Dance in America"*), PBS, 1989.
The Kennedy Center Honors: A Celebration of the Performing Arts, CBS, 1991.
Macy's Thanksgiving Day Parade, NBC, 1992.
Jammin': Jelly Roll Morton on Broadway (documentary), PBS, 1992.
Savion, *Sesame Street Stays Up Late!* (also known as *Sesame Street Stays Up Late! A Monster New Year's Eve Party*), PBS, 1993.
Sesame Street's All–Star 25th Birthday: Stars and Street Forever!, ABC, 1994.
In a New Light '94, ABC, 1994.
Savion, *Sesame Street Jam: A Musical Celebration*, 1994.
The Kennedy Center Honors: A Celebration of the Performing Arts, CBS, 1995.
Vanessa Williams & Friends: Christmas in New York, ABC, 1996.
It Just Takes One, USA Network, 1997.
53rd Presidential Inaugural Gala: An American Journey, CBS, 1997.
Stomp, Slide and Swing with Savion Glover, PBS, 1998.
Host, *Savion Glover's Nu York*, ABC, 1998.
Quincy Jones—The First 50 Years, ABC, 1998.
Host, *In Performance at the White House*, 1998.
Halftime performer, *Super Bowl XXXIII*, 1999.
Disney's Young Musicians Symphony Orchestra in Concert, The Disney Channel, 1999.
Voice of toy dancer, *The Steadfast Tin Soldier: An Animated Special from the "Happily Ever After: Fairy Tales for Every Child" Series* (animated), HBO, 2000.
Brother Time, *Barbra Streisand—Timeless* (also known as *Timeless: Live in Concert*), Fox, 2001.
Closing ceremony cast member, *2002 Olympic Winter Games*, NBC, 2002.
AFI Life Achievement Award: A Tribute to Tom Hanks, USA Network, 2002.
Michael Jackson: The One, CBS, 2004.
Apollo at 70: A Hot Night in Harlem, NBC, 2004.
An Evening at Stars: Tribute to Quincy Jones, Black Entertainment Television, 2005.
Newport Jazz Festival, 2006.

Television Appearances; Awards Presentations:
The 61st Annual Academy Awards Presentation, ABC, 1989.

16th Annual Black Filmmakers Hall of Fame, syndicated, 1989.
The ... Annual Tony Awards, 1996, CBS, 1997.
Presenter, *Broadway '97: Launching the Tonys*, PBS, 1997.
39th Grammy Awards, CBS, 1997.
The 13th Annual Stellar Gospel Music Awards, syndicated, 1998.
12th Annual Soul Train Music Awards, syndicated, 1998.
The ... NAACP Image Awards, Fox, 1999, 2001.
Presenter, *The 56th Annual Tony Awards*, CBS, 2002.
2004 Trumpet Awards, 2004.

Television Appearances; Pilots:
Chili, *Shangri–La Plaza*, CBS, 1990.

Television Appearances; Episodic:
Super Dave, 1987.
Himself, "Hall of Fame Day," *The All New Mickey Mouse Club* (also known as *MMC*), 1989.
Ebony/Jet Showcase, 1989.
Square One TV, 1990.
Savion, *Sesame Street* (also known as *Open Sesame*, *Sesame Street Unpaved*, and *The New Sesame Street*), PBS, 1990, 1995.
Showbiz Today, Cable News Network, 1996, 1997.
The Rosie O'Donnell Show, syndicated, 1996, 1998.
Late Show with David Letterman (also known as *Letterman* and *The Late Show*), 1997.
Sin City Spectacular (also known as *Penn & Teller's "Sin City Spectacular"*), FX Network, 1998.
"The New Jersey Performing Arts Center Opening Night Gala," *Great Performances*, PBS, 1998.
Nile, "Taps for Royal," *The Jamie Foxx Show*, The WB, 1999.
Saturday Night Live (also known as *SNL*), NBC, 1999.
America!, Hallmark Channel, 2000.
Bartholomew, *Cedric the Entertainer Presents*, Fox, 2003.
The Tonight Show with Jay Leno, NBC, 2005.
Russell Simmons Presents "Def Poetry" (also known as *Def Poetry* and *Def Poetry Jam*), HBO, 2005.
Special dance performer, "Round 1 Results," *Dancing with the Stars* (also known as *D.W.T.S.*), ABC, 2007.
"Savion Glover," *The Colbert Report*, Comedy Central, 2010.

Television Work; Movies:
Choreographer, *The Rat Pack*, HBO, 1998.

Television Work; Specials:
Executive producer and choreographer, *Savion Glover's Nu York*, ABC, 1998.
Choreographer, *The Rat Pack*, 1998.

Choreographer, *Barbara Streisand—Timeless* (also known as *Timeless: Live in Concert*), Fox, 2001.

Choreographer (tap), *Apollo at 70: A Hot Night Harlem,* NBC, 2003.

RECORDINGS

Music Videos:
Appeared in "Havana" by Kenny G. And "All about the Benjamins" by Puff Daddy and the Family.

Albums:
Black and Blue (original cast recording), DRG, 1989.
Jelly's Last Jam (original cast recording), Mercury, 1992.
Hot Jaz for Cool Yule, Pacific Vista Productions, 1995.
Bring in da Noise, Bring in da Funk (original cast recording), RCA Victor, 1996.

WRITINGS

Television Music; Specials:
Savion Glover's Nu York, ABC, 1998.

Other:
(With Bruce Weber) *Savion! My Life in Tap,* HarperCollins, 2000.

OTHER SOURCES

Books:
Contemporary Black Biography, Volume 14, Gale, 1997.
Encyclopedia of African–American Culture and History, Gale, 2006.
Newsmakers, Issue 4, Gale, 1997.

Periodicals:
Dance Magazine, November, 1994; April, 1996; May, 2004.
New Yorker, January 12, 2004.
New York Times, June 23, 2010.
TV Guide, May 23, 1998, p. 6.

GREENE, Billoah

PERSONAL

Born in Newark, NJ. *Education:* Otterbein College, B.F.A., acting.

Addresses: *Agent*—Stone Manners Salners Agency, 9911 West Pico Blvd., Suite 1400, Los Angeles, CA 90035. *Manager*—International Creative Management, 10250 Constellation Blvd., 9th Floor, Los Angeles, CA 90067.

Career: Actor.

Member: Alpha Phi Alpha.

Awards, Honors: Festival Prize, best supporting actor, Pocono Mountains Film Festival, 2004, for *Peoples.*

CREDITS

Film Appearances:
Don, *Levity,* Sony Pictures Classics, 2003.
Train station demo man, *Head of State,* DreamWorks, 2003.
Rashan, *Brother to Brother,* Wolfe Releasing, 2004.
Samel, *Everyday People,* HBO Films, 2004.
Teshawn Tucker/Zulunatic, *Preaching to the Choir* (also known as *On the One*), Codeblack Entertainment, 2005.
Jake Jackson, *The Minority,* 2006.
Sorn Jackson, *Peoples,* Strictly King Productions, 2009.
Vietnam soldier, *To the Wall,* 2011.

Film Stunt Coordinator:
The Minority, 2006.

Television Appearances; Series:
Dr. Greg Nash, *Jozi–H,* 2006–2007.

Television Appearances; Episodic:
Del Williams, "Crime and Punishment: Part 2," *Third Watch,* NBC, 2002.
Mr. Hanson, "Try Carter," *ER,* NBC, 2004.
Nooky, "I Did It All for the Nooky," *Jonny Zero,* Fox, 2005.
Rahsan, "Brother to Brother," *Independent Lens,* PBS, 2005.
Anton in 1954, "Committed," *Cold Case,* CBS, 2005.
Jeweller, *The Bold and the Beautiful* (also known as *Belleza y poder*), CBS, 2007.
Two–Man, "Bitches Brew," *The Shield,* FX Network, 2008.
Two–Man, "Parricide," *The Shield,* FX Network, 2008.
FBI Agent Alves, "Day 7: 11:00 a.m.–12:00 p.m.," *24,* Fox, 2009.
Charles Porter, "Collateral Damage," *CSI: Miami,* CBS, 2009.

Stage Appearances:
Booth, *Top Dog/Under Dog,* Philadelphia Theatre Company, 2003.

Also appeared as Charley, *Death of a Salesman;* Duke Orsino, *Twelfth Night;* PFC Melvin Peterson, *A Soldier's Play;* Picasso, *Picasso at the Lapin Agile.*

GRODNIK, Daniel 1952–
(Dan Grodnick, Dan Grodnik)

PERSONAL

Full name, Daniel Louis Grodnik; born May 30, 1952, in Minneapolis, MN; son of Stanley A. and Addie (maiden name, Luther) Grodnik; married; wife's name, Nancy; children: one. *Education:* University of Southern California, B.A., 1974.

Addresses: *Office*—Grodfilm, 4119 West Burbank Blvd., Burbank, CA 91505; Crazy Max Films, 1180 South Beverly Dr., Suite 700, Los Angeles, CA 90035; Mass Hysteria Entertainment, 5555 Melrose Ave., Swanson Bldg., Suite 400, Los Angeles, CA 90038.

Career: Producer, writer, and executive. Producer and chief executive officer at a number of companies in the Los Angeles area, including Daniel Grodnik Productions, 1974–76, Grodnik/Sharpe Productions, 1977–80, Weintraub/Grodnik Productions, 1981–83, the Grodnik Film Corporation, 1984–87, and The Grodnik Matheson Company, 1988–89. National Lampoon, chairman and chief executive officer, beginning 1989; Mass Hysteria Entertainment, Los Angeles, chairman and chief executive officer, beginning 2009; Grodfilm, Burbank, CA, principal; Crazy Max Films, Los Angeles, partner. Former president of Itasca Pictures. Gobbler Golf Invitational Golf Tournament, president, 1986. Also known as Dan Grodnik.

Member: Writers Guild of America, West.

Awards, Honors: Indie Memphis Film Festival Award, best narrative feature, and nomination for the Grand Jury Prize, Sundance Film Festival, both with others, 2006, for *Come Early Morning;* Golden Globe Award nomination, best motion picture—drama, and ALMA Award nomination, outstanding motion picture, American Latin Media Arts awards, both with others, 2007, for *Bobby.*

CREDITS

Film Executive Producer:
Starhops (also known as *Curb Service*), First American Films, 1978.

Terror Train (also known as *Terrible Train* and *Train of Terror*), Twentieth Century–Fox, 1980.
(Uncredited) *National Lampoon's "Christmas Vacation"* (also known as *Christmas Vacation*), Warner Bros., 1989.
Man's Best Friend, Alliance Atlantis Vivafilm, 1993.
The Thing Below (also known as *Ghost Rig 2: The Legend of the Sea Ghost, It Waits Below,* and *Sea Ghost*), DEJ Productions, 2004.
Thralls (also known as *Blood Angels*), Screen Media Ventures, 2004.
Glass Trap, Marla's Gardens Company/First Look International, 2005.
(As Dan Grodnik) *Bobby* (also known as *Bobby Kennedy*), Metro–Goldwyn–Mayer, 2006.
Come Early Morning, Bold Films/Roadside Attractions, 2006.
Mini's First Time (also known as *Sex, Lies & Murder*), First Independent Pictures, 2006.

Film Producer:
Out of Control, New World Pictures, 1985.
1969, Atlantic Entertainment Group, 1988.
Blind Fury, TriStar, 1989.
Powder (also known as *Arc*), Buena Vista, 1995.
The Nature of the Beast (also known as *Bad Company, Hatchet Man,* and *Nature of the Beast*), New Line Cinema, c. 1995.
The Rage (also known as *Word of Honor*), Miramax/Imperial Entertainment, 1997.
At Sachem Farm (also known as *Higher Love, Trade Winds,* and *Uncorked*), Itasca Pictures, 1998.
Zack & Reba (also known as *Zack and Reba*), LIVE International, 1998.
Lying in Wait (also known as *Fatal*), Itasca Pictures, 2000.
Who Is Cletis Trout? (also known as *Cletis Trout, Crime and Diamond,* and *Who the #@*?! Is Cletis Trout*), c. 2000, Paramount Classics, 2002.
(As Dan Grodnik) *Blue Demon,* Marla's Gardens Company/Regent Worldwide Sales, 2004.
Pursued, First Independent Pictures, 2004.
Camille, A–Mark Entertainment, 2007.
(As Dan Grodnik) *Safe Harbour* (also known as *Danielle Steel's "Safe Harbour"*), New Line Home Video, 2007.
Overnight, Red Eye Productions/Fusion Film Group/Phoenix Entertainment, c. 2010.
Stonerville (also known as *Brand Dead* and *Slam I Am*), Mass Hysteria Entertainment/Screen Media Ventures, c. 2010.

Film Coproducer:
Without Warning (also known as *Alien Encounters, Alien Shock, Alien Warning, It Came without Warning,* and *The Warning*), Filmways Pictures, 1980.
(Uncredited) *High Road to China,* Warner Bros., 1983.

Film Director:
Second unit director, *Zack & Reba* (also known as *Zack and Reba*), LIVE International, 1998.
(As Dan Grodnik) *Blue Demon,* Marla's Gardens Company/Regent Worldwide Sales, 2004.
Second unit director, *Camille,* A–Mark Entertainment, 2007.

Film Work; Other:
Assistant to producer, *For Pete's Sake* (also known as *July Pork Bellies*), Columbia, 1974.
(As Dan Grodnik) Consulting producer, *Slingshot,* Slingshot LLC, 2004, The Weinstein Company, 2005.

Worked on other projects.

Television Executive Producer; Movies:
Anna's Dream, PAX, 2002.
(As Dan Grodnik) *Another Pretty Face* (also known as *Time and Again*), PAX, 2002.
(As Dan Grodnik) *Mary Christmas,* PAX, 2002.
(As Dan Grodnik) *Book of Days,* PAX, 2003.
(As Dan Grodnik) *Deep Evil,* 2004.
Bloodsuckers (also known as *Vampire Wars: Battle for the Universe*), Sci–Fi Channel, 2005.
Never Cry Werewolf (also known as *The House next Door* and *School Girl vs. Wolfman*), Sci–Fi Channel, 2008.

Television Producer; Movies:
Hallowed Ground, Sci–Fi Channel, 2007.
Yeti: Curse of the Snow Demon (also known as *Yeti*), Sci–Fi Channel, 2008.

Television Director; Movies:
(As Dan Grodnik) Additional directing, *Another Pretty Face* (also known as *Time and Again*), PAX, 2002.

Second unit director, *Yeti: Curse of the Snow Demon* (also known as *Yeti*), Sci–Fi Channel, 2008.

Television Executive Producer; Specials:
National Lampoon's "Comedy Playoffs," Showtime, 1990.

Television Creator; Pilots:
Goldie and the Bears (also known as *Goldie and the Three Bears*), ABC, 1985.
Northstar, ABC, 1986.

Television Executive Producer; Pilots:
Goldie and the Bears (also known as *Goldie and the Three Bears*), ABC, 1985.
Northstar, ABC, 1986.
Sherlock Holmes Returns (also known as *1994 Baker Street: Sherlock Holmes Returns*), CBS, 1993.

WRITINGS

Screenplays; with Others:
(Uncredited) Story, *Terror Train* (screenplay by T. Y. Drake; also known as *Terrible Train* and *Train of Terror*), Twentieth Century–Fox, 1980.
(With Lyn Freeman, Ben Nett, and Steve Mathis) *Without Warning* (also known as *Alien Encounters, Alien Shock, Alien Warning, It Came without Warning,* and *The Warning*), Filmways Pictures, 1980.
(Uncredited; with Sandra Weintraub Roland, Vicangelo Bulluck, and Andrew J. Lederer) *Out of Control,* New World Pictures, 1985.
(As Dan Grodnik; with Brett Thompson, Lisa Morton, and Ron Oliver) *Blue Demon,* Marla's Gardens Company/Regent Worldwide Sales, 2004.

H

HAIGHT, Rip
    See CARPENTER, John

HALL, Philip Baker 1931–
    (Phillip Hall, Phillip Baker Hall)

PERSONAL

Born September 10, 1931, in Toledo, OH; married first wife (divorced, 1965); married Dianne Lewis, 1973 (divorced, 1976); married third wife, Holly Baker; children: (first marriage) two daughters; (third marriage) Anna Ruth. *Education:* Graduated from University of Toledo.

Addresses: *Agent*—Paradigm, 360 North Crescent Dr., North Bldg., Beverly Hills, CA 90210.

Career: Actor, director, and writer. South Coast Repertory Theatre, Costa Mesa, CA, guest artist, 1979–80; appeared in television commercials, including Holiday Inn hotels, 2008. *Military service:* Served in the U.S. Army after college.

Awards, Honors: Independent Spirit Award nomination, best male lead, Independent Features Project/West, 1996, for *Hard Eight;* Florida Film Critics Circle Award (with others), best ensemble cast, Screen Actors Guild Award nomination (with others), outstanding performance by a cast, 1998, both for *Boogie Nights;* Independent Spirit Award nomination, best male lead, 1998, for *Sydney;* Film Critics Circle Award (with others), best ensemble cast, Screen Actors Guild Award nomination (with others), outstanding performance by a cast in a theatrical motion picture, 2000, for *Magnolia;* Alan J. Pakula Award (with others), Broadcast Film

Critics Association, 2001, for *The Contender;* Satellite Award nomination, best actor in a supporting role in a series, miniseries, or motion picture made for television, International Press Academy, 2006, for *The Loop.*

CREDITS

Film Appearances:
Father Reis, *Cowards,* Jaylo, 1970.
Father Reis, *Love–In '72* (also known as *Love–in 1973*), 1971.
(As Phillip Hall) Ryan, *Throw Out the Anchor!,* 1974.
Dr. Inman, *The Man with Bogart's Face* (also known as *Sam Marlowe, Private Eye*), Twentieth Century–Fox, 1980.
Mike Sills, *The Last Reunion* (also known as *Revenge of the Bushido Blade* and *Ninja Nightmare*), 1980.
Dream On!, Magic Cinema, 1981.
Richard Nixon, *Secret Honor* (also known as *Lords of Treason, Secret Honor: The Last Testament of Richard M. Nixon,* and *Secret Honor: A Political Myth*), Vestron Video, 1984.
(Uncredited) Colonial Airlines executive, *Nothing in Common,* 1986.
Detective Mulvahill, *Three O'Clock High,* Universal, 1987.
Sidney, *Midnight Run,* Universal, 1988.
Judge Lavet, *An Innocent Man* (also known as *Hard Rain*), Buena Vista, 1989.
Dean Patterson, *How I Got into College,* Twentieth Century–Fox, 1989.
Police commissioner, *Ghostbusters II* (also known as *Ghostbusters 2*), Columbia, 1989.
IRS boss, *Say Anything ...* (also known as *... Say Anything ...*), Twentieth Century–Fox, 1989.
Joe, *Blue Desert* (also known as *Silent Victim*), Academy Entertainment, 1991.
Senator Thyme, *Live Wire,* New Line Cinema, 1992.
Sidney, *Cigarettes & Coffee,* 1993.
William T., *The Last Laugh,* 1994.
Detective Snyder, *The Little Death,* PolyGram, 1995.

Big Junior Brown, *Kiss of Death,* Twentieth Century–Fox, 1995.

(Uncredited) Chief justice, *The Rock,* Buena Vista, 1996.

Lenny Ish, *Hit Me,* Castle Hill Productions, 1996.

Sydney, *Hard Eight* (also known as *Sydney*), Columbia/TriStar, 1996.

Sidney Hughes, *Eye for an Eye,* Paramount, 1996.

Floyd Gondolli, *Boogie Nights,* New Line Cinema, 1997.

Minister, *Buddy,* Columbia, 1997.

U.S. Attorney General Ward, *Air Force One* (also known as *AFO*), Columbia, 1997.

John Sawyer, *Implicated* (also known as *Wishful Thinking*), Columbia/TriStar, 1998.

(Uncredited) Mark Silverberg, attorney, *Enemy of the State* (also known as *Enemy of America*), Buena Vista, 1998.

Mr. Bell, *Sour Grapes,* Columbia, 1998.

Christof's World network executive, *The Truman Show,* Paramount, 1998.

Captain Diel, *Rush Hour,* New Line Cinema, 1998.

Sheriff Al Chambers, *Psycho,* Universal, 1998.

Pobby Malavero, *Judas Kiss,* 1998.

Jimmy Gator, *Magnolia* (also known as *mag–no'li–a*), New Line Cinema, 1999.

Sol Hirsch, *Let the Devil Wear Black,* Trimark Pictures, 1999.

MacCarron, *The Talented Mr. Ripley* (also known as *The Mysterious Yearning Secretive Sad Lonely Troubled Confused Loving Musical Gifted Intelligent Beautiful Tender Sensitive Haunted Passionate Talented Mr. Ripley* and *Eclipse*), Paramount, 1999.

Gray Mathers, *The Cradle Will Rock,* Buena Vista, 1999.

Himself, *Psycho Path,* Universal Studios Home Video, 1999.

Don Hewitt, *The Insider,* Buena Vista, 1999.

A House on a Hill, 1999.

Himself, *That Moment: "Magnolia Diary"* (also known as *That Moment: "Magnolia Diary October 1998–March 2000"*), New Line Home Video, 2000.

General H. Lawrence Hodges, *Rules of Engagement* (also known as *Les regles d'engagement* and *Rules–Sekunden der entscheidung*), Paramount, 2000.

Oscar Billings, *The Contender* (also known as *Rufmord–Jenseits der moral*), DreamWorks, 2000.

Father James, *Lost Souls,* New Line Cinema, 2000.

Charlie Logan, *A Gentleman's Game,* First Look Home Entertainment, 2001.

Defense Secretary David Becker, *The Sum of All Fears* (also known as *Total Fears* and *Der Anschlag*), Paramount, 2002.

Sol Sussman, *Die, Mommie, Die,* Sundance Film Series, 2003.

Jack Keller, *Bruce Almighty,* Universal, 2003.

Tom Edison Sr., *Dogville* (also known as *The Film "Dogville" as Told in Nine Chapters and a Prologue*), Lions Gate Films, 2003.

Harry Mayfield, *A House on a Hill,* Calliope Films, 2003.

Eugene Kalb, *In Good Company,* Universal, 2004.

Mr. Randy, *The Matador,* Miramax, 2005.

Voice, *A Buck's Worth* (short film), 2005.

Arthur Pratt, *Duck,* Right Brained Releasing, 2005.

Father Callaway, *The Amityville Horror,* Metro–Goldwyn–Mayer, 2005.

Frank Perkins, *The Zodiac* (also known as *Zodiac*), THINKFilm, 2005.

Lance Strictland, *The Shaggy Dog,* Buena Vista, 2006.

Vernon Maxwell, *The TV Set,* THINKFilm, 2006.

Popper, *Islander,* Indican Pictures, 2006.

Roman Krzeminski, *You Kill Me,* IFC Films, 2007.

Sherwood Morrill, *Zodiac,* Paramount, 2007.

(Uncredited) Captain William Diel, *Rush Hour 3,* New Line Cinema, 2007.

Thesis: Work vs. Play (short film), Twentieth Century–Fox Home Entertainment, 2007.

Captain Smith, *The Lodger,* Stage 6 Films, 2009.

Coach Byrnes, *Fired Up!,* Screen Gems, 2009.

The man, *Wonderful World,* Magnolia Pictures, 2009.

Melvin Bump, *All Good Things,* Magnolia Pictures, 2010.

Judge Julius Hoffman, *The Chicago 8,* 2010.

Live With It, Summit Entertainment, 2010.

Himself, *Showing Up* (documentary), 2011.

Television Appearances; Series:
Superintendent James Malone, *Mariah,* ABC, 1987.
Ed Meyers, *Falcon Crest,* CBS, 1989–90.
William Vaughn, *Michael Hayes,* CBS, 1997.
George Greeley, *Pasadena,* Fox, 2001–2002.
Russ, *The Loop,* Fox, 2006–2007.

Television Appearances; Miniseries:
The Bastard (also known as *The Kent Chronicles*), syndicated, 1978.
Toddo Aurello, *Witness to the Mob,* NBC, 1998.
Aristotle Onassis, *Jackie Bouvier Kennedy Onassis,* CBS, 2000.

Television Appearances; Movies:
The Last Survivors, 1975.
First reporter, *Mayday at 40,000 Feet!,* CBS, 1976.
George, *Man from Atlantis,* NBC, 1977.
Phillips, *Kill Me If You Can* (also known as *The Caryl Chessman Story*), NBC, 1977.
Dr. Harvey Fess, *The Hostage Heart,* 1977.
Starrett, *Terror Out of the Sky* (also known as *The Revenge of the Savage Bees*), CBS, 1979.
Professor Gordon Owens, *Samurai,* ABC, 1979.
Warren Meech, *The Night the Bridge Fell Down,* NBC, 1980.
Clerk, *This House Possessed,* ABC, 1981.
Lester Greene, *Games Mother Never Taught You,* CBS, 1982.
Dean May, *Who Is Julia?,* CBS, 1986.

Sevrin, *The Spirit*, ABC, 1987.

Detective Charles, *The Goddess of Love*, NBC, 1988.

Judge Blumenfeld, *A Cry for Help: The Tracey Thurman Story*, NBC, 1989.

Dr. Leo Manus, *Incident at Dark River* (also known as *Dark River—A Father's Revenge*), TNT, 1989.

Sam Gochenour, *Crash Landing: The Rescue of Flight 232* (also known as *A Thousand Heroes*), ABC, 1992.

Ernie Horshack, *Stormy Weathers*, ABC, 1992.

Roswell general, *Roswell* (also known as *Roswell: The U.F.O. Cover–Up* and *Incident at Roswell*), Showtime, 1994.

Coroner Smitty, *M.A.N.T.I.S.* (also known as *Mantis*), Fox, 1994.

Dr. Kurt Lowden, *Without Warning*, CBS, 1994.

Dr. Bardwell, *Tempting Fate* (also known as *Parallels*), ABC, 1998.

Scarpatti, *Partners*, 1999.

Poppy Malavero, *The Judas Kiss*, Cinemax, 1999.

Senator Everett Dirksen, *Path to War*, HBO, 2002.

Arthur Schulte, *Mrs. Harris*, HBO, 2005.

Television Appearances; Specials:

Campus Culture Wars: Five Stories about P.C., PBS, 1993.

Television Appearances; Pilots:

George, *Man from Atlantis*, 1977.

Mr. Durfee, *Riding for the Pony Express*, CBS, 1980.

Bick Jack, reporter's dad, *Loomis*, CBS, 2001.

Television Appearances; Episodic:

Motel owner, "J. J.'s Fiancee: Part 2," *Good Times*, 1976.

Severson, "Gold Watch," *Visions*, 1976.

Sergeant Hacker, "The Light That Failed," *M*A*S*H*, CBS, 1977.

Boyle, "You Can Run, But You Can't Hide," *Visions*, 1977.

Oliver Warren, "The Steel Inferno," *Emergency!* (also known as *Emergencia* and *Emergency One*), 1978.

Bertram, "A Living Wage," *The Fitzpatricks*, 1978.

Major Gordon, "The Furlough," *The Waltons*, 1980.

Captain Rusmussen, "Smoke Screen," *Quincy* (also known as *Quincy M.E.*), 1982.

Deputy District Attorney Marty Shell, "Sleeping Dogs," *Quincy* (also known as *Quincy M.E.*), 1982.

Lieutenant Sweeney, "Hot Line," *Cagney & Lacey*, 1982.

Judge Wallace, "A Cry for Help," *T. J. Hooker*, ABC, 1982.

Prosecutor, "The Man in the White Hat," *Seven Brides for Seven Brothers*, 1982.

Wilcox, "Christmas Song," *Seven Brides for Seven Brothers*, 1982.

"Houston: Duffy's Choice," *Lottery!*, 1983.

Jack Marsh, "Too Rich and Too Thin," *Hardcastle and McCormick*, 1985.

Judge Delaponte, "Contempt of Court," *Miami Vice*, 1987.

Dr. Harrison, "Heartstrings: Parts 1, 2, & 3," *Family Ties*, 1988.

Judge, "The Mother," *Matlock*, NBC, 1990.

Herb, "This Bird Has Flown," *Bagdad Cafe*, 1990.

Tom Baker, "He's a Crowd," *L.A. Law*, NBC, 1991.

Judge Bianchi, "Daveja–Vu All Over Again," *Civil Wars*, ABC, 1991.

Lieutenant Bookman, "The Library," *Seinfeld*, NBC, 1991.

Len Costner, "Moving Violation," *Murder, She Wrote*, CBS, 1991.

Judge S. E. Cleveland, "Do the Wrong Thing," *Equal Justice*, 1991.

(As Phillip Baker Hall) Winchester Keller, "The Neutralizing Factor," *Dark Justice*, 1991.

Mr. Todd, "Playing Doctor," *Nurses*, NBC, 1992.

Judge Bianchi, "His Honor's Offer," *Civil Wars*, ABC, 1992.

Judge Bianchi, "A Bus Named Desire," *Civil Wars*, ABC, 1992.

City Councilman Kevin Fogerty, "Woody Gets an Election," *Cheers*, NBC, 1993.

Mr. Wellington, "You Gotta Have Heart," *Chicago Hope*, CBS, 1994.

Beanball McGee, "Lee's Bad, Bad Day," *Hardball*, Fox, 1994.

Mr. Humphreys, "Melissa the Thief," *The Good Life*, NBC, 1994.

Jerod, "Brotherly Shove," *Empty Nest*, NBC, 1994.

Oscar Kern, *Madman of the People*, NBC, 1994.

Judge Conklin, "Contempt," *Life's Work*, ABC, 1996.

President Dewey, "Proud Dick," *Third Rock from the Sun* (also known as *3rd Rock from the Sun*, *3rd Rock*, and *Encounters of the Personal Kind*), NBC, 1997.

Judge Joseph Vinocour, "Part I," *The Practice*, ABC, 1997.

Judge Joseph Vinocour, "Part V," *The Practice*, ABC, 1997.

Judge Joseph Vinocour, "Part VI," *The Practice*, ABC, 1997.

Judge Canker, "Betrayal," *The Practice*, ABC, 1997.

Mr. Frank, "Napping to Success," *The John Larroquette Show* (also known as *Larroquette*), NBC, 1997.

Group elder, "The Hand of Saint Sebastian," *Millennium*, 1997.

The Group Elder, "Owls," *Millennium*, Fox, 1998.

The Group Elder, "Roosters," *Millennium*, Fox, 1998.

Lieutenant Bookman, "The Finale: Part 1," *Seinfeld*, NBC, 1998.

Vincent Cattano, "Fear of Flying," *L.A. Doctors* (also known as *L.A. Docs*), CBS, 1998.

Charlie Rose (also known as *The Charlie Rose Show*), 2000.

Voice of Mr. Thompson, "Ugly Zoe," *Baby Blues* (animated), The WB, 2000.

Stuart Kimble, "St. Christopher's Prayer," *The Fugitive*, CBS, 2000.

Voice of Mr. Saunders, "Wanda Proof," *Baby Blues* (animated), The WB, 2002.

Dennis Brascom, "Cargo," *Night Visions* (also known as *Nightvision*), Fox, 2002.

Noah Ridder, "Silent Partner," *Without a Trace* (also known as *W.A.T.*), CBS, 2002.

Dr. Donald Douglas, "Home," *Everwood,* The WB, 2003.

Dr. Donald Douglas, "Do or Die," *Everwood,* The WB, 2004.

Dr. Donald Douglas, "Your Future Awaits," *Everwood,* The WB, 2004.

(As Phillip Baker Hall) Salvatore Lucarelli, "Mr. Monk Meets the Godfather," *Monk,* USA Network, 2004.

Ernie Dell, "Head Cases," *Boston Legal,* ABC, 2004.

Senator Matt Hunt, "An Khe," *The West Wing* (also known as *The White House*), NBC, 2004.

Senator Matt Hunt, "A Change Is Gonna Come," *The West Wing* (also known as *The White House*), NBC, 2004.

Dinner for Five, Independent Film Channel, 2004.

Doctor Morrison, "Mel's Offer," *Curb Your Enthusiasm,* HBO, 2004.

Up Close with Carrie Keagan, 2007.

Ned Johanssen, "Take Me as I Am," *Big Love,* HBO, 2007.

Irving Parker, "Dis–Lodged," *Psych,* USA Network, 2008.

Reverend Lowell, "The Vows," *Worst Week,* CBS, 2008.

Reverend Lowell, "The Wedding," *Worst Week,* CBS, 2008.

Doctor Morrison, "The Hot Towel," *Curb Your Enthusiasm,* 2009.

Mr. Jenkins, "The New Kid," *True Jackson, VP,* Nickelodeon, 2009.

Voice of Norman Walker, "London Calling/Novelist," *The Life & Times of Tim,* HBO, 2010.

"Rock Opera," *Warren the Ape,* MTV, 2010.

Walt Kleezak, *Modern Family,* ABC, 2011.

Stage Appearances:

Hucklebee, *The Fantasticks,* Sullivan Street Playhouse, New York City, 1960–62.

Leader, *Donogoo,* Greenwich Mews Theatre, New York City, 1961.

In White America, Players Theatre, New York City, 1965.

Prinz, *The World of Gunter Grass,* Pocket Theatre, 1966.

The Ecstasy of Rita, Washington Theatre Club, Washington, DC, 1972–73.

Ralph, *An Absence of Light,* Equity Library Theatre, New York Public Library at Lincoln Center, New York City, 1973.

Title role, *Gorky,* American Place Theatre, New York City, 1975.

Conjuring an Event, Center Theatre Group, Mark Taper Forum, Los Angeles, 1976–77.

Photographer, Pete Costas, *Hoagy, Bix, and Wolfgang Beethoven Bunkhaus,* Center Theatre Group, Mark Taper Forum, 1980–81.

Mr. Nixon, *Secret Honor: The Last Testament of Richard M. Nixon* (solo show), Provincetown Playhouse, New York City, 1983, then Los Angeles Actors' Theatre, Los Angeles, 1983–84.

Duke Mantee, *The Petrified Forest,* Los Angeles Theatre Center, Los Angeles, 1985–86.

All My Sons, Los Angeles Theatre Center, 1986–87.

The Crucible, Los Angeles Theatre Center, 1990–91.

A Map of the World, Odyssey Theatre Ensemble, Los Angeles, 1991–92.

Max, *The Homecoming,* Los Angeles, 1995.

Chertikov, *Sonya,* State University of New York, Purchase, New York, 1996.

Don, *American Buffalo,* Donmar Warehouse Theatre, London, then Atlantic Theatre, New York City, 2000.

Nick, *The Guys,* Actors' Gang, Hollywood, CA 2002.

Also appeared in *The Skin of Our Teeth; Death of a Salesman; Short Eyes.*

Major Tours:

In White America, U.S. cities, 1965.

Stage Work:

(With Andrew Frye) Director, *The Far Other Side of a Very Thin Line,* Center Theatre Group, Mark Taper Forum, Los Angeles, 1978–79.

WRITINGS

Plays:

(With James Shepard) *The Far Other Side of a Very Thin Line,* produced by Center Theatre Group, Mark Taper Forum, Los Angeles, 1978–79.

OTHER SOURCES

Periodicals:

Los Angeles Times, "Calendar," November 29, 1998, pp. 25–26.

HAMILTON, Linda 1956–

PERSONAL

Full name, Linda Carroll Hamilton; born September 26, 1956, in Salisbury, MD; father, a physician; married Bruce Abbot (an actor), December 19, 1982 (divorced,

1989); married James Cameron (a director and writer), March 24, 1997 (divorced, 1999); children: (first marriage) Dalton, (second marriage) Josephine Archer. *Education:* Attended Washington College, Chesterton, MD; studied acting at the Lee Strasberg Theatre Institute.

Addresses: *Agent*—United Talent Agency, 9560 Wilshire Blvd., 5th Floor, Beverly Hills, CA 90212; Writers and Artists Agency, 8383 Wilshire Blvd., Suite 550, Beverly Hills, CA 90211. *Manager*—Bobbie Edrick, Artist Circle Entertainment, 8955 Norma Place, Los Angeles, CA 90069.

Career: Actress.

Awards, Honors: Saturn Award nomination, best actress, Academy of Science Fiction, Fantasy, and Horror Films, 1985, for *The Terminator;* Golden Globe Award nominations, best actress in a dramatic television series, 1988 and 1989, Emmy Award nomination, outstanding lead actress in a drama series, 1989, for *Beauty and the Beast;* MTV Movie Awards, best female performance and most desirable female, Saturn Award, best actress, Academy of Science Fiction, Fantasy, and Horror Films, 1992, all for *Terminator 2: Judgment Day;* CableACE Award, actress in a movie or miniseries, 1995, Golden Globe Award nomination, best performance by an actress in a miniseries or motion picture made for television, 1996, for *A Mother's Prayer;* Blockbuster Entertainment Award, favorite actress—action/adventure, 1998, for *Dante's Peak;* Golden Satellite Award, best performance by an actress in a miniseries or a motion picture made for television, International Press Academy, 2000, for *The Color of Courage;* Video Premiere Award, best supporting actress, 2001, for *Skeletons in the Closet.*

CREDITS

Stage Appearances:
Reporter, *Looice,* New York Shakespeare Festival, Public Theatre, New York City, 1975.
Young Elizabeth, *Richard III,* Actors' Studio Theatre, New York City, 1977.
Title role, *Laura,* Los Angeles, 2000.
Ethel Rosenberg, *Worse than Murder: Ethel and Julius Rosenberg,* Ventura Cort Theatre, Studio City, CA, 2002.

Film Appearances:
Night–Flowers (also known as *Night Angels*), 1979.
Susan, *T.A.G.: The Assassination Game* (also known as *Tag: The Assassination Game, Everybody Gets It in the End,* and *Kiss Me, Kill Me*), New World, 1982.
Eva the Crescent Moon Lady, *The Stone Boy,* Twentieth Century–Fox, 1983.

Vicky Baxter, *Children of the Corn* (also known as *Stephen King's "Children of the Corn"*), New World, 1984.
Sarah Connor, *The Terminator,* Orion, 1984.
Nina, *Black Moon Rising,* New World, 1986.
Amy Franklin, *King Kong Lives,* De Laurentiis Entertainment Group, 1986.
Sticky Fingers, 1988.
Ellen Burrows, *Mr. Destiny,* Buena Vista, 1990.
Sarah Connor, *Terminator 2: Judgment Day* (also known as *T2, T2–Terminator 2: Judgment Day, T2: Extreme Edition, T2: Ultimate Edition, Terminator 2–Le jour du jugement dernier,* and *Terminator 2: le jugement dernier*), TriStar, 1991.
Herself, *T2: More than Meets the Eye,* 1993.
Karen Rainer, *Silent Fall,* Warner Bros., 1994.
Lauren Porter, *Separate Lives,* 1995.
Sarah Connor, *T2 3–D: Battle across Time* (also known as *T2: Terminator 2:3–D* and *Terminator 2: 3–D*), 1996.
Mayor Rachel Wando, *Dante's Peak,* Universal, 1997.
Amanda Givens, *Shadow Conspiracy,* Buena Vista, 1997.
Ruby Sanford, *The Secret Life of Girls,* 1999.
Tina Conway, *Skeletons in the Closet,* Artisan Entertainment, 2000.
Valerie, *Wholey Moses,* 2003.
June, *Jonah* (short film), 2004.
Bridgette, *Smile,* Dark Forest, 2005.
Kate, *Missing in America,* First Look, 2005.
Susan Mandeville, *The Kid & I,* Twentieth Century–Fox, 2005.
Karen, *Broken,* First Look, 2006.
Georgie, *In Your Dreams,* Magnet Films, 2007.
Sarah Connor, *Jeremiah Wright Painting a Picture of US Aggression,* Lyonspotter Pictures, 2008.
Sarah Connor, *Terminator Salvation,* 2009.
A Call to Arms, Scott Miller and Company, 2009.
Cory, *Holy Water,* Eyeline Entertainment, 2009.
Amelia Philips, *Refuge,* Westmark Prod., 2010.
DC Showcase: Jonah Hex, Warner Home Video, 2010.

Television Appearances; Series:
Lisa Rogers, *Secrets of Midland Heights,* CBS, 1980–81.
Lauren Hollister, *King's Crossing,* ABC, 1982.
Assistant District Attorney Catherine Chandler, *Beauty and the Beast,* CBS, 1987–89.
Carol, *The Line,* 2008.
Mary Bartowski, a recurring role, *Chuck,* NBC, 2010–11.

Television Appearances; Movies:
Greta Rideout, *Rape and Marriage—The Rideout Case,* CBS, 1980.
Anne Samoorian, *Reunion,* CBS, 1980.
Josie Greenwood, *Country Gold,* CBS, 1982.
Susan Decker, *Secrets of a Mother and Daughter,* CBS, 1983.

Mattie MacGregor, *Wishman,* 1983.
Elena Koslov, *Secret Weapons* (also known as *Secrets of the Red Bedroom* and *Sexpionage*), NBC, 1985.
Kate, *Club Med,* ABC, 1986.
Claire Madison, *Go toward the Light* (also known as *Go to the Light*), CBS, 1988.
Rosemary Holmstrom, *A Mother's Prayer,* USA Network, 1995.
Beth MacAlpine, *The Way to Dusty Death,* 1995.
Detective Jean Martin, *On the Line,* ABC, 1998.
Rachel Harrison, *Point Last Seen,* CBS, 1998.
Marie Taquet, "Marie Taquet," *Rescuers: Stories of Courage: Two Couples,* Showtime, 1998.
Tina, *Skeletons in the Closet,* 1998.
Anna Sipes, *The Color of Courage,* USA Network, 1999.
Ruby Sanford, *Unglued* (also known as *The Secret Life of Girls*), 1999.
Voice of Dr. Stephanie Lake, *Batman Beyond: The Movie* (animated), 1999.
Joanna Scott, *Sex & Mrs. X,* Lifetime, 2000.
Liz Donovan, *Bailey's Mistake,* ABC, 2001.
Elisabeth Vincken, *Silent Night,* 2002.
Kate, *Take 3,* 2006.
Julie Bedford, *Home by Christmas,* 2006.

Television Appearances; Miniseries:
Rachel Logan, "Unholy Alliances," *A Girl Thing,* Showtime, 2001.
Ultimate Sci–Fi Top 10, Sky Television, 2004.

Television Appearances; Specials:
The Making of "Terminator," 1984.
The Making of "Terminator 2: Judgment Day," 1992.
Toonces, the Cat Who Could Drive a Car, NBC, 1992.
The American Film Institute Salute to Steven Spielberg, NBC, 1995.
Narrator, *Robots Rising,* The Discovery Channel, 1998.
Saturday Night Live: The Best of Dana Carvey, NBC, 1999.
Saturday Night Live 25, NBC, 1999.
Other Voices: Creating "The Terminator," 2001.
Ultimate Super Heroes, Ultimate Super Villains, Ultimate Super Vixens, Bravo, 2005.
Arnold Schwarzenegger: I'll Be Back, Arts and Entertainment, 2007.

Television Appearances; Awards Presentations:
MTV's 1991 Video Music Awards, MTV and syndicated, 1991.
MTV Movie Awards, MTV, 1992.
Presenter, *The 17th Annual CableACE Awards,* 1995.
Presenter, *The Screen Actor's Guild Awards,* 1997.
Blockbuster Entertainment Awards, 1998.

Television Appearances: Pilots:
Mattie MacGregor, *Wishman,* ABC, 1983.
Roselyn Moore, *Thief,* 2006.

Television Appearances; Episodic:
Gloria, "Teddy Roosevelt Slept Here," *Shirley,* 1980.
Sandy Valpariso, "Fuchs Me? Fuchs You!," *Hill Street Blues,* NBC, 1984.
Sandy Valpariso, "Grace under Pressure," *Hill Street Blues,* NBC, 1984.
Sandy Valpariso, "The Other Side of Oneness," *Hill Street Blues,* NBC, 1984.
Sandy Valpariso, "Parting Is Such Sweet Sorrow," *Hill Street Blues,* NBC, 1984.
Carol McDermott, "Menace, Anyone?," *Murder, She Wrote,* CBS, 1986.
Host, *Saturday Night Live,* NBC, 1991.
Guest caller Claire, "The Good Son," *Frasier,* NBC, 1993.
Laura, "Odd Man Out," *Frasier,* NBC, 1997.
Voice of Nemesis, "Hercules and the King for a Day," *Disney's Hercules* (animated; also known as *Hercules*), ABC and syndicated, 1998.
Voice of Susan Maguire/Susan Wayne, "Chemistry," *Batman: Gotham Knights* (animated), Fox, 1998.
Voice of Nemesis, "Hercules and the Romans," *Disney's Hercules* (animated; also known as *Hercules*), ABC and syndicated, 1999.
Voice of Dr. Stephanie Lake, "Meltdown," *Batman Beyond* (animated), 1999.
Voice of Dr. Furbanna, "The Beasts of Karn," *Buzz Lightyear of Star Command* (animated), UPN and syndicated, 2000.
Voice of Dr. Furbanna, "Millennial Bugs," *Buzz Lightyear of Star Command* (animated), UPN and syndicated, 2000.
Voice of Dr. Furbanna, "Return to Karn," *Buzz Lightyear of Star Command* (animated), UPN and syndicated, 2000.
Corazon de ..., 2005.
Melissa, "Shall We Dance?," *According to Jim,* ABC, 2005.
Melissa Evans, "Lean on Me," *According to Jim,* ABC, 2005.
Roselyn Moore, "I Ain't Goin' to Jail for Anyone," *Thief,* 2006.
Guest, "Will and Linda," *Sidewalks Entertainment,* 2006.
Linda, "A Yippity Sippity," *Weeds,* Showtime, 2010.
Linda, "Bliss," *Weeds,* Showtime, 2010.

Television Talk Show Guest Appearances; Episodic:
Late Night with David Letterman, 1991.
So Graham Norton, Channel 4, 2002.
The View, ABC, 2004.
The Oprah Winfrey Show (also known as *Oprah*), syndicated, 2004.
Larry King Live, Cable News Network, 2005.
Breakfast, BBC, 2010.
This Morning, NBC, 2010.
The Wright Stuff, Channel 5, 2010.
Angela and Friends, Sky Television, 2010.

RECORDINGS

Video Games:

Voice of Sarah Connor, *Terminator 2: Judgment Day,* 1991.

Videos:

Getting Close to the Show (also known as *Getting Close to the Show: The Making of "Dante's Peak"*), 1998.

Other Voices: Creating "The Terminator," 2001.

Beauty and the Beast Season 2: Introductions with Ron Perlman and Linda Hamilton, Paramount Home Video, 2007.

Behind Your Dreams, Shoreline Entertainment, 2008.

It Was the Eighties!, Anchor Bay Entertainment, 2009.

Taped Readings:

Night Train by Martin Amis, Dove, 1998.

Otherwise Engaged by Suzanne Finnamore, Random House Audiobooks, 1999.

OTHER SOURCES

Periodicals:

People Weekly, May 11, 1998, p. 64.

HARRIS, Danielle 1977–

PERSONAL

Full name, Danielle Andrea Harris; born June 1, 1977, in Queens, New York, NY; daughter of Fran Harris.

Addresses: *Agent*—United Talent Agency, 9560 Wilshire Blvd., Suite 500, Beverly Hills, CA 90212; Don Buchwald and Associates, 6500 Wilshire Blvd., Suite 2200, Los Angeles, CA 90048. *Manager*—Felicia Sager, Sager Management, 260 South Beverly Dr., Suite 205, Beverly Hills, CA 90210; Immortal Entertainment, 1650 21st St., Santa Monica, CA 90404.

Career: Actress. Appeared in many television commercials.

Awards, Honors: Young Artist Award nominations, outstanding young actress costarring in a motion picture and outstanding young ensemble cast in a motion picture (with others), both 1992, for *Don't Tell Mom the Babysitter's Dead;* Young Artist Award nomination, outstanding young actress recurring in a television series, 1993, for *Roseanne.*

CREDITS

Film Appearances:

Jamie Lloyd, *Halloween 4: The Return of Michael Myers,* Galaxy International, 1988.

Jamie Lloyd, *Halloween 5* (also known as *Halloween 5: The Revenge of Michael Myers*), Galaxy International, 1989.

Tracey, *Marked for Death* (also known as *Screwface*), Twentieth Century–Fox, 1990.

Melissa Crandell, *Don't Tell Mom the Babysitter's Dead,* Warner Bros., 1991.

First classroom student, *City Slickers,* Columbia, 1991.

Darian Hallenbeck, *The Last Boy Scout,* Warner Bros., 1991.

Gwenie, *Free Willy,* Warner Bros., 1993.

Ashley Crighton, *Daylight,* Universal, 1996.

Hayley Wheaton, *Wish Upon a Star,* Warner Home Video, 1996.

Susan, *Shattered Image,* 1996.

Tosh Guaneri, *Urban Legend* (also known as *Mixed Culture*), TriStar, 1998.

Lulu, *Dizzyland,* 1998.

Young Charlene Silver, *Goosed,* 1999.

Suzi, *Poor White Trash,* Hollywood Independents, 2000.

Em & Me, 2000.

Totally Irresponsible, Trimark Pictures, 2000.

Barbie, *Killer Bud,* Trimark Pictures, 2001.

Voice of Debbie Thornberry, *The Wild Thornberrys Movie* (animated), Paramount, 2002.

Voice of Debbie Thornberry, *Rugrats Go Wild!* (animated), Paramount, 2003.

Freddy vs. Jason, New Line Cinema, 2003.

Leila, *The Partners,* Fox, 2003.

Liz Bronner, *Debating Robert Lee,* Radio London Films, 2004.

Carla, *Race You to the Bottom,* Regent Releasing, 2005.

Halloween: Faces of Fear, Monsters HD, 2007.

Annie Brackett, *Halloween* (also known as *Rob Zombie's "Halloween"*), Dimension, 2007.

Nancy, *Left for Dead,* Sunfilm Entertainment, 2007.

Olivia, *Burying the Ex,* Anemic Cinema, 2008.

Prank, Masimedia, 2008.

Felicia Freeze, *Super Capers,* Lions Gate Films, 2009.

Annie Brackett, *Halloween II* (also known as *Rob Zombie's "Halloween II"*), Dimension Films, 2009.

Alyssa, *Blood Night: The Legend of Mary Hatchet* (also known as *Blood Night*), Aspect Films, 2009.

Kathy, *The Black Waters of Echo's Pond,* Stardom Pictures, 2009.

Halfpipe, *Godkiller,* Gravitas Ventures, 2010.

Maria, *Cyrus,* Moonstone Entertainment, 2010.

Belle, *Stake Land,* Dark Sky Films, 2010.

Marybeth, *Hatchet 2,* Dark Sky Films, 2010.

Also appeared in *The Debate Club.*

Film Director:
Prank, 2008.

Television Appearances; Series:
Samantha "Sami" Garretson, *One Life to Live,* ABC, 1985–87.
Mollie Tilden (some sources cite Molly Tillman), a recurring role, *Roseanne,* ABC, 1992–93.
Cohost, *Brains and Brawn* (game show), NBC, 1993.
Voice of Debbie Thornberry, *The Wild Thornberrys* (animated), Nickelodeon, 1998–2000.
Plum Wilkinson DeLucca, *That's Life,* ABC, 2000–2001.
Voice of Sierra, *Father of the Pride,* NBC, 2004–2005.
Route 666: America's Scariest Home Haunts, FEARnet, 2007.
Susan, *Fear Clinic,* 2009.

Television Appearances; Movies:
Dana Hemmings, *Don't Touch My Daughter* (also known as *Nightmare*), NBC, 1991.
Young Isobel, *The Killing Mind,* Lifetime, 1991.
Priscilla "Cilla," *The Woman Who Loved Elvis,* ABC, 1993.
Jessica at age fifteen, *Roseanne: An Unauthorized Biography,* Fox, 1994.
Chelsea, *Back to Back* (also known as *Back to Back: American Yakuza 2*), HBO, 1996.
Young Charlene, *Goosed,* The Movie Channel, 1999.
Justine Sinclair, *Hard Time: Hostage Hotel* (also known as *Hostage Hotel*), TNT, 1999.
Leila, *The Partners,* ABC, 2003.

Television Appearances; Pilots:
Abby Proctor, *1776,* CBS, 1992.
Plum Wilkinson DeLucca, *That's Life,* ABC, 2000.

Television Appearances; Episodic:
Tara, "Thanksgiving," *Spenser: For Hire,* ABC, 1987.
Drug addict, "The Wrath of Farrakhan," *In Living Color,* 1990.
Melanie Monroe, "Heart on a Chain," *Eerie, Indiana,* NBC, 1991.
Susie Maxwell, "The Big Fix," *Growing Pains,* ABC, 1991.
Jennifer, "True Love Ways," *Jack's Place,* ABC, 1993.
Sheri Fisher, "Romeo and Juliet," *The Commish,* ABC, 1994.
Theresa "T. K." Keiner, "Sister Theresa," *Boy Meets World,* ABC, 1994.
Hollywood Lives, The Disney Channel, 1995.
Tiffany, "Camino High," *High Incident,* ABC, 1997.
Laura Quentin, "Something New," *ER,* NBC, 1997.
Laura Quentin, "Friendly Fire," *ER,* NBC, 1997.
Willow Mortner, "Clown without Pity," *Brooklyn South,* CBS, 1997.
Willow Mortner, "Tears on My Willow," *Brooklyn South,* CBS, 1998.
Noelle Landru, "An Education in Murder," *Diagnosis Murder,* CBS, 1998.
Eviva, "The Fourth Sister," *Charmed,* The WB, 1998.
Kiki, "20 Hours in America: Part 1," *The West Wing,* NBC, 2002.
Cohost, "Kids," *$9.99,* 2005.
Gina Carroll in 1976, "Yo, Adrian," *Cold Case,* CS, 2005.
"Teen Screamers," *Child Star Confidential,* E! Entertainment Television, 2006.
"Destiny's Child/Jonathan Brandis," *Boulevard of Broken Dreams,* E! Entertainment Television, 2007.
Dr. Phil, syndicated, 2007.
"Scotophobia," *Fear Clinic: Director Diaries,* 2010.
"Claustrophobia," *Fear Clinic: Director Diaries,* 2010.
"San Diego Comic–Con," *Fear Clinic: Director Diaries,* 2010.

Television Appearances; Specials:
Circus of the Stars Gives Kids the World, CBS, 1993.
Voice of Debbie Thornberry, *The Wild Thornberrys: The Origin of Donnie* (animated; also known as *The Origin of Donnie*), Nickelodeon, 2001.

Television Work; Series:
Provided additional voices for *The Wild Thornberrys* (animated), Nickelodeon.

Stage Appearances:
Cindy, *Civilization,* The Chandler Studio, North Hollywood, CA, 2004.

RECORDINGS

Videos:
Inside "Halloween 5," 2000.
"Halloween 4" Final Cut, 2001.
Halloween: 25 Years of Terror, Anchor Bay, 2006.
Michael Lives: The Making of "Halloween," The Weinstein Company, 2008.

Appeared in music video "The Bleeding" by Five Finger Death Punch, 2007.

Video Games:
Voice of Debbie Thornberry, *Rugrats Go Wild!,* THQ, 2003.

OTHER SOURCES

Periodicals:
Fangoria, January, 1999, pp. 20–25, 82.

HARRIS, Josie
See THACKER, Jossie

HAVINS, Alexa 1980–
(Alexa Havens)

PERSONAL

Full name, Alexa Carole Havins; born November 16, 1980, in Artesia, NM; raised in Chandler, AZ; married Justin Bruening (an actor), June 5, 2005; children: Lexington Grace. *Education:* Trained in singing at Bel Canto Studios; trained for the stage at Circle in the Square Theatre School, New York City; studied dance.

Addresses: *Agent*—The Gersh Agency, 41 Madison Ave., 33rd Floor, New York, NY 10010, and 9465 Wilshire Blvd., 6th Floor, Beverly Hills, CA 90212.

Career: Actress. Worked as a professional dancer.

Awards, Honors: Daytime Emmy Award nomination, outstanding younger actress in a drama series, and *Soap Opera Digest* Award nomination, outstanding younger lead actress, both 2005, for *All My Children.*

CREDITS

Television Appearances; Series:
Arabella "Babe" Carey Chandler, *One Life to Live* (also known as *Between Heaven and Hell, OLTL,* and *One Life to Live: The Summer of Seduction*), ABC, 2003–2005.
Arabella "Babe" Carey Chandler, *All My Children* (also known as *All My Children: The Summer of Seduction* and *La force du destin*), ABC, 2003–2007.

Television Appearances; Specials:
(In archive footage) Arabella "Babe" Carey Chandler, *SOAPnet Reveals ABC Soap Secrets,* ABC, 2004.

Television Appearances; Awards Presentations:
The 31st Annual Daytime Emmy Awards, NBC, 2004.
The 32nd Annual Daytime Emmy Awards, CBS, 2005.

Television Appearances; Episodic:
Georgia Durante, "Mafia Model," *Secret Lives,* Lifetime, 2003.
(As Alexa Havens) Gothic kid, "Halloween," *Reno 911!* (also known as *Reno 911*), Comedy Central, 2003.
Herself, "Havins/S. Damon" (also known as "Alexa Havins" and "Alexa Havins/Stuart Damon"), *Soapography,* SOAPnet, 2004.
Herself, *Extra* (also known as *Extra: The Entertainment Magazine*), syndicated, 2004.
Guest, *Soap Talk,* SOAPnet, multiple episodes, 2004.
Herself, "The Chemistry Set," *I Wanna Be a Soap Star,* SOAPnet, 2005.
Herself, "Oh Baby," *I Wanna Be a Soap Star,* SOAPnet, 2005.
Herself, *Entertainment Tonight* (also known as *Entertainment This Week, E.T., ET Weekend,* and *This Week in Entertainment*), syndicated, 2005.
Guest, *The Tony Danza Show,* syndicated, multiple episodes, 2005.
Guest, *The View,* ABC, 2005, 2006.
The talker, "Discovery," *Rescue Me* (also known as *Rescue Me: FDNY*), FX Network, 2006.
Elaine Beuliss, "In Treatment," *Law & Order: Criminal Intent* (also known as *Law & Order: CI*), USA Network, 2009.
Joannie Pogue in 1967, "The Brush Man," *Cold Case* (also known as *Anexihniastes ypothesis, Caso abierto, Cold case—affaires classees, Cold Case—Kein Opfer ist je vergessen, Doegloett aktak, Kalla spaar, Todistettavasti syyllinen,* and *Victims du passe*), CBS, 2009.
Kim Hewitt, "Dude, Where's My Groom?," *CSI: Miami* (also known as *CSI Miami* and *CSI: Weekends*), CBS, 2009.

Television Appearances; Pilots:
Appeared in *On and Off.*

Film Appearances:
Store owner, *Bank Brothers,* Maverick Entertainment Group, 2004.
(Uncredited) Interviewed fan, *Joe Killionaire,* ITN Distribution, 2005.
Samantha, *First Kiss* (short film), Big Step Productions, 2005.
Trish Unger, *Joshua,* Fangoria Magazine/Hart Sharp Video/Bedford Entertainment, 2006.
Tina, *Fat Girls,* 2006, Regent Releasing, 2007.
Blonde, *Brooklyn Rules* (also known as *Gang of Brooklyn* and *Nailed Right In*), City Lights Pictures, 2007.
Boat bride, *27 Dresses,* Twentieth Century–Fox, 2008.
(Uncredited) Fan, *Hancock* (also known as *Hidden from Earth, John Hancock,* and *Tonight, He Comes*), Columbia, 2008.
Daisy, *Desert Fox,* Negative Monkey Entertainment, 2009.
Maureen, *How to Seduce Difficult Women,* Quadrant Entertainment, 2009.
Second attractive waitress, *Old Dogs* (also known as *Daddy Sitter*), Walt Disney Studios Motion Pictures, 2009.

Lacy, *When in Rome,* Walt Disney Studios Motion Pictures, 2010.

Some sources cite appearances in other films, including an appearance as the title role in *Angie,* c. 2003; and an appearance in *The Crow: Wicked Prayer* (also known as *The Crow 4* and *Wicked Prayer*), Dimension Films, 2005.

Internet Appearances; Series:
Sarah, *Turbo Dates,* broadcast on *Fun Little Movies,* http://www.funlittlemovies.com and *Babelgum,* http://www.babelgum.com/turbodates, beginning 2008.

Stage Appearances:
Appeared as Laura Wingfield, *The Glass Menagerie;* and as Frankie Addams, *The Member of the Wedding.*

RECORDINGS

Videos:
Herself, *The Making of "Bank Brothers"* (short documentary), Madacy Entertainment/Maverick Entertainment Group, 2004.

OTHER SOURCES

Periodicals:
Soap Opera Digest, February 24, 2004, pp. 36–38, 40.

HAWKINS, Sally 1976–

PERSONAL

Born April 27, 1976, in Dulwich, England; daughter of Colin (a children's author and illustrator) and Jacqui (a children's author and illustrator) Hawkins. *Education:* Royal Academy of Dramatic Arts, London, graduated, 1998. *Avocational Interests:* Painting.

Addresses: *Agent*—International Creative Management, 10250 Constellation Way, 9th Floor, Los Angeles, CA 90067; John Grant, Conway Van Gelder, 18–21 Jermyn St., 3rd Floor, London SW1Y 6HP, England. *Manager*—Principal Entertainment, 1964 Westwood Blvd., Suite 400, Los Angeles, CA 90025.

Career: Actress.

Awards, Honors: Golden Nymph, best actress, Monte–Carlo Television Festival, 2007, and Royal Television Society award, best actress, 2008, both for *Persuasion;* Hollywood Breakthrough Award, actress of the year, Hollywood Film Festival, 2008; Spotlight Award, Mill Valley Film Festival, 2008, Silver Berlin Bear, Berlin International Film Festival, New York Film Critics Circle Award, Los Angeles Film Critics Association Award, San Francisco Film Critics Circle Award, Boston Society of Film Critics Award, Chicago Film Critics Association Award nomination, British Independent Film Award nomination, and European Film Award nomination, all best actress, 2008, Satellite Award, best actress in a motion picture comedy or musical, International Press Academy, 2008, Golden Globe Award, best actress in a motion picture comedy, 2009, National Society of Film Critics Award, London Critics Circle Film Award nomination, Empire Award nomination, Chlotrudis Award nomination, and Online Film Critics Society Award nomination, all best actress, 2009, and Peter Sellers Award for Comedy, *Evening Standard* British Film Awards, 2009, all for *Happy–Go–Lucky;* Virtuoso Award, Santa Barbara International Film Festival, 2009; Screen Actors Guild Award nomination (with others), outstanding cast in a motion picture, 2010, for *An Education.*

CREDITS

Film Appearances:
Girl at lamppost, *Post* (short film), FilmFour, 2002.
Samantha, *All or Nothing,* Metro–Goldwyn–Mayer/United Artists, 2002.
Susan, *Vera Drake,* Fine Line, 2004.
Slasher, *Layer Cake* (also known as *L4yer Cake*), Sony Pictures Classics, 2004.
Terri, *Hollow China* (short film), Soul Solution, 2006.
Kate, *Cassandra's Dream,* Weinstein Company, 2007.
Elly Carpenter, *w Delta z* (also known as *The Killing Gene* and *Waz*), Dimension Extreme, 2008.
Poppy Cross, *Happy–Go–Lucky,* Miramax, 2008.
Sarah, *An Education,* Sony Pictures Classics, 2009.
Marylin, *Desert Flower,* Majestic–Filmverleih, 2009, National Geographic Entertainment, 2011.
Maura, *Happy Ever Afters,* Hopscotch Films, 2009.
Linda, *It's a Wonderful Afterlife,* Bend It Films/Indian Film Company, 2010.
Rita O'Grady, *Made in Dagenham,* Sony Pictures Classics, 2010.
Never Let Me Go, Fox Searchlight, 2010.
Hill, *Submarine,* Optimum Releasing, 2010.
Mrs. Reed, *Jane Eyre,* Focus Features, 2011.

Television Appearances; Miniseries:
Zena Blake, *Tipping the Velvet,* BBC America, 2003.
Mary Shelley, *Byron,* BBC2, 2003, BBC America, 2005.
Sue Trinder, *Fingersmith,* BBC1, 2005.

Ella, *Twenty Thousand Streets Under the Sky,* BBC, 2005, BBC America, 2006.

Television Appearances; Movies:
Lisa, *Promoted to Glory,* ITV, 2003.
Rosalind, *The Young Visitors,* BBC1, 2003, BBC America, 2004.
Helen, *Bunk Bed Boys,* 2004.
Nathalie, *Shiny Shiny Bright New Hole in My Heart,* BBC, 2006.
Rebecca West, *H. G. Wells: War with the World,* 2006.
Anne Elliot, *Persuasion,* ITV, 2007, PBS, 2008.

Television Appearances; Episodic:
Emma Lister, "To Have and to Hold," *Casualty,* BBC1, 1999.
Sarah Carne, "Pretty Baby," *Doctors,* BBC, 2000.
"Domino Toppling," *Little Britain,* BBC America, 2003.
"Bath of Beans," *Little Britain,* BBC America, 2003.
Little Britain, BBC America, miscellaneous episodes, 2004, 2005.
Breakfast, BBC, 2005.
"Randolph Caer," *Man to Man with Dean Learner,* 2006.
Cinema 3, 2008.
(In archive footage) *Sky News: Sunrise,* Sky Television, 2009.

Television Appearances; Pilots:
The Everglades, 2007.

Television Appearances; Awards Presentations:
The 21st European Film Awards (also known as *The 2008 European Film Awards*), 2008.
Presenter, *The 14th Annual Critics' Choice Awards,* VH1, 2009.
The 66th Annual Golden Globe Awards, NBC, 2009.
Presenter, *The 67th Annual Golden Globe Awards,* NBC, 2010.

Television Work; Pilots:
Cocreator, *The Everglades,* 2007.

Stage Appearances:
Accidental Death of an Anarchist, Battersea Arts Centre, London, 1998.
Juliet, *Romeo and Juliet,* Theatre Royal, York, England, 1998.
Anya, *The Cherry Orchard,* Theatre Royal, York, 1999.
Kidnapped dog, *Svejk,* Gate Theatre, London, 1999.
Leah'le, *The Dybbuk,* Battersea Arts Centre, 1999.
Hero, *Much Ado about Nothing,* Regent's Park Open Air Theatre, London, 2000.
Hermia, *A Midsummer Night's Dream,* Regent's Park Open Air Theatre, 2000.

Zoe, *Misconceptions,* Octagon Theatre, Bolton, England, 2001.
The Way of the World, Wilton's Music Hall, London, 2003.
Lynsey Sargeant, *Country Music,* Royal Court Theatre, England, 2004.
Adela, *The House of Bernarda Alba,* Royal National Theatre, London, 2005.
Lue, *The Winterling,* Royal Court Theatre, 2006.

Also appeared in productions of *As You Like It,* Buckingham Palace, London; *Perapalas,* National Theatre Studio, London; and *The Whore of Babylon,* Globe Educational Centre.

Radio Appearances:
Voice, *Concrete Cow* (series), BBC4, 2002.
Think the Unthinkable, 2004.
War with the Newts, 2005.
The Party Line, 2005.
Ed Reardon's Week, BBC, 2005.

WRITINGS

Radio Series:
Concrete Cow, BBC4, 2002.

OTHER SOURCES

Books:
Newsmakers, Issue 4, Gale, 2009.

Periodicals:
Big Issue, April 7, 2008, pp. 13–14.
Evening Standard (London), July 29, 2010.
Telegraph Magazine (London), March 29, 2008, pp. 44–47.

HAWORTH, Jill 1945–2011
(Valerie Jill Haworth)

PERSONAL

Original name, Valerie Jill Haworth; born August 15, 1945, in Sussex, England; died January 3, 2011, in New York City. Actress. British actress Haworth, best known as the originator of the role of Sally Bowles in the musical *Cabaret,* was discovered by director Otto Preminger at the age of fourteen when she was cast as a young Jewish girl searching for her father in the in the 1960 world-war two epic *Exodus.* Haworth appeared in two other Preminger films, *The Cardinal* and *In Harm's Way* in the 1960s, followed by her leading role in the first Broadway production of *Cabaret,* which ran from 1966 to 1969. She then starred in a series of horror films, such as *Horror House* and *The Mutations,* and had a number of small roles on television series, including *Mission: Impossible, Bonanza, Baretta,* and *Vega$,* throughout the 1970s. She had a role in the 2001 comedy film *Mergers and Acquisitions.*

PERIODICALS

Guardian, January 12, 2011.
Los Angeles Times, January 9, 2011.
New York Times, January 4, 2011.
Telegraph, January 6, 2011.

HENDRIKSE, Maryke
(Maryke Hendrickse)

PERSONAL

Born in the Bahamas; immigrated to Canada at age two. *Education:* Trained as a dancer.

Career: Actress and voice artist. Performed on stage as a child in Toronto, Ontario, Canada; voice for radio presentations and commercials.

CREDITS

Television Appearances; Animated Series:
Voice of G. C., *Blaster's Universe,* CBS, 1999.
(English–language version) Voice of Anetta, *MegaMan: NT Warrior* (also known as *MegaMan: NT Warrior Axess* and *Rockman.exe;* originally broadcast in Japan in Japanese), The WB, 2001.
Voice of Hilary, *The Berenstain Bears,* PBS, 2003.
(English–language version) Voice of Myna, *Elemental gelade* (originally broadcast in Japan in Japanese), 2005.
Voice of Susan Test, *Johnny Test,* The WB, 2005–10.
(English–language version) Voice of Mitani's sister, *Hikaru no go* (originally broadcast in Japan in Japanese), Toonami, 2006.
(English–language version) Voice of Revy, *Black Lagoon* (also known as *Black Lagoon: The Second Barrage* and *Burakku ragun;* originally broadcast in Japan in Japanese), 2006.
(English–language version) Voice of Tabby, *.hack//Roots* (originally broadcast in Japan in Japanese), Cartoon Network, 2006.
Voice of Yasmin, *Bratz,* 2007.

(English–language version) Voice of Bubbles, *Demashita! Powerpuff Girls Z* (originally broadcast in Japan in Japanese), Cartoon Network, 2007.
Voice of Hideki, *Sushi Pack,* CBS, 2007.
Voice of Jenny, *Monster Buster Club,* Toon Disney, 2008.

Television Appearances; Animated Episodes:
Voice of first village girl, "Phaeton: The Chariot of Fire," *Mythic Warriors: Guardians of the Legend,* CBS, 1999.
Voice of Betty Butterworth, "The Good Old Days," *Moville Mysteries,* YTV, 2002.
Voices of Hannah and mirror, "Hannah and the Mirror," *Moville Mysteries,* YTV, 2002.
Voice of hot dog vendor, "Stupid over Cupid," *6Teen,* Teletoon, 2005.
(English–language version) Voice of Thunderblast, "Balance," *Transformers: Cybertron* (originally broadcast in Japan in Japanese), Cartoon Network and the WB, 2006.
(English–language version) Voice of Thunderblast, "Fury," *Transformers: Cybertron* (originally broadcast in Japan in Japanese), Cartoon Network and the WB, 2006.
Voice of Echo, "The Last Word," *Class of the Titans,* Teletoon, 2006.

Also voice of Genesis, "Genesis," *Braceface,* ABC Family; (English–language version) voice of Tsukiyomi, "The Great Duel at Shoun Falls" and "Eternal Love: The Naginata of Kenkon," *Inuyasha* (originally broadcast in Japan in Japanese), Cartoon Network; and voice of princess, "The Royal Rescue Hero," *Rescue Heroes* (also known as *Rescue Heroes: Global Response Team*), CBS.

Television Appearances; Live–Action Episodes:
Brooke, "More than Meets the Eye," *My Secret Identity,* syndicated, 1990.
Auditioner, "The Resurrection of May," *Wind at My Back,* CBC (later broadcast by Odyssey), 1996.

Film Appearances:
Married to It, 1991, Orion, 1993.
(English–language version) Voice of Miss Takamizawa, *Tetsujin 28* (animated; also known as *Tetsujin niju–nachigo;* originally broadcast in Japan in Japanese), 2005.
Nami, *Nana,* subtitled version, Viz Pictures, 2008.
Voice of tour guide Tammy, *The Legend of Silk Boy* (animated), 2010.

RECORDINGS

Animated Videos:
(English–language version) Voice of Lunamaria Hawke, *Kido senshi Gundam Seed Destiny* (also known as

Gundam Seed Destiny; originally broadcast in Japan as a Japanese television series), Bandai Entertainment, 2006.

Voices of Brights Brightly and second unicorn, *My Little Pony: A Very Pony Place,* Paramount Home Video, 2006.

Voice of Brights Brightly, *My Little Pony: The Runaway Rainbow,* 2006.

Voice of Regen, *Barbie Diaries,* Lions Gate Films Home Entertainment, 2006.

Voice of Yasmin, *Bratz: Babyz the Movie,* Fox Home Video, 2006.

(As Maryke Hendrickse) Voices of Lucia the Watilla and Sam Gilmore, *Dreamfall: The Longest Journey* (video game), Aspyr Media, 2007.

Voice of Yasmin, *Bratz: Super Babyz,* MGA Entertainment, 2007.

Voice of Amy Morris, *Holly Hobbie and Friends: Fabulous Fashion Show,* Sony Pictures Home Entertainment, 2008.

Voice of Melody, *Barbie and the Diamond Castle,* Universal Studios Home Entertainment, 2008.

Voices of Amy Morris and Nicky, *Holly Hobbie and Friends: Marvelous Makeover,* Sony Wonder, 2009.

Voice of Hadley, *Barbie in a Mermaid Tale,* Universal Studios Home Entertainment, 2010.

Voices of Teresa and others, *Barbie: A Fashion Fairytale,* Universal Studios Home Entertainment, 2010.

(English–language version) Voice of Sekimi, *The Girl Who Leapt through Time* (also known as *Toki o kakeru shojo;* originally broadcast in Japan in Japanese), Bandai Entertainment.

OTHER SOURCES

Electronic:

Toonarific Web Site, http://www.toonarific.com, October 13, 2010.

HENNER, Marilu 1952–

PERSONAL

Born April 6, 1952, in Chicago, IL; daughter of Joseph (a car salesman) and Loretta (a dance instructor) Henner; married Frederic Forrest (an actor), September 28, 1980 (divorced, 1982); married Rob Lieberman (a producer), 1990 (divorced, 2001); married Michael Brown, December 21, 2006; children: (second marriage) Nicholas Morgan, Joseph Marlon, two stepchildren. *Education:* Attended University of Chicago, c. 1969–72.

Addresses: *Agent*—William Morris Agency, 151 El Camino Dr., Beverly Hills, CA 90212. *Publicist*—Guttman Associates PR, 118 South Beverly Dr., Beverly Hills, CA 90212.

Career: Actress and producer. Appeared in television commercial for Wisk detergent, 1976.

Awards, Honors: Golden Globe Award nominations, best television actress in a supporting role, 1979, 1980, 1981, 1982, 1983, for *Taxi;* Joseph Jefferson Award, for *Annie Get Your Gun;* CableACE Award nomination, actress in a theatrical or dramatic special, 1987, for *Grown–Ups.*

CREDITS

Television Appearances; Series:

Elaine Nardo, *Taxi,* ABC, 1978–82, then NBC, 1982–83.

Match Game 73 (also known as *Match Game 78*), 1978.

Ava Evans Newton, *Evening Shade* (also known as *Arkansas*), CBS, 1990–94.

The Legend of Prince Valiant (animated), The Family Channel, 1991.

Host, *Marilu* (talk show), syndicated, 1994–95.

Guest panelist (20 episodes), *The Hollywood Squares,* syndicated, 1999–2004.

I Love the 80's 3–d, VH1, 2005.

I Love the '70s: Volume 2, VH1, 2006.

Host, *America's Ballroom Challenge,* 2006–2007.

Dancing With the Stars (also known as *D.W.T.S.*), ABC, 2006–2007.

The Apprentice (also known as *Celebrity Apprentice, The Apprentice 2, The Apprentice Los Angeles,* and *The Celebrity Apprentice*), NBC, 2008.

Television Appearances; Movies:

Laura Griffith, *Dream House,* CBS, 1981.

Victoria Ducane, *Love with a Perfect Stranger,* Showtime, 1986.

Freddy Grand, *Grand Larceny,* Lifetime, 1988.

Samantha Flannery, *Ladykillers,* ABC, 1988.

Jackie, *Chains of Gold,* 1991.

Nancy Conn, *Fight for Justice: The Nancy Conn Story,* 1995.

Mrs. Debbie Challender, *For the Children: The Irvine Fertility Scandal* (also known as *For the Future: The Irvine Fertility Scandal*), Lifetime, 1996.

Margaret Sutter, *My Son Is Innocent,* ABC, 1996.

Voice of Veronica Vreeland, *Batman & Mr. Freeze: Sub-Zero* (animated), The WB, 1998.

Miranda, *A Tale of Two Bunnies* (also known as *The Price of Beauty*), 2000.

Meg Baker, *Rocket's Red Glare* (also known as *The Mercury Project*), Fox Family, 2000.

Carol, *Love Rules!,* ABC, 2004.
Joint Custody, 2005.
Sydney Lake, *Good Behavior,* ABC, 2008.
Ann Danville, *The Governor's Wife,* Lifetime, 2008.

Also appeared in *The Blair Family Story,* Fox.

Television Appearances; Miniseries:
Margaret "Molly" Brown, *Titanic,* CBS, 1996.
Nancy Gordon, *Gone But Not Forgotten* (also known as *Phillip Margolin's "Gone But Not Forgotten"*), Lifetime, 2004.

Television Appearances; Pilots:
Janet, a student, *Off Campus,* CBS, 1977.
Ashley Walters, *Stark,* CBS, 1985.
Susan McDowell, *Channel 99,* NBC, 1988.
Marilu Henner, *The Comeback,* HBO, 2005.

Television Appearances; Specials:
Celebrity interviewer, *The Celebrity Football Classic,* NBC, 1979.
Nurse Girard, "Mr. Roberts," *NBC Live Theatre,* NBC, 1984.
Louise, *Grown Ups,* Showtime, 1985.
Host, *CBS All–American Thanksgiving Parade,* CBS, 1993.
Host, *Best of Taxi* (also known as *Hey Taxi*), CBS, 1994, *A Comedy Salute to Andy Kaufman,* 1995.
Comic Relief VII, HBO, 1995.
Disney's Most Unlikely Heroes, ABC, 1996.
Host, *We're Having a Baby!,* ABC, 1996.
Broadway '97: Launching the Tonys, PBS, 1997.
Macy's 21st Annual Fourth of July Fireworks Spectacular, 1997.
Andy Kaufman: The E! True Hollywood Story, E! Entertainment Television, 1998.
Broadway '98: Launching the Tony Awards, PBS, 1998.
Bob Fosse: The E! True Hollywood Story, E! Entertainment Television, 1999.
Celebrity Profile: Marilu Henner, 1999.
Stars Over Mississippi, with Prince Edward, PBS, 1999.
Intimate Portrait: Marilu Henner, 1999.
Andy Kaufman's Really Big Show, 1999.
Burt Reynolds: The E! True Hollywood Story, E! Entertainment Television, 2000.
Cohost, *Monaco Dancesport Championships,* Lifetime, 2001.
Host, *Latin Dancesport Championships,* Lifetime, 2001.
ABC's 50th Anniversary Bloopers Celebration, ABC, 2003.
A Life of Laughter: Remembering John Ritter, ABC, 2003.
Boomer Nation, Arts & Entertainment, 2004.
Mississippi Rising, 2005.
I Love the Holidays, VH1, 2005.
Great Things About the Holidays, Bravo, 2005.

National Health Test with Bryant Gumbel, NBC, 2006.
CMT: The Greatest–20 Sexiest Videos of 2006, Country Music Television, 2006.

Television Appearances; Awards Presentations:
The … Annual Primetime Emmy Awards Presentation, Fox, 1991, 1992.
The 17th Annual People's Choice Awards, CBS, 1991.
The … Annual Golden Globe Awards, TBS, 1993, 1995.
The … Annual Tony Awards, 1997, 1998.
The 25th International Emmy Awards, 1998.
The 1998 Creative Arts Emmy Awards, TV Land, 1998.
The 8th Annual TV Land Awards, TV Land, 2010.

Television Appearances; Episodic:
Susu, "Great Expectations," *The Paper Chase,* CBS, 1978.
Host, *The Midnight Special,* 1981.
Saturday Night Live, NBC, 1982.
Fridays, two episodes, 1982.
Claire, "Method Actor," *Alfred Hitchcock Presents,* NBC, 1985.
"Seductive Neighbor," *Who's the Boss?,* ABC, 1986.
Diane Wilmington, "Angela's New Best Friend," *Who's the Boss?,* ABC, 1986.
Pregnant woman overdue number three, "Segment: My Baby," *The Tracey Ullman Show,* 1989.
Voice of Veronica Vreeland, "Birds of a Feather," *Batman: The Animated Series* (animated), 1993.
Voice of Veronica Vreeland, "The Worry Men," *Batman: The Animated Series* (animated), 1993.
Late Show with David Letterman (also known as *Letterman* and *The Late Show*), CBS, 1993, 1997, 2001.
Voice of Veronica Vreeland, "Harley's Holiday," *Batman: The Animated Series* (animated), 1994.
Terry Belmont, "Since I Lost My Baby," *Cybill,* CBS, 1995.
Voice of Veronica Vreeland, "Catwalk," *Batman: The Animated Series* (animated), 1995.
"The Cameo Episode," *George & Leo,* CBS, 1997.
Voice of Veronica Vreeland, "Holiday Knights," *Batman: Gotham Knights* (animated), 1997.
Voice of Veronica Vreeland, "Chemistry," *Batman: Gotham Knights* (animated), 1998.
At Home With …, HGTV, 1999.
The Test, FX Network, 2001.
Georgia, "Great Expectations," *Providence,* NBC, 2002.
Georgia, "Things Have Changed," *Providence,* NBC, 2002.
Maggie Demontague, "Blah Bowls," *Greg the Bunny,* Fox, 2002.
"John Travolta," *Revealed with Jules Asner,* E! Entertainment Television, 2003.
"Bully the Kid," *Andy Richter Controls the Universe,* Fox, 2004.
Sharon Singleton, "Alarmed and Dangerous," *Center of the Universe,* 2004.

Donna Martin, "Riley's Parents," *Living with Fran*, The WB, 2005.

Marilu Henner, "Valerie Does Another Classic Leno," *The Comeback*, HBO, 2005.

"Small Screen, Big Stars," *TV Land's Top Ten*, TV Land, 2005.

"Greatest TV Romances," *TV Land's Top Ten*, TV Land, 2005.

"Sexiest Men," *TV Land's Top Ten*, TV Land, 2005.

"When Real Life and Screen Life Collide," *TV Land Confidential* (also known as *TV Land Confidential: The Untold Stories*), TV Land, 2005.

"Being Bad Behind the Scenes," *TV Land Confidential* (also known as *TV Land Confidential: The Untold Stories*), TV Land, 2005.

"Shape Up from the Inside Out," *Shape Up Your Life* (also known as *Marilu Henner's Shape Up Your Life*), 2005.

Grease: You're the One That I Want!, NBC, 2007.

Entertainment Tonight (also known as *E.T.* and *This Week in Entertainment*), syndicated, multiple episodes, 2007–10.

Elaine O'Connor–Nardo, *The O'Reilly Factor*, Fox News, 2008.

"Marilu Henner," *Who Are You Wearing*, The Learning Channel, 2008.

Melinda, *Roommates*, ABC Family, 2008.

"The Top Three Finalists Perform," *American Idol* (also known as *American Idol: The Search for a Superstar* and *Idol*), Fox, 2008.

Pamela Newman, "John, Cougar, Newman Camp," *My Boys*, TBS, 2008.

Linda, "And in the End," *ER*, NBC, 2009.

Pepper McMasters, "Pepper McMasters Singles Seminar," *Party Down*, Starz!, 2009.

Doc Talk, Documentary Channel, 2010.

Regina Landers, "And the Winner Is ...," *Numb3rs* (also known as *Num3ers*), 2010.

Television Talk Show Guest Appearances; Episodic:

Late Night with David Letterman, NBC, 1982, 1985, 1989, 1990.

The Tonight Show Starring Johnny Carson, NBC, 1990, 1991, 1992.

The Tonight Show with Jay Leno, NBC, 1992, 1993, 2008.

Late Night with Conan O'Brien, 1995, 1998.

The Daily Show with Jon Stewart (also known as *The Daily Show, A Daily Show with Jon Stewart*, and *The Daily Show with Jon Stewart Global Edition*), 1996, 1997, 1998.

Howard Stern, 1997.

The Rosie O'Donnell Show, syndicated, 1997, 1998, 1999.

The Martin Short Show, syndicated, 1999.

Politically Incorrect (also known as *P.I.*), 2001.

The View, ABC, 2001, 2002.

The Tony Danza Show, syndicated, 2004, 2005.

Today (also known as *NBC News Today* and *The Today Show*), NBC, 2004, 2008.

The Late Late Show with Craig Ferguson, CBS, 2005.

CW 11 Morning News (also known as *The WB 11 Morning News*), The CW, 2008.

Jimmy Kimmel Live!, ABC, 2008.

Ellen: The Ellen DeGeneres Show, syndicated, 2009.

Television Executive Producer; Series:

Marilu, syndicated, 1994–95.

Medicine Ball, Fox, 1995.

Television Producer; Series:

Shape Up Your Life (also known as *Marilu Henner's "Shape Up Your Life"*), 2005.

Television Executive Producer; Movies:

Abandoned and Deceived, 1995.

A Vision of Murder: The Story of Donielle, CBS, 2000.

Film Appearances:

(Film debut) Danielle, *Between the Lines*, Midwest Film, 1977.

Annette, *Blood Brothers* (also known as *A Father's Love*), Warner Bros., 1978.

Kit Conger and Sue Alabama, *Hammett*, Orion/Warner Bros., 1982.

Agnes Chapman, *The Man Who Loved Women*, Columbia, 1983.

Sister Betty, *Cannonball Run II*, Warner Bros., 1983.

Lil, *Johnny Dangerously*, Twentieth Century–Fox, 1984.

Sally, *Perfect*, Columbia, 1984.

Miss Tracy, *Rustlers' Rhapsody* (also known as *Esos locos cuatreros*), Paramount, 1985.

"Freddy" Grand, *Grand Larceny*, 1987.

Jackie, *Chains of Gold*, 1991.

Trudi, *L.A. Story*, TriStar, 1991.

Belinda Blair/Flavia Brent, *Noises Off ...*, Buena Vista, 1992.

Herself, *I'm From Hollywood*, 1992.

Lil (This Is The Life), *The Weird Al Yankovic Video Library: His Greatest Hits*, 1992.

Voice of Veronica Vreeland, *Batman: Mask of the Phantasm* (animated; also known as *Batman: Mask of the Phantasm: The Animated Movie, Batman: The Animated Movie*, and *Mask of the Phantasm: Batman the Animated Movie*), 1993.

Katie, *Chasers*, Warner Bros., 1994.

Lil, "This Is the Life," *Weird Al Yankovic: The Videos*, 1996.

Voice of Veronica Vreeland, *SubZero* (animated; also known as *Batman & Mr. Freeze: SubZero* and *Subzero*), 1998.

Mrs. Stuart While, *The Titanic Chronicles*, 1999.

Herself/Elaine Nardo, *Man on the Moon* (also known as *Der Mondmann*), MCA/Universal, 1999.

Mother, *Lost in the Pershing Point Hotel,* Northern Arts Entertainment, 2000.

Dani, *Enemies of Laughter,* Eternity Pictures, 2000.

Lil, "This Is The Life," *Weird Al Yankovic: The Ultimate Video Collection,* Volcano Entertainment Group, 2003.

Stage Appearances:

Marty, *Grease,* Royale Theatre, New York City, 1972. (Broadway debut) Donna, *Over Here!,* Shubert Theatre, 1974.

Marilu, *Pal Joey,* Circle in the Square, New York City, 1976.

Sonia Walsk, *They're Playing Our Song,* Burt Reynolds' Dinner Theatre, Jupiter, FL, 1984.

Barbara Kahn, *Social Security,* Ethel Barrymore Theatre, New York City, 1987.

Roxie Hart, *Chicago,* Broadway production, 1997.

The Tale of the Allergist's Wife, Broadway production, 2002.

Also appeared in *Carnal Knowledge,* Los Angeles; *Super Sunday; Grown–Ups; Once upon a Mattress; The Roar of the Greasepaint, the Smell of the Crowd.*

Major Tours:

Grease, U.S. cities, 1971.

Annie Get Your Gun, U.S. cities, 2000.

RECORDINGS

Videos:

American Idol: Unauthorized, Crystal Entertainment Group, 2007.

WRITINGS

Books:

(With Jim Jerome) *By All Means Keep on Moving* (autobiography), Pocket Books, 1994.

(With Laura Morton) *Marilu Henner's Total Health Makeover,* 1998.

(With Morton) *The 30 Day Total Health Makeover,* 2001.

I Refuse to Raise a Brat: Straightforward Advice on Parenting in an Age of Overindulgence, 1999.

(With Lorin Henner) *Healthy Life Kitchen,* 2000.

(With Lorin Henner) *Healthy Kids: Help Them Eat Smart and Stay Active,* 2001.

Wear Your Life Well: Use What You Have to Get What You Want, 2008.

Television Series:

Shape Up Your Life (also known as *Marilu Henner's "Shape Up Your Life"*), 2005.

OTHER SOURCES

Periodicals:

Redbook, April, 1993, p. 32.

WWD, October 9, 1997, p. 19.

HERZOG, Werner 1942–

PERSONAL

Original name, Werner H. Stipetic; born September 5, 1942, in Munich (some sources say Sachrang), Germany; son of Elizabeth Herzog; married Martje Grohmann (a journalist and actress), 1967 (divorced, 1987); married Christine Ebenberger, August 19, 1989, (divorced, 1994); married Lena, 1999; children: Rudolph Amos Herzog, Hanna Mattes. *Education:* Attended University of Munich, University of Pittsburgh, and Duquesne University.

Addresses: *Agent*—International Creative Management, 8942 Wilshire Blvd., Beverly Hills, CA 90211; Gersh, 9465 Wilshire Blvd., 6th Floor, Beverly Hills, CA 90212.

Career: Director, producer, writer, and actor. Werner Herzog Filmproduktion, founder, 1963; Werner Herzog Foundation, founder; staged several operas. Worked for National Aeronautics and Space Administration (NASA), 1966; previously worked as a dockworker in Manchester, England; and steel factory worker, parking lot attendant, and rodeo hand, Pittsburgh, PA.

Awards, Honors: Oberhausen Film Festival Prize, 1968, for *Letzte Worte;* Bundesfilmpreis Award and Silver Berlin Bear Award, best first film, Golden Berlin Bear Award nomination, Berlin International Film Festival, Filmstrip in Silver, outstanding feature film, German Film Awards, 1968, all for *Lebenszeichen;* Interfilm Award, 1971, for *Land des Scheweigens und der Dunkelheit;* FIPRESCI, Grand Prize of the Jury, Prize of the Ecumenical Jury, Golden Palm Award nomination, Cannes International Film Festival, Film Strip in Silver, best shaping of a feature film, German Film Awards, 1975, all for *Jeder fuer sich und gott gegen alle;* Cesar Award nomination, best foreign film, Critics Award, best foreign film, French Syndicate of Cinema Critics, 1976, both for *Aguirre, der zorn gottes;* German Film Critics Prize, 1977, for *Stroszek;* Rauriser Literaturpreis, 1978, for *Vom Gehen im Eis;* Special Mention Award, Cracow Film Festival, Film Strip in Silver, outstanding short film, German Film Awards, 1978, for *La soufriere;* Golden Palm Award nomination, Cannes Film Festival, 1979, Silver Guild Film Award, Guild of German Art

House Cinemas, 1981, for *Woyzeck;* Golden Berlin Bear Award nomination, 1979, for *Nosferatu: Phantom der Nacht;* Best Director Award and Golden Palm Award nomination, Cannes International Film Festival, OCIC Award, San Sebastian International Film Festival, 1982, Film Award nomination, best foreign language film, British Academy of Film and Television Arts, 1983, Gold Guild Film Award, German film, Guild of German Art House Cinemas, 1984, all for *Fitzcarraldo;* Golden Palm Award nomination, Cannes Film Festival, 1984, for *Wo die gruenen Ameisen traeumen;* Bavarian Film Award (with Lucki Stipetic), best production, 1988, for *Cobra Verde;* Filmcritica "Bastone Bianco" Award—Special Mention, Venice Film Festival, 1990, for *Echos aus einem dusteren Reich;* Golden Osella Award, Venice Film Festival, 1991, for *Cerro Torre: Schrei aus Stein;* Prize of the City of Hof, Hof International Filmdays, 1993; Grand Prix, Melbourne International Film Festival, 1993, for *Lektionen in Finsternis;* Special Jury Award, Amsterdam International Documentary Film Festival, 1997, International Documentary Association Award (with others), best feature documentary, 1998, Emmy Award nomination (with others), outstanding nonfiction special, Golden Spire Award, television—history, San Francisco International Film Festival, Sierra Award nomination, best documentary, Las Vegas Film Critics Society, Silver FIPA Award, documentary and essay, Biarritz International Festival of Audiovisual Programming, 1999, all for *Little Dieter Needs to Fly;* Audience Award, best documentary, Sao Paulo International Film Festival, European Film Awards nomination, best documentary award, 1999, both for *Mein liebster feind–Klaus Kinski;* Dragon of Dragons Honorary Award, Cracow Film Festival, 2002; Gotham Award nomination, best documentary, Los Angeles Film Critics Association Award, best documentary/non–fiction film, New Visions Award—Special Mention, Sitges Catalonian International Film Festival, Alfred P. Sloan Feature Film Prize and Grand Jury Prize nomination, Sundance Film Festival, 2005, Independent Spirit Award nomination, best documentary, Independent Features Project/West, Chlotrudis Award nomination, best director, Directors Guild of America, outstanding directorial achievement in documentary, 2006, for *Grizzly Man;* Best Film Award nomination and Carnet Jove Special Mention Award, Sitges Catalonian International Film Festival, FIPRESCI Prize Award, parallel sections, Venice Film Festival, 2005, Best Film Award nomination, Mar del Plata Film Festival, 2006, for *The Wild Blue Yonder;* Outstanding Achievement Award, Hot Docs Canadian International Documentary Festival; Gotham Award nomination, best documentary, 2008, Academy Award nomination (with Henry Kaiser), best documentary—features, Independent Spirit Award nomination, best documentary, 2009, for *Encounters at the End of the World;* Career Award, Sant Jordi Awards, 2009; Golden Lion Award nomination, Venice Film Festival, 2009, for *My Son, My Son, What Have Ye Done;* Christopher D. Smithers Foundation Special Award and Golden Lion Award nomination, Venice Film Festival, 2009, Chlotrudis Award nomination, best director,

Dublin Film Critics Special Jury Prize, Dublin International Film Festival, 2010, for *The Bad Lieutenant: Port of Call—New Orleans.*

CREDITS

Film Producer and Director:
(And sound and editor) *Herakles* (short film) 1962.
(And editor) *Spiel im sand* (also known as *Playing in the Sand* and *Game in the Sand;* uncompleted), 1964.
(And editor) *Die beispiellose verteidigung der festung Deutschkreuz* (also known as *The Unparalleled Defense of the Fortress of Deutschkreuz*), Werner Herzog Filmproduktion, 1966.
Letzte Worte (short film; also known as *Last Words*), Werner Herzog Filmproduktion, 1968.
Lebenszeichen, Werner Herzog Filmproduktion, 1968, released in the United States as *Signs of Life,* New Yorker, 1981.
Massnahmen gegen fanatiker (also known as *Measures Against Fanatics* and *Precautions Against Fanatics*), Werner Herzog Filmproduktion, 1969.
Auch Zwerge haben klein angefangen (also known as *Even Dwarfs Started Small*), New Line Cinema, 1970.
(And sound) *Behinderte Zukunft* (documentary; also known as *Frustrated Future, Handicapped Future,* and *Impeded Future*), Werner Herzog Filmproduktion, 1970.
(And sound) *Fata Morgana,* Werner Herzog Filmproduktion, 1970.
(And sound) *Land des schweigens und der dunkelheit* (documentary; also known as *Land of Silence and Darkness*), New Yorker, 1971.
(And sound) *Aguirre, der zorn Gottes,* 1973, released in the United States as *Aguirre, the Wrath of God,* 1977.
Die grosse ekstase des bildschnitzers Steiner (short documentary; also known as *The Great Ecstasy of the Sculptor Steiner* and *The Strange Ecstasy of Woodcarver Steiner*), New Yorker, 1974.
Jeder fuer sich und Gott gegen alle (also known as *Every Man for Himself and God Against All, The Enigma of Kaspar Hauser,* and *The Mystery of Kaspar Hauser*), Cine International/Cinema V, 1974.
(And sound) *How Much Wood Would a Woodchuck Chuck?* (short documentary), Werner Herzog Filmproduktion, 1976.
Mit mir will keiner spielen (short film; also known as *No One Will Play with Me* and *Nobody Wants to Play With Me*), Werner Herzog Filmproduktion, 1976.
Herz aus glas (also known as *Heart of Glass*), Cine International Filmvertrieb, 1976.
Stroszek, Werner Herzog Filmproduktion, 1977.
(And sound) *La soufriere* (short documentary), New Yorker, 1977.

Nosferatu–Phantom der nacht (also known as *Nosferatu, the Vampire, Nosferatu—fantome de la nuit, Nosferatu the Vampyre,* and *Nosferatu, Phantom of the Night*), Twentieth Century–Fox, 1979.

Werner Herzog's "Woyzeck" (also known as *Woyzeck*), Werner Herzog Filmproduktion, 1979.

Huie's Predigt (short documentary; also known as *Huie's Sermon*), New Yorker, 1980.

Fitzcarraldo, New World, 1982.

Ballade vom kleinen soldaten (also known as *Ballad of the Little Soldier*), New Yorker, 1984.

Gasherbrum—Der leuchtende berg (documentary; also known as *The Dark Glow of the Mountains*), New Yorker, 1984.

Echos aus einem duesteren reich (also known as *Echo d'un sombre empire* and *Echoes from a Somber Empire*), 1990.

Lektionen in Finsternis (also known as *Lessons in Darkness*), 1992.

Bells from the Deep: Faith and Superstition in Russia (also known as *Glocken aus der tiefe*), 1993.

Little Dieter Needs to Fly, 1997.

Invincible (also known as *Unbesiegbar*), Fine Line, 2001.

Pilgrimage, 2001.

"Ten Thousand Years Older," *Ten Minutes Older: The Trumpet,* 2002.

Wheel of Time, 2002.

The White Diamond, Fandango, 2004.

Rescue Dawn, Metro–Goldwyn–Meyer, 2006.

Nosferatu, 2008.

My Son, My Son, What Have Ye Done, First Look, 2009.

Film Director:

Glaube und wahrung (also known as *God's Angry Man*), New Yorker, 1980.

Werner Herzog Eats His Shoe (short film), Les Blank, 1980.

Wo die gruenen ameisen traeumen (also known as *Where the Green Ants Dream*), Orion, 1985.

Portrait Werner Herzog, 1986.

Cobra Verde (also known as *Slave Coast*), De Laurentiis Entertainment Group, 1988.

Les gauloises, 1988.

Herdsmen of the Sun (documentary; also known as *Wodaabe–Die Hirten der Sonne. Nomaden am sudrand der shara, Wodaabe, les bergers du soleil,* and *Wodaabe: Herdsman of the Sun*), Interama, 1989.

Schrei aus Stein (also known as *Cerro Torre: Schrei aus Stein, Cerro Torre–Scream of Stone, Cerro Torre, le cri de la roche,* and *Scream of Stone*), 1991.

Mexico, 1999.

Mein liebster feind—Klaus Kinski (also known as *25. tunti: Klaus Kinski* and *My Best Friend*), New Yorker Films, 1999.

Grizzly Man, Lions Gate Films, 2005.

The Wild Blue Yonder, Fandango, 2005.

Encounters at the End of the World, Image Entertainment, 2007.

Cobra Verde, 518 Media, 2007.

The Bad Lieutenant: Port of Call—New Orleans (also known as *Bad Lieutenant: Port of Call New Orleans* and *Bad Lieutenant*), First Look, 2009.

La boheme, Sky Arts, 2009.

The Cave, Werner Herzog Filmproduktion, 2010.

Film Producer:

Wo die grunen ameisen traumen, 1984.

The Making of "Hulk," Universal Studios Home Video, 2003.

Incident at Loch Ness, 2004.

Film Work:

Sound, *Herakles,* 1962.

Sound, *Massnahmen gegen fanatiker,* 1969.

Encounters at the End of the World, 2007.

Film Appearances:

Himself, *NDF–Report,* 1966.

Soldat, *Lebenszeichen* (also known as *Signs of Life*), 1968.

Geschichten vom kuebelkind, 1970.

Narrator, *Die grobe ekstase des bildschnitzers Steiner,* 1974.

(Uncredited) Glass carrier, *Herz aus Glas* (also known as *Heart of Glass*), Cine International Filmvertrieb, 1976.

Narrator, *La soufriere* (short documentary), New Yorker, 1977.

Himself, *Was Ich bin, sind meine filme* (documentary; also known as *I Am My Films: A Portrait of Werner Herzog, I Am My Films,* and *I Am What My Films Are*), Filmwelt verleib/New Yorker, 1978.

Monk, *Nosferatu—Phantom der nacht* (also known as *Nosferatu, the Vampire* and *Nosferatu, Phantom of the Night*), Twentieth Century–Fox, 1979.

The Making of "Nosferatu" (also known as *Werner Herzog Talks About the Making of His New Film "Nosferatu the Vampyre"*), 1979.

Himself, *Garlic Is As Good As Ten Mothers,* Les Blank, 1980.

Himself, *Werner Herzog Eats His Shoe* (short film), Les Blank, 1980.

Burden of Dreams (documentary about the making of *Fitzcarraldo;* also known as *Die Last der traume*), Contemporary Films Ltd., 1982.

Werner Herzog in Peru (short film), Les Blank, 1982.

Chambre 666 (documentary; also known as *Chambre 666 n'importe quand ...* and *Room 666*), Gray City, 1982.

Narrator, *Ballade vom kleinen soldaten* (also known as *Ballad of the Little Soldier*), New Yorker, 1983.

The father, *Man of Flowers,* International Spectrafilm, 1984.

Himself, *Tokyo–Ga* (documentary), Filmverlag der Autoren, 1984.

Lawyer, *Wo die grunen ameisen traumen,* 1984.

Portrait Werner Herzog, 1986.

Gemeindeschreiber Businger, *Gekauftes Glueck* (also known as *Bride of the Orient* and *La fiancee thailandaise*), 1988.

Mita, *Hard to Be a God* (also known as *Es ist nicht leicht ein Gott zu sein, Trudno Byt Bogom,* and *Un dieu rebelle*), 1989.

Lightning Over Braddock: A Rustbowl Fantasy, Zeitgeist, 1989.

Echos aus einem dusteren reich, 1990.

Himself, *Schneeweissrosenrot* (also known as *SnowwhiteRosered*), 1991.

TV–Regisseur, *Cerro Torre: Schrei aus stein* (also known as *Cerro Torre Scream of Stone*), 1991.

Brennendes Herz (also known as *Burning Heart*), 1995.

The Night of the Film–makers, 1995.

Narrator, *Little Dieter Needs to Fly,* 1997.

Face, *What Dreams May Come,* PolyGram Filmed Entertainment, 1998.

Himself, *Mein liebster feind–Klaus Kinski* (also known as *25.tunti: Klaus Kinski* and *My Best Friend*), 1999.

Himself, *Der Ball ist ein sauhund,* 1999.

Father, *Julien Donkey–Boy* (also known as *Dogme #6–Julien Donkey–Boy* and *Julien Donkey–Boy*), Fine Line, 1999.

Der Letzte Dokumentarfilm, 1999.

A Brief History of Errol Morris, 2000.

Klaus Kinski—Ich bin kein Schauspieler, 2000.

Curtain puller/spectator, *Invincible,* 2001.

Himself, *Der Boxprinz* (also known as *The Boxing Prince*), 2002.

Wheel of Time, 2003.

Dribble (short film), Troma Team Video, 2004.

Incident at Loch Ness, Twentieth Century–Fox, 2004.

Narrator, *The White Diamond,* Fandango, 2004.

Narrator, *Grizzly Man,* Lions Gate Films, 2005.

Perpetuum mobile—Voces en el espacio azul (short film), 2005.

Walking to Werner, Linas Films, 2006.

All in This Tea, Flower Films, 2007.

Encounters at the End of the World, 2007.

Pierre Rissient: Man of Cinema (also known as *Man of Cinema: Pierre Rissient*), DeepFocus Productions, 2007.

Bierbichler, Real Fiction, 2007.

Father Umbrillo, *Mister Lonely,* Canana Films, 2007.

The German, *The Grand,* Anchor Bay, 2007.

Gegenschuss—Aufbruch der filmemacher (also known as *Reverse Angle: Rebellion of the Filmmakers*), Kinowelt Fimverleih, 2008.

BLAST!, Louise Rosen, 2008.

Capturing Reality (also known as *Capturing Reality: The Art of Documentary*), First Run Features, 2008.

Monk, *Nosferatu,* 2008.

The Lonely, O'Salvation, 2009.

Narrator, *Plastic Bag,* Gigantic Pictures, 2009.

Narrator, *The Cave,* Werner Herzog Filmproduktion, 2010.

Television Work; Specials:

Producer, *Location Africa,* 1987.

Opera director and director, *Giovanna d'Arco,* 1989.

Coproducer and director, *Wodaabe: Herdsmen of the Sun* (also known as *Wodaabe—Die Hirten der sonne. Nomaden am sudrand der Sahara*), 1989.

Opera director, *Lohengrin,* 1991.

Opera director and director, *La donna del lago,* 1992.

Producer and director, *Lessons of Darkness* (documentary; also known as *Lektionen in Finsternis*), The Discovery Channel, 1992.

Director, *Die Verwandlung der welt in musik: Bayreuth vor der premiere,* 1996.

Director, *Julianes Sturz in den dschungel* (also known as *Wings of Hope*), 2000.

Television Work; Movies:

Sound, *Die fliegenden Arzte von Ostafrika,* 1969.

Sound, *Handicapped Future* (also known as *Behinderte Zukunft?*), 1971.

Television Director; Movies:

Die fliegenden aarzte von Ostafrika (short documentary; also known as *The Flying Doctors of East Africa*), 1969.

God's Angry Man, 1980.

Glaube und Waehrung, 1980.

Jag Mandir: Das excentrische privattheater des Maharadscha von Udaipur, 1991.

The Transformation of the World into Music (also known as *Die Verwandlung der welt in musik*), 1994.

(And producer) *Tod fuer fuenf stimmen* (also known as *Death for Five Voices, Gesualdo: Death for Five Voices,* and *Gesualdo–Tod fuer fuenf stimmen*), 1995.

Television Director; Miniseries:

(With others) *Les francais vus par ...* (also known as *The French as Seen By ...*), 1988.

Television Director; Episodic:

"Flucht aus Laos," *Hollenfahrten,* 1998.

"Neue Welten—Hinter dem europaischen horizont," *2000 Jahre Christentum* (also known as *2000 Years of Christianity*), 2000.

Television Appearances; Specials:

Interviewer, *Handicapped Future* (also known as *Behinderte Zukunft?*), 1971.

How Much Wood Would a Woodchuck Chuck ... Beobachtngen zu einer neuen Sprache, 1976.

Room 666 (also known as *Chambre 666*), 1982.

Ballade vom kleinen soldaten, 1984.

Gasherbrum—Der leuchtende berg, 1985.

Location Africa, 1987.

Giovanna d'Arco, 1989.

Bis ans Ende … und dann noch weiter. Die ekstatische welt des filmemachers Werner Herzog, 1989.

Narrator, *Wodaabe: Herdsmen of the Sun* (also known as *Wodaabe—Die Hirten der sonne. Nomaden am sudrand der Sahara*), 1989.

Jag Mandir: Das exzentrische privattheater des maharadscha von udaipur, 1991.

Narrator, *Lessons of Darkness* (documentary; also known as *Lektionen in Finsternis*), The Discovery Channel, 1992.

La donna del lago, 1992.

Narrator, *Death for Five Voices* (also known as *Tod fur funf stimmen* and *Gesualdo: Death for Five Voices*), 1995.

Die Verwandlung der welt in musik: Bayreuth vor der premiere, 1996.

Himself, *Julianes Sturz in den Dschungel* (also known as *Wings of Hope*), 2000.

50 Films to See Before You Die, Channel 4, 2006.

Munchner (Filmfest)–Geschichten—25 Jahre Filmfest Munchen, 2007.

Back to Room 666, V2 Cinema, 2008.

81st Annual Academy Awards, ABC, 2009.

Television Appearances; Episodic:

Cinema 3, 1991.

Miradas 2, Television Espanola, 2006.

"Werner Herzog/Frank Black," *The Henry Rollins Show,* Independent Film Channel, 2006.

"Steve Zahn/Werner Herzog," *Shootout* (also known as *Sunday Morning Shootout* and *Hollywood Shootout*), AMC, 2007.

Up Close with Carrie Keagan, 2007.

Late Night with Conan O'Brien, NBC, 2008.

"Werner Herzog: Beyond Reason," *Imagine,* BBC, 2008.

Charlie Rose (also known as *The Charlie Rose Show*), PBS, 2009.

Dias de cine, 2009.

"It's a Black President, Huey Freeman," *The Boondocks* (animated), Cartoon Network, 2010.

Television Appearances; Miniseries:

Director of opera "Il Guarany," *Tales from the Opera,* 1994.

Stage Director:

Tannhauser, 2000.

Fidelio, La Scala, Milan, Italy, 2000.

Also directed operas in Bayreuth, Germany, and Washington, DC.

RECORDINGS

Videos:

Meeting with Werner Herzog, Dreamlight Entertainment, 2004.

In the Edges: The "Grizzly Man" Session, Lions Gate Films, 2005.

WRITINGS

Screenplays:

Herakles (short film) 1962.

Spiel im sand (also known as *Playing in the Sand* and *Game in the Sand;* uncompleted), 1964.

Die beispiellose verteidigung der festung Deutschkreuz (also known as *The Unparalleled Defense of the Fortress of Deutschkreuz*), Werner Herzog Filmproduktion, 1966.

Lebenszeichen (based on the story "Der tolle Invalide auf dem Fort Ratonneau" by Achim von Armin; also known as *Signs of Life*), Werner Herzog Filmproduktion, 1968.

Letzte Worte (short film; also known as *Last Words*), Werner Herzog Filmproduktion, 1968.

Massnahmen gegen fanatiker (also known as *Measures against Fanatics*), Werner Herzog Filmproduktion, 1969.

Die fliegenden arzte von Ostafrika (short documentary; also known as *The Flying Doctors of East Africa*), Werner Herzog Filmproduktion, 1970.

Auch Zwerge haben klein angefangen (also known as *Even Dwarfs Started Small*), New Line Cinema, 1970.

Behinderte Zukunft (documentary; also known as *Frustrated Future, Handicapped Future,* and *Impeded Future*), Werner Herzog Filmproduktion, 1970.

Fata Morgana, Werner Herzog Filmproduktion, 1970.

Land des schweigens und der dunkelheit (documentary; also known as *Land of Silence and Darkness*), New Yorker, 1971.

Aguirre, der zorn Gottes (also known as *Aguirre, the Wrath of God;* dialogue and cutting continuity published as "Aguirre, la colere de Dieu" in *Avant–Scene du Cinema,* June 15, 1978, New Yorker, 1972.

Die grosse ekstase des bildschnitzers Steiner (short documentary; also known as *The Great Ecstasy of the Sculptor Steiner, The Great Ecstasy of Woodcarver Steiner,* and *The Strange Ecstasy of Woodcarver Steine*), New Yorker, 1974.

Jeder fuer sich und Gott gegen alle (also known as *Every Man for Himself and God Against All, The Enigma of Kaspar Hauser,* and *The Mystery of Kaspar Hauser;* dialogue and cutting continuity published as "L'enigme de Kaspar Hauser" in *Avant–Scene du cinema,* June, 1976, Cine International/Cinema V, 1974.

How Much Wood Would a Woodchuck Chuck? (Short documentary), Werner Herzog Filmproduktion, 1976.

(With Herbert Achternbusch) *Mit mir will keiner spielen* (short film; also known as *No One Will Play with Me* and *Nobody Wants to Play with Me*), Werner Herzog Filmproduktion, 1976.

(With others) *Herz aus Glas* (also known as *Heart of Glass;* based in part on Achternbusch's novel *Die Stunde des Todes*), Cine International Filmvertrieb, 1976.

La soufriere (short documentary), New Yorker, 1977.

Stroszek, Werner Herzog Filmproduktion, 1977, published in *2 Filmerzahlungen,* 1979.

Nosferatu—Phantom der Nacht (also known as *Nosferatu, the Vampire, Nosferatu–fantome de la nuit, Nosferatu, the Vampyre,* and *Nosferatu, Phantom of the Night*), Twentieth Century–Fox, 1979, published in *2 Filmerzahlungen,* 1979.

Werner Herzog's "Woyzeck" (also known as *Woyzeck*), Werner Herzog Filmproduktion, 1979.

Huie's Predigt (short documentary; also known as *Huie's Sermon*), New Yorker, 1980.

Glaube und Wahrung (also known as *God's Angry Man*), New Yorker, 1980.

Werner Herzog Eats His Shoe (short film), Les Blank, 1980.

Fitzcarraldo, New World, 1982, published as *Fitzcarraldo: The Original Story,* translated by Martje Herzog and Alan Greenberg, Fjord Press, 1982.

Ballade vom kleinen soldaten (also known as *Ballad of the Little Soldier*), New Yorker, 1984.

Gasherbrum—Der leuchtende berg (documentary; also known as *The Dark Glow of the Mountains*), New Yorker, 1984.

(With Bob Ellis) *Wo die gruenen ameisen traeumen* (also known as *Where the Green Ants Dream*), Orion, 1985.

Portrait Werner Herzog, 1986.

Cobra Verde (also known as *Slave Coast*), De Laurentiis Entertainment Group, 1988.

Echos aus einem dustern reich (also known as *Echo d'un sombre empire* and *Echoes from a Somber Empire*), 1990.

Glocken aus der tiefe—glaube und aberglaube in Rubland, 1995.

The Mystery of Kaspar Hauser, Almi Cinema 5, 1996.

Little Dieter Needs to Fly, 1997.

Mein liebster feind–Klaus Kinski (also known as *25. tunti: Klaus Kinski* and *My Best Friend*), New Yorker Films, 1999.

Invincible (also known as *Unbesiegbar*), Fine Line, 2001.

"Ten Thousand Years Older," Ten Minutes Older: The Trumpet, 2002.

Wheel of Time, Hemispheric Pictures, 2003.

Incident at Loch Ness, Twentieth Century–Fox, 2004.

The White Diamond, Fandango, 2004.

Grizzly Man, Lions Gate, 2005.

The Wild Blue Yonder, Fandango, 2005.

Rescue Dawn, Metro–Goldwyn–Meyer, 2006.

Encounters at the End of the World, Image Entertainment, 2007.

Cobra Verde, 518 Media, 2007.

Nosferatu, 2008.

My Son, My Son, What Have Ye Done, First Look, 2009.

The Cave, Werner Herzog Filmproduktion, 2010.

Film Composer:

Auch Zwerge haben klein angefangen (also known as *Even Dwarfs Started Small*), 1971.

Television Specials:

Wodaabe: Herdsmen of the Sun (also known as *Wodaabe—Die Hirten der sonne. Nomaden am sudrand der Sahara*), 1989.

Lektionen in finsternis (also known as *Lessons in Darkness*), The Discovery Channel, 1992.

El hambre en el mundo explicada a mi hijo, 2002.

Television Movies:

Jag Mandir: Das excentrische privattheater des Maharadscha von Udaipur, 1991.

Tod fuer fuenf stimmen (also known as *Death for Five Voices, Gesualdo—Tod fuer fuenf stimmen,* and *Gesualdo: Death for Five Voices*), 1995.

Die Verwandlung der welt in musik: Bayreuth vor der premiere, 1996.

Julianes Sturz in den Dschungel (also known as *Wings of Hope*), 2000.

Television Episodic:

"Flucht aus Laos," Hollenfahrten, 1998.

"Neue Welten—Hinter dem europaischen Horizont," 2000 Jahre Christentum (also known as *2000 Years of Christianity*), 2000.

Other Writings:

Werner Herzog: Drehbucher I, 1977.

Werner Herzog: Drehbucher II, 1977.

Vom Gehen im Eis, 1978, translation by Alan Greenberg published as *Walking on Ice,* Tanan Press, 1980.

Sur la chemin des glaces: Munich–Paris 23.11 au 14.12 1974, 1979.

Screenplays (collection), translation by Greenberg, Tanan Press, 1980.

Also contributed articles to film magazines.

OTHER SOURCES

Books:

Corrigan, Timothy, *The Films of Werner Herzog,* Routledge, 1990.

Cronin, Paul, *Herzog on Herzog*, 2003.
International Dictionary of Films and Filmmakers, Volume 2: *Directors*, St. James Press, 1996.

Periodicals:
Cineaste, fall, 1999, p. 32.
Interview, November, 1997, p. 88.
Journal of European Studies, September, 1996, p. 239.
New Republic, October 14, 2002, p. 24.

HOFFMAN, Dustin 1937–
(Stan Etic)

PERSONAL

Full name, Dustin Lee Hoffman; born August 8, 1937, in Los Angeles, CA; son of Harry (a set decorator and furniture salesman) and Lillian (a jazz pianist; maiden name, Gold) Hoffman; married Anne Byrne (a ballet dancer), May 3, 1969 (divorced, 1980); married Lisa Gottsegen, October 21, 1980; children: (first marriage) Karina (stepdaughter), Jenna (an actress and photographer); (second marriage) Jacob, Rebecca, Max, Alexandra. *Education:* Trained for the stage at the Pasadena Playhouse, 1958, and with Barney Brown, Lonny Chapman, and Lee Strasberg; studied at Los Angeles Conservatory of Music and Santa Monica College.

Addresses: *Office*—c/o Punch Productions, 11661 San Vicente Blvd., Suite 222, Los Angeles, CA 90049; c/o Neverland Production Office, Shepperton Studios, Shepperton, Middlesex TW17 0QD, England. *Agent*—Creative Artists Agency, 9830 Wilshire Blvd., Beverly Hills, CA 90212; Endeavor, 9701 Wilshire Blvd., 10th Floor, Beverly Hills, CA 90212. *Manager*—c/o Firm, 9465 Wilshire Blvd., Suite 212, Beverly Hills, CA 90212. *Publicist*—Wolf, Kasteler and Associates, 335 N. Maple Dr., Suite 351, Beverly Hills, CA 90210. *Contact*—c/o 31054 Broadbeach Rd., Malibu, CA 90265; c/o 335 N. Maple Dr., Suite 351, Beverly Hills, CA 90210.

Career: Actor, director, producer, and writer. First Artists Productions, founder (with Steve McQueen, Paul Newman, Sidney Poitier, and Barbra Streisand), 1969; appeared in television commercial for Volkswagen automobiles, 1966, and E! Entertainment Television, 2002; previously worked as an attendant at a psychiatric institution, a toy demonstrator at a department store, janitor, typist, dishwasher, demonstrator at Macy's toy department, and a waiter.

Awards, Honors: Obie Award, best actor, *Village Voice*, 1966, for *The Journey of the Fifth Horse*; Drama Desk Award, Vernon Rice Award, and *Theatre World* Award, 1967, all for *Eh?*; Academy Award nomination, best actor, Golden Globe Award, best new male film star of the year, Golden Globe Award nomination, best motion picture actor—musical/comedy, Golden Laurel Award nomination, male comedy performance, 1968, Film Award, best newcomer, British Academy of Film and Television Arts, 1969, all for *The Graduate*; Golden Laurel 2nd place, male new face, 1968; Golden Laurel 2nd place, male star, 1970; Drama Desk Award, outstanding performance, 1969, for *Jimmy Shine*; Golden Globe Award nomination, best motion picture actor—musical/comedy, 1970, for *John and Mary*; Academy Award nomination, best actor, Golden Globe Award nomination, best motion picture actor—drama, Golden Laurel Award, male dramatic performance, David Award, best foreign actor, David di Donatello Awards, 1970, all for *Midnight Cowboy*; Film Award, best film actor in a leading role, British Academy of Film and Television Arts, 1970, for *Midnight Cowboy* and *John and Mary*; Hasting Pudding Theatricals, Man of the Year, Harvard University, 1972; Golden Laurel Award, best star—male, 1971; Golden Laurel 3rd place, best comedy performance—male, 1971, Film Award nomination, best actor, British Academy of Film and Television Arts, 1972, both for *Little Big Man*; Academy Award nomination, best actor, Golden Globe Award nomination, best motion picture actor—drama, 1975, Film Award nomination, best actor, British Academy of Film and Television Arts, 1976, both for *Lenny*; Golden Globe Award nomination, best motion picture actor—drama, 1977, for *Marathon Man*; Film Award nominations, best actor, British Academy of Film and Television Arts, 1977, for *All the President's Men* and *Marathon Man*; Los Angeles Film Critics Association Award, best actor, 1979, Kansas City Film Critics Circle Award, best actor, 1980, Academy Award, Los Angeles Film Critics Association Award, New York Film Critics Circle Award, National Society of Film Critics Award, all best actor, Golden Globe Award, best motion picture actor—drama, David Award, best foreign actor, David di Donatello Awards, 1980, Film Award nomination, best actor, British Academy of Film and Television Arts, 1981, all for *Kramer vs. Kramer*; Academy Award nomination, best actor, New York Film Critics Circle, best actor, Golden Globe Award, best actor in a motion picture—comedy/musical, National Society of Film Critics, Film Award (with others), best film actor in a leading role, British Academy of Film and Television Arts, Boston Society of Film Critics Award, best actor, 1983, all for *Tootsie*; Drama Desk Award, best actor in a play, 1984, for the stage version of *Death of a Salesman*; Emmy Award, outstanding actor in a miniseries or special, Emmy Award nomination (with others), outstanding drama/comedy special, Golden Globe award, best actor in a miniseries or motion picture made for television, 1986, all for the television version of *Death of a Salesman*; Academy Award, Golden Berlin Bear, Berlin Film Festival, both best actor, Golden Globe Award, best performance by an actor in a motion picture—drama, David Award, best foreign actor, David di Donatello Awards, Kansas City Film Critics Circle Award, best actor, 1989, and Film Award nomination, best actor, British Academy of Film and Television Arts, 1990, all for *Rain Man;* People's Choice Award, favorite dramatic motion picture actor, 1989; Honorary Golden Berlin Bear, 1989; People's Choice Award, world–favorite motion picture actor, 1990; honorary A.A. degree, Santa Monica College, 1989; Golden Globe Award nomination, best performance by an actor in a motion picture—comedy/musical, 1992, for *Hook;* decorated Officer, Order of Arts and Letters, France, 1995; Golden Lion Award, Venice Film Festival, 1996; Cecil B. DeMille Award, Golden Globe Awards, 1997; Britannia Award, 1997, for excellence in film; Academy Award nomination, best actor, Golden Globe Award nomination, best performance by an actor in a motion picture—comedy/musical, Golden Satellite Award nomination, best performance by an actor in a motion picture—comedy or musical, International Press Academy, Screen Actors Guild Award nomination, outstanding performance by a male actor in a leading role, 1998, all for *Wag the Dog;* Life Achievement Award, American Film Institute, 1999; Daytime Emmy Award nomination (with others), outstanding children's special, 2000, for *The Devil's Arithmetic;* Barrymore Award, Hollywood Makeup Artist and Hair Stylist Guild, 2002; Marquee Award, CineVegas International Film Festival, 2002; Distinguished Actor Award, Costume Designers Guild Award, 2002; Golden Camera Lifetime Achievement Award, 2003; Empire Award, 2003, for lifetime achievement; Peter Owens Award, San Francisco International Film Festival, 2003; MTV Movie Award, best comedic performance, 2005, for *Meet the Fockers;* Screen Actors Guild Award nomination, outstanding performance by a cast in a motion picture (with others), 2005, for *Finding Neverland;* Gala Tribute, Film Society of Lincoln Center; Career Achievement Award, Chicago International Film Festival, 2006; Annie Award, best voice acting in an animated feature production, International Animated Film Society, 2009, for *Kung Fu Panda;* Lifetime Achievement Awards, Cesar Awards, 2009; Golden Globe Award nomination, best performance by an actor in a motion picture—comedy or musical, 2009, for *Last Chance Harvey;* Chairman's Award, career achievement, Palm Springs International Film Festival, 2009.

CREDITS

Film Appearances:
Hap, *The Tiger Makes Out,* Columbia, 1967.
Ben Braddock, *The Graduate,* Embassy, 1967.
Jack Fisher, *Madigan's Millions* (also known as *El millon de Madigan, Madigan's Million,* and *Un dollaro per 7 vigliacci*), American International, 1968.
John, *John and Mary,* Twentieth Century–Fox, 1969.
Enrico "Ratso" Rizzo, *Midnight Cowboy,* United Artists, 1969.

Jack Crabb, *Little Big Man,* National General, 1970.
Arthur Penn: The Director, 1970.
On Location: Dustin Hoffman, 1971.
Georgie Soloway, *Who Is Harry Kellerman, and Why Is He Saying Those Terrible Things About Me?,* National General, 1971.
David Sumner, *Straw Dogs,* Cinerama, 1971.
Title role, *Alfredo, Alfredo,* Paramount, 1973.
Louis Dega, *Papillon,* Allied Artists, 1973.
The Magnificent Rebel, 1973.
Lenny Bruce (title role), *Lenny,* United Artists, 1974.
Carl Bernstein, *All the President's Men,* Warner Bros., 1976.
Thomas Babington "Babe" Levy, *Marathon Man,* Paramount, 1976.
Benjamin Braddock, *America at the Movies,* 1976.
The Magic of Hollywood … Is the Magic of People, 1976.
Pressure and Press: The Making of "All the President's Men," 1976.
Max Dembo, *Straight Time,* Cinerama, 1978.
Wally Stanton, *Agatha,* Warner Bros., 1979.
Ted Kramer, *Kramer vs. Kramer,* Columbia, 1979.
Michael Dorsey/Dorothy Michaels, *Tootsie,* Columbia, 1982.
(In archive footage) Thomas Levy (segment *Marathon Man*), *Terror in the Aisles* (also known as *Time for Terror*), 1984.
Private Conversations: On the Set of "Death of a Salesman," 1985.
Private Conversations, 1986.
Chuck Clark, *Ishtar,* Columbia, 1987.
Raymond Babbitt, *Rain Man,* Metro–Goldwyn–Mayer/United Artists, 1988.
Vito McMullen, *Family Business,* TriStar, 1989.
Narrator, *Common Threads: Stories from the Quilt,* 1989.
Mumbles, *Dick Tracy,* Buena Vista, 1990.
Captain James Hook (title role), *Hook,* TriStar, 1991.
Dutch Schultz, *Billy Bathgate,* Buena Vista, 1991.
Waldo Salt: A Screenwriter's Journey, 1991.
Bernie LaPlante, *Hero* (also known as *Accidental Hero*), Columbia, 1992.
Oscar's Greatest Moments, 1992.
The Graduate at 25, 1992.
Reader, *Earth and the American Dream,* 1992.
(In archive footage) Peter, *La class americaine* (also known as *Le grand detournement*), 1993.
Himself, *Jonas in the Desert,* 1994.
Himself, *Midnight Cowboy Revisited,* 1994.
Colonel Sam Daniels, M.D., *Outbreak,* Warner Bros., 1995.
Walt "Teach" Teacher, *American Buffalo,* Samuel Goldwyn, 1996.
Danny Snyder, *Sleepers,* Warner Bros., 1996.
Max Brackett, *Mad City,* Warner Bros., 1997.
Stanley Motss, *Wag the Dog,* New Line Cinema, 1997.
Dr. Norman Goodman, *Sphere,* Warner Bros., 1998.
(In archive footage) Himself/Shylock, *Shylock,* 1999.
Himself, *Film–Fest DVD: Issue 1–Sundance,* 1999.

(Uncredited; in archive footage) Willy Loman, *Being John Malkovich,* USA Films, 1999.

The conscience, *The Messenger: The Story of Joan of Arc* (also known as *Joan of Arc* and *Jeanne d'Arc*), Columbia, 1999.

In Action, 2000.

Voice, *Tuesday* (animated short film), 2001.

Himself, *Finding the Truth: The Making of "Kramer vs. Kramer,"* 2001.

Himself, *The Directors: Wolfgang Petersen,* Wellsprung Media, 2001.

(Uncredited; in archive footage) *The Kid Stays in the Picture,* USA Films, 2002.

Ben Floss, *Moonlight Mile,* Buena Vista, 2002.

The Weather Underground, 2002.

King, *Confidence,* 2003.

Wendell Rohr, *The Runaway Jury,* Twentieth Century–Fox, 2003.

Sex at 24 Frames Per Second, Image Entertainment, 2003.

The Shakespeare Sessions, PBS, 2003.

Freedom2speak v2.0, Freedom2Speak International, 2004.

The Best of "So Graham Norton," United Film and Television Productions, 2004.

Charles Frohman, *Find Neverland,* Miramax, 2004.

Bernard, *I Heart Huckabees* (also known as *I Love Huckabees*), Twentieth Century–Fox, 2004.

Bernie Focker, *Meet the Fockers,* Universal, 2004.

The critic, *Lemony Snicket's "A Series of Unfortunate Events,"* Paramount, 2004.

Voice of Tucker, *Racing Stripes,* Independent Films, 2005.

Meyer Lansky, *The Lost City,* 2005.

Benjamin Braddock, *Rumor Has It …,* Warner Bros., 2005.

Ban the Sadist Videos! Part 2 (documentary), Anchor Bay Films, 2006.

Michael Dorsey/Dorothy Michaels, *Boffo! Tinseltown's Bombs and Blockbusters,* HBO Films, 2006.

Who Is Harry Nilsson (And Why Is Everybody Talkin' about Him?), LSL Productions, 2006.

The Holiday, Universal, 2006.

Giuseppe Baldini, *Perfume: The Story of a Murderer* (also known as *Perfume*), Paramount, 2006.

Professor Jules Hilbert, *Stranger Than Fiction,* Sony, 2006.

Mr. Edward Magorium, avid shoe–wearer, *Mr. Magorium's Wonder Emporium,* 2007.

Trumbo, Samuel Goldwyn, 2007.

Narrator, *Visual Acoustics,* Arthouse Films, 2008.

Voice of Shifu, *Kung Fu Panda* (animated; also known as *Kung Fu Panda: The IMAX Experience*), Paramount, 2008.

Narrator, *Belonging,* Free–Will Productions, 2008.

Harvey Shine, *Last Chance Harvey,* Anchor Bay Films, 2008.

Voice of Roscuro, *The Tale of Despereaux,* Universal, 2008.

Voice of Shifu, *Kung Fu Panda: Secrets of the Furious Five* (animated), 2008.

Narrator, *Jews and Baseball: An American Love Story,* 2010.

Izzy, *Barney's Version,* Fandango, 2010.

Film Work:

Director and producer, *Straight Time,* Cinerama, 1978.

Producer, *A Walk on the Moon,* Miramax, 1999.

Producer, *The Furies,* 1999.

Producer, *The Wide Blue Road,* Milestone Films, 2001.

Television Appearances; Series:

Antenas no Ar, 1997.

Voice of Benedict Arnold, *Liberty's Kids* (animated; also known as *Liberty Kid*), PBS, 2002.

Television Appearances; Miniseries:

Host of introductory segments, *Strokes of Genius,* 1984.

30 Years of Billy Connolly, 1998.

Bravo Profiles: The Entertainment Business, 1998.

Television Appearances; Movies:

Narrator/father, *The Point,* ABC, 1971.

Willy Loman, *Death of a Salesman,* 1985.

Milquetoast the cross–dressing cockroach, *A Wish for Wings That Work,* 1991.

(Uncredited) Presenter, *The Devil's Arithmetic,* Showtime, 1999.

Chester "Ace" Bernstein, *Luck,* HBO, 2011.

Television Appearances; Pilots:

Arthur Greene, *Higher and Higher, Attorneys at Law,* CBS, 1968.

New York at the Movies, Arts and Entertainment, 2002.

Television Appearances; Specials:

Arthur Penn, 1922–: Themes and Variants, 1970.

Marlo Thomas and Friends in Free to Be … You and Me, ABC, 1974.

Ihr braucht Narren wie mich, 1976.

Bette Midler—Ol' Red Hair Is Back, NBC, 1977.

The American Film Institute Salute to James Stewart, 1980.

Margret Dunser, auf der suche nach den besonderen, 1981.

Night of 100 Stars, 1982.

TV's Censored Bloopers, 1984.

The Night of 100 Stars II, 1985.

Private Conversations: On the Set of "Death of a Salesman," (also known as *Private Conversations: The Making of the Television Adaptation of "Death of a Salesman"* with Dustin Hoffman), PBS, 1985.

Willy Loman, *Death of a Salesman* (also known as *Der Tod eines handlungreisenden*), CBS, 1985.

The Ultimate Stuntman: A Tribute to Dar Robinson, 1987.

"Rain Man" Featurette, 1988.

The 3rd Annual Hollywood Insider Academy Awards Special, USA Network, 1989.

Narrator, *Common Threads: Stories from the Quilt,* HBO, 1989.

Time Warner Presents the Earth Day Special, ABC, 1990.

Oprah: Behind the Scenes, ABC, 1992.

Muhammad Ali's 50th Birthday Celebration, ABC, 1992.

In a New Light, ABC, 1992.

In a New Light '93, ABC, 1993.

Aretha Franklin: Duets, Fox, 1993.

Voice, *Earth and the American Dream,* HBO, 1993.

La classee americaine, 1993.

Comic Relief VI, HBO, 1994.

The American Film Institute Salute to Jack Nicholson, 1994.

Inside the Academy Awards, 1995.

The American Film Institute Salute to Steven Spielberg, NBC, 1995.

The First Hundred Years: A Celebration of American Movies, HBO, 1995.

Barbra: The Concert, 1995.

Himself, *The American Film Institute Salute to Clint Eastwood,* 1996.

Benjamin Braddock, *Comic Relief,* 1997.

Antes de ser famosos, 1998.

Interviewee, *Gene Hackman: Portrait of an Artist,* Arts and Entertainment, 1998.

Himself, *AFI's 100 Years ... 100 Movies,* CBS, 1998.

To Life! America Celebrates Israel's 50th, CBS, 1998.

Host, *Warner Bros. Story: No Guts, No Glory: 75 Years of Award Winners,* TNT, 1998.

Beneath the Surface: The Making of "Sphere," 1998.

Honoree, *A Salute to Dustin Hoffman* (also known as *The 27th American Film Institute Life Achievement Award: A Salute to Dustin Hoffman*), 1999.

Himself, *AFI's 100 Years ... 100 Stars,* CBS, 1999.

Interviewee, *The Messenger: The Story of Joan of Arc,* History Channel, 1999.

Hollywood Screen Tests: Take 1, 1999.

Twentieth Century Fox: The Blockbuster Years, 2000.

Himself, *AFI's 100 Years, 100 Laughs: America's Funniest Movies,* CBS, 2000.

A Home for the Holidays with Mariah Carey, CBS, 2001.

Narrator, *Goldwyn,* PBS, 2001.

Interviewee, *Dustin Hoffman: First in His Class,* Arts and Entertainment, 2001.

Come Together: A Night for John Lennon's Words & Music, TNT and The WB, 2001.

AFI Life Achievement Award: A Tribute to Barbra Streisand, Fox, 2001.

(Uncredited; in archive footage) Himself, *Reel Radicals: The Sixties Revolution in Film,* 2002.

(Uncredited) Himself, *Inside the Playboy Mansion,* Arts and Entertainment, 2002.

There's Only One Paul McCartney, BBC, 2002.

Moonlight Mile: A Journey to Screen, 2002.

Once Upon a Time in Utah, Sundance, 2003.

75 Years of the Academy Awards: An Unofficial History, BBC, 2003.

The Award Show Awards Show, Trio Network, 2003.

Introducing Graham Norton, Comedy Central, 2004.

Steve McQueen: The Essence of Cool, AMC, 2005.

Happy Birthday, Peter Pan, BBC, 2005.

Earth to America, TBS, 2005.

Penelope, camino a los Oscar, 2007.

Benjamin, *Memoirs of a Cigarette,* Channel 4, 2007.

AFI's 100 Years ... 100 Movies: 10th Anniversary Edition, 2007.

Micael Ballhaus—Eine Reise durch mein leben, 2008.

Raymond Babbitt, *Oscar, que empiece el espectaculo,* 2008.

Stanley Motss, *President Hollywood,* BBC4, 2008.

Ted Kramer, *Ceremonia de inauguracion—56 festival internacional de cine de San Sebastian,* 2008.

Ted Kramer, *Premio Donstia a Meryl Streep,* 2008.

AFI Life Achievement Award: A Tribute to Warren Beatty, USA Network, 2008.

Hollywood Habitat for Humanity, DIY Network, 2008.

A Night at the Movies: The Suspenseful World of Thrillers, TCM, 2009.

2009 Golden Globe Awards Red Carpet Special, 2009.

AFI Life Achievement Award: A Tribute to Mike Nichols, TV Land, 2010.

Television Appearances; Awards Presentations:

The ... Tony Awards, 1968, 1969, CBS, 1990.

The ... Annual Academy Awards, 1980, 1983, ABC, 1989, 1990, 1996, 1998, 2000, 2001, 2003.

Presenter, *The ... Annual Academy Awards,* 1981, 1987, ABC, 1991, 1993, 2005, 2006.

Presenter, *Walt Disney Presents the American Teacher Awards,* The Disney Channel, 1992.

The 54th Annual Golden Globe Awards, 1997.

Presenter, *The 24th Annual People's Choice Awards,* 1998.

Presenter, *The 13th Annual American Comedy Awards,* Fox, 1999.

Presenter, *Sports Illustrated's Sportsman of the Year 2000,* CBS, 2000.

The Orange British Academy Film Awards, 2000, 2002.

Presenter, *The 2001 Blockbuster Entertainment Awards,* Fox, 2001.

Keynote speaker, *AFI Awards 2001,* CBS, 2002.

The 45th Annual Grammy Awards, CBS, 2003.

Presenter, *The ... Annual Golden Globe Awards,* 2005, 2007, 2009.

2005 MTV Movie Awards, 2005.

2006 BAFTA/LA Cunard Britannia Awards, 2006.

Presenter, *The 14th Annual Critics' Choice Awards,* 2009.

The British Academy Film Awards, BBC America, 2010.

Television Appearances; Episodic:

"Sweet Prince of Delancey Street," *Naked City,* ABC, 1961.

Robert Burke, "The Voices of Death," *The Defenders,* 1962.

"Barefoot on a Bed of Coals," *Naked City,* ABC, 1963.

"A Matter of Law and Disorder," *The Defenders,* CBS, 1965.

"The Heroine," *The Doctors and the Nurses* (also known as *The Nurses*), CBS, 1965.

"The Star Wagon," *N.E.T. Playhouse,* National Educational Television (now PBS), 1966.

Zoditch, "The Journey of the Fifth Horseman," *N.E.T. Playhouse,* National Educational Television (now PBS), 1966.

The Dragon, "A Christmas Masque," *Hallmark Hall of Fame,* 1966.

"The Trap of Solid Gold," *ABC Stage '67,* ABC, 1967.

Team captain, *The Match Game,* 1968.

Arthur Greene, "Higher and Higher," *Premiere,* 1968.

V.I.P.–Schaukel, 1972, 1980.

Aspel & Company, 1988.

"Dustin Hoffman/Sir Peter Hall," *The South Bank Show,* 1989.

Champlin on Film, syndicated, 1989.

(As Sam Etic) Voice of Mr. Bergstrom, "Lisa's Substitute," *The Simpsons* (animated), Fox, 1991.

"Waldo Salt: A Screenwriter's Journey," *American Masters,* PBS, 1992.

Wogan, 1992.

"Outbreak," *HBO First Look,* HBO, 1995.

"Very Important Pennis: Part 1," *Anyone for Pennis?,* 1996.

Before They Were Famous, 1997.

The Entertainment Business, Bravo, 1998.

Talk Soup, E! Entertainment Television, 1998.

"Sphere," *HBO First Look,* HBO, 1998.

Himself, "Today Is a Good Day: Remembering Chief Dan George," *Life and Times,* CBC, 1999.

"Shirley MacLaine: This Time Around," *Biography,* 2000.

Mad TV, Fox, 2001.

"Wetten dass ...? aus Leipzig," *Wetten, dass ...?,* 2002.

Festival Pass with Chris Gore, 2002.

Tinseltown TV, International Channel, two episodes, 2003.

"Runaway Jury," *HBO First Look,* HBO, 2003.

Shootout (also known as *Sunday Morning Shootout* and *Hollywood Shootout*), AMC, 2003, 2004.

Festival di Sanremo, 2004.

"Dustin Hoffman," *Hollywood Greats* (also known as *The Hollywood Greats*), BBC1, 2004.

"Pavarotti: The Last Tenor," *Arena,* ABC, 2004.

GMTV, ITV, 2005.

Cinema mil, Televisio de Catalunya, 2005.

80s, TV3 (Televisio de Catalunya), two episodes, 2005.

La azotea de Wyoming, 2005.

20h10 petantes, 2005.

Larry's first guide, "The End," *Curb Your Enthusiasm,* HBO, 2005.

The Bigger Picture (also known as *The Bigger Picture with Graham Norton*), BBC, 2006.

Entertainment Tonight (also known as *E.T.* and *This Week in Entertainment*), syndicated, 2006, 2007, 2008, 2009, 2010.

Parkinson, BBC, 2006.

Film '72, BBC, 2006.

Ben Braddock, "Sexiest Movie Moments," *20 to 1,* Nine Network, 2007.

"The Films of Wolfgang Petersen," *The Directors,* Encore, 2008.

"The Films of Barry Levinson," *The Directors,* Encore, 2008.

"The Films of David O. Russell," *The Directors,* Encore, 2008.

Le grand journal de Canal+, 2008.

"Prepare for Pandamonium ... The Making of 'Kung Fu Panda,'" *HBO First Look,* HBO, 2008.

Miradas 2, 2008.

"Dustin Hoffman," *Private Sessions,* 2008.

"34eme nuit des Cesars," *La nuit des Cesars,* 2009.

Xpose, TV3 (Ireland), 2009.

Nyhetsmorgon, 2009.

"First Assistant Director," *Eiga no tatsujin 2: End Credits,* 2009.

Television Talk Show Guest Appearances; Episodic:

The Mike Douglas Show, 1968, 1971.

The Tonight Show Starring Johnny Carson, NBC, 1971.

The Tonight Show with Jay Leno, NBC, 1992, 1994, 2004, 2006, 2008, 2009, 2010.

The Rosie O'Donnell Show, syndicated, 1999.

Charlie Rose (also known as *The Charlie Rose Show*), PBS, 1999, 2004, 2008.

Howard Stern, 2000.

Himself/Jonny Regan, *V Graham Norton,* Channel 4, 2002, 2003.

Live with Regis and Kelly, syndicated, 2004, 2006, 2007, 2008.

Late Show with David Letterman (also known as *Letterman* and *The Late Show*), CBS, 2004, 2006, 2008, 2010.

Today (also known as *NBC News Today* and *The Today Show*), NBC, 2005.

This Morning, ITV, two episodes, 2005, 2009.

Ellen: The Ellen DeGeneres Show, syndicated, 2005, 2006, 2009.

"Dustin Hoffman," *Inside the Actors Studio* (also known as *Inside the Actors Studio: The Craft of Theatre and Film* and *Actors Interview*), Bravo, 2006.

The Daily Show with Jon Stewart (also known as *The Daily Show, A Daily Show with Jon Stewart,* and *The Daily Show with Jon Stewart Global Edition*), Comedy Central, 2006.

The Graham Norton Show, BBC2, BBC America, 2007, 2008.

Rachael Ray, syndicated, three episodes, 2007.

Tavis Smiley, PBS, 2009.

Jimmy Kimmel Live!, ABC, 2009.

Friday Night with Jonathan Ross, BBC1, BBC America, 2009.

Television Work:

Executive producer, *Death of a Salesman* (special), CBS, 1985.

Executive producer, *Devil's Arithmetic* (movie), Showtime, 1999.

Stage Appearances:

Ridzinski, *A Cook for Mr. General,* Playhouse Theatre, New York City, 1961.

Clov, *Endgame,* Theatre Company of Boston, Boston, MA, 1964.

Dunlavin, *The Quare Fellow,* Theatre Company of Boston, 1964.

C. Couch (Babboon), *In the Jungle of Cities,* Theatre Company of Boston, 1964.

Nicholas Trilestski, *A Country Scandal,* Theatre Company of Boston, 1964.

Ben, *The Dumbwaiter,* Theatre Company of Boston, 1964.

Bert Hudd, *The Room,* Theatre Company of Boston, 1964.

Pozzo, *Waiting for Godot,* Theatre Company of Boston, 1964.

Zapo, *Picnic on the Battlefield,* Theatre Company of Boston, 1964.

Hugo, *Dirty Hands,* Theatre Company of Boston, 1964.

Peter, *The Cocktail Party,* Theatre Company of Boston, 1964.

Frankie, *Three Men on a Horse,* McCarter Theatre, Princeton, NJ, 1964.

The Subject Was Roses, Royal Theatre, 1964–64, then Helen Hayes Theatre, New York City, 1965, then Henry Miller's Theatre, New York City, 1965–66, then Belasco Theatre, New York City, 1966.

A View from the Bridge, Sheridan Square Playhouse, New York City, 1965–66.

Immanuel, *Harry, Noon and Night,* American Place Theatre, New York City, 1966.

Zoditch, *The Journey of the Fifth Horse,* American Place Theatre, 1966.

Title role, "The Old Jew," Max, "Reverberations," and Jax, "Fragments," *Fragments* (triple–bill), Berkshire Theatre Festival, Stockbridge, MA, 1966.

Valentine Bross, *Eh?,* Circle in the Square, New York City, 1966.

Title role, *Jimmy Shine,* Brooks Atkinson Theatre, New York City, 1968.

Willy Loman, *Death of a Salesman,* Broadhurst Theatre, New York City, 1984.

The Night of 100 Stars II, Radio City Music Hall, New York City, 1985.

Shylock, *The Merchant of Venice,* Phoenix Theatre, London, 1989, then 46th Street Theatre, New York City, 1989–90.

Stage Work:

Assistant director, *A View from the Bridge,* Sheridan Square Playhouse, New York City, 1965–66.

Director, *Jimmy Shine,* Brooks Atkinson Theatre, New York City, 1968.

Director, *All Over Town,* Booth Theatre, New York City, 1974.

Coproducer, *Death of a Salesman,* Broadhurst Theatre, New York City, 1984.

RECORDINGS

Albums:

Young Ben, *Death of a Salesman,* Caedmon, 1968.

Videos:

The Graduate: One on One with Dustin Hoffman, 1992.

"Midnight Cowboy" Revisited, 1994.

The Making of "Sphere," 1998.

Film–Fest DVD: Issue 1—Sundance, 1999.

Finding the Truth: The Making of "Kramer vs. Kramer," 2001.

Going the Distance: Remembering "Marathon Man," 2001.

Graham Norton: Erect for 30 Years, 2003.

Host, *Now Showing: Unforgettable Moments from the Movies* (documentary), Andrews McMeel Publishing, 2003.

A Terrible Tragedy: Alarming Evidence from the Making of Film—Costumes and Other Suspicious Disguises, Paramount, 2004.

I Heart Huckabees: Production Surveillance, Twentieth Century–Fox, 2005.

The Making of "Runaway Jury," Twentieth Century–Fox, 2005.

Finding Neverland: On the Red Carpet (short film), 2005.

The Magic of "Finding Neverland," Buena Vista, 2005.

After Midnight: Reflecting on a Classic 35 Years Later, Sony, 2006.

Celebrating Schlesinger, Sony, 2006.

Controversy and Acclaim (also known as *Controversy and Acclaim: The Timelessness of a Groundbreaking Film*), Sony, 2006.

Passion & Poetry: Sam Peckinpah's Straw Dogs, EuroVideo, 2007.

The Story of "Perfume," DreamWorks, 2007.

The Making of "The Tale of Despereaux," Universal, 2009.

WRITINGS

Television Specials:

Additional written material, *Time Warner Presents the Earth Day Special,* ABC, 1990.

Soundtracks:

Ishtar, 1987.

Songs:

"Shooting the Breeze," *Last Chance Harvey,* Overture Films, 2008.

OTHER SOURCES

Books:

Brode, Douglas, *The Films of Dustin Hoffman,* Citadel Press, 1988.

Dworkin, Susan, *Making Tootsie: A Film Study with Dustin Hoffman and Sydney Pollack,* NewMarket Press, 1983.

Lenburg, Jeff, *Dustin Hoffman, Hollywood's Anti–Hero,* St. Martin's Press, 1983.

St. James Encyclopedia of Popular Culture, St. James Press, 2000.

Periodicals:

American Film, December, 1988, p. 20.

Entertainment Weekly, March 4, 1994, p. 46; fall, 1996, p. 69.

New York Times, December 16, 1979; December 21, 1982; December 10, 1989.

New York Times Magazine, March 18, 1984.

People Weekly, January 17, 1983; May 25, 1987; March 20, 1995, p. 144; March 16, 1998, p. 138.

Rolling Stone, February 3, 1983.

Saturday Review, January/February, 1986.

Time, December 3, 1979.

World Press Review, April, 1997, p. 37.

HOFFMAN, Philip Seymour 1967–
(Phil Hoffman, Philip Hoffman, Philip S. Hoffman)

PERSONAL

Born July 23, 1967, in Fairport, NY; son of Gordon S. Hoffman (a Xerox employee) and Marilyn (a lawyer, civil rights activist, and family court judge) Hoffman Connor; children: (with girlfriend Mimi O'Donnell) Cooper Alexander, Tallulah, and Willa. *Education:* New York University, B.F.A., theatre, 1989; attended Circle in the Square Professional Theatre School, New York City.

Addresses: *Agent*—Paradigm Talent Agency, 10100 Santa Monica Blvd., Suite 2500, Los Angeles, CA 90067. *Publicist*—Image Management PR, 8271 Melrose Ave., Suite 208, Los Angeles, CA 90046. *Manager*—Davien Littlefield Management, 939 Eighth Ave., Suite 609, New York, NY 10019.

Career: Actor, producer, and director. Labyrinth Theatre Company, co–artistic director; previously worked as a waiter, a lifeguard, and with children.

Member: Screen Actors Guild.

Awards, Honors: Screen Actors Guild Award nomination (with others), outstanding performance by a cast, Florida Film Critics Circle Award (with others), best ensemble cast, 1998, for *Boogie Nights;* San Diego Film Critics Society Award, best supporting actor, 1999, Screen Actors Guild Award nomination, outstanding performance by a male actor in a leading role, Golden Satellite Award, best performance by an actor in a motion picture, comedy or musical, International Press Academy, Verona Love Screens Film Festival Award, best actor, 2000, all for *Flawless;* National Board of Review Award (with others), best acting by an ensemble, 1998, Independent Spirit Award nomination, best supporting male, Independent Features Project/West, Chlotrudis Award nomination, best supporting actor, 1999, for *Happiness;* National Board of Review Awards, best supporting actor and best acting by an ensemble (with others), 1999, Screen Actors Guild Award nomination (with others), outstanding performance by a cast in a theatrical motion picture, Chlotrudis Award, best actor, Florida Film Critics Circle (with others), best ensemble cast, 2000, for *Magnolia;* Antoinette Perry Award nomination, Theatre World Award, outstanding new performer, Outer Critics Circle Award (with John C. Reilly), special achievement, 2000, all for *True West;* National Board of Review Award (with others), best acting by an ensemble, 2000, Florida film Critics Circle Award (with others), best ensemble, Online Film Critics Society Award, best ensemble cast performance (with others), 2001, for *State and Main;* Screen Actors Guild Award nomination (with others), outstanding performance by the cast of a theatrical motion picture, Online Film Critics Society Award, best supporting actor, ALFS Award nomination, actor of the year, London Critics Circle Film Awards, Golden Satellite Award nomination, best performance by an actor in a supporting role, comedy or musical, Chicago Film Critics Association Award, best supporting actor, Blockbuster Entertainment Award nomination, favorite supporting actor—drama/romance, Online Film Critics Society Awards, best ensemble cast performance (with others) and best supporting actor, 2001, all for *Almost Famous;* Golden Satellite Award nomination, best performance by an actor in a supporting role, comedy or musical, 2003, for *Punch–Drunk Love;* Lucille Lortel Award nomination, outstanding director, Drama Desk Award nomination, outstanding director of a play, 2003, both for *Our Lady of 121st St.;* Genie Award nomination, performance by an actor in a leading role, Academy of Canadian Cinema and Television, 2003, Chlotrudis Award, best actor, Vancouver Film Critics Circle Award, best actor—Canadian film, 2004, for *Owning Mahowny;* Emmy Award nomination, outstanding supporting actor in a miniseries or movie, 2005, for *Empire Falls;* Riviera Award, Santa Barbara International Film Festival, 2006; Satellite Award, outstanding actor in a motion picture, drama, Florida Film Critics Circle Award, best actor, Boston Society of Film Critics Award, best actor, Dallas–Fort Worth Film Critics Association Award, best actor, Los Angeles Film Critics Association Award, best actor, National Board of Review Award, best actor, San Diego Film Critics

Society Award, best actor, Toronto Film Critics Association Award, best performance—male, Southeastern Film Critics Association Award, best actor, Washington DC Area Film Critics Association Award, 2005, National Society of Film Critics Award, best actor, Academy Award, best performance by an actor in a leading role, Austin Film Critics Award, best actor, Film Award nomination, best performance by an actor in a leading role, British Academy of Film and Television Arts, Critics Choice Award, best actor, Chicago Film Critics Association Award, best actor, Chlotrudis Award, best actor, Golden Globe Award, best performance by an actor in a supporting role in a motion picture, Independent Spirit Award, best male lead, Kansas City Film Critics Circle Award, best actor, Online Film Critics Society Award, best actor, Screen Actors Guild Award nomination (with others), outstanding performance by a cast in a motion picture, Screen Actors Guild Award, outstanding performance by a male actor in a leading role, Vancouver Film Critics Circle Award, best actor, 2006, ALFS Award nomination, actor of the year, London Critics Circle Film Awards, 2007, for *Capote;* Saturn Award nomination, best supporting actor, Academy of Science Fiction, Horror, and Fantasy Films, 2007, for *Mission: Impossible III;* Jury Award, best actor, Ft. Lauderdale International Film Festival, Golden Globe Award nomination, best performance by an actor in a motion picture—musical or comedy, Gotham Award nomination (with others), best ensemble cast, 2007, Independent Spirit Award, best male lead, 2008, for *The Savages;* Chicago Film Critics Association Award, best supporting actor, 2007, Academy Award nomination, best performance by an actor in a supporting role, Film Award nomination, best supporting Actor, British Academy of Film and Television Arts, Critics Choice Award nomination, best supporting actor, Golden Globe Award nomination, best performance by an actor in a supporting role in a motion picture, Online Film Critics Society Award nomination, best supporting actor, 2008, for *Charlie Wilson's War;* Central Ohio Film Critics Association Award, actor of the year, Chlotrudis Award nomination, best actor, Gotham Award (with others), best ensemble cast, 2008, Sant Jordi Award, best foreign actor, 2009, for *Before the Devil Knows You're Dead;* Gotham Award (with others), best ensemble cast, 2008, Robert Altman Award, Independent Spirit Awards, 2009, for *Synecdoche, New York;* Chicago Film Critics Association Award, best supporting actor, Satellite Award nomination, best actor in a supporting role, 2008, Academy Award nomination, best performance by an actor in a supporting role, Film Award, best supporting actor, British Academy of Film and Television Arts, Critics Choice Award nominations, best acting ensemble (with others) and best supporting actor, Golden Globe Award nomination, best performance by an actor in a supporting role in a motion picture, Online Film Critics Society Award nomination, best supporting actor, Screen Actors Guild Award nominations, outstanding performance by a cast in a motion picture (with others) and outstanding performance by a male actor in a supporting role, 2009, for *Doubt.*

CREDITS

Film Appearances:

(As Phil Hoffman) Klutch, *Triple Bogey on a Par Five Hole,* Poe Productions, 1991.

(As Phil Hoffman) *Szuler* (also known as *Cheat*), 1992.

(As Philip S. Hoffman) George Willis, Jr., *Scent of a Woman,* Universal, 1992.

Chris, *My New Gun,* I.R.S. Media, 1992.

(As Philip S. Hoffman) Matt, *Leap of Faith,* Paramount, 1992.

(As Philip Hoffman) Chuck, *My Boyfriend's Back* (also known as *Johnny Zombie*), Buena Vista, 1993.

(As Philip S. Hoffman) Cochran, *Money for Nothing,* Hollywood Pictures, 1993.

Wiley McCall, *Joey Breaker* (also known as *Agent Breaker*), Skouras Pictures, 1993.

(As Philip S. Hoffman) Reporter, *Sliver* (also known as *Sliver—Gier der augen*), Paramount, 1993.

Officer Raymer, *Nobody's Fool,* Paramount, 1994.

(As Philip Hoffman) Frank Hansen, *The Getaway,* Twentieth Century–Fox/Universal, 1994.

Gary, *When a Man Loves a Woman* (also known as *Significant Other* and *To Have and to Hold*), Buena Vista, 1994.

(As Philip S. Hoffman) Bernardo, Horatio, and Laertes, *The Fifteen Minute Hamlet,* Cin–Cine 19, 1995.

Young craps player, *Hard Eight* (also known as *Sydney*), Samuel Goldwyn, 1996.

Dusty, *Twister* (also known as *Catch the Wind* and *Wind Devils*), Universal/Warner Bros., 1996.

Scotty J., *Boogie Nights,* New Line Cinema, 1997.

Mitch Roman, *Patch Adams,* Universal, 1998.

(As Phil Hoffman) Sean, *Next Stop Wonderland* (also known as *Last Train to Wonderland*), Miramax, 1998.

Brandt, *The Big Lebowski,* Gramercy, 1998.

Allen, *Happiness,* Good Machine, 1998.

Bill, *Culture,* 1998.

Duncan, *Montana,* 1998.

Freddie Miles, *The Talented Mr. Ripley* (also known as *The Strange Mr. Ripley* and *The Mysterious Yearning Secretive Sad Lonely Troubled Confused Loving Musical Gifted Intelligent Beautiful Tender Sensitive Haunted Passionate Talented Mr. Ripley*), Miramax/Paramount, 1999.

Phil Parma, Partridge's male nurse, *Magnolia* (also known as *mag–no'li–a*), New Line Cinema, 1999.

Rusty Zimmerman, *Flawless,* Metro–Goldwyn–Mayer, 1999.

Himself, *That Moment: Magnolia Diary* (also known as *That Moment: Magnolia Diary October 1998–March 2000*), New Line Home Video, 2000.

Joseph Turner White, *State and Main* (also known as *Sequences et consequences*), New Line Cinema, 2000.

Lester Bangs, *Almost Famous* (also known as *Untitled: Almost Famous the Bootleg Cut*), DreamWorks, 2000.

Himself, *The Reflections on "The Talented Mr. Ripley,"* 2000.

Himself, *Last Party 2000,* 2001.

Wilson Joel, *Love Liza,* Sony Pictures Classics, 2002.

Dean Trumbell, *Punch–Drunk Love,* Sony Pictures Entertainment, 2002.

Freddy Lounds, *Red Dragon* (also known as *Roter Drache*), MCA/Universal, 2002.

Jacob Elinsky, *25th Hour,* Buena Vista, 2002.

Dan Mahowny, *Owning Mahowny,* Sony Pictures Classics, 2003.

Himself, *A Director's Journey: The Making of "Red Dragon,"* Universal Home Video, 2003.

Dean Trumbell, *Mattress Man Commercial,* Columbia, 2003.

Cold Mountain, Miramax, 2003.

Sandy, *Captured,* Universal, 2003.

Host, *Party's Over,* 2003.

Film Trix, Cornukopia Entertainment, 2004.

Sandy Lyle, *Along Came Polly,* Universal, 2004.

Henry, *Strangers with Candy,* THINKFilm, 2005.

Truman Capote, *Capote,* Metro–Goldwyn–Mayer, 2005.

Owen Davian, *Mission: Impossible III* (also known as *M:i:III*), Paramount, 2006.

Jon Savage, *The Savages,* Twentieth Century–Fox, 2007.

Andy Hanson, *Before the Devil Knows You're Dead,* Sony, 2007.

Gust Avrakotos, *Charlie Wilson's War,* Universal, 2007.

A World for Inclusion, UNESCO, 2008.

Caden Cotard, *Synecdoche, New York,* Sony Pictures Classics, 2008.

Father Brendan Flynn, *Doubt,* Miramax, 2008.

I Knew It Was You: Rediscovering John Cazale (documentary), HBO, 2009.

Voice of Max Jerry Horovitz, *Mary and Max,* Mongrel Media, 2009.

The Count, *Pirate Radio* (also known as *The Boat That Rocked* and *Pirates Rock*), Focus Features, 2009.

Jim the bartender, *The Invention of Lying,* Warner Bros., 2009.

Jack, *Jack Goes Boating,* Overture Films, 2010.

Salinger (documentary), 2010.

Film Director:

Jack Goes Boating, Overture Films, 2010.

Film Producer:

Capote, Metro–Goldwyn–Mayer, 2005.
Jack Goes Boating, Overture Films, 2010.

Television Appearances; Miniseries:

Joseph Plumb Martin, *Liberty! The American Revolution,* PBS, 1997.

Charlie Mayne, *Empire Falls,* HBO, 2005.

Television Appearances; Movies:

Buck Forrester, *The Yearling,* CBS, 1994.

Duncan, *Montana* (also known as *Nothing Personal*), HBO, 1998.

Television Appearances; Specials:

Steward and performer of songs "Into the Woods," "First Midnight," "Second Midnight," and "Ever After," *Into the Woods,* PBS, 1991.

30 by 30: Kid Flicks—Party Animals, HBO and HBO Family, 2001.

The 26th Annual Kennedy Center Honors: A Celebration of the Performing Arts, CBS, 2003.

Once Upon a Time in Utah, Sundance, BBC, 2003.

A Journey to "Cold Mountain," Miramax, 2003.

Como conseguir un papel en Hollywood, Canal+ Espana, 2007.

Penelope, camino a los Oscar, Canal+ Espana, 2007.

Buscando a Penelope, 2009.

I Knew It Was You: Rediscovering John Cazale, HBO, 2010.

AFI Life Achievement Award: A Tribute to Mike Nichols, TV Land, 2010.

Television Appearances; Awards Presentations:

2000 Blockbuster Entertainment Awards, 2000.

The ... Annual Screen Actors Guild Awards, TNT, 2001, 2006.

The WIN Awards, PAX, 2005.

MTV Woodie Awards, MTV, 2005.

The 11th Annual Critics' Choice Awards, The WB, 2006.

The 63rd Annual Golden Globe Awards, NBC, 2006.

2006 Independent Spirit Awards, 2006.

The ... Annual Academy Awards, ABC, 2006, 2008, 2009.

Presenter, *The 64th Annual Golden Globe Awards,* NBC, 2007.

Presenter, *The 79th Annual Academy Awards,* ABC, 2007.

The 17th Annual Gotham Awards, 2007.

Television Appearances; Episodic:

Steven Hanauer, "The Violence of Summer," *Law & Order,* NBC, 1990.

Eddie Feldman, *Law & Order,* NBC, 1993.

"Filmen 'The Big Lebowski'/Nyheter och vader," *Nyhetsmorgon,* 1998.

The Rosie O'Donnell Show, syndicated, two episodes, 2000.

The Charlie Rose Show, PBS, 2000, 2002, 2005, 2007, 2008.

Inside the Actors Studio, Bravo, 2000.

The Daily Show with Jon Stewart (also known as *The Daily Show, A Daily Show with Jon Stewart,* and *The Daily Show with Jon Stewart Global Edition*), Comedy Central, 2003, 2004, 2005, 2008.

Late Night with Conan O'Brien, NBC, 2003, 2005.

Celebrity Charades, AMC, 2004.

Tavis Smiley, PBS, 2004, 2010.

Henry's Film Corner, Independent Film Channel, 2005.

Shootout (also known as *Sunday Morning Shootout* and *Hollywood Shootout*), AMC, 2005.

Live with Regis and Kelly, syndicated, 2005.

The Early Show, CBS, 2005.

Today (also known as *NBC News Today* and *The Today Show*), NBC, 2005.

The Tonight Show with Jay Leno, NBC, 2006.

Corazon de ..., two episodes, 2006.

Film '72, BBC, 2006.

Late Show with David Letterman (also known as *Letterman* and *The Late Show*), CBS, 2006.

Miradas 2, 2006.

"Oprah's After–Oscar Party," *The Oprah Winfrey Show* (also known as *Oprah*), syndicated, 2006.

HypaSpace (also known as *HypaSpace Daily* and *HypaSpace Weekly*),SPACE, 2006.

"Charlie Wilson's War," *HBO First Look,* HBO, 2007.

Cinema 3, Televisio de Catalunya, 2008, 2009.

Entertainment Tonight (also known as *E.T.* and *This Week in Entertainment*), syndicated, 2008.

"Radio Rock Revolution," *Cinetipp,* Pro 7, 2009.

"Radio Rock Revolution," *Der Kabel 1 Kinotipp,* Kabel 1, 2009.

"Radio Rock Revolution," *Kinotipp,* 2009.

"Strong Women," *Moving Pictures Live!,* 2010.

Live from Studio Five, Channel 5, 2010.

The Late Late Show with Craig Ferguson, CBS, 2010.

Also appeared in "The Films of Anthony Minghella," *The Directors.*

Television Executive Producer; Pilots:
Emma Dial, HBO, 2010.

Stage Appearances:
Earl, *Food and Shelter,* Vineyard 15th Street Theatre, New York City, 1991.

Launcelot, *The Merchant of Venice,* Goodman Theatre, Chicago, IL, 1994–95.

Greensboro (A Requiem), McCarter Theatre, Princeton, NJ, 1995–96.

RawHeadAndBloodyBones, *The Skriker,* New York Shakespeare Festival, Public Theatre, Newman Theatre, New York City, 1996.

C. B., *Defying Gravity,* American Place Theatre, New York City, 1997–98.

Mark, *Shopping and Fucking,* New York Theatre Workshop, New York City, 1998.

The Author's Voice & Imagining Brad, Drama Department, Greenwich House Theatre, New York City, 1999.

Austin/Lee, *True West,* Circle in the Square Theatre, New York City, 2000.

Treplev, Konstantin Gavrilovich, *The Seagull,* Joseph Papp Public Theatre, New York Shakespeare Festival, New York City, 2001.

Long Days Journey into Night, Broadway production, 2003.

Jack, *Jack Goes Boating,* Joseph Papp Public Theatre, Martinson Hall, New York City, 2007.

Iago, *Othello,* Jack H. Skirball Center for the Performing Arts, New York City, 2009.

Also appeared in *King Lear; The Merchant of Venice.*

Major Tours:
Appeared in touring productions, European cities.

Stage Director:
Jesus Hopped the A Train, Labyrinth Theatre Company, East 13th Street Theatre, New York City, 2000.

The Glory of Living, Manhattan Class Company, New York City, 2001.

Our Lady of 121st Street, Labyrinth Theatre Company, Union Square Theatre, New York City, 2003.

The Last Days of Judas Iscariot, Joseph Papp Public Theatre, New York City, 2005.

The Little Flower of East Orange, Joseph Papp Public Theatre, 2008.

Also directed *In Arabia; We'd All Be Kings.*

Stage Production Designer:
Dutch Heart of Man, Joseph Papp Public Theatre, New York City, 2003.

Guinea Pig Solo, Joseph Papp Public Theatre, 2004.

The Last Days of Judas Iscariot, Joseph Papp Public Theatre, 2005.

School of the Americas, Joseph Papp Public Theatre, 2006.

A Small, Melodramatic Story, Joseph Papp Public Theatre, 2006.

Jack Goes Boating, Joseph Papp Public Theatre, 2007.

A View From 151st Street, Joseph Papp Public Theatre, 2007.

Unconditional, Joseph Papp Public Theatre, 2008.

Stage Work; Other:
Executive director, *Sailor's Song,* Joseph Papp Public Theatre, New York City, 2004.

RECORDINGS

Videos:
Inside "The Talented Mr. Ripley," 1999.

Spike Lee's "25th Hour": The Evolution of an American Filmmaker, Touchstone Home Video, 2003.

Truman Capote: Answered Prayers, Sony, 2006.

Making Capote: Concept to Script, Sony, 2006.

Missing Action: Inside the Action Unit, 2006.

The Making of the Mission, 2006.

Scoring the Mission, 2006.

Mission: Metamorphosis, 2006.

Visualizing the Mission, Paramount, 2006.

Inside the IMF, Paramount, 2006.
Directed by Sidney Lumet: How the Devil Was Made, Image, 2008.
Scoring "Doubt," Miramax, 2009.
Doubt: Stage to Screen, Miramax, 2009.

OTHER SOURCES

Periodicals:
Back Stage West, March 12, 1998, p. 4.
Entertainment Weekly, June 26, 1998, p. 24.
Interview, February, 1999, pp. 98–101; December, 1999, p. 36.
Los Angeles Times, April 5, 1998, pp. 28–32.
Time, November 22, 1999, p. 100.
Variety, January 3, 2000, p. 57.

HYNES, Tyler 1986–

PERSONAL

Born May 6, 1986, in Toronto, Ontario, Canada.

Career: Actor, producer, and director. All Logic (a rap band), member.

Awards, Honors: Young Artist Award, best performance in a television movie (comedy)—supporting young actor, Young Artist Award nomination (with others), best ensemble in a television movie, 2001, both for *The Other Me;* Young Artist Award nomination, best performance in a television drama series—leading young actor, 2002, for *Tales from the Neverending Story;* Gemini Award nomination, best performance by an actor in a leading role in a dramatic program or miniseries, Academy of Canadian Cinema and Television, 2002, Young Artist Award nomination, best performance in a television movie, miniseries, or special—leading young actor, 2003, both for *Tagged: The Jonathan Wamback Story.*

CREDITS

Film Appearances:
Demi Brooke, *Little Men,* Legacy Releasing, 1997.
Chip, *Home Team,* 1998.
Ripple, *Levity,* Sony Pictures Classics, 2003.
Frank, *The Last Sign,* First Look International, 2005.
Rebel stoner, *Citizen Duane,* MTI Home Video, 2006.
Ricky, *Camille,* A–Mark Entertainment, 2007.
Ian French, *Impossible* (short film), 2010.
Slave, *Immortals,* Universal, 2011.

Film Work:
Producer and director, *Doug.* (short film), 2010.

Television Appearances; Series:
Will Bauer, *Amazon* (also known as *Peter Benchley's "Amazon"*), syndicated, 1999–2000.
Nate Bates, *15/Love,* YTV, 2005–2006.
Christian Parker, *Sophie,* CBC, 2008, ABC Family, 2009.

Television Appearances; Movies:
Scottie DeSota, *The Other Me,* The Disney Channel, 2000.
Jonathan Wamback, *Tagged: The Jonathan Wamback Story,* CTV, 2001.
Malky McDowell, *While I Was Gone,* CBS, 2004.
Rusty, *I Do, They Don't,* ABC Family, 2005.
Brad, *Mom at Sixteen,* Lifetime, 2005.

Television Appearances; Episodic:
Gary Epps, "The Haunted House Mystery," *The Mystery Files of Shelby Woo,* Nickelodeon, 1998.
Darren, "Breakout," *Lassie,* Animal Planet and YTV, 1999.
Billy Riddle, "Tethered Goat," *Soldier of Fortune, Inc.* (also known as *S.O.F. Special Ops Forces*), syndicated, 1999.
Jimmy Miller, "The Tale of the Wisdom Glass," *Are You Afraid of the Dark?,* Nickelodeon, 1999.
Atreyu, "Deleting Mr. Blank," *Tales from the Neverending Story,* Hallmark Channel, 2001.
Atreyu, "The Gift of the Name," *Tales from the Neverending Story,* Hallmark Channel, 2001.
R J Strachan, "He Knows His Brother," *Flashpoint,* CTV and CBS, 2008.
Joshua Donovan, "Claudia," *Warehouse 13,* Syfy, 2009.
Joshua Donovan, "Elements," *Warehouse 13,* Syfy, 2009.
Joshua Donovan, "Time Will Tell," *Warehouse 13,* Syfy, 2009.

Also appeared as Darren, "Dad's Watch," *Lassie,* Animal Planet and YTV; Atreyu, "The Luck Stops Here," *Tales from the Neverending Story,* Hallmark Channel.

Internet Appearances; Web Series:
Gabriel, *Valemont,* www.mtv.com, 2009.

RECORDINGS

Albums:
Recorded (with Brandon Hynes) *Don't Hold Back: The Story of Jarvo.*

J

JAENADA, Oscar 1975–

PERSONAL

Full name, Oscar Jaenada Gajo; born May 4, 1975, in Esplugues de Llobregat, Barcelona, Spain.

Addresses: *Agent*—International Creative Management, 10250 Constellation Blvd., 9th Floor, Los Angeles, CA 90067.

Career: Actor. Appeared in advertisements.

Awards, Honors: Toulouse Cinespana Award, best actor, Award of the Spanish Actors Union nomination, film: lead performance—male, Butaca Award nomination, best Catalan film actor, Goya Award nomination, best new actor, CEC Award nomination, best new artist, Cinema Writers Circle, and Newcomer Award nomination (male), Spanish Actors Union, all 2004, for *Noviembre;* Goya Award, best actor, CEC Award, best actor, Cinema Writers Circle, Fotogramas de Plata, best movie actor, Award of the Spanish Actors Union nomination, film: lead performance—male, and Butaca Award nomination, best Catalan film actor, all 2006, for *Camaron;* Silver Biznaga, Malaga Spanish Film Festival, best supporting actor, and Toulouse Cinespana Award, best actor, both 2008, for *Todos estamos invitados.*

CREDITS

Film Appearances:
El arbol (short film), 1996.
Droga (short film), 1997.
Colaboracion ciudadana (short film), 1999.
Cacique, *Aunque tu no lo sepas* (also known as *What You Never Knew*), Wanda Vision, 2000.

El juego (short film), 2000.
Domestos, *Lisistrata* (also known as *Lysistrata*), Bogeyman Licensing, 2002.
Aitor (a director), *Descongelate!* (also known as *Chill Out!*), Warner Sogefilms, 2003.
Alfredo, *Noviembre* (also known as *November*), Alta Films, 2003.
Fali, *XXL,* TriPictures, 2004.
Juan, *Aloe* (short film), Sergio Delgado, 2004.
Alberto, *El juego de la verdad,* Manga Films, 2004, Domain Entertainment, 2005.
Title role, *Camaron* (also known as *Camaron: When Flamenco Became Legend*), Filmanova/Monoria Films, 2005.
Gabriel, *Somne,* Lotus Films/Vaca Films/Yacare Films, 2005.
Ricky, *Carne de neon* (short film; also known as *Neon Flesh*), Jaleo Films/Morena Films, 2005.
Crimenes ejemplares de Max Aub (short film), 2005.
Boris, *Dias azules* (also known as *Blue Days*), Nirvana Films, c. 2005.
Ivan, *Skizo,* Bainet Zinema, 2006.
Pablo, *El efecto Rubik (& el poder del color rojo)* (short film), Los Chicos del Banko, 2006.
Redondeo (short film), 2006.
El chino, *La vida abismal* (also known as *Life in the Abyss* and *Life on the Edge*), Els Films de la Rambla, 2007.
Josu Jon, *Todos estamos invitados* (also known as *Who's Next*), Alta Films, 2008.
Young man, *Sub–Way* (short film), Fundacion Inquietudes, 2008.
Dario (David Ardiazola), *Che: Part Two* (also known as *Che, Che: Guerilla, Che: Part Two—Guerilla, Guerilla,* and *La Guerilla*), IFC Films, 2008, URD Pictures, 2009.
David, *Trash,* Escandalo Films/Just Films, 2009.
Waiter, *The Limits of Control* (also known as *No Limits No Control*), Focus Features, 2009.
Sukalde kontuak, Barton Films, 2009.
Cougar, *The Losers,* Warner Bros., 2010.

Nicolas Tremel, *La herencia Valdemar* (also known as *The Valdemar Legacy* and *La herencia Waldemar*), Universal Pictures International, 2010.

Nicolas Tremel, *La herencia Valdemar II: La sombra prohibida* (also known as *The Valdemar Legacy II* and *La herencia Valdemar II*), Universal/Universal Pictures International, 2010.

Circuit, Actividades Mediaticas Audiovisuales Singulares, 2010.

Spaniard, *Pirates of the Caribbean: On Stranger Tides* (also known as *Pirates 4* and *P.O.T.C. 4*), Walt Disney Pictures, 2011.

The Cold Light of Day, Summit Entertainment, 2011.

Television Appearances; Series:

Trives, *Ciudad sur,* [Spain], 2001.

Marcos, *Javier ya no vive solo,* Telecinco, 2002.

Alvaro Mondego, *Piratas,* Telecinco, beginning c. 2010.

Television Appearances; Movies:

Damian, *La vida aqui,* Televisio de Catalunya (TV3), 2003.

Television Appearances; Specials:

Himself, *Ceremonia de clausura Seminci 08,* Television Espanola (TVE), 2008.

Himself, *Ceremonia de inauguracion—56 festival internacional de cine de San Sebastian,* Television Espanola (TVE), 2008.

Himself, *Ceremonia de clausura–58 festival internacional de cine de San Sebastian,* Television Espanola (TVE), 2010.

Television Appearances; Awards Presentations:

Presenter, *50 premios Sant Jordi de cinematografia,* Television Espanola (TVE), 2006.

XX premios Goya, Television Espanola (TVE), 2006.

Presenter, *XXI premios anuales de la academia* (also known as *XXI premios Goya*), Television Espanola (TVE), 2007.

51 premis Sant Jordi de cinematografia, Television Espanola (TVE) Catalunya, 2007.

Presenter, *XXIV premios anuales de la academia,* Television Espanola (TVE), 2010.

II premis Gaudi de l'academia del cinema catala, Televisio de Catalunya (TV3), 2010.

(Uncredited) *XXII premios anuales de la academia* (also known as *XXII premios Goya*), Television Espanola (TVE), 2010.

Television Appearances; Episodic:

Estacio d'Enllac (also known as *Estaciodenllac*), Televisio de Catalunya (TV3), c. 1998.

"Descolocados," *A las once en casa,* Television Espanola (TVE), 1999.

Mario, "Fuera de juego," *Hospital central,* Telecinco, 2000.

"Declaracion de amor," *Al salir de clase,* Telecinco, 2000.

"Mareos matutinos," *Al salir de clase,* Telecinco, 2000.

"Un cadaver inquieto," *El comisario,* Telecinco, 2000.

"Un virus de primavera," *Al salir de clase,* Telecinco, 2000.

Fer, "La gente cambia," *Companeros,* Antena 3 de Television, 2001.

Fer, "Ser un buen colega," *Companeros,* Antena 3 de Television, 2001.

"Cachorros," *El comisario,* Telecinco, 2001.

Jorge, *7 vidas* (also known as *Siete vidas*), Telecinco, 2003.

(And in archive footage) Himself, *Magacine,* multiple episodes, Canal+ Espana, 2004 and 2005.

Himself, *Silenci?,* Televisio de Catalunya (TV3), 2004, 2006.

Himself, *Corazon, corazon,* Television Espanola (TVE), 2005.

Himself, *Corazon de …,* Television Espanola (TVE), multiple episodes, 2005 and 2006.

Himself, *Continuara …,* Television Espanola (TVE) Catalunya, 2005, 2006, 2007, 2009, 2010.

Himself, *Banda sonora,* Barcelona Televisio, 2007.

Himself, *Miradas 2,* Television Espanola (TVE), 2007.

Himself, *Exit,* Barcelona Televisio, 2008.

Himself, *Taller Canal+,* Canal+ Espana, 2008.

Himself, *Cinema 3* (also known as *Cinema tres* and *Informatiu cinema*), Televisio de Catalunya (TV3), multiple episodes in 2008, 2009.

Himself, *Dias de cine,* Television Espanola (TVE), 2009, 2010.

Himself, *Mark at the Movies,* 2010.

Himself, *Tvist,* Televisio de Catalunya (TV3), 2010.

Television Talk Show Guest Appearances; Episodic:

Lo + plus, Canal+ Espana, 2004.

Channel no 4 (also known as *Channel Fresh*), Cuatro, 2005.

La mirada critica, Telecinco, 2005.

Buenafuente, Antena 3 de Television, 2005, La Sexta, 2007.

Toni Rovira y tu, 25 TV, 2005, 2007.

Version espanola, Television Espanola (TVE), 2005, multiple episodes in 2008.

En directe, Televisio de Catalunya (TV3), 2006.

Noche hache, Cuatro, multiple episodes, 2006.

D–Calle, Television Espanola (TVE), 2007.

Senyores i senyors (also known as *S & S*), Television Espanola (TVE) Catalunya, 2007.

El club, Televisio de Catalunya (TV3), 2009.

Divendres, Televisio de Catalunya (TV3), 2010.

Made in Hollywood, syndicated, 2010.

Up Close with Carrie Keagan, 2010.

Stage Appearances:

Aprobado en inocencia, 1991.

Aqui hi ha mullader, 1991.

Bajarse al moro, 1992.

Traficantes de placer (also known as *Pleasure Dealers*), 1992.

Esperando a Godot, 1994.

Las cartas de Hercules Poirot, 1995.

Mucho ruido y pocas nueces (de Tatan Club) (also known as *Much Ado about Nothing*), 1996.

Danny y Roberta (also known as *Danni y Roberta*), 1997.

Escuadra hacia la muerte, 1997.

Perversidad sexual en Chicago (also known as *Sexual Perversity in Chicago*), 1998.

Appeared in various productions, beginning c. 1988.

OTHER SOURCES

Electronic:
Oscar Jaenada, http://www.oscarjaenada.com/, August 25, 2010.

JAMES, Gary
    See CAIRNS, Gary

JENKINS, Jody K.
    (Jody Jenkins)

PERSONAL

Born in London, England; son of Karl Jenkins (a composer).

Addresses: *Agent*—Air Edel Associates, Ltd., 18 Rodmarton St., London W1U 8BJ, England.

Career: Composer and music programmer.

Awards, Honors: Emmy Award nomination (with others), outstanding individual achievement in a craft—music and sound, News and Documentary Emmy Award, 2009, for *When We Left Earth: The NASA Missions.*

CREDITS

Film Music Programmer:
Nanny McPhee, Universal, 2005.
(As Jody Jenkins) *Atonement,* Focus Features, 2007.
(Uncredited) *The Soloist,* Paramount, 2009.

(As Jody Jenkins) *Agora,* Newmarket Films, 2009.
Everybody's Fine, Miramax, 2009.
The Nutcracker in 3D (also known as *Nutcracker: The Curse of the Rat King*), Freestyle Releasing, 2010.
Hippie Hippie Shake, Universal, 2010.
The Cabin in the Woods, Metro–Goldwyn–Mayer, 2011.

Film Work; Other:
Sound, *What Barry Says* (animated short film), 2004.
Musician: percussion programming, *V for Vendetta* (also known as *V for Vendetta: The IMAX Experience*), Warner Bros., 2006.
Score synthesizer programmer, *The Brave One* (also known as *Brave One*), Warner Bros., 2007.
Music technical engineer, *The Chronicles of Narnia: Prince Caspian* (also known as *Prince Caspian*), Walt Disney Studios Motion Pictures, 2008.

WRITINGS

Film Scores:
What Barry Says (animated short film), 2004.
The Sound of Mumbai: A Musical, 2010.
Lipstikka, 2011.

Film Additional Music:
Pas de Trois (short film), 2002.
Shrooms, Magnolia Pictures, 2007.

Film Background Music:
Aladin, Films International, 2009.

Television Scores; Series:
Ladette to Lady, ITV, 2006–2008.
Aussie Ladette to Lady, ITV and Nine Network, 2009.
Clash of the Dinosaurs, 2009.

Television Additional Music: Miniseries:
"Mercury: Ordinary Supermen," *When We Left Earth: The NASA Missions* (documentary), The Discovery Channel, 2008.

Television Additional Music; Movies:
(Uncredited) *Dying to Dance,* NBC, 2001.

Television Scores; Episodic:
(As Jody Jenkins) *The Convent,* BBC, 2006.

JENKINS, Karl 1944–

PERSONAL

Full name, Karl William Pamp Jenkins; born February 17, 1944, in Penclawdd, Wales; children: Jody K. (a composer and music programmer).

Addresses: *Agent*—Air Edel Associates, Ltd., 18 Rodmarton St., London W1U 8BJ, England.

Career: Composer. Also composed music for television commercials, including Delta Air Lines, Levi's jeans, Speedo swim wear, Jaguar automobiles, DeBeers jewelry, and Pepsi; (with son, Jody K. Jenkins) composed music for television commercials, including Samsung electronics, Morgan Stanley Dean Witter investments, and BMW automobiles.

Awards, Honors: Decorated Officer of the Order of the British Empire, 2005; Golden Goblet Award, Shanghai International Film Festival, 2006; decorated Commander of the Order of the British Empire, 2010.

CREDITS

Film Work:
Music conductor and music orchestrator, *River Queen*, Weinstein Company, 2005.

Television Work; Specials:
Music conductor, *The Violent Earth*, The Discovery Channel, 1999.

Television Appearances; Episodic:
Himself, *Full House*, BBC2, 1973.
Himself, *Breakfast*, BBC, 2010.

WRITINGS

Film Scores:
Shadows (short film), 1982.
River Queen, Weinstein Company, 2005.

Film Songs:
"The Hurricane," *The Hurricane*, 1999.

Television Scores; Movies:
The Bad Sister, Channel 4, 1983.
Dying to Dance, NBC, 2001.

Television Scores; Specials:
The Violent Earth, The Discovery Channel, 1999.

JOHNSON, Geordie 1953–

PERSONAL

Born February 25, 1953, in Claresholm, Alberta, Canada. *Education:* University of Calgary, B.F.A., drama.

Career: Actor.

Awards, Honors: Stage Door Award, best supporting actor, 1997; Gemini Award, best performance by an actor in a guest role in a dramatic series, Academy of Canadian Cinema and Television, 2000, for *Deep in the City.*

CREDITS

Television Appearances; Series:
Alexander Lucard, *Dracula: The Series*, syndicated, 1990–91.
Daniel Booth, *Traders*, Global TV, 1999–2000.
Daniel Harmon, *Canada: A People's History*, CBC, 2000.
Georgy Kerensky, *Largo Winch*, Mystery Channel, 2001–2003.
Jonathan Verrity, *Durham County*, The Movie Network, Movie Central, Ion Television, 2009.

Also appeared as Will Forrester, *The Campbells*, syndicated.

Television Appearances; Episodic:
Ivan Zukov, "The Dancing Lesson," *Adderly*, CBS, 1986.
Dave Lawrence, "User Deadly," *Alfred Hitchcock Presents*, USA Network, 1988.
Robert Farlane, "Mondo Condo," *Street Legal*, CBC, 1988.
Vince, "Cinema Verite," *Counterstrike*, USA Network, 1990.
Doug Mather, "Secrets," *E.N.G.*, CTV, Lifetime, 1991.
Greg, "Our Boyfriends Ourselves," *Material World*, CBC, 1991.
Tom McIntire, "Let Death Do Us Part," *The Hidden Room*, Lifetime, 1991.
Arnold Hodis, "Presumed Toxic," *Street Legal*, CBC, 1991.
Arnold Hodis, "Breach of Trust," *Street Legal*, CBC, 1992.
Arnold Hodis, "November" *Street Legal*, CBC, 1992.
Arnold Hodis, "After the Fall," *Street Legal*, CBC, 1992.
Daniel Barker, "The Color of Mad," *Beyond Reality*, USA Network, 1992.
Writer, "By the Numbers," *The Ray Bradbury Theater*, USA Network, 1992.
Sam Leaver, "Betrayed," *Counterstrike*, USA Network, 1993.
George Malkovich, "Sunday at the Hotel with George," *Kung Fu: The Legend Continues*, syndicated, 1993.
Ben Shore, *Free Willy*, ABC, 1994.
George Vladpallin, "Sunday at the Museum with George," *Kung Fu: The Legend Continues*, syndicated, 1994.
Dragon, "The Fire Inside," *Forever Knight*, syndicated, 1995.

Jerry Tate, "My Boyfriend Is a Vampire," *Forever Knight,* USA Network, syndicated, 1995.

Police Commissioner Bob Neville, "Skin Deep," *TekWar* (also known as *TekWar: The Series*), USA Network, 1996.

Konstantine Malikov, "From Russia with Love," *Taking the Falls,* 1996.

Samuel, "The Two Headed Man," *Spoken Art,* Bravo, 1996.

Hedeon Mishenka, "The Fog/House on Garden Street," *PSI Factor: Chronicles of the Paranormal,* syndicated, 1997.

Desmond Happy, "The Director Files," *Once a Thief* (also known as *John Woo's "Once a Thief"*), syndicated, 1998.

Victor Hansen, "The Devil You Know," *Highlander: The Raven,* syndicated, 1999.

Stephen de Bekke, "The Painting," *Poltergeist: The Legacy,* Sci–Fi Channel, 1999.

Oliver Martin, "Bed Fellows," *Deep in the City* (also known as *The City*), CTV, 2000.

Lord Tyrol, "Royalty," *The Secret Adventures of Jules Verne,* Sci–Fi Channel, syndicated, 2000.

Bartolome Naz, "And Your Heart Will Fly Away," *Andromeda* (also known as *Gene Roddenberry's "Andromeda"*), syndicated, 2002.

Tristan Catchpole, "The Prisoner," *Starhunter,* syndicated, 2003.

Tristan Catchpole, "Hyperspace 1," *Starhunter,* syndicated, 2004.

Tristan Catchpole, "Hyperspace 2," *Starhunter,* syndicated, 2004.

Barclay Blake, "Dinosaur Fever," *Murdoch Mysteries,* Bravo, 2009.

Television Appearances; Movies:

Interpreter, *Bridge to Silence,* CBS, 1989.

Antipholus of Ephesus/Antipholus of Syracuse, *The Comedy of Errors,* 1989.

Brookw, *The Diviners,* CBC, 1993.

David Kenyon, *A Stranger in the Mirror,* ABC, 1993.

Jacques, *A Change of Place,* CBS, 1994.

Miles Kendrick, *Bionic Ever After?,* CBS, 1994.

Paul, *Spenser: The Judas Goat,* Lifetime, 1994.

Franz Liszt, *Liszt's Rhapsody,* HBO, 1996.

Gary Myers, *Dangerous Evidence: The Lori Jackson Story,* Lifetime, 1999.

Richard Baines, *Charms for the Easy Life,* Showtime, 2002.

Lex Allbright, *The Dark Room,* CBC, 2007.

Television Appearances; Pilots:

Georgy Kerensky, *Largo Winch: The Heir,* 2001.

Television Appearances; Miniseries:

Orin Hunter, *Too Rich: The Secret Life of Doris Duke,* CBS, 1999.

Film Appearances:

Jake, *Skullduggery,* Media Home Video, 1983.

Sean, *Chautauqua Girl,* 1983.

Andrew Bothwell, *The Boy in the Blue,* Twentieth Century–Fox, 1986.

Gordie, *The Circle Game,* Shadowlife Films, 1994.

Oliver, *The English Patient,* Miramax, 1996.

Albert, *The Absence of Emily,* Sideview Productions Inc., 2003.

Stage Appearances:

Hector, *Troilus and Cressida,* Stratford Festival, Canada, 2003.

Nathan Detroit, *Guys & Dolls,* Stratford Festival, 2004.

The prince, *Dirty Rotten Scoundrels,* Theatre Calgary, Calgary, Alberta, Canada, 2009.

JOINER, Christy Bella

PERSONAL

Original name, Christybella Cannon Joiner; raised in Georgia; daughter of Jerry Cannon (a banking official) and Brenda Joiner. *Education:* Attended University of Georgia and Valdosta State University; trained as a classical pianist.

Career: Actress. Performed as a child pianist with Atlanta Symphony Orchestra. Model with Elite Modeling Agency and Click, beginning 2000; Nevichi Cosmetics, international model and spokesperson, 2008. Volunteer at charity events, including Stand Up to Cancer.

CREDITS

Television Appearances; Episodic:

Hot girl, "Vegas Baby, Vegas!," *Entourage,* HBO, 2006.

Jane Seymour's lady in waiting, "Matters of State," *The Tudors,* Showtime, 2008.

Jane Seymour's lady in waiting, "The Northern Uprising," *The Tudors,* Showtime, 2009.

Television Appearances; Other:

Lana's friend, *Wicked Minds,* 2002.

Film Appearances; Uncredited:

Fashion model, *Another Nine & a Half Weeks* (also known as *Love in Paris* and *Nine Half 2*), Trimark Pictures, 1997.

Bar patron, *Underestimating Jake,* Big Star Pictures, 2001.

(In archive footage) Runway model, *On Last Thing,* Magnolia Pictures, 2006.

Model at party, *Perfect Stranger,* Columbia, 2007.

Dream girl, *Succubus: Hell Bent,* Screen Media Ventures, 2007.

(In archive footage) Fashion model, *Lagerfeld Confidential* (documentary), Koch Lorber, 2007.

Nurse, *Veronika Decides to Die,* Umbrella Entertainment, 2009.

Waitress, *Wall Street: Money Never Sleeps* (also known as *Wall Street*), Twentieth Century–Fox, 2010.

RECORDINGS

Videos:
(Uncredited) Stripper, *8MM 2,* Sony Pictures Home Entertainment, 2005.

JORDAN, James 1979–

PERSONAL

Born March 14, 1979, in Houston, TX. *Education:* Missouri Theatre University, B.A., theatre, 2002; University of California, Los Angeles, M.F.A., 2005.

Addresses: *Agent*—Stone Manners Salners Agency, 9911 West Pico Blvd., Suite 1400, Los Angeles, CA 90035.

Career: Actor. Daftcollective, cofounder and partner.

Member: Screen Actors Guild.

Awards, Honors: Sir Ian McKellen Award, University of California Los Angeles, 2004.

CREDITS

Film Appearances:
Vicious Circle (short film), 2005.
Rubin Aquino, *Til Parole Do Us Part* (short film), 2005.
Himself, *A Day on the Set with "Veronica Mars"* (short documentary), 2006.
Little brother, *Seraphim Falls,* Destination Films, 2006.

Also appeared as Private Mills, *Dust.*

Television Appearances; Series:
Thomas "Lucky" Dohanic, *Veronica Mars,* UPN, 2006.
Tim Foyle, *Veronica Mars,* UPN, 2006–2007.

Television Appearances; Episodic:
Young soldier, "Spoils of War," *Over There,* FX Network, 2005.
Ryan, "Shooting Stars," *CSI: Crime Scene Investigation* (also known as *CSI: Las Vegas* and *C.S.I.*), CBS, 2005.
Derek, "Suburban Prostitution," *Close to Home,* CBS, 2005.
Nick "Stump" Fanelli, "Frank's Best," *Cold Case,* CBS, 2005.
Claude Osteen, "The Code," *Just Legal,* The WB, 2006.
Doug Berry, "All for One," *Without a Trace* (also known as *W.A.T.*), CBS, 2006.
Clint Gilmore, "Sunblock," *CSI: Miami,* CBS, 2007.
Chris Dunlap, "Power of Attorney," *The Closer,* TNT, 2009.
Phillips, "Day 8: 5:00 a.m.–6:00 a.m.," *24,* Fox, 2010.

Stage Appearances:
Bean, *Money Shot,* DAFT and Company of Angels, Los Angeles, 2008.

Also appeared as Alan, *Kindred,* Los Angeles Theatre Ensemble, Los Angeles; Benny, *Hot,* DAFT and the Ark Theatre Company.

JULYAN, David

PERSONAL

Education: Studied at University College, London.

Addresses: *Agent*—Soundtrack Music Associates, 2229 Cloverfield Blvd., Santa Monica, CA 90405; Air Edel Associates, 18 Rodmarton St., London W1U 8BJ, England.

Career: Composer and score producer.

CREDITS

Film Work:
Sound, *Following,* Zeitgeist Films, 1998.
Electronic music programmer, *Insomnia,* Warner Bros., 2002.
Orchestrator, *Happy Here and Now,* IFC Films, 2002.
Score producer, *The Last Drop,* 2005.
Score producer, *Eden Lake,* Weinstein Company, 2008.
Score producer, *Hurt,* Monterey Media, 2009.
Score producer, *The Descent: Part 2* (also known as *Descent 2*), Pathe, 2009.

Film Appearances:
Following, Zeitgeist Films, 1998.

Television Production Assistant; Series:
The Cruise, BBC, 1998.

Television Production Assistant; Specials:
Jane's Cruise to the Stars (documentary), BBC, 1998.

Television Appearances; Episodic:
Film 2006 (also known as *The Film Programme*), BBC, 2006.

WRITINGS

Film Scores:
Doodlebug (short film), 1997.
Following, Zeitgeist Films, 1998.
Memento, Newmarket Films, 2000.
Insomnia, Warner Bros., 2002.
Happy Here and Now, IFC Films, 2002.
Spivs, Image Entertainment, 2004.
Return to Sender, 2004.
Rory O'Shea Was Here (also known as *Inside I'm Dancing*), Universal, 2004.

The Descent, Lions Gate Films, 2005.
Dungeons & Dragons: Wrath of the Dragon God (also known as *Dungeons & Dragons 2: The Elemental Might*), Warner Home Video, 2005.
The Last Drop, 2005.
Die trojanische kuh (short film; also known as *The Trojan Cow*), 2006.
The Prestige, Newmarket Films, 2006.
Outlaw, Magnolia Pictures, 2007.
w Delta z (also known as *War* and *The Killing Gene*), Weinstein Company, 2007.
Eden Lake, Weinstein Company, 2008.
The Daisy Chain, Image Entertainment, 2008.
The Descent: Part 2 (also known as *Descent 2*), Pathe, 2009.
Heartless, IFC Midnight, 2009.
The Cabin in the Woods, Metro–Goldwyn–Mayer, 2011.

Television Scores; Series:
The Secret Rulers of the World, Channel 4, 2001.
Matrioshki (also known as *Matroesjka's*), 2005.

Television Additional Music; Episodic:
Matrioshki (also known as *Matroesjka's*), 2005.
"Van Gogh," *Simon Schama's Power of Art,* 2006.

K

PERSONAL

Education: Attended the University of California, Santa Barbara, and the University of California, Los Angeles, beginning 1997.

Addresses: *Office*—Rogue Pictures, 8899 Beverly Blvd., Suite 510, Los Angeles, CA 90048.

Career: Producer and executive. Chief executive officer of Relativity Management, 2002—, Relativity Media, 2004—, Rogue Pictures, 2008—, and Relativity Capital, 2008—, as well as Relativity Media Holdings, Relativity Media India, and Single Picture Business.

Awards, Honors: Hollywood Film Festival Award, producer of the year, 2009; named to the Film Power 100 list by the *Guardian* online, http://www.guardian.co.uk, 2010.

CREDITS

Film Executive Producer:

Jerry V. Death (short film), Relativity Media/Madrik Multimedia/Paisley Lane Films, 2005.

Land of the Dead (also known as *Dead Reckoning, George A. Romero's "Land of the Dead,"* and *Twilight of the Dead*), Universal, 2005.

All the King's Men, Columbia, 2006.

(And unit production manager) *The Fast and the Furious: Tokyo Drift* (also known as *The Fast and the Furious, Fast & Furious: Tokyo Drift, The Fast and the Furious 3, Fast & Furious 3: Tokyo Drift,* and *Wild Speed X3: Tokyo Drift*), Universal, 2006.

Gridiron Gang (also known as *Gang Gridiron* and *Redemption*), Columbia, 2006.

RV (also known as *Camping Car, Recreational Vehicle, Runaway Vacation, R.V., RV: Runaway Vacation,* and *VR*), Columbia, 2006.

Talladega Nights: The Ballad of Ricky Bobby (also known as *High, Wide, and Handsome, Talladega Nights,* and *Untitled Will Ferrell NASCAR Comedy*), Columbia, 2006.

Catch and Release (also known as *Catch & Release*), Columbia, 2007.

Charlie Wilson's War, Universal, 2007.

Full of It (also known as *Big Liar on Campus, The Life and Lies of Sam Leonard, Nothing but the Truth,* and *The Whole Truth*), New Line Cinema, 2007.

I Now Pronounce You Chuck & Larry, Universal, 2007.

The Kingdom (also known as *Operation: Kingdom*), Universal, 2007.

3:10 to Yuma (also known as *Three Ten to Yuma* and *3:10 Yuma*), Lions Gate Films, 2007.

Baby Mama (also known as *Rent–a–Mama*), Universal, 2008.

The Bank Job (also known as *Baker Street, Bank Job,* and *D–Notice*), Lions Gate Films, 2008.

Death Race (also known as *Death Race 3000*), Universal, 2008.

The Forbidden Kingdom (also known as *Dragon Kingdom, Jackie Chan/Jet Li Project, King of Kung Fu,* and *Untitled J&J Project*), Lions Gate Films/The Weinstein Company, 2008.

Made of Honor (also known as *Made of Honour*), Columbia, 2008.

The Tale of Despereaux (animated), Universal, 2008.

21 (also known as *Las Vegas 21, 21 Blackjack, 21: Black Jack, 21: Las Vegas, 21—The Movie,* and *Untitled Blackjack Picture*), Columbia, 2008.

Yes Man, Warner Bros., 2008.

Brothers (also known as *My Brother*), Lions Gate Films, 2009.

Did You Hear about the Morgans? (also known as *Untitled Hugh Grant/Sarah Jessica Parker Project*), Columbia, 2009.

Duplicity, Universal, 2009.

The International (also known as *The Bank*), Columbia, 2009.

Land of the Lost, Universal, 2009.

Love Happens (also known as *Brand New Day* and *Traveling*), Universal, 2009.

Nine (musical; also known as *Untitled Rob Marshall Project*), The Weinstein Company, 2009.

The Taking of Pelham 1 2 3 (also known as *The Taking of Pelham 123*), Columbia, 2009.

Zombieland, Columbia, 2009.

The Bounty Hunter (also known as *The Bounty* and *Untitled Sarah Thorp Project*), Columbia, 2010.

Catfish, Universal/Rogue Pictures, 2010.

Live with It (also known as *I'm with Cancer*), Summit Entertainment, 2010.

MacGruber, Universal, 2010.

Piranha 3D (also known as *Piranha* and *Piranha 3–D*), Dimension Films, 2010.

Robin Hood, Universal, 2010.

Season of the Witch, Lions Gate Films, 2010.

Skyline, Universal/Rogue Pictures, 2010.

The Spy Next Door (also known as *Double Mission, Kung Fu Nanny,* and *Spy Daddy*), Lions Gate Films, 2010.

The Wolfman (also known as *Wolfman*), Universal, 2010.

Film Producer:

A Perfect Getaway (also known as *Perfect Getaway*), Universal/Rogue Pictures, 2009.

Dear John, Screen Gems, 2010.

The Fighter, Paramount, 2010.

Little Fockers (also known as *Meet the Fockers Sequel, Meet the Little Fockers, Meet These Little Fockers,* and *Meet the Parents: Little Fockers*), Universal, 2010.

Untitled Comedy (also known as *Movie 43*), Relativity Media, c. 2010.

Sanctum (also known as *James Cameron's "Sanctum"*), 2010, Rogue Pictures, 2011.

The Dark Fields, Rogue Pictures/Relativity Media, 2011.

Haywire (also known as *Knockout*), Lions Gate Films, 2011.

Immortals, Universal, 2011.

Contractors, Relativity Media, c. 2011.

The Low Dweller, Relativity Media/Energy Entertainment/Appian Way/Scott Free Productions, c. 2011.

Worked on other projects.

Television Appearances; Episodic:

Guest, "Michael Keaton/Rob Schneider/Ryan Kavanaugh," *In the House with Peter Bart & Peter Guber* (also known as *In the House*), Starz!, 2010.

OTHER SOURCES

Periodicals:

New York Times, May 5, 2008, p. C8.

Electronic:

Guardian http://www.guardian.co.uk, September 24, 2010.

Relativity Media, http://www.relativitymediallc.com, August 7, 2010.

KAY, Vernon 1974–

PERSONAL

Full name, Vernon Charles Kay; born April 27, 1974, in Bolton, England; son of Norman and Gladys Kay; married Tess Daly (a television host), September 12, 2003; children: Phoebe Elizabeth, Amber Isabella. *Education:* Manchester Metropolitan University, diploma.

Addresses: *Agent*—George Ashton, James Grant Media, 94 Strand on the Green, Chiswick, London W4 3NN, England.

Career: Actor and television host. Worked as a model; appeared in a commercial for JD Sports, 2002. Prince's Trust, ambassador.

Member: British Model Flying Association, Fifty Club, Solo House.

Awards, Honors: Honorary doctorate, University of Bolton, 2009.

CREDITS

Television Appearances; Series:

Presenter, *FBi,* 2000.

Presenter, *T4,* Channel 4, 2000–2005.

Presenter, *Boys and Girls,* 2003.

Presenter, *A Wife for William,* 2004.

Presenter, *HeadJam,* 2004.

Presenter, *Celebrities Under Pressure,* ITV, 2004.

Host, *Hit Me Baby 1 More Time,* ITV, 2005.

Host, *Hit Me, Baby, One More Time,* NBC, 2005.

Contestant, *Gameshow Marathon,* CBS, 2005.

Presenter, *Just the Two of Us,* BBC, 2006–2007.

Host, *All Star Family Fortunes,* ITV, 2006–10.

Host, *The 5 O'clock Show,* 2010.

Presenter, *The Whole 19 Yards,* ITV1, 2010.

Also presenter for *Top of the Pops Plus.*

Television Appearances; Specials:

The 100 Greatest Kids TV Shows, Channel 4, 2001.

Britney Laid Bare, 2002.

Presenter, *Smash Hits Poll Winners Party,* Channel 4, 2002, 2005.
Presenter, *Prince's Trust Urban Music Festival: A Tribute to Jay–Z,* 2004.
Bruce Forsyth: A BAFTA Tribute, 2005.
Avenue of the Stars: 50 Years of ITV, ITV, 2005.
Presenter, *The Record of the Year 2005,* 2005.
Host, *The Prince's Trust 30th Birthday: Live,* ITV, 2006.
Presenter, *T4 on the Beach 2006,* Channel 4, 2006.
Presenter, *T4 on the Beach: The Cheeky Highlights,* Channel 4, 2006.
Contestant, *Celebrity Pot Black,* 2006.
Presenter, *Duet Impossible,* 2006.
Host, *2006 Greatest Hits,* 2006.
World's Greatest Elvis, 2007.
Happy Birthday Brucie!, BBC, 2008.

Television Appearances; Miniseries:
I Love 1980's, 2001.
I Love 1990's, 2001.
Host, *Beat the Star,* 2008.

Television Appearances; Pilots:
Presenter, *California Dreaming,* BBC, 2005.

Television Appearances; Episodic:
Babewatch, ITV, 1998.
Liquid News, BBC, 2001, 2002, 2003.
It's Only TV … but I Like It, 2002.
Shooting Stars, BBC, 2002.
They Think It's All Over, BBC, 2003.
Friday Night with Jonathan Ross, BBC America, 2003.
Bo' Selecta!, Channel 4, 2003, 2004.
The Terry and Gaby Show, Channel 5, 2004.
The Paul O'Grady Show, ITV, multiple appearances, including some as guest host, between 2005 and 2009.
This Morning, ITV, 2005, 2006.
A Question of Sport, BBC, 2006.
How Do You Solve a Problem Like Maria?, CBC, 2006.
Strictly Come Dancing, BBC, 2006.
Davina, BBC, 2006.
Presenter, "The Price Is Right," *Gameshow Marathon,* CBS, 2007.
Presenter, "Mr. and Mrs.," *Gameshow Marathon,* CBS, 2007.
(Uncredited) *Hell's Kitchen,* ITV, 2007.
"The Extra Special Series Finale," *Extras,* HBO, 2007.
Thank God You're Here, NBC, 2008.
Loose Women, ITV, 2009.
Voice, *Top Gear,* BBC, 2009.
(In archive footage) *Live from Studio Five,* Channel 5, 2010.

Appeared in *Clothes Show Live,* BBC, and *The Big Breakfast,* Channel 4; presenter for *The Mag,* Channel 5; also reporter for Trouble Television.

Television Appearances; Awards Presentations:
Presenter, *Brit Awards,* 2003.
Host, *British Academy Video Games Awards,* 2006.
The British Comedy Awards 2006 Live, ITV, 2006.
The National Television Awards, ITV, audience member, 2006, then 2007.

Film Appearances:
Himself, *Shaun of the Dead,* Focus Features, 2004.

Radio Appearances; Series:
Presenter, *Xfm,* BBC1, beginning 2006.

Presenter of entertainment programming for BBC1, beginning 2004.

RECORDINGS

Videos:
Men in Black Training Video: UK, Columbia TriStar Home Video, 2002.
Presenter, *Family Fortunes* (video games), Universal, Volumes 2–4, 2006–2008.

OTHER SOURCES

Periodicals:
Independent (London), January 4, 2007, p. 16.

Electronic:
Vernon Kay Official Site, http://www.officialvernonkay.com, August 4, 2010.

KEATING, Trish

PERSONAL

Born in Quebec, Canada; raised in Nova Scotia, Canada; father, a professor. *Education:* St. Francis Xavier University, B.S., clothing and textiles, 1968; certificate from the British Columbia Academy of Fashion; diploma in costume studies from Dalhousie University.

Career: Costume designer. Also worked as a set dresser and in other capacities. Worked as an assistant costume designer for CBC Television. Designed costumes for television commercials.

CREDITS

Film Costume Designer:
Dead Wrong (also known as *The Columbia Connection, Death Fighter,* and *Entrapment*), Heritage/Sounder Productions, 1983.
Walls (also known as *Lock Up*), Jerico Films, 1984.
The Boy Who Could Fly, Twentieth Century–Fox, 1986.
The Accused, Paramount, 1988.
Run, Buena Vista, 1991.
Arctic Blue, New City Productions, 1993.
White Fang 2: Myth of the White Wolf (also known as *White Fang 2* and *White Fang II*), Buena Vista, 1994.
Tales from the Crypt Presents: "Demon Knight" (also known as *Demon Keeper* and *Tales of the Crypt: Demon Knight*), MCA/Universal, 1995.
Carpool, Warner Bros., 1996.
Tales from the Crypt Presents: "Bordello of Blood" (also known as *Bordello of Blood* and *Dead Easy*), Universal, 1996.
Disturbing Behavior (also known as *Disturbing Behaviour*), Metro–Goldwyn–Mayer, 1998.
The 6th Day (also known as *On the Sixth Day* and *The Sixth Day*), Columbia, 2000.
Spooky House, R.S. Entertainment/ECG Worldwide Entertainment, 2000, Entertainment Highway, 2002.
Hope Springs (also known as *New Cardiff*), Buena Vista, 2003.
Man about Town, Media 8 Entertainment, c. 2005.
Good Luck Chuck (also known as *The Warm–Up Guy*), Lions Gate Films, 2007.
In the Land of Women, Warner Bros., 2007.
Trick 'r Treat (also known as *Trick or Treat*), Warner Bros., 2008.
Love Happens (also known as *Brand New Day* and *Traveling*), Universal, 2009.
The Uninvited (also known as *Apparition* and *A Tale of Two Sisters*), Paramount, 2009.

Film Assistant Costume Designer:
Rainbow War (short film), Pyramid Media, 1985.
Reindeer Games (also known as *Deception* and *Wild Christmas*), Dimension Films, 2000.

Film Set Dresser:
Beyond My Reach, Boulevard Films, 1990.
What the Moon Saw, Boulevard Films/Century Park Pictures, 1990.

Film Work; Other:
Costume supervisor: British Columbia, *The Thing* (also known as *John Carpenter's "The Thing"*), Universal, 1982.
Seamstress, *Ladies and Gentlemen, the Fabulous Stains* (also known as *All Washed Up* and *The Professionals*), Paramount, 1982.

Costumer, *Never Cry Wolf,* Buena Vista, 1983.
Wardrobe supervisor, *Running Brave,* Buena Vista/Paramount, 1983.
Associate costume designer, *Knight Moves* (also known as *Enigma mortal* and *Face to Face*), Warner Bros., 1992.
Financial contributor, *Tilt* (short film), Starstruck Pictures, 2003.

Television Costume Designer; Series:
Murphy's Law, ABC, 1988–89.
The Odyssey, CBC and other channels, 1992–94.
John Doe (also known as *Der Fall John Doe!* and *Mies vailla nimeae*), Fox, 2002–2003.
Killer Instinct (also known as *Deviant Behavior, The Gate,* and *Pahuuden jaeljillae*), Fox, 2005.

Television Costume Designer; Miniseries:
Intensity (also known as *Dean Koontz's "Intensity"*), Fox, 1997.
Living with the Dead (also known as *Talking to Heaven*), CBS, 2002.

Television Costume Designer; Movies:
The People across the Lake, NBC, 1988.
The Death of the Incredible Hulk (also known as *The Death of the Incredible Hulk: The Movie* and *Hulk*), NBC, 1990.
Christmas on Division Street, CBS, 1991.
Fatal Memories (also known as *The Eileen Franklin Story*), NBC, 1992.
The Amy Fisher Story (also known as *Beyond Control* and *Lolita story*), ABC, 1993.
Liar, Liar (also known as *Daddy's Little Secret* and *Liar, Liar: Between Father and Daughter*), CBC and CBS, 1993.
A Christmas Romance, CBS, 1994.
Seasons of the Heart, NBC, 1994.
Broken Trust (also known as *Court of Honor*), TNT, 1995.
Johnny's Girl, ABC, 1995.
Mother, May I Sleep with Danger? (also known as *The Stalker*), NBC, 1996.
Night Visitors (also known as *Area 51*), NBC, 1996.
The Advocate's Devil, ABC, 1997.
A Call to Remember, Starz!, 1997.
Baby Monitor: Sound of Fear (also known as *Sound of Fear*), USA Network, 1998.
Killers in the House (also known as *Captivity*), USA Network, 1998.
Wilder Days, part of *Johnson & Johnson Spotlight Presentations,* TNT, 2003.
Meltdown (also known as *American Meltdown*), FX Network, 2004.

Television Work; Other; Movies:
Women's costumer, *Consenting Adult,* ABC, 1985.

Set dresser, *Bushfire Moon* (also known as *The Christmas Visitor* and *Miracle Down Under*), [Australia], also broadcast on *WonderWorks,* PBS, c. 1987.

Television Costume Designer; Specials:
Visitors from the Unknown, CBS, 1992.

Television Costume Designer; Episodic:
"Shattered Vows," *The Hitchhiker* (also known as *Deadly Nightmares* and *Le voyageur*), HBO, 1983.
"Cabin Fever," *The Hitchhiker* (also known as *Deadly Nightmares* and *Le voyageur*), HBO, 1987.
"Dead Heat," *The Hitchhiker* (also known as *Deadly Nightmares* and *Le voyageur*), HBO, 1987.
"Minuteman," *The Hitchhiker* (also known as *Deadly Nightmares* and *Le voyageur*), HBO, 1987.
"A Day in the Life," *Saved,* TNT, 2006.
"Baptiste," *Human Target,* Fox, 2010.
"Christopher Chance," *Human Target,* Fox, 2010.
"Corner Man," *Human Target,* Fox, 2010.
"Victoria," *Human Target,* Fox, 2010.

Television Costumer Designer; Pilots:
Secrets of the Unknown, CBS, 1991.
Beer Money, USA Network, 2001.
Tru Calling (also known as *Heroine, Tru,* and *True Calling*), Fox, 2003.
V, ABC, 2009.

KELEGIAN, Sylva 1962–
(Silva Kelegian, Sylvia Kelegian)

PERSONAL

Born February 22, 1962, in New York, NY; father, a pianist; mother, a ballet dancer; married Jude Ciccolella (an actor), December 20, 1997. *Avocational Interests:* Animals.

Addresses: *Agent*—Ellis Talent Group, 4705 Laurel Canyon Rd., Valley Village, CA 91607.

Career: Actress. Actors Studio, life member. The Forgotten Dog Foundation, cofounder. Also known as Sylvia Kelegian.

CREDITS

Film Appearances:
Denise Ventoula (The Angel), *The Devil & the Angel,* Big Fun Productions/Miracle Pictures, 1997.
Drug user, *Bringing out the Dead,* Paramount, 1999.

Marcia, *Sometime in August,* 1999.
Mother at fire, *Spider–Man* (also known as *Spiderman, Spider–Man: The Motion Picture, El hombre arana, Homem–Aranha, Omul paianjen, Pokember, Spider–Man—Haemaehaekkimies,* and *Spindelmannen*), Columbia, 2002.
Nurse Hodges, *Crash* (also known as *Collision* and *L.A. Crash*), Lions Gate Films/Arclight Films, 2004.
Office assistant, *Coach Carter* (also known as *All Day Long*), Paramount, 2005.
(As Silva Kelegian) Shopper, *Going Shopping* (also known as *Shopping*), Rainbow Releasing, 2005.
Ivy Starnes, *Atlas Shrugged,* The Strike Productions, 2011.

Television Appearances; Movies:
Ellie Carver, *Desperation* (also known as *Desolation* and *Stephen King's "Desperation"*), ABC, 2006.

Television Appearances; Episodic:
Second technician, "Infection," *Babylon 5* (also known as *B5, Babylon 5.,* and *Spacecenter Babylon 5*), syndicated, 1994.
Sandra Lawlor, "Burned," *Law & Order* (also known as *Law & Order Prime*), NBC, 1997.
Margo Grayson, "Disciple," *Law & Order* (also known as *Law & Order Prime*), NBC, 1999.
Margaret Custance, "A Hole in Juan," *NYPD Blue* (also known as *New York Blues, New York Cops—NYPD Blue, New York Police, New York Police Blues, New York Police Department, N.Y.P.D,* and *N.Y.P.D.*), ABC, 2000.
Lindsay Branson (some sources cite role as Lindsay Bramson), "Victims," *Law & Order: Special Victims Unit* (also known as *Law & Order's Sex Crimes, Law & Order: SVU,* and *Special Victims Unit*), NBC, 2001.
Caroline Tytell, "Only Schmucks Pay Income Tax," *NYPD Blue* (also known as *New York Blues, New York Cops—NYPD Blue, New York Police, New York Police Blues, New York Police Department, N.Y.P.D,* and *N.Y.P.D.*), ABC, 2003.
Margie, "Addicted to Love," *Strong Medicine,* Lifetime, 2003.
Roz Kempf, "Hazel Park," *The Guardian* (also known as *El guardia, The Guardian—Retter mit Herz, Le protecteur, O allos mou eaftos, Ochita bengoshi Nick Fallin, Ochita bengoshi Nick Fallin 2,* and *Oikeuden puolesta*), CBS, 2003.
Stephanie Minkowski, "Human Error," *Mister Sterling,* NBC, 2003.
Lauren Andrews–Dardis, "Lost and Found," *Without a Trace* (also known as *Vanished* and *W.A.T.*), CBS, 2004.
Marie Danaher, "Predictive Neglect," *Judging Amy,* CBS, 2004.
Lucy McKittrick, "The Hunt," *Invasion,* ABC, 2005.
Lucy McKittrick, "Unnatural Selection," *Invasion,* ABC, 2005.

Meg Wheeler, "Dance with Me," *Blind Justice*, ABC, 2005.

Denise, "The Killing Box," *Prison Break* (also known as *The Break, Prison Break: Manhunt, Prison Break: On the Run, Grande evasion, I apodrasi, Pako, Pogenemine,* and *Prison Break—Em busca da verdade*), Fox, 2006.

Lucy McKittrick, "All God's Creatures," *Invasion*, ABC, 2006.

Federal agent, "Kingdom Come," *Big Love*, HBO, 2007.

Federal agent, "Oh, Pioneers," *Big Love*, HBO, 2007.

Diane, "Welcome to Kanagawa," *Desperate Housewives* (also known as *Beautes desespereees, Desperate housewives—I segreti di Wisteria Lane, Desupareto na tsuma tachi, Esposas desesperadas, Frustrerte fruer, Gotowe na wszystko, Kucanice, Meeleheitel koduperenaised, Mujeres desesperadas, Noikokyres se apognosi, Szueletett felesegek,* and *Taeydelliset naiset*), ABC, 2008.

Rita Gratton, "The He in the She," *Bones* (also known as *Brennan, Bones—Die Knochenjaegerin, Dr. Csont,* and *Kondid*), Fox, 2008.

Donna, "A Long, Strange Trip," *ER* (also known as *Emergency Room* and *E.R.*), NBC, 2009.

Pam Bayer, "Lotto Fever," *Cold Case* (also known as *Anexihniastes ypothesis, Caso abierto, Cold case—affaires classees, Cold Case—Kein Opfer ist je vergessen, Doegloett aktak, Kalla spaar, Todistettavasti syyllinen,* and *Victimes du passe*), CBS, 2009.

Stage Appearances:

Mabel Codd, *The Soul of an Intruder*, Theatre 3, New York City, 2000.

KELLY, David 1929–
(Dave Kelly)

PERSONAL

Original name, Daithi O Ceallaigh; born July 11, 1929, in Dublin, Ireland; married Laurie Morton (an actress), February 2, 1961; children: David, Miriam. *Education:* Trained at Abbey Theatre School, Dublin, Ireland; also trained as a drafter and calligrapher. *Avocational Interests:* Painting with watercolors.

Career: Actor. Performed at age eight as a child actor in Ireland, including appearances at Gaiety Theatre, Dublin, c. 1937. Also worked at an advertising agency early in his career.

Awards, Honors: Screen Actors Guild Award nominations, outstanding supporting actor and outstanding cast performance (with others), Golden Satellite Award, best actor in a comedy or musical motion picture, International Press Academy, and Chlotrudis Award nomination, best supporting actor, all 1999, for *Waking Ned Devine;* Lifetime Achievement Award, *Irish Times,* 2003; Irish Film and Television Award nomination, best supporting actor in a feature film, 2005, for *Charlie and the Chocolate Factory;* Lifetime Achievement Award, Irish Film and Television Awards, 2005; Helen Hayes Award, Washington Theatre Awards Society, for *Moon for the Misbegotten;* ESB National Media Award (of Ireland), lifetime achievement.

CREDITS

Film Appearances:

Fenton, *The Mail Van Murder* (short film), Anglo–Amalgamated Film Distributors, 1957.

First customer, *Dublin Nightmare*, J. Arthur Rank, 1958.

Reception clerk, *The Quare Fellow* (also known as *The Condemned Man*), Astor Pictures, 1962.

(As Dave Kelly) Ticket collector, *The Girl with Green Eyes,* Lopert, 1964.

(As Dave Kelly) Garrett Deasy, *Ulysses,* Continental Distributing, 1967.

Vicar, *The Italian Job,* Paramount, 1969.

Maguire, *Quackser Fortune Has a Cousin in the Bronx,* 1970.

(Uncredited) Adjutant, *The McKenzie Break* (also known as *Escape*), United Artists, 1970.

Murphy, *Never Mind the Quality: Feel the Width,* Metro–Goldwyn–Mayer, 1973.

Conan O'Byrne, *Philadelphia, Here I Come,* 1975.

Chauffeur in Ireland, *The Next Man,* Allied Artists, 1976.

Dean of studies, *A Portrait of the Artist as a Young Man,* Contemporary Films, 1977, Howard Mahler Films, 1979.

Little person, *The Purple Taxi* (also known as *Un taxi mauve*), dubbed version, Quartet Films, 1980.

Cameron, *The Jigsaw Man,* United Film Distribution, 1983.

Dr. Trevor, *Anne Devlin,* COW, 1984.

Stryker's War (also known as *Thou Shalt Not Kill ... Except*), Film World, 1985.

Surgeon, *Pirates,* Cannon, 1986.

Daniel Tracey, *Joyriders,* Cannon, 1989.

Grandfather, *Into the West,* Miramax, 1993.

Seamus, *The Barber Shop* (short film), Mainstream Films/Paradox Pictures, 1993.

Christy Ward, *A Man of No Importance,* Sony Pictures Classics, 1994.

Mr. Dunwoody, *Moondance,* Buena Vista Home Video, 1995.

Father Gaynor, *The Run of the Country,* Columbia, 1995.

O'Connor, *The MatchMaker,* Gramercy, 1997.

Michael O'Sullivan, *Waking Ned Devine* (also known as *Wake Up! Ned* and *Waking Ned*), Fox Searchlight, 1998.

Father Grogan, *Ordinary Decent Criminal,* Miramax, 2000.

Fergus Wilks, *Greenfingers* (also known as *Jailbuds*), Metro–Goldwyn–Mayer/Samuel Goldwyn, 2001.

Doc, *Mean Machine,* Paramount, 2002.

Dave, *Mystics,* Momentum Pictures Home Entertainment, 2002.

Walter, *The Last,* 67 Pictures, 2002.

O'Toole, *Puckoon,* United Artists, 2002.

Trival, *Agent Cody Banks 2: Destination London,* Metro–Goldwyn–Mayer, 2004.

Priest/Michael, *Laws of Attraction,* New Line Cinema, 2004.

Paddy O'Flannagan, *The Calcium Kid,* Universal, 2004.

Seamus Kerrigan, *Dutch Bird* (short film), Catchlight Productions/One Take Pictures, 2004.

Grandpa Joe, *Charlie and the Chocolate Factory* (also released as *Charlie and the Chocolate Factory: The IMAX Experience*), Warner Bros., 2005.

Frank Kovak, *The Kovak Box,* First Look International, 2007.

Mr. Toole, *The Martyr's Crown* (short film), Park Films, 2007.

Guard, *Stardust,* Paramount, 2007.

Narrator, *Poetic License* (short film), Great Western Films, 2007.

The doctor, *The Good Doctor* (short film), I–Wire Films, 2009.

Television Appearances; Series:

Mick Cavan, *Emmerdale Farm,* YTV, 1973.

Albert Riddle, *Robin's Nest,* ITV, 1977–81, syndicated, 1982–83.

Wobbly Ron, *Cowboys,* 1980–81.

Upwardly Mobile, 1998.

Also appeared as Sylvie Dolan in *Glenroe,* and as Fred, *Slinger's Day.*

Television Appearances; Miniseries:

The Passing Show, 1951.

Matthew, *The Ronnie Barker Playhouse,* 1968.

The thief, *For Amusement Only,* BBC, 1968.

Voice of dead man, *Tales from the Lazy Acre,* 1972.

Walter, *Oh, Father!,* 1973.

Rashers, *Strumpet City,* RTE, 1980.

Abdab, *Whoops Apocalypse,* ITV, 1982.

Hall porter, *Scarlett,* CBS, 1994.

Angus the gunsmith, *Kidnapped,* ABC Family, 1995.

Television Appearances; Movies:

Sergo, *Red Monarch,* 1983.

Balthazar, "The Comedy of Errors," *The Complete Dramatic Works of William Shakespeare,* BBC, 1983.

Poet, *Merlin of the Crystal Cave,* BBC, 1991.

Rough for Theatre I, RTE, broadcast in the U.S. by PBS, 2001.

Howard Mather, *The Front,* Lifetime, 2010.

Television Appearances; Specials:

(As Dave Kelly) "No Skin Off Me," *G.E. True Theatre* (also known as *General Electric Theatre* and *G.E. Theatre*), 1957.

Sean Kelly, "The Iron Harp," *ITV Play of the Week,* ITV, 1958.

Sergeant Hanna, "Rest in Violence," *ITV Television Playhouse,* ITV, 1958.

"I Loved You Last Summer," *Armchair Theatre,* 1965.

"The Big Blonde," *Armchair Theatre,* 1966.

Finbar, "The Retreat," *The Wednesday Play,* BBC, 1966.

Miko, "A Crucial Week in the Life of a Grocer's Assistant," *The Wednesday Play,* BBC, 1967.

Joe, "A Young Man in Trouble," *Armchair Theatre,* ABC England and Thames Television, 1970.

Mr. Casey and director of the college, "Stephen D," *BBC Play of the Month,* BBC, 1972.

Cloggy Moore, "The Virgins," *Armchair Theatre,* ABC England and Thames Television, 1974.

Mark, "Fugitive," *Play for Today,* BBC1, 1974.

Judge, "The Legion Hall Bombing," *Play for Today,* BBC1, 1978.

Voice, *The Light Princess,* BBC, 1978.

Tavern keeper, "The Hunchback of Notre Dame," *Hallmark Hall of Fame,* CBS, 1982.

The … Irish Film and Television Awards, (presenter) 2005, then 2009.

Fawlty Exclusive: Basil's Best Bits, 2009.

Television Appearances; Episodic:

Kennefick, "Death in England," *Undermind,* 1965.

Con, "It's a Terrible Way to Be," *Public Eye,* ITV, 1966.

Whistler, "One for Sorrow," *The Informer,* BBC, 1966.

Furrier, "A Sinister Sort of Service," *Adam Adamant Lives!,* BBC, 1967.

Mr. Perry, "The Casting Session," *Half Hour Story,* 1968.

McDara, "The Assassin," *The Jazz Age,* BBC, 1968.

Sean O'Riordan, "Blood Is Thinner than Water," *Never Mind the Quality, Feel the Width,* 1970.

Cousin Enda, "The Sacred Chemise of Miss Argyll," *Me Mammy,* 1971.

Cedric Jackson, "A Neighbour's Goods: Parts 1 & 2," *Z Cars,* BBC, 1972.

Carlson, "To the Lowest Bidder," *The Adventurer,* syndicated, 1973.

Mr. O'Leary, "Radio Activity," *Doctor on the Go,* 1975.

O'Reilly, "The Builders," *Fawlty Towers,* BBC, 1975.

Inky Smith, "Easy Money," *Mr. Big,* BBC, 1977.

Paddy, "Rebel without a Pause," *Citizen Smith,* BBC, 1978.

Tramp, *Time of My Life,* 1980.

Dooley, "One of Those Days," *The Gentle Touch,* London Weekend Television, 1982.

Smiling Smiley, "The Muse in Skebawn," *The Irish R.M.,* PBS, 1985.

Rummy, "Rummy's Cut," *Yellowthread Street,* 1990.

Paddy, "When the Going Gets Tough, the Tough Go Shopping," *2point4 Children,* BBC, 1991.

Paddy, "Dirty Bowling," *2point4 Children,* BBC, 1991.

Pa Deighton, "Substitute," *Heartbeat,* 1997.

Plunkett O'Reilly, "He Healeth the Sick," *Ballykissangel*, BBC1, 1998.

"Charlie and the Chocolate Factory," *HBO First Look*, HBO, 2005.

(Uncredited) *Big Brother's Efourum*, E4, 2005.

Stage Appearances:

Willie Garvey, *Career Angel*, National Theatre, New York City, 1944.

Appeared in productions of *The Crucible; Krapp's Last Tape* (solo show), New York City and other cities; *The Quare Fella; They Might Be Giants;* and *Waiting for Godot*, Joan Littlewood's Theatre Workshop. Also appeared at Nottingham Playhouse, Nottingham, England.

Major Tours:

Toured European cities in productions of *Candida, The Countless Cathleen, Mrs. Warren's Profession,* and *Stephen D.*

Radio Appearances:

Guest on the series *Baldi*, BBC4; also appeared in many other radio presentations.

RECORDINGS

Videos:

The Making of "Puckoon," 2004.

Charlie and the Chocolate Factory: Different Faces, Different Flavors, Warner Home Video, 2005.

Voice of Grandpa Joe, *Charlie and the Chocolate Factory* (video game), Take Two Interactive Software, 2005.

40 Myles On: A Night of Irish Comedy, Park Films, 2007.

(In archive footage) *An Island's Legacy: Preparing for TT*, Spooks Studio Film Distribution, 2007.

OTHER SOURCES

Periodicals:

Independent (London), July 30, 2005.

KELLY, Minka 1980–

PERSONAL

Full name, Minka Dumont Kelly; born June 24, 1980, in Los Angeles, CA; daughter of Rick Dufay (a guitarist) and Maureen (a nightclub showgirl) Kelly.

Addresses: *Agent*—Tracy Brennan, Creative Artists Agency, 2000 Avenue of the Stars, Los Angeles, CA 90067. *Manager*—Nicole King, Management 360, 9111 Wilshire Blvd., Beverly Hills, CA 90210.

Career: Actress. Appeared in commercials for Old Navy stores and Johnson & Johnson health care and medicinal products; Madge Cosmetics, worked as model.

CREDITS

Television Appearances; Series:

Lyla Garrity, *Friday Night Lights* (also known as *F.N.L.*), NBC, 2006–2008, DirecTV, 2009, NBC, 2009–10.

Television Appearances; Pilots:

Lyla Garrity, *Friday Night Lights*, NBC, 2006.
Hope, *Body Politic*, The CW, 2009.

Television Appearances; Episodic:

Monica, "Panic House," *Cracking Up*, Fox, 2004.
Stacey, "Movie Job," *Drake & Josh*, Nickelodeon, 2004.
Bonnie, "Home Again," *American Dreams* (also known as *Our Generation*), NBC, 2005.
Ricki, "The Kid, the Cake, and the Chemistry," *What I Like about You*, The WB, 2005.
Ricki, "Enough Is Enough," *What I Like about You*, The WB, 2005.
Ricki, "I Want My Baby Back," *What I Like about You*, The WB, 2005.
Last Call with Carson Daly, NBC, 2006.
The Bonnie Hunt Show, NBC, 2009.
The Late Late Show with Craig Ferguson, CBS, 2009.
Gaby Moss, "The Big 'O,'" *Parenthood*, NBC, 2010.
Gaby Moss, "What's Goin' On Down There?," *Parenthood*, NBC, 2010.
"Parenthood," *Infanity*, TV Guide Channel, 2010.

Television Appearances; Specials:

"Gift from the Gods Award" winner, *Guys Choice*, Spike TV, 2006.
The Teen Choice Awards, Fox, 2008.
Stand Up to Cancer, multiple networks, 2010.

Film Appearances:

River, *Devil's Highway*, 2005, Image Entertainment, 2007.
Tammy, *The Pumpkin Karver*, First Look International, 2006.
State's Evidence, Push, 2006.
Miss Ross, *The Kingdom*, Universal, 2007.
Autumn, *(560) Days of Summer*, Fox Searchlight, 2009.
Eden Mercer, *Searching for Sonny*, Red Productions, 2010.
Sara, *The Roommate*, Screen Gems, 2011.

OTHER SOURCES

Periodicals:
TV Guide, June 30, 2008, p. 38.

KIBERD, James 1949–

PERSONAL

Born July 6, 1949, in Providence, RI; married Susan Keith (an actress and director), May 17, 1986. *Education:* Studied art at the University of Pennsylvania; studied art in several European cities.

Addresses: *Agent*—(art) MB Modern, 41 East 57th St., 8th Floor, New York, NY 10022.

Career: Actor and director. Worked as an artist, with solo and group exhibitions throughout New York State and in Texas; artist–in–residence at the America the Beautiful Fund, National Endowment for the Arts, and New York State Council on the Arts, all 1979, Rockland Center for the Arts, 1980, and Pouch Cove Foundation, Newfoundland, Canada, 1999. Worked as an acting teacher, public speaker, management consultant, chef, carpenter, and roofer. Named national ambassador for UNICEF.

Member: Screen Actors Guild, Actors' Equity Association, American Federation of Television and Radio Artists.

Awards, Honors: *Soap Opera Digest* Award nomination, outstanding comic performance: daytime, 1992, for *All My Children;* Danny Kaye Award from UNICEF, 1994; Gold Medal of Honor, Houston branch of UNICEF, 1998; Meyer Schapiro Artist Award, Augusta State University, 2002; ariZoni Award (also known as Zony Award), best actor in a major role in a play, 2004, for *The Taming of the Shrew.*

CREDITS

Television Appearances; Series:
Michael "Mike" Donovan, *Loving* (also known as *Love without End;* later known as *The City*), ABC, 1983–85.
Dustin Trent, *Another World* (also known as *Another World: Bay City* and *AW: Bay City*), NBC, 1989.
Trevor Dillon, *All My Children* (also known as *All My Children: The Summer of Seduction* and *La force du destin*), ABC, 1989–2000.

Television Appearances; Specials:
Detective Ben Lawson, "Teenage Confidential," *ABC Afterschool Specials,* ABC, 1996.

Television Appearances; Awards Presentations:
The 17th Annual Daytime Emmy Awards, ABC, 1990.
Presenter, *The 19th Annual Daytime Emmy Awards,* NBC, 1992.

Television Appearances; Episodic:
Lewis Johnson, "One If by Land, Two If by Sea," *Spenser: For Hire* (also known as *Spenser*), ABC, 1986.
Dollar, "Unfinished Business," *Third Watch,* NBC, 2001.
Hal Munson, *As the World Turns,* CBS, 2001.
(In archive footage) Trevor Dillon, "All My Children," *Biography* (also known as *A&E Biography: All My Children*), Arts and Entertainment, 2003.

Television Appearances; Pilots:
Michael "Mike" Donovan, *Loving* (also known as *Love without End;* later known as *The City*), ABC, 1983.

Film Appearances:
Liquor store owner, *Queenie in Love,* Pyramide Distribution, 2001.
Dr. Samuel Hirsch, *Demon under Glass,* BCI Eclipse, 2002.
Al Walker, *Survival of the Fittest* (short film), 2005.
Walter, *Sunset Tuxedo* (short film), American Film Institute, 2005.
Sheriff, *Jack* (short film), Black Hat Productions, 2006.
Bob the backpacker, *Hunter–Gatherer* (short film), 2008.
Elliot, *Soldier's Heart,* 2008.

Some sources cite appearances in other films.

Stage Appearances:
Colonel Kercelick, *Veterans Day* (also known as *Veteran's Day* and *Veterans' Day*), Denver Center for the Performing Arts, Denver, CO, c. 1987–88.
Whirling Joe Ferguson, *The Male Animal,* Equity Library Theatre, New York City, c. 1988.
Taylor Lydell, *Quiet on the Set,* Westbeth Theatre, New York City, 1990.
Duncan McFee, *Double Double,* The Cape Playhouse, Dennis, MA, 1992.
Title role, *Macbeth,* Pennsylvania Shakespeare Festival, Allentown College, Labuda Center for the Performing Arts, Center Valley, PA, 1993.
Ty Cobb (title role), *Cobb,* Penguin Rep Theatre, Stony Point, NY, 1995.
Leontes, *The Winter's Tale,* The West End Theatre Company, Church of St. Paul and St. Andrew, New York City, c. 1999.

Seward, *Defending the Light: Seward for the Defense* (also known as *Defending the Light*), New Federal Theatre, Tribeca Performing Arts Center, New York City, 2000.

Dr. Treves, *The Elephant Man*, Pacific Repertory Theatre, Carmel–by–the–Sea, CA, 2002.

Fluellen and member of the chorus, *Henry V*, Pacific Repertory Theatre, 2002.

Henry IV, *Henry IV, Part 1*, Pacific Repertory Theatre, 2002.

Henry IV, *Henry IV, Part 2*, Pacific Repertory Theatre, 2002.

Klowne Launcelot Gobbo, *The Merchant of Venice*, Pacific Repertory Theatre, 2002.

The stage manager, *Our Town*, Culver–Stockton College, Robert W. Brown Performing Arts Center, Mabee Little Theatre, Canton, MO, 2002.

Greg, *Sylvia*, The Miles Memorial Playhouse, Norris Center for the Performing Arts, Rolling Hills Estates, CA, c. 2003.

Petruchio, *The Taming of the Shrew*, Southwest Shakespeare Company, AZ, c. 2003–2004.

Capulet, *Romeo and Juliet* (also known as *Romeo&Juliet* and *Romeo & Juliet*), Shakespeare Santa Monica, Santa Monica, CA, c. 2005.

John Casey, *Manhattan Casanova*, Hudson Stage, Pace University, The Woodward Hall, Woodward Hall Theater, Briarcliff Manor, NY, 2006.

Appeared as Biff, *Death of a Salesman*, as Andrew Makepeace Ladd III, *Love Letters*, as Crumblish and J. C., *Recent Developments in Southern Connecticut*, as Trigorin, *The Seagull*, and as Nick, *Who's Afraid of Virginia Woolf?*, all Penguin Rep Theatre; as Larry Parks, *Are You Now or Have You Ever Been?*, New Federal Theatre; as Chuck, *Fluorescent Hunger*, Home Theatre, NY; as Gouverneur Morris, *Founding Fathers*, New York Historical Society; and as Claudius, ghost, and player king, *Hamlet*, Sande Shurin Theatre, New York City.

Stage Director:

(With Susan Keith) *Our Town*, Norris Center for the Performing Arts, Rolling Hills Estates, CA, and Culver–Stockton College, Robert W. Brown Performing Arts Center, Mabee Little Theatre, Canton, MO, 2002.

A Perfect Ganesh, Synaptic Productions, Chappaqua Crossing Auditorium, Chappaqua, NY, 2008.

RECORDINGS

Videos:

(And in archive footage) Trevor Dillon and himself, *All My Children: Behind the Scenes* (short documentary), ABC Studios, 1994.

(In archive footage) Trevor Dillon, *Daytime's Greatest Weddings*, Buena Vista Home Video, 2004.

OTHER SOURCES

Periodicals:
New York Times, October 26, 2008, p. 10L.
Soap Opera Digest, March 5, 1991, pp. 28–30, 32.

Electronic:
James Kiberd http://www.jameskiberd.com, August 7, 2010.

KOFFLER, Pamela
   (Pamela R. Koffler)

PERSONAL

Daughter of a dentist; married Russell Lee Fine (a cinematographer). *Education:* Yale University, B.A., 1987.

Addresses: *Office*—Killer Films, 526 West 26th St., Suite 715, New York, NY 10001. *Agent*—Craig Gering, Creative Artists Agency, 2000 Avenue of the Stars, Los Angeles, CA 90067.

Career: Producer. Killer Films, New York City, partner and executive in charge of production. Also worked as script supervisor, post–production supervisor, production coordinator, line producer, and assistant director, in some cases credited as Pam Koffler.

Awards, Honors: Producers Award, Independent Spirit Awards, Independent Features Project/West, 2000, for *I'm Losing You;* Independent Spirit Award nomination (with others), best feature, 2002, for *Hedwig and the Angry Inch;* Emmy Award nomination, outstanding made–for–television movie, 2006, and Producers Guild of America Award nomination, television producer of the year in long–form category, 2007, both (with others) for *Mrs. Harris.*

CREDITS

Film Producer:
Office Killer, Miramax, 1997.
I'm Losing You, Lions Gate Films, 1999.
Crime and Punishment in Suburbia, United Artists, 2000.
Hedwig and the Angry Inch, Fine Line, 2001.

Women in Film, Lions Gate Films, 2001.
The Grey Zone, 2001, Lions Gate Films, 2003.
(As Pamela R. Koffler) *Chelsea Walls,* Lions Gate Films, 2002.
One Hour Photo (also known as *Stalker*), Fox Searchlight, 2002.
Camp, IFC Films, 2003.
The Company, Sony Pictures Classics, 2003.
A Home at the End of the World, Warner Independent Pictures, 2004.
The Notorious Bettie Page, Picturehouse Entertainment, 2005.
Savage Grace, IFC Films, 2008.
Then She Found Me, THINKFilm, 2008.
Motherhood, Freestyle Releasing, 2009.

Film Executive Producer:
Boys Don't Cry, Fox Searchlight, 1999.
The Safety of Objects, 2001, IFC Films, 2003.
An American Crime, First Look International, 2007.
Dirty Girl, Weinstein Company, 2010.

Film Associate Producer:
Post Cards from America, Strand Releasing, 1995.
Series 7: The Contenders (also known as *Series 7* and *Series 7: The Battle Royal*), USA Films, 2001.

Film Appearances:
Phrenology head, *Swoon,* Fine Line, 1992.

Television Executive Producer:
Mrs. Harris (movie), HBO, 2005.
Mildred Pierce (miniseries), HBO, 2010.

Television Work; Episodic:
Associate producer, "Romantic Comedy" and "Film in the Television Age" segments, *American Cinema,* PBS.

Television Appearances; Episodic:
Appeared in "One Hour Photo," *Anatomy of a Scene,* Sundance Channel.

RECORDINGS

Videos:
The Making of "One Hour Photo," Twentieth Century–Fox, 2002.

KURTZMAN, Alex 1973–
   (Alex Kurtzman–Counter)

PERSONAL

Full name, Alexander Hilary Kurtzman; born September 7, 1973, in Los Angeles, CA; married Samantha Counter (a director, producer, and cinematographer).

Addresses: *Office*—Kurtzman/Orci, 100 Universal City Plaza, Bldg. 5125, Universal City, CA 91608. *Agent*—Creative Artists Agency, 2000 Avenue of the Stars, Los Angeles, CA 90067. *Publicist*—I/D Public Relations, 8409 Santa Monica Blvd., West Hollywood, CA 90069.

Career: Producer and writer. Kurtzman/Orci (also known as K/O and Kurtzman Orci Paper Products), Universal City, CA, principal. Participated in entertainment conventions, including serving as a panelist.

Member: Writers Guild of America, West, Directors Guild of America.

Awards, Honors: Writers Guild of America Award nominations (television), new series and long form—original, both with others, 2009, for *Fringe;* Writers Guild of America Award nomination (screen), best adapted screenplay, and Saturn Award nomination, best writing, Academy of Science Fiction, Fantasy & Horror Films, both with Roberto Orci, 2010, for *Star Trek.*

CREDITS

Film Executive Producer:
The Proposal, Walt Disney Studios Motion Pictures, 2009.
Star Trek (also known as *Christa & Christian's Big Adventure, Corporate Headquarters, Corporate HQ, The Ernest Castlehun Chronicles, Star Trek: The Beginning, Star Trek XI, Star Trek: The Future Begins, Star Trek Zero, Untitled Blake Allen Project, Untitled Paramount Project,* and *Untitled Walter Lace Project;* IMAX versions known as *Star Trek: (IMAX DMR Version)* and *Star Trek: The IMAX Experience*), Paramount, 2009.

Film Producer:
Eagle Eye (also known as *Control total;* IMAX version known as *Eagle Eye: The IMAX Experience*), DreamWorks, 2008.
Cowboys & Aliens, DreamWorks, 2011.

Film Work; Other:
Production assistant, *Bodies, Rest & Motion* (also known as *Bodies, Rest and Motion*), Fine Line, 1993.

Worked on other projects.

Television Executive Producer; Series:
Jack of All Trades, syndicated, 2000.
Alias, ABC, 2003–2004.
Fringe, Fox, 2008–2009.

Hawaii Five–O, CBS, 2010—.
Transformers Prime (animated; also known as *Transformers: Prime*), The Hub, beginning c. 2010.

Television Co–executive Producer; Series:
Hercules: The Legendary Journeys (also known as *Hercules*), syndicated, beginning c. 1999.
Alias, ABC, 2002–2003.

Television Work; Other; Series:
Supervising producer, *Alias,* ABC, 2001–2002.
Creator, *Fringe,* Fox, 2008—.
Consulting producer, *Fringe,* Fox, 2009—.
Developer, *Hawaii Five–O,* CBS, 2010—.

Also worked as a creative associate, *Hercules: The Legendary Journeys* (also known as *Hercules*), syndicated.

Television Co–executive Producer; Episodic:
"City of the Dead," *Hercules: The Legendary Journeys* (also known as *Hercules*), syndicated, 1999.
"Seeds of Faith," *Xena: Warrior Princess* (also known as *Xena* and *Zina*), syndicated, 2000.

Television Creative Associate; Episodic:
"The Giant Killer," *Xena: Warrior Princess* (also known as *Xena* and *Zina*), syndicated, 1996.
"Girls Just Wanna Have Fun," *Xena: Warrior Princess* (also known as *Xena* and *Zina*), syndicated, 1996.
"Orphan of War," *Xena: Warrior Princess* (also known as *Xena* and *Zina*), syndicated, 1996.
"Remember Nothing," *Xena: Warrior Princess* (also known as *Xena* and *Zina*), syndicated, 1996.

Television Work; Other; Episodic:
Creative consultant, "Punch Lines," *Xena: Warrior Princess* (also known as *Xena* and *Zina*), syndicated, 2000.
(As Alex Kurtzman–Counter) Director, "A Free Agent," *Alias,* ABC, 2003.

Television Executive Producer; Pilots:
The Secret Service, ABC, 2004.
Fringe, Fox, 2008.
Hawaii Five–O, CBS, 2010.
Fox/Eid/Kurtzman/Orci Prosecutor Drama, Fox, c. 2010.
Locke & Key, Fox, c. 2011.

Television Work; Other; Pilots:
Creator, *Fringe,* Fox, 2008.
Developer, *Hawaii Five–O,* CBS, 2010.

Television Appearances; Episodic:
Himself "'Transformers': Their War, Our World," *HBO First Look,* HBO, 2007.

Himself, "The Making of 'Eagle Eye'" (also known as "Eagle Eye"), *HBO First Look,* HBO, 2008.

RECORDINGS

Video Appearances; as Himself; Documentaries:
From Script to Sand: The Skorponok Desert Attack (short documentary), Paramount Home Entertainment/DreamWorks Home Entertainment, 2007.
Our World, Paramount Home Entertainment/DreamWorks Home Entertainment, 2007.
Their War, Paramount Home Entertainment/DreamWorks Home Entertainment, 2007.
"Kurtzman–Orci," *The Dialogue* (part of a documentary series; also known as *The Dialogue: An Interview with Screenwriters Alex Kurtzman and Roberto Orci* and *The Dialogue: Learning from the Masters*), released on DVDs as part of collections, c. 2007.
The Human Factor: Exacting Revenge of the Fallen, Paramount Home Entertainment, 2009.
Villains of "Star Trek" (short documentary), Paramount Home Entertainment, 2009.
Beyond Words (recording of convention panel), 2010.

WRITINGS

Screenplays:
(With Roberto Orci and Caspian Tredwell–Owen; story by Tredwell–Owen) *The Island,* DreamWorks, 2005.
(With Orci; and story with Orci, Ted Elliott, and Terry Rossio) *The Legend of Zorro* (related to other films, television series, and other treatments and the character of Zorro, created by Johnston McCulley; also known as *The Mask of Zorro 2, The Return of Zorro, Z, Zorro 2,* and *Zorro Unmasked*), Columbia, 2005.
(With Orci and J. J. Abrams) *Mission: Impossible III* (related to other films and television series; also known as *Heyday, M:i:III, M: i: III,* and *Mission: Impossible 3*), Paramount, 2006.
(With Orci; and story with Orci and John Rogers) *Transformers* (related to other films, television series, and other projects; also known as *Prime Directive, The Transformers,* and *Transformers: The Movie 2;* IMAX version known as *Transformers: The IMAX Experience*), Paramount, 2007.
(With Orci) *Star Trek* (related to other films, television series, and other projects; also known as *Christa & Christian's Big Adventure, Corporate Headquarters, Corporate HQ, The Ernest Castlehun Chronicles, Star Trek: The Beginning, Star Trek XI, Star Trek: The Future Begins, Star Trek Zero, Untitled Blake Allen Project, Untitled Paramount Project,* and *Untitled Walter Lace Project;* IMAX versions known as *Star Trek: (IMAX DMR Version)* and *Star Trek: The IMAX Experience*), Paramount, 2009.

(With Orci and Ehren Kruger) *Transformers: Revenge of the Fallen* (related to other films, television series, and other projects; also known as *Prime Directive, Transformer: Revenge,* and *Transformers 2;* IMAX versions known as *Transformers: Revenge of the Fallen (IMAX DMR Version)* and *Transformers: Revenge of the Fallen—The IMAX Experience*), DreamWorks, 2009.

(With others) *Cowboys & Aliens* (based on a graphic novel by Fred Van Lente, Andrew Foley, Scott Mitchell Rosenberg, Luciano Lima, and Dennis Calero), DreamWorks, 2011.

With Orci, wrote *The Goonies 2* (also known as *The Goonies II*) and *The Twenty–Eighth Amendment* (also known as *The 28th Amendment*); with Orci and Jody Lambert, wrote *Welcome to People,* DreamWorks; with Orci and Damon Lindelof, wrote *Untitled Star Trek Sequel* (related to other films, television series, and other projects; also known as *Star Trek 2, Star Trek XII,* and *Untitled (Paramount Pictures/Star Trek Sequel)*), Paramount.

Teleplays; Episodic:

(With others) *Hercules: The Legendary Journeys* (related to myths; also known as *Hercules*), syndicated, multiple episodes, 1997–99.

(With Roberto Orci) "The Floundering Father," *Jack of All Trades* (related to characters created by Eric Morris), syndicated, 2000.

(With Orci; story by Chris Manheim) "God Fearing Child," *Xena: Warrior Princess* (also known as *Xena* and *Zina*), syndicated, 2000.

(With Orci) "The Morning After," *Jack of All Trades* (related to characters created by Eric Morris), syndicated, 2000.

(With Orci) "Raging Bully," *Jack of All Trades* (related to characters created by Eric Morris), syndicated, 2000.

(As Alex Kurtzman–Counter; with others) *Alias* (characters created by J. J. Abrams), ABC, multiple episodes, 2001–2003.

(With Orci, Abrams, and Jeff Pinkner) "The Same Old Story," *Fringe,* Fox, 2008.

(With Orci, Abrams, and Pinkner) "Bound," *Fringe,* Fox, 2009.

(With Orci and Peter M. Lenkov) "Lanakila," *Hawaii Five–O* (related to other television series), CBS, 2010.

Teleplays; Pilots:

(With Roberto Orci) *The Secret Service,* ABC, 2004.

(With Orci and J. J. Abrams) *Fringe,* Fox, 2008.

(Story with Orci and Peter M. Lenkov) *Hawaii Five–O* (related to other television series), CBS, 2010.

Wrote other pilots, including *Darkside,* Fox.

L

LAGA'AIA, Jay 1963–

PERSONAL

Full name, Jay Lavea Laga'aia; born September 10, 1963, in Auckland, New Zealand; married; wife's name, Sandra Jane (a high school teacher), August 16, 1990; children: (from previous relationship) Jeremy; (with wife) Matthew, Iosefa, Jessica, Nathaniel, Georgia Rose.

Addresses: *Agent*—Johnson and Laird, PO Box 78340, Grey Lynn, Auckland 1245, New Zealand.

Career: Actor, singer, and songwriter.

Awards, Honors: *Bolinda Rave Review* Award, 2002, for *The Whale Rider;* New Zealand Television Award nomination, best actor, 2002, and *New Zealand TV Guide* Award, best actor, 2003, both for *Street Legal;* Sydney Theatre Award, best production for children, 2007.

CREDITS

Television Appearances; Series:
Ron Ualesi, *Heroes* (also known as *Heroes II*), TV New Zealand, 1984–86.
Host, *Spot On!,* 1987.
Sete, *Marlin Bay,* 1993–94.
Senior Constable Tommy Tavita, *Water Rats,* Nine Network, 1996–2001.
Himself, *Play School,* ABC Australia, beginning 2000.
David Silesi, *Street Legal,* 2000–2003.
Host, *Starstruck,* Nine Network, 2001.
Host, *The Big Time,* beginning 2001.
Narrator, *Larry the Lawnmower,* Seven Network, 2008.

Nick Pickering, *Bed of Roses,* ABC Australia, 2008–10.
Elijah Johnson, *Home and Away,* Seven Network, 2010.

Television Appearances; Miniseries:
Mana, *The Other Side of Paradise,* Ten Network, 1992.
Jean–Christian, *The Violent Earth,* Nine Network, 1998.
Contestant, *Celebrity Big Brother for Charity Live,* 2002.

Television Appearances; Movies:
Maru, *Green Sails,* 2000.

Television Appearances; Episodic:
Sergeant Bob Gilligan, "Shifting Sands," *Soldier Soldier,* ITV, 1993.
Sergeant Bob Gilligan, "Live Fire," *Soldier Soldier,* ITV, 1993.
Buck Walton, "Hot Rocks," *High Tide,* syndicated, 1994.
Tenape, "No One Rules Me," *The Mysterious Island,* The Family Channel, 1995.
Tenape, "He's Not Heavy," *The Mysterious Island,* The Family Channel, 1995.
Draco, "Sins of the Past," *Xena: Warrior Princess,* 1995.
Draco, "A Comedy of Errors," *Xena: Warrior Princess,* 1997.
Warrior, "Paradise Regained," *Tales of the South Seas,* Ten Network, 1998.
Host, *Surprise Surprise,* ITV, 2000.
Russell Gilbert Live, 2000.
Draco, "Lyre, Lyre, Hearts on Fire," *Xena: Warrior Princess,* 2000.
(In archive footage) Draco, "Punch Lines," *Xena: Warrior Princess,* 2000.
Michael Stevenson, "In Sickness and in Health," *All Saints,* 2005.
Michael Stevenson, "Till Death Do Us Part," *All Saints,* 2006.
(In archive footage) "Hoaxes, Cheats, and Liars," *20 to 1,* Nine Network, 2006.

Gabriel, "A Spark from Heaven," *McLeod's Daughters,* Nine Network, 2007.

Himself, *Spicks and Specks,* ABC Australia, 2007.

Joe Tahore/Frogman, *The Strip,* Nine Network, 2008.

Chase Brandstone, "Prophecy," *Legend of the Seeker,* 2008.

Chase Brandstone, "Destiny," *Legend of the Seeker,* 2008.

Chase Brandstone, "Hartland," *Legend of the Seeker,* 2009.

Chase Brandstone, "Conversion," *Legend of the Seeker,* 2009.

Good News Week, 2010.

Television Appearances; Specials:

(In archive footage) *Look Who's Famous Now,* TV2 New Zealand, 1999.

(Uncredited) *52 Annual TV Week Logie Awards,* 2010.

Television Appearances; Other:

The Civic, TV New Zealand, 1988.

Constable Locie Campbell, *Strangers,* TV New Zealand, 1988.

Open House, TV New Zealand, 1988.

Simon, *Gloss,* TV New Zealand, 1988.

Demo worker, *Arcadia Factor,* TV New Zealand, 1988.

Presenter, *Your Choice,* TV New Zealand, 1988.

Presenter, *Telequest,* TV New Zealand, 1988.

Presenter and translator, *Crime Watch,* TV New Zealand, 1988.

Theatresports, TV New Zealand, 1988.

Comedian, *Laugh Inz,* TV3, 1989.

Presenter, *Cyclone Ofa,* TV New Zealand, 1991.

Derek, *The Further Adventures of the Black Stallion,* 1992.

Mana, *Late for School,* Ten Network, 1992.

Presenter, *Robot Wars,* Nine Network, 1999.

Cohost, *TV2 Big Time,* TV2 New Zealand, 2001.

Film Appearances:

Bruce, *Never Say Die,* Kings Road Entertainment, 1988.

Jay, *The Navigator: A Mediaeval Odyssey* (also known as *The Navigator: An Odyssey across Time*), Circle Films, 1988.

Captain Typho, *Star Wars: Episode II—Attack of the Clones* (also known as *Attack of the Clones, Attack of the Clones: The IMAX Experience, Stars Wars II,* and *Star Wars II: Attack of the Clones*), Twentieth Century–Fox, 2002.

Narrator, *The Whale Rider,* Newmarket Films, 2003.

Captain Typho, *Star Wars: Episode III—Revenge of the Sith* (also known as *Revenge of the Sith, Stars Wars II: Revenge of the Sith,* and *Star Wars III: Revenge of the Sith*), Twentieth Century–Fox, 2005.

Vincent, *Solo,* Dendy Films, 2006.

Helicopter pilot, *Nim's Island,* Fox–Walden, 2008.

Pickaxe, *Crooked Business,* Nyst Entertainment, 2008.

Car park victim, *Zombies! Zombies! Zombies!* (also known as *Zombies! Zombies! Zombies!—Strippers vs. Zombies*), Passion River Films, 2008.

Bo, *Lightswitch* (short film), Down Dere Films, 2009.

Narrator, *Makazie One* (short film), Clutch Master Rocketship, 2009.

Senator Turner, *Daybreakers,* Lions Gate Films, 2010.

Stage Appearances:

Sweet Charity (musical), Mercury Theatre, 1984.

Pirate, *Pirates of Penzance* (musical), Mercury Theatre, 1984.

Chino, *West Side Story* (musical), 1985.

Multiple roles, *The Rink,* Mercury Theatre, 1985.

Athol Fugard, *The Island,* Mercury Theatre, 1988.

Woza Albert, Mercury Theatre, 1988.

Macheath, *Threepenny Opera* (musical), Inside Out Theatre, 1993.

Levee, *Ma Rainey's Black Bottom,* Pacific Theatre, 1995.

Eddie/Dr. Scott, *The New Rocky Horror Picture Show,* Paul Dainty Productions, 1998.

Mufasa, *The Lion King* (musical), Disney Theatrical Productions, Sydney, Australia, 2003.

Jay, *Jay's Place,* Sydney Theatre, Sydney, 2007.

Also performed in recital with Western Australian Symphony Orchestra, 2007.

Major Tours:

Wesley, *Ladies Night Gateway,* Australian cities, 1993.

Judas and Simon, *Jesus Christ Superstar,* Australian cities, 1994.

Jay, *Come Dance and Sing with Jay and Friends,* Australian cities, 2008.

Radio Appearances:

Host, *Breakfast Show,* Aotearoa Radio, 1989.

Cohost, *Breakfast Radio,* Mai FM Radio, 2002.

RECORDINGS

Albums:

(And songwriter) *Come Dance and Sing,* ABC for Kids Music, 2007.

I Can Play Anything, 2010.

Audio Books:

Reader, *The Whale Rider,* 2007.

LANDESBERG, Steve 1936–2010

PERSONAL

Original name, Steve Landesberg; born November 23, 1936, in New York City; died of complications from colon cancer, December 20, 2010, in Los Angeles, California. Actor. Best known as Sgt. Arthur P. Dietrich from the popular sitcom *Barney Miller,* Landesberg was thrice nominated for Emmy Awards for his portrayal of the contemplative detective. He began his career as a stand-up comic in 1969 in New York City and became a regular performer in television variety shows such as *The David Frost Show, The Dean Martin Comedy Hour,* and *The Tonight Show Starring Johnny Carson* in the early 1970s. Landesberg had small roles in the TV series *Black Bart, When Things Were Rotten* and *On The Rocks* before being cast as Sgt. Dietrich in 1975. He appeared in 130 episodes of *Barney Miller* until the show's final episode in 1982. Roles in shows such as *Seinfeld, The Golden Girls, Law and Order, That 70's Show,* and *Everybody Hates Chris* followed, and Landesberg had recurring parts in the sitcom *Conrad Bloom,* the animated series *Harvey Birdman, Attorney at Law,* and the comedy series *Head Case.* His most recent film role was as the pediatrician Dr. Rosenbaum in the 2008 comedy *Forgetting Sarah Marshall.*

PERIODICALS

Los Angeles Times, December 21, 2010.
New York Times, December 10, 2010.
San Francisco Gate, December 22, 2010.
Variety, December 20, 2010.

LANDIS, Angela
(Angie Landis, Angela Tubman)

PERSONAL

Career: Actress, producer, and writer.

CREDITS

Film Appearances:
Susan, *Guns on the Clackamas: A Documentary,* 1995.
"Miss" Grace Martin, *Bicentennial Man* (also known as *Andrew NDR114*), Buena Vista, 1999.
Dayna, *Best Friends,* EmFran Films, 2001.
Second hooker, *The Gray in Between,* Barry Katz Productions, 2002.
British female, *Asleep at the Wheel on the Road to Nowhere,* Asleep On the Road, 2004.
(As Angie Landis) Josephine Taylor, *Anna's Eve,* 2004.
(As Angela Tubman) Nurse White, *Alien Abduction,* The Asylum, 2005.
Eve, *Megaconda,* 2009.
Angela, *Awaken,* The 48 Hour Film Project, 2009.
Rachel, *The Echo Game,* Psychic Bunny, 2009.
Foxy, *George's Intervention,* Tavix Pictures, 2009.

London, *He Who Finds a Wife 2: Thou Shall Not Covet,* BlackChristianMovies.com, 2010.
First reporter, *Airline Disaster,* The Asylum, 2010.

Television Appearances; Episodic:
Kathy, "Such Sweet Sorrow," *ER,* NBC, 2000.

Television Appearances; Movies:
First person, *Turbulent Skies,* 2010.

Television Appearances; Pilots:
Gretchen, *1000 Ways to Lie,* Spike TV, 2010.
Anika, *Milf Money,* 2011.

Internet Appearances; Web Series:
Jen, *Misadventures in Matchmaking,* http://misadventuresinmatchmaking.com, 2009.
Kourtney, *Keeping up with the Kartrashians,* http://www.funnyordie.com/videos/1fb3a54ced/keeping-up-with-the-kartrashians-ep-1, 2011.

Internet Producer; Web Series:
Misadventures in Matchmaking, http://misadventuresinmatchmaking.com, 2009.
Executive producer, *Keeping up with the Kartrashians,* http://www.angelalandis.com/kartrashians.html, 2011.

Stage Appearances:
Appeared as Kitty, *Amy Gets Her Man,* Actors Playpen, Los Angeles; Robin, *Mud,* NoHo Actor's Studio, Los Angeles; Izzy, *Becoming Diana,* The Secret Rose, Los Angeles; Allegra, *Damaged Goods,* The Complex, Los Angeles; Jess/Dr., *5 Funny Scenes,* Lillian Theatre, Los Angeles; Julie, *Pizza Man,* Jewel Box Theatre, Los Angeles; Nina, *The Seagull,* Anderson Theatre; Cavale, *Cowboy Mouth,* Anderson Theatre; Helen, *Laughter on the 23rd Floor,* Lakewood Theatre; wife, *LaRonde,* Fireside Theatre; Scarlet, *Coyote Ugly,* Fireside Theatre; Betsy, *Murder On the Rerun,* CoJe Theatre; Bianca, *Let's Murder Marsha,* CoJe Theatre; and Allison, *Romantic Comedy,* CoJe Theatre.

WRITINGS

Internet Web Series:
Misadventures in Matchmaking, http://misadventuresinmatchmaking.com, 2009.
Keeping up with the Kartrashians, http://www.angelalandis.com/kartrashians.html, 2011.

OTHER SOURCES

Electronic:
Angela Landis Official Site, http://www.angelalandis.com, March 8, 2011.

LANDIS, John 1950–
(John Landie)

PERSONAL

Full name, John David Landis; born August 3, 1950, in Chicago, IL; son of Marshall David (an interior decorator) and Shirley (maiden name, Magaziner) Landis; married Deborah Nadoolman (a costume designer), July 27, 1980; children: Rachel, Max.

Addresses: *Agent*—Gersh Agency, 9465 Wilshire Blvd., 6th Floor, Beverly Hills, CA 90210. *Manager*—Gold/Miller Division, Mosaic Media Group, 9200 Sunset Blvd., 10th Floor, Los Angeles, CA 90069.

Career: Producer, director, writer, actor, and stunt performer. St. Claire Entertainment, partner and chair; Twentieth Century–Fox, worked as a mail person. American Lung Association of Los Angeles County, member of board of directors.

Member: Writers Guild of America, Directors Guild of America, Screen Actors Guild, Academy of Motion Picture Arts and Sciences.

Awards, Honors: Best Film Award, Fantafestival, 1982, for *Schlock;* Saturn Award nomination, best writing, Academy of Science Fiction, Horror, and Fantasy Films, 1982, for *An American Werewolf in London;* International Fantasy Film Award nomination (with others), best film, Fantasporto, 1984, for *Twilight Zone: The Movie;* Special Jury Prize, Cognac Festival du Film Policier, 1985, for *Into the Night;* decorated chevalier, French Order of Arts and Letters, 1985; CableAce Award nominations (with others), comedy series, National Cable Television Association, 1991, 1993, 1994, CableAce Award (with others), comedy series, for *Dream On;* Tim–Machine Honorary Award, Sitges–Catalonia International Film Festival, 2004; Copper Wing Tribute Award, Phoenix Film Festival, 2004; Emmy Award (with others), outstanding variety, music or comedy special, 2008, for *Mr. Warmth: The Don Rickles Project;* Image Awards from National Association for the Advancement of Colored People, W. C. Handy Award, People's Choice awards, and other awards.

CREDITS

Film Director:
Schlock (also known as *The Banana Monster*), Jack Harris, 1973.
The Kentucky Fried Movie, United Film, 1977.

National Lampoon's "Animal House" (also known as *Animal House*), Universal, 1977.
The Blues Brothers, Universal, 1980.
An American Werewolf in London (also known as *American Werewolf*), Universal, 1981.
(And producer) *Coming Soon,* 1982.
(And producer, with Steven Spielberg) Segments "Prologue" and "Back There," *Twilight Zone: The Movie,* Warner Bros., 1983.
Trading Places, Paramount, 1983.
Into the Night, Universal, 1985.
Spies Like Us, Warner Bros., 1985.
Three Amigos!, Orion, 1986.
(With Joe Dante, Carl Gottlieb, Peter Horton, and Robert K. Weiss; and executive producer) *Amazon Women on the Moon* (also known as *Cheeseburger Film Sandwich*), Universal, 1987.
Coming to America (also known as *Prince in New York*), Paramount, 1988.
Oscar, Buena Vista, 1991.
Black or White, 1991.
Innocent Blood (also known as *A French Vampire in America*), Warner Bros., 1992.
Beverly Hills Cop III, Paramount, 1994.
The Stupids, New Line Cinema, 1996.
(And producer and music executive producer) *Blues Brothers 2000,* Universal, 1998.
The Great Sketch Experiment, JibJab Media, 2006.
Mr. Warmth: The Don Rickles Project, 2007.
Burke and Hare, Maple Pictures, 2010.
Epic Proportions, 2010.

Film Executive Producer:
Clue (also known as *Clue: The Movie*), Paramount, 1985.
The Lost World (also known as *Sir Arthur Conan Doyle's "The Lost World"*), 1998.
Some Guy Who Kills People, Level 10 Films, 2010.

Film Producer:
The Making of "Thriller," 1983.
Mr. Warmth: The Don Rickles Project, 2007.

Film Stunt Performer:
The Good, the Bad and the Ugly (also known as *Il buono, il brutto, il cattivo.* and *The Good, the Ugly, the Bad*), 1966.
The Charge of the Light Brigade, 1968.
Once Upon a Time in the West (also known as *C'era una volta il West*), 1968.
Schlock (also known as *The Banana Monster*), Jack Harris, 1973.
An American Werewolf in London, Universal, 1981.

Film Work; Other:
Assistant director, *Kelly's Heroes,* 1970.

Automated dialogue replacement (ADR), *Oscar,* Buena Vista, 1991.

Executive music producer, *Blues Brothers 2000,* 1998.

Film Appearances:

The T.A.M.I. Show (also known as *The Rock Revival of 1964*), 1964.

The tallest nun, *Kelly's Heroes,* 1970.

Schlockthropus, *Schlock* (also known as *The Banana Monster*), Jack Harris, 1973.

Jake's friend, *Battle for the Planet of the Apes* (also known as *Colonization of the Planet of the Apes*), Twentieth Century–Fox, 1973.

Mechanic, *Death Race 2000,* New World, 1975.

Extra, *Jaws,* 1975.

(Uncredited) Studio crew member fighting with gorilla, *The Kentucky Fried Movie,* United Film, 1977.

Cafeteria dishwasher, *Animal House* (also known as *National Lampoon's "Animal House"*), 1978.

Voice of Grover, *The Muppet Movie,* 1979.

Corporal Mizerany, *1941,* Universal, 1979.

Trooper La Fong, *The Blues Brothers,* Universal, 1980.

(Uncredited) Man hit by a car, *An American Werewolf in London* (also known as *American Werewolf*), Universal, 1981.

(Uncredited) Man in bank, *Eating Raoul,* Twentieth Century–Fox, 1982.

Leonard Winesop, *The Muppets Take Manhattan,* TriStar, 1984.

Savak, *Into the Night,* Universal, 1985.

Physician, *Darkman,* Universal, 1990.

Radio technician, *Spontaneous Combustion,* Taurus Entertainment, 1990.

Director, *Black or White,* 1991.

Lab technician, *Stephen King's "Sleepwalkers"* (also known as *Sleepstalkers* and *Sleepwalkers*), Columbia, 1992.

Himself, *Venice/Venice,* International Rainbow Pictures, 1992.

Dr. Edwards, *Body Chemistry II: Voice of a Stranger* (also known as *Voice of a Stranger*), Columbia TriStar Home Video, 1992.

FBI Agent, *Silence of the Hams* (also known as *Il silenzio dei prosciutti*), October Films, 1994.

Himself, *Who Is Henry Jaglom?,* 1995.

First astronaut, *Vampirella,* Concorde, 1996.

Doctor, *Mad City,* Warner Bros., 1997.

Judge Trevino, *Laws of Deception,* 1997.

Narrator, *Hollywood Rated "R"* (also known as *Les deniers du culte*), 1997.

Himself, *Chicago Filmmakers on the Chicago River,* 1998.

Gambler, *Diamonds,* Miramax, 1999.

Judge Kaltenbrenner, *Freeway II: Confessions of a Trickbaby,* Full Moon Entertainment, 1999.

Himself, *The American Nightmare,* 2000.

Professor Ackerman, *2001 Maniacs,* Rhino Films/Tuffin Entertainment, 2003.

Michael Jackson: Number Ones, 2003.

Edgar G. Ulmer–The Man Off–screen, Kino International, 2004.

Doctor Levine, *Surviving Eden,* Good Films Releasing, 2004.

Doctor, *Spider–Man 2* (also known as *Spider–Man 2.1* and *Spider–Man 2: The IMAX Experience*), Columbia, 2004.

Pere copain Maxime, *Le couperet* (also known as *The Ax*), Mars Distributing, 2005.

Arabian ambassador, *Torrente 3: El Protector,* Amiguetes Entertainment, 2005.

The Sci–Fi Boys, Universal, 2006.

Famous Monster: Forrest J Ackerman, Space: The Imagination Station, 2007.

Look, Anchor Bay Films, 2007.

Sister Rosa Stigmata, *Mr. Warmth: The Don Rickles Project,* 2007.

Spine Tingler! The William Castle Story, Sony, 2007.

Dead On: The Life and Cinema of George A. Romero, New Eye Films, 2008.

Trailers from Hell, Metaluna Productions, 2008.

Department store manager, *Parasomnia,* Eagle Films, 2008.

Judge Paxton B. Johnston, *The Scenesters,* Midwinter Studios, 2009.

The Boys: The Sherman Brothers' Story, Walt Disney, 2009.

Tattoos: A Scarred History, 4Digital Media, 2009.

Into the Pit: The Shocking Story of Deadpit.com, Rusty Robot Productions, 2009.

Beware the Moon: Remembering "An American Werewolf in London," Universal, 2009.

American Grindhouse, Lorber Films, 2010.

Machete Maidens Unleashed!, ABC Australia, 2010.

Television Executive Producer; Series:

Dream On, HBO, 1990–96.

Weird Science, USA Network, 1994.

Sliders, Fox, 1995–96.

Campus Cops, USA Network, 1996.

Disney's Honey, I Shrunk the Kids: The TV Show, syndicated, 1997–99.

The Lost World (also known as *Sir Arthur Conan Doyle's "The Lost World"*), 1999.

Also executive producer of *Topper,* CBS.

Television Director; Series:

Dream On, 1990–95.

Also director of *Topper,* CBS.

Television Executive Producer; Movies:

Here Come the Munsters, 1995.

The Munsters' Scary Little Christmas, Fox, 1996.

(And director) *Susan's Plan* (also known as *Dying to Get Rich*), Cinemax, 1998.

The Lost World (also known as *Sir Arthur Conan Doyle's "The Lost World"*), 1999.

Television Producer; Movies:
(And director) *Thriller* (also known as *Michael Jackson's "Thriller"*), 1983.

Television Director; Movies:
Slasher, 2004.

Television Director; Episodic:
"Disaster at Buzz Creek," *George Burns Comedy Week,* CBS, 1985.
Premiere episode, *Dream On,* HBO, 1990.
"Disneyland's 35th Anniversary Celebration," *Walt Disney's Wonder World of Color* (also known as *Disneyland, Disney's Wonderful World, The Disney Sunday Movie, The Magical World of Disney, The Wonderful World of Disney, Walt Disney,* and *Walt Disney Presents*), 1990.
"The Second Greatest Story Ever Told," *Dream On,* HBO, 1991.
"Black or White," *Dangerous,* Fox, 1991.
"Muskrat Ramble," *Campus Cops,* USA Network, 1996.
"Honey, Name That Tune," *Disney's "Honey, I Shrunk the Kids: The TV Show,"* syndicated, 1999.
"Deer Woman," *Masters of Horror,* 2005.
"Family," *Masters of Horror,* 2006.
"Scary Sherry: Bianca's Toast," *Psych,* 2007.
"American Duos," *Psych,* USA Network, 2007.
"In Sickness and in Health," *Fear Itself,* 2008.
"Christmas Joy," *Psych,* USA Network, 2008.

Television Work; Pilots:
Director, *Tropical Heat,* Fox, 1993.
Executive Producer, *Sir Arthur Conan Doyle's "The Lost World"* (also known as *The Lost World*), syndicated, 1999.

Television Work; Specials:
Director, *Disneyland's 30th Anniversary Celebration,* 1985.
Executive producer, *Fuzzbucket,* ABC, 1986.
Director, *Mr. Warmth: The Don Rickles Project,* HBO, 2007.
Executive producer, *Starz Inside: Ladies or Gentlemen,* Starz!, 2008.

Also associated with the special *B. B. King: Into the Night.*

Television Appearances; Specials:
The Making of "An American Werewolf in London," 1981.
MTV 1st Annual Video Music Awards, 1984.

Stephen King's World of Horror (also known as *This Is Horror*), 1986.
Stand–up Comics Take a Stand!, The Family Channel, 1989.
Presenter, *The Horror Hall of Fame,* 1990.
Heartstoppers: Horror at the Movies, 1992.
Jerry Lewis, Total Filmmaker (also known as *Martin and Lewis: Their Golden Age of Comedy*), The Disney Channel, 1994.
Leonard Winesop, *The World of Jim Henson,* 1994.
The Abbey Road Story, 1998.
Don Ameche: Hollywood's Class Act, Arts and Entertainment, 1999.
Andy Kaufman's Really Big Show, Arts and Entertainment, 1999.
Video Killed the Radio Star, VH1, 2000.
It's Black Entertainment, Showtime, 2000.
The American Nightmare, Independent Film Channel, 2000.
It's Burlesque, Arts and Entertainment, 2001.
Boogeymen II: Masters of Horror (also known as *Masters of Horror*), 2002.
Forever Ealing, 2002.
Screen Tests of the Stars, 2002.
The Essential Michael Jackson, 2002.
Michael Jackson's Private Home Movies, Fox, 2003.
101 Most Shocking Moments in Entertainment, E! Entertainment Television, 2003.
The Michael Jackson Story, ITV, 2003.
Night Bites: Women and Their Vampires, WE, 2003.
Unseen + Untold: National Lampoon's Animal House, Universal Studios, 2003.
The 100 Greatest Scary Moments, Channel 4, 2003.
The 100 Greatest Musicals, Channel 4, 2003.
Unseen + Untold: The Blues Brothers, Spike TV, 2004.
Mario Bava: Operazione paura, Sky Television, 2004.
Movie's Greatest Cars, Sky One, 2005.
Hollywood's Master Storytellers: The Blues Brothers, 2005.
The Perfect Scary Movie, Channel 4, 2005.
The 50 Greatest Comedy Films, Channel 4, 2006.
Animal Hooves: An Interview with John Landis, 2006.
Greatest Ever Comedy Movies, 2006.
Bloodsucking Cinema, Starz!, 2007.
Ciak Point Torino, 2007.
Greatest Ever 80s Movies, Channel 5, 2007.
Thou Shalt Not: Sex, Sin and Censorship in Pre–Code Hollywood, TCM, 2008.
Animal House: The Inside Story, 2008.
Starz Inside: Fantastic Flesh, Starz!, 2008.
Starz Inside: The Face Is Familiar, Starz!, 2009.

Television Appearances; Movies:
Mike Calvecchio, *Psycho IV: The Beginning,* Showtime, 1990.
Surgical assistant, *Quicksilver Highway,* Fox, 1997.
The judge, *Laws of Deception,* Cinemax, 1999.

Television Appearances; Miniseries:
Russ Dorr, *Stephen King's "The Stand"* (also known as *The Stand*), ABC, 1994.
A–Z of Horror, 1997.
The 100 Scariest Movie Moments, Bravo, 2004.

Television Appearances; Episodic:
The Tonight Show Starring Johnny Carson, 1972.
Michael, "The Pal–Mir Escort," *The Six Million Dollar Man,* 1974.
Good Morning America (also known as *G.M.A.*), 1978.
Entertainment Tonight (also known as *E.T.* and *This Week in Entertainment*), syndicated, 1990, 2005.
Herb, "Futile Attraction," *Dream On,* HBO, 1991.
(As John Landie) Additional voices, *Eek! The Cat* (animated; also known as *Eek! and the Terrible Thunderlizards* and *Eek!stravaganza*), 1992.
Dr. Edwards, "Femme Fatale Month: Part 3," *Joe Bob's Drive–In Theater,* 1993.
Herb, "Where There's Smoke, You're Fired," *Dream On,* HBO, 1994.
The Big Scary Movie Show, Sci–Fi Channel, 1996.
Himself, "Caroline and the Movie," *Caroline in the City* (also known as *Caroline*), NBC, 1996.
"Bud Abbott & Lou Costello: Abbott & Costello Meet Biography," *Biography,* 1996.
"Don Ameche: Hollywood's Class Act," *Biography,* 1999.
"New Years Compilation," *I Love 1980's,* BBC, 2001.
The Big Breakfast, Seven Network, 2002.
"Animal House," *VH–1 Behind the Movie,* VH1, 2002.
Dinner for Five, Independent Film Channel, 2003.
Breakfast, BBC, 2004, 2009.
"Hollywood's Prehistoric Superstars," *Animal Icons,* Animal Planet, 2005.
The Late Late Show with Craig Ferguson, CBS, 2006.
The Tonight Show with Jay Leno, NBC, 2006.
"Halloween Theme," *Secret's Out,* 2006.
"Amazing Moments in Music," *20 to 1,* Nine Network, 2007.
"Movies," *TV Land Confidential* (also known as *TV Land Confidential: The Untold Stories*), TV Land, 2007.
"Guns, Gangsters and Getaways: The Story of the British Crime Thriller," *British Film Forever,* BBC, 2007.
"Magic, Murder and Monsters: The Story of British Horror and Fantasy," *British Film Forever,* BBC, 2007.
"Sauce, Satire and Silliness: The Story of British Comedy," *British Film Forever,* BBC, 2007.
"Penelope," *Secret's Out,* 2008.

RECORDINGS

Videos:
Producer, director, writer (with others), and performer, *Making Michael Jackson's "Thriller"* (also known as *Michael Jackson: Making Michael Jackson's "Thriller"*), Palace/Virgin Vision/Gold, 1983.

Himself, *Dangerous: The Short Films* (also known as *Michael Jackson—Dangerous: The Short Films*), 1993.
Director and performer, *HIStory* (also known as *Michael Jackson: Video Greatest Hits—HIStory*), 1994.
Jason and the Argonauts: An Interview with Ray Harryhausen, 1995.
Producer, *Michael Jackson: HIStory on Film–Volume II,* 1997.
The Making of "Blues Brothers 2000," 1998.
The Stories Behind the Making of "The Blues Brothers," 1998.
The Yearbook: An "Animal House" Reunion, 1998.
Narrator, *Monster by Moonlight! The Immortal Saga of "The Wolf Man,"* 1999.
Where Are They Now?: A Delta Alumni Update, Universal, 2003.
Michael Jackson: Number Ones, 2003.
Ray Harryhausen: The Early Years Collection, Sony, 2005.
Shadows in the Dark: The Val Lewton Legacy, Warner Home Video, 2005.
RKO Production 601: The Making of "Kong, the Eighth Wonder of the World," Warner Home Video, 2005.
Footlight Parade: Music for the Decades, Warner Home Video, 2006.
Busby Berkeley's Kaleidoscopic Eyes, Warner Home Video, 2006.
Inside The Asylum: The Making of "2001 Maniacs," Lions Gate Films, 2006.
Amazing! Exploring the Far Reaches of Forbidden Planet, Warner Home Video, 2006.
Insider Trading: The Making of "Trading Places," Paramount Home Video, 2007.
Prince–ipal Photography: The Coming Together of America, Paramount Home Video, 2007.
Bob Burns' Hollywood Halloween, Bob's Basement Productions, 2009.
Pure in Heart: The Life and Legacy of Lon Chaney, Jr., Universal Studios Home Video, 2010.

Coproducer, director, and writer (with others), "Thriller" (music video; also known as "Michael Jackson's Thriller"), by Michael Jackson, 1983; director, "Black or White" (music video), by Michael Jackson, 1991.

WRITINGS

Screenplays:
(And song lyrics) *Schlock* (also known as *The Banana Monster*), Jack Harris, 1973.
(With Dan Aykroyd) *The Blues Brothers,* Universal, 1980.
An American Werewolf in London (also known as *American Werewolf;* also based on characters created by Landis), Universal, 1981.
Coming Soon, 1982.

"Prologue" and "Back There," *Twilight Zone: The Movie,* Warner Bros., 1983.

Into the Night, Universal, 1985.

Clue (also known as *Clue: The Movie*), 1985.

Jason and the Argonauts: An Interview with Ray Harryhausen, 1995.

Michael Jackson: Video Greatest Hits–HIStory, 1995.

Michael Jackson: HIStory on Film, 1997.

An American Werewolf in Paris, 1997.

(And song lyrics, with others) *Blues Brothers 2000,* Universal, 1998.

Susan's Plan (also known as *Dying to Get Rich* and *Dying to Get Rich!*), 1998.

Also wrote *Making Michael Jackson's Thriller.*

Television Series:
Fear Itself, NBC, 2007.

Television Movies:
Thriller (also known as *Michael Jackson's "Thriller"*), 1983.

Susan's Plan (also known as *Dying to Get Rich*), Cinemax, 1998.

Television Episodic:
"Key Witness," *Homes and Yo–Yo,* 1976.

"Deer Woman," *Masters of Horror,* 2005.

ADAPTATIONS

The film *Clue,* released by Paramount in 1985, was based on a story by Landis and Jonathon Lynn; the 1997 film *An American Werewolf in Paris* (also known as *American Werewolf 2* and *Le loup–garou de Paris*), was based on characters created by Landis for *An American Werewolf in London.*

OTHER SOURCES

Books:
Farber, Stephen, and Marc Green, *Outrageous Conduct: Art, Ego, and the Twilight Zone Case,* Ballantine Books (New York City), 1988.

LeBrecque, Ron, *Special Effects: Disaster at "Twilight Zone," the Tragedy and the Trial,* Scribner–Macmillan (New York City), 1988.

Periodicals:
American Film, May, 1982.

Cinefantastique, November, 1997, p. 20.

Entertainment Weekly, July 25, 1997, p. 86.

People Weekly, August 4, 1980; July 18, 1983; February 26, 1985.

Rolling Stone, August 7, 1980; July 7, 1983.

LAZAR, Aaron

PERSONAL

Full name, Aaron S. Lazar; born in Cherry Hill Township, NJ; son of Paul and Cheryl Lazar; married; wife's name, LeAnn (a model). *Education:* Duke University, B.A.; University of Cincinnati, M.F.A.

Addresses: *Agent*—Robert Attermann, Abrams Artists Agency, 275 Seventh Ave., 26th Floor, New York, NY 10001.

Career: Actor. Actor's Center Workshop Company, member of company, 2006—; performed in concert with Barry Manilow in New York City and Las Vegas, NV; guest artist with various orchestras in the United States and abroad.

Member: American Federation of Television and Radio Artists, Actors' Equity Association, Screen Actors Guild.

Awards, Honors: Drama Desk Award nomination, outstanding featured actor in a musical, 2007, for *Les Miserables.*

CREDITS

Stage Appearances:
Joe and understudy for the role of Curly, *Oklahoma!* (musical), George Gershwin Theatre, New York City, 2002–2003.

Fabrizio Naccarelli, *The Light in the Piazza* (musical), Vivian Beaumont Theatre, Lincoln Center, New York City, 2005–2006.

Enjolras, *Les Miserables* (musical), Broadhurst Theatre, New York City, 2006–2008.

Charles Darnay, *A Tale of Two Cities* (musical), Al Hirschfeld Theatre, New York City, 2008.

Terry, *SideShow* (workshop), 2008.

Major Eric Fenton, *Death Takes a Holiday* (workshop), 2008.

Ben Joplin, *Impressionism,* Gerald Schoenfeld Theatre, New York City, 2009.

Count Carl–Magnus Malcolm, *A Little Night Music* (musical), Walter Kerr Theatre, New York City, 2009—.

Appeared as fireman and understudy for the role of Raoul, *The Phantom of the Opera* (musical), Majestic Theatre, New York City, early in his career; more recently appeared as Billy Bigelow, *Carousel* (musical), with Boston Pops Orchestra; Adam, *Imagine This,* with Jerusalem Philharmonic Orchestra, Jerusalem, Israel; Gabey, *On the Town,* English National Opera; and Lieutenant Cable, *South Pacific* (musical), with Hollywood Bowl Orchestra; workshops and readings include appearances as Robbie, *The Baby and Johnnie Project;* in title role, *Dillinger;* and as Bobby, *Harmony;* concerts include *The After Party,* Laurie Beechman Theatre, New York City; *Broadway by the Year,* Town Hall Theatre, New York City; *Broadway Backwards III,* American Airlines Theatre, New York City; *Leading Men III,* Birdland venue, New York City.

Major Tours:
Appeared as Dewhurst and understudy for the role of Percy, *The Scarlet Pimpernel,* U.S. cities.

Film Appearances:
Roy, *One Man's Castle* (short film), Hypnotic, 2003.
Jake, *The Notorious Bettie Page,* Picturehouse Entertainment, 2006.
Jason Hart, *The Shallow End of the Ocean* (short film), 2007.
Landlord, *The Roofer* (short film), Buffalo Run Productions, 2009.

Other films include *Johnny Moment,* Nascent Entertainment, and *Mahogany Pipe,* Mantra Pictures.

Television Appearances; Specials:
Fabrizio Naccarelli, "The Light in the Piazza" (broadcast of stage production), *Live from Lincoln Center,* PBS, 2006.

Television Appearances; Episodic:
Ben Robbins, "Honor," *New Amsterdam,* Fox, 2008.
Claudio, "Bad Amanda," *Ugly Betty,* ABC, 2008.
Today (also known as *NBC News Today* and *The Today Show*), NBC, 2008.
Producer, *All My Children* (also known as *AMC*), ABC, 2009.
Ron Lipkin, *All My Children* (also known as *AMC*), ABC, 2009.
Father D'Allesio, "Book of Hours," *White Collar,* USA Network, 2009.

OTHER SOURCES

Electronic:
Aaron Lazar Official Site, http://www.aaronlazar.com, October 14, 2010.

LETSCHER, Matt 1970–
    (Mathew Letscher, Matthew Letscher)

PERSONAL

Born June 26, 1970, in Grosse Pointe, MI. *Education:* University of Michigan, graduated, 1992. *Avocational Interests:* Biking, camping, fishing, golf, hiking, rock climbing.

Addresses: *Manager*—Mark Armstrong, Saunders Armstrong Caserta Management, 2120 Colorado Blvd., Suite 120, Santa Monica, CA 90404.

Career: Actor. Purple Rose Theatre Company, Chelsea, MI, actor.

Awards, Honors: Blockbuster Entertainment Award nomination, favorite villain, 1999, for *The Mask of Zorro;* Los Angeles Drama Critics Circle Award, outstanding lead performance, 2007, for *Anatol.*

CREDITS

Television Appearances; Series:
(As Matthew Letscher) Rob Paley, *Almost Perfect,* CBS, 1995–97.
Will Marek, *Living in Captivity,* Fox, 1998.
Gavin Stone, *Good Morning, Miami,* NBC, 2002–2004.
Eric Garrett, a recurring role, *Joey,* NBC, 2004–2005.
Burton Schaefer, a recurring role, *The New Adventures of the Old Christine,* CBS, 2006–2007.
Nathan Stone, *Eli Stone,* ABC, 2008–2009.
Alex Tyler, a recurring role, *Brothers & Sisters,* ABC, 2009–10.

Television Appearances; Movies:
(As Matthew Letscher) Eddie Shea, *Stolen Innocence,* CBS, 1995.
Needlemeyer, *Prehysteria! 3,* HBO, 1995.
(As Mathew Letscher) Voice of Eddie, *Power 98,* HBO, 1995.
Larry King, *When Billie Beat Bobby,* ABC, 2001.
David, *Count Me In,* 2001.
This Could Work, 2001.
Emmett Westover, *King of Texas* (also known as *Boss Lear*), TNT, 2002.
Dr. Mark Bloom, *Fertile Ground,* 2005.
Gideon Graber, *Amish Grace,* Lifetime, 2010.

Television Appearances; Miniseries:
Mike Love, *The Beach Boys: An American Family,* ABC, 2000.

Ted Kennedy, *Jackie, Ethel, Joan: The Women of Camelot* (also known as *Jackie, Ethel, Joan: The Kennedy Woman,* NBC, 2001.
I Love the '80s, 2002.

Television Appearances; Pilots:

Ned, "Love in the Old South," *Love, American Style,* ABC, 1999.
Matt, *52 Fights,* ABC, 2006.
Nathan Stone, *Eli Stone,* ABC, 2008.
Bob Randall, *Awkward Situations for Men,* ABC, 2010.

Television Appearances; Specials:

Nathan, "Long Shadows," *American Playhouse,* PBS, 1994.

Television Appearances; Episodic:

Rick, "Rush Week," *Saved by the Bell: The College Years,* NBC, 1993.
(As Matthew Letscher) Tom Jennings, "Life and Death," *Dr. Quinn, Medicine Woman,* CBS, 1994.
Harley Eastlake, "Head 'n' Tail," *Silk Stalkings,* USA Network, 1994.
(As Matthew Letscher) Daniel Pryor, "The Fourteenth Floor," *The Larry Sanders Show,* HBO, 1994.
Steven Morgan, "The Toast," *Ellen* (also known as *These Friends of Mine*), ABC, 1994.
Jeff Chadwick, "I Know What Scares You," *Silk Stalkings,* USA Network, 1995.
Johnny Payne, "Heartburned," *The Watcher,* UPN, 1995.
(As Matthew Letscher) "Holy Ghosts," *Vanishing Son,* 1995.
John Leary, "What's Up, Chuck?," *NYPD Blue,* ABC, 1999.
Kevin Norris, "Things Have Changed," *Providence,* NBC, 2002.
Kevin Norris, "Smoke and Mirrors," *Providence,* NBC, 2002.
Kevin Norris, "Out of Control," *Providence,* NBC, 2002.
(As Matthew Letscher) Vincent Shyer, "Broken Mirror," *Criminal Minds,* CBS, 2005.
(As Matthew Letscher) Mr. Blake, "Welcome to Wherever You Are," *The West Wing,* NBC, 2006.
Robbie Cole, "Family," *Saved,* TNT, 2006.
Will Bechtel, "Shark Week," *Justice,* Fox, 2006.
Assistant District Attorney Adam Mersel, "Angel of Death," *Boston Legal,* ABC, 2007.
Dr. Mike Lasker, "Broken Home," *CSI: Miami,* CBS, 2007.
Dad, "Pinata Hustler," *The Hustler,* 2009.
Dan Coakley, "Murphy's Lie," *Entourage,* HBO, 2009.
Dan Coakley, "No More Drama," *Entourage,* HBO, 2009.
Dan Coakley, "Berried Alive," *Entourage,* HBO, 2009.
Dr. Erik Westphal, "You Give Me Fever," *Medium,* CBS, 2009.

A. J. Fowler, "Good Grief," *Drop Dead Diva,* Lifetime, 2010.

Film Appearances:

(As Matthew Letscher) Young second Maine man, *Gettysburg,* New Line Cinema, 1993.
Not This Part of the World, 1994.
David, *The Golem* (also known as *The Golem of L.A.*), 1995.
(As Matthew Letscher) Danny, *Lovelife,* Trimark Home Video, 1997.
Captain Harrison Love, *The Mask of Zorro,* TriStar, 1998.
John Clairborne, *John John in the Sky* (also known as *I'll Wave Back*), Monarch Home Video, 2000.
Owen Henderson, *Madison,* Premiere Marketing & Distribution, 2001, Metro–Goldwyn–Mayer, 2005.
Howard Butterworth, *Super Sucker,* Purple Rose Films, 2002.
Colonel Adelbert Ames, *Gods and Generals,* Warner Bros., 2002.
Assistant district attorney, *Identity,* Columbia, 2003.
Guy Stone, *Straight–Jacket.* Regent Releasing, 2004.
Mike Howard, *Heart of the Beholder,* 2005, Vanguard Cinema, 2008.
Gil Hines, *Nothing Is Private* (also known as *Towelhead*), Warner Independent Pictures, 2007.
Mr. Brady, *Radio Free Albemuth,* 2010.

Stage Appearances:

Ray Dolenz, *Proposals,* Ahmanson Theatre, Los Angeles, 1997, then (Broadway debut) Broadhurst Theatre, 1997–98.
Rain Dance, Purple Rose Theatre, Chelsea, MI, 2001.
Captain Jack Absolute, *The Rivals,* Vivian Beaumont Theatre, Lincoln Center, New York City, 2004–2005.
Anatol, Los Angeles, c. 2007.
George, *The Language Archive,* Roundabout Theatre Company, Laura Pels Theatre, New York City, 2010.

Also appeared in *Absolution,* Court Theatre; as Orlando, *As You Like It,* Antony, *Julius Caesar,* and Buckingham, *Richard III,* all Idaho Shakespeare Festival, Boise, ID; in *Love's Labour's Lost,* Old Globe Theatre; in *On Approval* and *Tonight at 8:30,* both Pacific Resident Theatre; as Konstantin, *The Seagull,* Fountain Theatre; and in *The Sisters,* Pasadena Playhouse, Pasadena, CA, and *The Tropical Pickle,* Purple Rose Theatre, Chelsea, MI.

LEWIS, Clea 1965–

PERSONAL

Born July 19, 1965, in Cleveland Heights, OH; daughter of Robert Lewis (a lawyer and former vaudeville performer); mother, a writer; married Peter Ackerman (an actor), 2000; children: Stanley Keats. *Education:* Brown University, B.A., 1987; University of California, San Diego, M.F.A., 1990; attended Royal Academy of Dramatic Arts, London, and London Academy of Music and Drama; also trained at Cleveland Playhouse and with Second City, Chicago.

Addresses: *Agent*—Nevin Dolcefino, Innovative Artists, 1505 10th St., Santa Monica, CA 90401; and Allison Levy, Innovative Artists, 235 Park Ave. S., 10th Floor, New York, NY 10003. *Manager*—Steven Levy, Framework Entertainment, 9057 Nemo St., Suite C, West Hollywood, CA 90069.

Career: Actress. Second City, Chicago, IL, member of company, 1987–90; also appeared at Body Politic, Chicago.

CREDITS

Film Appearances:
Sylvia, *Hero* (also known as *Accidental Hero*), Columbia, 1992.
Lisa Campos, *Diabolique,* Warner Bros., 1996.
Nora Golden, *The Rich Man's Wife,* Buena Vista, 1996.
Ilsa, *Scotch and Milk,* 1998.
Grace, *The Office Party,* 2000.
Joan, *Superstore* (short film), Sazam Productions, 2004.
Voices of female mini–sloth and dung beetle mom, *Ice Age: The Meltdown* (animated; also known as *Ice Age 2*), Twentieth Century–Fox, 2006.
Gina, *Perfect Stranger,* Columbia, 2007.
Lily, *Motherhood,* Freestyle Releasing, 2009.
Miss Ptaszinski, *Confessions of a Shopaholic,* Walt Disney, 2009.
Voice of start mom, *Ice Age: Dawn of the Dinosaurs* (animated; also known as *Ice Age 3*), Twentieth Century–Fox, 2009.

Television Appearances; Series:
Megan Traynor, *Flying Blind,* Fox, 1992–93.
Audrey Penney, *Ellen* (also known as *These Friends of Mine*), ABC, 1994–98.
Voice of Nicky, *Pepper Ann* (animated; also known as *Disney's "Pepper Ann"*), ABC, 1998–2000.
Rachel Tomlinson, *Maggie Winters,* CBS, 1998–99.
Jenny Barker, *Andy Barker, P.I.,* NBC, 2007.

Television Appearances; Pilots:
Megan Traynor, *Flying Blind,* Fox, 1992.
Wendy Lipton, *Madigan Men,* ABC, 2000.
Jenny Barker, *Andy Barker, P.I.,* NBC, 2007.

Television Appearances; Episodic:
Lyla, "It's a Wonderful Laugh," *Doogie Howser, M.D.,* ABC, 1991.

Krista, "Hilary Gets a Life," *The Fresh Prince of Bel–Air,* NBC, 1991.
Franny, "The One Where Monica Gets a Roommate," *Friends,* NBC, 1994.
Glove salesgirl, "Purseona," *Mad About You,* NBC, 1995.
Danielle, "Love Letters," *Double Rush,* CBS, 1995.
The Daily Show (also known as *The Daily Show with Jon Stewart* and *The Daily Show with Jon Stewart Global Edition*), 1996.
The Rosie O'Donnell Show, syndicated, 1996, 1999.
Carol, "Road Rage," *Tracey Takes On …,* HBO, 1999.
Voices of Wanda and actress, "Tough Love/A Little Dad'll Do," *The Angry Beavers* (animated), 1999.
My Big Fat Greek Life, CBS, 2003.
Heaven Moscowitz, "Trade," *Law & Order: Special Victims Unit* (also known as *Law & Order: SVU* and *Special Victims Unit*), NBC, 2008.
Emily, "Truth or Dare," *The New Adventures of the Old Christine,* CBS, 2010.

Television Appearances; Other:
Voice of Amy Lawrence, *Tom Sawyer* (movie), The Nashville Network, 2000.
TV's Greatest Sidekicks (special), Lifetime, 2004.

Stage Appearances:
Emma, *Pterodactyls,* South Coast Repertory, Costa Mesa, CA, 1994–95.
All in the Timing, Geffen Playhouse, Hartford, CT, 1998.
(New York debut) Grace, *Things You Shouldn't Say Past Midnight,* Promenade Theatre, 1999.
Maria Fenwick, *An Experiment with an Air Pump,* Manhattan Theatre Club Stage I, New York City, 1999.
Heidi, *Fuddy Meers,* Manhattan Theatre Club Stage II, 1999–2000, and Minetta Lane Theatre, New York City, 2000.
Miss Leighton, *Once in a Lifetime,* Adams Memorial Theatre, Williamstown, MA, 2002.
Sandy, *Writer's Block,* Atlantic Theatre Company, Linda Gross Theatre, New York City, 2003.
Leah, *Last Easter,* Manhattan Class Company, Lucille Lortel Theatre, New York City, 2004.
Jane, *Absurd Person Singular,* Biltmore Theatre (now Samuel J. Friedman Theatre), New York City, 2005.

Also appeared in *The My House Play,* Wisdom Bridge Theatre, Chicago, IL; and *Othello,* Chicago Shakespeare Company.

RECORDINGS

Audio Books:
Reader, "The Princess Diaries" series, Random House Listening Library, 2004–2008.

LONG, Matt 1980–

PERSONAL

Full name, Matthew Clayton Long; born May 18, 1980, in Winchester, KY; married Lora Chaffins, April 23, 2005. *Education:* Graduated from Western Kentucky University. *Avocational Interests:* The outdoors, hiking, and backpacking.

Addresses: *Agent*—United Talent Agency, 9560 Wilshire Blvd., Suite 500, Beverly Hills, CA 90212. *Manager*—Authentic Talent and Literary Management, 45 Main St., Suite 1004, Brooklyn, NY 11201.

Career: Actor.

Awards, Honors: Prism Award nomination, performance in a drama series storyline, 2006, for *Jack & Bobby.*

CREDITS

Film Appearances:
Private Smith, *The Greatest Adventures of My Life* (also known as *American Drummer Boy*), KOAN, 2001.
Young Johnny Blaze, *Ghost Rider* (also known as *Spirited Rider*), Sony, 2007.
Tyler, *Sydney White,* Universal, 2007.
Nathan, *Reflections,* 2008.
Mike Donaldson, *Homecoming,* Paper Street Films, 2009.
Michael, *Blue Nude* (short film), 2010.

Television Appearances; Series:
Jack McCallister, *Jack & Bobby,* The WB, 2004–2005.
Dylan Hewitt, *The Deep End,* ABC, 2010.
Joey Baird, *Mad Men,* AMC, 2010.

Television Appearances; Movies:
Dave Ford, *Deceit,* Lifetime, 2006.

Television Appearances; Specials:
The 6th Annual Family Television Awards, The WB, 2004.

Television Appearances; Pilots:
Jack McCallister, *Jack & Bobby,* The WB, 2004.
Chad Wilson, *Secrets of a Small Town,* 2006.
Dylan Hewitt, *The Deep End,* ABC, 2010.

Television Appearances; Episodic:
Live with Regis and Kelly, syndicated, 2005.

LOPEZ, George 1961–

PERSONAL

Full name, George Edward Lopez; born April 23, 1961, in Mission Hills, CA; raised by grandparents, Refugil (a builder) and Benita (a factory worker) Gutierrez; married Ann Serrano (a producer), September 18, 1993; children: Mayan.

Addresses: *Office*—George Lopez Presents, 4000 Warner Blvd., Bldg. 8, Suite 10, Burbank, CA 91522. *Agent*—Creative Artists Agency, 2000 Avenue of the Stars, Los Angeles, CA 90067. *Publicist*—Slate PR, 8322 Beverly Blvd., Suite 201, Los Angeles, CA 90048.

Career: Actor, comedian, writer, and producer. George Lopez Presents, Burbank, CA, principal. Worked as a stand–up comedian; worked as a disc jockey on MEGA 92.3, Los Angeles; appeared in television commercials for Nextel communications, 2003. George and Ann Lopez–Richie Alarcon Care Foundation (charity providing arts resources for education), founder; spokesperson for charities, including Los Angeles Police Department's Stop the Violence. Also worked in an airplane parts plant.

Awards, Honors: ALMA Award nomination, outstanding performance by an individual or act, American Latino Media Arts Awards, 1999, for *2nd Annual Latino Laugh Festival;* ALMA Award nomination, outstanding supporting actor in a motion picture, 2002, for *Bread and Roses;* Teen Choice Award nomination, choice television breakout star—male, 2003, BET Comedy Award nomination, outstanding lead actor in a comedy series, Black Entertainment Television, Imagen Award, best actor in a television comedy, Imagen Foundation, Young Artist Award nomination (with Constance Marie), most popular mom and pop in a television series, 2004, Image Award nominations, outstanding actor in a comedy series, National Association for the Advancement of Colored People, 2004, 2005, 2006, 2007, ALMA Award nomination, outstanding actor in a television series, 2006, Imagen Award nominations, best actor in a television comedy, Imagen Foundation, 2006, 2007, all for *George Lopez;* star on the Hollywood Walk of Fame, 2006; Imagen Award, best actor/feature film, Imagen Foundation, Kids' Choice Award nomination, favorite movie actor, 2009, for *Beverly Hills Chihuahua;* received awards for charitable work, including National Hispanic Media Coalition Impact Award, the Manny Mota Foundation Community Spirit Award, and named Honorary Mayor of Los Angeles.

CREDITS

Film Appearances:

Tomado, *Fist of Fear, Touch of Death* (also known as *The Dragon and the Cobra* and *Fist of Fear*), Ace Video, 1980.

Eddie Martinez, *Ski Patrol,* Triumph, 1990.

Murder investigator, *Fatal Instinct,* United International, 1993.

Perez, *Bread and Roses* (also known as *Pan y rosas*), Lions Gate Films, 2000.

Mr. Guzman, *Real Women Have Curves,* Newmarket Film Group, 2002.

Felix, *Outta Time* (also known as *The Courier* and *Out of Time*), Artisan Entertainment, 2002.

Gangster, *Ali G Indahouse,* Universal, 2002.

(Uncredited) Detective number two, *Frank McKlusky, C.I.,* Buena Vista, 2002.

The Original Latin Kings of Comedy, Paramount, 2002.

Mr. Electric, Tobor, Ice Guardian, and Mr. Electricdad, *The Adventures of Sharkboy and Lavagirl 3–D,* Dimension Films, 2005.

Caddy #101, *Where's Marty?,* 2006.

Everado, *Tortilla Heaven,* 2007.

Rodriguez, *Balls of Fury,* Rogue Pictures, 2007.

Himself, *Mr. Warmth: The Don Rickles Project* (documentary), Vivendi Entertainment, 2007.

Himself, *Balls Out: The Making of "Balls of Fury,"* 2007.

Father Salazar, *Henry Poole Is Here,* Overture Films, 2008.

John Sweeney, *Swing Vote,* Walt Disney Studios Motion Pictures, 2008.

Voice of Papi, *Beverly Hills Chihuahua,* Walt Disney Studios Motion Pictures, 2008.

Himself, *Loco Comedy Jam Volume 1,* 2008.

Narrator, *Viva la causa* (documentary), Southern Poverty Law Center, 2008.

Himself, *President Barack Obama: The Man and His Journey,* 2009.

Glaze, *The Spy Next Door* (also known as *Double Mission*), Lions Gate Films, 2010.

Alphonso, *Valentine's Day,* New Line Cinema, 2010.

Voice of Carlos, *Marmaduke,* Twentieth Century–Fox, 2010.

Beverly Hills Chihuahua 2, Walt Disney Studios, 2010.

Himself, *Jackie Chan: Stunt Master and Mentor* (short documentary), Lions Gate Films, 2010.

Voice of Bobo the Toucan, *Rio* (animated), Twentieth Century–Fox, 2011.

Voice of Grouchy Smurf, *The Smurfs,* Columbia, 2011.

Film Work:

Executive producer, *El Superstar: The Unlikely Rise of Juan Frances* (also known as *Juan Frances: Live*), Cinema Libre Studio, 2008.

Television Appearances; Series:

Title role, *George Lopez,* ABC, 2002–2007.

Mayor Hernandez, *Reno 911!,* Comedy Central, 2008–2009.

Host, *Lopez Tonight,* TBS, 2009—.

Television Appearances; Miniseries:

Chucho Osorio, *Fidel,* Showtime, 2002.

Television Appearances; Movies:

Henry Ramiro, *Naughty or Nice,* ABC, 2004.

Eddie Serrano, *Mr. Troop Mom,* Nickelodeon, 2009.

Television Appearances; Specials:

A Pair of Jokers: George Lopez & Tom Parks, Showtime, 1994.

Latino Laugh Festival, pay–per–view, 1997.

The 2nd Annual Latino Laugh Festival, Showtime, 1998.

ABC's Christmas in Aspen, ABC, 2002.

"1982," *I Love the '80s,* VH1, 2002.

The View: His & Her Body Test, ABC, 2003.

The Disco Ball (also known as *The Disco Ball ... A 30–Year Celebration*), ABC, 2003.

All ABC Bloopers, ABC, 2003.

Presenter, *ABC 50th Anniversary Celebration,* ABC, 2003.

"1973," *I Love the '70s,* VH1, 2003.

Intimate Portrait: Constance Marie, Lifetime, 2003.

The Mark Twain Prize: Lily Tomlin, 2003.

Richard Pryor: I Ain't Dead Yet, #%$#@!!* (also known as *Richard Pryor: I Ain't Dead Yet, #*%$#@!!—Uncensored*), Comedy Central, 2003.

Host, *Walt Disney World Christmas Day Parade,* ABC, 2003.

An American Celebration at Ford's Theatre, ABC, 2003.

The Original Latin Kings of Comedy, Showtime, 2003.

A Merry Mickey Celebration, ABC, 2003.

George Lopez: Why Are You Crying?, Showtime, 2004.

Bar Mitzvah Bash! (also known as *Comedy Central's "Bar Mitzvah Bash"*), Comedy Central, 2004.

50 Most Awesomely Bad Songs ... Ever, VH1, 2004.

TV Land Landmarks: Breaking the Mold, TV Land, 2004.

Host, *The 2004 NFL Opening Kickoff,* ABC, 2004.

The 101 Most Unforgettable SNL Moments, E! Entertainment Television, 2004.

"TV Guide" Close–Up: From Comedy Club to Prime-time, TV Guide Channel, 2004.

Host, *TV Guide's Greatest Moments 2003,* ABC, 2004.

ABC Extreme Bloopers, ABC, 2004.

Commentator, *Countdown to the Emmys,* ABC, 2004.

ReAct Now: Music & Relief, MTV and VH1, 2005.

Forbes Celebrity 100: Who Made Bank?, E! Entertainment Television, 2006.

Stand Up or Sit Down Comedy Challenge, 2006.

Comic Relief 2006, HBO and TBS, 2006.

The 75th Annual Hollywood Christmas Parade, The CW, 2006.

Host, *The Sierra Mist Stand Up or Sit Down Comedy Challenge,* TBS, 2006.

Reel Comedy: "Balls of Fury," Comedy Central, 2007.

George Lopez: America's Mexican, HBO, 2007.

Brown Is the New Green: George Lopez and the American Dream (documentary), PBS, 2007.

AFI Life Achievement Award: A Tribute to Al Pacino, USA Network, 2007.

The 9th Annual A Home for the Holidays, CBS, 2007.

Idol Gives Back 2, Fox, 2008.

The Samuel L. Jackson American Cinematheque Tribute, AMC, 2008.

Kids' Inaugural: We Are the Future, The Disney Channel, 2009.

We Are One: The Obama Inaugural Celebration at the Lincoln Memorial, HBO, 2009.

Mario Lopez: The E! True Hollywood Story, E! Entertainment Television, 2009.

Eva Longoria Parker: The E! True Hollywood Story, E! Entertainment Television, 2009.

George Lopez: Tall, Dark & Chicano, HBO, 2009.

Host, *In Performance at the White House: Fiesta Latina,* 2009.

CNN Presents: Latino in America, Cable News Network, 2009.

Host, *Christmas in Washington,* TNT, 2009.

Presenter, *CNN Heroes: An All–Star Tribute,* Cable News Network, 2009.

Bill Cosby: Mark Twain Prize, PBS, 2009.

Presenter, *The 3rd Annual CNN Heroes: An All–Star Tribute,* Cable News Network, 2009.

Make 'Em Laugh: The Funny Business of America, PBS, 2009.

Presenter, *The Grammy Nominations Concert Live! Countdown to Music's Biggest Night,* CBS, 2009.

Back from Hell: A Tribute to Sam Kinison, 2010.

The Battle for Late Night, Arts and Entertainment, 2010.

Idol Gives Back 3, Fox, 2010.

America Celebrates July 4th at Ford's Theatre, ABC, 2010.

Television Appearances; Awards Presentations:

Host, *7th Annual Florida Sports Awards,* 2002.

The … Annual Family Television Awards, 2002, The WB, 2003, 2005.

Presenter, *The 30th Annual American Music Awards,* ABC, 2003.

Presenter, *The 29th Annual People's Choice Awards,* CBS, 2003.

Cohost, *The 55th Annual Primetime Emmy Awards,* Fox, 2003.

Spike TV VGA Video Game Awards, Spike TV, 2003.

Presenter, *The 2003 ESPY Awards,* ESPN, 2003.

Host, *The … Annual Latin Grammy Awards,* CBS, 2003, 2004.

The 46th Annual Grammy Awards, CBS, 2004.

The 2nd Annual TV Land Awards, TV Land, 2004.

Host, *The 2004 Primetime Creative Arts Emmy Awards,* 2004.

Presenter, *Nickelodeon's 17th Annual Kids' Choice Awards,* Nickelodeon, 2004.

Presenter, *The 56th Annual Primetime Emmy Awards,* ABC, 2004.

Presenter, *The 10th Annual Critics' Choice Awards,* 2005.

Presenter, *Nickelodeon's 18th Annual Kids' Choice Awards,* Nickelodeon, 2005.

The … Annual People's Choice Awards, CBS, 2006, 2010.

Presenter, *The 2006 ALMA Awards,* ABC, 2006.

Nickelodeon's … Annual Kids' Choice Awards, Nickelodeon, 2007, 2009, 2010.

The 2007 ALMA Awards, ABC, 2007.

Presenter, *The 50th Annual Grammy Awards,* CBS, 2008.

The Teen Choice Awards 2009, Fox, 2009.

Host, *The 2009 ALMA Awards,* ABC, 2009.

The 2010 VH1 Do Something Awards, VH1, 2010.

Kougar Kardashian, *Teen Choice Awards 2010,* Fox, 2010.

Television Appearances; Episodic:

Comedy Club, 1987.

Stand–Up Spotlight, VH1, 1988.

Caroline's Comedy Hour, Arts and Entertainment, 1989.

Tompkins Square, Comedy Central, 1996.

Resurrection Blvd., Showtime, 2000.

Mr. Fender, "Cold Turkey," *The Brothers Garcia,* Nickelodeon, 2001.

Mr. Fender, "The Student Buddy," *The Brothers Garcia,* Nickelodeon, 2001.

"Sandra Bullock," *Revealed with Jules Asner,* 2002.

Hollywood Squares (also known as *H2* and *H2: Hollywood Squares*), syndicated, 2003.

"Top 10 TV Cars," *TV Land's Top Ten,* TV Land, 2004.

"Greatest TV Romances," *TV Land's Top Ten,* TV Land, 2005.

Unscripted, HBO, 2005.

Punk'd, MTV, 2005.

(Uncredited) Himself, "Valerie Stands Out on the Red Carpet," *The Comeback,* 2005.

The Big Idea with Donny Deutsch, CNBC, 2005.

Showbiz Tonight, Cable News Network, 2005.

Himself, "The Ski Lift," *Curb Your Enthusiasm,* HBO, 2005.

George, "Freddie Gets Cross Over George," *Freddie,* ABC, 2006.

"All in the Family Episodes," *TV Land's Top Ten,* TV Land, 2006.

"George Lopez," *Sit Down Comedy with David Steinberg,* TV Land, 2006.

Dancing with the Stars (also known as *D.W.T.S.*), ABC, 2006, 2007.

Himself, "Nat Is a Stand Up Guy," *The Naked Brothers Band,* Nickelodeon, 2007.

De La Hoya/Mayweather 24/7, 2007.

Sports Unfiltered with Dennis Miller, 2007.

"Best of 2007: The 25th Edition," *Just for Laughs* (also known as *Ed Byrne's "Just for Laughs," Just for Laughs Comedy Festival,* and *Just for Laughs Montreal Comedy Festival*), CBC, 2007.

Entertainment Tonight (also known as *E.T.*), syndicated, 2007, 2008, 2009, 2010.

"Ben Kingsley/George Lopez," *Shootout* (also known as *Sunday Morning Shootout* and *Hollywood Shootout*), AMC, 2008.

Himself, "Polar Bears," *The Naked Brothers Band,* Nickelodeon, 2008.

Himself, "Everybody Cried at Least Once," *The Naked Brothers Band,* Nickelodeon, 2008.

Comedian, "Would Ya Hit a Guy with Glasses?: Nerds, Jerks & Oddballs," *Make 'Em Laugh: The Funny Business of America,* PBS, 2009.

The Movie Loft, 2009.

Extra (also known as *Extra: The Entertainment Magazine*), syndicated, 2010.

Made in Hollywood, 2010.

Voice of himself, *The Bob & Tom Show,* WGN, 2010.

Cupcake Wars, Food Network, 2010.

Also appeared in *Resurrection Blvd.,* Showtime.

Television Talk Show Guest Appearances; Episodic:
The Tonight Show Starring Johnny Carson, NBC, 1991.
The Tonight Show with Jay Leno, NBC, 2002, 2005.
The View, ABC, 2002, 2003, 2005, 2007, 2010.
The Late Late Show with Craig Kilborn, CBS, 2003.
The Sharon Osbourne Show (also known as *Sharon*), syndicated, 2003, 2004.
Late Night with Conan O'Brien, NBC, 2003, 2004, 2005.
Jimmy Kimmel Live!, ABC, 2003, 2004, 2005, 2006, 2007.
Good Day Live, syndicated, 2003, 2004.
On-Air with Ryan Seacrest, syndicated, 2004.
Dennis Miller, CNBC, 2004.
Live with Regis and Kelly, syndicated, 2004, 2005, 2007, 2008.
Ellen: The Ellen DeGeneres Show, syndicated, 2004, 2005, 2006, 2007, 2008, 2009.
Good Morning America, ABC, 2005.
Howard Stern, E! Entertainment Television, 2005.
The Tony Danza Show, syndicated, 2005.
Last Call with Carson Daly, MTV, 2005, 2006.
The Megan Mullally Show, syndicated, 2006.
Up Close with Carrie Keagan, 2007, 2008.
Tavis Smiley, PBS, 2008.
The Bonnie Hunt Show, NBC, 2008.
The Oprah Winfrey Show (also known as *Oprah*), syndicated, 2009.
The Late Late Show with Craig Ferguson, CBS, 2009.
Larry King Live, Cable News Network, 2009, 2010.

Television Work; Series:
Producer and cocreator, *George Lopez,* ABC, 2002–2004.

Consulting producer, *Freddie,* ABC, 2005–2006.
Executive producer, *Lopez Tonight,* TBS, 2009—.

Television Work; Movies:
Executive producer, *Mr. Troop Mom,* Nickelodeon, 2009.

Television Executive Producer; Specials:
George Lopez: Why Are You Crying?, Showtime, 2004.
George Lopez: America's Mexican, HBO, 2007.
George Lopez: Tall, Dark & Chicano, HBO, 2009.

Television Director; Episodic:
"George Discovers Benny's Sili–Con Job," *George Lopez,* ABC, 2005.
"Sabes Gay, It's George's Fantasy Episode," *George Lopez,* ABC, 2007.

RECORDINGS

Video Games:
Stand–up performances #12, *Don't Quit Your Day Job,* 1996.

Albums:
Tall, Dark & Chicano, 2009.

Also recorded *Right Now Right Now* (a comedy album); *Team Leaders* (a comedy album).

WRITINGS

Film Scripts:
Loco Comedy Jam Volume 1, 2008.

Television Specials:
George Lopez: America's Mexican, HBO, 2007.
George Lopez: Tall, Dark & Chicano, HBO, 2009.

Television Episodes:
George Lopez, ABC, 2002–2007.

Autobiography:
Why You Crying?: My Long, Hard Look at Life, Love, and Laughter, Touchstone Books, 2004.

OTHER SOURCES

Books:
Newsmakers, Gale, 2003.

Periodicals:
New York Times, November 22, 2002; November 1, 2009, p. 12.
New York Post, December 26, 2002.
Parade, May 4, 2003, p. 22.
People, October 21, 2002; June 13, 2005, p. 83.
Time, August 22, 2005, p. 45.
TV Guide, April 5, 2003, pp. 34–35.
USA Today, May 9, 2005, p. 3C.

LUSTIG, Branko 1932–

PERSONAL

Born June 10, 1932, in Osijek, Croatia; married Mirjana, c. 1970. *Education:* Attended the Akademija dramske umjetnosti (Academy of Dramatic Art), Zagreb, Croatia. *Religion:* Judaism.

Career: Producer, production manager, assistant director, and actor. Jadran Film, assistant director. Six Point Films, Encino, CA, founder and chairman; also the founder and honorary president of the Jewish Film Festival Zagreb in Zagreb, Croatia. Akademija dramske umjetnosti (Academy of Dramatic Art), Zagreb, Croatia, instructor of film production.

Member: Directors Guild of America.

Awards, Honors: Emmy Award (with others), outstanding miniseries, 1990, for *Drug Wars: The Camarena Story;* Directors Guild of America Award (with others), outstanding directorial achievement in dramatic specials, 1990, for *War and Remembrance;* Academy Award, best picture, Film Award, best film, British Academy of Film and Television Arts, Motion Picture Producer of the Year Award, Producers Guild of America, and Directors Guild of America Award, outstanding directorial achievement in motion pictures, all with others, and Studio Crystal Heart Award, Heartland Film Festival, all 1994, for *Schindler's List;* Academy Award, best picture, and Film Award, best film, British Academy of Film and Television Arts, both with others, and Motion Picture Producer of the Year Award (with Douglas Wick), Producers Guild of America, all 2001, for *Gladiator;* Libertas Award, Dubrovnik International Film Festival, 2004; Lifetime Achievement Award, Israel Film Festival, 2009; honorary doctorate, University of Zagreb, 2009; other awards and honors include an award from the Los Angeles Museum of the Holocaust, 2009.

CREDITS

Film Executive Producer:
Dogadjaj (also known as *An Event*), Jadran Film, 1969, subtitled version, Continental Distributing, 1970.

Black Hawk Down, Columbia, 2001.
Hannibal (also known as *The Silence of the Lambs 2*), Metro–Goldwyn–Mayer, 2001.
Kingdom of Heaven (also known as *The Crusades*), Twentieth Century–Fox, 2005.
A Good Year, Fox 2000, 2006.
American Gangster (also known as *The Return of Superfly* and *Tru Blu*), Universal, 2007.

Film Producer:
Schindler's List (also known as *Steven Spielberg's "Schindler's List"*), Universal, 1993.
The Peacemaker (also known as *Peacemaker*), DreamWorks, 1997.
Gladiator (also known as *The Gladiators*), DreamWorks, 2000.

Film Assistant Director:
Die Blechtrommel (also known as *The Tin Drum*), 1979, subtitled version, New World, 1980.
Memed My Hawk (also known as *The Lion and the Hawk*), Jadran Film/The Focus Group, 1984, Filmworld, 1987.

Film Production Manager:
... und ewig knallen die Raeuber (also known as *The Bandit and the Princess* and *... und ewig knallen die Rauber*), Columbia–Bavaria Filmgesellschaft, 1962.
Little Mother (also known as *Blood Queen, Don't Cry for Me Little Mother, Immoral Mistress, Mother,* and *Woman of the Year*), Jadran Film/Audubon Films/ Peter Cartsen Produktion, 1973.
Score (also known as *The Score*), Jadran Film/Audubon Films/Danton Films, 1974.
Seljacka buna 1573 (subtitled; also known as *Anno Domini 1573*), Jadran Film/Croatia Film, 1975.
American Gangster (also known as *The Return of Superfly* and *Tru Blu*), Universal, 2007.

Film Unit Production Manager:
Ne okreci se sine (also known as *Don't Look Back, My Son* and *My Son Don't Turn Round*), Jadran Film, 1956, VEB Progress Film–Vertrieb, 1958.
Schindler's List (also known as *Steven Spielberg's "Schindler's List"*), Universal, 1993.
Additional unit production manager, *The Saint,* Paramount, 1997.
The Peacemaker (also known as *Peacemaker*), DreamWorks, 1997.
Gladiator (also known as *The Gladiators*), DreamWorks, 2000.
Black Hawk Down, Columbia, 2001.
Kingdom of Heaven (also known as *The Crusades*), Twentieth Century–Fox, 2005.
A Good Year, Fox 2000, 2006.

Film Unit Manager:

As the Sea Rages (also known as *Dynamite*), Columbia Film–Verleih, 1959, dubbed version, Columbia, 1960.

Kozara, Bosna Film, 1962.

Ann och Eve—de erotiska (also known as *Ann and Eve, Ann & Eve,* and *Anybody's*), Jadran Film/Omega Film, dubbed version, Chevron Pictures, 1970, dubbed version released as *Anne and Eve,* Astral Films, 1971.

Film Work; Other:

Production assistant, *Skopje 63* (documentary; also known as *Skopje, Skopje 1963,* and *Skopje '63*), Jadran Film/Vardar Film, 1964.

Location manager, *Fiddler on the Roof* (musical; also known as *Anatevka*), United Artists, 1971.

Production designer, *Nije daleko* (short film), Jadran Film, 1979.

Production supervisor: Yugoslavia, *Sophie's Choice,* Universal, 1982.

Worked on other projects; some sources cite work on additional projects.

Film Appearances:

Kozara, Bosna Film, 1962.

Seljacka buna 1573 (subtitled; also known as *Anno Domini 1573*), Jadran Film/Croatia Film, 1975.

Nightclub maitre d', *Schindler's List* (also known as *Steven Spielberg's "Schindler's List"*), Universal, 1993.

Man with poodle, *The Peacemaker* (also known as *Peacemaker*), DreamWorks, 1997.

(In archive footage) Himself, *Imaginary Witness: Hollywood and the Holocaust* (documentary), 2004, Shadow Distribution, 2007, Koch Lorber Films, 2009.

Television Work; Series:

Production manager, *Mathias Sandorf,* 1979.

Television Producer; Miniseries:

Coproducer, *The Great Escape II: The Untold Story,* NBC, 1988.

Drug Wars: The Camarena Story (also known as *The Drug Wars: Camarena*), NBC, 1990.

Intruders, CBS, 1992.

Television Associate Producer; Miniseries:

The Winds of War (also known as *Herman Wouk's "The Winds of War"*), ABC, 1983.

War and Remembrance, ABC, 1988–89.

Television First Assistant Director; Miniseries:

(And production consultant and production manager: Yugoslavia) "The Winds Rise," *The Winds of War* (also known as *Herman Wouk's "The Winds of War"*), ABC, 1983.

The Great Escape II: The Untold Story, NBC, 1988.

Drug Wars: The Camarena Story (also known as *The Drug Wars: Camarena*), NBC, 1990.

Intruders, CBS, 1992.

Television Work; Movies:

Production supervisor: Yugoslavia, *Nadia,* syndicated, 1984.

First assistant director, *On Thin Ice: The Tai Babilonia Story,* NBC, 1990.

Producer and assistant director, *Wedlock,* HBO, 1991.

Television Producer; Pilots:

DEA (also known as *DEA: Special Task Force*), Fox, 1990.

Television Appearances; Movies:

Onbaschi, *Mit Karl May im Orient* (also known as *With Karl May in the Orient*), Zweites Deutsches Fernsehen (ZDF), 1963.

Television Appearances; Awards Presentations:

The 66th Annual Academy Awards, ABC, 1994.

The 73rd Annual Academy Awards, ABC, 2001.

Presenter, *Lola—Der Deutsche Filmpreis 2010,* [Germany], 2010.

Television Appearances; Episodic:

Himself, "Gladiator," *HBO First Look,* HBO, 2000.

RECORDINGS

Video Appearances; as Himself; Documentaries:

Breaking the Silence: The Making of "Hannibal," Metro–Goldwyn–Mayer Home Entertainment, 2001.

The Essence of Combat: Making "Black Hawk Down," Columbia TriStar Home Entertainment, 2002.

(In archive footage) *Strength and Honor: Creating the World of "Gladiator,"* DreamWorks Home Entertainment, 2005.

Unholy War: Mounting the Siege (short), Twentieth Century–Fox Home Entertainment, 2006.

Fallen Empire: Making "American Gangster," MCA/Universal Home Video, 2008.

LYALL, Susan

PERSONAL

Education: Studied at the Fashion Institute of Technology.

Addresses: *Agent*—Doug Apatow Agency, 12049 Jefferson Blvd., Suite 200, Culver City, CA 90230.

Career: Costume Designer.

CREDITS

Film Costume Designer:
Fear, Anxiety & Depression, Samuel Goldwyn, 1989.
Men of Respect, Columbia, 1990.
End of the Night, In Absentia, 1990.
Mississippi Masala, Samuel Goldwyn, 1991.
Blowback, Northern Arts Entertainment, 1991.
Little Man Tate, Orion, 1991.
Thunderheart, TriStar, 1992.
King of the Hill, Universal, 1993.
For Love or Money (also known as *Concierge*), Universal, 1993.
Trevor (also known as *Ellen DeGeneres Presents "Trevor"*), Peccadillo Pictures, 1994.
Blink, New Line Cinema, 1994.
Imaginary Crimes, Warner Bros., 1994.
Nell, Twentieth Century–Fox, 1994.
Empire Records, Warner Bros., 1995.
Home for the Holidays, Paramount, 1995.
She's the One, Twentieth Century–Fox, 1996.
Extreme Measures (also known as *Body Bunk*), Columbia, 1996.
The Spanish Prisoner, Columbia TriStar Home Video, 1997.
Just the Ticket, United Artists, 1999.
200 Cigarettes, Paramount, 1999.
Music of the Heart, Miramax, 1999.
State and Main, New Line Cinema, 2000.
The Mothman Prophecies (also known as *Prophecy*), Sony, 2002.
Flightplan, Buena Vista, 2005.
Invincible, Buena Vista, 2006.
Music and Lyrics, Warner Bros., 2007.
Rachel Getting Married, Sony Picture Classics, 2008.
Motherhood, National Entertainment Media, 2009.
Remember Me, Summit Entertainment, 2010.
The Beaver, Summit Entertainment, 2010.
Red, Summit Entertainment, 2010.

Film Appearances:
Woman at party, *Home for the Holidays,* Paramount, 1995.

Television Costume Designer; Movies:
Caught in the Act, 1993.

Television Costume Designer; Episodic:
"Angst for the Memories," *Dream On,* HBO, 1990.
" … And Sheep Are Nervous," *Dream On,* HBO, 1990.
"Three Coins in the Dryer," *Dream On,* HBO, 1990.

Television Costume Designer; Pilots:
Only Living Boy in NY, Fox, 2000.
Washingtonienne, HBO, 2009.

Stage Costume Designer:
The Musical Comedy Murders of 1940, Circle Repertory Theatre, New York City, 1987.
As Is, Circle Repertory Theatre, 1987.
Dalton's Back, Circle Repertory Theatre, 1989.
Sunshine, Circle Repertory Theatre, 1989–90.
Red Diaper Baby, McGinn–Cazale Theatre, New York City, then Actor's Playhouse, New York City, both 1992.

M

MacCORKINDALE, Simon 1952–2010

PERSONAL

Original name, Simon Charles Pendered MacCorkindale; born February 12, 1952, in Ely, Cambridgeshire, England; died of complications from bowel and lung cancer, October 14, 2010, in London, England. Actor. Dashing British actor MacCorkindale made a career playing suave, often pedantic authority figures on television and the silver screen. His early television parts included a recurring role as Lieutenant Carter in the 1973 adventure mini-series *Hawkeye, the Pathfinder* and appearances in productions of *I, Claudius; Romeo and Juliet;* and *Jesus of Nazareth.* In 1978 MacCorkindale gained wide recognition for his performance in the Agatha Christie thriller *Death on the Nile.* He starred in the American sci-fi series *Manimal* in 1983 and was featured in 59 episodes of *Falcon Crest* in the mid-1980s. Refusing to Americanize his accent for US audiences, MacCorkindale returned to Britain and formed the production company Amy International with his second wife, Susan George, in 1987. The duo produced the films *Stealing Heaven, Djavolji raj,* and *Such a Long Journey* in the 1990s. Following roles in the television series *Counterstrike* and *Poltergeist, the Legacy,* MacCorkindale undertook his best-known role in 2002, playing medical consultant Harry Harper in 229 episodes of the BBC series *Casualty* and in the spinoffs *Holby City* and *Casualty @ Holby City.* Toward the end of his career, MacCorkindale appeared in stage productions of *The Sound of Music* and *Sleuth* and was a regular panelist on the talk-show *The Wright Stuff.*

PERIODICALS

Guardian, October 17, 2010.
Independent, October 18, 2010.
Los Angeles Times, October 17, 2010.
New York Times, October 15, 2010.

MACMURRAY, Sam
See MCMURRAY, Sam

MANDYLOR, Costas 1965–

PERSONAL

Original name, Costas Theodosopoulos; born September 3, 1965, in Melbourne, Victoria, Australia; son of Yannis (a taxi driver) and Louise (maiden name, Mandylaris) Theodosopoulos; brother of Louis Mandylor (an actor); married Talisa Soto (an actress), May, 1997 (divorced, 2000). *Avocational Interests:* Boxing.

Addresses: *Agent*—Innovative Artists, 1505 10th St., Santa Monica, CA 90401. *Manager*—Evolution Entertainment, 901 North Highland Ave., Los Angeles, CA 90038. *Publicist*—Anderson Group Public Relations, 8060 Melrose Ave., 4th Floor, Los Angeles, CA 90046.

Career: Actor. Worked as a model; appeared in television commercials, including Coors Light, 2001. Worked as a professional soccer player with the Green Gully, Melbourne, Australia; trained with Panathinaikos team in Greece.

Awards, Honors: Screen Actors Guild Award nominations (with others), outstanding performance by an ensemble in a drama series, 1995, 1996, both for *Picket Fences.*

CREDITS

Film Appearances:
Avram Arouch, *Triumph of the Spirit,* Triumph, 1989.
Italian Count, *The Doors,* TriStar, 1991.

Frank Costello, *Mobsters* (also known as *The Evil Empire*), Universal, 1991.

Mark, *Soapdish,* Paramount, 1991.

Costello, *Fatal Past,* Skouras, 1994.

John Donovan, *Virtuosity,* Paramount, 1995.

Vegas, *Venus Rising,* IRS Releasing, 1995.

Martin Niconi, *Crosscut,* 1995, A–Pix Entertainment, 1996.

George G. Kendall, *Portraits of a Killer* (also known as *Portraits of Innocence*), Live Entertainment, 1996.

Mark, *Shame,* 1996.

Jack Turner, *Stand–Ins,* Overseas Filmgroup, 1997.

Rich Adams, *Just Write,* Curb Entertainment, 1997.

Hector Stroessner and Ray Soldado, *Double Take,* Twice Removed Productions, Inc., 1997.

Conversations in Limbo, Limbo Productions, 1998.

Cicero, *My Brother Cicero* (short film), 1998.

Alan Decker, *Intrepid* (also known as *Deep Water*), Starlight, 1999.

Jared, *Gangland,* Dominion International, 2000.

Monash deputy, *The Pledge* (also known as *Pledge*), Warner Bros., 2001.

Michael Amorosa, *Above & Beyond,* Green/Epstein/Bacino, 2001.

Bobby Giordano, *Turn of Faith,* CAOH Enterprises, 2001.

Kevin Dodd, *Cover Story,* First Look Media, 2002.

Instructor, *The Real Deal,* Dream Rock/Moonstone Entertainment, 2002.

Tony, *Hitters,* Fries Film Group, 2002.

Ray, *The Shore,* Nile River Pictures, 2003.

Aiden Porter, *Patient 14,* Gemstar Pictures, 2003.

(Uncredited) Charley "Gloves" Columbo, *The Game of Their Lives* (also known as *The Miracle Match*), Crusader Entertainment, 2003, IFC Films, 2005.

Dick Sydney, *Dinocroc* (also known as *DinoCroc*), Buena Vista Home Entertainment, 2004.

Aiden Porter, *The Eavesdropper,* Freestyle Home Entertainment, 2004.

Raymond, *The Shore,* 2005.

Terrell, *Dr. Chopper,* 2005.

John Deckert, *Sub Zero,* Lions Gate Films Home Entertainment, 2005.

Billy, *Payback* (also known as *Redemption Factor*), 2006.

Forensic Hoffman, *Saw III,* Lions Gate Films, 2006.

Joey, *Made in Brooklyn,* 2007.

Mortemain and Noe, *Nobody,* 2007.

Hoffman, *Saw IV,* Lions Gate Films, 2007.

Hondshew, *Beowulf* (also known as *Beowulf: An IMAX 3D Experience* and *Beowulf: The IMAX Experience*), Paramount, 2007.

Steve, *Toxic,* Weinstein Company, 2008.

Del, *Emma Blue,* 2008.

Jesus, *The Drum Beats Twice,* Vivendi Entertainment, 2008.

Mark Hoffman, *Saw V,* Lions Gate Films, 2008.

Frank Lazaridis, *Golden Goal!* (also known as *The Ball Is Round*), Plus Entertainment, 2008.

Frank Bisner, *Lost Warrior: Left Behind,* Gorilla Pictures, 2008.

Rex, *Immortally Yours* (also known as *Kiss of the Vampire*), MTI Home Video, 2009.

Congressman Donaldson, *In the Eyes of a Killer,* Film Planet Entertainment, 2009.

Mark Hoffman, *Saw VI* (also known as *Saw 6*), Lions Gate Films, 2009.

Himself, *The Fatal Five,* Lions Gate Films Home Entertainment, 2009.

Steve Clay, *Torn,* Instinct Eden Rock International, 2010.

Raymond Crowe, *Sinners & Saints* (also known as *Sinners and Saints*), 2010.

Jimmy Muldoon, *The Cursed,* TriCoast Studios, 2010.

Gannon, *Hyenas,* 2010.

Matthew, *An Affirmative Act,* Palisades Tartan, 2010.

Hoffman, *Saw 3D* (also known as *Saw VII 3D* and *Saw: The Final 3D*), Lions Gate Films, 2010.

Sheriff O'Connor, *513,* 2010.

Mason, *Should've Been Romeo,* 2011.

Also appeared in *Bitter Sweet.*

Television Appearances; Series:

Kenny Lacos, *Picket Fences,* CBS, 1992–96.

Alphonse Royo, *Players,* NBC, 1997–98.

Monk, *Secret Agent Man,* UPN, 2000.

Flatland, 2002.

Television Appearances; Miniseries:

Salvatore Bonanno, *Bonanno: A Godfather's Story,* Showtime, 1999.

Television Appearances; Movies:

Lawrence, *Delta of Venus,* Showtime, 1995.

Paul Blankenship/Eric, *Falling for You,* CBS, 1995.

Lord Shin, *Fist of the North Star* (also known as *Hokuto no Ken*), HBO, 1996.

Dominic Delaserra, *Almost Dead,* HBO, 1996.

Captain Jaid, *Roger Corman Presents "Last Exit to Earth"* (also known as *Last Exit to Earth*), Showtime, 1996.

Cupid on Earth, *Love–Struck,* The Family Channel, 1997.

Mike Hanlon, *The Fury Within,* USA Network, 1998.

Gianni Uzielli, *Exiled: A "Law & Order" Movie* (also known as *Exiled*), NBC, 1998.

Nikos Kostantinos, *Shelter,* HBO, 1998.

McCarthy, *Shame, Shame, Shame* (also known as *Climax*), The Movie Channel, 1999.

Ryan Mitchell, *Stealth Fighter,* HBO, 1999.

Salvatore Bonanno, *Bonanno: A Godfather's Story* (also known as *The Youngest Godfather*), 1999.

Nathan Delaney, *Sanctuary* (also known as *Nora Roberts' "Sanctuary"*), CBS, 2001.

Chris Milos, *Scent of Danger* (also known as *Scent of Murder*), Animal Planet, 2002.

Marco Poloni, *Just Desserts,* Hallmark Channel, 2003.

Matt McLaughlin, *Disaster Zone: Volcano in New York,* Sci–Fi Channel, 2006.

Chase Harper, *Primal Doubt* (also known as *Personal Indiscretions*), Lifetime, 2007.

Television Appearances; Specials:
The 17th Annual People's Choice Awards, CBS, 1991.
Half Way Horrible, HBO, 1993.

Television Appearances; Pilots:
Ernesto, "For Whom the Bells Toll," *The Wedding Bells,* Fox, 2007.

Television Appearances; Episodic:
Late Night with David Letterman, 1991.
Dan King, "Half–Way Horrible," *Tales from the Crypt,* HBO, 1993.
Lee, "The Heist," *The Outer Limits* (also known as *The New Outer Limits*), Showtime, 1996.
Jerry Tamblin, "Get Fast," *F/X: The Series,* 1997.
"Cholitas," *Resurrection Blvd.,* 2000.
"Luchando," *Resurrection Blvd.,* 2000.
Vincent Corell, "Something Borrowed," *Nash Bridges,* CBS, 2001.
Franciscan brother, "The Agony and the Ex–tacy," *Sex and the City* (also known as *S.A.T.C.* and *Sex and the Big City*), HBO, 2001.
Bobby Jensen, "Be All My Sins Remembered," *Andromeda* (also known as *Gene Roddenberry's "Andromeda"*), syndicated, 2002.
Greg, "Behind the Words," *Sacred Ground,* 2002.
Greg, "Walk Like a Man," *Sacred Ground,* 2002.
Rick Lang, "Saving Private Leo," *Charmed,* The WB, 2002.
Mica Divornak, "Poster Girl," *She Spies,* NBC, 2002.
Reno Castelli, "Slippery Slope," *Fastlane,* Fox, 2003.
Bill Brewer, "Healing Old Wounds," *7th Heaven,* The WB, 2004.
Bill Brewer, "Mi Familia: Part 2," *7th Heaven,* The WB, 2004.
Beau Brewer, "Soup's On," *7th Heaven,* The WB, 2005.
Beau Brewer, "Chicken Noodle Heads," *7th Heaven,* The WB, 2005.
Beau Brewer, "And Baby Makes Three," *7th Heaven,* The WB, 2006.
Ernesto, "Wedding from Hell," *The Wedding Bells,* Fox, 2007.
Ernesto, "The Fantasy," *The Wedding Bells,* Fox, 2007.
The 7PM Project, Ten Network, 2009.
Made in Hollywood, 2009.

MARCIL, Vanessa 1969(?)–
(Vanessa Marcil Giovinazzo)

PERSONAL

Original name, Sally Vanessa Ortiz; born October 15, 1969 (some sources cite 1968), in Indio, CA; daughter of Peter (a contractor) and Patricia (an herbalist; maiden name, Marcil) Ortiz; married Corey Feldman (an actor and producer), August 6, 1989 (divorced January 1, 1993); married Carmine Giovinazzo (an actor and writer), July 11, 2010; children: (with actor Brian Austin Green) Kassius Lijah. *Education:* Attended College of the Desert. *Avocational Interests:* Volunteering at rehabilitation centers.

Addresses: *Agent*—Adena Chawke, Innovative Artists, 1505 10th St., Santa Monica, CA 90401.

Career: Actress. Former member of Circle Theatre Acting Company, Indio, CA; appeared in television commercials, including one for Head and Shoulders shampoo. Designer of Kass (children's clothing line); Patricia House (support organization and telephone hotline for women who can no longer care for their children), Los Angeles, founder.

Awards, Honors: *Soap Opera Digest* Award nominations, outstanding female newcomer, 1994, and hottest soap couple (with Maurice Benard), 1995, *Soap Opera Digest* Awards, hottest female star, 1997, and outstanding lead actress, 1998, Daytime Emmy Award nominations, 1997 and 1998, and Daytime Emmy Award, 2003, all outstanding supporting actress in a drama series, and *Soap Opera Digest* Award, favorite return, 2003, all for *General Hospital.*

CREDITS

Television Appearances; Series:
Brenda Barrett, *General Hospital,* ABC, 1992–98, 2000, 2002–2003, then (as Vanessa Marcil Giovinazzo) 2010—.
Host, a recurring role, *ABC in Concert* (also known as *In Concert*), ABC, between 1995 and 1998.
Gina Kincaid, *Beverly Hills, 90210* (also known as *Class of Beverly Hills*), Fox, 1998–2000.
Samantha Jane "Sam" Marquez, *Las Vegas,* NBC, 2003–2008.

Television Appearances; Movies:
Sydney Carpenter, *To Love, Honor and Deceive* (also known as *The Protected Wife*), ABC, 1996.
Kate Hewitt, *The Nanny Express,* Hallmark Channel, 2008.
Margarita Silva Santos, *One Hot Summer,* Lifetime, 2009.

Television Appearances; Specials:
Brenda Barrett, *General Hospital: Twist of Fate,* ABC, 1996.
Host, *The Superstars,* 1998.
(In archive footage) *ABC Soaps' Most Unforgettable Love Stories,* ABC, 1998.

Sex with Cindy Crawford, ABC, 1998.
The General Hospital 35th Anniversary Show, ABC, 1998.
Beverly Hills 90210: The E! True Hollywood Story, E! Entertainment Television, 2001.
Intimate Portrait: Vanessa Marcil, Lifetime, 2003.
A Dr. Phil Primetime Special: Family First, CBS, 2004.
Host, *NBC Premiere Week Preview,* NBC, 2005.

Television Appearances; Miniseries:
Host, *Blush: The Search for America's Greatest Makeup Artist,* Lifetime, 2008.

Television Appearances; Episodic:
Kerry Andrews, "Hot Wire," *High Incident,* ABC, 1996.
Kerry Andrews, "Remote Control," *High Incident,* ABC, 1996.
Crazy Kara, "A Shot in the Dark: Part 2," *Spin City,* ABC, 2001.
Detective Carmen Olivera, "Johnny Got His Gold," *NYPD Blue* (also known as *N.Y.P.D.*), ABC, 2001.
Detective Carmen Olivera, "Shear Stupidity," *NYPD Blue* (also known as *N.Y.P.D.*), ABC, 2002.
Sam Marquez, "What Happens in Vegas Dies in Boston," *Crossing Jordan,* NBC, 2004.
Sam Marquez, "Luck Be a Lady," *Crossing Jordan,* NBC, 2005.
Herself, "Variety Is the Spice of Life," *My First Time,* Showtime, 2006.
Josie Scotto, "Chapter Fourteen: Let the Games Begin," *Lipstick Jungle,* NBC, 2008.
Josie Scotto, "Chapter Sixteen: Thanksgiving," *Lipstick Jungle,* NBC, 2008.
Josie Scotto, "Chapter Eighteen: Indecent Exposure," *Lipstick Jungle,* NBC, 2008.
Kim Marcus, "Voir Dire," *Without a Trace* (also known as *W.A.T.*), CBS, 2009.
Kim Marcus, "Daylight," *Without a Trace* (also known as *W.A.T.*), CBS, 2009.
Kim Marcus, "Hard Landing," *Without a Trace* (also known as *W.A.T.*), CBS, 2009.

Television Appearances; Pilots:
Dr. Emma Ryder, *L.A. Med,* ABC, 1997.
Samantha Jane, *Las Vegas,* NBC, 2003.

Television Talk Show Guest Appearances; Episodic:
The Rosie O'Donnell Show, syndicated, multiple appearances, between 1996 and 2000.
Late Night with Conan O'Brien, NBC, 2003.
SoapTalk, SoapNet, 2003.
The Sharon Osbourne Show (also known as *Sharon*), syndicated, 2003, 2004.
Today (also known as *NBC News Today* and *The Today Show*), NBC, 2004.
Last Call with Carson Daly, NBC, 2004.
Jimmy Kimmel Live!, ABC, 2004.

The Tony Danza Show, syndicated, 2004, 2005.
Ellen: The Ellen DeGeneres Show, syndicated, multiple appearances, between 2004 and 2006.
Martha, syndicated, 2006.
(As Vanessa Marcil Giovinazzo) *The View,* ABC, 2010.
(As Giovinazzo) *The Wendy Williams Show,* 2010.

Television Appearances; Awards Presentations:
Presenter, *The ... Annual Soap Opera Awards,* NBC, 1993, 1998.
Presenter, *The ... Annual Daytime Emmy Awards,* ABC, 1994, NBC, 1998, and (as Vanessa Marcil Giovinazzo) CBS, 2010.
The 18th Annual Soap Opera Digest Awards, SoapNet, 2003.
Host, *The 31st Annual Daytime Emmy Awards,* NBC, 2004.
The WIN Awards, PAX, 2005.

Film Appearances:
The Undertaker, 1995.
Carla Pestalozzi, *The Rock,* Buena Vista, 1996.
Danielle, *976–WISH,* David Bertman Productions, 1997.
Maggie Harty, *This Space Between Us,* Atmosphere Entertainment, 1998.
Erin, *Nice Guys Sleep Alone,* Asylum Entertainment, 1999.
Tess Woodward, *Storm Watch* (also known as *Code Hunter* and *Virtual Storm*), Velocity Home Entertainment, 2002.
Madison, *The Bannen Way,* Sony Pictures Home Entertainment, 2010.

Stage Appearances:
Cat on a Hot Tin Roof, Los Angeles, 1992.
Southern Rapture, Los Angeles, 1993.
Starfire, Los Angeles, 1999.

Appeared in productions of *Fools, The Miracle Worker, Pygmalion,* and *Sweet Bird of Youth.*

RECORDINGS

Videos:
Appeared in the music video "The Most Beautiful Girl in the World" by Prince, 1994.

OTHER SOURCES

Periodicals:
ABC Soaps in Depth, September 3, 2002, pp. 28–34.
Bikini, September, 1999, pp. 58–59.
Entertainment Weekly, February 17, 1995, p. 50; June 13, 1998, p. 16; May 4, 1999.

FHM, September, 2000, pp. 106–10.
Maxim, June, 2005, pp. 144, 146, 148, 150.
People Weekly, May 8, 1995, p. 144; June 17, 1996,
   pp. 178–79.
Soap Opera Digest, May 20, 1997, pp. 28–31.
Stuff, October, 2003, pp. 114–18.
TV Guide, February 1, 2003, p. 42.

Other:
Intimate Portrait: Vanessa Marcil (television special),
   Lifetime, 2003.

MARIANELLI, Dario 1963–
   (Dario Marionelli)

PERSONAL

Born June 21, 1963, in Pisa, Italy. *Education:* Graduated from the National Film and Television School, 1997; spent a year as postgraduate composer at the Guildhall School of Music and Drama.

Addresses: *Agent*—Air Edel Associates, Ltd., 18 Rodmarton St., London W1U 8BJ, England.

Career: Composer, conductor, and orchestrator.

Member: Academy of Motion Pictures Arts and Sciences.

Awards, Honors: Film Composer of the Year Award nominations, International Film Music Critics Association, 2005, 2007; Academy Award nomination, best achievement in music written for motion pictures—original scores, European Film Award nomination, best composer, World Soundtrack Award nominations, best original soundtrack of the year and soundtrack composer of the year, 2006, all for *Pride & Prejudice;* Chicago Film Critics Association Award nomination, best original score, Phoenix Film Critics Society Award, best original score, Satellite Award nomination, best original score, International Press Academy, 2007, Academy Award, best achievement in music written for motion pictures—original scores, Film Award nomination, best music, British Academy of Film and Television Arts, Critics Choice Award nomination, best composer, Broadcast Film Critics Association, European Film Award nomination, best composer, Golden Globe Award, best original score—motion picture, Online Film Critics Society Award nomination, best score, World Soundtrack Award, best original score of the year, World Soundtrack Award nomination, film composer of the year, 2008, all for *Atonement;* Cinema Writers Circle Award nomination, best score, Goya Award nomination, best original score, 2010, both for *Agora.*

CREDITS

Film Work:
Music conductor and orchestrator, *I Went Down,*
   Artisan Entertainment, 1997.
Music conductor and orchestrator, *Pandaemonium,*
   USA Films, 2000.
Conductor and orchestrator, *The Warrior,* Miramax,
   2001.
Conductor and orchestrator, *In This World,* Lions Gate
   Films, 2002.
Music conductor and orchestrator, *I Capture the Castle,*
   Samuel Goldwyn, 2003.
Song publisher, *Code 46,* United Artists, 2003.
Conductor and orchestrator, *Beyond the Gates* (also
   known as *Shooting Dogs*), Renaissance Films,
   2005.
Conductor and orchestrator, *Sauf le respect que je vous
   dois,* Haut et Court, 2005.
Conductor and music producer, *Opal Dream,* Strand
   Releasing, 2005.
Music conductor and orchestrator, *The Warrior,* Miramax, 2005.
Music conductor and orchestrator, *The Return,* Rogue
   Pictures, 2006.
Conductor and orchestrator, *Goodbye Bafana* (also
   known as *The Color of Freedom*), 2007.
Orchestrator, *Atonement,* Focus Features, 2007.
Conductor and orchestrator, *Far North,* Image Entertainment, 2007.
Orchestrator, *The Brave One* (also known as *Brave
   One*), Warner Bros., 2007.
Music orchestration, *Shrooms,* Magnolia Pictures,
   2007.
Song performer, *A Very British Gangster* (documentary),
   Echo Bridge Home Entertainment, 2007.
Song performer, *Capitalism: A Love Story* (documentary), Overture Films, 2009.
Orchestrator, *Agora,* Newmarket Films, 2009.

Television Appearances; Specials:
The 80th Annual Academy Awards, ABC, 2008.

WRITINGS

Film Scores:
Models Required (short film), 1994.
Ailsa, 1994.
The Long Way Home, 1995.
(As Dario Marionelli) *The Sheep Thief* (short film),
   1997.
I Went Down, Artisan Entertainment, 1997.

Southpaw (documentary; also known as *Southpaw: The Francis Barrett Story*), Shooting Gallery, 1999.
The Funeral of the Last Gypsy King (short film), 1999.
Being Considered, Storm Entertainment, 2000.
Pandaemonium, USA Films, 2000.
The Man Who Bought Mustique, First Run Features, 2001.
Happy Now, 2001.
The Warrior, Miramax, 2001.
The Visitor (short film), National Film and Television School, 2001.
In This World, Lions Gate Films, 2002.
I Capture the Castle, Samuel Goldwyn, 2003.
September, 2003.
The Bypass (short film), 2003.
Cheeky, 2003.
Beyond the Gates (also known as *Shooting Dogs*), Renaissance Films, 2005.
Pride & Prejudice, Focus Features, 2005.
The Brothers Grimm, Miramax, 2005.
Sauf le respect que je vous dois, Haut et Court, 2005.
Opal Dream, Strand Releasing, 2005.
The Warrior, Miramax, 2005.
V for Vendetta (also known as *"V for Vendetta": The IMAX Experience*), Warner Bros., 2006.
The Return, Rogue Pictures, 2006.
We Are Together (Thina Simunye) (documentary), Palm Pictures, 2006.
Shrooms, Magnolia Pictures, 2007.
Goodbye Bafana (also known as *The Color of Freedom*), 2007.
Atonement, Focus Features, 2007.
Far North, Image Entertainment, 2007.
The Brave One (also known as *Brave One*), Warner Bros., 2007.
Beyond the Gates, IFC Films, 2007.
Trancity (short film), 2008.
My World (short film), 2008.
We Are Together: The Children of Agape Choir, Palm Pictures, 2008.
The Soloist, Paramount, 2009.
Agora, Newmarket Films, 2009.
Everybody's Fine, Miramax, 2009.
Eat Pray Love, Columbia, 2010.
Hippie Hippie Shake, Universal, 2010.

Also scored *This Little Life; Meerkats.*

Film Songs:
"Tehran," *Code 46,* United Artists, 2003.
A Very British Gangster (documentary), Echo Bridge Home Entertainment, 2007.
"Two Figures by a Fountain," *Capitalism: A Love Story* (documentary), Overture Films, 2009.
"Mrs. Darcy," *Wild Child,* Universal, 2009.

Film Segments:
Uneternal City (documentary), 2008.

Television Scores; Miniseries:
Blood Strangers, Granada Television, 2002.

Television Scores; Movies:
This Little Life, BBC, 2003.
Passer By, BBC, 2004.

Television Scores; Specials:
Preserve, 1999.
On the Trail of Mark Twain with Peter Ustinov (documentary), PBS, 1999.
Secrets of the Pharaohs (documentary), PBS, 2001.
Into the Great Pyramid (documentary), 2002.
9/11: The Falling Man (documentary), Channel 4, 2006.

Television Songs; Specials:
"Dawn" and "Geogina," *Pride and Prejudiced Revisited,* BBC, 2005.

MARSHALL, Amber 1988–

PERSONAL

Born June 2, 1988, in London, Ontario, Canada (some sources say Toronto, Ontario, Canada). *Education:* Studied acting with the Original Kids Theatre Company. *Avocational Interests:* Riding horses, animals.

Career: Actress. Appeared in television commercials, including TD Canada Trust. Previously worked as a veterinary assistant.

Awards, Honors: Young Artist Award nomination, best performance in a television movie, miniseries or special—leading young actress, 2004, for *The Elizabeth Smart Story.*

CREDITS

Film Appearances:
Daughter, *Resident Evil: Apocalypse* (also known as *Biohazard 2: Apocalypse*), Screen Gems, 2004.

Television Appearances; Series:
Ally, *Super Rupert,* YTV, 2001.
Tracey Battle, *The Power Strikers,* 2005.
Amy Fleming, *Heartland,* CBS then syndicated, 2007—.

Also appeared as Rebecca, *Dark Oracle,* YTV.

Television Appearances; Miniseries:
Lorna at age six, *Life with Judy Garland: Me and My Shadows,* ABC, 2001.

Television Appearances; Movies:
Lily, *The Christmas Shoes,* CBS, 2002.
Title role, *The Elizabeth Smart Story* (also known as *Kidnapped: The Elizabeth Smart Story*), CBS, 2003.

Television Appearances; Episodic:
Renetta Moore, "Daddy's Girl," *Twice in a Lifetime,* CTV and PAX, 2001.
"Karate Kid," *Doc,* PAX, 2002.
Second girl, "Mr. Monk Meets Dale the Whale," *Monk,* USA Network, 2002.

MARSHALL, Rob 1960–

PERSONAL

Born October 17, 1960, in Madison, WI; raised in Pittsburgh, PA. *Education:* Graduated from Carnegie–Mellon University, 1982.

Addresses: *Agent*—International Creative Management, 8942 Wilshire Blvd., Beverly Hills, CA 90211; Creative Artists Agency, 2000 Avenue of the Stars, Los Angeles, CA 90067. *Contact*—Lucamar Productions, 584 Broadway, Suite 1003, New York, NY 10012.

Career: Dancer, choreographer, and director. Began his acting career with Civic Light Opera, Pittsburgh, PA; Asolo State Theatre, Sarasota, FL, guest artist, 1987–88.

Awards, Honors: Antoinette Perry Award nomination, best choreography, 1993, for *Kiss of the Spider Woman;* Antoinette Perry Award nomination, best choreography, Outer Critics Circle Award, and Los Angeles Drama Critics Award, 1994, all for *Damn Yankees;* Antoinette Perry Award nomination, best choreography, Outer Critics Circle Award, Laurence Olivier Theatre Award nomination, Society of London Theatre, and Drama Desk Award nomination, 1994, all for *She Loves Me;* Outer Critics Circle Award nomination, c. 1995, for *Victor/Victoria;* Outer Critics Circle Award nomination, c. 1996, for *A Funny Thing Happened on the Way to the Forum;* Emmy Award nomination, outstanding choreography, 1996, for *Mrs. Santa Claus;* Emmy Award nomination, outstanding choreography, 1997, for *Cinderella;* Laurence Olivier Theatre Award nomination, best choreography, 1998, Outer Critics Circle Award nomination, Los Angeles Drama Critics Award, all for *Damn Yankees;* Antoinette Perry Award nomina-

tions, best choreography and best director of a musical, 1998, Drama Desk Award nomination, Outer Critics Circle Award nomination, all for *Cabaret;* Emmy Award, outstanding choreography, Emmy Award nomination, outstanding directing for a miniseries, movie or a special, Directors Guild of American Award nomination, outstanding directorial achievement in musical/variety, American Choreography Award, outstanding achievement in television—variety or special, 2000, all for *Annie;* National Board of Review Award, best debut director, 2002, Academy Award nomination, best achievement in directing, Golden Globe Award nomination, best director—motion picture, Directors Guild of America Award (with others), outstanding directorial achievement in motion pictures, David Award nomination, best foreign film, David di Donatello Awards, David Lean Award for Direction nomination, British Academy of Film and Television Arts, Online Film Critics Society Award nomination, best breakthrough filmmaker, PFCS Award nomination, best director, best newcomer, Phoenix Film Critics Society, Amanda Award nomination, best foreign feature film, American Choreography Award (with others), outstanding achievement in feature film, 2003, all for *Chicago;* Dora Mavor Moore Award, outstanding choreography in a play or musical, Toronto Alliance for the Performing Arts, Drama–Logue Award, both for *Chicago;* Antoinette Perry Award nomination, Drama Desk Award nomination, and Outer Critics Circle Award nomination, all for *Little Me;* Outer Critics Circle Award nomination, for *Company;* Satellite Award nomination, outstanding director, International Press Academy, 2005, for *Memoirs of a Geisha;* Emmy Awards, outstanding choreography (with John DeLuca), outstanding directing for a variety, music or comedy program and outstanding variety, music or comedy special (with others), Directors Guild of America Award, outstanding directorial achievement in musical/variety, 2007, for *Tony Bennett: An American Classic;* Satellite Award nomination, best director, 2009, for *Nine;* Distinguished Director Collaborator, 2010.

CREDITS

Stage Work:
Choreographer, *Bells Are Ringing,* Goodspeed Opera House, East Haddam, CT, 1990.
Choreographer, *Eleanor,* Pittsburgh Public Theatre, Pittsburgh, PA, 1990–91.
Choreographer and director, *Chess,* Paper Mill Playhouse, Millburn, NJ, 1991–92.
The 1940's Radio Hour, Repertory Theatre of St. Louis, St. Louis, MO, 1991–92.
Director and (with sister, Kathleen Marshall) Choreographer, *A Chorus Line,* Westchester Broadway Theatre, Elmsford, NY, 1991–92.
Choreographer, *A Christmas Carol,* McCarter Theatre, Princeton, NJ, 1992–93.

Musical staging, *She Loves Me,* Criterion Theatre, then Roundabout Theatre, both New York City, 1993, then Brooks Atkinson Theatre, New York City, 1993–94, later London production, c. 1996.

Contributor, *Kiss of the Spider Woman,* Broadhurst Theatre, New York City, 1993–95, then London production, c. 1996.

Choreographer, *Damn Yankees,* Marquis Theatre, New York City, 1994–95, then London production, 1997.

Musical staging, *The Petrified Prince,* New York Shakespeare Festival, Joseph Papp Public Theatre, Martinson Hall, New York City, 1994–95.

Musical staging, *Company,* Criterion Theatre, 1995.

Choreographer, *Victor/Victoria,* Marquis Theatre, 1995–97.

Choreographer, *A Funny Thing Happened on the Way to the Forum,* St. James Theatre, New York City, 1996–98.

Choreographer and codirector, *Cabaret,* Kit Kat Club, New York City, 1998–99.

Choreographer and director, *Little Me,* Criterion Theatre, 1998–99.

Uncredited direction, *Seussical,* Richard Rogers Theatre, New York City, 2000.

Director, *Chicago,* Long Beach, CA, 2003.

Also worked as director and choreographer, *Promises, Promises;* choreographer of Pittsburgh productions of *Brigadoon, Camelot, Oliver,* and *South Pacific.*

Major Tours:
Choreographer, *Drood!,* 1988.
Director, *Cabaret,* U.S. cities, 2000.

Stage Appearances:
Understudy for the role of Munkustrap, *Cats,* Winter Garden Theatre, New York City, between 1982 and 1987.

Boogie–Woogie Rumble of a Dream Deferred, off–Broadway production, 1982.

Marsalis and monk, *Zorba,* Broadway Theatre, New York City, 1983–84.

Understudy for the roles of Lino, Lucky, and Tony, *The Rink,* Martin Beck Theatre, New York City, 1984.

Ann Reinking ... Music Moves Me, Joyce Theatre, New York City, 1984–85.

Christopher Lyon, *The Mystery of Edwin Drood,* Delacorte Theatre, Central Park, New York City, 1985, then Imperial Theatre, New York City, 1985–86.

Major Tours:
A Chorus Line, 1980.
Marsalis and monk, *Zorba,* U.S. cities, 1983.

Television Choreographer; Specials:
"Victor/Victoria," *Julie Andrews: Back on Broadway,* PBS, 1995.

America's Millennium, CBS, 1999.
Victor/Victoria, Bravo, 2000.
Chita Rivera tribute conceiver, *The 25th Anniversary Kennedy Center Honors: A Celebration of the Performing Arts,* CBS, 2002.
Artistic supervisor (*Chicago* dance performance), *The 75th Annual Academy Awards,* ABC, 2003.

Television Director; Specials:
The Kennedy Center Honors: A Celebration of the Performing Arts, 2001.

Television Work; Movies:
Choreographer, *Mrs. Santa Claus,* CBS, 1996.
Choreographer and musical staging, "Cinderella" (also known as "Rodgers and Hammerstein's 'Cinderella'"), *The Wonderful World of Disney,* ABC, 1997.
Director and choreographer, *Annie,* ABC, 1999.
Producer, director, and choreographer, *Tony Bennett: An American Classic,* 2006.

Also directed and choreographed *Mame,* ABC.

Television Appearances; Specials:
On the Move: The Central Ballet of Canada, PBS, 1988.
On the Move: The Central Ballet of China, PBS, 1988.
The 75th Annual Academy Awards, ABC, 2003.
The 100 Greatest Musicals, Channel 4, 2003.
Presenter, *The 58th Annual Tony Awards* (also known as *The 2004 Tony Awards*), CBS, 2004.
On the Set: Memoirs of a Geisha, Starz!, 2005.
MovieReal: Memoirs of a Geisha, Arts and Entertainment, 2005.
The 59th Primetime Emmy Awards, Fox, 2007.
Roman Polanski: Wanted and Desired, Wide Pic, 2008.
Oscar, que empiece el espectaculo, Canal+ Espana, 2008.
Hollywood Singing and Dancing: A Musical Treasure, PBS, 2008.
Streisand: Live in Concert, 2009.

Television Appearances; Episodic:
"Chicago," *VH–1 Behind the Movie,* VH1, 2002.
Charlie Rose (also known as *The Charlie Rose Show*), PBS, 2003, 2005.
"From Screen to Stage: Kristin Chenoweth and Rob Marshall," *Evening at the Pops,* PBS, 2004.
"Richard Gere," *Biography,* Arts and Entertainment, 2004.
Cinema mil, Televisio de Catalunya, 2005.
Breakfast, BBC, 2006.
Grease: You're the One That I Want!, NBC, 2007.
"Renee Zellweger," *E! True Hollywood Story,* E! Entertainment Television, 2008.
"Italian Every Time," *Barefoot Contessa,* 2008.
"The Cast of Nine!," *Larry King Live,* Cable News Network, 2009.

This Morning, ITV, 2009.

Entertainment Tonight (also known as *E.T.* and *This Week in Entertainment*), syndicated, three episodes, 2009.

In the House, NBC, 2009.

Cinema 3, 2010.

Film Work:

Choreographer, *Cradle Will Rock,* Buena Vista, 1999.

Codirector and choreographer, *Loser,* Sony, 2000.

Director and choreographer, *Chicago,* Miramax, 2002.

Director, *Memoirs of a Geisha,* Columbia, 2005.

Executive producer, director, and choreographer, *Nine,* Sony, 2009.

Film Appearances:

ShowBusiness: The Road to Broadway (documentary), Regent Releasing, 2007.

RECORDINGS

Video Appearances:

The Music of "Memoirs," Sony, 2006.

A Day with Chef Nobu Matsuhisa, Sony, 2006.

The Road to Japan, Sony, 2006.

The Way of the Sumo, Sony, 2006.

Portrait of a Choreographer, Twentieth Century–Fox, 2007.

Hollywood Singing and Dancing: 1920s—The Dawn of the Hollywood Musical, Passport Video, 2008.

Hollywood Singing and Dancing: A Musical History, KOCH International, 2008.

Hollywood Singing and Dancing: A Musical History—The 1940s: Stars, Stripes and Singing, KOCH International, 2009.

Hollywood Singing and Dancing: A Musical History—1950's, KOCH International, 2009.

Hollywood Singing and Dancing: A Musical History—1960's, KOCH International, 2009.

Hollywood Singing and Dancing: A Musical History—1970's, KOCH International, 2009.

Hollywood Singing and Dancing: A Musical History—1980's, 1990's and 2000's, KOCH International, 2009.

OTHER SOURCES

Periodicals:

Dance Magazine, March, 1994, p. 70; August, 1996, p. 62.

Newsweek, January 27, 2003, p. 67.

Playbill, February 28, 2003, p. 21.

MASTROIANNI, Chiara 1972–

PERSONAL

Born May 28, 1972, in Paris, France; daughter of Marcello Mastroianni (an actor) and Catherine Deneuve (an actress); half–sister of Christian Vadim (an actor); married Benjamin Biolay (a singer, composer, and writer), May 11, 2002 (divorced, 2005); children: (with Pierre Torreton, a sculptor) Milo; (with Biolay) Anna.

Addresses: *Agent*—Zelig, 57 Rue Reaumur, Paris 75002, France.

Career: Actress.

Awards, Honors: Cesar Award nomination, most promising actress, Academie des Arts et Techniques du Cinema, 1994, for *Ma saison preferee;* National Board of Review Award (with others), best acting by an ensemble, 1994, for *Pret–a–Porter.*

CREDITS

Film Appearances:

(Uncredited) The little girl, *A nous deux* (also known as *An Adventure for Two* and *Us Two*), 1979.

Claire, *A la belle etoile,* Bac Films, 1993.

Anne, *Ma saison preferee* (also known as *My Favorite Season*), Vertigo Films, 1993.

Sophie Choiset, *Pret–a–Porter* (also known as *Pret–a–Porter: Ready to Wear* and *Ready to Wear*), Miramax, 1994.

Claudia, *N'oublie pas que tu vas mourir* (also known as *Don't Forget You're Going to Die*), La Sept Cinema, 1995.

Claire Conti, *Le journal du seducteur* (also known as *Diary of a Seducer*), Gemini Films, 1995.

Francoise, *All Men Are Mortal,* Warner Bros., 1995.

Hillbilly Chainsaw Massacre, 1995.

Cecile, *Trois vies et une seule mort* (also known as *Three Lives and Only One Death* and *Tres vidas e uma so morte*), Laurenfilm, 1996.

Graduate student, *Les voleurs* (also known as *The Child of the Night* and *Thieves*), Sony Pictures Classics, 1996.

Lea, *Cameleone* (also known as *Chameleon*), Rezo Films, 1996.

Patricia, *Comment je me suis dispute ... (ma vie sexuelle)* (also known as *My Sex Life ... or How I Got into an Argument*), Zeitgeist Films, 1997.

Viviane, *On a tres peu d'amis,* Gemini Films, 1997.

Kriss, *Nowhere,* Fine Line, 1997.

Mireille, *A vendre* (also known as *For Sale*), Golem Distribucion/Pyramide, 1998.

Madame de Cleves, *A carta* (also known as *The Letter, La lettre, A princesa de Cleves,* and *La princesse de Cleves*), Atalanta Filmes/Mikado/Gemini Films, 1999.

Albertine, *Le temps retrouve* (also known as *Time Regained, O tempo reencontrado, Il tempo ritrovato,* and *Marcel Proust's "Time Regained"*), Artificial Eye, 1999.

Rosa Agnello, *Libero Burro,* Twentieth Century–Fox Italia/UGC–Fox Distribution, 1999.

Marine, *Six–Pack,* Pathe, 2000.

"La faute au vent," *Scenario sur la drogue* (also known as *Drugs!*), 2000.

Hotel nurse, *Hotel,* 2001, Innovation Film Group, 2003.

Ada, *Le parole di mio padre* (also known as *The Words of My Father* and *Zeno—Le parole di mio padre*), Mikado/Pierre Grise Distribution, 2001.

Carlotta, *Carnages* (also known as *Carnage*), Diaphana Films, 2002.

Bianca, *Il est plus facile pour un chameau …* (also known as *It's Easier for a Camel …*), New Yorker Films, 2004.

Barbara, *Akoibon,* 2005.

Herself, *Marcello, una vita dolce* (documentary), Surf Film, 2006.

Aude Neuville, *Towards Zero* (also known as *L'heure zero*), Studio Canal, 2007.

Jeanne, *Love Songs* (also known as *Les chansons d'amour*), IFC Films, 2007.

(French–and English–language versions) Voice of Marjane "Marji" Satrapi as a teenager and a woman, *Persepolis* (animated), Sony Pictures Classics, 2007.

Sylvia—Ivan's wife, *A Christmas Tale* (also known as *Un conte de Noel* and *Christmas Story*), IFC Films, 2008.

Le jeune femme dans le cafe, *La belle personne* (also known as *The Beautiful Person*), Le Pacte, 2008, IFC Films, 2009.

Emma Charpentier, *Le crime est notre affaire* (also known as *Crime Is Our Business*), Studio Canal, 2008.

Nathalie/Celimene, *Un chat un chat* (also known as *Pardon My French*), Les Films du Losange, 2009.

La mere de Marianne/La cliente aux lunettes, *Park Benches* (also known as *Bancs publics*), UGC Distribution, 2009.

Lena, *Making Plans for Lena* (also known as *Non ma fille, tu n'iras pas danser*), Le Pacte, 2009, IFC Films, 2010.

L'actrice, *Man at Bath* (also known as *Homme au bain*), Le pacte, 2010.

Lili, adulte, *Chicken with Plums* (also known as *Poulet aux prunes*), Celluloid Dreams, 2011.

Television Appearances; Movies:
Brigitte, *Reveuse jeunesse* (also known as *Shattered Lives*), 1994.

Herself, *Searching for Debra Winger,* Showtime, 2002.

Television Appearances; Specials:
Herself, *French Beauty,* 2005.

Television Appearances; Episodic:
V.I.P.—Schaukel, 1976.
"Bavardages en SIDA minteur," *3000 scenarios contre un virus,* 1994.
En directe, Mari Pau, 1999.
Mundo VIP, 1999.
"La faute au vent," *Scenarios sur la drogue,* 2000.
"La 27eme nuit des Cesars," *La nuit des Cesars,* 2002.
On ne peut pas plaire a tout le monde, 2002, 2004.
The ou cafe, 2005.
Le grand journal de Canal+, 2005, 2008, 2010.
"31eme nuit des Cesars," *La nuit des Cesars,* 2006.
Ce soir (ou jamais!), 2007.
L'hebdo cinema, 2007.
Cinema 3, 2009.

RECORDINGS

Video Games:
(English–language version) Voice, *Beyond Atlantis II* (also known as *Atlantis 3: The New World*), 2001.

Albums:
(With Benjamin Biolay) *Home,* 2004.

OTHER SOURCES

Periodicals:
People Weekly, May 8, 1995, p. 156.
Time, February 23, 1993, p. 75.

MAZZARINO, Joseph
(Joe Mazzarino, Joey Mazzarino)

PERSONAL

Married Kerry Butler (an actress), 1997; children: one. *Education:* Studied economics and theatre at Fordham University.

Career: Writer, puppeteer, and voice performer. Jim Henson Pictures, puppeteer and muppet performer for television series and specials and for feature films.

Awards, Honors: Daytime Emmy (with others), outstanding writing in a children's series, 1994, 1995, 1998, 1999, 2001, 2002, 2003, 2006, 2009 and Daytime Emmy Award nominations (with others), outstanding writing in a children's series, 2000, 2004, 2005, 2007, 2008, 2009, Daytime Emmy Award nomination, outstanding original song, 2005, Writers Guild Award nomination, children's episodic and specials, 2010, all for *Sesame Street.*

CREDITS

Television Appearances; Series; As Joey Mazzarino:
Stinky the Stinkweed and Joey Monkey, *Sesame Street* (also known as *Canadian Sesame Street, The New Sesame Street, Open Sesame, Sesame Park,* and *Les amis de Sesame*), PBS, 1993–97.
Artie, *Dog City,* Fox, 1993.
Voices of Chelli and Lyle Sock, *Big Bag* (animated), Cartoon Network, 1995–98.
Voice of Spit, *Aliens in the Family,* ABC, 1995–96.

Television Appearances; Specials:
The Muppets Celebrate Jim Henson, CBS, 1990.
Voice of monster, *It Came from Beneath the Bed or Nightmare on Magellan Street,* Nickelodeon, 1991.
Voice of monster, *Don't Touch That Box!,* Nickelodeon, 1991.
Sesame Street Stays Up Late! A Monster New Year's Eve Party, PBS, 1993.
Voice of two–headed monster, "Sesame Street's Peter and the Wolf," *Sesame Street,* PBS, 2000.
Jamie Fox/Mary/Matt Lauer Chicken/sheep, *The 36th Annual Daytime Emmy Awards,* The CW, 2009.

Television Appearances; Movies:
(As Joe Mazzarino) Voice of Joey Monkey, *Sesame Street Jam: A Musical Celebration,* 1994.
Voice of King Fred, *Cinderelmo,* 1999.
(As Joey Mazzarino) Goggles and first turtle, *Kermit's Swamp Years: The Real Story behind Kermit the Frog's Early Years* (also known as *Kermit's Swamp Years*), Starz!, 2002.
Roary/Boogie Woogie, *Blue's Room,* Nickelodeon, 2006.
Stan the Snowball, *Elmo's Christmas Countdown,* 2007.

Television Appearances; Episodic:
CityKids, ABC, 1993.
"15 Muttons of Fame," *Sheep in the Big City,* 2001.
"Agony of De–Bleat," *Sheep in the Big City,* 2001.
"A Star Is Shorn," *Sheep in the Big City,* 2001.
"To Sheep, Perchance to Dream," *Sheep in the Big City,* 2001.
(As Joseph Mazzarino) Muppet doctor, "Eppur Si Muove," *The West Wing* (also known as *The White House*), 2004.

Voice of Henry the Monster, "The Music Monster," *Jack's Big Music Show,* 2005.
Tube, Smelly, "The Crook," *Nick Jr.'s Play Along* (also known as *Nick Jr. Playalong Adventures, Nick Jr. Playalong DVD, Nick Jr. Playalong Fun, Nick Jr. Playalong Games,* and *Nick Jr. Playalong PC*), Nick Jr., 2007.
Voice of Muppet Matt Lauer/Rat, "The Muppets Take Over Today," *Today* (also known as *NBC News Today* and *The Today Show*), NBC, 2008.
Puppeteer, "Apollo, Apollo," *30 Rock,* 2009.

Television Director; Series:
Sesame Street, PBS, 2007–2008.

Television Work; Specials:
Elmo's Christmas Countdown, ABC, 2007–2008.

Film Appearances:
Voice of Artie, *Jim Henson's Dog City: The Movie,* 1989.
Voice of Wesley/coffee guy, *Muppet Breaking Point,* 1992.
Muppet Know How, 1993.
(As Joseph Mazzarino) Voice of John–Boy, *Sesame Songs: Sing–Along Earth Songs* (also known as *Sing–Along Earth Songs*), 1993.
Gimley's boss, *Muppet Breakout,* 1993.
Lightning, *Elmo Saves Christmas,* 1996.
Bug, *The Adventures of Elmo in Grouchland,* Columbia, 1999.
Sesame Street: Computer Caper, 2002.
(As Joseph Mazzarino) Voice of Goggles and first turtle, *Kermit's Swamp Years,* 2002.
Voice of Papa Bear, *Sesame Street: Three Bears and a New Baby,* Sony Wonder, 2003.
Chicken, *Lights, Camera, Imagination!* (short; also known as *Sesame Street: 4–D Movie Magic*), 2003.
Bobby, *Sesame Street: Happy Healthy Monsters,* Genius Products, 2004.
Sesame Street: Friends to the Rescue, Genius Products, 2005.
Sesame Street: All–Star Alphabet, Sesame Workshop, 2005.
Elmo Visits the Doctor, Sony Wonder, 2005.
Elmo's World: Reach for the Sky, 2006.
Guess That Shape and Color, 2006.
Elmo's World: Pets!, Genius Products, 2006.
Voice of Joe Marley/Joey Dickens/Lightning, *A Sesame Street Christmas Carol,* Genius Products, 2006.
Elmo's World: What Makes You Happy?, Genius Products, 2007.
Ready for School, Sesame Workshop, 2007.
Plaza Sesamo: A mi me gusta contar!, Warner Home Video, 2008.
Food delivery guy, *Ghost Town,* Paramount, 2008.

WRITINGS

Television Series; As Joey Mazzarino:
Sesame Street (also known as *Canadian Sesame Street, The New Sesame Street, Open Sesame, Sesame Park,* and *Les amis de Sesame*), PBS, 1998–2007.
Sheep in the Big City (animated), Cartoon Network, 2000.

Television Movies:
Kermit's Swamp Years: The Real Story Behind Kermit the Frog's Early Years (also known as *Kermit's Swamp Years*), Starz!, 2002.

Television Specials:
Elmopalooza, ABC, 1998.
Elmo's Magic Cookbook, Food Network, 2001.
Sesame Street Presents: The Street We Live On (also known as *Sesame Street: Elmo's World–The Street We Live On!*), 2004.
Elmo's Christmas Countdown, ABC, 2007–2008.

Screenplays:
The Adventures of Elmo in Grouchland, Columbia, 1999.
(With Jerry Juhl and Ken Kaufman) *Muppets from Space,* Columbia, 1999.
Lights, Camera, Imagination! (short film; also known as *Sesame Street: 4–D Movie Magic*), 2003.
Kid's Favorite Country Songs, 2007.
Ready for School, 2007.

Television Lyrics, Specials:
Elmo's Christmas Countdown, ABC, 2007–2008.

McCALLUM, Rick 1952–
    (Rick Mccallum)

PERSONAL

Born in Heidelberg, Germany; stepson of Michael York (an actor).

Addresses: *Contact*—c/o Lucasfilm Ltd., PO Box 2009, San Rafael, CA 94912.

Career: Producer and actor.

Awards, Honors: Video Premiere Award nomination (with others), best audio commentary, 2001, for *Star Wars: Episode I—The Phantom Menace.*

CREDITS

Film Producer:
Star Wars: Episode VI—Return of the Jedi (also known as *Return of the Jedi* and *Star Wars VI: Return of the Jedi*), 1983.
Dreamchild, Universal, 1985.
(With others) *Link,* Cannon, 1986.
Castaway, Warner Home Video, 1986.
Track 29, Island Releasing, 1988.
Strapless, Gavin, 1989.
Blackeyes, 1989.
The Adventures of Young Indiana Jones: Daredevils of the Desert, 1992.
Radioland Murders, Universal, 1994.
Star Wars: Episode IV—A New Hope (also known as *Star Wars, La guerra de las estrellas,* and *Star Wars IV: A New Hope*), Twentieth Century–Fox, 1997.
Star Wars: Episode V—The Empire Strikes Back (also known as *Star Wars V: The Empire Strikes Back* and *The Empire Strikes Back*), Twentieth Century–Fox, 1997.
Return of the Jedi–Special Edition, Twentieth Century–Fox, 1997.
The Pirates and the Prince (also known as *Star Wars Animated Adventures: Droids*), 1997.
Treasure of the Hidden Planet, 1997.
Star Wars: Episode 1—The Phantom Menace (also known as *The Phantom Menace* and *Star Wars I: The Phantom Menace*), Twentieth Century–Fox, 1999.
The Adventures of Young Indiana Jones: The Trenches of Hell, 1999.
The Adventures of Young Indiana Jones: Spring Break Adventure, 1999.
The Adventures of Young Indiana Jones: Masks of Evil, 1999.
The Adventures of Young Indiana Jones: Adventures in the Secret Service, Paramount, 1999.
The Adventures of Young Indiana Jones: Oganga, the Giver and Taker of Life, 1999.
The Adventures of Young Indiana Jones: The Phantom Train of Doom, 1999.
(As Rick Mccallum) *The Adventures of Young Indiana Jones: Daredevils of the Desert,* 1999.
Star Wars: Episode II—Attack of the Clones (also known as *Attack of the Clones: The IMAX Experience, Star Wars II,* and *Star Wars II: Attack of the Clones*), Twentieth Century–Fox, 2002.
Star Wars: Episode III—Revenge of the Sith (also known as *Revenge of the Sith, Star Wars III: Revenge of the Sith,* and *Star Wars: Revenge of the Sith*), Twentieth Century–Fox, 2005.
The Adventures of Young Indiana Jones: My First Adventure, Paramount, 2007.
The Adventures of Young Indiana Jones: Passion for Life, Paramount, 2007.
The Adventures of Young Indiana Jones: The Perils of Cupid, Paramount, 2007.

The Adventures of Young Indiana Jones: Journey of Radiance, Paramount, 2007.

The Adventures of Young Indiana Jones: Love's Sweet Song, Universal, 2007.

The Adventures of Young Indiana Jones: Espionage Escapades, Universal, 2007.

The Adventures of Young Indiana Jones: Demons of Deception, Universal, 2007.

The Adventures of Young Indiana Jones: Scandal of 1920, Universal, 2008.

The Adventures of Young Indiana Jones: Winds of Change, Paramount, 2008.

Red Tails, Lucasfilm, 2010.

Film Work:

Executive producer, *Pennies from Heaven,* Metro–Goldwyn–Mayer, 1981.

Production manager, *Track 29,* 1988.

Unit manager, *The Adventures of Young Indiana Jones: Spring Break Adventure,* 1999.

Production manager, *The Adventures of Young Indiana Jones: Scandal of 1920,* 2008.

Film Appearances:

(Uncredited) Stormtrooper, *Star Wars—Special Edition,* Twentieth Century–Fox, 1997.

The Unauthorized Star Wars Story, Visual Entertainment, 1999.

(Uncredited) Naboo courier, *Star Wars: Episode I—The Phantom Menace* (also known as *The Phantom Menace* and *Star Wars I: The Phantom Menace*), Twentieth Century–Fox, 1999.

(Uncredited; in archive footage) *R2–D2: Beneath the Dome,* Twentieth Century–Fox, 2001.

Television Work; Miniseries:

Executive producer, *The Singing Detective,* BBC, then PBS, 1988.

Television Work; Series:

Production manager, *The Young Indiana Jones Chronicles,* 1992–93.

Executive producer, *Star Wars: Clone Wars* (animated), Cartoon Network, 2003.

Executive producer, *The Adventures of Young Indiana Jones Documentaries,* Lucasfilm, 2007.

Television Producer; Movies:

On Tidy Endings, HBO, 1988.

Heading Home, Arts and Entertainment, 1992.

Young Indiana Jones and the Hollywood Follies, The Family Channel, 1994.

Young Indiana Jones and the Attack of the Hawkmen, The Family Channel, 1995.

Young Indiana Jones and the Treasure of the Peacock's Eye, The Family Channel, 1995.

Young Indiana Jones: Travels with Father, The Family Channel, 1996.

Television Producer; Series:

The Young Indiana Jones Chronicles, ABC, 1992–93.

Television Producer; Pilots:

Lucasfilm Live Action Star Wars Series, 2009.

Television Producer; Episodic:

"Heading Home," *Screen Two,* 1991.

Television Appearances; Specials:

Star Wars: The Magic and the Mystery, Fox, 1997.

Taet pa troldmanden George Lucas, 1997.

From Star Wars to Star Wars: The Story of Industrial Light & Magic, 1999.

The Inside Reel: Digital Filmmaking (documentary), PBS, 2001.

R2–D2: Beneath the Dome, 2001.

Star Wars at 30, G4, 2007.

Television Appearances; Episodic:

"Troldsejlet special: Bag Klonernes angreb," *Troldspejlet* (also known as *Magic Mirror*), 2002.

RECORDINGS

Videos:

The Unauthorized "Star Wars" Story, 1999.

The Beginning: Making Episode I (also known as *The Beginning: Making Star Wars Episode I*), 2001.

Films Are Not Released, They Escape, 2002.

State of the Art: The Pre–Visualization of Episode II (also known as *State of the Art: The Pre–Visualization of Star Wars Episode II*), 2002.

It's All for Real: The Stunts of Episode III, Twentieth Century–Fox, 2005.

Within a Minute: The Making of Episode III (documentary), Twentieth Century–Fox, 2005.

Music Videos:

Produced the music video "Undercover" by the Rolling Stones.

OTHER SOURCES

Periodicals:

Cinema, October, 1999, pp. 32–34.

Empire, 1997, pp. 80–81.

SFX, May, 2002, pp. 64–70.

McCULLUM, Julito 1990–

PERSONAL

Original name, Uriel De–Jesus Amanza–McCullum; born December 16, 1990, in Brooklyn, New York, NY; son of Glynis and Uriel Almanza.

Addresses: *Manager*—J. Mitchell Management, 70 West 36th St., Suite 1006, New York, NY 10018.

Career: Actor.

CREDITS

Television Appearances; Series:
Namond Brice, *The Wire,* HBO, 2006–2008.

Television Appearances; Episodic:
"Becoming P. Diddy & Usher," *Becoming,* MTV, 2002.
Cal, "Out of the Ashes," *Hack,* CBS, 2003.
Jason Young, "Underbelly," *Law & Order: Special Victims Unit* (also known as *Law & Order: SVU* and *Special Victims Unit*), NBC, 2006.
Darnell Thomson, "Maltese Cross," *Law & Order: Criminal Intent* (also known as *Law & Order: CI*), NBC, 2006.
Alpha, "Rock Star," *Law & Order: Criminal Intent* (also known as *Law & Order: CI*), USA Network, 2009.
Calvin Stokes, "Four Cops Shot," *Law & Order,* NBC, 2010.

Television Appearances; Movies:
Jamal, *The Wool Cap,* TNT, 2004.

Television Appearances; Miniseries:
Lafayette, *Miracle's Boys,* The N, 2005.

Television Appearances; Specials:
The Wire: It's All Connected, HBO, 2006.
Bring That Year Back 2006: Laugh Now, Cry Later, Black Entertainment Television, 2006.

Television Appearances; Pilots:
Cal Milton, *Hack,* CBS, 2002.

Film Appearances:
Jamal, *God's Forgotten House,* WonderPhil Prod., 2005.
Ball player, *Preaching to the Choir* (also known as *On the One*), Codeblack Entertainment, 2005.

Terrence, *Akeelah and the Bee,* Sony, 2006.
Kid, *Parting Words,* Schofield Films, 2008.
Detective Johnson's son, *You're Nobody 'til Somebody Kills You,* Blackfoot Films, 2010.

RECORDINGS

Music Videos:
Appeared in "Runaway Love" by Ludacris, 2006.

McMURRAY, Sam 1952–
(Sam MacMurray, Sam Mcmurray)

PERSONAL

Born April 15, 1952, in New York, NY; son of Richard (an actor) and Jane (an actress; maiden name, Hoffman) McMurray; stepson of Lesley Woods; married Elizabeth Collins (an actress); children: two daughters. *Education:* Washington University, B.A., literature.

Addresses: *Agent*—AKA Talent Agency, 6310 San Vicente Blvd., Suite 200, Los Angeles, CA 90048. *Manager*—Opus Entertainment, 5225 Wilshire Blvd., Suite 905, Los Angeles, CA 90036.

Career: Actor and producer. Appeared in television commercials, including Bud Light, 1997. O'Neill Playwrights Conference, New London, CT, member for seven years.

Awards, Honors: Daytime Emmy Award nomination, outstanding performer in a children's special, 1997, for "Teenage Confidential," *ABC Afterschool Specials;* two Drama–Logue Awards.

CREDITS

Film Appearances:
(Film debut) Young man at party, *The Front,* Columbia, 1976.
Young vagrant, *Union City,* Kinesis, 1980.
Mr. McManus, *Baby, It's You,* Paramount, 1983.
Officer Crespi, *C.H.U.D.,* New World, 1984.
Clem Friedkin, *Fast Forward,* Columbia, 1985.
Glen, *Raising Arizona,* Twentieth Century–Fox, 1987.
Peter Harriman, *Ray's Male Heterosexual Dance Hall* (short film), Discovery Program/Chanticleer, 1988.
Bateman, *The Wizard,* Universal, 1989.
Bill, *National Lampoon's "Christmas Vacation"* (also known as *Christmas Vacation* and *National Lampoon's "Winter Holiday"*), Warner Bros., 1989.

Kreimach, *Little Vegas* (also known as *Little Vegas: A Desert Story*), IRS Releasing, 1990.

Lance, *Stone Cold,* Columbia, 1991.

Morris Frost, *L.A. Story,* TriStar, 1991.

Skip Wankman, *Class Act,* Warner Bros., 1992.

Don Buckman, *Addams Family Values,* Paramount, 1993.

Alex, *Getting Even with Dad,* Metro–Goldwyn–Mayer/United Artists, 1994.

Federal prosecutor, *Dear God,* Paramount, 1996.

Edgar Wallace, *Savage,* Conquistador Entertainment, 1997.

Boccoli, *Slappy and the Stinkers* (also known as *Free Slappy*), TriStar, 1998.

Tricky, *The Mod Squad,* Metro–Goldwyn–Mayer/United Artists, 1999.

Goon Bob, *Baby Geniuses* (also known as *Baby Talking*), Sony Pictures Entertainment, 1999.

Lester Leeman, *Drop Dead Gorgeous* (also known as *Gnadenlos schoen*), New Line Cinema, 1999.

Jerry Brock, *Carlo's Wake,* 1999.

Chief Troutman, *Lucky Numbers* (also known as *Lucky Number* and *Le bon numero*), Paramount, 2000.

Todd Northup, *Sunshine State,* Sony Pictures Classics, 2002.

Dad Bumpers, *Wishcraft,* 2002.

Mr. Smith, *Lone Star State of Mind* (also known as *Coyboys and Idiots* and *Road to Hell*), TriStar, 2002.

Voice of Lieutenant Griswald, *Recess: All Growed Down* (animated), 2003.

Jack Rumpkin, *Confessions of an Action Star* (also known as *Sledge: The Untold Story*), Lightyear Entertainment, 2005.

Roger Dugan, *Tennis, Anyone ...?,* Fireside Entertainment, 2005.

Apartment manager, *Cruel But Necessary,* Koch Entertainment, 2005.

Harry, *A Christmas Too Many,* Lions Gate Films, 2007.

Fire marshall, *Killer Pad,* Lions Gate Films, 2008.

Ronnie, *Meet Monica Velour,* Anchor Bay Films, 2010.

Big Bad Dan, *A Little Help,* 2010.

Hale Everwright, *Miss Nobody,* 2010.

Dick Stevens, *The A Plate,* 2011.

Film Work:

Coproducer, *Slappy and the Stinkers* (also known as *Free Slappy*), TriStar, 1998.

Television Appearances; Series:

Wes Leonard, *Ryan's Hope,* ABC, 1975.

Phil, *The Edge of Night* (also known as *Edge of Night*), 1979.

Officer Harvey Schoendorf, *Baker's Dozen,* CBS, 1982.

Regular, *The Tracey Ullman Show,* Fox, 1987–90.

Voice of Roy Hess and others and puppeteers, *Dinosaurs,* ABC, 1991–95.

Roger Dumphy, *Stand by Your Man,* Fox, 1992.

Detective Marshak, *Likely Suspects,* Fox, 1992–93.

Coach Jimmy Dugan, *A League of Their Own,* CBS, 1993.

Dr. Douglas McGill, *Medicine Ball,* Fox, 1995.

Charlie Sweet, *Matt Waters,* CBS, 1995–96.

Voice of Lieutenant Griswald and others, *Recess* (animated; also known as *Disney's "Recess: Created by Paul and Joe"*), 1997–2000.

Supervisor Patrick O'Boyle, *The King of Queens,* CBS, 2001–2006.

Douglas Jenkins, *Free for All,* Showtime, 2003.

Various voices, *The Boondocks* (animated), Cartoon Network, 2005–10.

Dr. Goode's father, *Head Case,* CBS, 2008–2009.

Various, *State of the Union* (also known as *Tracey Ullman's "State of the Union"*), Showtime, 2009–10.

Warden, *Raising Hope,* Fox, 2010.

Television Appearances; Miniseries:

Pearson, *Hands of a Stranger,* CBS, 1987.

Television Appearances; Movies:

The trendy liberal, *Mom's On Strike,* 1984.

Morrison, *Out of the Darkness* (also known as *Zigo's Choice*), CBS, 1985.

Police lieutenant, *Adam: His Song Continues,* NBC, 1986.

David Thomas, *Take My Daughters, Please* (also known as *All My Darling Daughters*), NBC, 1988.

Dick Langley, "He Never Game Me Orgasm," in *National Lampoon's Attack of the 5 Ft. 2 In. Woman* (also known as *Attack of the 5 Ft. 2 Woman*), Showtime, 1994.

Herman Munster, *The Munsters' Scary Little Christmas,* Fox, 1996.

Wilson McQuaid, *Boys & Girls,* 1996.

Soccer Dog: The Movie, HBO, 1999.

Voice of Harry Tully, *Batman Beyond: The Movie* (animated), 1999.

Coach Shaw, *Soccer Dog: The Movie,* HBO, 1999.

Brian, *The Amati Girls,* Fox, 2000.

(As Sam Mcmurray) Agent Stameck, *Stealing Sinatra,* Showtime, 2003.

Skip Westland, *Ruby Romaine Trailer Tales,* 2003.

Arnie, *McBride: Anybody Here Murder Marty?,* Hallmark Channel, 2005.

Jack Struthers, *Lake Placid 2,* Sci–Fi Channel, 2007.

Wheaton, *Ring of Death,* Spike TV, 2008.

Television Appearances; Specials:

Trendy liberal, "Mom's on Strike," *ABC Afterschool Specials,* ABC, 1984.

Tracey Ullman Backstage, Fox, 1988.

Various parts, *The Best of "The Tracey Ullman Show,"* 1990.

Glen Mattson, "Teenage Confidential," *ABC Afterschool Specials,* ABC, 1996.

Skip Westland, *Tracey Ullman in the Trailer Tales,* HBO, 2003.

Television Appearances; Pilots:
Regular, *Not Necessarily the News,* HBO, 1982.
Frank McGee, *The Hope Division,* ABC, 1987.
Chaos Theory, NBC, 1999.
Vince, Sr., *Those Who Can,* NBC, 2000.

Also appeared in *Dads,* ABC.

Television Appearances; Episodic:
Duke Peter Dushan, "The Pride and the Princess," *Kojak,* CBS, 1976.
Ned, "The Devil's Work," *Ourstory,* PBS, 1976.
Howard Benson, "Louise's Convention," *The Jeffersons,* 1979.
Charles Remington, "All Around the Clock," *The Ropers,* 1979.
Jimmy Walters, "Calderon's Demise," *Miami Vice,* NBC, 1984.
Gann, "More Skinned Against than Skinning," *Hill Street Blues,* NBC, 1986.
Stu Angry, "The D.J.," *You Again?,* NBC, 1986.
Michael Saxon, *O'Hara,* ABC, 1987.
(Uncredited) Moe Hyman, "Blonde on Blonde," *Moonlighting,* ABC, 1987.
Lieutenant Tony Brandt, "Raising Marijuana," *21 Jump Street,* Fox, 1988.
Coach Finelli, "The Refrigerator of Filmore High," *Head of the Class,* ABC, 1988.
Mike, "Dear Mike," *Dear John,* NBC, 1988.
Brent, *Empty Nest,* NBC, 1988.
Mike, "Something on the Side," *Dear John,* NBC, 1989.
Mark Howard Haper, "Heather Can Wait," *Who's the Boss?,* NBC, 1989.
Bart Hess, "The Model," *Matlock,* NBC, 1989.
Steven Ehrhardt, "Roamers and Rumors," *Grand,* 1990.
Mr. Kane, "Cheaters," *The Golden Girls,* NBC, 1990.
Voice of Gulliver Dark, "Homer's Night Out," *The Simpsons* (animated), Fox, 1990.
Andy, "Dance Show," *Married ... with Children* (also known as *Married with Children*), Fox, 1990.
Voice of SNPP employee and Duff commercial voice, "Homer's Odyssey," *The Simpsons* (animated), Fox, 1990.
Rondall Kittleman, "Satellite on a Hot Tim's Roof," *Home Improvement,* ABC, 1991.
Mark Harper, "Party Politics," *Who's the Boss?,* 1991.
Sergio, "Run for the Border," *Blossom,* NBC, 1991.
Walter Herrigan, "Have Gun, Will Unravel," *Civil Wars,* ABC, 1991.
"Lily Makes a Move," *Sibs,* 1992.
"The Best Years of My Life," *Sibs,* 1992.
Ron, *Down the Shore,* Fox, 1992.
Mr. Rips, "Goodbye Mr. Rips," *Parker Lewis Can't Lose* (also known as *Parker Lewis*), Fox, 1992.
Pierce, "Birds of a Feather," *Batman: The Animated Series* (animated; also known as *Batman* and *The Adventures of Batman & Robin*), 1993.
The Tonight Show with Jay Leno, NBC, 1993.

Ron, "Life's a Drag," *Down the Shore,* 1993.
Thomas, "Change Partners ... and Dance," *Party of Five,* Fox, 1995.
Detective Dorn, "Car Mechanic," *Deadly Games,* UPN, 1995.
Voice of Cyrus, "Sherman, Woman and Child," *The Critic* (animated), Fox, 1995.
Gary, "Maybe This Time," *Maybe This Time,* ABC, 1995.
Detective Dorn, "Camp Counselor: Parts 1 & 2," *Deadly Games,* UPN, 1995.
Voice of Shawn, "TV or Not TV," *Steven Spielberg Presents "Pinky and the Brain"* (animated), The WB, 1995.
Voice of first tax man, "The Mummy/Robin Brain," *Steven Spielberg Presents "Pinky and the Brain"* (animated), The WB, 1996.
Voice of video teacher, "Brain's Bogie/Say What, Earth?," *Steven Spielberg Presents "Pinky and the Brain"* (animated), The WB, 1997.
Morris Clancy, "Prison Story," *The Pretender,* NBC, 1997.
Dr. David Stockton, "Take My Wife, Please," *Chicago Hope,* CBS, 1997.
Dr. David Stockton, "Missed Conception: Part 1," *Chicago Hope,* CBS, 1997.
(As Sam MacMurray) Chandler's boss Doug, "The One with the Ultimate Fighting Champion," *Friends,* NBC, 1997.
Voice of Robby Fisher, "Steely Phil/Quantity Time," *Hey Arnold!* (animated), Nickelodeon, 1997.
Dennis Lundy, "Hosed," *Wings,* NBC, 1997.
Oliver Marley, "Cinderella and the Funeral," *Soul Man,* ABC, 1997.
Marco McCulloch, "Misleading Lady," *Living Single,* 1997.
Freddy Rizzo, "The Two Mrs. Rizzos," *Pearl,* CBS, 1997.
Detective Dorn, "The Ex–Girlfriend," *Deadly Games,* UPN, 1997.
Voice of Keith Doll, "Beach Blanket Bravo/The Day the Earth Didn't Move Around Much/Aisle of Mixed–Up Toys," *Johnny Bravo* (animated), Cartoon Network, 1997.
Voice of Keith Doll, "The Man Who Cried 'Clown!'/Johnny, Real Good/Little Talky Tabitha!," *Johnny Bravo* (animated), Cartoon Network, 1997.
Ken, *Cosby,* CBS, 1997.
Voice of Ernie, "Joker's Millions," *The New Batman Adventures* (animated), 1998.
Marco McCulloch, "To Catch a Thief," *Living Single,* Fox, 1998.
Bob Bare, "Baby Boom," *Diagnosis Murder* (also known as *Dr. Mark Sloan*), CBS, 1998.
Voice of Rodrick Snootwell, "Open Wide for Zombies/Dumbwaiters," *The Angry Beavers* (animated), Nickelodeon, 1998.
Doug, "The One with Chandler's Work Laugh," *Friends,* NBC, 1999.
Dentist, "Scandal," *Tracey Takes On ...,* HBO, 1999.

Voice of Harry Tully, "Rebirth: Part 1," *Batman Beyond* (animated; also known as *Batman of the Future*), The WB, 1999.

Voice of Chelsea's dad, "Spellbound," *Batman Beyond* (animated; also known as *Batman of the Future*), The WB, 1999.

Voice of bum, "Bloodsport," *Batman Beyond* (animated; also known as *Batman of the Future*), The WB, 1999.

Voice of Buckley Lord, "Grudge Match/Polishing Rhonda," *Hey Arnold!* (animated), Nickelodeon, 1999.

Voice of Flip, "You Otter Know," *The Wild Thornberrys* (animated), Nickelodeon, 1999.

Voice of Chelsea's dad, "The Last Resort," *Batman Beyond* (animated; also known as *Batman of the Future*), The WB, 2000.

Dr. Vic Schweiber, "The Diary," *Freaks and Geeks,* NBC, 2000.

Dr. Vic Schweiber, "The Garage Door," *Freaks and Geeks,* NBC, 2000.

Dr. Vic Schweiber, "Noshing and Moshing," *Freaks and Geeks,* NBC, 2000.

Voice of Buckley Lloyd, "Stuck in a Tree/Rhonda Goes Broke," *Hey Arnold!* (animated), Nickelodeon, 2001.

Milton Maxwell, "The Accident," *The Lot,* AMC, 2001.

Officer Stockton, "Traffic Ticket," *Malcolm in the Middle,* Fox, 2001.

Dr. Bernstein, "Doctor, Doctor," *Yes, Dear,* CBS, 2001.

"Somebody's Fool," *Deadline,* NBC, 2001.

Dr. John Kennedy, "Second Opinion," *The Sopranos,* HBO, 2001.

Supervisor O'Boyle, "Package Deal," *The King of Queens,* CBS, 2001.

Supervisor O'Boyle, "S'no Job," *The King of Queens,* CBS, 2001.

Supervisor O'Boyle, "Pregnant Pause," *The King of Queens,* CBS, 2001.

Daniel Bryant, "You've Got Male," *Spin City,* ABC, 2001.

The Immortal, "The Funeral," *The Tick,* Fox, 2001.

Doug, "The One with Ross's Step Forward," *Friends,* NBC, 2001.

Voice of Larry Lux, "Ro's Reunion," *The Zeta Project* (animated), 2001.

Chef, "Hoop Dreams," *It's Like, You Know ...,* 2001.

Mr. Montgomery, "Tea and Antipathy," *Reba,* The WB, 2001.

Supervisor O'Boyle, "Double Downer," *The King of Queens,* CBS, 2002.

Supervisor O'Boyle, "Hero Worship," *The King of Queens,* CBS, 2002.

Supervisor O'Boyle, "Screwed Driver," *The King of Queens,* CBS, 2002.

Norris, "The Sixteenth Minute," *Touched by an Angel,* CBS, 2002.

Jim Modica, *Greetings from Tucson,* The WB, 2002.

Voice of Buckley Lloyd, "The Racing Mule/Curly's Girl," *Hey Arnold!* (animated), Nickelodeon, 2002.

Voice of Dad, *Free For All,* Showtime, 2003.

Supervisor O'Boyle, "Driving Reign," *The King of Queens,* CBS, 2003.

Mr. Modica, "Student Council," *Greetings from Tucson,* The WB, 2003.

Voice of Gilbert Halestrom, "Fearful Symmetry," *Justice League* (animated; also known as *JL* and *Justice League Unlimited*), Cartoon Network, 2004.

Lieutenant Jeff Henry, "Bale to the Chief," *NYPD Blue* (also known as *N.Y.P.D.*), ABC, 2005.

Al Girard, "S(elf) Help," *Head Cases,* Starz!, 2005.

Larry, "My Fairy King," *That '70s Show,* Fox, 2006.

Dr. Hoffman, "Used, Abused and Unenthused," *Huff,* Showtime, 2006.

Dr. Hoffman, "A Cornfield Grows in L.A.," *Huff,* Showtime, 2006.

Tom "Z" Zimmerman in 2007, "Blood on the Tracks," *Cold Case,* CBS, 2007.

Lou, "The Suite Life Goes Hollywood: Parts 1 & 2," *The Suite Life of Zack and Cody* (also known as *TSL* and *Suite Life*), The Disney Channel, 2007.

General Mark "Fitz" Fitzgerald, "Do Tell," *Boston Legal,* ABC, 2007.

Mike Landry, "Tandem Repeats," *ER,* NBC, 2008.

Dr. Victor Bravenec, "Mandala," *Breaking Bad,* AMC, 2009.

Dr. Victor Bravenec, "ABQ," *Breaking Bad,* AMC, 2009.

Voice of Tucker Wade, "From Here to Fraternity," *Glenn Martin DDS* (animated), Nickelodeon, 2009.

"The Sounds of Silence," *The Secret Life of an American Teenager,* ABC Family, 2010.

Also appeared in *Easy Street,* CBS.

Stage Appearances:

The Merry Wives of Windsor, Delacorte Theatre, Joseph Papp Public Theatre, New York Shakespeare Festival, New York City, 1974.

(Off–Broadway debut) Lonnie, *The Taking of Miss Janie,* New York Shakespeare Festival, Mitzi E. Newhouse Theatre, 1975.

Otis Fitzhugh, *Ballymurphy,* Manhattan Theatre Club, New York City, 1976.

Bobby Wheeler, *Clarence,* Roundabout Theatre, New York City, 1976.

Doalty, *Translations,* Manhattan Theatre Club, 1981.

The Great Magoo, Hartford Stage Company, Hartford, CT, 1982.

Mick Connor, *Comedians,* Manhattan Punch Line Theatre, New York City, 1983.

Man Overboard, Sargent Theatre, New York City, 1983.

Benjamin "Kid Purple" Schwartz, *Kid Purple,* Manhattan Punch Line Theatre, 1984.

Homesteaders, Long Wharf Theatre, New Haven, CT, 1984.

Phil, "Desperadoes," in *Marathon '85,* Ensemble Studio Theatre, New York City, 1985.

Mike Connor, *The Philadelphia Story,* Hartman Theatre, Stamford, CT, 1985.

Union Boys, Yale Repertory Theatre, New Haven, CT, 1985.

L.A. Freewheeling, Hartley House Theatre, New York City, 1986.

Savage in Limbo, O'Neill Theatre Center, New London, CT, 1987, then Cast Theatre, Los Angeles.

Also appeared as Phil, *The Dumping Ground,* in *Welfare, The Store,* and *Lucky Star,* all Ensemble Studio Theatre, New York City; *A Soldier's Play,* New York City; *The Connection,* New York City.

Radio Appearances:

Appeared as voice of Commander Naru and others, *The Empire Strikes Back Radio Drama,* National Public Radio.

RECORDINGS

Video Games:

Voice of BBC newscaster and American newscaster, *Command & Conquer: Red Alert 2* (also known as *Command & Conquer: Red Alert 2—Yuri's Revenge*), 2001.

Voice, *Command & Conquer: Yuri's Revenge* (also known as *Red Alert 2 Expansion Pack: Yuri's Revenge*), Electronic Arts, 2001.

Voice of Jack Foster and Henry Haskins, *Law & Order: Justice Is Served,* Legacy Interactive, 2004.

True Crime: New York City, Activision, 2005.

WRITINGS

Television Additional Material; Episodic:

Wrote for *Head Cases,* Starz!.

MEADOW, Lynne 1946–

PERSONAL

Full name, Lynne Carolyn Elizabeth Meadow; born November 12, 1946, in New Haven, CT; daughter of Franklin Raymond and Virginia (maiden name, Ribakoff) Meadow. *Education:* Bryn Mawr College, B.A., 1968; Yale University School of Drama, 1968–70. *Avocational Interests:* Tennis and skiing.

Addresses: *Office*—Manhattan Theatre Club, 311 West 43rd St., New York, NY 10036–6413.

Career: Artistic director, director, and producer. Manhattan Theatre Club, New York City, artistic director, 1972—; State University of New York at Stony Brook, adjunct professor, 1975–76; Eugene O'Neill Playwrights' Conference, Waterford, CT, director, 1975–77; New York Shakespeare Festival, New York City, director, 1977; Yale University and Circle in the Square, New York City, director, 1977–80; National Endowment for the Arts, theatre and music theatre panelist, 1977–88; Fund for New American Plays, artistic advisor, 1988–90.

Awards, Honors: Citation of Merit, National Council of Women, 1976; Outer Circle Critics Award, Drama Desk Award, and Obie Award, *Village Voice,* all 1977, for *Ashes;* Margo Jones Award for Continued Encouragement for New Playwrights, 1981; Critics Circle Award, outstanding revival on or off Broadway, 1986, for *Loot;* Lucille Lortel Award, 1987, for outstanding achievement; Special Drama Desk Award, 1989; New York Drama Critics Circle Award, best foreign play, 1989, for *Aristocrats;* Northwood Institute of Distinguished Women of Year, 1990; Person of the Year Award, National Theatre Conference, 1992; Manhattan Magazine Award, 1994; Lee Reynolds Award, League of Professional Theatre Women, 1994; Antoinette Perry Award, best play, 1995, for *Love! Valour! Compassion!;* Antoinette Perry Award nomination, best play, 1996, for *Seven Guitars;* Antoinette Perry Award nomination, best play, 2001, for *King Hedley II;* Antoinette Perry Award nomination, best play, 2001, for *The Tale of the Allergist's Wife;* Antoinette Perry Award, best play, 2001, for *Proof;* Antoinette Perry Award nomination, best musical, 2001, for *A Class Act;* Mr. Abbott Award, Stage Directors and Choreographers Foundation, 2003.

CREDITS

Stage Director:

Jesus as Seen by His Friends, Manhattan Theatre Club, New York City, 1973.

Shooting Gallery, Manhattan Theatre Club, 1973.

The Wager, Manhattan Theatre Club, 1974.

Bits and Pieces, Manhattan Theatre Club, 1974.

Golden Boy, Manhattan Theatre Club, 1975.

Marco Polo, Phoenix Theatre, New York City, 1976.

The Pokey, Manhattan Theatre Club, 1976.

Ashes, Manhattan Theatre Club, 1976.

Chez Nous, Manhattan Theatre Club, 1977.

Catsplay, Manhattan Theatre Club, 1978.

Artichoke, Manhattan Theatre Club, 1979.

The Jail Diary of Albie Sachs, Manhattan Theatre Club, 1979.

Biography, Manhattan Theatre Club, 1980.

Vikings, Manhattan Theatre Club, 1980.

Close of Play, Manhattan Theatre Club, 1981.

Sally and Marsha, Manhattan Theatre Club, 1982.

The Three Sisters, Manhattan Theatre Club, 1982.

Park Your Car in Harvard Yard, Manhattan Theatre Club, 1984.

Principia Scriptoriae, Manhattan Theatre Club Stage I, New York City, 1986.

Bloody Poetry, Manhattan Theatre Club Stage I, 1987.

Woman in Mind, Manhattan Theatre Club Stage I, 1988.

Eleemosynary, 1989.

Absent Friends, Manhattan Theatre Club Stage I, 1991.

A Small Family Business, Music Box Theatre, New York City, 1992.

The Loman Family Picnic, Manhattan Theatre Club Stage I, 1993–94.

Nine Armenians, Manhattan Theatre Club Stage I, 1996–97.

Captains Courageous—The Musical, Manhattan Theatre Club Stage I, 1999.

The Tale of the Allergist's Wife, Ethel Barrymore Theatre, New York City, 2000.

Blur, 2001.

Gone Home, Manhattan Theatre Club Stage II, New York City, 2002–2003.

Last Dance, Manhattan Theatre Club Stage II, 2003.

Fear of Flying, City Center, New York City, 2003.

Rose's Dilemma, Manhattan Theatre Club Stage I, 2003–2004.

Sarah, Sarah, Manhattan Theatre Club Stage II, 2004.

Moonlight and Magnolias, Manhattan Theatre Club Stage I, 2005.

The American Pilot, Manhattan Theatre Club Stage II, 2006.

Our Leading Lady, Manhattan Theatre Club Stage II, 2007.

Also directed *Athens,* Manhattan Theatre Club Stage I, New York City.

Stage Artistic Director:

Chez Nous, Manhattan Theatre Club, New York City, 1977.

Play and Other Plays, Stage 73, New York City, 1977–78.

Scenes from Soweto, Stage 73, 1978.

Statements After an Arrest Under the Immorality Act, Stage 73, 1978.

Strawberry Fields, Stage 73, 1978.

The Rear Column, Stage 73, 1978.

Catsplay, Manhattan Theatre Club, 1978.

Ain't Misbehavin', Longacre Theatre, New York City, 1978–79, then Plymouth Theatre, New York City, 1979–81, later Belasco Theatre, New York City, 1981–82, then Ambassador Theatre, New York City, 1988–89.

Grand Magic, Stage 73, 1978–79.

Don Juan Comes Back from the War, Stage 73, 1979.

Losing Time, Stage 73, 1979.

The Jail Diary of Albie Sachs, Manhattan Theatre Club, 1979.

Biography, Manhattan Theatre Club Stage I, New York City, 1980.

Vikings, Manhattan Theatre Club, 1980.

Endgame, Stage 73, 1980.

Mass Appeal, Stage 73, 1980, then Booth Theatre, New York City, 1981–82.

Crimes of the Heart, Stage 73, 1980–81.

American Days, Stage 73, 1980–81.

Translations, Stage 73, 1981.

Hunting Scenes from Lower Bavaria, Stage 73, 1981.

Harry Ruby's Songs My Mother Never Sang, Stage 73, 1981.

No End of Blame, Stage 73, 1981–82.

The Three Sisters, Manhattan Theatre Club, 1982.

Gardenia, Stage 73, 1982.

The Singular Life of Albert Nobbs, Manhattan Theatre Club Stage I, 1982.

Talking With, Manhattan Theatre Club Stage I, 1982.

Standing on My Knees, Stage 73, 1982.

Skimishes, Stage 73, 1982–83.

Summer, Manhattan Theatre Club Stage I, 1983.

Triple Feature, Stage 73, 1983.

Elba, Manhattan Theatre Club Stage I, 1983.

Early Warnings, Manhattan Theatre Club Stage I, 1983.

The Philanthropist, Stage 73, 1983.

Blue Plate Special, Stage 73, 1983.

Friends, Stage 73, 1983–84.

Mensch Meier, Stage 73, 1984.

Other Places, Stage 73, 1984.

The Miss Firecracker Contest, Stage 73, 1984.

In Celebration, Manhattan Theatre Club Stage I, 1984.

Hunsbandry, Stage 73, 1984.

Messiah, Manhattan Theatre Club Stage I, 1984–85.

Hang on to the Good Times, Manhattan Theatre Club Stage I, 1985.

What's Wrong with This Place?, Stage 73, 1985.

Digby, Manhattan Theatre Club Stage I, 1985.

California Dog Fight, Manhattan Theatre Club Stage I, 1985.

Oliver Oliver, Stage 73, 1985.

It's Only a Play, Manhattan Theatre Club Stage I, 1986.

Loot, Manhattan Theatre Club Stage I, 1986.

Principia Scriptoriae, Manhattan Theatre Club Stage I, 1986.

Women of Manhattan, Manhattan Theatre Club Stage I, 1986.

The Hands of Its Enemy, Manhattan Theatre Club Stage I, 1986.

Bloody Poetry, Manhattan Theatre Club Stage I, 1987.

Hunting Cockroaches, Manhattan Theatre Club Stage I, 1987.

Death of a Buick, Manhattan Theatre Club Stage I, 1987.

The Lucky Spot, Manhattan Theatre Club Stage I, 1987.

Claptrap, Manhattan Theatre Club Stage I, 1987.

Tea, Manhattan Theatre Club Stage I, 1987.

Frankie and Johnny in the Clair de Lune, Manhattan Theatre Club Stage I, 1987.

One Two Three Four Five, Manhattan Theatre Club Stage II, New York City, 1987, then Manhattan Theatre Club Stage I, 1988–89.

The Day Room, Manhattan Theatre Club Stage I, 1987–88.

Woman in Mind, Manhattan Theatre Club Stage I, 1988.

April Snow, Manhattan Theatre Club Stage II, 1988.

Emily, Manhattan Theatre Club Stage I, 1988.

The Debutante Ball, Manhattan Theatre Club Stage II, 1988.

Urban Blight, Manhattan Theatre Club Stage I, 1988.

Italian American Reconciliation, Manhattan Theatre Club Stage II, 1988.

What the Butler Saw, Manhattan Theatre Club Stage I, 1989.

Eleemosynary, Manhattan Theatre Club Stage II, 1989.

The Talented Tenth, Manhattan Theatre Club Stage II, 1989.

The Loman Family Picnic, Manhattan Theatre Club Stage II, 1989.

Aristocrats, Theatre Four, 1989.

Wolf–Man, Manhattan Theatre Club Stage II, 1989.

Eastern Standard, John Golden Theatre, New York City, 1989.

The Art of Success, Manhattan Theatre Club Stage I, 1989–90.

The Lisbon Traviata, Manhattan Theatre Club Stage I, 1989, then Promenade Theatre, New York City, 1989–90.

The American Plan, Manhattan Theatre Club Stage II, 1990–91.

Bad Habits, Manhattan Theatre Club Stage I, 1990.

Mi Vida Loca, Manhattan Theatre Club Stage II, 1990.

Prin, Manhattan Theatre Club Stage I, 1990.

Abundance, Manhattan Theatre Club Stage I, 1990.

The Wash, Manhattan Theatre Club Stage II, 1990.

The Piano Lesson, Walter Kerr Theatre, New York City, 1990–91.

Absent Friends, Manhattan Theatre Club Stage I, 1991.

Life During Wartime, Manhattan Theatre Club Stage II, 1991.

Black Eagles, Manhattan Theatre Club Stage II, 1991.

Reassurance: Stories by Allan Gurganus, Manhattan Theatre Club Stage I, 1991.

The Stick Wife, Manhattan Theatre Club Stage II, 1991.

Lips Together, Teeth Apart, Manhattan Theatre Club Stage I, 1991, then Lucille Lortel Theatre, New York City, 1992.

Beggars in a House of Plenty, Manhattan Theatre Club Stage II, 1991.

A Piece of My Heart, Union Square Theatre, 1991.

Sight Unseen, Manhattan Theatre Club Stage II, 1992.

Boesman and Lena, Manhattan Theatre Club Stage I, 1992.

Groundhog, Manhattan Theatre Club Stage II, 1992.

The Extra Man, Manhattan Theatre Club Stage I, 1992.

Innocent's Crusade, Manhattan Theatre Club Stage II, 1992.

Mad Forest, Manhattan Theatre Club Stage I, 1992.

Joined at the Head, Manhattan Theatre Club Stage II, 1992.

A Small Family Business, Music Box Theatre, 1992.

The Years, Manhattan Theatre Club Stage I, 1992–93.

The Last Yankee, Manhattan Theatre Club Stage II, 1993.

Putting It Together, Manhattan Theatre Club Stage I, 1993.

Jenny Keeps Talking, Manhattan Theatre Club Stage II, 1993.

Pretty Fire, Manhattan Theatre Club Stage II, 1993.

Playland, Manhattan Theatre Club Stage II, 1993.

A Perfect Ganesh, Manhattan Theatre Club Stage I, 1993.

Four Dogs and a Bone, Manhattan Theatre Club Stage II, 1993, then Lucille Lortel Theatre, 1993–94.

The Loman Family Picnic, Manhattan Theatre Club Stage I, 1993–94.

Day Standing on Its Head, Manhattan Theatre Club Stage II, 1993–94.

Three Birds Alighting on a Field, Manhattan Theatre Club Stage I, 1994.

The Arabian Nights, Manhattan Theatre Club Stage II, 1994.

Kindertransport, Manhattan Theatre Club Stage I, 1994.

Durang/Durang, Manhattan Theatre Club Stage II, 1994.

Love! Valour! Compassion!, Manhattan Theatre Club Stage I, 1994–95, then Walter Kerr Theatre, New York City, 1995.

After–Play, Manhattan Theatre Club Stage II, 1995.

Holiday Heart, Manhattan Theatre Club Stage I, 1995.

Three Viewings, Manhattan Theatre Club Stage II, 1995.

Night and Her Stars, Manhattan Theatre Club Stage II, 1995.

Sylvia, Manhattan Theatre Club Stage I, 1995.

The Radical Mystique, Manhattan Theatre Club Stage II, 1995.

Full Gallop, Manhattan Theatre Club Stage II, 1995.

New England, Manhattan Theatre Club Stage I, 1995.

Valley Song, Manhattan Theatre Club Stage II, 1995–96.

Blue Window, Manhattan Theatre Club Stage I, 1996.

Overtime, Manhattan Theatre Club Stage II, 1996.

By the Sea, By the Sea, By the Beautiful Sea, Manhattan Theatre Club Stage II, 1996.

The Blues are Running, Manhattan Theatre Club Stage II, 1996.

Seven Guitars, Walter Kerr Theatre, 1996.

Nine Armenians, Manhattan Theatre Club Stage I, 1996–97.

Neat, Manhattan Theatre Club Stage II, 1997.

Psychopathia Sexualis, Manhattan Theatre Club Stage I, 1997.

Dealer's Choice, Manhattan Theatre Club Stage II, 1997.

The Green Heart, Variety Arts Theatre, 1997.

Collected Stories, Manhattan Theatre Club Stage I, 1997.

Seeking the Genesis, Manhattan Theatre Club Stage II, 1997.

Alligator Tales, Manhattan Theatre Club Stage II, 1997.

Three Days of Rain, Manhattan Theatre Club Stage II, 1997–98.

Eyes for Consuela, Manhattan Theatre Club Stage II, 1998.

Mizlansky/Silnsky or Schmucks, Manhattan Theatre Club Stage I, 1998.

Labor Day, Manhattan Theatre Club Stage I, 1998.

Corpus Christi, Manhattan Theatre Club Stage I, 1998.

The Memory of Water, Manhattan Theatre Club Stage II, 1998.

Captains Courageous—The Musical, Manhattan Theatre Club Stage I, 1999.

Red, Manhattan Theatre Club Stage II, 1999.

East is East, Manhattan Theatre Club Stage I, 1999.

La Terrasse, Manhattan Theatre Club Stage II, 1999.

An Experiment with an Air Pump, Manhattan Theatre Club Stage I, 1999.

The Weir, Walter Kerr Theatre, 1999.

Y2K, Lucille Lortel Theatre, 1999–2000.

Putting It Together, Ethel Barrymore Theatre, New York City, 1999–2000.

The Tale of the Allergist's Wife, Ethel Barrymore Theatre, 2000–2002.

The Wild Party, Manhattan Theatre Club Stage II, 2000.

Proof, Manhattan Theatre Club Stage II, Walter Kerr Theatre, 2000.

Comic Potential, Manhattan Theatre Club Stage I, 2000.

A Class Act, Manhattan Theatre Club Stage II, Ambassador Theatre, New York City, 2000–2001.

Time and Again, Manhattan Theatre Club Stage II, 2001.

Boy Gets Girl, Manhattan Theatre Club Stage I, 2001.

Newyorkers, Manhattan Theatre Club Stage II, 2001.

Glimmer, Glimmer & Shine, Manhattan Theatre Club Stage I, 2001.

King Hedley II, Virginia Theatre, New York City, 2001.

Wonder of the World, Manhattan Theatre Club Stage I, 2001–2002.

Where's My Money?, Manhattan Theatre Club Stage II, 2001–2002.

Further Than the Furthest Thing, Manhattan Theatre Club Stage I, 2002.

Four, Manhattan Theatre Club Stage II, 2002.

Garden, Manhattan Theatre Club Stage II, 2002.

House, Manhattan Theatre Club Stage I, 2002.

In Real Life, Manhattan Theatre Club Stage II, 2002.

Yellowman, Manhattan Theatre Club Stage I, 2002.

The Elephant Man, Royale Theatre, 2002.

Gone Home, Manhattan Theatre Club Stage II, 2002–2003.

Frankie and Johnny in the Clair de Lune, Belasco Theatre, 2002–2003.

Kimberly Akimbo, Manhattan Theatre Club Stage I, 2003.

Polish Joke, Manhattan Theatre Club Stage II, 2003.

Humble Boy, Manhattan Theatre Club Stage I, 2003.

Last Dance, Manhattan Theatre Club Stage II, 2003.

Iron, Manhattan Theatre Club Stage II, 2003.

The Violet Hour, Biltmore Theatre, New York City, 2003.

Sarah, Sarah, Manhattan Theatre Club Stage II, 2004.

Between Us, Manhattan Theatre Club Stage I, 2004.

Five By Tenn, Manhattan Theatre Club Stage II, 2004.

Drowning Crow, Biltmore Theatre, 2004.

Sight Unseen, Biltmore Theatre, 2004.

Reckless, Biltmore Theatre, 2004.

Brooklyn Boy, Biltmore Theatre, 2005.

Moonlight and Magnolias, Manhattan Theatre Club Stage I, 2005.

A Picasso, Manhattan Theatre Club Stage I, 2005.

After the Night and the Music, Biltmore Theatre, 2005.

Absurd Person Singular, Biltmore Theatre, 2005.

The Other Side, Manhattan Theatre Club Stage I, 2005–2006.

Beauty of the Father, Manhattan Theatre Club Stage II, 2006.

Defiance, Manhattan Theatre Club Stage I, 2006.

Based on a Totally True Story, Manhattan Theatre Club Stage II, 2006.

Regrets Only, Manhattan Theatre Club Stage I, 2006.

Rabbit Hole, Biltmore Theatre, 2006.

Three Days of Rain, Bernard B. Jacobs Theatre, New York City, 2006.

Shining City, Biltmore Theatre, 2006.

Losing Louie, Biltmore Theatre, 2006.

Doubt, Walter Kerr Theatre, 2005–2006.

Our Leading Lady, Manhattan Theatre Club Stage II, 2007.

Blackbird, Manhattan Theatre Club Stage I, 2007.

The Receptionist, Manhattan Theatre Club Stage I, 2007.

Pumpgirl, Manhattan Theatre Club Stage II, 2007.

Translations, Biltmore Theatre, 2007.

Lovemusik, Biltmore Theatre, 2007.

Mauritius, Biltmore Theatre, 2007.

The Four of Us, Manhattan Theatre Club Stage II, 2008.

From Up Here, Manhattan Theatre Club Stage I, 2008.

Romantic Poetry, Manhattan Theatre Club Stage I, 2008.

Back Back Back, Manhattan Theatre Club Stage II, 2008.

Come Back, Little Sheba, Biltmore Theatre, 2008.

Top Girls, Biltmore Theatre, 2008.

To Be Or Not To Be, Samuel J. Friedman Theatre, New York City, 2008.

The 24 Hour Plays 2008, American Airlines Theatre, New York City, 2008 and 2009.

The American Plan, Samuel J. Friedman Theatre, 2009.

Accent on Youth, Samuel J. Friedman Theatre, 2009.

The Royal Family, Samuel J. Friedman Theatre, 2009.

Ruined, Manhattan Theatre Club Stage I, 2009.

Humor Abuse, Manhattan Theatre Club Stage II, 2009.

Nightingale, Manhattan Theatre Club Stage I, 2009.

Equivocation, Manhattan Theatre Club Stage I, 2010.

That Face, Manhattan Theatre Club Stage I, 2010.

Time Stands Still, Samuel J. Friedman Theatre, 2010.

Collected Stories, Samuel J. Friedman Theatre, 2010.

The Pitmen Painters, Samuel J. Friedman Theatre, 2010.

Stage Producer:
Starting Here, Starting Now, 1977.
Ain't Misbehavin', 1978.
Crimes of the Heart, 1981.
Miss Firecracker Contest, 1984.
Franky and Johnny, 1987.
Eastern Standard, 1988.
Lisbon Traviata, 1989.
Lips Together, Teeth Apart, 1991.
Four Dogs and a Bone, 1993.
Love! Valour! Compassion!, 1994.
Proof, Walter Kerr Theatre, New York City, 2000.

Stage Production Supervisor:
Boy Gets Girl, Manhattan Theatre Club Stage I, New York City, 2001.

Major Tours:
Director, *The Tale of the Allergist's Wife,* U.S. cities, 2002.

MICHAEL, Sean
    See AFABLE, Sean Michael

MIKO, Izabella 1981–
    (Izabela Mikolajczyk)

PERSONAL

Full name, Izabella Anna Mikolajczak; born January 21, 1981, in Lodz, Poland; daughter of Aleksander Mikolajczak (an actor) and Grazyna Dylag (an actress). *Education:* Studied acting at the Lee Strasberg Institute; ballet at the National Ballet School, Warsaw, Poland, and the School of American Ballet. *Avocational Interests:* Environmental issues.

Addresses: *Agent*—Fortitude, 8619 Washington Blvd., Culver City, CA 90232; Special Artists Agency, 9465 Wilshire Blvd., Suite 470, Beverly Hills, CA 90212. *Manager*—Affirmative Entertainment and Productions, 425 North Robertson Blvd., Los Angeles, CA 90048.

Career: Actress. Appeared in television commercials, including Starbuck's coffee houses. Also worked as a fashion model. Previously a ballet dancer. EkoMiko (an ecology project), creator.

CREDITS

Film Appearances:
The girl with the matches, *Mr. Blob in the Universe* (also known as *Pan Kleks w kosmosie*), 1988.

(Uncredited) Kuba's daughter, *Niech zyje milosc,* 1991.
Cammie, *Coyote Ugly,* Buena Vista, 2000.
Megan, *The Forsaken* (also known as *Desert Vampires, Vampires of the Desert,* and *Vampire Hunter*), Screen Gems, 2001.
Renee, *Minimal Knowledge* (also known as *Murder Reincarnated*), York Entertainment, 2002.
Kaliope, *The Shore,* 2005.
Alice, *Bye Bye Blackbird,* 2005.
Krysta, *Park,* Monarch Home Video, 2006.
Jill Michaelson, *The House of Usher,* THINKFilm, 2006.
Sara, *Save the Last Dance 2,* Paramount Home Entertainment, 2006.
Kristen, *Crashing,* Image Entertainment, 2007.
Strawberry, *Flakes,* IFC Films, 2007.
Young woman, *Waiting* (short film), 2007.
Madelaine, *Dark Streets,* Samuel Goldwyn Films, 2008.
Hania, *Love and Dance* (also known as *Kochaj I tancz*), ITI Cinema, 2009.
Katrine, *Double Identity,* 2009.
Athena, *Clash of the Titans,* Warner Home Video, 2009.
Timmy, *Repo,* 2010.
Jensen, *Age of Heroes,* ContentFilm International, 2010.

Television Appearances; Miniseries:
(As Izabela Mikolajczyk) Zuzia Szymanko, *Kuchnia polska,* 1993.

Television Appearances; Movies:
Ludmila, *Skip Tracer,* 2008.

Television Appearances; Specials:
The 5th Annual GQ Men of the Year Awards, Fox, 2000.

Television Appearances; Pilots:
Sophie Mansour, *Gramercy Park,* ABC, 2004.
Raia, *The Cape,* NBC, 2011.

Television Appearances; Episodic:
Carrie, "Requiem for a Gleet," *Deadwood,* HBO, 2005.
Carrie, "Complications," *Deadwood,* HBO, 2005.
Carrie, "Something Very Expensive," *Deadwood,* HBO, 2005.

RECORDINGS

Music Videos:
Appeared in "Mr. Brightside" by The Killers, 2004.

WRITINGS

Film Songs:
"I Can't Ignore," *The House of Usher,* THINKFilm, 2006.

"In Between Your Breaths and Your Words," *Love and Dance,* ITI Cinema, 2009.

OTHER SOURCES

Electronic:
Izabella Miko Official Site, http://www.izabellamiko. com, September 3, 2010.

MIKOLAJCZYK, Izabela
    See MIKO, Izabella

MINTER, Kristin 1965–

PERSONAL

Born 1965, in Miami, FL; daughter of Charlie (a financial firm executive) and Dottie (a horse trainer) Minter. *Education:* Studied at the Philadelphia College of Performing Arts, and with Kate McGregor–Stewart, Richard Peterson, James Walker, Bob Carnegie, and Cameron Thor.

Addresses: *Agent*—Visionary Artists Agency, 5503 Denny Ave., North Hollywood, CA 91601; Sovereign Talent Group, 10474 Santa Monica Blvd., Suite 301, Los Angeles, CA 90025. *Manager*—The Marshak/ Zachary Co., 8840 Wilshire Blvd., 1st Floor, Beverly Hills, CA 90211.

Career: Actress. Worked as a model in Europe after completing high school. Appeared in television commercials, including Allegra medications, California horse racing, and Rainier beer.

CREDITS

Film Appearances:
Heather McCallister, *Home Alone,* Twentieth Century–Fox, 1990.
Kathy Winslow, *Cool As Ice,* Universal, 1991.
Cousin Karen, *Passed Away,* Buena Vista, 1992.
Agent Xan, *Bayscape 2042,* 1992.
Tracy, *There Goes My Baby* (also known as *The Last Days of Paradise*), Orion, 1994.
Cheryl, *Lover's Knot,* Astra Cinema, 1995.
Marie Belot, *Savage,* Sogepaq, 1995.
Drunken neighbor, *Dick Richards,* 1996.
Monica, *The Temple of Phenomenal Things,* 1997.
Dean's fiancee, *Soulmates,* 1997.

Zebrah, *The Effects of Magic,* Cricket Releasing/Vision Films, 1998.
Stella, *Tyrone* (also known as *Bad Trip*), Tyrone Productions, 1999.
Joy, *Behind the Seams,* 2000.
Gina, *King of Open Mics,* 2000.
Susie, *American Virgin* (also known as *Live Virgin*), Granite Releasing, 2000.
Carla, *Tick Tock* (also known as *A Friendship to Die For*), Avalanche Home Entertainment, 2000.
Cherry, *Diamond Men,* Panorama Entertainment, 2001.
Claire, *Myopia* (also known as *From the Hip*), Lost Dog Productions/Speedway Films, 2001.
Lucca, *The Bread, My Sweet* (also known as *A Wedding for Bella*), Panorama Entertainment, 2001.
Title role, *Waiting for Anna,* Hypnotic, 2002.
Suzie, *The Gray in Between,* Barry Katz Productions, 2002.
Stephanie, *March 1st,* 2002.
Helen, *Straighten Up America* (short film), 2003.
Parole officer Reina, *In the Blink of an Eye* (also known as *Pissed*), Artist View Entertainment, 2005.
Oblivious mom, *Friends with Money,* Sony Pictures Classics, 2006.
Regan Price, *Six Sex Scenes and a Murder,* Panorama Entertainment, 2008.
Candace, *Blur,* Tavix Pictures, 2009.
Sara, *Dead in Love,* Wild Range Productions, 2009.
Cynthia, *What If ...,* Pure Flix Entertainment, 2010.

Television Appearances; Series:
Sheila, *The Outsiders,* Fox, 1990.
Miranda "Randi" Fronczak, *ER,* NBC, 1995–2003.

Also appeared as Jordan Baines, *General Hospital,* ABC.

Television Appearances; Miniseries:
Valerie Thayer, *Danielle Steele's "Family Album"* (also known as *Family Album*), NBC, 1994.

Television Appearances; Movies:
Lisa Cates, *Flashfire* (also known as *August Fires*), HBO, 1994.
Rita, *Dad, the Angel & Me,* The Family Channel, 1995.
Charlotte, *Michael Angel* (also known as *The Apostate*), Cinemax, 1998.

Television Appearances; Pilots:
Rebecca, *Moon Over Miami,* ABC, 1993.
Tracy Hart, *Seattle Emergency,* The WB, 1997.

Television Appearances; Episodic:
Jenna, "The Flash Is Always Greener," *Living Dolls,* 1989.

Christine, " ... And This Little Piggy Moved Out," *Pig Sty,* UPN, 1994.

Christine, "Erin Go Barf," *Pig Sty,* UPN, 1994.

Debra Vaughn, "Secrets Great and Small," *University Hospital,* 1995.

Debra Vaughn, "Endings and Beginnings," *University Hospital,* 1995.

Sue Hambleton, "Fly Paper," *Fallen Angels,* Showtime, 1995.

Rachel MacLeod, "Homeland," *Highlander,* syndicated, 1995.

Rachel MacLeod, "Promises," *Highlander,* syndicated, 1996.

Rachel MacLeod, "Deliverance," *Highlander,* syndicated, 1996.

Emma, "Black Widow," *Kung Fu: The Legend Continues,* 1996.

Gianna, "Trackdown," *Nash Bridges,* NBC, 1996.

Janice Nowack, "Encore," *Brimstone,* Fox, 1998.

Annalise, "Nurse Evil," *G vs. E* (also known as *Good vs. Evil*), USA Network, 2000.

Annalise, "Immigrant Evil," *G vs. E* (also known as *Good vs. Evil*), USA Network, 2000.

Alex, "Trial and Error," *Providence,* NBC, 2001.

Candy Moran, "Two Clarks and a Bar," *NYPD Blue* (also known as *N.Y.P.D.*), ABC, 2001.

Charlotte Williams, "Tone Dead," *John Doe,* Fox, 2003.

Herself, *SoapTalk,* SoapNet, 2005.

Cheryl Vitti, "Marlon's Brando," *Blind Justice,* ABC, 2005.

Sara, "Enlightenment," *Crossing Jordan,* NBC, 2005.

Bambi, "Dennis, Bulgari, Big Losers at ACoRNS: Film at Eleven," *Pepper Dennis,* The WB, 2006.

Hooker, "Living Legend," *CSI: Crime Scene Investigation* (also known as *CSI: Las Vegas* and *C.S.I.*), CBS, 2006.

Dana Pritchard, "The Thing Under the Bed," *Dirt,* FX Network, 2007.

Kitty, "Gene Shelly," *Nip/Tuck,* FX Network, 2009.

Sugar, "Red Sky at Night," *The Mentalist,* CBS, 2010.

Stage Appearances:

Appeared in *Freeway Strangler; Play It Again Sam; Arron Guilespi Will Make You a Star.*

RECORDINGS

Video Games:

(Uncredited) Voice of ILB: Sophia Bossedon, *Halo 2,* Microsoft Game Studios, 2004.

OTHER SOURCES

Periodicals:

Femme Fatales, April, 2002, pp. 56–57.

Electronic:

Kristin Minter Official Site, http://www.kristinminster. net, October 20, 2010.

MODER, Julia
  See ROBERTS, Julia

MOK, Ken 1960–
  (Kenneth Mok)

PERSONAL

Born July 5, 1960, in Larchmont, NY; children: one daughter. *Education:* Boston University, B.S./B.A., business administration and minor in journalism.

Addresses: *Office*—10x10 Entertainment, 1640 South Sepulveda Blvd., Suite 450, Los Angeles, CA 90025. *Agent*—Paradigm, 360 North Crescent Dr., North Bldg., Beverly Hills, CA 90210.

Career: Producer. Worked as a production assistant and in other capacities. 10x10 Entertainment (also known as Ten by Ten Entertainment and 10 by 10 Entertainment), Los Angeles, principal; KM2 (company specializing in programing and Internet ventures), cofounder. Worked as a news producer and a writer for Cable News Network (CNN)'s CNN Headline News and for NBC News; member of a junior executives program and worked as a creative executive for NBC, a director of comedy series development for ABC, and a vice president of MTV Productions. Involved with CAPE (Coalition of Asian Pacifics in Entertainment). Worked as an assistant buyer.

Awards, Honors: Daytime Emmy Award nomination (with Dawn Parouse), outstanding children's special, 1999, for *The Tiger Woods Story.*

CREDITS

Television Creator; Series:

Australia's Next Top Model (also known as *Top Model*), Foxtel Digital, 2004, Fox 8, beginning 2005.

The Shot (also known as *Click!*), VH1, 2007.

Television Developer; Series:

All–American Girl (also known as *All American Girl*), ABC, 1994–95.

America's Next Top Model (also known as *America's Next Top Model 2, America's Next Top Model with Tyra Banks, ANTM,* and *Top Model*), UPN, 2003–2006, The CW, 2006—.

Codeveloper, *Pussycat Dolls Present: "Girlicious"* (also known as *Pussycat Dolls Present*), The CW, 2008.

Television Executive Producer; Series:

Tough Enough (also known as *$1,000,000 Tough Enough, Tough Enough 2, Tough Enough III, WWE Tough Enough,* and *WWF Tough Enough*), MTV, 2001–2004.

Sorority Life (also known as *Sorority Life Los Angeles, Sorority Life SUNY Buffalo,* and *Sorority Life, UC Davis*), MTV, c. 2002–2004.

America's Next Top Model (also known as *America's Next Top Model 2, America's Next Top Model with Tyra Banks, ANTM,* and *Top Model*), UPN, 2003–2006, The CW, 2006—.

Australia's Next Top Model (also known as *Top Model*), Foxtel Digital, 2004, Fox 8, beginning 2005.

Made in the USA (also known as *Made in the U.S.A.*), USA Network, beginning 2005.

ego trip's "(White) Rapper Show" (also known as *Egotrip Presents "The White Rapper Show," Egotrips: The White Rapper Show, Ego Trips: The (White) Rapper Show,* and *The White Rapper Show*), VH1, 2006.

Twentyfourseven (also known as *twentyfourseven* and *24-7*), MTV, beginning 2006.

Pussycat Dolls Present (also known as *The Pussycat Dolls Present: "The Search for the Next Doll"*), The CW, 2007.

The Shot (also known as *Click!*), VH1, 2007.

ego trip's "Miss Rap Supreme" (also known as *egotrip's "Miss Rap Supreme"* and *Miss Rap Supreme*), VH1, 2008.

Pussycat Dolls Present: "Girlicious" (also known as *Pussycat Dolls Present*), The CW, 2008.

Stylista (also known as *Untitled Tyra Banks Project*), The CW, 2008.

Changing Lanes, Black Entertainment Television, beginning 2010.

Television Producer; Series:

Making the Band, ABC, 2000–2001, MTV, 2002.

Benelux' Next Top Model (also known as *Benelux Next Top Model*), 2BE and RTL5, beginning 2009.

Television Production Assistant; Series:

(As Kenneth Mok) *The Chair,* ABC, 2002.

The Wayne Brady Show, syndicated, 2002.

Closer to Truth, PBS, beginning 2002.

On the Spot (also known as *Improv Sitcom* and *Untitled Jeff Davis Project*), The WB, 2003.

Eve (also known as *The Opposite Sex*), UPN, 2003–2004.

Television Work; Other; Series:

Wardrobe driver, *The Cosby Show* (also known as *Bill Cosby, Bill Cosby Show,* and *Cosby Show*), NBC, c. 1980.

(As Kenneth Mok) Assistant to the producer, *Haunted,* UPN, 2002.

Assistant production office coordinator, *Eve* (also known as *The Opposite Sex*), UPN, 2004–2005.

(As Kenneth Mok) Assistant to writer, *Eve* (also known as *The Opposite Sex*), UPN, 2005–2006.

Television Executive Producer; Movies:

The Tiger Woods Story, Showtime, 1998.

Television Developer; Specials:

America's Next Top Model: Return to the Runway, UPN, 2005.

America's Next Top Model: Where the Girls Are, UPN, 2006.

America's Next Top Model: Exposed, UPN, 2008.

Television Executive Producer; Specials:

America's Next Top Model: The Runway Ahead, UPN, 2004.

T.H.E.M. (also known as *Them*), NBC, 2004.

America's Next Top Model: Return to the Runway, UPN, 2005.

America's Next Top Model: What the Divas Are Doing Now, UPN, 2005.

America's Next Top Model: Exposed, UPN, 2008.

Television Work; Other; Specials:

Development executive and director, *T.H.E.M.* (also known as *Them*), NBC, 2004.

Worked on other projects.

Television Work; Developer; Pilots:

All–American Girl (also known as *All American Girl*), ABC, 1994.

Who's Your Daddy?, Fox, 2005.

Television Executive Producer; Pilots:

Even the Losers, ABC, 1998.

Chaos Theory, NBC, 1999.

Cooked 1 (also known as *Cooked, Humor Me,* and *UPN/Michael Curtis/Dane Cook Easy Life Comedy*), UPN, 2004.

The High Life, NBC, 2004.

Love in Two Cities, TBS, 2004.

Who's Your Daddy?, Fox, 2005.

Stylista (also known as *Untitled Tyra Banks Project*), The CW, 2008.

Teen Dream, 2008.

Operation Fabulous, The CW, c. 2008.
The Love Shaq, Arts and Entertainment, 2009.

Television Production Assistant; Pilots:
Father Lefty (also known as *Lefty*), CBS, 2002.
Eddie's Father (also known as *The Courtship of Eddie's Father*), The WB, c. 2003.

Television Appearances; Episodic:
Himself, *People in the News,* Cable News Network, 2003.
(As Kenneth Mok) Background pimp, "Pimps Up, Diva-Style Down," *Eve* (also known as *The Opposite Sex*), UPN, 2004.
Himself, "Tyra Banks," *The E! True Hollywood Story* (also known as *THS* and *Tyra Banks: The E! True Hollywood Story*), E! Entertainment Television, 2005.
Himself, "'America's Next Top Model,'" *The E! True Hollywood Story* (also known as "*America's Next Top Model*": *The E! True Hollywood Story* and *THS*), E! Entertainment Television, 2006.
Himself, "Pussycat Dolls," *The E! True Hollywood Story* (also known as *Pussycat Dolls: The E! True Hollywood Story* and *THS*), E! Entertainment Television, 2008.

Some sources cite appearances in other programs.

Film Work:
(Uncredited) Deejay and assistant to crowd controller, *The New Guy,* Columbia, 2002.
(Uncredited) Production assistant, *Team America: World Police* (also known as *American Heroes, Team America,* and *Untitled Trey Parker/Matt Stone Project*), Paramount, 2004.
Producer, *Invincible* (also known as *Who's Nuts Invincible*), Buena Vista, 2006.

WRITINGS

Teleplays:
Wrote a comedy program about an Asian American family, 1980s.

MORGAN, Michelle 1981–

PERSONAL

Born July 16, 1981, in Calgary, Alberta, Canada. *Education:* Studied theatre and classical literature at the University of Toronto. *Avocational Interests:* Cooking, board sports like snowboarding and surfing.

Career: Actress. Performed sketch comedy at the Laugh Sabbath comedy nights, Toronto, Ontario, Canada. Volunteered at women's shelters; designed and conducted workshops called *Be Heard!* for women at a Calgary–based shelter.

Member: Canadian Actors' Equity Association, Alliance of Canadian Cinema Television and Radio Artists.

CREDITS

Film Appearances:
Debra Moynihan, *Diary of the Dead* (also known as *George A. Romero's "Diary of the Dead"* and *"The Death of Death"*), Third Rail Releasing, 2007.
The wrong Felice, *Confessions of a Porn Addict,* Kinosmith, 2008.

Television Appearances; Series:
Samantha Louise "Lou" Fleming, *Heartland,* CBC and syndicated, 2007—.

Television Appearances; Movies:
Rebecca, *Road Rage,* NBC, 1999.
Jaclyn Kennedy Colberson, *Nancy Drew,* ABC, 2002.
Donna Marks, *Fire Serpent,* Sci–Fi Channel, 2007.

Television Appearances; Episodic:
Tiffany Heitzenrader, *CSI: Miami,* CBS, 2002.
Teresa, "Old Enough to Fight," *American Dreams,* NBC, 2003.
Voice, "French Take Woodland," *Kid Notorious,* Comedy Central, 2003.
Onyangos Tochter, "11," *Die Patriarchin,* 2005.
Counter waitress, "Happy Birthday, Mr. President," *Across the River to Motor City,* CityTV, 2007.
Counter waitress, "Stranger in the House," *Across the River to Motor City,* CityTV, 2007.
Abigail, "Look Out, Here They Come!," *The L Word,* Showtime, 2008.
F.R.A.N., "Be All My Sings Remember'd," *Stargate: Atlantis* (also known as *Atlantis*), 2008.
F.R.A.N., "Ghost in the Machine," *Stargate: Atlantis* (also known as *Atlantis*), 2008.
Leftcoast TV, 2010.

Internet Appearances; Episodic:
Celeste, "Hot Coffee," *Bunny Hug* (a web series), koldcast.tv and channelflip.com, 2010.
Celeste, "After Math," *Bunny Hug* (a web series), koldcast.tv and channelflip.com, 2010.
Celeste, "Resolute Bay," *Bunny Hug* (a web series), koldcast.tv and channelflip.com, 2010.

OTHER SOURCES

Electronic:
Michelle Morgan Official Site, http://www.
    michellemorgan.net, October 30, 2010.

MOUNT, Thom 1948–

PERSONAL

Full name, Thomas Henderson Mount; born May 26, 1948, in Durham, NC; son of Lillard H. and Bonnie M. Mount; married Katrina Woodard (marriage ended); married Chloe King; children: (second marriage) Cooper. *Education:* Attended Bard College, 1968–70; California Institute of Arts, B.F.A., 1971, M.F.A., 1973.

Addresses: *Office*—Reliant Pictures, 5555 Melrose Ave., Dressing Room Building, 3rd Floor, Hollywood, CA 90038.

Career: Producer. Metro–Goldwyn–Mayer, assistant to the producer; Universal Studios, Studio City, CA, production executive, 1975–79, executive vice president in charge of production, 1976–78, head of theatrical division, c. 1979–80, president and head of production, 1979–83, president of worldwide motion picture production, 1982–83; Mount Co. (also known as Mount Film Group and Mount/Kramer Co.), Beverly Hills, CA, principal and independent film producer, beginning 1983; Reliant Pictures, Hollywood, CA, chief executive officer. Entertainment Internet, Inc., cochair, beginning 1998, and creator of the casting service CastNet.com; Hollywood Broadcasting.com, managing partner; consultant to RKO Pictures. California Institute for the Arts, member of board of trustees, 1971–72; Bard College, member of board of trustees, 1980–92; Duke University, National Endowment for the Humanities artist in residence, 1990; Columbia University, adjunct professor, 1995–96; Los Angeles Film School, managing partner.

Member: Producers Guild of America (member of board of trustees, 1995; president, 1998–2001).

Awards, Honors: Golden Satellite Award, special achievement for a career of outstanding service in the entertainment industry, International Press Academy, 2001; Louis B. Mayer Award, motion picture business leader of the year, DeSantis Center for Motion Picture Industry Studies, Florida Atlantic University, 2001.

CREDITS

Film Producer:
(With Tim Hampton) *Frantic,* Warner Bros., 1987.
Can't Buy Me Love (also known as *Boy Rents Girl*), Buena Vista, 1987.
(With Mark Burg) *Bull Durham,* Orion, 1988.
(With Hank Moonjean) *Stealing Home,* Warner Bros., 1988.
Tequila Sunrise, Warner Bros., 1988.
Frankenstein Unbound (also known as *Roger Corman's "Frankenstein Unbound"*), Warner Bros., 1990.
Death and the Maiden, Fine Line, 1994.
Night Falls on Manhattan, Paramount, 1997.
Bathory, Bontonfilm/Tatrafilm/Central Partnership (Russia), 2008.
Cheri, Miramax, 2009.

Film Executive Producer:
My Man Adam (also known as *Inside Adam Swit*), TriStar, 1985.
Pirates (also known as *Roman Polanski's "Pirates"*), Cannon, 1986.
Terms of Enrollment (also known as *Charlie Barnett's "Terms of Enrollment"*), 1986.
The Indian Runner, Metro–Goldwyn–Mayer, 1991.
Natural Born Killers, Warner Bros., 1994.

Film Appearances:
Mackendrick on Film (documentary), Sticking Place Films, 2004.

Television Work; Specials:
Producer, *Son of the Morning Star,* 1987.
Executive producer, *The Neville Brothers: Tell It Like It Is,* Cinemax, 1989.
Co–executive producer, *The Kennedy Center Mark Twain Prize Celebrating the Humor of Richard Pryor,* Comedy Central, 1999.

Television Work; Other:
Producer, *Cinemax Comedy Experiment* (series), Cinemax, 1987.
Executive producer, *Open Admissions* (movie), 1988.

Television Appearances; Specials:
"Richard Pryor: Comic on the Edge," *Biography,* Arts and Entertainment, 1996.
Unseen + Untold: The Blues Brothers, Spike TV, 2004.
Hollywood's Master Storytellers: The Blues Brothers, 2005.
Animal House: The Inside Story, 2008.

Stage Work:
Coproducer, *Death and the Maiden,* Brooks Atkinson Theatre, New York City, 1992.

RECORDINGS

Videos:
The Yearbook: An "Animal House" Reunion, Universal Studios Home Video, 1998.

Between the Lines: The Making of "Bull Durham," 2001.

MULHERN, Stephen 1977–

PERSONAL

Full name, Stephen Daniel Mulhern; born April 4, 1977.

Career: Actor. Also performed as a magician.

CREDITS

Television Appearances; Series:
The Quick Trick Show, 1996.
Presenter, *Brilliant Creatures,* 1998.
Presenter, *CiTV,* ITV1, 1998–2002.
Presenter, *Finger Tips,* 2002.
Globo Loco, ITV, 2003.
Presenter, *SM:TV Live,* ITV1, 2003.
Presenter, *Animals Do the Funniest Things,* ITV, 2004–2006.
Presenter, *Britain's Got More Talent,* ITV, 2007–10.

Television Appearances; Episodic:
The Big Big Talent Show, ITV, 1997.
"Live Final 2004," *Stars in Their Eyes Kids,* ITV, 2004.
Celebrities under Pressure, ITV, 2004.
Presenter, *Ministry of Mayhem,* ITV, 2004, 2006.
"Live Grand Final 2005," *Stars in Their Eyes,* ITV, 2005.
The Paul O'Grady Show, ITV, 2005, 2009.
"2005 Celebrity Special 3," *Stars in Their Eyes,* ITV, 2005.
Today with Des and Mel, ITV, 2006.
GMTV, ITV, 2006.
Presenter, *Tricky TV,* ITV, three episodes, 2006.
This Morning, ITV, two episodes, 2006.
The Slammer, BBC, 2006.
Loose Women, ITV, 2006, 2007.
Ant & Dec's Saturday Night Takeaway, ITV, 2006, 2007.
The Xtra Factor, ITV2, 2006, 2009.
The Great Mulhern, *The Slammer,* BBC, 2006.
Dancing on Ice: Defrosted, ITV, two episodes, 2007.
All Star Family Fortunes, ITV, 2007.
Host, *The 5 O'Clock Show,* Channel 4, two episodes, 2010.

Also appeared as Merlin, "No Time Like the Present," *Timmy Towers,* ITV.

Television Appearances; Specials:
Presenter, *The National Music Awards 2003,* ITV, 2003.
The Record of the Year 2004, ITV, 2004.
Host, *Harry Potter at the Castle: Magic at Midnight,* ITV, 2005.
An Audience with Coronation Street, ITV, 2006.
Tiswas Reunited, ITV, 2007.
An Audience with Jeremy Beadle, ITV, 2008.
Ad of the Decade, ITV, 2009.
Host, *The All Star Impressions Show,* ITV, 2009.

MURRAY, Joel 1963–

PERSONAL

Born April 17, 1963, in Wilmette, IL; brother of Bill Murray (an actor, comedian, and writer), John Murray (a writer), and Brian Doyle–Murray (an actor and writer); married Eliza Coyle (an actress), 1989; children: Hank, Gus, Louie, Annie. Educational: Studied with Del Close at the Improv Olympics and with Don DePollo, Michael Gelman, Bernie Sahlins, and Del Close at Second City. *Avocational Interests:* Writing, playing golf, coaching sons in baseball and basketball.

Addresses: *Agent*—Diverse Talent Group, 9911 West Pico Blvd., Suite 350 West, Los Angeles, CA 90035; Innovative Artists Agency, 1505 Tenth St., Santa Monica, CA 90401.

Career: Actor, director, and producer. Second City (comedy group), Chicago, IL, member of company for five years; also performed with Harold (improvisational group), Chicago. Caddyshack (restaurant), co–owner.

Member: American Federation of Television and Radio Artists, Actors Equity Association, Screen Actors Guild, Directors Guild of America.

CREDITS

Film Appearances:
George Calamari, *One Crazy Summer,* Warner Bros., 1986.
Guest, *Scrooged,* Paramount, 1988.
Shopping Elvis and Paul, *Elvis Stories,* 1989.
Bert, *Only You,* 1992.
Milkman, *Shakes the Clown,* IRS Releasing, 1992.
Basketball player, *The Cable Guy,* Columbia TriStar, 1996.
Bartender, *The Thin Pink Line* (also known as *Pink Pink Line*), PARCO Co./Tokyo Theatres Co., 1998.
Taxi driver, *It's All about You,* 2002.

First robber, *Nobody Knows Anything!,* Stargazer Entertainment, 2003.
Mr. Randall, *See Anthony Run* (short film), 2005.
Shapiro, *Hatchet,* Anchor Bay Entertainment, 2006.
Mr. Reynolds, *The Tiffany Problem* (short film), 2008.
Doug Shapiro, *Hatchet II,* Dark Sky Films, 2010.

Film Work:
Executive producer, *Ballhawks* (short film), 2009.

Television Appearances; Series:
Norris Weldon, *Grand,* NBC, 1990.
Captain Ken Epstein, *Pacific Station,* NBC, 1991–92.
Ray Litvak, *Love and War* (also known as *Love Is Hell*), CBS, 1992–95.
Voice of Beethoven, *Beethoven* (animated), CBS, 1994.
Peter James "Pete" Cavanaugh, *Dharma & Greg,* ABC, 1997–2002.
Voice of Carl Bitterman and other characters, *Baby Blues* (animated), The WB, 2000.
Voices, *3–South,* MTV, 2002.
Himself, *The Sweet Spot,* Comedy Central, 2002.
Danny "Fitz" Fitzsimmons, *Still Standing,* CBS, 2003–2006.
Fred Rumsen, *Mad Men,* AMC, 2007—.
Eddie Jackson, *Shameless,* Showtime, 2011—.

Television Appearances; Movies:
Bart Polonski, *Long Gone,* HBO, 1987.
Jerry, *Men Will Be Boys,* 1990.
Dick Durkee, *Road Warriors,* 1995.
Mr. Jones, *Encino Woman* (also known as *California Woman*), ABC, 1996.
Sam Bridgewater, *Mending Fences,* 2009.

Television Appearances; Specials:
Voice of Carl Bitterman, *A Baby Blues Christmas Special* (animated), Cartoon Network, 2002.
Himself, *Windy City Memories,* 2008.

Television Appearances; Pilots:
Lieutenant, *Family Beat,* The WB, 1996.
Jack, *Titletown,* Fox, 2003.
Eddie, *Shameless,* Showtime, 2011.

Television Appearances; Episodic:
The Tonight Show Starring Johnny Carson, 1990.
Doug LeMuere, "House Guests," *Blossom,* NBC, 1992.
Ron Wolfe, "Who's Afraid of Ron and Cindy Wolfe?," *Partners,* Fox, 1995.
Bob Myers, "The Bob Episode," *Mr. & Mrs. Smith,* 1996.
Vince Chandler, "The Fifth Wheel," *The Nanny,* CBS, 1997.
Voice, *Disney's "Hercules"* (animated; also known as *Hercules*), ABC, 1998.

Voice of Professor Triffid, "Little Secrets," *Buzz Lightyear of Star Command* (animated; also known as *Disney/Pixar's "Buzz Lightyear of Star Command"*), UPN and syndicated, 2000.
Voice of Professor Triffid, "Dirty Work," *Buzz Lightyear of Star Command* (animated; also known as *Disney/Pixar's "Buzz Lightyear of Star Command"*), UPN and syndicated, 2000.
(Uncredited) Bob, *The Drew Carey Show,* ABC, 2001.
Hollywood Squares (also known as *H2* and *H2: Hollywood Squares*), syndicated, 2001.
Dante Langenhan, "Mind Games," *John Doe,* Fox, 2002.
Larry, "Hal's Friend," *Malcolm in the Middle,* Fox, 2003.
Balloon sculptor/God, "Vanity, Thy Name Is Human," *Joan of Arcadia,* CBS, 2004.
Bank manager, "Shop for Sale," *American Body Shop,* Comedy Central, 2007.
Petey, "Mr. McGlue's Feedbag," *Two and a Half Men,* CBS, 2007.
Danny Tackle, *Factory,* Spike TV, 2007.
Attorney general, "Minimal Loss," *Criminals Minds,* CBS, 2008.
Bobby Kent in 2008, "One Small Step," *Cold Case,* CBS, 2008.
Petey, "Baseball was Better with Steroids," *Two and a Half Men,* CBS, 2009.
Crowley, "My Men," *My Boys,* TBS, 2010.
Crowley, "Extreme Mike–Over," *My Boys,* TBS, 2010.

Television Work; Series:
Creator and executive producer, *The Sweet Spot,* Comedy Central, 2002.

Television Director; Episodic:
Dharma & Greg, ABC, 2001–2002.
The Sweet Spot, Comedy Central, 2002.
"Still Bonding," *Still Standing,* CBS, 2005.
"Still Sweet," *Still Standing,* CBS, 2005.
"Still Flunking," *Still Standing,* CBS, 2005.
"The Cooper–Hofstadter Polarization," *The Big Bang Theory,* CBS, 2008.
Funny or Die Presents …, HBO, 2010.

RECORDINGS

Video Games:
Additional voices, *Ghost Busters* (also known as *Ghostbusters: The Video Game*), Atari, 2009.

WRITINGS

Television Series:
(With brothers Bill Murray, John Murray, and Brian Doyle–Murray) *The Sweet Spot,* Comedy Central, 2002.

N–O

NADAL, Lymari 1978–

PERSONAL

Born February 11, 1978, in Ponce, PR; married Edward James Olmos (an actor, director, and producer), 2002; stepchildren: Mico Olmos, Bodie James Olmos. *Education:* Universidad de Puerto Rico (University of Puerto Rico), master's degree, chemistry; also studied acting at the Universidad de Puerto Rico (University of Puerto Rico) and the London Academy of Music and Dramatic Art.

Addresses: *Agent*—International Creative Management, 10250 Constellation Blvd., 9th Floor, Los Angeles, CA 90067. *Manager*—Schiff Company, 9465 Wilshire Blvd., Suite 480, Beverly Hills, CA 90212.

Career: Actress and writer. Participated in various events, including awards presentations and fund–raising benefits.

Member: Screen Actors Guild, Writers Guild of America, West.

Awards, Honors: Screen Actors Guild Award nomination (with others), outstanding performance by a cast in a motion picture, 2008, for *American Gangster.*

CREDITS

Film Appearances:

Marisol, *Ladrones y mentirosos* (also known as *Thieves and Liars*), 2006.

Eva, *American Gangster* (also known as *The Return of Superfly* and *Tru Blu*), Universal, 2007.

Giana O'Neill, *The Plan* (also known as *Battlestar Galactica Movie* and *Battlestar Galactica: The Plan*), Universal Studios Home Entertainment, 2009, broadcast by Syfy, 2010.

Title role, *America,* Isla Films, c. 2010.

Television Appearances; Series:

Linda, *Te amare en silencio,* Univision, beginning c. 2003.

Television Appearances; Miniseries:

Giana, *Battlestar Galactica* (also known as *Battlestar Galactica: The Miniseries, BSG,* and *Galactica*), Sci–Fi Channel, 2003.

Television Appearances; Movies:

Giana O'Neill, *The Plan* (also known as *Battlestar Galactica Movie* and *Battlestar Galactica: The Plan*), Syfy, 2010, also released by Universal Studios Home Entertainment, 2009.

Television Appearances; Episodic:

Linda, "The Barber Shop," *American Family* (also known as *American Family: Journey of Dreams*), PBS, 2002.

Herself, *Mas vale tarde,* Telemundo, 2008.

Hazel Ortega, "Sangre por Sangre," *CSI: NY* (also known as *CSI: New York, CSI: New York 2, C.S.I. New York, C.S.I.: New York, C.S.I.: NY,* and *CSI: Weekends*), CBS, 2010.

Stage Appearances:

Title role, *Yerma,* Bilingual Foundation of the Arts, Los Angeles, 2006.

Appeared in productions in Puerto Rico.

RECORDINGS

Videos:
Herself, *Fallen Empire: Making "American Gangster"* (documentary), MCA/Universal Home Video, 2008.

WRITINGS

Screenplays:
(With Sonia Fritz and Miguel Machalski) *America,* Isla Films, c. 2010.

Teleplays:
Wrote different versions of a program about her experiences in graduate school.

NEAL, Elise 1970–

PERSONAL

Born March 14, 1970, in Memphis, TN; father, a construction worker; mother's name, Arletha Neal. *Education:* Studied at University of the Arts in Philadelphia; trained as a dancer.

Addresses: *Manager*—Vincent Cirrincione, Vincent Cirrincione and Associates, 1516 North Fairfax Ave., Los Angeles, CA 90046.

Career: Actress. Appeared in television commercials; performed as a dancer. Assorted Flavors (female rhythm and blues group), producer.

Awards, Honors: Image Award nominations, outstanding actress in a comedy series, National Association for the Advancement of Colored People, 2000 and 2001, for The Hughleys; Image Award nomination, outstanding supporting actress in a motion picture, Screen Actors Guild Award nomination, and Black Reel Award nomination, both best ensemble (with others), all 2006, for *Hustle & Flow*; Trailblazer Award, 2006.

CREDITS

Television Appearances; Series:
Janey Sinclair, *Loving,* ABC, 1994.
Lieutenant J. J. Fredricks, *SeaQuest DSV* (also known as *SeaQuest 2032*), NBC, 1995–96.
Yvonne Hughley, *The Hughleys,* ABC, 1998–99, then UPN, 2000–2002.
Tia Jewel, *All of Us,* UPN, 2003–2005.
Ayana Boulet, *K–Ville,* Fox, 2007.
Jennifer, *My Manny,* TBS, 2009.

Television Appearances; Movies:
Young woman, *There Was a Little Boy,* CBS, 1993.
Amy, *Chance of a Lifetime,* CBS, 1998.
Carlita, *Let It Be Me* (also known as *Love Dance*), Starz!, 1998.
Linda Sayers, *Brian's Song,* ABC, 2001.

Television Appearances; Specials:
Alicia, "Daddy's Girl," *ABC Afterschool Specials,* ABC, 1996.
Host from Las Vegas, *Dick Clark's New Year's Rockin' Eve,* ABC, 1998.
Host, *Bloopers,* ABC, 1999.
E! Rack–N–Roll: Behind the Scenes, E! Entertainment Television, 1999.
The 2nd Annual Soul Train Christmas Starfest, syndicated, 1999.
Scream: The E! True Hollywood Story, E! Entertainment Television, 2001.
Guest judge, *Iron Chef USA: Showdown in Las Vegas* (also known as *Iron Chef USA: Holiday Showdown*), UPN, 2001.
25 Strong! The BET Silver Anniversary Special, Black Entertainment Television, 2005.

Television Appearances; Miniseries:
Spa instructress, *Armistead Maupin's "Tales of the City"* (also known as *Tales of the City*), 1993.
Heroes of Black Comedy, 2002.
The 100 Scariest Movie Moments, Bravo, 2004.
Black in the 80s, VH1, 2005.

Television Appearances; Pilots:
Yvonne Hughley, *The Hughleys,* ABC, 1998.
Tia Jewel, *All of Us,* UPN, 2003.
Jill David, *A.U.S.A.,* NBC, 2003.
Josephine Jean, *Wyclef Jean in America,* HBO, 2006.
Ayana Boulet, *K–Ville,* Fox, 2007.
Christie, *Jack and Janet Save the Planet* (also known as *Janet Saves the Planet*), The Disney Channel, 2010.

Television Appearances; Episodic:
Charlayne Ward, "Cradle to Grave," *Law & Order,* NBC, 1991.
Pandora, *Out All Night,* NBC, c. 1992.
Debbie, *Getting By,* ABC, c. 1992.
Heather, "Car Wars," *Family Matters,* ABC, 1993.
Miss Jackie, "High Plains Dreamer," *California Dreams,* 1993.
Lisa, "Boyz in the Woodz," *Hangin' with Mr. Cooper,* ABC, 1993.
Heather, "Car Wars," *Family Matters,* 1993.

Wendy Robertson, "M Is for the Many Things She Gave Me," *The Fresh Prince of Bel–Air,* NBC, 1994.

Tamara Parnett, "Cutting Edge," *Chicago Hope,* CBS, 1995.

Millie, "Take the Points," *Pointman,* syndicated, 1995.

Lisa, "Here Comes the Groom," *Hangin' with Mr. Cooper,* 1995.

Sharon, "School's Out Forever," *Living Single,* Fox, 1996.

Juanita Du'Shea, "Pool Sharks Git Bit," *The Steve Harvey Show,* The WB, 1996.

Arial, *High Incident,* ABC, c. 1996.

"You Can Almost Go Home Again," *Hitz,* MTV, 1997.

"Coming to Chicago," *The Steve Harvey Show,* The WB, 1997.

Tanya Cooper, "The Rich Girl," *The Wayans Bros.,* The WB, 1998.

Catherine, "Wishboned," *Fantasy Island,* ABC, 1998.

Hollywood Squares (also known as *H2* and H2: Hollywood Squares), several appearances, 2002.

Pyramid (also known as *The $100,000 Pyramid*), 2002.

Brenda, "Something about Brenda," *Method & Red,* Fox, 2004.

The Sharon Osbourne Show (also known as *Sharon*), syndicated, 2004.

Giselle, "Bodies in Motion," *CSI: Crime Scene Investigation* (also known as *C.S.I.* and *CSI: Las Vegas*), CBS, 2005.

Weekends at the DL, Comedy Central, 2005.

Janine, "What You Do for Love," *Private Practice,* ABC, 2009.

The Brian McKnight Show, The CW, 2010.

The Mo'Nique Show, Black Entertainment Television, 2010.

"Elise Neal," *Life After,* 2010.

Television Appearances; Awards Presentations:

The ... Annual Stellar Gospel Music Awards, syndicated, 1997, 2000.

Presenter, *The 26th Annual American Music Awards,* ABC, 1999.

6th Annual Soul Train Lady of Soul Awards, syndicated, 2000.

Presenter, *The Source Hip–Hop Music Awards 2001,* UPN, 2001.

3rd Annual BET Awards, Black Entertainment Television, 2003.

2003 Vibe Awards: Beats, Style, Flavor, UPN, 2003.

The 18th Annual Soul Train Music Awards, The WB, 2004.

The 2nd Annual Vibe Awards, UPN, 2004.

The Black Movie Awards, TNT, 2005.

Presenter, *The 21st Annual Soul Train Music Awards,* The CW, 2007.

Film Appearances:

Hooker, *Malcolm X* (also known as *X*), Warner Bros., 1992.

Beulah (Scrappie), *Rosewood,* Warner Bros., 1997.

Nadine, *Def Jam's "How to Be a Player"* (also known as *How to Be a Player*), Gramercy, 1997.

Paula, *Money Talks* (also known as *Runaway*), New Line Cinema, 1997.

Hallie McDaniel, *Scream 2,* Dimension Films, 1997.

Jeanine, *Restaurant,* Palisades Pictures, 1998.

Wilma Watson, *The Rising Place,* Flatland Pictures, 1999.

Debra Graham, *Mission to Mars* (also known as *M2M*), Buena Vista, 2000.

Gabi Paige, *Sacred Is the Flesh* (also known as *Sacred*), Strange Fruit, 2001.

Aunt June, *Paid in Full,* Dimension Films, 2002.

Summer Twitty, *Playas Ball,* Ventura, 2003.

Yevette, *Hustle & Flow,* Paramount, 2005.

Herself, *My Nappy Roots: A Journey through Black Hair–itage* (documentary), Virgin Moon Entertainment, 2005.

Jare, *4 Life,* Codeblack Entertainment/Vivendi Entertainment, 2007.

Passion, *Who's Deal?,* Select Media Productions, 2008.

Monica, *Preaching to the Pastor,* Digital Media Production House, 2009.

Let God Be the Judge, Phase 4 Films, 2010.

Alana, *Love Ranch,* E1 Entertainment, 2010.

Monique, *Love Chronicles: Secrets Revealed,* Melee Entertainment/Swirl Films, 2010.

Rich's mom, *Gun,* Image Entertainment, 2010.

Leslie, *N–Secure,* Bluff City Films, 2010.

Kim, *School of Hard Knocks,* School of Hard Knocks, c. 2010.

Gloria, *Mama Used to Say ...* (short film), c. 2010.

According to some sources, also appeared in the film *Wing Commander,* Twentieth Century–Fox, 1999.

Stage Appearances:

Member of ensemble, *Uptown ... It's Hot!* (musical), Lunt–Fontanne Theatre, New York City, 1986.

Member of ensemble, *Oh, Kay!* (musical), Richard Rodgers Theatre, New York City, 1990–91.

Andree, "Mixed Babies," *Class 1 Acts: '91–'92,* Manhattan Class Company Theatre, New York City, 1992.

Major Tours:

Sophisticated Ladies, world cities, 1989.

RECORDINGS

Videos:

Behind the "Scream," 2000.

Appeared in the music videos "Strobelite Honey" by Black Sheep, 1992, and "A Rose Is Still a Rose" by Aretha Franklin.

OTHER SOURCES

Periodicals:
USA Today, July 29, 2005, p. 4D.

NO–BIZZI
See YATES, Reggie

NUCCI, Danny 1968–

PERSONAL

Born September 15, 1968, in Klagenfurt, Austria; immigrated to the United States, c. 1974; naturalized U.S. citizen, 1990; father, a salesman of textile machinery; brother of Natalie Nucci (an actress); married Terre Bridgham, 1995 (divorced, 1998); married Paula Marshall (an actress and producer), October 12, 2003; children: (first marriage) Savannah Pauline; (second marriage) Maya.

Addresses: *Agent*—Suzanne Wohl, TalentWorks, 3500 West Olive Ave., Suite 1400, Burbank, CA 91505.

Career: Actor. Worked as a valet parking attendant for celebrity affairs.

Awards, Honors: Young Artist Award nomination, best young guest actor in a television series, 1986, for "Wins and Losses," *Hotel;* Young Artist Award nomination, exceptional young supporting actor in a television special or movie, 1987, for *The Children of Times Square;* Young Artist Award nomination, best young actor starring in a television drama special, movie, or variety show, 1988, for "An Enemy Among Us," *CBS Schoolbreak Special;* Young Artist Award nomination, best young actor in a nighttime drama series, 1989, for *Falcon Crest;* Screen Actors Guild Award nomination (with others), outstanding performance by a cast, 1997, for *Titanic.*

CREDITS

Film Appearance:
Tommy, *American Drive–in,* 1985.
Nasty kid at school, *Explorers,* Paramount, 1985.
Spider Bomboni, *Book of Love,* New Line Cinema, 1991.
Hector Morales, *Roosters,* Astra Cinema, 1993.

Hugo Diaz, *Alive* (also known as *Alive: The Miracle of the Andes*), Buena Vista, 1993.
Todd, *Rescue Me* (also known as *The Infernal Venture* and *Street Hunter*), Cannon, 1993.
Gilbert Tellez, *Homage,* Arrow Releasing, 1995.
Danny Rivetti, *Crimson Tide,* Buena Vista, 1995.
Rico Sanchez, *In the Flesh* (also known as *Deadly Measures, Desperate Measures, Nanny's Nightmare,* and *Im Sog des Boesen*), 1995.
Lieutenant Shephard, *The Rock,* Buena Vista, 1996.
Deputy Monroe, *Eraser,* Warner Bros., 1996.
Jesse Torrejo, *The Big Squeeze* (also known as *Body of a Woman*), First Look Pictures, 1996.
Gaetano Amador, *The Unknown Cyclist,* Trident Releasing, 1997.
Fabrizio De Rossi, *Titanic,* Twentieth Century–Fox, 1997.
Joey Donna, *That Old Feeling,* Universal, 1997.
Guy Normal, *Shark in a Bottle,* 7.23 Productions, 1998.
Cousin Matt, *Love Walked In,* TriStar, 1998.
Sugar: The Fall of the West, 1998.
Tuesday's Letters, 1999.
David/"Dave", *Friends and Lovers,* Lions Gate Films, 1999.
Oscar, *Do It for Uncle Manny,* 2002.
Gino, *American Cousins,* Bard Entertainments/Icon Film Distribution, 2003.
E. J. Inglewood, *Break a Leg,* Catchlight, 2003, MTI Home Video, 2006.
Officer Giraldi, *World Trade Center,* Paramount, 2006.
Paul Reeds, *The Way Back Home,* 2006, Bridgestone Multimedia, 2008.
Benny Rodriguez, *The Sandlot 3* (also known as *The Sandlot: Heading Home*), Twentieth Century–Fox Home Entertainment, 2007.
Avery Goldman, *Totally Baked: A Pot–u–mentary,* Salient Media/Vivendi Entertainment, 2007.
John Gotti, *Sinatra Club,* Ubatz Productions/San Pietro Productions, 2010.
Freddie Pagano (The Cat), *Pizza with Bullets,* Radmks/ D'Artagnan Entertainment/Mpire Films, 2010.
Dan, *Monster Heroes,* Tarnol Group Pictures, 2010.

Television Appearances; Series:
Freddy, *Pryor's Place,* CBS, 1984.
Marvin, *Days of Our Lives* (also known as *Days* and *DOOL*), 1987.
Gabriel Ortega, *Falcon Crest,* CBS, 1988–89.
Manny Lott, *Snoops,* ABC, 1999–2000.
Frankie Zito, *Some of My Best Friends,* CBS, 2001.
Deputy Rico Amonte, *10–8: Officers On Duty* (also known as *10–8*), ABC, 2003–2004.

Television Appearances; Movies:
Jai, *Combat High* (also known as *Combat Academy*), NBC, 1986.
Luis Sotavento, *The Children of Times Square,* ABC, 1986.

Willie, *The Brotherhood of Justice,* ABC, 1986.
Airon Ayala, *For the Love of My Child: The Anissa Ayala Story,* NBC, 1993.
Paul Garcia, *Ray Alexander: A Taste for Justice,* NBC, 1994.
Roberto, *Blind Justice* (also known as *Canaan's Way*), HBO, 1994.
Stuart Dempsey, *Sublet* (also known as *Codename: Jaguar*), Cinemax, 1999.
P. D. Mitjans, *The Outfitters,* Sundance Channel, 1999.
Frank Siena, *Mafia Doctor,* CBS, 2003.
Perry Walters, *Backwoods* (also known as *Naked: Survival Game*), Spike TV, 2008.

Television Appearances; Miniseries:
Vince Grella, *A Matter of Justice* (also known as *Final Justice*), NBC, 1993.
Vincent Sforza, *Firestarter 2: Rekindled* (also known as *Firestarter: Rekindled*), Sci–Fi Channel, 2002.

Television Appearances; Specials:
Scott Fischer, "An Enemy Among Us," *CBS Schoolbreak Special,* CBS, 1987.
Leo, *Missing Parents,* Showtime, 1991.
Intimate Portrait: Lea Thompson, Lifetime, 1998.

Television Appearances; Pilots:
Dennis Ferrand, *Home Free,* NBC, 1988.
Paul Minetti, *The High Life,* ABC, 1990.
Manny Lott, *Snoops,* ABC, 1999.
Frankie Zito, *Some of My Best Friends,* CBS, 2001.
Father Robert "Lefty" Lefrack, *Father Lefty,* CBS, 2002.

Television Appearances; Episodic:
General Hospital, ABC, c. 1982.
Hell Town, NBC, 1985.
Evan, "Wins and Losses," *Hotel,* 1985.
Boy, "Pinball," *Mr. Belvedere,* 1985.
Rick, "Designated Hitter," *Family Ties,* NBC, 1985.
First boy, "JFK: Part 2," *Call to Glory,* 1985.
Buddy, "The Leprechaun–Artist," *The Twilight Zone,* CBS, 1986.
"Choices," *Our House,* 1986.
Budge, "The Great Hawaiian Adventure Company," *Magnum, P.I.,* 1988.
Scooter Krassner, "Employee of the Month," *Growing Pains,* ABC, 1988.
Dominick/"D. J.", "Private School," *Brand New Life,* 1989.
Eddie Morano, "Symphony," *A Peaceable Kingdom,* 1989.
Tony Pronti, "Leap of Faith—August 19, 1963," *Quantum Leap,* NBC, 1990.
Greg Knecht, "Baby You Can't Drive My Car," *Ferris Bueller,* NBC, 1990.
Private Wozniak, "Acceptable Losses," *Tour of Duty,* 1990.

Ramon Escobar, "Goodbye, Judge Green," *Equal Justice,* 1990.
Moose, "Heck's Angels," *Out of This World,* 1991.
Lou Campanella, "Three O'Clock and All Is Hell," *Blossom,* NBC, 1992.
Pizza guy, "Red All Over," *Dream On,* HBO, 1992.
Marco Espinoza, "Father Eddie," *The Commish,* ABC, 1994.
Pete, "That Burning Passion," *Just Shoot Me!,* NBC, 2002.
Pete, "Watch Your Backdraft," *Just Shoot Me!,* NBC, 2003.
The Sharon Osbourne Show (also known as *Sharon*), syndicated, 2003.
The Wayne Brady Show, syndicated, 2003.
Jimmy Kimmel Live!, ABC, 2003.
The Best Damn Sports Show Period, 2003.
Ron, "Joey and the Dream Girl: Part 2," *Joey,* NBC, 2004.
Bill Arnello, "Mob Rules," *House M.D.* (also known as *Dr. House* and *House*), Fox, 2005.
(Uncredited; in archive footage) Fabrizio, *Today Tonight,* Seven Network, 2007.
Scott Lucas, "4G," *Without a Trace* (also known as *W.A.T.*), CBS, 2008.
Ben Machado, "Flame Red," *The Mentalist,* CBS, 2008.
Burke Manning, "Normal," *Criminal Minds,* CBS, 2008.
Gilbert Mazzara, "Love Me Dead," *Castle,* ABC, 2009.
Gilbert Mazzara, "Sucker Punch," *Castle,* ABC, 2010.
Officer Nicholas Henderson, "Vacation Getaway," *CSI: NY,* CBS, 2010.

RECORDINGS

Videos:
Voice of Alberto, *The Brave Little Toaster to the Rescue* (animated), 1997.

O'CONNELL, Jerry 1974–

PERSONAL

Full name, Jeremiah O'Connell; born February 17, 1974, in New York, NY; son of Michael O'Connell (an advertising agency art director) and Linda Witkowski (an art teacher); brother of Charlie O'Connell (an actor and model); married Rebecca Romjin (an actress and producer), July 14, 2007; children: Dolly Rebecca Rose and Charlie Tamara Tulip (twins). *Education:* New York University, B.F.A., 1995; student at Southwestern Law School, 2009; trained at HB Studio, New York City.

Addresses: *Agent*—United Talent Agency, 9560 Wilshire Blvd., Suite 500, Beverly Hills, CA 90212.

Manager—Michael Rotenberg, 3 Arts Entertainment, 9460 Wilshire Blvd., 7th Floor, Beverly Hills, CA 90212. *Publicist*—Nicki Fioravante, PMK*BNC, 8687 Melrose Ave., 8th Floor, Los Angeles, CA 90069.

Career: Actor, producer, and director. Appeared in commercials for Duncan Hines cookie mix, 1980, and Ritz Bits crackers, 1987.

Awards, Honors: Jackie Coogan Award (with others), Young Artist Awards, 1987, for *Stand by Me;* Young Artist Award nominations, best young actor in a family syndicated show, 1989, and best young actor in an off–primetime family series, 1990, both for *My Secret Identity.*

CREDITS

Television Appearances; Series:
Andrew Clements, *My Secret Identity,* syndicated, 1988–91.
Brody Wilder, *Camp Wilder,* ABC, 1992–93.
Quinn Mallory, *Sliders,* Fox, 1995–97, Sci–Fi Channel, 1998–99.
Detective Woodrow "Woody" Hoyt, *Crossing Jordan,* NBC, 2002–2007.
Detective Woody Hoyt, a recurring role, *Las Vegas,* NBC, 2004–2006.
Laird, *Carpoolers,* ABC, 2007.
Neal Danner, *Do Not Disturb,* Fox, 2008.
Pete Kaczmarek, *The Defenders,* CBS, 2010.

Television Appearances; Movies:
Carl, "The Room Upstairs," *Hallmark Hall of Fame,* CBS, 1987.
Young Ralphie Parker, *Ollie Hopnoodle's Haven of Bliss,* PBS, 1988.
Mac, *The Ranger, the Cook and a Hole in the Sky* (also known as *A Hole in the Sky*), ABC, 1995.
Lawrence Sellars, *Blue River,* Fox, 1995.
Reverend Perry Ray Pruitt, *What the Deaf Man Heard,* CBS, 1997.
David Collins, *Buying the Cow* (also known as *Unlucky Happy*), Starz!, 2002.
Declan Fitzpatrick, *Midnight Bayou* (also known as *Nora Roberts' "Midnight Bayou"*), Lifetime, 2009.

Television Appearances; Pilots:
Quinn Mallory, *Sliders,* 1995.
Voice of Tony, *Clayton* (animated), UPN, 2000.
Ryan Wheeler, *Romeo Fire,* NBC, 2002.
Detective Woodrow "Woody" Hoyt, *Sunset Division,* NBC, 2003.
Laird, *Carpoolers,* ABC, 2007.
Neal Danner, *Do Not Disturb,* Fox, 2008.

Bruce Sweet, *Rex Is Not Your Lawyer,* NBC, 2010.
Pete Kaczmarek, *The Defenders,* CBS, 2010.

Television Appearances; Specials:
Scream: The E! True Hollywood Story, E! Entertainment Television, 2001.
Rock 'n Jock Super Bowl XXXV, MTV, 2001.
The 2002 Blockbuster Hollywood Christmas Spectacular, NBC, 2002.
Favorite Stars: Then & Now, ABC, 2003.
E! Entertainer of the Year, E! Entertainment Television, 2003.
Maxim Hot 100, VH1, 2004.
(In archive footage) *E! 101 Most Starlicious Makeovers,* E! Entertainment Television, 2004.
100 Greatest Kid Stars, VH1, 2005.
Breakfast at Churchill Downs, 2005.
Speechless, 2008.
The 2008 Teen Choice Awards, Fox, 2008.
Host, *VH1 Pepsi Smash Super Bowl Bash,* VH1, 2008, 2009.

Television Appearances; Miniseries:
Brian Herlihy, *The '60s,* NBC, 1999.

Television Appearances; Episodic:
Bobby, "The Child Broker," *The Equalizer,* CBS, 1988.
Super Sloppy Double Dare, 1988.
David Landon, "The Organization Man," *Charles in Charge,* CBS, 1989.
Oddville, MTV, 1997.
Nyhetsmorgon, 1997.
The Martin Short Show, 2000.
Blockbuster Entertainment, 2001.
Andy, "Rest Stop," *Night Visions* (also known as *Nightvision*), Fox, 2001.
"Lost City of Peru," *Celebrity Adventures,* E! Entertainment Television, 2001.
Pete Rossock, "Searching for Eddie Van Halen," *Going to California,* Showtime, 2002.
Ted Levins, *MADtv,* Fox, 2003.
Joe Gibson, "Hawks and Handsaws," *Without a Trace* (also known as *W.A.T.*), CBS, 2004.
Singer, *The Screaming Cocktail Hour,* 2004.
Pyramid (also known as *The $100,00 Pyramid*), syndicated, 2004.
Voice of Captain Marvel, "Clash," *Justice League* (animated; also known as *JL* and *Justice League Unlimited*), Cartoon Network, 2005.
The Bachelor (also known as *The Bachelor: London Calling* and *The Bachelor: On the Wings of Love*), ABC, 2005.
The Apprentice (also known as *The Apprentice Los Angeles, The Apprentice 2,* and *Celebrity Apprentice*), NBC, 2005.
(In archive footage) Bianca's date, *Video on Trial,* MuchMusic, 2005.
Joel, "Derailed," *Ugly Betty,* ABC, 2007.

Voice of Nightwing, "Artifacts," *The Batman* (animated), The CW, 2007.

Voice of Nightwing, "The Metal Race of Comedy," *The Batman* (animated), The CW, 2007.

On the Lot, Fox, 2007.

Dancing with the Stars, ABC, 2007.

Entertainment Tonight (also known as *E.T.* and *This Week in Entertainment*), syndicated, multiple appearances, beginning 2007.

(Uncredited; in archive footage) Quinn Mallory, "Parallel Worlds: A User's Guide," *Time Shift,* BBC, 2007.

Craig, "The Gallery Show," *Samantha Who?,* ABC, 2008.

Colin Friesen, "Magic Snow and Creepy Gene," *Eastwick,* ABC, 2009.

Colin Friesen, "Pampered and Tampered," *Eastwick,* ABC, 2010.

Appeared as Brody in an episode of *ABC TGIF,* ABC; as guest host, *In the Mix,* PBS; and in *MTV Cribs,* MTV.

Television Talk Show Guest Appearances; Episodic:
Late Night with David Letterman, NBC, 1986.

Guest host, *Later,* NBC, 1994.

Late Show with David Letterman, CBS, 1996.

Late Night with Conan O'Brien, NBC, multiple appearances, between 1997 and 2008.

The Tonight Show with Jay Leno, NBC, 1998, 2000, 2005, 2008.

The Daily Show with Jon Stewart (also known as *The Daily Show* and *The Daily Show with Jon Stewart Global Edition*), Comedy Central, 1999.

The Howard Stern Radio Show, 1999.

Howard Stern, 1999.

The Rosie O'Donnell Show, syndicated, 1999.

Pajama Party, Oxygen, 2000.

The Late Late Show with Craig Kilborn (also known as *The Late Late Show*), CBS, 2001.

Rove Live, Ten Network, 2001.

TRL, 2003.

The View, ABC, 2003.

The Caroline Rhea Show, syndicated, 2003.

The Michael Essany Show, E! Entertainment Television, 2003.

RI:SE, 2003.

V Graham Norton, Channel 4, 2003.

Jimmy Kimmel Live!, ABC, 2003, 2010.

Guest cohost, *The Sharon Osbourne Show* (also known as *Sharon*), syndicated, 2004.

On–Air with Ryan Seacrest, syndicated, 2004.

The Tony Danza Show, syndicated, 2004, 2005.

Last Call with Carson Daly, NBC, 2004, 2005, 2007.

Ellen: The Ellen DeGeneres Show, syndicated, between 2004 and 2009.

The Late Late Show with Craig Ferguson, CBS, 2005, 2009.

Rachael Ray, syndicated, 2007, 2008.

Howard Stern on Demand (also known as *Howard TV on Demand*), 2007.

Live with Regis and Kelly, syndicated, 2007, 2009.

MADtv, Fox, 2008.

Late Night with Jimmy Fallon, NBC, 2009.

Television Work; Series:
Director, *Sliders,* Fox, 1997, then Sci–Fi Channel, between 1998–99.

Producer, *Sliders,* Sci–Fi Channel, 1998–99.

Film Appearances:
Vern Tessio, *Stand by Me,* Columbia, 1986.

Scott "The Dood" Foreman, *Calendar Girl,* Columbia, 1993.

Title role, *Joe's Apartment,* Warner Bros., 1996.

Frank Cushman, *Jerry Maguire* (also known as *The Agent*), TriStar, 1996.

Derek Feldman, *Scream 2,* Dimension Films, 1997.

(Uncredited) Trip McNeely, *Can't Hardly Wait,* Columbia/TriStar, 1998.

NYC tree buyer, *Tree Weeks,* 1998.

Michael Penorisi, *Body Shots,* New Line Cinema, 1999.

Phil Ohlmyer, *Mission to Mars* (also known as *M2M*), Buena Vista, 2000.

Michael Delany, *Tomcats,* Columbia, 2001.

(Uncredited) Second twin at Highland High party, *The New Guy,* Columbia, 2002.

Charlie Carbone, *Kangaroo Jack,* Warner Bros., 2003.

Himself, *Overnight* (documentary), THINKFilm, 2004.

Sean Cooley, *Fat Slags,* Entertainment Film Distributors, 2004.

Max, *Yours, Mine, and Ours,* Metro–Goldwyn–Mayer, 2005.

Businessman, *Lies & Alibis* (also known as *The Alibi*), Sony Pictures Home Entertainment, 2006.

David Lilly, *Man About Town,* Lions Gate Films Home Entertainment, 2006.

Lucas Dylan, *Room 6,* Anchor Bay Entertainment, 2006.

Himself, *Wet Dreams* (documentary), 2006.

Curtis Marks, *Baby on Board,* Angry Monkey Entertainment, 2009.

Ben, *Obsessed,* Screen Gems, 2009.

Derrick Jones, *Piranha* (also known as *Piranha 3D*), Dimension Films, 2010.

Voice of Biscuit, *Cat Tale* (animated), Imagi Entertainment, 2010.

Film Executive Producer:
First Daughter, Twentieth Century–Fox, 2004.

Internet Appearances; Videos:
Tom Cruise, *The Parody Video Tom Cruise Wants You to See,* FunnyOrDie.com, 2008.

Worst Wedding DJ Ever, FunnyOrDie.com, 2010.

Piranha 3D: For Your Consideration, FunnyOrDie.com, 2010.

Internet Producer; Videos:
The Parody Video Tom Cruise Wants You to See, FunnyOrDie.com, 2008.

Stage Appearances:
Appeared in a production of *Worldly Acts,* Tiffany Theatre.

RECORDINGS

Videos:
The Making of "Sliders," 1998.
"Heartbreaker," Mariah's #1's, 1999.
Behind the "Scream," 2000.
Vern Tessio, *Walking the Tracks: The Summer of "Stand by Me,"* 2002.
Voice of Captain Marvel, *DC Showcase: Superman/ Shazam!—The Return of Black Adam* (animated), Warner Home Video, 2010.

Appeared in the music video "Heartbreaker" by Mariah Carey, 1999.

Audio Books; Reader:
Quantum, by Tom Grace, Time Warner, 2000.
6–321, by Michael Laser, Listening Library, 2001.

ADAPTATIONS

"Way Out West," an episode of *Sliders,* broadcast by the Sci–Fi Channel in 1999, was based on a story by O'Connell. The film *First Daughter,* released by Twentieth Century–Fox in 2004, was also based on a story by O'Connell.

OTHER SOURCES

Periodicals:
Entertainment Weekly, June 12, 1998, p. 57.
People Weekly, July 15, 1996, pp. 133–34.
Playboy, October, 2004, p. 44.
TV Guide, January 25, 2003, p. 8; November 7, 2005, p. 29; April 24, 2006, pp. 30–31.

OGILVY, Ian 1943–

PERSONAL

Full name, Ian Raymond Ogilvy; born September 30, 1943, in Woking, Surrey, England; son of Franis Ogilvy (an advertising executive) and Aileen Raymond (an

actress); married Diane (a model; marriage ended); married Kathryn "Kitty" Holcomb (an actress), 1992; children: (first marriage) Emma (stepdaughter), Titus; (second marriage) two stepsons. *Education:* Attended Royal Academy of Dramatic Art. *Avocational Interests:* Skiing, scuba diving, playing computer games, gardening, building things out of wood, riding his motorcycle.

Addresses: *Agent*—The Gage Group, 14724 Ventura Blvd., Suite 505, Sherman Oaks, CA 91403.

Career: Actor and writer. Appeared in television commercials, including Evergood coffee, c. late 1990s—. Also worked as a student stage manager at the Royal Court Theatre, London.

Awards, Honors: Three DramaLogue Awards; *Los Angeles Times* Critics Award.

CREDITS

Film Appearances:
Philip, *La sorella di Satana* (also known as *Revenge of the Blood Beast, Satan's Sister, The She Beast, Sister of Satan,* and *Il lago di Satana*), Europix Consolidated, 1966.
Desmond Flower, *Stranger in the House* (also known as *Cop–Out*), Cinerama 68, 1967.
Peter, *The Day the Fish Came Out* (also known as *Otan ta psaria vgikan sti steria*), Twentieth Century–Fox, 1967.
Mike Roscoe, *The Sorcerers,* Allied Artists, 1968.
Richard Marshall, *Matthew Hopkins: Witchfinder General* (also known as *The Conqueror Worm, Edgar Allan Poe's "Conqueror Worm," Matthew Hopkins: Conquerer Worm,* and *Witchfinder General*), American International Pictures, 1968.
Ronald, *The Invincible Six* (also known as *The Heroes*), 1968, International Film Distributors, 1970.
William De Lancey, *Waterloo,* Paramount, 1970.
Edgar Linton, *Wuthering Heights,* American International Pictures, 1971.
Charles Fengriffen, *... And Now the Screaming Starts!* (also known as *Bride of Fengriffen, Fengriffen,* and *I Have No Mouth but I Must Scream*), Cinerama/ Lara Classics, 1973.
William Seaton, "The Door," *From Beyond the Grave* (also known as *Creatures, Creatures from Beyond the Grave, Tales from Beyond the Grave, Tales from the Beyond,* and *The Undead*), Warner Bros., 1973.
David Hunter, *No Sex Please: We're British,* 1973, Columbia, 1979.
Simon Templar, *The Saint and the Brave Goose* (also known as *Collision Course*), 1979.
Chagall, *Death Becomes Her,* Universal, 1992.
Brian, *Invasion of Privacy,* 1992.

Starch, *Eddie Presley,* Raven Pictures International, 1993.

Dr. Jennings, *Puppet Master 5: The Final Chapter* (also known as *The Final Chapter: Puppet Master 5* and *Puppet Master V*), Paramount Home Video, 1994.

Gary, *The Disappearance of Kevin Johnson,* 1996.

Grace, *Fugitive Mind,* Royal Oaks Communications, 1999.

Himself, *Blood Beast: The Films of Michael Reeves* (documentary), Boum Productions/Pagan Films, 1999.

Tigon Tales of Terror (short documentary), Anchor Bay Entertainment, 2005.

The Story of Upstairs Downstairs (documentary), Network, 2005.

Narrator, *The Saint Steps in ... To Colour* (documentary), Network, 2006.

Dennis, *After Midnight,* 2007.

Himself and narrator, *The Saint Steps in ... to Television* (documentary), Network, 2008.

Mr. Tullen, *My Life in Ruins,* Fox Searchlight, 2009.

Television Appearances; Series:

Lying narrator, *The Liars,* Granada Television, 1966.

Moz, *Orlando,* ITV, 1966.

Lawrence Kirbridge, *Upstairs, Downstairs,* ITV, 1972, also broadcast on *Masterpiece Theatre,* PBS, c. 1975.

Simon Templar, *Return of the Saint* (also known as *The Son of the Saint*), CBS, 1978–79.

Richard Maddison, *Tom, Dick and Harriet,* ITV, 1983.

Reginald Hewitt, *Generations,* NBC, 1990.

Marc Delacourt, *Malibu Shores,* CBS, 1996.

Geoffrey, *Dharma & Greg,* ABC, 2000.

Television Appearances; Miniseries:

Owen Gereth, *The Spoils of Poynton,* BBC, 1970, broadcast on *Masterpiece Theatre,* PBS, 1971.

Wolfgang Buck, *Man of Straw,* BBC, 1972.

Humphrey Oliver, *Moll Flanders,* BBC and PBS, 1975.

Drusus, "A Touch of Murder," *I, Claudius,* BBC2, 1976, broadcast on *Masterpiece Theatre,* PBS, 1977.

Duncan Free, *Menace Unseen,* Independent Television, 1988.

Television Appearances; Movies:

Edward VIII, "The Gathering Storm" (also known as "Churchill, the Gathering Storm" and "Walk with Destiny"), *Hallmark Hall of Fame,* NBC, 1974.

Dominic Allardyce, *The Haggard Fashion,* 1974.

Stiva, *Anna Karenina,* CBS, 1985.

Max Donaldson, *Mister Cly, Mister Clay,* 1985.

Daniel Portman, *Maigret,* Harlech Television and syndicated, 1988.

Jason Stone, *Grand Theft Hotel* (also known as *B. L. Stryker: "Grand Theft Hotel"*), ABC, 1990.

Brian, *Invasion of Privacy,* USA Network, 1992.

Talk show host, *Shattered Image,* USA Network, 1994.

Miles, *Horse Sense,* The Disney Channel, 1999.

Johnny Restarick, *Marple: They Do It With Mirrors,* Arts and Entertainment, 2009.

Television Appearances; Specials:

Alban Torel, *The Door of Opportunity* (also known as *W. Somerset Maugham's "The Door of Opportunity"*), BBC, 1970.

Comedy Tonight, ITV, 1980.

Night of One Hundred Stars, 1980.

Apeal: CARE, 1982.

Backstage at "Masterpiece Theatre": A 20th Anniversary Special, PBS, 1991.

Carol Leifer: Gaudy, Bawdy & Blue, Showtime, 1992.

Heart–throbs of the 70s, Sky Television, 2001.

Television Appearances; Pilots:

Denholm Sinclair, *Maggie,* CBS, 1986.

Giancarlo Rinaldi, *Three of a Kind,* ABC, 1989.

Television Appearances; Episodic:

Tom Olliphant, "Celebration Dinner," *ITV Play of the Week,* ITV, 1964.

David Easton, "Sweets to the Sweet," *The Hidden Truth,* 1964.

Franz, "Ironhand," *Theatre 625,* BBC, 1965.

Pedro Da Silva, "Safe Conduct," *The Man in Room 17,* Granada Television, 1965.

Viscount Ballantyne, "The Connoisseur," *The Wednesday Play,* BBC, 1966.

"A Man of His Time," *The Golden Age,* 1967.

Ed, "What Will You Do About Christmas?," *Half Hour Story,* 1967.

Andre, "Goodnight Pelican," *Boy Meets Girl,* BBC, 1967.

Lord Windermere, "Lady Windermere's Fan," *ITV Playhouse,* ITV, 1967.

Baron von Curt, "They Keep Killing Steed," *The Avengers,* ITV, 1968.

Inspector Appleby, "Lesson in Anatomy," *Detective,* BBC, 1968.

"Child's Play," *Thirty–Minute Theatre,* BBC2, 1968.

Herbie (RB–34), "Liar!," *Out of the Unknown,* BBC2, 1969.

David Baurmarez–Smith, "The Brophy Story," *Armchair Theatre,* 1969.

Toby, "Kidnap: Whose Pretty Girl Are You?," *Strange Report,* ITV, 1969.

Sam, "Wine of India," *The Wednesday Play,* BBC, 1970.

"Helen," *Thirty–Minute Theatre,* BBC2, 1970.

Hector Robinson, "English Family Robinson Summer 1910," *Seasons of the Year,* 1971.

Arthur Gower, "Trelawny of the Wells," *BBC Play of the Month,* BBC, 1972.

Title role, "Candide," *BBC Play of the Month,* BBC, 1973.

A man, "Alfred Potter's Story," *Armchair 30,* 1973.

Martin Seacombe, "Saturn's Rewards," _Zodiac,_ Thames Television, 1974.

Morris Townsend, "Catherine," _Affairs of the Heart,_ 1974.

Reverend Gain Dishart, "The Little Minister," _BBC Play of the Month,_ BBC, 1975.

"For Richer or Poorer," _Comedy Premiere,_ 1975.

Grayson, "Tomkinson's Schooldays," _Ripping Yarns,_ BBC2, 1976.

It's Childsplay, BBC, 1976.

Call My Bluff, BBC, 1977, 1979, 1980, 1981, 1982, 1984, 1985, 1987, 1988.

Thomas Aimwell, "The Beaux Stratagem," _BBC Play of the Month,_ BBC, 1978.

Himself, "Ian Ogilvy," _This Is Your Life,_ NBC, 1979.

"1981 Christmas Show," _The Morecambe and Wise Show,_ Thames Television, 1981.

"Ian Ogilvy," _Look Who's Talking,_ 1981.

Your 100 Best Hymns, 1981.

South East at Six, 1982.

"Infernal Device," _Q.E.D.,_ CBS, 1982.

Nationwide, 1983.

Give Us a Clue, 1983.

Breakfast Time, 1983, 1984, 1986.

Saturday Review, 1984.

Vintage Quiz, ITV, 1985.

The Two Ronnies, 1986.

Lord Edgar, "Rutterkin," _Robin of Sherwood_ (also known as _Robin Hood_), ITV and Showtime, 1986.

Harold Baines, "Appointment in Athens," _Murder, She Wrote,_ CBS, 1989.

"The Mystery of Tears," _QED,_ 1989.

Inspector Miles Cottrell, "A Passing Inspection," _Over My Dead Body,_ 1990.

Jimmy Sutane, "Dancers in Mourning," _Campion,_ BBC, 1989, PBS, 1990.

Peter Baines, "The Sicilian Encounter," _Murder, She Wrote,_ CBS, 1990.

Jimmy Sutane, "Dancers in Mourning: Parts 1 & 2," _Mystery!: Campion_ (also known as _Campion_), PBS, 1990.

Archibald Bond, "Smile, You're Dead," _P.S. I. Luv U,_ CBS, 1991.

Peter Templeton, "The Monte Carlo Murders," _Murder, She Wrote,_ CBS, 1992.

Lawson Childress, "Murder in White," _Murder, She Wrote,_ CBS, 1993.

Poindexter Bond, _Phenom,_ ABC, 1993.

Romeo, "Who Killed Romeo?," _Burke's Law,_ CBS, 1994.

Shredder Stoneham, "Rampage," _Walker, Texas Ranger,_ CBS, 1994.

Sterling, "Dragonswing II," _Kung Fu: The Legend Continues,_ syndicated, 1994.

Travor Furlong, "Bounty Hunters' Convention," _The Adventures of Brisco County, Jr._ (also known as _Brisco County, Jr._), Fox, 1994.

Wade Foster, "Murder of the Month Club," _Murder, She Wrote,_ CBS, 1994.

Lyle Fairbanks, "The New Healers," _Diagnosis Murder_ (also known as _Dr. Mark Sloan_), CBS, 1995.

Dan Hollingsworth, "The Romanoff Affair," _One West Waikiki,_ syndicated, 1996.

David Kirkwood, "A Sentimental Education," _Hope & Gloria,_ NBC, 1996.

Marion Michaels, "Opportunity Knockers," _The Faculty,_ ABC, 1996.

Pebble Mill, 1996.

Voices of Dr. Smallwood and second techie, "Village of the Doomed," _The Real Adventures of Jonny Quest_ (animated), Cartoon Network and syndicated, 1996.

Duncan Briggs, "How to Marry a Billionaire," _Murphy Brown,_ CBS, 1997.

Jeffrey Mason, "The Good of the Service," _JAG,_ CBS, 1997.

Lionel Spencer, "Caroline and Richard & Julia," _Caroline in the City_ (also known as _Caroline_), NBC, 1997.

Mr. Spencer, "Caroline and the Ombudsman," _Caroline in the City_ (also known as _Caroline_), NBC, 1997.

Clive Harbison, "Show Me the Monet," _Early Edition,_ CBS, 1998.

Larry Duggin, "Talked to Death," _Diagnosis Murder_ (also known as _Dr. Mark Sloan_), CBS, 1998.

Lord Jano, "In the Kingdom of the Blind," _Babylon 5_ (also known as _B5_), TNT, 1998.

Himself, "The Blood Beast: The Films of Michael Reeves," _Eurotika!,_ 1999.

Jack Campbell, "Other People's Business," _The Love Boat: The Next Wave,_ UPN, 1999.

Jerry Lane, "Trash TV: Parts 1 & 2," _Diagnosis Murder_ (also known as _Dr. Mark Sloan_), CBS, 1999.

Leo Turnlow, "Saving Ryan's Privates," _Melrose Place,_ Fox, 1999.

Leo Turnlow, "They Shoot Blanks, Don't They?," _Melrose Place,_ Fox, 1999.

Miles Clayton, "Water Dance," _Baywatch,_ syndicated, 1999.

Seymour, "And the Winner Is ...," _The Parkers,_ UPN, 2002.

"Crime–fighters," _After They Were Famous,_ 2005.

This Morning, ITV, 2005.

Breakfast, BBC, 2005, 2006.

"Magic, Murder and Monsters: The Story of British Horror and Fantasy," _British Film Forever,_ BBC, 2007.

Stage Appearances:

Aladdin, Northampton Repertory Theatre, Northampton, Northamptonshire, England, 1964.

Hamlet, Thorndike Theatre, Leatherhead, Surrey, England, 1970.

Three Sisters, Albery Theatre, London, 1978.

The Millionairess, Theatre Royal Haymarket, London, 1978–79.

Design for Living, Globe Theatre, London, 1982.

The Common Pursuit, Lyric Theatre, London, 1984.

Rookery Nook, Shaftesbury Theatre, London, 1986.

Rough Crossing, Matrix Theatre, Los Angeles, 1993.

Professor Henry Higgins, _My Fair Lady_ (musical), Pacific Coast Civic Light Opera, 1999.

Andrew, _Sleuth,_ Apollo Theatre, London, 2002–2003.

Also appeared as John/James, *Love! Valour! Compassion!,* U.S. production; *The Devil's Disciple,* Liverpool, England; *Happy Family,* London production; *The Importance of Being Earnest,* London production; *One of Us,* London production; *Run for Your Wife,* London production; *Stagestruck,* London production; *Waltz of the Toreadors,* London production.

Major Tours:
Howard Booth, *Snakes and Ladders,* British cities, 2002.
Andrew, *Sleuth,* British cities, 2003.

Stage Work:
Director of the revised version of *A Slight Hangover,* Mill at Sonning.

RECORDINGS

Taped Readings:
Present Laughter, L.A. Theatre Works, 1996.

Reader for other taped readings, including readings featuring the character of James Bond.

WRITINGS

Screenplays:
The Stud Farm (also known as *The Male Farm, Fun Farm,* and *The Stud(y) Farm*), McAbee Pictures, 1969.

Stage Plays:
A Slight Hangover, Churchill Theatre, Bromley, England, c. 1985, revised version, Mill at Sonning, also produced at other venues, including Howick Little Theatre, Pakuranga, New Zealand, c. 2004.

Novels:
Loose Chippings, Headline, 1996.
The Polkerton Giant, Headline, 1997.
A Slight Hangover (based on his stage play), Writer's Club Press, 2000.

Novels for Children:
Measle and the Wrathmonk, HarperCollins, 2004.
Measle and the Dragon, HarperCollins, 2005.
Measle and the Mallockee, HarperCollins, 2006.
Measle and the Slitherghoul, Oxford University Press, 2006.
Measle and the Doompit, Oxford University Press, 2007.

Contributor to periodicals.

OTHER SOURCES

Periodicals:
TV Zone, March, 1999, p. 38–41.

Electronic:
Ian Ogilvy Official Site, http://www.ianogilvy.com, October 20, 2010.

O'HALLORAN, Brian 1969–
(Brian C. O'Halloran, Brian Christopher O'Halloran)

PERSONAL

Full name, Brian Christopher O'Halloran; born December 20, 1969, in New York, NY; father was an automotive engineer.

Career: Actor.

CREDITS

Film Appearances:
Dante, *Clerks* (also known as *Clerks X: Tenth Anniversary Edition* and *cLeRKs*), Miramax, 1994.
Gill, *Mallrats,* Gramercy, 1995.
Groupies, The Weston Group, 1997.
First executive Jim Hicks, *Chasing Amy,* Miramax, 1997.
(As Brian Christopher O'Halloran) Reporter, *Dogma,* Lions Gate Films, 1999.
(As Brian Christopher O'Halloran) Will Carlson/Flappy/Vulgar, *Vulgar,* Lions Gate Films, 2000.
(As Brian Christopher O'Halloran) Dante Hicks, *Jay and Silent Bob Strike Back,* Dimension Films, 2001.
(As Brian C. O'Halloran) Shawn, *Drop Dead Roses,* York Entertainment, 2001.
Narrator, *Maybe Means No* (short film), 2002.
Clerk, *Moby Presents: Alien Sex Party,* Music Video Distributors, 2003.
Oh, What a Lovely Tea Party, View Askew Productions, 2004.
Dante Hicks, *Clerks: The Lost Scene,* Miramax, 2004.
Dante, *Clerks II,* Paramount, 2006.
Mitch Stone, *The Junior Defenders,* Warner Home Video, 2007.
Jason "Jay" Daly, *Brutal Massacre: A Comedy,* Anchor Bay, 2007.
(As Brian C. O'Halloran) Jeep driver, *The Happening,* Twentieth Century–Fox, 2008.
Dr. Jordan, *Hooking Up* (also known as *Clusterfuck*), Sony, 2009.

The Emperor Wears No Clothes, The Brookturn Co., 2009.

Television Appearances; Specials:
Dante Hicks, *The Flying Car* (short film), 2002.
Clerks II: Unauthorized, VH1, 2006.

Television Appearances; Series:
Dante Hicks, *Clerks* (also known as *Clerks: Uncensored*), ABC, 2000, Comedy Central, 2001.

RECORDINGS

Videos:
Snowball Effect: The Story of "Clerks," Miramax, 2004.
"Clerks" 10th Anniversary Q & A, Miramax, 2004.
Back to the Well: "Clerks II," Paramount, 2006.
Train Wreck!, Paramount, 2006.

OLDMAN, Gary 1958–
  (Maurice Escargot)

PERSONAL

Full name, Leonard Gary Oldman; born March 21, 1958, in London, England; son of Leonard (a welder) and Kathleen (a homemaker) Oldman; married Lesley Manville (an actress), 1988 (divorced, 1990); married Uma Thurman (an actress, producer, and writer), October 1, 1990 (divorced, 1992); married Donya Fiorentino (a model and photographer), February 16, 1997 (divorced, 2001); married Alexandra Edenborough, December 31, 2008; children: (first marriage) Alfred; (third marriage) Gulliver Flynn, Charlie John. *Education:* Rose Bruford College of Speech and Drama, B.A. (with honors), 1979; trained for the stage at Greenwich Young People's Theatre.

Addresses: *Agent*—Jim Osborne, Paradigm, 360 North Crescent Dr. N., Beverly Hills, CA 90210; (voice work and commercials) Alix Gucovsky, Special Artists Agency, 9465 Wilshire Blvd., Suite 470, Beverly Hills, CA 90212. *Manager*—Douglas J. Urbanski, Douglas Management Group, 504 North Robertson Blvd., Los Angeles, CA 90048.

Career: Actor, producer, director, and writer. SE8 Group (production company), principal. Previously a member of Theatre Royal, York, England; appeared in television commercials for DKNY apparel, 2000, One 2 One, 2001, and Nokia cell phones, 2006; also appeared in print advertisements. Cannes Film Festival, member of jury, 1993.

Awards, Honors: *Drama Magazine* Award, best actor, British Theatre Association, 1985, and Fringe Award, best newcomer, *Time Out,* 1985–86, both for *The Pope's Wedding;* Evening Standard Award, most promising newcomer in a film, 1986, for *Sid and Nancy;* Film Award nomination, best actor, British Academy of Film and Television Arts, London Critics Circle Film Award, actor of the year, 1988, for Prick Up Your Ears; Independent Spirit Award nomination, best male lead, Independent Features Project/West, 1992, for *Rosencrantz and Guildenstern Are Dead;* Annual CableACE Award, best actor in a dramatic series, National Cable Television Association, 1993, for *Sydney Pollack's "Fallen Angels";* Saturn Award, best actor, Academy of Science Fiction, Fantasy, and Horror Films, MTV Movie Award nomination (with Winona Ryder), best kiss, 1993, for *Dracula;* Channel 4 Director's Award, Edinburgh International Film Festival, 1997, and MTV Film Award, best original screenplay, and Alexander Korda Award (with others), best British film, British Academy of Film and Television Arts, British Independent Film Award nominations, best British director of an independent film and best original screenplay by a British writer of a produced independent film, Channel 4 Director's Award, Edinburgh International Film Festival, and nomination for Golden Palm, Cannes Film Festival, all 1997, and Empire Award, best debut, all 1998, all for *Nil by Mouth;* Movie Award nominations, best fight (with Harrison Ford) and best villain, and Blockbuster Entertainment Award nomination, favorite supporting actor in an action or adventure, all 1998, for *Air Force One;* Saturn Award nomination, best supporting actor, 1999, for Lost in Space; Alan J. Pakula Award (with others), Broadcast Film Critics Association Awards, Independent Spirit Award nomination and Screen Actors Guild Award nomination, both best supporting actor, all 2001, for *The Contender;* Emmy Award nomination, outstanding guest actor in a comedy series, 2001, for Friends; Master Screen Artist Tribute, USA Film Festival, 2001; DVDX Award nomination, best supporting actor in a DVD premiere movie, DVD Exclusive Awards, 2003, for *Interstate 60;* Saturn Award nomination, best supporting actor, 2005, for Harry Potter and the Prisoner of Azkaban; Critics Choice Award nomination, best acting ensemble, Broadcast Film Critics Association, and People's Choice Award, favorite cast, both (with others) 2009, for The Dark Knight.

CREDITS

Film Appearances:
Sid Vicious, *Sid and Nancy* (also known as *Love Kills* and *Sid and Nancy: Love Kills*), Samuel Goldwyn, 1986.
Joe Orton, *Prick Up Your Ears,* Samuel Goldwyn, 1987.
Martin, *Track 29,* Island, 1988.
Johnny, *We Think the World of You,* Cinecom, 1988.
Ben Chase, *Criminal Law,* TriStar, 1988.
Emmett Foley, *Chattahoochee,* Hemdale, 1990.

Jackie Flannery, *State of Grace,* Orion, 1990.

(As Maurice Escargot) Pop, *Henry & June,* Universal, 1990.

Rosencrantz, *Rosencrantz and Guildenstern are Dead,* Cinecom, 1990.

Lee Harvey Oswald, *JFK,* Warner Bros., 1991.

Count Dracula/Vlad III Draculea, *Dracula* (also known as *Bram Stoker's "Dracula"*), Columbia, 1992.

Beyond JFK: The Question of Conspiracy (documentary), 1992.

Drexl Spivey, *True Romance* (also known as *Breakaway*), Warner Bros., 1993.

Ludwig van Beethoven, *Immortal Beloved,* Columbia, 1994.

Agent Norman Stansfield, *The Professional* (also known as *The Cleaner, Leon,* and *Leon: The Professional*), Columbia, 1994.

Jack Grimaldi, *Romeo Is Bleeding,* Gramercy, 1994.

Milton Glenn, *Murder in the First,* Warner Bros., 1995.

Reverend Arthur Dimmesdale, *The Scarlet Letter,* Buena Vista, 1995.

Albert Milo, *Basquiat* (also known as *Build a Fort, Set It on Fire*), Miramax, 1996.

Ivan Korshunov, *Air Force One* (also known as *AFO*), Columbia, 1997.

Jean–Baptiste Emmanuel Zorg, *The Fifth Element* (also known as *The Fifth Man*), Columbia, 1997.

Dr. Zachary Smith (Spider Smith), *Lost in Space* (also known as *LS*), New Line Cinema, 1998.

Voice of Sir Ruber, *Quest for Camelot* (also known as *Camelot* and *The Magic Sword: Quest for Camelot*), Warner Bros., 1998.

Representative Sheldon "Shelly" Runyon, *The Contender,* DreamWorks, 2000.

Buford Dill, *Nobody's Baby,* Millenium, 2001.

(Uncredited) Mason Verger, *Hannibal,* Metro–Goldwyn–Mayer, 2001.

O. W. Grant, *Interstate 60* (also known as *I–60* and *Interstate 60: Episodes of the Road*), Samuel Goldwyn, 2002.

The devil, *Beat the Devil* (also known as *The Hire: Beat the Devil*), 2002.

Rolfe, *Tiptoes,* Reality Check, 2003.

Charlie Strom, *Sin,* Columbia TriStar, 2003.

Lynch, *Dead Fish,* Mobius International, 2004.

Sirius Black, *Harry Potter and the Prisoner of Azkaban* (also released as *Harry Potter and the Prisoner of Azkaban: The IMAX Experience*), Warner Bros., 2004.

Sirius Black, *Harry Potter and the Goblet of Fire* (also known as *The Goblet of Fire;* also released as *Harry Potter and the Goblet of Fire: The IMAX Experience*), Warner Bros., 2005.

Scouse, *Who's Kyle?* (short film), Vanguard Cinema, 2005.

Jim Gordon, *Batman Begins* (also released as *Batman Begins: The IMAX Experience*), Warner Bros., 2005.

Me and Graham: The Soundtrack of Our Lives (documentary), Humanity Entertainment/Jeffrey Butscher Entertainment, 2005.

Sirius Black, *Harry Potter and the Order of the Phoenix* (also known as *The Order of the Phoenix;* also released as *Harry Potter and the Order of the Phoenix: The IMAX Experience*), Warner Bros., 2007.

Paul, *BackWoods* (also known as *Bosque de sombras* and *Spiral Violence*), Lions Gate Films, 2007.

James "Jim" Gordon, *The Dark Knight* (also known as *Batman: The Dark Knight;* also released as *The Dark Knight: The IMAX Experience*), Warner Bros., 2008.

The Secret World of Superfans (documentary), Sam Okun Productions, 2008.

Rabbi Sendak, *The Unborn,* Rogue Pictures, 2009.

William Holtzer, *Rain Fall,* Grindstone Entertainment Group, 2009.

Voices of Bob Cratchit, Marley, and Tiny Tim, *A Christmas Carol* (animated; also known as *Disney's "A Christmas Carol," Disney's "Christmas Carol'';* also released as *A Christmas Carol: An IMAX 3D Experience*), Walt Disney, 2009.

Voice of General Grawl, *Planet 51* (animated), TriStar, 2009.

Take Flight: Gary Oldman Directs Chutzpah (short documentary), Miss Juliet Productions, 2009.

Carnegie, *The Book of Eli* (also known as *The Walker*), Warner Bros., 2010.

Criminal Empire for Dummy's, Sony Pictures Entertainment, 2010.

Narrator, *Countdown to Zero,* Magnolia Pictures, 2010.

Narrator, *One Night in Turin,* Kaleidoscope Home Entertainment, 2010.

Elvis, *Guns, Girls, and Gambling,* Ascot Elite Entertainment, 2011.

Father Solomon, *Red Riding Hood,* Warner Bros., 2011.

George Smiley, *Tinker, Tailor, Soldier, Spy,* Studio Canal/Working Title Films, 2011.

Film Work:

Producer and director, *Nil by Mouth,* Sony Pictures Classics, 1997.

Executive producer, *Plunkett and MaCleane,* Gramercy, 1999.

Executive producer, *The Contender,* DreamWorks, 2000.

Cinematographer, *Take Flight: Gary Oldman Directs Chutzpah* (short documentary), Miss Juliet Productions, 2009.

Television Appearances; Movies:

Daniel, *Remembrance,* Channel 4, released in the United States as a film, Mainline, 1982.

Coxy, *Meantime,* Channel 4, 1983, released in the United States as a film, Film 4, 1984.

Morgan's Boy, 1984.

Derek Bates, "Honest, Decent, and True," *Screen Two,* BBC, 1986.

Bex Bissek, "The Firm," *Screen Two,* BBC, 1989.

Ian Tyson, "Heading Home," *Screen Two,* BBC, 1991, then Arts and Entertainment, 1992.
Charlie Strom, *Sin,* Starz!, 2001.

Television Appearances; Specials:
Blood Lines: Dracula—The Man, the Myth, the Movies, 1992.
In Search of Dracula with Jonathan Ross, London Weekend Television, 1996.
Lost in Space: A Behind the Scenes Journey, 1998.
Lost in Space Forever, Fox, 1998.
Alan Clarke: His Own Man, 2000.
Narrator, *Tales of Edgar Allen Poe* (also known as *Great Books: Poe's Tales of Terror*), The Learning Channel, 2001.
Anthony Hopkins: A Taste for Hannibal, 2002.
The 100 Greatest Movie Stars, Channel 4, 2003.
Batman Begins: Behind the Mask, ITV, 2005.
The Hidden Secrets of Harry Potter, 2007.
Nubes y claros—Rodando "Bosque de sombras," 2007.
(In archive footage) Ivan Korshunov, *President Hollywood,* BBC4, 2008.

Television Appearances; Miniseries:
Voice of Lee Harvey Oswald, "Who Was Lee Harvey Oswald?," *Frontline,* 1993.
Pontius Pilate, *Jesus,* CBS, 1999.
(In archive footage) *British Film Forever,* BBC, 2007.

Television Appearances; Episodic:
The Kenny Everett Video Show, 1979.
Ben, "On Your Tod," *Dramarama,* ITV, 1984.
Gary, "Rachel and the Roarettes," *Summer Season,* 1985.
Don Ross, "Close Call," *Knots Landing,* CBS, 1989.
Pat Kelly (some sources cite the role as Pat Keiley), "Dead–End for Delia," *Sydney Pollack's "Fallen Angels,"* Showtime, 1993.
"The Best Man for the Job: The Making of 'The Professional,'" *HBO First Look,* HBO, 1994.
Nyhetsmorgon, 1997.
Hairdresser, "Hair," *Tracey Takes On ...,* HBO, 1999.
"'The Contender': The Making of a Political Thriller," *HBO First Look,* HBO, 2000.
Richard Crosby, "The One with Monica and Chandler's Wedding: Parts 1 & 2," *Friends,* NBC, 2001.
"Piddler on the Roof," *Greg the Bunny,* Fox, 2002.
"'Harry Potter and the Prisoner of Azkaban': Something Wicked This Way Comes," *HBO First Look,* HBO, 2004.
"Planet Potter," *Planet Voice,* 2005.
"Batman Begins: An Origin Story," *HBO First Look,* HBO, 2005.
"'Harry Potter and the Order of the Phoenix': Fulfilling a Prophecy," *HBO First Look,* HBO, 2007.
(In archive footage) "Film Locations in NYC," *Filmania: Eiga no tatsujin,* 2009.
(In archive footage) *Cinemaholic,* 2009.

Made in Hollywood, 2010.
The 7PM Project, Ten Network, 2010.

Also appeared in *Backstory,* AMC; as Ruber in episodes of various animated series, including *The Cartoon Characters Villains, Devon and Cornwall: The Series, Mickey & Bugs' House of Villains,* and *Villain Toon Jam.*

Television Talk Show Guest Appearances; Episodic:
Late Show with David Letterman, CBS, 1994.
Charlie Rose (also known as *The Charlie Rose Show*), PBS, 1995.
"Intolerance," *Dennis Miller Live,* HBO, 2001.
The Tonight Show with Jay Leno, NBC, 2001.
V Graham Norton, Channel 4, 2003.
Today (also known as *NBC News Today* and *The Today Show*), NBC, 2004.
The View, ABC, 2008.
Late Night with Conan O'Brien, NBC, 2008.
Up Close with Carrie Keagan, ABC, 2008, 2010.
The Tonight Show with Conan O'Brien, NBC, 2010.

Television Appearances; Awards Presentations:
The ... Annual Screen Actors Guild Awards, E! Entertainment Television, 2001, TBS and TNT, 2009.
Presenter, *2001 Creative Arts Emmy Awards,* E! Entertainment Television, 2001.
(Uncredited) *The 2001 IFP/West Independent Spirit Awards,* Independent Film Channel, 2001.
Presenter, *17th Annual IFP/West Independent Spirit Awards,* Independent Film Channel, 2002.

Television Work; Movies:
Producer, *Sin,* Starz!, 2001.

Stage Appearances:
Massacre at Paris, Glasgow Citizens Theatre, Glasgow, Scotland, 1980.
Chinchilla, Glasgow Citizens Theatre, 1980.
Desperado Corner, Glasgow Citizens Theatre, 1980.
A Waste of Time, Glasgow Citizens Theatre, 1980.
Soldier, *Summit Conference,* Lupton Theatre Company, Lyric Theatre, London, 1982.
Entertaining Mr. Sloane, 1983.
P. C. Naylor, *Rat in the Skull,* Royal Court Theatre, London, 1984.
Scopey, *The Pope's Wedding,* Royal Court Theatre, 1984.
Mike, *Saved,* Royal Court Theatre, 1984.
Son, "Red, Black, and Ignorant," third man, "Tin Can People," and son and man, "Great Peace," *The War Plays,* Royal Shakespeare Company, Pit Theatre, London, 1985.
Major Carp and Petko, *The Desert Air,* Royal Shakespeare Company, Pit Theatre, 1985.
Abel, *Abel and Cain,* Royal Shakespeare Company, Almeida Theatre, London, 1985.

Sordido, *Women Beware Women,* Royal Court Theatre, 1986.

Jack, *Real Dreams,* Royal Shakespeare Company, Pit Theatre, 1986.

The Dumb Waiter, Royal Shakespeare Company, Almeida Theatre, 1986.

Grimes and Billy Corman, *Serious Money,* Royal Court Theatre, 1987.

The Country Wife, 1987.

Also appeared in *Minnesota Moon,* London.

Major Tours:

Toured in *Chinchilla, Desperado Corner,* Massacre at Paris, and A Waste of Time, all with Glasgow Citizens Theatre, European and South American cities.

Radio Appearances:

Performer as an anonymous Londoner, *Walk Right by Me* (monologue), BBC4.

RECORDINGS

Videos:

(Uncredited; in archive footage) The devil, "Since I Don't Have You," *Guns n' Roses: Welcome to the Videos,* 1998.

Beloved Beethoven, 1999.

"The Contender": The Making of a Political Thriller, 2001.

Breaking the Silence: The Making of "Hannibal," 2001.

Memories of: Elephant, Blue Underground, 2004.

Head to Shrunken Head, 2004.

Conjuring a Scene, 2004.

(Uncredited; in archive footage) Sirius Black, *Creating the Vision,* 2004.

Cape and Cowl, Warner Home Video, 2005.

(Uncredited) *Batman: The Tumbler,* Warner Home Video, 2005.

Chutzpah, This Is?, Jewish Music Group, 2005.

The Costumes Are the Sets: The Design of Eiko Ishioka, Sony Pictures Home Entertainment, 2007.

The Blood Is the Life: The Making of "Bram Stoker's Dracula," Sony Pictures Home Entertainment, 2007.

(In archive footage) *In Camera: The Naive Visual Effects of "Bram Stoker's Dracula,"* Sony Pictures Home Entertainment, 2007.

Appeared in the music video "Since I Don't Have You" by Guns n' Roses, 1994.

Video Games:

Voice of Jean Baptiste Emanuel Zorg, *The Fifth Element,* Activision, 1998.

Voices of Rocky and Agent Masterson, *True Crime: Streets of LA,* 2003.

Voice of Sergeant Jack Barnes, *Medal of Honor: Allied Assault—Spearhead,* Electronic Arts, 2003.

Voice of Ignitus, *The Legend of Spyro: A New Beginning,* Sierra Entertainment, 2006.

Voice of Ignitus, *The Legend of Spyro: The Eternal Night,* Sierra Entertainment, 2007.

Voice of Ignitus, *The Legend of Spyro: Dawn of the Dragon,* 2008.

Voice of Sergeant Reznov, *Call of Duty: World at War* (also known as *Final Fronts*), Activision, 2008.

Albums:

Song performer, "I Wanna Be Your Dog" and "My Way," *Sid and Nancy* (original soundtrack recording), 1986.

Also contributor to the album *Every Silver Lining Has a Cloud* by Julian Schnabel, and (in the duet with David Bowie "You've Been Around") to *The Sacred Squall of Now.* Appeared in the music video "Love Kills" by Joe Strummer.

WRITINGS

Screenplays:

Nil by Mouth, Sony Pictures Classics, 1997.

OTHER SOURCES

Books:

International Dictionary of Films and Filmmakers, Volume 3: *Actors and Actresses,* St. James Press, 1996.

Newsmakers 1998, Gale, 1998.

Periodicals:

American Film, April, 1988.

Entertainment Weekly, February 10, 1995, p. 14.

Harper's Bazaar, February, 1998, p. 196.

Interview, January, 1992, p. 84; February, 1998, p. 60.

New York Times, November 8, 1992.

OLYPHANT, Timothy 1968–
    (Tim Olyphant)

PERSONAL

Full name, Timothy David Olyphant; born May 20, 1968, in Honolulu, HI; son of Katherine Wright; brother of Andy Olyphant (a artist and repertory executive for a record label); married Alexis Knief, 1999; children: Grace Katherine, Henry, Vivian. *Education:* Attended University of Southern California; trained at William Esper Studio, New York City.

Addresses: *Agent*—Creative Artists Agency, 2000 Avenue of the Stars, Los Angeles, CA 90067. *Manager*—Cotton Gramm, Brillstein Entertainment Partners, 9150 Wilshire Blvd., Suite 350, Beverly Hills, CA 90212.

Career: Actor and producer. Indie 103.1 Radio, Los Angeles, sports reporter for morning show anchored by Joe Escalante, until 2008.

Awards, Honors: *Theatre World* Award, outstanding debut performance, 1996, for *The Monogamist;* Young Hollywood Award, best bad boy, *Movieline,* 2000, for *Go;* Screen Actors Guild Award nomination (with others), outstanding ensemble in a drama series, 2007, for *Deadwood.*

CREDITS

Film Appearances:
Brett Artounian, *The First Wives Club,* Paramount, 1996.
Hiker, *A Life Less Ordinary,* Twentieth Century–Fox, 1997.
Mickey Altieri, *Scream 2,* Dimension Films, 1997.
Hooks, *1999* (also known as *Girls & Boys*), 1998.
Luke, *No Vacancy,* 1999.
Todd Gaines, *Go,* TriStar, 1999.
Dennis, *The Broken Hearts Club: A Romantic Comedy,* Sony Pictures Classics, 2000.
Roy Mason, *Auggie Rose* (also known as *Beyond Suspicion*), Warner Bros., 2000.
Detective Drycoff, *Gone in Sixty Seconds,* Buena Vista, 2000.
Brat, *Advice from a Caterpillar,* 2001.
Guitarist Rob Malcolm, *Rock Star,* Warner Bros., 2001.
Michael, *Head over Heels,* Universal, 2001.
Brian, *Doppelganger,* 2001.
Randy, *The Safety of Objects,* IFC Films, 2001.
Sonny Mann, *Coastlines,* Curb Entertainment, 2001.
Pete, *Dreamcatcher,* Warner Bros., 2003.
Hollywood Jack Slayton, *A Man Apart,* New Line Cinema, 2003.
Kelly, *The Girl Next Door,* Twentieth Century–Fox, 2004.
Fritz, *Catch and Release,* Columbia, 2007.
Thomas Gabriel, *Live Free or Die Hard* (also known as *Die Hard 4.0* and *Die Hard 4: Live Free or Die Hard*), Twentieth Century–Fox, 2007.
Agent 47, *Hitman,* Twentieth Century–Fox, 2007.

Chip Johnson, *Meet Bill* (also known as *Bill*), First Look International, 2008.
Lieutenant Colonel Boot Miller, *Stop–Loss,* Paramount, 2008.
Dick, *High Life,* Union Pictures, 2009.
Nick, *A Perfect Getaway,* Rogue Pictures/Universal, 2009.
David Dutten, *The Crazies,* Overture Films, 2010.
Elektra Luxx, Myriad Pictures, 2010.
Henri, *I Am Number Four,* DreamWorks, 2011.
Voice of The Spirit of the West, *Rango* (animated), Paramount, 2011.

Television Appearances; Series:
Seth Bullock, *Deadwood,* HBO, 2004–2006.
Wes Krulik, *Damages,* FX Network, 2009–10.
Marshal Raylan Givens, *Justified,* FX Network, 2010—.

Television Appearances; Movies:
Lieutenant Lukas, *When Trumpets Fade* (also known as *Hamburger Hill 2*), HBO, 1998.
Eli West, *Shadow Realm,* Sci–Fi Channel, 2002.

Television Appearances; Specials:
Roy Hobbs, *Ellen Foster,* CBS, 1997.
Making *"Deadwood":* The Show Behind the Show, HBO, 2004.
(As Tim Olyphant) Making *"Deadwood":* Season Two, HBO, 2005.

Television Appearances; Pilots:
Scooby, *Mr. & Mrs. Smith,* CBS, 1996.

Television Appearances; Episodic:
Brett Farraday, "Camino High," *High Incident,* ABC, 1997.
Brett Farraday, "Starting Over," *High Incident,* ABC, 1997.
Brett Farraday, "Shootout," *High Incident,* ABC, 1997.
Sam, "Valley of the Twenty–Something Guys," *Sex and the City* (also known as *S.A.T.C.* and *Sex and the Big City*), HBO, 1998.
Eli, "Harmony," *Night Visions* (also known as *Nightvision*), Fox, 2002.
"'Dreamcatcher': Unraveling the Nightmare," *HBO First Look,* HBO, 2003.
Dinner for Five, Independent Film Channel, 2005.
Billy Reed, "Dad's Car," *My Name Is Earl,* NBC, 2006.
Amazon Fishbowl with Bill Maher, 2006.
The Late Late Show with Craig Ferguson, CBS, 2006.
Jimmy Kimmel Live!, ABC, 2007.
Up Close with Carrie Keagan, 2007.
Late Night With Conan O'Brien, NBC, 2007.
Winston Funk, "The Boss," *Samantha Who?,* ABC, 2008.

The Office, NBC, 2010.
The Hour (also known as *CBC News: The Hour*), CBC, 2010.
Entertainment Tonight (also known as *E.T.* and *This Week in Entertainment*), syndicated, 2010.
Rachael Ray, syndicated, 2010.
The Bonnie Hunt Show, NBC, 2010.
The Tonight Show with Jay Leno, NBC, 2011.
Late Night with Jimmy Fallon, NBC, 2011.
Made in Hollywood, 2011.

Television Producer; Episodic:
"The Moonshine War," *Justified,* FX Network, 2011.

Stage Appearances:
The Monogamist, Playwrights Horizons Theatre, New York City, 1995.
The Santaland Diaries, Atlantic Theatre Company, Linda Gross Theatre, New York City, 1996.

RECORDINGS

Videos:
Film–Fest DVD: Issue 2—Cannes, 1999.
Analog Hero in a Digital World: Making of "Live Free or Die Hard," Twentieth Century–Fox Home Entertainment, 2007.
Voice of cowboy, *Turok* (video game), Touchstone Games, 2008.

OTHER SOURCES

Periodicals:
Cosmopolitan, January, 1998, p. 39.
Entertainment Weekly, June 16, 2006, p. 31.
Premiere, April, 1999, p. 96; April, 2003, p. 23.
Seventeen, January, 1998, p. 76.
TV Guide, January 19, 2009, pp. 42–43.

P

PALMINTERI, Chazz 1952(?)–

PERSONAL

Full name, Calogero Lorenzo Palminteri; born May 15, 1952 (some sources cite 1946 or 1951), in the Bronx, New York, NY; son of Lorenzo (a bus driver) and Rose (a homemaker) Palminteri; married Gianna Ranaudo (an actress), June 6, 1992; children: Dante Lorenzo, Gabriella Rose. *Education:* Graduate of Bronx Community College of the City University of New York; studied acting with Lee Strasberg at Actors Studio and with Paul Austin.

Addresses: *Agent*—WME Entertainment, 9601 Wilshire Blvd., 3rd Floor, Beverly Hills, CA 90210. *Manager*— Creative Film Management, 430 West 14th St., Suite 402B, New York, NY 10014.

Career: Actor, producer, director, and writer. Toured Europe with New York Comedy Players, 1975–80; appeared in a commercial for Vanilla Coke soft drinks, 2002. Singer and songwriter; performed as a singer with the band RassmaChazz; also worked as a nightclub doorman at LimeLight, New York City, and 20/20 Club, Los Angeles. Cooley's Anemia Foundation, national spokesperson.

Awards, Honors: *DramaLogue* Awards, outstanding performance and best play, 1988, and (New York) Outer Critics Circle Award nominations, outstanding performance and best play, all for *A Bronx Tale;* Independent Spirit Award, Independent Features Project/West, Academy Award nomination, and Screen Actors Guild Award nomination, all best supporting actor, National Board of Review Award (with others), best acting by an ensemble, and American Comedy Award nomination, all 1995, for *Bullets over Broadway;* award from Coalition of Italo–American Associations, 1995, for leadership in entertainment; Sant Jordi Award, best foreign actor, 1996, for *The Usual Suspects, A Bronx Tale,* and *Bullets over Broadway;* special achievement award for the performing arts, National Italian American Foundation, 1996; Indie Hero Award, Method Fest, 2004; Special Jury Prize (with others), outstanding ensemble in a dramatic film, 2006, for *A Guide to Recognizing Your Saints; DramaLogue* Award, outstanding performance, for *Faithful.*

CREDITS

Film Appearances:
Truck hijacker, *Home Free All,* Almi, 1984.
Second hood, *The Last Dragon* (also known as *Berry Gordon's "The Last Dragon"*), TriStar, 1985.
Frank Livorno, *An Even Break,* 1989.
Connie, *Oscar,* Buena Vista, 1991.
Tony, *Innocent Blood* (also known as *A French Vampire in America*), Warner Bros., 1992.
Lyle Corrente, *There Goes the Neighborhood* (also known as *Paydirt*), Paramount, 1993.
Sonny LoSpecchio, *A Bronx Tale,* Savoy Pictures, 1993.
Cheech, *Bullets over Broadway,* Miramax, 1994.
Lieutenant John Pirelli, *The Perez Family,* Samuel Goldwyn, 1995.
Matt Gavin, *Jade,* Paramount, 1995.
David "Dave" Kujan, *The Usual Suspects,* Gramercy, 1995.
Ellory Coolidge, *Mulholland Falls,* Metro–Goldwyn–Mayer, 1996.
Guy Baran, *Diabolique,* Warner Bros., 1996.
Tony, *Faithful,* New Line Cinema, 1996.
(Uncredited) Mr. Bunny Zadir, *A Night at the Roxbury,* Paramount, 1998.
Phil, *Hurlyburly* (also known as *Casting Director*), Fine Line, 1998.
The Book that Wrote Itself (documentary), 1999.
Primo Sidone (some sources spell the name "Sindone"), *Analyze This* (also known as *Analyze Me*), Warner Bros., 1999.

Voice of Smokey, *Stuart Little* (animated), Sony Pictures Entertainment, 1999.

Eddie Dugan, *One Eyed King,* Splendid Pictures, 2001.

Mr. King, *Down to Earth,* Paramount, 2001.

Speaking voice of Buster, *Lady and the Tramp II: Scamp's Adventure* (animated), Buena Vista Home Video, 2001.

Joe, *Poolhall Junkies,* Samuel Goldwyn, 2002.

Just Like Mona, Moonstone Entertainment/Regent, 2003.

Tweat, *One Last Ride,* Eclectic Entertainment, 2004.

Arizona, *Noel,* Screen Media Films, 2005.

Voice of Woolworth, *Hoodwinked!* (animated; also known as *Little Red*), Weinstein Company, 2005.

Frank Pacelli, *In the Mix,* Lions Gate Films, 2005.

Kassada, *Animal,* DEJ Productions, 2005.

Monty, *A Guide to Recognizing Your Saints,* First Look International, 2006.

Detective Rydell, *Running Scared* (also known as *Wild Bullet*), New Line Cinema, 2006.

Vince, *Push,* Peach Arch Entertainment Group, 2006.

Walken, *Little Man* (also known as *Perfect Gem & Valuable*), Revolution Studios, 2006.

The travel agent, *Arthur and the Invisibles* (also known as *Arthur and the Minimoys*), Metro–Goldwyn–Mayer, 2006.

Lee Maxwell, *Body Armour,* Darclight Films International, 2007.

George Zucco, *The Dukes,* Cavu Releasing, 2008.

Title role, *Yonkers Joe,* Magnolia Pictures, 2008.

Beyond Wiseguys: Italian Americans & the Movies (documentary), Beachcomber Films/Pacific Street Films, 2008.

Sal, *Jolene,* Screen Media Films, 2009.

Frank Gregorio, *Once More with Feeling,* Sundance Selects, 2009.

Journey to Sundance (documentary), Hollywood Filmmakers, 2009.

Marvin Milkshake, *The Oogieloves in the Big Balloon Adventure,* Big Balloon Adventure Movie, 2010.

Geno Scarpacci, *Hollywood & Wine,* Eagle Films, 2010.

Voice of Babe Ruth, *Henry and Me* (animated), Creative Group, 2010.

Voice of pigeon, *Cat Tale* (animated), Imagi Entertainment, 2010.

Film Work:

Director, *Noel,* Screen Media Films, 2005.

Coproducer, *The Dukes,* Cavu Releasing, 2008.

Executive producer, *Yonkers Joe,* Magnolia Pictures, 2008.

Television Appearances; Movies:

Drummond, *Glory Years,* 1987.

Soldier, *Peter Gunn,* ABC, 1989.

Ricky Benzone, *The Last Word* (also known as *Cosa Nostra: The Last Word*), Showtime, 1995.

Giovanni Falcone, *Excellent Cadavers* (also known as *Falcone*), HBO, 1998.

Lieutenant Laine Devon, *Scar City* (also known as *S.C.A.R.* and *Scarred City*), HBO, 1998.

Paul Castellano, *Boss of Bosses,* TNT, 2001.

Joseph DiCaro, *Drift,* 2006.

Television Appearances; Specials:

Inside the Academy Awards, TNT, 1995.

Sinatra: 80 Years My Way, ABC, 1995.

(In archive footage) *50 Years of Funny Females,* 1995.

Little Italy, PBS, 1996.

(In archive footage) *40 premios Sant Jordi de cinematografia,* 1996.

Italians in America, Arts and Entertainment, 1998.

(Uncredited; in archive footage) *Sharon Stone—Una mujer de 100 caras,* 1998.

(Uncredited; in archive footage) *Femmes Fatales: Sharon Stone,* 1998.

(In archive footage) *... y otras mujeres de armas tomar,* 1998.

Guns for Hire: The Making of "The Magnificent Seven," Channel 4, 2000.

Host, *An All–Star Tribute to Brian Wilson,* TNT, 2001.

I Love New York, 2002.

"Humphrey Bogart," *Biography,* Arts and Entertainment, 2003.

Presenter, *2003 AFI Life Achievement Award: A Tribute to Robert De Niro,* USA Network, 2003.

A Tribute to Joe Mantegna, 2004.

Bullets over Hollywood, Starz!, 2005.

All*Star Cup, 2006.

Speechless, 2008.

Judge, *The 2010 Miss Universe Pageant,* NBC, 2010.

Television Appearances; Episodic:

Sonny Cappelito, "Bald Ambition," *Hill Street Blues,* NBC, 1986.

Sergeant Marcy, "The Court Martial: Parts 1 & 2," *Matlock,* NBC, 1987.

Frank, "He–e–ere's Papa!," *Dallas,* CBS, 1989.

Leslie, "Viva Las Vegas," *Valerie's Family* (also known as *The Hogan Family* and *Valerie*), NBC, 1989.

Peter Alatorre, "Sins of the Father," *Wiseguy,* CBS, 1989.

Peter Alatorre, "Heir to the Throne," *Wiseguy,* CBS, 1989.

Sal Roselli, "How Will They Remember Me?," *Wiseguy,* CBS, 1989.

Tommy Esposito, "Pursued," *The Fanelli Boys,* NBC, 1990.

Tony, "Love Ya, Babe," *Sydney,* CBS, 1990.

The Chevy Chase Show, 1993.

Lo + plus, 1996.

Voice of Leonardo da Vinci, "Art," *Dilbert* (animated), UPN, 1999.

"Rod Steiger," *Bravo Profiles,* Bravo, 2001.

Darrell "Duke" Walcott, "Lust for Life," *Dr. Vegas,* USA Network, 2004.

Captain Frank McNeil, "Kind of Blue," *Kojak,* USA Network, 2005.

Captain Frank McNeil, "Music of the Night," *Kojak,* USA Network, 2005.

Captain Frank McNeil, "All Bets Off: Parts 1 & 2," *Kojak,* USA Network, 2005.

Shorty, "Fifteen Percent," *Modern Family,* ABC, 2010.

Frank Rizzoli, Sr., "Boston Strangler Redux," *Rizzoli & Isles,* TNT, 2010.

Frank Rizzoli, Sr., "Born to Run," *Rizzoli & Isles,* TNT, 2010.

Frank Rizzoli, Sr., "The Beast in Me," *Rizzoli & Isles,* TNT, 2010.

Frank Rizzoli, Sr., "When the Gun Goes Bang, Bang, Bang," *Rizzoli & Isles,* TNT, 2010.

Celebrity Ghost Stories, Biography Channel, 2010.

Television Talk Show Guest Appearances; Episodic:

The Tonight Show with Jay Leno, NBC, 1993, 2008.

The Late Show with David Letterman (also known as *The Late Show* and *Letterman*), CBS, 1995.

The Rosie O'Donnell Show, syndicated, 1999.

Late Night with Conan O'Brien, NBC, multiple appearances, between 2003 and 2008.

Last Call with Carson Daly, NBC, 2005.

The Tony Danza Show, syndicated, 2006.

The Late Late Show with Craig Ferguson, CBS, 2006.

Tavis Smiley, PBS, 2008.

Shootout (also known as *Hollywood Shootout* and *Sunday Morning Shootout*), 2008.

Television Appearances; Awards Presentations:

Presenter, *The Blockbuster Entertainment Awards,* CBS, 1995.

Presenter, *The 1995 MTV Movie Awards,* MTV, 1995.

The 67th Academy Awards Presentation, ABC, 1995.

The Third Annual Vibe Awards on UPN, UPN, 2005.

Presenter, *50 premios Sant Jordi de cinematografia,* 2006.

Television Appearances; Pilots:

Captain Frank McNeil, *Kojak,* USA Network, 2005.

Television Director; Movies:

Women vs. Men (also known as *Oooph!*), Showtime, c. 2001.

Television Director; Episodic:

"Unnatural Disasters," *Oz,* HBO, 1999.

Stage Appearances:

Randy, *22 Years,* Stage 73, New York City, 1971–72.

The Guys in the Truck (some sources cite title as *The Guy in the Truck*), 1982, then Broadway production, 1983.

Mr. Connolly, Mr. Papp, Rodney, and Mountain, *The Flatbush Faithful,* Judith Anderson Theatre, New York City, 1985.

A Bronx Tale (solo show), Ensemble Theatre, Los Angeles, 1988, then Playhouse 91, New York City, 1989.

The Resistible Rise of Arturo Ui, National Actors Theatre, Michael Schimmel Center for the Arts, Pace University, New York City, 2002.

A Bronx Tale (solo show; revised and expanded version), Walter Kerr Theatre, New York City, 2007–2008.

Also appeared in productions of *Faithful* and *The Kings Men.*

Major Tours:

A Bronx Tale (solo show), U.S. cities, c. 2008.

RECORDINGS

Videos:

The Making of "Lady and the Tramp II:" From Tramp to Scamp, 2001.

Keyser Soeze: Lie or Legend?, Metro–Goldwyn–Mayer Home Entertainment, 2002.

Round Up: Deposing "The Usual Suspects," 2002.

In the Mix: 25 Days and Not a Minute More, Lions Gate Films Home Entertainment, 2006.

Running Scared: Through the Looking Glass, Media 8 Entertainment, 2006.

WRITINGS

Screenplays:

A Bronx Tale (solo show; based on his stage play), Savoy Pictures, 1993.

Faithful (based on his stage play), New Line Cinema, 1996.

Stage Plays:

Faithful, c. 1985.

A Bronx Tale (solo show), Ensemble Theatre, Los Angeles, 1988, then Playhouse 91, New York City, 1989, revised and expanded version, Walter Kerr Theatre, New York City, 2007–2008.

OTHER SOURCES

Periodicals:

Boston Globe, May 14, 1995, p. 41.

Cosmopolitan, January, 1995, p. 98.

Entertainment Weekly, October 15, 1993, pp. 19–20.

Interview, November, 1994, p. 22.

Los Angeles Times, May 18, 1989, p. 13.

New York, September 11, 1995, p. 50.

New York Times, September 13, 1993, pp. C13–C14; July 9, 1995, p. C11.

People Weekly, January 18, 1999, p. 87; January 28, 2002, p. 81.

Playboy, April, 1999, p. 117.

PARKER, Tom 1977–
(Thomas Scott Parker)

PERSONAL

Born July 23, 1977, in Walnut Creek, CA. *Education:* Carnegie Mellon University, B.F.A., 1999. *Avocational Interests:* Travel, world cultures.

Addresses: *Agent*—David Rose, Innovative Artists Talent and Literary Agency, 1505 10th St., Santa Monica, CA 90401; (advertisements) Beverly Kline, Independent Artists Agency, 9601 Wilshire Blvd., Suite 750, Beverly Hills, CA, 90210–5213. *Manager*—Steven Levy, Framework Entertainment, 9057 Nemo St., Suite C, Los Angeles, CA 90069–5511.

Career: Actor. Worked as a travel writer and photographer, with artwork in exhibitions.

Member: Screen Actors Guild, American Federation of Television and Radio Artists, Actors' Equity Association.

Awards, Honors: John Arthur Kennedy Acting Award for undergraduate excellence in acting or music theatre, Carnegie Mellon University.

CREDITS

Television Appearances; Series:
Host and travel journalist, *5 Takes: Latin America* (also known as *5 Takes*), Travel Channel, 2007.

Television Appearances; Movies:
Robert, *Partner(s),* Lifetime, 2005.

Jackson Sumner, *McBride: Requiem,* Hallmark Channel, 2006.

Young Johnny, *Desperation* (also known as *Desolation* and *Stephen King's "Desperation"*), ABC, 2006.

Television Appearances; Episodic:
Carter, "Surprise Party," *North Shore,* Fox, 2004.

Dr. Riley, "Split Ends," *What I Like about You,* The WB, 2004.

Matt Gillespie, "NICU," *ER* (also known as *Emergency Room* and *E.R.*), NBC, 2004.

Rick Adams, "Dead Ringer," *CSI: Crime Scene Investigation* (also known as *C.S.I., CSI, CSI: Las Vegas, CSI: Weekends,* and *Les experts*), CBS, 2004.

Brian Hartman, "Acceptance," *Everwood* (also known as *Our New Life in Everwood*), The WB, 2005.

Brian Hartman, "Getting to Know You," *Everwood* (also known as *Our New Life in Everwood*), The WB, 2005.

Todd Kipling, "More Than This," *Without a Trace* (also known as *Vanished* and *W.A.T.*), CBS, 2006.

Jamie, "What about … Finding Your Place (also known as "What about Finding Your Place … "), *What about Brian,* ABC, 2007.

Jamie, "What about … Marjorie" (also known as "What about Marjorie … "), *What about Brian,* ABC, 2007.

Jamie, "What about … Strange Bedfellows" (also known as "What about Strange Bedfellows … "), *What about Brian,* ABC, 2007.

Jamie, "What about … Temptations" (also known as "What about Temptations … "), *What about Brian,* ABC, 2007.

Jerry, "Whistleblower," *Eyes,* ABC, 2007.

Luke, "Karma," *Eyes,* ABC, 2007.

Grant Lawson, "Flight Risk," *CSI: Miami* (also known as *CSI Miami* and *CSI: Weekends*), CBS, 2009.

Liam McBride, "Roles of Engagement" (some sources cite episode title as "Rolls of Engagement"), *Mental,* Fox, 2009.

Allen Greenway, "Flag on the Play," *CSI: NY* (also known as *CSI: New York, CSI: New York 2, C.S.I. New York, C.S.I.: New York, C.S.I.: NY,* and *CSI: Weekends*), CBS, 2010.

Ryan, "Dog Fight," *'Til Death* (also known as *Eddie & Jeff*), Fox, 2010.

Tim, "Are You Romantic?," *100 Questions* (also known as *100 Questions for Charlotte Payne*), NBC, 2010.

Television Appearances; Pilots:
Plumb, *Traveling in Packs,* ABC, 2007.

Blair Wilson, *The More Things Change,* ABC, 2008.

Film Appearances:
Actor, *Happy End* (also known as *All the Way to the Top, I Want to Be Famous,* and *Nowhere to Go but Up*), Forensic Films, 2003.

(As Thomas Scott Parker) Billy, *Special Breakfast Eggroll: 99 Cents* (also known as *No Sure Thingz* and *The Sure Thing Effect*), 2003.

Michael Cattrall, *Cruel Intentions 3,* Columbia TriStar, 2004.

Reece, *Greener Mountain* (also known as *Inn Trouble*), 2005, Allumination Filmworks, 2008.

George Christensen, *J–ok'el* (also known as *Curse of the Weeping Woman: J–ok'el, Curse of the Weep-*

ing Woman: J'okel, and *J'okel*), Grupo Mercamedia, 2007, Maverick Entertainment Group, 2008.

Stage Appearances:

Romeo, *Romeo and Juliet,* Utah Shakespearean Festival, Cedar City, UT, 1998.

(As Thomas Scott Parker) Matt, *The Fantasticks* (musical), Utah Shakespearean Festival, 2001.

Sebastian, *Twelfth Night* (also known as *Twelfth Night, or What You Will*), Long Wharf Theatre, New Haven, CT, 2002.

Appeared in other productions of the Utah Shakespearean Festival, including appearances as Fortinbras, *Hamlet,* and as the boy, *Henry V.* Appeared in other productions, including appearances as Joe Hardy, *Damn Yankees* (musical), Riverside Theatre; as a member of the ensemble, *A Midsummer Night's Dream,* Tyrone Guthrie Theater, Minneapolis, MN; as Stephen, *Sorrows of Stephen,* Blue Heron Arts Center, New York City; and as Henry Lee Stafford, *Valhalla* (workshop production), New York Theatre Workshop, New York City. Appeared as soloist, *Hair* (musical), as Longaville, *Love's Labour's Lost,* as Ian, *Pre Paradise, Sorry Now,* and as Bobby Joe, *Welcome Home, Bobby Joe,* all Carnegie Mellon University.

WRITINGS

Teleplays; with Others; Episodic:

5 Takes: Latin America (also known as *5 Takes*), Travel Channel, 2007.

Writings for the Internet:

Author of material posted on *Big Welcome!,* http://www.bigwelcome.net.

Nonfiction:

Worked as a travel writer and photographer.

OTHER SOURCES

Electronic:

Big Welcome!, http://www.bigwelcome.net, September 28, 2010.

YouTube, http://www.youtube.com/user/tomparker230, September 29, 2010.

PATTERSON, Scott 1958–

PERSONAL

Full name, Scott Gordon Patterson; born September 11, 1958, in Philadelphia, PA; raised in Haddonfield, NJ, and Baltimore, MD; son of Frank (an advertising executive and former boxer) and Hope Patterson; married Vera Davich, 1983 (divorced, 1985). *Education:* Studied comparative literature at Rutgers University; attended community colleges in Florida and Arizona; trained at Actors' Studio, New York City, and with acting coaches Sondra Lee and Robert Lewis. *Avocational Interests:* Playing guitar, writing music, painting, skiing, and collecting art, artifacts, and rare writings.

Addresses: *Agent*—Independent Artists Agency, 9601 Wilshire Blvd., Suite 750, Beverly Hills, CA 90210. *Manager*—Laina Cohn Management, 15066 Sutton St., Sherman Oaks, CA 91403. *Publicist*—S/W PR Shop, 1000 North Clark Dr., #104, Los Angeles, CA 90048.

Career: Actor and stunt performer. The Complex, Hollywood, CA, teacher of acting classes; also appeared in commercials. Former professional baseball player (pitcher) in minor league teams affiliated with the Atlanta Braves, Los Angeles Dodgers, Texas Rangers, and New York Yankees, 1980–88. Also worked in construction and as a musician.

CREDITS

Film Appearances:

Al, *Intent to Kill,* PM Entertainment Group, 1993.

Mike McGrevey, *Little Big League,* Warner Home Video, 1994.

Scott's father, *Three Wishes,* Savoy Pictures, 1995.

California Highway Patrol officer, *A Boy Called Hate,* Dove, 1996.

Mark Bradley, *Highway 395,* 2000.

Gil, *Her Best Move,* Metro–Goldwyn–Mayer, 2007.

Agent Strahm, *Saw IV,* Lions Gate Films, 2007.

Agent Peter Strahm, *Saw V,* Lions Gate Films, 2008.

(Uncredited) Agent Peter Strahm, *Saw VI* (also known as *Saw 6*), Lions Gate Films, 2009.

George, *The Frankenstein Brothers,* 2010.

Film Work:

Stunt performer, *Blank Check* (also known as *Blank Cheque*), Buena Vista, 1994.

Television Appearances; Series:

Lucas "Luke" Danes, *Gilmore Girls* (also known as *Gilmore Girls: Beginnings*), The WB, 2000–2007.

Gary Tolochuck, *Aliens in America,* The CW, 2007–2008.

Michael Bucanan, *The Event,* NBC, 2010–11.

Television Appearances; Movies:

The Return of "Ironside," NBC, 1993.

Ahpossno, *Alien Nation: Dark Horizon,* Fox, 1994.

Simon Trent, *Them,* UPN, 1996.

Phil, *Rhapsody in Bloom,* Starz!, 1998.
Ben Sloane, *Concrete Canyons,* 2010.

Television Appearances; Specials:
The 4th Annual Family Television Awards, 2002.
"Gilmore Girls" Backstage Special, ABC Family, 2004.

Television Appearances; Pilots:
Lucas "Luke" Danes, *Gilmore Girls* (also known as *Gilmore Girls: Beginnings*), The WB, 2000.
Gary Tolochuck, *Aliens in America,* The CW, 2007.

Television Appearances; Episodic:
Billy, "The Sponge," *Seinfeld,* NBC, 1995.
Chick Chandler, "Pre–Judgement Day," *Silk Stalkings,* USA Network, 1996.
Mickey, "Where There's Smoke," *Fired Up,* NBC, 1997.
Dan Manville, "The Real Thing," *Arli$$,* HBO, 1997.
Mickey, "Fire and Nice," *Fired Up,* NBC, 1998.
Detective Thomas "Tom" Swain, "Justice," *Vengeance Unlimited,* ABC, 1998.
Detective Thomas "Tom" Swain, "Noir," *Vengeance Unlimited,* ABC, 1998.
Ted, "The Client," *It's Like, You Know ...,* ABC, 1999.
Jacob Perryhill, "Performance Anxiety," *Get Real,* Fox, 1999.
John Gregorio/Donald Dorio, "Das Boob," *Will & Grace,* NBC, 1999.
Carl, "Love Conquers Evil," *Good vs Evil,* 2000.
Hollywood Squares (also known as *H2* and *H2: Hollywood Squares*), syndicated, 2002.
Pyramid (also known as *The $100,000 Pyramid*), syndicated, 2002, 2003.
Voice of Agent King Faraday and Franco Bertinelli, "Double Date," *Justice League* (animated; also known as *JL* and *Justice League Unlimited*), Cartoon Network, 2005.
Voice of Agent King Faraday, "I Am Legion," *Justice League* (animated; also known as *JL* and *Justice League Unlimited*), Cartoon Network, 2005.
Voice of Agent King Faraday, "To Another Shore," *Justice League* (animated; also known as *JL* and *Justice League Unlimited*), Cartoon Network, 2005.
Up Close with Carrie Keagan, 2007.
Finnigan "Finn" Court, "Another, Another Chance," *90210,* The CW, 2010.
Finnigan "Finn" Court, "Multiple Choices," *90210,* The CW, 2010.
Finnigan "Finn" Court, "Meet the Parent," *90210,* The CW, 2010.

OTHER SOURCES

Periodicals:
New York Daily News, February 1, 2002.
People Weekly, January 28, 2002, pp. 121–22.
Soap Opera Weekly, January 8, 2002.

PETZEL, Christopher 1971–

PERSONAL

Full name, Christopher Joerg Daniel Petzel; born July 30, 1971, in Frankfurt, Germany.

Addresses: *Contact*—Clandestine Service, 7656 Sunset Blvd., Los Angeles, CA 90046. *Office*—Fierce Entertainment, 8306 Wilshire Blvd., Suite 904, Beverly Hills, CA 90211.

Career: Producer. Founder and CEO of Fierce Entertainment.

CREDITS

Film Producer:
The Unscarred, Arclight Films, 1999.
Man–Thing, Artisan, 2005.
War (also known as *Rogue Assassin*), Maple Pictures, 2007.

Film Executive Producer:
To Kill a King, Anchor Bay, 2003.
Carolina, Miramax, 2003.
Shadows in the Sun (also known as *The Shadow Dancer*), Elephant Films, 2005.
Good Old Fashioned Orgy, Fierce Entertainment, 2010.
The Hungry Rabbit Jumps, Ascot Elite Entertainment, 2010.

PODESTA, Patti

PERSONAL

Addresses: *Agent*—Paradigm, 360 N. Crescent Dr., North Bldg., Beverly Hills, CA 90210.

Career: Production designer.

Awards, Honors: Emmy Award nomination (with others), outstanding art direction for a miniseries or movie, 2008, Excellence in Production Design Award nomination (with others), television movie or miniseries, Art Directors Guild, 2009, both for *Recount.*

CREDITS

Film Production Designer:
Driven, Driven Productions Inc., 1996.
Nowhere, Fine Line, 1997.

Locust Valley, MTV Productions, 1999.
Swap Meet, 1999.
Operation Splitsville, Cineville, 1999.
Splendor, Samuel Goldwyn, 1999.
Angel's Dance, York Entertainment, 1999.
Memento, Columbia TriStar, 2000.
Scorched, Twentieth Century–Fox, 2003.
Spin, Universal Studios Home Video, 2003.
The Chumscrubber, Eagle Films, 2005.
Annapolis, Buena Vista, 2006.
Bobby, Metro–Goldwyn–Mayer, 2006.
Smart People, Miramax, 2008.
Tell Tale (also known as *Tell–Tale*), CTV International, 2009.
Love and Other Drugs, Twentieth Century–Fox, 2010.

Film Costume Designer:
Driven, Driven Productions Inc., 1996.

Film Work:
Assistant production designer, *A Dangerous Woman,* MCA/Universal Home Video, 1993.

Television Production Designer; Movies:
Recount (also known as *Recount: The Story of the 2000 Presidential Election*), HBO, 2008.
Until Proven Innocent, HBO, 2010.

Television Production Designer; Pilots:
This Is How the World Ends, MTV, 2000.
Andy Barker, P.I., NBC, 2007.

Television Production Designer; Series:
Kathy's So–Called Reality, MTV, 2001.
Spyder Games, MTV, 2001.

Television Appearances; Episodic:
Also appeared in "Momento," *Anatomy of a Scene,* Sundance Channel.

POSTLETHWAITE, Pete 1946–2011
(Peter Postlethwaite)

PERSONAL

Original name, Peter William Postlethwaite; born February 7, 1945 (some sources cite 1946), in Warrington, England; died of complications from pancreatic cancer, January 2, 2011, in Shropshire, England. Actor. Prolific British actor Postlethwaite was well known for his ability to play a diverse range of characters, from murderous villains to mild-mannered priests. He enjoyed a successful career as a stage and television actor in the United Kingdom in the 1970s, appearing in the series *Last of the Summer Wine, Going Straight,* and *Horse in the House* and performing at the Everyman Theater in Liverpool. After a stint with the Royal Shakespeare Company in the mid-1980s, Postlethwaite earned recognition as a film actor in the comedy *A Private Function* and the 1988 drama *Distant Voices, Still Lives.* These roles led to appearances in the hit films *Alien3, The Last of the Mohicans, The Usual Suspects, Romeo + Juliet, Jurassic Park,* and *Amistad* in the 1990s. Postlethwaite was nominated for an Oscar for his supporting performance in *In the Name of the Father,* in which he played the father of a young man falsely accused of bombing a pub during the Irish Troubles. His recent film credits include *on Flux, The Omen, Clash of the Titans, Inception,* and *The Town,* as well as recurring parts in the television series *The Sins* and *Criminal Justice.*

PERIODICALS

Guardian, January 3, 2011.
Los Angeles Times, January 4, 2011.
New York Times, January 3, 2011.
Telegraph, January 3, 2011.
Washington Post, January 3, 2011.

POTTS, Michael

PERSONAL

Education: Yale University, degree, drama.

Addresses: *Manager*—Blue Ridge Entertainment, 450 W. 17th St., Suite 318, New York, NY 10011.

Career: Actor.

Awards, Honors: Obie Award, outstanding performance, *Village Voice,* 1994, for *The America Play.*

CREDITS

Stage Appearances:
Brazil, *The America Play,* New York Shakespeare Festival, Joseph Papp Public Theatre, Martinson Hall, New York City, 1994.
Gratiano, *Overtime,* Manhattan Theatre Club Stage II, New York City, 1996.
David Bradley, *Mud, River, Stone,* Playwrights Horizons Theatre, New York City, 1997.

Sir Lucius O'Trigger, *The Rivals,* Adams Memorial Theatre, Williamstown Theatre Festival, Williamstown, MA, 1998.

Julius Snaith, *A Cup of Coffee,* Yale Repertory Theatre, New Haven, CT, 1999.

Nicola, *Arms and the Man,* Roundabout Theatre Company, Gramercy Theatre, New York City, 2000.

Ray and doctor, *Joe Fearless (A Fan Dance),* New York Performance Works, Atlantic Theatre, New York City, 2000.

Brooklyn Bridge (staged reading), National Arts Club, New York City, 2000.

Benvolio, *Romeo and Juliet,* Center Theatre Group, Ahmanson Theatre, Los Angeles, 2001.

Revivalist minister, *Salome* (staged reading), Falconworks Artists Group, New York City, 2001.

Rudy, *Once Around the City* (musical), Second Stage Theatre, New York City, 2001.

Feste, *Twelfth Night,* New York Shakespeare Festival, Delacorte Theatre, New York City, 2002.

"Golden Boy," *Encores!,* City Center Theatre, New York City, 2002.

"Haiti," *Brave New World: American Theatre Responds to 9/11,* Town Hall Theatre, New York City, 2002.

Counselor to the king, *The Persians,* National Actors Theatre, Michael Schimmel Center for the Arts, New York City, 2003.

Member of ensemble, *Highway Ulysses,* American Repertory Theatre Company, Loeb Drama Center, Cambridge, MA, 2003.

Kreon/messenger, *Oedipus,* American Repertory Theatre Company, Loeb Drama Center, 2004.

The Mysteries, East 13th Street, Classic Stage Company Theatre, New York City, 2004.

John Lennon, *Lennon,* Orpheum Theatre, San Francisco, CA, 2005.

Brooks Sr./Brooks Jr., *Grey Garden's,* Playwrights Horizons Theatre, 2006.

Duke of Buckingham, *Richard III,* East 13th Street, Classic Stage Company Theatre, 2007.

Alonso, *The Tempest,* East 13th Street, Classic Stage Company Theatre, 2008.

Homer/Priam, *The Age of Iron,* East 13th Street, Classic Stage Company Theatre, 2009.

Appeared in *Jocasta,* Voice and Vision Company, New York City; appeared in New York City productions of *The 52nd Street Project, Playboy of the West Indies,* and *Rent;* appeared in regional productions of *The Hostage, Love's Labour's Lost, Othello,* and *Randy Newman's Faust;* also appeared in *The Death of the Last Black Man in the Whole Entire World* and *St. Joan of the Stockyards.*

Film Appearances:

Bill, *Halloween Night* (also known as *The Damning, Death Mask,* and *Hack–o–Lantern*), Atlantic Video, 1990.

Tow truck driver, *Hackers,* Metro–Goldwyn–Mayer/United Artists, 1995.

First DOE technician, *The Peacemaker,* DreamWorks, 1997.

Justice guard, *Conspiracy Theory,* Warner Bros., 1997.

Black People Hate Me and They Hate My Glasses (short film), 2000.

South Shell pot buyer, *Diggers,* Magnolia Pictures, 2006.

Oedipus, *Jocasta,* Ishtar Records, 2008.

Also appeared in *George: A True Story* and *Stonewall.*

Television Appearances; Series:
Brother Mouzone, *The Wire,* HBO, 2003–2004.

Television Appearances; Episodic:
Mel, "Yes, We Have NO Cannolis," *NYPD Blue,* ABC, 1996.

Reggie Dobbs, "Entrapment," *Law & Order,* NBC, 1997.

Detective Jackson, "No Secrets," *Trinity,* NBC, 1998.

Floyd, "The Wedding," *Cosby,* CBS, 1999.

Reinhardt, "Medium Rare," *Oz,* HBO, 2001.

"The Eyes Have It," *Queens Supreme,* CBS, 2004.

Dr. Bertand, "Three Boys and a Gun," *The Jury,* Fox, 2004.

Lester Wilkes, "New York Minute," *Law & Order,* NBC, 2005.

Malcolm Young, "Captive," *Law & Order,* NBC, 2007.

"Grey Gardens: From East Hampton to Broadway," *Independent Lens,* PBS, 2007.

Nigel Saladu, "A New Cup," *The Flight of the Conchords* (also known as *Flight of the Conchords*), HBO, 2009.

Yusef, "The Alanon Case," *Bored to Death,* HBO, 2009.

Horatio Emanuel, "You Haven't Replaced Me," *Damages,* FX Network, 2010.

Horatio Emanuel, "All That Crap about Your Family," *Damages,* FX Network, 2010.

Stokes's attorney, "Four Cops Shot," *Law & Order,* NBC, 2010.

Also appeared in *As the World Turns,* CBS; *Comic Strip Live,* Fox; and *One Life to Live,* ABC.

Television Appearances; Miniseries:
Voice, *The West,* PBS, 1996.

Television Appearances; Specials:
Voice of Isaac, *Thomas Jefferson,* PBS, 1997.

RECORDINGS

Video Games:
Cyrus, *The Warriors,* Rockstar Games, 2005.

PRESSMAN, David 1965–

PERSONAL

Born November 6, 1965, in New York, NY; son of Lawrence Pressman (an actor) and Lanna Saunders (an actress).

Addresses: *Agent*—Pakula, King and Associates, 9229 West Sunset Blvd., Suite 315, Los Angeles, CA 90069.

Career: Actor.

CREDITS

Film Appearances:
Boy with envelope, *Paradise Motel,* Saturn International, 1984.
Kid at grocery store, *Black Moon Rising,* 1986.
Carlton, *Pyrates,* Vestron Video, 1991.
Old man, *Teenage Mutant Ninja Turtles II: The Secret of Ooze,* New Line Cinema, 1991.
Hospital prison ward guard, *The Rocketeer,* Walt Disney, 1991.
First gambler, *Father Hood,* Walt Disney Studios, 1993.
Assistant lieutenant, *Stargate* (also known as *Stargate, la porte des etoiles*), Metro–Goldwyn–Mayer, 1994.
Alex, *Independence Day* (also known as *ID4*), Twentieth Century–Fox, 1996.
Second protester, *Volcano,* Twentieth Century–Fox, 1997.
Anchorage captain, *Godzilla,* TriStar, 1998.
Kat and Allison, 2000.
Brian, *Lip Service,* Artist View Entertainment, 2001.
Maori tribesman, *Zoolander,* Paramount, 2001.
Assistant director, *Gigli,* Columbia, 2003.
Poker player, *Nobody's Perfect* (short film), 2004.
Terence Meyers, *Starsky & Hutch,* Warner Bros., 2004.
Reporter in Montreal, *Blades of Glory,* Paramount, 2007.
Melvin "Murph Murph" Murphy, *The Grand,* Anchor Bay, 2007.
First assistant director—Vietnam crew, *Tropic Thunder,* Paramount, 2008.
Doctor number one, *Little Fockers,* Paramount, 2010.

Television Appearances; Series:
Mr. Rusnak, *Newhart,* 1989–1990.
Coozman, *Imagine That,* NBC, 2002.

Television Appearances; Movies:
Sacrificial lamb, *Police Story: The Freeway Killings,* NBC, 1987.

Officer Gilbert, *Merry Christmas, Drake & Josh,* Nickelodeon, 2008.
Keith, *No Heroics,* 2009.

Television Appearances; Episodic:
Roy, "Take My Ex–Wife Please," *Eisenhower & Lutz,* CBS, 1988.
Teenager, "The Whiplash Kid Returns: Part 1," *Eisenhower & Lutz,* CBS, 1988.
Fraternity boy, "Animal Frat—October 19, 1967," *Quantum Leap,* NBC, 1990.
Mr. Miller, "The Christmas Mystery," *Father Dowling Mysteries,* ABC, 1990.
Tino, "Love Ya, Babe," *Sydney,* CBS, 1990.
Waiter, "Rose Loves Miles" (also known as "Ro$e Love$ Mile$"), *The Golden Girls,* NBC, 1991.
Larry, "Once I Had a Little Secret," *Dear John,* 1991.
Second guy, "Kids," *Blossom,* NBC, 1992.
Gasmer, "The Good, the Bad, and the Pharmacist," *Grace under Fire* (also known as *Grace under Pressure*), ABC, 1993.
Michael Walker, "And the Heat Goes On," *The John Larroquette Show,* NBC, 1995.
Recording engineer, "Attraction," *The Single Guy,* NBC, 1995.
Mike, "Kelly's Gotta Habit," *Married ... with Children,* Fox, 1996.
Nino, "Lockdown," *Malcolm & Eddie,* UPN, 1997.
Recruiter, "Romeo and Julie," *Working,* NBC, 1999.
Tony, "The Royal Flush," *Unhappily Ever After,* The WB, 1999.
Sailor, *The Amanda Show,* 2000.
David, *The Amanda Show,* 2000.
Ed Miller, "Witches in Tights," *Charmed,* The WB, 2002.
Ed Miller, "Crimes & Witch Demeanors," *Charmed,* The WB, 2002.
Elliot Sperling, "Lullaby," *Judging Amy,* 2004.
Mickey, "My Unicorn," *Scrubs* (also known as *Scrubs: Med School*), 2004.
James Cameron's assistant, "The Bat Mitzvah," *Entourage,* HBO, 2005.
Insurance adjuster, "Lude Awakening," *Weeds,* 2005.
Walsh, " ... 1 ...," *Alias,* ABC, 2005.
Walsh, "The Shed," *Alias,* ABC, 2005.
Walsh, "Mockingbird," *Alias,* ABC, 2005.
Marty, "Mr. Monk Goes to the Dentist," *Monk,* 2006.
Mexican Freddy, "Baseball Myths," *My Boys,* 2006.
Mexican Freddy, "Opportunity Knocks," *My Boys,* 2006.
Voice of shovin' buddy, "Peters Progress," *Family Guy* (animated; also known as *Padre de familia*), Fox, 2009.
Mexican Freddy, "Addition by Subtraction," *My Boys,* 2010.
Daniel Arkin, "Final Curtain," *Hawthorne,* TNT, 2010.

Television Appearances; Pilots:
Sam Durkin, Jr., *FM,* NBC, 1989.
Carl, *Girl's Best Friend,* CBS, 1994.

Elliot Tanny (some sources spell name Tenney), *Can't Hurry Love,* CBS, 1995.

Jonathan, *World on a String,* Fox, 1997.

Fuddy's coworker, *What's Up, Peter Fuddy?,* Fox, 2001.

RECORDINGS

Videos:

(In archive footage) Alex, *Independence Day: The ID4 Invasion,* 1996.

Playboy: Hef's Halloween Spooktacular (documentary), 2005.

PRIKRYL, Sarah 1977–

PERSONAL

Born August 4, 1977, in Austin, TX. *Education:* University of St. Thomas, B.A. (cum laude), drama and communications; studied acting at the Sharon Chatten Studio; studied photography at the Glassell School of Art.

Addresses: *Agent*—Circle Talent Associates, 520 Broadway, Suite 350, Santa Monica, CA 90401.

Career: Actress. Participated in college acting competitions. Performed voice work. Worked as a model. Operator of Incito Photography, an independent photography studio, and contributed photographs to periodicals.

Member: Screen Actors Guild, Actors' Equity Association.

Awards, Honors: Named outstanding communications graduate, University of St. Thomas; member of a number of college honor societies, including Alpha Psi Omega (national honorary theatre society, president of chapter).

CREDITS

Stage Appearances:

Fairy, *A Midsummer Night's Dream,* Alley Theatre, Large Stage, Houston, TX, c. 2000.

Madame Darbel, *Eating Crow,* Main Street Theatre, Houston, c. 2000–2001.

Fran Briggs, *House,* Alley Theatre, Large Stage [and] *Garden,* Alley Theatre, Neuhaus Arena Stage, Houston, both plays staged simultaneously, 2002.

Helen Trent, *The 13th Chair* (also known as *The Thirteenth Chair*), Alley Theatre, Houston, 2002.

Sandra, *One Flew over the Cuckoo's Nest,* Alley Theatre, 2002.

Ghost of Christmas Past, *A Christmas Carol,* Alley Theatre, 2002, 2004.

Ghost of Christmas Past and Mrs. O'Mally, *A Christmas Carol,* Alley Theatre, 2003.

Hero, *Much Ado about Nothing,* Houston Shakespeare Festival, University of Houston, School of Theatre & Dance, Houston, 2003.

Perdita, *A Winter's Tale,* Houston Shakespeare Festival, University of Houston, School of Theatre & Dance, 2003.

Player queen, *Hamlet,* Alley Theatre, 2003.

Traveler, *The Trip to Bountiful,* Alley Theatre, 2003.

Hermione, *A Winter's Tale,* Will & Company, Ricardo Montalban Theatre, Hollywood, CA, c. 2006.

Portia, *The Merchant of Venice,* Will & Company, Ricardo Montalban Theatre, c. 2006.

Appeared in other productions, including an appearance as Jo March, *Little Women,* and as Hippolyta, *A Midsummer Night's Dream,* both Main Street Theatre; as Annie, *All My Sons;* as Shirley, *Lady Be Good* (musical); as Lady Macduff and a witch, *Macbeth,* Los Angeles Theatre Center, Los Angeles; as Pavane, *New York Minutes;* as Estelle Rigault, *No Exit;* as Athena and a member of the ensemble, *The Odyssey,* Geffen Playhouse, Los Angeles; as Shelby, *Steel Magnolias;* and as Dawn, *The Universal Language.* Member of the Alley Theatre; associate artist of Will & Company.

Major Tours:

Toured in *Faces of America* (solo show), Will & Company, U.S. cities.

Film Appearances:

Lead role, *Culture of Silence* (short film), National Education Institute, 2001.

IKYLM: The Shannon Douglas Story (also known as *I Know You Love Me: The Who Is Shannon Douglas Story* and *Shannon Douglas Story*), Robertson Street Productions, c. 2004.

Beauty, *My Demon Within,* Demon Partners, 2005.

Josie, *TV Face,* Bloodstream Media, 2007.

Susan, *11 Minutes Ago,* Cinetic Rights Management/Fly High Films, 2007.

The blind girl, *Spiderfly* (short film; also known as *SpiderFly*), Little Gorilla Films, 2008.

Deborah, *The Sit Down* (short film), Hollywood Fightclub Productions, 2008.

Korean Czech woman, *An Urgent Announcement from the GCPFRC* (short film), Out of Exile Films, 2008.

Emergency room nurse, *Stellina Blue,* Panorama Entertainment, 2009.

Dorothy Stewart, *The Damage Done* (short film), Rainfall Films, 2010.

Jen McKenzie, *Playing House,* UV Lite Productions, 2010.

Jessica, *Sails Men* (short film), 2010.

Sara, *Goodbye Promise,* Glimpse of Dreams Studios, 2010.

Paracusia (short film), OCD Films, 2010.

Appeared in other films, including *The Angst Bunny,* Y–Guys Productions; *Arrival at Esgaroth,* Rainfall Films; *Madison High,* Force Majeure Productions; and *Mr. Snow* (also known as *Mister Snow*), Camday Entertainment.

Film Work:
Coproducer, *Ten Seconds to Midnight* (short film), Elevate Films, 2007.

Television Appearances; Series:
Host of *Animal Talk,* HCC–TV.

Television Appearances; Episodic:
(Uncredited) Janet, "Halloween," *Freddie,* ABC, 2005.

(Uncredited) Tiffany Jordon, "Bikini Wax," *Navy NCIS: Naval Criminal Investigative Service* (also known as *Naval CIS, Navy CIS, Navy NCIS, NCIS,* and *NCIS: Naval Criminal Investigative Service*), CBS, 2005.

(Uncredited) Young Katya, "Ice," *Alias,* ABC, 2005.

Television Appearances; Pilots:
Rick's Place, c. 2008.

Also appeared in *Forever Winter.*

Internet Appearances:
Company member, *The Showcase,* posted on the web page associated with the Third Coast Theatre, at http://www.thirdcoasttheatre.com, c. 2007.

Exodus 3 (animated webisode pilot), c. 2008.

WRITINGS

Screenplays:
Wrote screenplays.

OTHER SOURCES

Electronic:
Sarah Prikryl, http://www.sarahprikryl.com, August 25, 2010.

PROBST, Nicholas
See **PRYOR, Nicholas**

PRYOR, Nicholas 1935–
(Nicholas Probst)

PERSONAL

Original name, Nicholas David Probst; born January 28, 1935, in Baltimore, MD; son of J. Stanley (a pharmaceutical manufacturer) and Dorothy (maiden name, Driskill) Probst; married Joan Epstein (an actress), December 21, 1958 (divorced, 1968); married Melinda Plank (an actress and dancer), February 27, 1968 (divorced); married Pamela (divorced); married Christina Belford, 1993 (divorced); children: (third marriage) Stacey. *Education:* Yale University, B.A., drama, 1956.

Addresses: *Contact*—SBD Partners, 1801 Avenue of the Stars, Suite 902, Los Angeles, CA 90067.

Career: Actor. Worked as a cabinet maker and inventor; developed and patented an accessory that improves the usefulness and storage capacity of household closets.

Member: Actors' Equity Association, American Federation of Television and Radio Artists, Screen Actors Guild, Writers Guild of America East.

Awards, Honors: National scholar, Oregon Shakespeare Festival, 1953; RCA–NBC acting scholar, Yale University, 1955–56.

CREDITS

Television Appearances; Series:
Ernest Cooper, *Young Dr. Malone,* NBC, 1959.

Rex Stern, *The Brighter Day,* CBS, c. 1960–61.

Johnny Ellis, *The Secret Storm,* CBS, 1962–63.

Search for Tomorrow, CBS, 1963.

As the World Turns, 1965.

Ken Cora (some sources cite Ken Alexander), *The Nurses,* ABC, 1965–67.

Paul Bradley, *Love Is a Many Splendored Thing,* CBS, 1967.

Lincoln "Linc" Tyler III, *All My Children,* ABC, 1971–72.

Joel Gantry, *The Edge of Night,* CBS, 1973–74 and 1981–82.

John Quincy Adams II, *The Adams Chronicles,* PBS, 1975–76.

Jeffrey Trout, a recurring role, *Eight Is Enough,* 1979–81.

Jack Felspar, *The Bronx Zoo,* NBC, 1986.

Chancellor Milton Arnold, a recurring role, *Beverly Hills, 90210,* Fox, 1993–97.

Victor Collins, *Port Charles,* ABC, 1997–2003.

Victor Collins, *General Hospital,* 1997.

Television Appearances; Miniseries:

John Quincy Adams II, *The Adams Chronicles,* 1976.

Hank Ferris, *Washington: Behind Closed Doors,* ABC, 1977.

James Grew, *East of Eden* (also known as *John Steinbeck's "East of Eden"*), ABC, 1981.

Noble House (also known as *James Clavell's "Noble House"*), 1988.

Bert Yeager, *Ruby Ridge: An American Tragedy* (also known as *Every Knee Shall Bow: The Siege at Ruby Ridge* and *The Siege at Ruby Ridge*), CBS, 1996.

Gerry Uelman, *American Tragedy,* CBS, 2000.

Television Appearances; Movies:

David, *Summer of Decision,* 1959.

Art Beresford, *Fear on Trial,* CBS, 1975.

James T. O'Neil, *Force Five* (also known as *Final Tactic*), CBS, 1975.

Mack, *Widow,* NBC, 1976.

Manners, *The Life and Assassination of the Kingfish* (also known as *Every Man a King*), NBC, 1977.

Man in a sports car, *Night Terror,* NBC, 1977.

Jeff Kramer, *Having Babies II,* ABC, 1977.

Ellsworth, *Martinelli, Outside Man,* 1977.

Bill Gilmore, *Rainbow,* NBC, 1978.

Dick Owens, *Reunion,* CBS, 1980.

Dave Gildea, *The Plutonium Incident,* CBS, 1980.

Larry Wax, *Marriage Is Alive and Well,* NBC, 1980.

Ryan, *The Last Song,* CBS, 1980.

Jacob, *Gideon's Trumpet,* CBS, 1980.

Ed Lissik, *The $5.20 an Hour Dream,* CBS, 1980.

Ralph Dortlund, *Desperate Voyage,* CBS, 1980.

Ed Lissick, *The $5.20 an Hour Dream,* 1980.

Elwin Potter, *A Few Days in Weasel Creek,* CBS, 1981.

Dr. Judd, *Splendor in the Grass,* NBC, 1981.

Greg Baker, Sr., *The Kid from Nowhere,* NBC, 1982.

John Cye Cheasty, *Blood Feud,* syndicated, 1983.

Dr. Thompson, *Amazons,* ABC, 1984.

Mitchell McKay, *Second Sight: A Love Story,* CBS, 1984.

Larry Walker, *Into Thin Air,* CBS, 1985.

Freddie Dayton, *Murder in Three Acts* (also known as *Agatha Christie's "Murder in Three Acts"*), CBS, 1986.

Richard Baxter, *A Stoning in Fulham County* (also known as *The Amish Story, Incident at Tile Mill Road,* and *The Stoning*), NBC, 1988.

Mr. Exeter, *The Diamond Trap* (also known as *The Great Diamond Robbery*), CBS, 1988.

Colonel William Devereaux, *Nightbreaker* (also known as *Advance to Ground Zero*), TNT, 1989.

Gordon Padway, *The Hit Man,* 1991.

Majority Rule, Lifetime, 1992.

Philip Carlyle, *Love Can Be Murder* (also known as *Kindred Spirits*), NBC, 1992.

Judge Lamartine, *Murder Between Friends,* NBC, 1994.

Don Barnett, *Trial by Fire,* ABC, 1995.

Paul Coster, *Cagney & Lacey: Together Again,* CBS, 1995.

Paul Cleary, *Broken Trust* (also known as *Court of Honor*), TNT, 1995.

Perry Davies, *Betrayed: A Story of Three Women,* ABC, 1995.

Ralph Gilchrist, *A Walton Wedding,* CBS, 1995.

Frank Sanborn, *Carriers* (also known as *Virus X—Die toedliche falle*), CBS, 1998.

Walter Burkett, *Without Warning* (also known as *Diagnosis Murder: Without Warning*), CBS, 2002.

Stuart Janney, *Ruffian,* ABC, 2007.

Television Appearances; Episodic:

Kraft Television Theatre, NBC, 1955.

The U.S. Steel Hour, CBS, 1958.

Omnibus, ABC, 1958.

Dave McComber, "Ah, Wilderness," *Hallmark Hall of Fame,* NBC, 1959.

The DuPont Show of the Month, NBC, 1960.

Robert, "Dear Arthur," *Ford Startime,* NBC, 1960.

Dane Ross, "The Changing Heart," *Alfred Hitchcock Presents,* NBC, 1961.

Tom Baxter, premiere episode, *Another World* (also known as *Another World: Bay City*), NBC, 1964.

The guard, "Faces," *Coronet Blue,* 1967.

"A Little Shuck and a Whole Lotta Jive," *Kaz,* 1978.

Clint Reilly, "Passport to Murder," *Hart to Hart,* ABC, 1979.

Al Mitchell, "Kids," *Lou Grant,* 1979.

Jacob, "Gideon's Trumpet," *Hallmark Hall of Fame,* NBC, 1980.

Major Nathaniel Burnham, "Rumor at the Top," *M*A*S*H,* CBS, 1981.

"Brain Child," *Trapper John, M.D.,* 1981.

"A Time of Peril," *McClain's Law,* 1981.

Horace Simmons, "The Late Sarah White," *Tales of the Gold Monkey,* ABC, 1982.

Royal Wilder, "Times Are Changing: Parts 1 & 2," *Little House on the Prairie* (also known as *Little House: A New Beginning*), NBC, 1982.

Victor Farrell, "Double Entry," *Simon & Simon,* 1982.

Dr. Braft, "Matthew Star D.O.A.," *The Powers of Matthew Star,* 1983.

Franklin Delano Roosevelt, "Destiny's Choice," *Voyagers!,* 1983.

"Dutton's Choice," *Insight,* 1983.

Dr. Miller, "The Hospital," *Silver Spoons,* 1983.

Norman MacClafferty, "Golden Opportunity," *Cover Up,* 1984.

Harry Parmel, "Capitol Offense," *Murder, She Wrote,* CBS, 1985.

Mr. Ardrey, "The Life and Time of Dominic Florio, Jr.," *Hill Street Blues,* NBC, 1985.

Vince, "Many Happy Returns," *Knight Rider,* NBC, 1985.

Nathan Billings, "The Ewing Connection," *Dallas,* CBS, 1985.

Nathan Billings, "Sentences," *Dallas,* CBS, 1985.

Nathan Billings, "The Verdict," *Dallas,* CBS, 1985.

Dr. Maurice Boland, "The Californians," *Dynasty,* 1985.

Howard McBride, "Does Not Compute," *Riptide,* 1985.

Dr. Maurice Boland, "Moment of Truth," *The Colbys,* 1985.

Mr. Conner, "Free Advice," *The Paper Chase,* 1985.

Ryan, "Four O'Clock," *Alfred Hitchcock Presents,* NBC, 1986.

Prison doctor, "Cheek to Cheek," *St. Elsewhere,* NBC, 1986.

Dr. Fetlock, "One for the Books," *Amazing Stories,* 1986.

Scott Cunningham, "My Dad's Bigger Than Yours," *Sidekicks,* 1986.

Ben Crawley, "When the Bough Breaks," *Falcon Crest,* CBS, 1987.

The Tonight Show Starring Johnny Carson, NBC, 1987.

Jary Mallot, "First Love," *Rags to Riches,* 1987.

Professor Darnell, "My Fair Tony," *Who's the Boss?,* 1988.

Dr. Simon Brill, "Plastic Fantastic Lovers," *Moonlighting,* ABC, 1989.

Porter, "Conflict of Interest," *Mancuso, FBI,* 1989.

Zach Bennett, "The Perfume Game," *227,* 1989.

Mr. Prescott, "Breaking in Is Hard to Do," *Sugar and Spice,* 1990.

Ray Albertson, "The Hawkins Family," *Lifestories,* 1990.

David Kingston, "O'Malley's Luck," *Murder, She Wrote,* CBS, 1990.

Theo Cayle, "The Committee," *Murder, She Wrote,* CBS, 1991.

Dr. Frankovich, "Like Father, Like Son," *Growing Pains,* 1991.

"The Amazing Lassie," *The New Lassie,* 1991.

Dr. Birch, "There Goes the Judge," *L.A. Law,* NBC, 1991.

Dr. Birch, "Monkey on My Back Lot," *L.A. Law,* NBC, 1991.

Dr. Birch, "P.S. Your Shrink Is Dead," *L.A. Law,* NBC, 1992.

Jack, "Tippecanoe and Georgie, Too!," *Sisters,* NBC, 1992.

Mr. Simpson, *Jack's Place,* ABC, 1992.

Moriarty, *Picket Fences,* CBS, 1993.

Doctor, *The Mommies,* NBC, 1993.

George Lazlo, *Jack's Place,* ABC, 1993.

Dr. Paul Dodge, "The Obsession," *Matlock,* ABC, 1993.

Senator George Stewart, "The Washington Affair: Parts 1 & 2," *Dr. Quinn, Medicine Woman,* CBS, 1994.

Dr. Harold Halpern, *Chicago Hope,* CBS, 1994.

David Robinson, "System Down," *Picket Fences,* CBS, 1994.

Board member, "Growth Pains," *Chicago Hope,* CBS, 1995.

Phil, "The Spider Webb," *Nowhere Man,* UPN, 1995.

Alvin Felton, "Miracle," *Live Shot,* UPN, 1995.

Eugene "Gene" Bennett, "Analogies," *Party of Five,* Fox, 1995.

Eugene "Gene" Bennett, "The Wedding," *Party of Five,* Fox, 1995.

Dr. Raymond Huxley, "A History of Murder," *Diagnosis Murder,* CBS, 1996.

Eugene "Gene" Bennett, "Going Home," *Party of Five,* Fox, 1996.

Eugene "Gene" Bennett, "Don't Let Go," *Party of Five,* Fox, 1996.

Joe Hockhowser, "Buried in Peace," *The Cape,* 1996.

Dr. Kloves, "The Pursuit of Dignity," *The Practice,* ABC, 1998.

Dr. Llewellyn Young, "The Crash," *Gideon's Crossing,* ABC, 2001.

Bart Shell, "Paternity," *The Guardian,* CBS, 2001.

Special Prosecutor Clement Rollins, "Ways and Means," *The West Wing,* NBC, 2001.

Father Tom, "Bad Chemistry," *That's Life,* ABC, 2001.

"Admissions," *Strong Medicine,* Lifetime, 2002.

John Colohan, "Meet the Grandparents," *NYPD Blue,* ABC, 2003.

John Colohan, "Maybe Baby," *NYPD Blue,* ABC, 2003.

John Colohan, "Yo, Adrian," *NYPD Blue,* ABC, 2003.

Wild Card, Lifetime, 2003.

"Revelations," *Without a Trace* (also known as *W.A.T*), CBS, 2003.

Joel's father, "Sexiest Movie Moments," *20 to 1,* Nine Network, 2007.

Television Appearances; Pilots:

Ellsworth, *The Outside Man,* CBS, 1977.

Harry Featherstone, *Revenge of the Gray Gang,* NBC, 1981.

Scott Thomas, *Homeroom,* ABC, 1981.

Walker Garrett, *The Big Easy,* ABC, 1982.

Crazy Like a Fox, 1984.

Nelson Sturgess, *Starting Now,* CBS, 1989.

Captain Barrisford, *Angie, the Lieutenant* (also known as *Angie*), ABC, 1992.

Eugene "Gene" Bennett, *Party of Five,* Fox, 1994.

Richard, *Dark Angel,* Fox, 1996.

Bennett Goldman, *October Road,* ABC, 2007.

Television Appearances; Specials:

Tom, *Star for Tonight,* NBC, 1955.

Film Appearances:

Lionel Aldridge, *The Way We Live Now,* United Artists, 1970.

Paul Kearney, *Man on a Swing,* Paramount, 1974.

Andy DiCarlo, *Smile,* United Artists, 1975.

Carl Gordon, *The Happy Hooker,* Cannon, 1975.

Professor Samuel Graves, *The Gumball Rally,* Warner Bros., 1976.

Dr. Charles Warren, *Damien: Omen II* (also known as *Omen II* and *Omen II: Damien*), Twentieth Century–Fox, 1978.

George Brockington, *The Fish That Saved Pittsburgh,* United Artists, 1979.

Jim Hammen, *Airplane!* (also known as *Flying High*), Paramount, 1980.

Joel's father, *Risky Business,* Warner Bros., 1983.

Eddie, *The Falcon and the Snowman,* Orion, 1984.

John Pilgrim, *Choke Canyon* (also known as *On Dangerous Ground*), United Film Distribution, 1986.

Senator Tom Stewart, *Morgan Stewart's Coming Home* (also known as *Home Front*), New Century/Vista, 1987.

Benjamin Wells, *Less Than Zero,* Twentieth Century–Fox, 1987.

Ramsen Conklin and man in bloody white suit, *Brain Dead* (also known as *Paranoia*), Metro–Goldwyn–Mayer, 1990.

Hotel manager, *Pacific Heights,* Twentieth Century–Fox, 1990.

Hoffa's attorney, *Hoffa,* Twentieth Century–Fox, 1992.

Peter Farrell, *Sliver* (also known as *Sliver—Gier der augen*), Paramount, 1993.

Bidwell, *Hail Caesar,* Crystal Sky Communications, 1994.

Judge Flynn F. Slattery, *The Chamber,* Universal, 1996.

Secretary of State Jack Douglas, *Executive Decision* (also known as *Critical Decision*), Warner Bros., 1996.

Paul Moran, *Murder at 1600* (also known as *Murder at 1600 Pennsylvania Avenue*), Warner Bros., 1997.

Dr. Prentice, *Molly,* Metro–Goldwyn–Mayer, 1999.

Dale, *The Bachelor,* New Line Cinema, 1999.

Senator Delich, *Collateral Damage,* Warner Bros., 2002.

Harold Smithfield, *The List,* Twentieth Century–Fox, 2007.

Tander Welch, *The Four Children of Tander Welch,* 2008.

Stage Appearances:

Peter, *Light Up the Sky,* Drummond Players, Baltimore, MD, 1951.

Trock, *Winterset,* Drummond Players, 1951.

Haimon, *Antigone,* Drummond Players, 1951.

John, *John Loves Mary,* Drummond Players, 1951.

Loevborg, *Hedda Gabler,* Drummond Players, 1951.

The Father, Drummond Players, 1951.

Peg o' My Heart, Drummond Players, 1951.

Lord Chancellor, *Iolanthe,* Camden Hills Theatre, Camden, ME, 1952.

Arthur Kindred, *Detective Story,* Camden Hills Theatre, 1952.

Randy Curtis, *Lady in the Dark,* Camden Hills Theatre, 1952.

Singer, *My Heart's in the Highlands,* Camden Hills Theatre, 1952.

Cromwell, *Henry VIII,* Camden Hills Theatre, 1952.

Gremio, *The Taming of the Shrew,* Camden Hills Theatre, 1952.

Owen, *Jenny Kissed Me,* Camden Hills Theatre, 1952.

Launcelot Gobbo, *The Merchant of Venice,* Oregon Shakespeare Festival, Ashland, OR, 1953.

Hortensio, *The Taming of the Shrew,* Oregon Shakespeare Festival, 1953.

Suffolk, *Henry IV, Part I,* Oregon Shakespeare Festival, 1953.

Coriolanus, Oregon Shakespeare Festival, 1953.

Paul Verrall, *Born Yesterday,* Star Theatre, Minneapolis, MN, 1954.

Ernest, *The Importance of Being Earnest,* Star Theatre, 1954.

Turk, *Come Back, Little Sheba,* Star Theatre, 1954.

Arthur, *Detective Story,* Star Theatre, 1954.

Don, *The Moon Is Blue,* Star Theatre, 1954.

Simon, *Hay Fever,* Star Theatre, 1954.

John, *The Old Maid,* Drew Theatre, East Hampton, NY, 1957.

(As Nicholas Probst) Captain Dupont, *Small War on Murray Hill,* Ethel Barrymore Theatre, New York City, 1957.

Roger Parson, *The Egghead,* Ethel Barrymore Theatre, 1957.

Bill, *Love Me Little,* Helen Hayes Theatre, New York City, 1958.

Bezano, *He Who Gets Slapped,* Falmouth Playhouse, Falmouth, MA, 1958.

Jimmie Keefe, *Howie,* Forty–Sixth Street Theatre, New York City, 1958.

Buzz, *The Highest Tree,* Longacre Theatre, New York City, 1959.

Borak, Martinique Theatre, 1960.

Fredricks, *Craig's Wife,* Tappan Zee Playhouse, Nyack, NY, 1960.

Schuyler Grogan, *Invitation to a March,* Ogunquit Playhouse, Ogunquit, ME, 1961.

Ed Hughes, *The Advocate,* Bucks County Playhouse, New Hope, PA, 1962.

James Keller, *The Miracle Worker,* Bucks County Playhouse, 1962.

Romeo, *Romeo and Juliet,* Casino Park Playhouse, Holyoke, MA, 1963.

Young man, *Moments of Love,* Westport County Playhouse, Westport, CT, 1963.

Understudy for the role of Nick, *Who's Afraid of Virginia Woolf?,* Billy Rose Theatre, New York City, 1964.

Barney, *A Party for Divorce,* Provincetown Playhouse, New York City, 1966.

Tiger, *The Rehearsal,* Theatre of Living Arts, Philadelphia, PA, 1968.

James Daley, *That Championship Season,* Booth Theatre, New York City, 1974.

Gordon, *Thieves,* Broadhurst Theatre, New York City, 1974.

Mr. Webb, *Our Town,* 1990–91.

Major Tours:

Alan, *The Boys in the Band,* U.S. cities, 1969–70.

WRITINGS

Television Episodes:

"The Overnight Case," *Way Out,* 1961.

Q

QUAID, Dennis 1954–

PERSONAL

Full name, Dennis William Quaid; born April 9, 1954, in Houston, TX; son of William Rudy (an electrical contractor) and Juanita B. "Nita" (a real estate agent) Quaid; brother of Randy Quaid (an actor); married P. J. Soles (an actress and producer), November, 1978 (divorced, 1983); married Meg Ryan (an actress), February 14, 1991 (divorced, 2001); married Kimberly Buffington (a real estate agent), July 4, 2004; children: (second marriage) Jack Henry; (third marriage) Thomas Boone and Zoe Grace (twins). *Education:* Attended University of Houston, 1972–75. *Avocational Interests:* Fishing, horseback riding, golfing, aviation (licensed private pilot).

Addresses: *Agent*—WME Entertainment, 9601 Wilshire Blvd., 3rd Floor, Beverly Hills, CA 90212. *Publicist*—WKT Public Relations, 9350 Wilshire Blvd., Suite 405, Beverly Hills, CA 90212.

Career: Actor. Summers/Quaid Productions, cofounder, 1989; appeared in public service announcements and print ads; voice for Visa credit card commercials. Member of the rock bands the Eclectics and Dennis Quaid and the Sharks. Dennis Quaid Charity Weekend, founder, 2003. Formerly worked as a standup comedian, clown, singing waiter, and encyclopedia salesperson.

Awards, Honors: Best Actor Award, Valladolid International Film Festival, 1987, and Independent Spirit Award, best male lead, Independent Features Project/West, 1988, both for *The Big Easy;* Screen Actors Guild Award (with others), outstanding performance by the cast of a theatrical motion picture, 2001, for *Traffic;* Saturn Award, best supporting actor, Academy of Science Fiction, Fantasy, and Horror Films, and Blockbuster Entertainment Award nomination, favorite actor in a suspense film, both 2001, for *Frequency;* New York Film Critics Circle Award, best supporting actor, 2002, Golden Globe Award nomination, best supporting actor in a motion picture, Independent Spirit Award, Screen Actors Guild Award nomination, Chicago Film Critics Association Award, Phoenix Film Critics Society Award nomination, and Online Film Critics Society Award, all best supporting actor, and Golden Satellite Award nomination, best performance by an actor in a supporting role in a drama, International Press Academy, all 2003, all for *Far from Heaven;* Camie Award (with others), Character and Morality in Entertainment Awards, 2003, for *The Rookie;* received star on Hollywood Walk of Fame, 2005; inducted into Texas Hall of Fame, 2005; ShoWest Award, male star of the year, National Association of Theatre Owners, 2009; Emmy Award nomination, outstanding lead actor in a miniseries or movie, 2010, for *The Special Relationship.*

CREDITS

Film Appearances:

(Uncredited) Bellhop, *Crazy Mama,* New World, 1975.

Shark, *I Never Promised You a Rose Garden,* New World, 1977.

Alan, *The Seniors* (also known as *The Senior*), Cinema Shares, 1978.

Frank, *September 30, 1955* (also known as *24 Hours of the Rebel*), Universal, 1978.

Paul Fleishauer, *Our Winning Season,* American International Pictures, 1978.

Mike, *Breaking Away* (also known as *Bambino*), Twentieth Century–Fox, 1979.

Ed Miller, *The Long Riders,* United Artists, 1980.

Mad Grossman, *G.O.R.P.* (also known as *Gorp*), Filmways, 1980.

Freddie Dupler, *All Night Long,* Universal, 1981.

Lar, *Caveman,* United Artists, 1981.

Travis Child, *The Night the Lights Went Out in Georgia,* Avco Embassy, 1981.

Art Long, *Tough Enough,* Twentieth Century–Fox, 1983.

Captain Leroy Gordon "Gordo" Cooper, Jr. (Hot Dog), *The Right Stuff,* Warner Bros., 1983.

Michael "Mike" Brody, *Jaws 3–D* (also known as *Jaws 3*), Universal, 1983.

Alex Gardner, *Dreamscape,* Twentieth Century–Fox, 1984.

Willis Davidge, *Enemy Mine,* Twentieth Century–Fox, 1985.

Detective Remy McSwain, *The Big Easy* (also known as *The Big Crackdown*), Columbia, 1987.

Eddie Sanger, *Suspect,* TriStar, 1987.

Lieutenant Tuck Pendleton, *Innerspace,* Warner Bros., 1987.

Dexter Cornell, *D.O.A.,* Buena Vista, 1988.

Gavin Grey, *Everybody's All–American* (also known as *When I Fall in Love*), Warner Bros., 1988.

Jerry Lee Lewis, *Great Balls of Fire!,* Orion, 1989.

Jack Faulkner, *Postcards from the Edge,* Columbia, 1990.

Jack McGurn, *Come See the Paradise,* Twentieth Century–Fox, 1990.

Arlis Sweeney, *Flesh and Bone,* Paramount, 1993.

Jefferson "Jeff" Blue, *Undercover Blues* (also known as *Cloak and Diaper*), Metro–Goldwyn–Mayer, 1993.

Wallace Foudroyant/Biff the clown, *Wilder Napalm,* TriStar, 1993.

John "Doc" Holliday, *Wyatt Earp,* Warner Bros., 1994.

Kidnapped, 1994.

Edward "Eddie" Bichon, *Something to Talk about* (also known as *The Game of Love, Grace Under Pressure, The King of Carolina,* and *Sisters*), Warner Bros., 1995.

Bowen, *DragonHeart,* Universal, 1996.

Agent Frank LaCrosse, *Switchback* (also known as *Going West, Going West in America,* and *Zig Zag*), Paramount, 1997.

William "Joe Doe" McCall, *Gang Related* (also known as *Criminal Intent* and *Gang City*), Metro–Goldwyn–Mayer/Orion, 1997.

Hugh, *Playing by Heart* (also known as *Dancing about Architecture, If They Only Knew, Intermedia,* and *My Heart, My Love*), Miramax, 1998.

Joshua Rose and Guy, *Savior,* Initial Entertainment Group, 1998.

Nicholas "Nick" Parker, *The Parent Trap* (also known as *Disney's "The Parent Trap"* and *Family Game*), Buena Vista, 1998.

Jack "Cap" Rooney, *Any Given Sunday* (also known as *Gridiron, The League, Monday Night, On Any Given Sunday,* and *Playing Hurt*), Warner Bros., 1999.

Arnie Metzger, *Traffic,* USA Films, 2000.

Frank Sullivan, *Frequency,* New Line Cinema, 2000.

Frank Whitaker, *Far from Heaven,* Focus Features, 2002.

James "Jim"/"Jimmy" Morris, Jr., *The Rookie* (also known as *Old Rookie*), Buena Vista, 2002.

Cooper Tilson, *Cold Creek Manor,* Buena Vista, 2003.

General Sam Houston, *The Alamo,* Buena Vista, 2004.

Professor Jack Hall, *The Day after Tomorrow,* Twentieth Century–Fox, 2004.

Captain Frank Townes, *The Flight of the Phoenix,* Twentieth Century–Fox, 2004.

Dan Foreman, *In Good Company,* Universal, 2004.

Frank Beardsley, *Yours, Mine, and Ours,* Metro–Goldwyn–Mayer, 2005.

President Staton, *American Dreamz,* Universal, 2006.

Voice of Roven, *Battle for Terra* (animated; also known as *Terra*), Lions Gate Films/Roadside Attractions, 2007.

Lawrence Wetherhold, *Smart People,* Miramax, 2008.

Thomas Barnes, *Vantage Point,* Columbia, 2008.

Ben Schwartzwalder, *The Express* (also known as *The Express: The Ernie David Story*), Universal, 2008.

Detective Aidan J. Breslin, *Horsemen* (also known as *Horsemen of the Apocalypse*), Lions Gate Films, 2009.

General Abernathy (Hawk), *G.I. Joe: The Rise of Cobra* (also known as *G.I. Joe*), Paramount, 2009.

Payton, *Pandorum,* Overture Films, 2009.

From Hollywood to Syracuse: The Legacy of Ernie Davis (documentary), Universal, 2009.

Bob Hanson, *Legion,* Screen Gems, 2010.

Reverend Shaw Moore, *Footloose,* Paramount, 2011.

Tom Hamilton, *Soul Surfer,* Affirm Films, 2011.

According to some sources, appeared in a film titled *Stranger than the Wheel,* 2001.

Film Work:

Song performer, "Game I Can't Win," *Modern Girls,* 1986.

Television Appearances; Movies:

Phil Lawver, *Are You in the House Alone?,* CBS, 1978.

Roy, *Amateur Night at the Dixie Bar and Grill,* NBC, 1979.

Barry Morrow, *Bill,* CBS, 1981.

Kyle Hager, *Johnny Belinda,* CBS, 1982.

Barry Morrow, *Bill: On His Own,* CBS, 1983.

Jim Clay, *Everything that Rises,* TNT, 1998.

Gabe, *Dinner with Friends,* HBO, 2001.

Bill Clinton, *The Special Relationship,* HBO, 2010.

Television Appearances; Specials:

The Making of "Jaws 3–D": Sharks Don't Die, 1983.

"The Big Bang" (also known as Robert Wuhl's "The Big Bang"), *Cinemax Comedy Experiment,* Cinemax, 1986.

Texas 150: A Celebration Special, ABC, 1986.

The Neville Brothers: Tell It Like It Is, Cinemax, 1989.

The American Film Institute Salute to Elizabeth Taylor, ABC, 1993.

Himself, *A Century of Cinema* (also known as *Hollywood Stars: A Century of Cinema*), The Disney Channel, 1994.

Host, *The Blue Angels*, Arts and Entertainment, 1994.

Wyatt Earp: Walk with a Legend, 1994.

Narrator, *Panama Canal: The Eighth Wonder of the World*, The Discovery Channel, 1998.

(Uncredited; in archive footage) *Warner Bros. 75th Anniversary: No Guts, No Glory*, 1998.

Inside Traffic: The Making of "Traffic," 2000.

(In archive footage) Mike, *Twentieth Century–Fox: The Blockbuster Years*, 2000.

The Making of "Far From Heaven," 2002.

American Bandstand's 50th Anniversary Celebration, 2002.

(In archive footage) *Jaws: The E! True Hollywood Story*, E! Entertainment Television, 2002.

I Walk the Line: A Night for Johnny Cash, CBS, 2005.

ReAct Now: Music & Relief, MTV and VH1, 2005.

Lindsay Lohan: The E! True Hollywood Story, E! Entertainment Television, 2005.

(In archive footage) *Meg Ryan: The E! True Hollywood Story*, E! Entertainment Television, 2005.

(In archive footage) Jack Faulkner, *Premio Donostia a Meryl Streep*, 2008.

Chasing Zero: Winning the War on Healthcare Reform, The Discovery Channel, 2010.

Television Appearances; Miniseries:

Voices, *Freedom: A History of Us*, PBS, 2003.

Television Appearances; Episodic:

Scott Martin, "The Sky Is Falling," *Baretta*, ABC, 1977.

Guest host, *Saturday Night Live* (also known as *SNL*), NBC, 1990.

Magacine, 1996.

Dias de cine, 1996.

Himself, *Muppets Tonight!*, ABC, 1997.

Lo + plus, 1998.

Continuara, 1998.

"Full Contact: The Making of 'Any Given Sunday,'" *HBO First Look*, HBO, 1999.

Celebrity Wings, 2003.

(In archive footage) *Coming Attractions*, E! Entertainment Television, 2003.

(In archive footage) "John Ritter Remembered," *Larry King Live*, Cable News Network, 2003.

"The Making of 'The Day after Tomorrow,'" *HBO First Look*, HBO, 2004.

Corazon de ..., 2005.

"The Girls Who Go to Texas," *America's Next Top Model* (also known as *America's Next Top Model 2*, *America's Next Top Model with Tyra Banks*, *ANTM*, and *Top Model*), UPN, 2006.

Ben Schwartzwalder, "The Express," *HBO First Look*, HBO, 2008.

Celebrity traveler, *Getaway*, 2008.

Access Hollywood, syndicated, 2008.

Entertainment Tonight (also known as *E.T.* and *This Week in Entertainment*), syndicated, several appearances, beginning 2008.

Extra (also known as *Extra: The Entertainment Magazine*), syndicated, 2008.

(In archive footage) Jerry Lee Lewis, *Banda sonora*, 2008.

(In archive footage) *The O'Reilly Factor*, Fox News Channel, 2008.

Voice of Grandpa Redbeard, "Grandpappy the Pirate," *SpongeBob SquarePants* (animated; also known as *SpongeBob*), Nickelodeon, 2009.

CMT Insider, Country Music Television, 2009.

Made in Hollywood, 2010.

"The Book of Eli/The Spy Next Door/Fish Tank," *The Rotten Tomatoes Show*, Current TV, 2010.

Also interviewee for *On the Record with Bob Costas*, HBO.

Television Talk Show Guest Appearances; Episodic:

The Late Show with David Letterman (also known as *The Late Show* and *Letterman*), CBS, multiple appearances, between 1996 and 2008.

The Rosie O'Donnell Show, syndicated, 1998, 2000, 2001.

The View, ABC, 2000, 2002, 2005.

Inside the Actors Studio (also known as *Actors Interview* and *Inside the Actors Studio: The Craft of Theatre and Film*), Bravo, 2002.

The Tonight Show with Jay Leno, NBC, 2002, 2006, 2008.

Shootout (also known as *Hollywood Shootout* and *Sunday Morning Shootout*), AMC, 2004.

Live with Regis and Kelly, syndicated, 2004, 2008, 2009.

Late Night with Conan O'Brien, NBC, 2005.

The Daily Show with Jon Stewart (also known as *The Daily Show* and *The Daily Show with Jon Stewart Global Edition*), Comedy Central, 2005, 2006.

The Late Late Show with Craig Ferguson, CBS, 2005, 2006, 2010.

Ellen: The Ellen DeGeneres Show, syndicated, 2005, 2006, 2008.

Good Morning America (also known as *G.M.A.*), ABC, 2008.

Rachael Ray, syndicated, 2008.

Today (also known as *NBC News Today* and *The Today Show*), NBC, 2008.

The Bonnie Hunt Show, NBC, 2008, 2009.

The Tonight Show with Conan O'Brien, NBC, 2009.

Late Night with Jimmy Fallon, NBC, 2009.

Tavis Smiley, PBS, 2010.

In the House with Peter Bart & Peter Guber (also known as *In the House*), 2010.

Jimmy Kimmel Live!, ABC, 2010.

Television Appearances; Awards Presentations:

Presenter, *The 61st Annual Academy Awards Presentation*, ABC, 1989.

Presenter, *The 11th Annual Kids' Choice Awards,* Nickelodeon, 1998.

Annual Screen Actors Guild Awards, TNT, 1998.

2000 Blockbuster Entertainment Awards, Fox, 2000.

Presenter, *The ... Annual Golden Globe Awards,* NBC, 2000, 2005.

The ... Independent Spirit Awards, Independent Film Channel, 2002, 2006.

Presenter, *The ... Independent Spirit Awards,* Independent Film Channel and Bravo, 2005.

The 62nd Primetime Emmy Awards, NBC, 2010.

Television Work; Movies:

Executive producer and director, *Everything that Rises,* TNT, 1998.

Stage Appearances:

Uncle Jocko, *Gypsy,* community theatre production, c. 1970.

Lee, *True West,* Cherry Lane Theatre, New York City, beginning c. 1982, later Los Angeles Stage Company, Los Angeles, c. 1984.

Tom, *The Last of the Knucklemen,* American Theatre of Actors, 1983.

RECORDINGS

Videos:

The Making of "DragonHeart," 1997.

The Science & Technology behind "Frequency," 2000.

Realizing "The Right Stuff," Warner Bros., 2003.

Gordon Cooper, *T–20 Years and Counting,* Warner Bros., 2003.

Cooper's Documentary, Buena Vista Home Entertainment, 2004.

Rules of the Genre, Buena Vista Home Video, 2004.

Return of the Legend: The Making of "The Alamo," Touchstone Home Video, 2004.

(In archive footage) Himself and Doc Holliday, *It Happened That Way,* Warner Home Video, 2004.

Phoenix Diaries, Twentieth Century–Fox, 2005.

Meat Loaf: In Search of Paradise, D&E Entertainment, 2007.

The Express: Making History—The Story of Ernie Davis, Mob Scene Creative Productions, 2009.

The Express: Making of "The Express," Mob Scene Creative Productions, 2009.

(In archive footage) *Hollywood Singing & Dancing: A Musical History—1980s, 1990s, and 2000s,* Koch International, 2009.

Legion: From Pixels to Picture, Sony Pictures Home Entertainment, 2010.

Legion: Creating the Apocalypse, Sony Pictures Home Entertainment, 2010.

Humanity's Last Line of Defense, Sony Pictures Home Entertainment, 2010.

Appeared in the music videos "Great Balls of Fire" by Jerry Lee Lewis; and "Thing Called Love" by Bonnie Raitt.

WRITINGS

Songs Featured in Films:

"Amanda," "Hound Dog," and "If You Don't Know by Now," *The Night the Lights Went Out in Georgia,* Avco–Embassy, 1981.

"The Jungle," *Tough Enough,* Twentieth Century–Fox, 1983.

(Uncredited) "Closer to You," *The Big Easy,* Columbia, 1987.

OTHER SOURCES

Books:

International Dictionary of Films and Filmmakers, Volume 3: *Actors and Actresses,* St. James Press, 1996.

Periodicals:

AARP, September/October, 2010.

American Film, June, 1989.

Cosmopolitan, August, 1998, p. 188; June, 1994.

Entertainment Weekly, May 12, 2000, pp. 40–42; February 16, 2001, p. 104; April 19, 2002, pp. 32–34; December 20, 2002, p. 83.

Interview, June, 1989, p. 42.

Men's Health Best Life, April, 2006, pp. 72–75.

New York Times, November 6, 1988.

Parade Magazine, July 5, 1998, p. 22; December 14, 2003, pp. 6–7.

People Weekly, July 13, 1998, p. 27; August 17, 1998, p. 110; July 17, 2000, pp. 82–83; April 15, 2002, pp. 63–64.

Playboy, December, 1987, p. 128.

Premiere, August, 1989, p. 46; April, 2004, p. 112; June, 2005, pp. 122–23.

Rolling Stone, July 13, 1989, p. 118.

Sports Illustrated, May 31, 2010, p. 16.

Texas Monthly, June, 2000, p. 204.

Time, November 18, 2002, pp. 131–32.

USA Today, December 20, 2004; February 20, 2008; April 30, 2010.

USA Weekend, July 24, 2009, pp. 6–7.

Vogue, November, 1993.

Washington Post, April 11, 2008, pp. 33, 36.

QUATERMASS, Martin
    See CARPENTER, John

QUINN, Declan 1957–

PERSONAL

Born 1957; raised in Chicago, IL; father, a college professor; brother of Aidan Quinn (an actor), James Quinn (an actor), Marian Quinn (an actress), and Paul Quinn (an actor); married Etta; children: four daughters, Stella, Sarah, Rae, and Alice. *Education:* Columbia College, Chicago, IL, graduated, 1979. *Religion:* Roman Catholic.

Addresses: *Agent*—Peters, Fraser, and Dunlop, Drury House, 34–43 Russell St., London WC2B 5HA, England; Dattner, Dispotto and Associates, 10635 Santa Monica Blvd., Suite 165, Los Angeles, CA 90025.

Career: Cinematographer and producer. Began career at Windmill Land Studios in Ireland. Photographer for commercials and public service announcements, including an AIDS awareness series for MTV, c. 1991, and commercials for Radio Shack electronics stores, Avis car rental agencies, Aruba Travel Board, Children's Advil pain reliever, Pizza Hut restaurants, Unique Boutique, Coca Cola soft drinks, and Lee jeans.

Awards, Honors: Clio Award, best cinematography, 1991, for "MTV AIDS Campaign"; Annual CableACE Award, best cinematography, National Cable Television Association, c. 1993, for "Dead–End for Delia," *Fallen Angels;* Independent Spirit Award, best cinematography, Independent Features Project/ West, 1996, for *Leaving Las Vegas;* Cinematography Award, dramatic category, Sundance Film Festival, 1998, for *2 by 4;* Independent Spirit Award, best cinematography, 1998, for *Kama Sutra: A Tale of Love;* Emmy Award nomination, outstanding cinematography for a miniseries or movie, 2003, for *Hysterical Blindness;* Independent Spirit Award, best cinematography, 2004, for *In America;* IFTA Award nomination, best cinematography, Independent Film and Television Alliance, 2007, for *Breakfast on Pluto.*

CREDITS

Film Cinematographer:
The Kill–Off, Cabriolet, 1989.
Blood and Concrete—A Love Story (also known as *Blood and Concrete*), IRS Releasing, 1991.
Freddy's Dead: The Final Nightmare (also known as *A Nightmare on Elm Street 6*), New Line Cinema, 1991.
Cousin Bobby, Cinevista, 1992.

The Bargain Shop, 1992.
The Ballad of Little Joe, Fine Line, 1993.
All Things Bright and Beautiful, 1994.
Vanya on 42nd Street, Sony Pictures Classics, 1994.
Leaving Las Vegas, Metro–Goldwyn–Mayer, 1995.
Carried Away (also known as *Acts of Love*), Fine Line, 1996.
Kama Sutra: A Tale of Love, Trimark Pictures, 1997.
One Night Stand, New Line Cinema, 1997.
Sheet Rock, Sheet Rock Productions, 1997.
One True Thing, MCA/Universal, 1998.
2 by 4, Strand Releasing, 1999.
(And co–executive producer) *This Is My Father* (also known as *L'histoire de mon pere*), Sony Pictures Classics, 1999.
Flawless, Metro–Goldwyn–Mayer, 1999.
28 Days, Columbia, 2000.
Monsoon Wedding (also known as *Le mariage des moussons*), USA Films, 2002.
In America, Twentieth Century–Fox, 2002.
(With others) *City by the Sea,* Warner Bros., 2002.
"India," in *11'09"01—September 11* (also known as *11 minutes 9 seconds 1 image* and *Onze minutes, neuf secondes, un cadre*), Empire Pictures, 2003.
Cold Creek Manor, Buena Vista, 2003.
Vanity Fair, Focus Features, 2004.
Breakfast on Pluto, A–Film Distribution, 2005.
Get Rich or Die Tryin', Paramount, 2005.
Jimmy Carter Man from Plains, Sony Pictures Classics, 2007.
The Lucky Ones, Lions Gate Films, 2008.
Rachel Getting Married, Sony Pictures Classics, 2008.
Pride and Glory (also known as *Pride & Glory*), New Line Cinema, 2008.
8, IPA Asia Pacific, 2008.
New York, I Love You, Vivendi Entertainment, 2009.
The Private Lives of Pippa Lee, Maple Pictures, 2009.
Neil Young Trunk Show, Abramorama, 2009.
Marley, Wild Side Films, 2010.

Also cinematographer for *Clash of Ash.*

Film Appearances:
On Location With: All Things Bright and Beautiful, 1994.

Television Cinematographer; Movies:
Clash of the Ash, RTE, 1987, then PBS, 1992.
Lapsed Catholic, RTE, 1988.
Lies of the Twins, USA Network, 1991.
The Heart of Justice, TNT, 1993.
Hysterical Blindness, HBO, 2002.

Television Cinematographer; Specials:
"Over the Limit," *ABC Afterschool Special,* ABC, 1990.
"The Hollow Boy," *American Playhouse,* PBS, 1991.

Out of Order: Rock the Vote Targets Health Care, MTV, 1995.

Television Cinematographer; Episodic:
"Dead–End for Delia," *Fallen Angels,* Showtime, 1993.
"The Quiet Room," *Fallen Angels,* Showtime, 1993.
"All Things Bright and Beautiful," *Screen Two,* 1994.

RECORDINGS

Video Cinematographer:
The Jim Rose Circus Sideshow, 1993.

Also cinematographer for the music videos "Rocky World" by Daniel Lanois, 1983, "U2: Unforgettable Fire," 1984, "U2: Outside It's America," 1987, "Christy" by Christy Moore, 1994, "Tonight, Tonight" by Smashing Pumpkins, and concert videos for REM, 1988 and 1994.

OTHER SOURCES

Periodicals:
Elle, June, 1999, pp. 106–08, 110.
Premiere, March, 1997, p. 38.

R

RACK, Tom

PERSONAL

Children: Two.

Career: Actor and writer.

CREDITS

Film Appearances:

Sol Silver, *The Bay Boy* (also known as *Bad Company* and *Un printemps sous la neige*), 1984, Orion, 1985.

Discussions in Bioethics: The Courage of One's Convictions (short film; also known as *La bioethique: une question de choix–Le courage de ses convictions*), National Film Board of Canada, 1985.

Faulkner, *Toby McTeague* (also known as *Toby*), Filmline International, 1986.

Automated Lovers (short film), National Film Board of Canada, 1986.

Braindrain, *Wild Thing,* Atlantic Releasing, 1987.

Dr. Rudge, *Whispers* (also known as *Dean R. Koontz's "Whispers"*), International Video Entertainment, 1989.

Mick, *Mindfield,* Allegro Films Distribution, 1989.

William Green, *Jacknife,* Cineplex–Odeon, 1989.

Jesus de Montreal (also known as *Jesus of Montreal*), 1989, subtitled version, Orion Classics, 1990.

Sexton, *Cursed* (also known as *Pouvoir obscur*), Pax Film International, 1990.

Rostrovitch, *Lola Zipper,* Acteurs Auteurs Associes, 1991.

Zigesfeld, *If Looks Could Kill* (also known as *Teen Agent*), Warner Bros., 1991.

Dr. Bork, *Stalked,* Republic, 1994.

Locust, *Strip Search,* A–Pix Entertainment, 1997.

Kurt's uncle, *Provocateur* (also known as *Agent provocateur*), Via Appia Communications, 1998.

Governor Lawrence, *Chasing Holden,* Lions Gate Films, 2001.

Bobcat, *The Human Stain,* Miramax, 2003.

Also appeared as Edward, *Young Ivanhoe.*

Television Appearances; Miniseries:

Hurlstone (some sources cite Hartstone), *Spearfield's Daughter,* syndicated, 1986.

Robert Oppenheimer, *Race for the Bomb,* CBC, 1986.

John Dodge, *Ford: The Man and the Machine,* CBS, 1987.

Abraham Lincoln, *Champagne Charlie,* syndicated, 1989.

Vito, *Vendetta II: The New Mafia* (also known as *Bride of Violence 2* and *Donna d'onore 2*), HBO, 1993.

Bard, *Hiroshima,* Showtime, 1995.

Dr. Weinrich, *The Sleep Room,* Lifetime, 1998.

Hans Fritzsche, *Nuremberg,* TNT, 2000.

Television Appearances; Movies:

Slepak (some sources cite Stepak), *Secret Weapons* (also known as *Secrets of the Red Bedroom* and *Sexpionage*), NBC, 1985.

Vito, *Bride of Violence 2* (also known as *Vendetta II: The New Mafia*), 1993.

Edward, *Young Ivanhoe,* WIN, 1995.

Mirak, *For Love Alone: The Ivana Trump Story* (also known as *Ivana Trump's For Love Alone*), CBS, 1996.

Reverend Schmidt, *Free Money,* Starz!, 1998.

Windsor Protocol (also known as *Jack Higgins' "Windsor Protocol"*), Showtime, 1998.

Gilbert Miller, *The Audrey Hepburn Story,* ABC, 2000.

Mr. Finerman, *X Change,* HBO, 2000.

Mr. Walters, *Someone Is Watching,* Lifetime, 2000.

Dr. Caldwell, *The Killing Yard,* Showtime, 2001.

Reinhold Neibuhr, *Varian's War,* Showtime, 2001.

Brother Abel, *The Case of the Whitechapel Vampire*, Hallmark Channel, 2002.
Elie Wiesel, *The Reagans*, Showtime, 2003.
Dr. Schneider, *Her Perfect Spouse* (also known as *The Perfect Husband*), USA Network, 2004.
Evan, *A Teacher's Crime*, 2008.

Television Appearances; Episodic:
Sheriff and security guard, "The Tale of the Pinball Wizard," *Are You Afraid of the Dark?*, Nickelodeon, 1992.
Boyfriend, "The Needle and the Damage Done," *Sirens*, syndicated, 1994.
Watcher, "The Tale of Watcher's Woods," *Are You Afraid of the Dark?*, Nickelodeon, 1994.
"Klondike Mice," *The Country Mouse and the City Mouse Adventures* (animated), 1998.
"Matador Mice," *The Country Mouse and the City Mouse Adventures* (animated), 1998.
John, "The Lord Is My Shepherd," *Soldier of Fortune, Inc.* (also known as *Special Ops Force*), syndicated, 1999.
Piotr Grishenko, "Endgame," *Largo Winch*, 2001.

Television Appearances; Specials:
Dr. Meister, *The Blue Man* (also known as *Eternal Evil*), 1985.
Philippe Cameron, *The Final Heist* (also known as *L'etrange rancon*), 1991.
Robert Oppenheimer, *Einstein: Light to the Power of 2*, HBO, 1996.

Televison Appearances; Pilots:
Mr. Winchwood, *The Warden*, TNT, 2001.

WRITINGS

Teleplays; Episodic:
(With Louise Lamarre) "The Tale of the Pinball Wizard," *Are You Afraid of the Dark?*, Nickelodeon, 1992.

Screenplays:
Where Are You My Lovelies, 1986.

REESE, Rhett

PERSONAL

Raised in Phoenix, AZ.

Addresses: *Agent*—William Morris Endeavor Entertainment (WmEE2), One William Morris Place, Beverly Hills, CA 90212.

Career: Writer and producer. Writing and producing partner of Paul Wernick.

Member: Writers Guild of America, West.

CREDITS

Television Creator; with Paul Wernick; Series:
The Joe Schmo Show (also known as *The Joe and Jane Schmo Show, Joe Schmo 2,* and *Lap of Luxury*), Spike TV, 2003–2004.
Stuck on Dirty (also known as *Stuck to ODB*), Spike TV, 2005.

Television Executive Producer; with Others; Series:
The Joe Schmo Show (also known as *The Joe and Jane Schmo Show, Joe Schmo 2,* and *Lap of Luxury*), Spike TV, 2003–2004.
Invasion Iowa, Spike TV and ITV4, 2005.
Stuck on Dirty (also known as *Stuck to ODB*), Spike TV, 2005.

Television Production Assistant; Specials:
James Cagney: Top of the World, TNT, 1992.

Television Producer; with Paul Wernick; Pilots:
The Tomatos (animated), MTV, c. 2006.
ABC/Reese/Wernick Freshman Coma Comedy, Fox, 2007.
Executive producer, *Fox/Reese/Wernick Vet Clinic Drama*, Fox, 2007.

Television Appearances; as Himself; Specials:
40 Greatest Reality TV Moments (also known as *The Greatest*), VH1, 2004.
40 Greatest Pranks (also known as *The Greatest*), VH1, 2005.

Television Appearances; Episodic:
(In archive footage) Himself, "Hoaxes, Cheats and Liars," *20 to 1* (also known as *20 to 01*), Nine Network, 2006.

Film Work:
Executive producer, *Zombieland*, Columbia, 2009.

Worked on other films.

WRITINGS

Teleplays; with Paul Wernick; Concepts for Series:
Living the Dream, TVNZ, beginning 2004.

Teleplays; with Others; Episodic:
The Joe Schmo Show (also known as *The Joe and Jane Schmo Show, Joe Schmo 2,* and *Lap of Luxury*), Spike TV, 2003–2004.
Gloire et fortune: la grande imposture, M6 Metropole Television, 2004.
Invasion Iowa, Spike TV and ITV4, 2005.
El show de Candido, Spike TV, 2006.

Teleplays; with Paul Wernick; Pilots:
Zombieland, CBS, 2005, later produced as film for Columbia, 2009.
The Tomatos (animated), MTV, c. 2006.
ABC/Reese/Wernick Freshman Coma Comedy, Fox, 2007.
Fox/Reese/Wernick Vet Clinic Drama, Fox, 2007.

Screenplays:
Additional story material, *Dinosaur* (animated), Buena Vista, 2000.
Additional screenplay material, *Monsters, Inc.* (animated; also known as *Hidden City* and *Monsters & Co.*), Buena Vista, 2000.
(With Robert C. Ramirez) *Clifford's Really Big Movie* (animated; based on the book series by Norman Bridwell), Warner Bros./Scholastic Productions, 2004.
Cruel Intentions 3, Columbia TriStar, 2004.
Additional story material, *Tarzan II* (animated; also known as *Tarzan 2*), Buena Vista Home Video/Walt Disney Home Video, 2005.
(With Paul Wernick) *Zombieland* (originally a television pilot, CBS, 2005, Columbia, 2009.
(With Wernick) *Earth vs. Moon,* Universal, c. 2009.
(With Wernick) *Venom* (related to comic books), Sony, c. 2009.

With Wernick, worked on other screenplays, including *Deadpool* (related to comic books; also known as *X–Men: Deadpool* and *X–Men Origins: Deadpool*), Twentieth Century–Fox; *Untitled G.I. Joe Sequel* (related to toys and other films and programs; also known as *Untitled (Paramount Pictures/G.I. Joe Sequel)*), Paramount; and *Zombieland 2* (also known as *Zombieland 3D*).

REEVES, Matt 1966–
  (Matthew Reeves)

PERSONAL

Full name, Matthew George Reeves; born April 27, 1966, in Rockville Centre, NY; raised in Los Angeles,

CA. *Education:* University of Southern California, degree in film.

Addresses: *Agent*—John Lesher, Endeavor Agency, 9701 Wilshire Blvd., 10th Floor, Beverly Hills, CA 90212; Creative Artists Agency, 2000 Avenue of the Stars, Los Angeles, CA 90067. *Manager*—Keepers Financial Corporation, 269 S. Beverly Dr., Suite 363, Beverly Hills, CA 90212.

Career: Director, writer, and producer.

Awards, Honors: Filmmaker's Showcase Award, Academy of Science Fiction, Fantasy, and Horror Films, 2008.

CREDITS

Film Work:
Director, "Mr. Petrified Forest," *Future Shock,* Hemdale Home Video, 1994.
Director, *The Pallbearer,* Miramax, 1996.
Coproducer, *The Yards,* Miramax, 1999.
Director, *Cloverfield* (also known as *1–18–08, Monstrous,* and *Cloverfield: Hakaisha*), Paramount, 2008.
Director, *Let Me In,* Overture Films, 2010.

Film Appearances:
Bunker soldier, *28 Weeks Later,* Twentieth Century–Fox, 2007.

Television Director; Episodic:
"Billable Hours," *Relativity,* ABC, 1997.
"All Is Bright", *Homicide: Life on the Street* (also known as *H:LOTS* and *Homicide*), NBC, 1997.
"The Last Stand," *Felicity,* The WB, 1998.
"Felicity Was Here," *Felicity,* The WB, 1999.
"The Slump," *Felicity,* The WB, 2000.
"The Declaration," *Felicity,* The WB, 2001.
(With Richard Hatem) "The Ferguson Syndrome," *Miracles,* ABC, 2003.

Television Work; Series:
Creator (with Jeffrey Abrams) and executive producer, *Felicity,* The WB, 1998–2002.

Television Work; Pilots:
Director, *Felicity,* The WB, 1998.
Director, *Gideon's Crossing,* ABC, 2000.
Director, *Conviction,* 2006.
Executive producer, *Ordinary Joe,* ABC, 2008.

Television Appearances; Specials:
(As Matthew Reeves) *Spotlight: David Schwimmer,* Comedy Central, 1996.

Television Appearances; Movies:
Greg Satch, *Bloodmonkey,* Sci–Fi Channel, 2008.

Television Appearances; Episodic:
Ed Salter, *Footballers Wives: Overtime,* ITV, BBC America, 2004.

RECORDINGS

Videos:
The VFX of "Cloverfield," Paramount, 2008.

WRITINGS

Screenplays:
Future Shock, 1994.
Under Siege 2: Dark Territory (also known as *Under Siege 2*), Warner Bros., 1995.
(With Jason Katims) *The Pallbearer,* Miramax, 1996.
(With others) *The Yards,* Miramax, 1999.
Let Me In, Overture Films, 2010.

Television Series:
Felicity, The WB, 1998–2002.

Television Pilots:
Ordinary Joe, ABC, 2008.

REILLY, Damara
(Daamara Reilly, Damara C. Reilly, Damara Riley)

PERSONAL

Education: California State University, B.S.; attended San Francisco State University; trained with A Contemporary Theatre (also known as ACT), Seattle, WA.

Addresses: *Agent*—DDO Artists Agency, 6725 West Sunset Blvd., Suite 230, Los Angeles, CA 90028.

Career: Actress and voice performer; comedian; voice performer for commercials; also worked as a dancer and choreographer.

Member: American Federation of Television and Radio Artists, Actors' Equity Association, Screen Actors Guild.

CREDITS

Television Appearances; Movies:
Dr. Daniels's nurse, *Babies,* NBC, 1990.

(As Damara Riley) Secretary *Mrs. Lambert Remembers Love,* CBS, 1991.
Lucy Wainswright, *For My Daughter's Honor* (also known as *Indecent Seduction*), CBS, 1996.

Television Appearances; Miniseries:
Lillian "Lil" Tinker, *Murder in Small Town "X",* Fox, 2001.

Television Appearances; Episodic:
Ms. Pell, "Protection," *Midnight Caller,* NBC, 1990.
Sheila, "Out with the Old," *Family Matters,* CBS, 1997.
HMO attorney, "First Do No Harm," *Diagnosis Murder* (also known as *Dr. Mark Sloan*), CBS, 1998.
First croupier, "Dealer's Choice," *Beverly Hills, 90210* (also known as *Class of Beverly Hills*), Fox, 1998.
Alien surgeon, "Workforce: Part 2," *Star Trek: Voyager* (also known as *Voyager*), UPN, 2001.
Estelle, "It Takes Two to Tangle," *Frasier,* NBC, 2001.
(Uncredited) Estelle, "April Showers," *ER,* NBC, 2001.
Captain Bouchard, "Redemption," *JAG,* CBS, 2001.
Judge Judy Koharski, "My Brother's Keeper," *Family Law,* CBS, 2001.
Judge Judy Koharski, "Big Brother," *Family Law,* CBS, 2002.
Janice, "Angel Work," *The Division,* Lifetime, 2002.
Lita Gibbons, "Revenge Is Best Served Cold," *CSI: Crime Scene Investigation* (also known as *C.S.I.* and *CSI: Las Vegas*), CBS, 2002.
Mrs. Koppleman, "My Monster," *Scrubs* (also known as *Scrubs: Med School*), NBC, 2002.
Diane, "Underground Railroad," *Without a Trace* (also known as *W.A.T.*), CBS, 2003.
(As Damara C. Reilly) Female guard, "Mr. Monk Goes to the Theater," *Monk,* USA Network, 2003.
Gail Hopper, "Cold Cash," *Threat Matrix,* ABC, 2003.
Cafeteria cashier, "Election Night," *Jack & Bobby,* The WB, 2004.
Reenacter, "What a Day," *Untold Stories of the ER,* The Learning Channel, 2005.
Mattie in 2005, "A Perfect Day," *Cold Case,* CBS, 2005.
Meredith Johnson, "Ghost in the Machine," *Medium,* NBC, 2006.
Madge, "Everybody Hates Driving," *Everybody Hates Chris,* The CW, 2007.
Madge, "Everybody Hates the Port Authority," *Everybody Hates Chris,* The CW, 2008.
(As Damara C. Reilly) Housekeeper, "Adventures in the Skin Trade," *Las Vegas,* NBC, 2008.
(As Daamara Reilly) "Jazz," *Tim and Eric Awesome Show, Great Job!,* Cartoon Network, 2008.

Appeared in an episode of *American Dreams,* NBC; appeared as receptionist, *For Your Love,* The WB; in *Homeland Security,* as Miss Rossi, *Moesha,* UPN; Nancy Rebeiro, *Moloney,* CBS; theatre manager, *Rescue 77,* The WB; waitress, *To Have and to Hold,* CBS; and "911" administrator, *Trauma,* NBC.

Television Appearances; Specials:
Lee, *Uncommon Heroes,* CBS, 1996.

Film Appearances:
(As Damara Riley) Charlie Rose, *The Making of " ... And God Spoke,"* Live Entertainment, 1994.
Cat lady, *Rusty: A Dog's Tale* (also known as *Rusty: The Great Rescue*), Twentieth Century–Fox Home Entertainment, 1998.
Pat, *Year of the Scapegoat* (short film), 2005.
Nurse, *Neighborhood Watch* (also known as *Deadly End*), Cafe Productions, 2005.
(Uncredited) Mom Natwick, *Art School Confidential,* Sony Pictures Classics, 2006.
Chris, *The Last Guy* (short film), 310 Productions/About Time Filmworks, 2006.
Julie, *Johnny Goner* (short film), Black Shadow Films, 2008.
Mad "SONJA" Vicke, *Dandelion Dharma* (short film), Crunch Entertainment, 2009.
Carla, *Maneater,* Arsenal Pictures, 2009.
Ruby, *Riding Hoods* (short film), 2010.
Carla, *Small Town Saturday Night,* Grindstone Entertainment Group, 2010.
Voice of Madame Boa, *Welcome to the Throne Room* (animated short film), 2010.
Dance teacher Mrs. Streidell, *After Always* (short film), 2010.

Other film appearances include role of Joanne, *Wildfire.*

Stage Appearances:
Appeared as Sheila, *A Chorus Line,* Marin Civic Light Opera, Marin, CA; Joanne, *Company,* Shakespeare Santa Cruz, Laguna Playhouse, Laguna Beach, CA; Adelaide, *Guys and Dolls,* Marin Civic Light Opera; Mama Rose, *Gypsy,* Lambo's Theatre; Bernarda, *The House of Bernarda Alba,* Theatre of Note; Nat, *Rabbit Hole,* Union Square Studio 300, San Francisco, CA; and Martha, *Who's Afraid of Virginia Woolf?,* CitiArts Theatre.

REYNOLDS, Ryan 1976–

PERSONAL

Full name, Ryan Rodney Reynolds; born October 23, 1976, in Vancouver, British Columbia, Canada; son of Jim (a food wholesaler and former semi–professional boxer) and Tammy (in retail sales) Reynolds; married Scarlett Johansson (an actress), September 27, 2008 (filed for divorce, 2011). *Education:* Attended Kwantlen College in Canada.

Addresses: *Office*—Dark Trick Films, 421 North Beverly Dr., Suite 280, Beverly Hills, CA 90210. *Agent*—Creative Artists Agency, 2000 Avenue of the Stars, Los Angeles, CA 90067. *Manager*—Jonathan Perry, Original Film Management, 2045 South Barrington Ave., Los Angeles, CA 90025. *Publicist*—42West, 220 West 42nd St., 12th Floor, New York, NY 10036.

Career: Actor and producer. Dark Trick Films, Beverly Hills, CA, partner. Formerly worked in a grocery store.

Awards, Honors: Young Artist Award nomination, best young actor costarring in a cable series, 1993, and Youth in Film Award nomination, best young actor, both for *Fifteen;* Young Hollywood Award, next generation male, 2003; MTV Movie Award nomination, breakthrough male performance, 2003, for *Van Wilder;* Teen Choice Award, choice movie scary scene, 2005, for *The Amityville Horror;* Gotham Award nomination (with others), best ensemble cast, 2009, for *Adventureland;* Teen Choice Award nomination, choice summer movie star—male, 2009, People's Choice Award nomination (with Sandra Bullock), favorite on–screen team, MTV Movie Award nominations, best kiss (with Bullock) and best comedic performance, 2010, for *The Proposal;* MTV Movie Award nomination (with others), best fight, People's Choice Award nomination (with others), favorite on–screen team, 2010, for *X–Men Origins: Wolverine;* People's Choice Award nominations, favorite comedy star and favorite movie actor.

CREDITS

Film Appearances:
Ganesh/Jeffrey, *Ordinary Magic* (also known as *Ganesh*), Triboro Entertainment, 1993.
Howard Ancona, *Life During Wartime* (also known as *The Alarmist*), Columbia TriStar Home Video, 1997.
Chip, *Dick* (also known as *Dick, les coulisses de la presidence*), Columbia/TriStar, 1999.
Henry Lipschitz, *Coming Soon,* Unapix Entertainment, 2000.
Karl O'Reilly, *Big Monster on Campus* (also known as *Boltneck*), 2000.
Red Shoes, *We All Fall Down,* Road Cone, 2000.
Quigley, *Finder's Fee,* Lions Gate Films, 2001.
Mike Hanson, *Buying the Cow,* Destination Films, 2001.
Title role, *Van Wilder* (also known as *National Lampoon's "Van Wilder"* and *Van Wilder: Party Liaison*), Artisan Entertainment, 2002.
Mark Tobias, *The In–Laws,* Warner Bros., 2003.
Kevin, *Foolproof,* Odeon Films, 2003.
Quentin, *Standing Still,* 2003.
Michael D'Angelo, *School of Life,* School of Life Productions, 2003.
Monty, *Waiting ...,* Media Ventures Pictures/Wisenheimer Films, 2003.
Male nurse, *Harold & Kumar Go to White Castle* (also known as *Harold & Kumar Get the Munchies*), New Line Cinema, 2004.

Hannibal King, *Blade: Trinity,* New Line Cinema, 2004.
George Lutz, *The Amityville Horror,* Sony, 2005.
Chris Brander, *Just Friends,* New Line Cinema, 2005.
Richard Messner, *Smokin' Aces,* Universal, 2006.
Gary/Gavin/Gabriel, *The Nines,* Sony, 2007.
Frank Allen, *Chaos Theory,* Warner Bros., 2007.
Will Hayes, *Definitely, Maybe* (also known as *Love Diaries*), Universal, 2008.
Michael Waechter, *Fireflies in the Garden,* Mars Entertainment, 2008.
Mike Connell, *Adventureland,* Miramax, 2009.
Wade Wilson, *X–Men Origins: Wolverine* (also known as *Wolverine: X–Men Zero*), Twentieth Century–Fox, 2009.
Andrew Paxton, *The Proposal,* Buena Vista, 2009.
Captain Excellent, *Paper Man,* Kimmel International, 2009.
Paul Conroy, *Buried,* Warner Bros., 2010.
Hal Jordan/Green Lanter, *Green Lantern,* Warner Bros., 2011.

Also appeared in *The Light–house.*

Film Executive Producer:
The Whale (documentary), Mountainside Films, 2011.

Television Appearances; Movies:
Kevin Bannister, *My Name Is Kate,* ABC, 1994.
Andy, *Serving in Silence: The Margarethe Cammermeyer Story* (also known as *Serving in Silence*), ABC, 1995.
Ben Colson, *A Secret between Friends: A Moment of Truth Movie* (also known as *When Friendship Kills*), NBC, 1996.
Wade Early, *Tourist Trap,* ABC, 1998.
Karl O'Reilly, *Big Monster on Campus* (also known as *Boltneck* and *Teen Monster*), Cinemax, 1998.
Buying the Cow, Starz!, 2002.
Mr. D, *School of Life,* ABC, 2005.

Television Appearances; Series:
Billy Simpson, *Fifteen* (also known as *Hillside*), Nickelodeon, 1991–94.
Macro, a recurring role, *The Odyssey,* Sci–Fi Channel, 1993–94.
MuchOnDemand, Much Music, 1997.
Michael Leslie "Berg" Bergen, *Two Guys, a Girl and a Pizza Place* (also known as *Two Guys and a Girl*), ABC, 1998–2001.
Voice of Ty Cheese, *Zeroman* (animated), Teletoon, 2004–2005.

Television Appearances; Episodic:
Derek Tillman, "If These Walls Could Talk," *The Outer Limits,* Showtime, 1995.
"Redemption," *Lonesome Dove: The Outlaw Years,* 1995.
"The Heartbreak Kid," *The Marshal,* ABC, 1995.
Jay "Boom" DeBoom, "Syzygy," *The X–Files,* Fox, 1996.
Tony Hemingway, "Napping to Success," *The John Larroquette Show,* 1996.
Paul Nodel, "Double Helix," *The Outer Limits,* Showtime and syndicated, 1997.
Paul Nodel, "The Origin of Species," *The Outer Limits,* Showtime and syndicated, 1998.
Guest, *SM:TV Live,* ITV1, 2002.
Spence, "My Dream Job," *Scrubs,* NBC, 2003.
MTV Hits (also known as *Beat Seekers*), MTV, 2003.
Total Request Live (also known as *TRL, TRL Weekend,* and *Total Request with Carson Daly*), MTV, 2004.
MADtv, Fox, two episodes, 2005.
Tan a gustito, 2006.
Hams, "Douchebag in the City," *My Boys,* TBS, 2007.
Extra (also known as *Extra: The Entertainment Magazine*), syndicated, 2008.
Entertainment Tonight (also known as *E.T.* and *This Week in Entertainment*), syndicated, multiple episodes between 2008–10.
On the Road Weekly, 2009.
Punkt 12, 2009.
Host, "Ryan Reynolds/Lady Gaga," *Saturday Night Live* (also known as *SNL*), NBC, 2009.

Television Talk Show Guest Appearances; Episodic:
The View, 2003.
Late Night with Conan O'Brien, NBC, 2003, 2004, 2005, 2007, 2008.
Live with Regis and Kelly, syndicated, 2004, 2005, 2007, 2008.
The Tony Danza Show, syndicated, 2004.
Jimmy Kimmel Live!, ABC, 2004, 2005, 2007, 2010.
Ellen: The Ellen DeGeneres Show, syndicated, 2005, 2009.
The Late Late Show with Craig Ferguson, CBS, 2005, 2009.
Up Close with Carrie Keagan, 2007, 2008, 2009.
The Tonight Show with Jay Leno, NBC, 2007.
Rachael Ray, syndicated, 2008.
Late Show with David Letterman (also known as *Letterman* and *The Late Show*), CBS, 2009.
This Morning, ITV, 2009.
Xpose, TV3, 2009.
Nyhetsmorgon, 2009, 2010.
Late Night with Jimmy Fallon, NBC, two episodes, 2009.

Television Appearances; Awards Presentations:
Young Hollywood Awards, 2003.
2003 MTV Movie Awards, MTV, 2003.
2003 Much Music Video Music Awards, Much Music, 2003.
The Teen Choice Awards 2005, Fox, 2005.
The Teen Choice Awards 2007, Fox, 2007.
2009 MTV Movie Awards, MTV, 2009.
The 36th Annual People's Choice Awards, CBS, 2010.

Presenter, *The 82nd Annual Academy Awards* (also known as *2010 Academy Awards, The 2010 Oscars,* and *The Oscars*), ABC, 2010.
The 64th Annual Tony Awards, CBS, 2010.

Television Appearances; Miniseries:
Bobby Rupp, *In Cold Blood,* CBS, 1996.

Television Appearances; Pilots:
Seth, *Sabrina, the Teenage Witch,* ABC, 1996.

Television Appearances; Specials:
Reel Comedy: National Lampoon's Van Wilder, Comedy Central, 2002.
101 Sexiest Celebrity Bodies, E! Entertainment Television, 2005.
Richard Messner, *Behind the Scenes with Joe Carnahan,* 2010.
Canada for Haiti, 2010.
25 Years of Sexy: People Magazine's Sexist Man Alive!, 2010.

RECORDINGS

Videos:
The Making of "We All Fall Down," Universal Studios, 2002.
On Location: The Amityville Horror, Metro–Goldwyn–Mayer, 2005.
Nightstalkers, Daywalkers and Familiars: Inside the World of "Blade Trinity," New Line Cinema, 2005.
The Source of Evil, Metro–Goldwyn–Mayer, 2005.
Monty, *That Little Extra,* Lions Gate Films, 2007.

Appeared in the music video "Bouncing off the Walls" by Sugarcult.

OTHER SOURCES

Periodicals:
TV Guide, May 27, 2000, pp. 26–28.

RICE, Jeff

PERSONAL

Married; children: three. *Education:* Graduate of University of California, Los Angeles. *Avocational Interests:* Building furniture.

Addresses: *Office*—Jeff Rice Films/Imprint Entertainment, 100 Universal City Plaza, Suite 7152, Universal City, CA 91608; LMNO Productions, 15821 Ventura Blvd., Suite 320, Encino, CA 91436.

Career: Producer and executive. LMNO Productions, Encino, CA, senior vice president for production and general manager of RH Studios, 1998—. Affiliate of Jeff Rice Films/Imprint Entertainment; formerly worked as a post–production manager, supervisor, and coordinator for Kane Productions International and others; also worked as an actor.

CREDITS

Film Executive Producer:
Future Shock, Hannover House, 1994.
The Badge, Gold Circle Films/Lions Gate Films/Millennium Films, 2002.
Kiss the Bride, 2002, Metro–Goldwyn–Mayer, 2004.
I Love Your Work, 2003, THINKFilm, 2005.
Slingshot, Weinstein Company, 2005.
Chasing Ghosts (also known as *Mad Dog*), Sony Pictures Home Entertainment, 2005.
Borderland, After Dark Films/Lions Gate Films, 2007.
Kentucky Rhapsody, Mint Entertainment, 2008.
The Last Word, Image Entertainment, 2009.
The Tomb (also known as *Ligeia*), Lightning Media, 2010.
My Son, My Son, What Have Ye Done, First Look Pictures, 2010.
Locked Down, Lions Gate Films/Grindstone Entertainment Group, 2010.

Film Co–executive Producer:
Grizzly Mountain, Legacy Releasing, 1997.
Two Weeks, Metro–Goldwyn–Mayer, 2006.
White Air, Monarch Home Video, 2007.
Finding Rin Tin Tin, Nu Image, 2007.
While She Was Out (also known as *Alive*), Anchor Bay Films, 2008.
Cabin Fever 2: Spring Fever, Lions Gate Films, 2009.

Film Producer:
Goldilocks and the Three Bears, Mama Papa Baby Productions/Santa Monica Pictures, 1995.
Speedway Junky, 1999, Regent Releasing, 2001.
After Sex, Cutting Edge Entertainment/Lantern Lane Entertainment, 2000.
The Watcher, MCA/Universal, 2001.
The Theory of the Leisure Class, The Asylum/Vanguard Cinema, 2001.
Arizona Summer, Skyline West Pictures, 2003.
Standing Still (also known as *Amy Adams in Night Before Wedding*), Freestyle Releasing, 2006.
Unbeatable Harold, Lg Entertainment, 2006.
Finding Bliss, Phase 4 Films, 2010.
Slightly Single in L.A., Helios Productions/Most–Rice Films/Imprint Entertainment/Game Face Entertainment, 2010.

Film Coproducer:
Dancer, Texas Pop. 81, TriStar, 1998.
Escape to Grizzly Mountain, Metro–Goldwyn–Mayer Home Entertainment, 2000.

Blonde Ambition (also known as *Working Blonde*), First Look International, 2007.

Film Associate Producer:
The Legend of Wolf Mountain, KOAN, 1993.

Television Executive Producer; Series:
The Industry (also known as *B InTune* and *Josh and JB in the Industry*), 2009.

Television Executive Producer; Other:
The Courageous Heart of Irena Sendler (movie), CBS, 2009.
House of Jazmin (miniseries), MTV, 2009.

OTHER SOURCES

Electronic:
LMNO Productions Web Site, http://www.lmnotv.com, August 24, 2010.

ROBERTS, Julia 1967–
(Julia Moder)

PERSONAL

Original name, Julie Fiona Roberts; born October 28, 1967, in Smyrna, GA; daughter of Walter Grady Roberts (an acting workshop proprietor, actor, writer, and salesperson) and Betty Lou Bredemus (an acting workshop proprietor, actress, real estate agent, and church secretary); sister of Eric Roberts (an actor) and Lisa Roberts (an actress); aunt of Emma Roberts (an actress); married Lyle Lovett (a singer and songwriter), June 27, 1993 (divorced, 1995); married Daniel "Danny" Moder (a camera operator and photographer), July 4, 2002; children: (second marriage) Hazel and Phinneaus (twins), Henry Daniel. *Education:* Studied acting at the Lee Strasberg Institute. *Avocational Interests:* Animals, knitting.

Addresses: *Office*—Red Om Films, 3000 West Olympic Blvd., Bldg. 3, Suite 2330, Santa Monica, CA 90404. *Agent*—Creative Artists Agency, 2000 Avenue of the Stars, Los Angeles, CA 90067. *Publicist*—Engelman and Company, 156 Fifth Ave., New York, NY 10010.

Career: Actress and producer. Red Om Films (a production company), Santa Monica, CA, partner; Click Agency, worked as a model; affiliated with YMA Productions and Shoelace Productions. Appeared in television commercials, including America Online, 2004; appeared in print ads for Gianfranco Ferre, 2006,

and Lancome Paris' cosmetics. Spokesperson to raise funds for awareness of Rett Syndrome; served as goodwill ambassador to UNICEF; The Hole in the Wall Gang Camp, member of board of directors. Associated with the Four Corners Animal League.

Awards, Honors: Independent Spirit Award nomination, best female lead, Independent Features Project/West, 1988, Young Artist Award nomination, best young actress in a motion picture—drama, 1989, both for *Mystic Pizza;* Golden Globe Award, best performance by an actress in a supporting role in a motion picture, and Academy Award nomination, best supporting actress, both 1989, for *Steel Magnolias;* Golden Globe Award, best performance by an actress in a motion picture—comedy/musical, Academy Award nomination, best actress, and Film Award nomination, best actress, British Academy of Film and Television Arts, 1990, all for *Pretty Woman;* Hollywood Women's Press Club Award (with others), discovery of the year, 1990; People's Choice Award, favorite all–around female entertainer, 1991; People's Choice Awards, favorite motion picture actress, 1991, 1998, 2000, 2001, 2002, 2003, 2004; ShoWest Convention Award, female star of the year, National Association of Theatre Owners, 1991; MTV Movie Award nominations, best female performance and most desirable female, 1992, both for *Dying Young;* People's Choice Award, favorite comedy motion picture actress, 1992; People's Choice awards, favorite dramatic motion picture actress, 1992 and 1994; MTV Movie Award nomination, best female performance, 1994, for *The Pelican Brief;* Blockbuster Entertainment Award, favorite actress—comedy, Golden Globe Award nomination, best performance by an actress in a motion picture–comedy/musical, Golden Satellite Award nomination, best performance by an actress in a motion picture—comedy or musical, International Press Academy, and MTV Movie Award nomination, best female performance, all 1997, for *My Best Friend's Wedding;* Blockbuster Entertainment Award, favorite actress—suspense, 1997, for *Conspiracy Theory;* Hasty Pudding woman of the year, Hasty Pudding Theatricals, Harvard University, 1997; named one of the "top 100 movie stars of all time," *Empire* magazine, 1997; Blockbuster Entertainment Award, favorite actress—drama, 1998, for *Stepmom;* Special Award, international star of the year, ShoWest Convention, National Association of Theatre Owners, 1998; People's Choice Award, favorite motion picture actress, 1998; Emmy Award nomination, outstanding guest actress in a drama series, 1999, for "Empire," *Law & Order;* Blockbuster Entertainment Award nomination, favorite actress—comedy/romance, MTV Movie Award nomination, best female performance, and Golden Slate nomination, best female performance, Csapnivalo awards, all 2000, for *Runaway Bride;* Golden Globe Award nomination, best performance by an actress in a motion picture—comedy/musical, Golden Satellite Award nomination, best performance by an actress in a motion picture—comedy or musical, and Blockbuster Entertainment Award nomination, favorite actress—

comedy/romance, all 2000, for *Notting Hill;* National Board of Review Award, Los Angeles Film Critics Association Award, San Diego Film Critics Society Award (with Laura Linney), and New York Film Critics Online Award (with Ellen Burstyn), all best actress, Sierra Award nomination, Las Vegas Film Critics Society, best actress, and Golden Slate Award nomination, Csapnivalo awards, best female performance, Teen Choice Award, film—choice actress, all 2000, Academy Award, best actress in a leading role, Golden Globe Award, best performance by an actress in a motion picture—drama, Film Award, best performance by an actress in a leading role, British Academy of Film and Television Arts, Screen Actors Guild Award, outstanding performance by a female actor in a leading role, Broadcast Film Critics Association Award, best actress, Blockbuster Entertainment Award, favorite actress—drama, Online Film Critics Society Award, best actress, ALFS Award, actress of the year, London Critics Circle, MTV Movie Award, best female performance, Golden Satellite Award nomination, best performance by an actress in a motion picture—drama, Chicago Film Critics Association Award nomination, best actress, Empire Award nomination, best actress, MTV Movie Award nomination, best line from a movie, 2001, all for *Erin Brockovich;* named one of the "twenty–five most intriguing people of 2001," *People Weekly,* 2001; named one of the "top 20 entertainers of 2001," E! Entertainment Television, 2001; named number eighteen in Hollywood power, *Premiere,* 2002; named number sixteen in Hollywood power, *Premiere,* 2003; National Board of Review Award (with others), best acting by an ensemble, 2004, Critics Choice Award nomination (with others), best acting ensemble, 2005, both for *Closer;* Critics Choice Award nomination (with others), best acting ensemble, 2005, for *Ocean's Twelve;* People's Choice Award, favorite female star, 2005; American Cinematheque Award, 2007; Kids' Choice Award nomination, favorite voice from an animated movie, 2007, for *The Ant Bully;* Golden Globe Award nomination, best performance by an actress in a supporting role in a motion picture, 2008, for *Charlie Wilson's War;* Golden Globe Award nomination, best performance by an actress in a motion picture—musical or comedy, 2010, for *Duplicity;* named number one in Hollywood power and number twelve in financial power, "Power 100," *Forbes;* also named a top box office star in other polls.

CREDITS

Film Appearances:
Tracks, 1976.
(Uncredited) Babs, *Firehouse,* 1987.
Daisy Arujo, *Mystic Pizza,* Samuel Goldwyn, 1988.
Daryle Shane, *Satisfaction* (also known as *Girls of Summer*), Twentieth Century–Fox, 1988.
Call girl, *Off the Boulevard,* Touchstone, 1989.
Shelby Eatenton Latcherie, *Steel Magnolias,* TriStar, 1989.

Maria Collogero, *Blood Red,* 1989.
Rachel Mannus, *Flatliners* (also known as *L'experience interdite, Linea mortale,* and *Morte imminente*), Columbia, 1990.
Vivian "Viv" Ward, *Pretty Woman,* Buena Vista, 1990.
Hilary O'Neil, *Dying Young* (also known as *The Choice of Love*), Twentieth Century–Fox, 1991.
Sara Waters/Laura Burney, *Sleeping with the Enemy* (also known as *Les nuits avec mon ennemi* and *Feind in meinem bett*), Twentieth Century–Fox, 1991.
Tinkerbell, *Hook,* TriStar, 1991.
(Uncredited) Herself, *The Player,* Fine Line, 1992.
Darby Shaw, *The Pelican Brief,* Warner Bros., 1993.
Anne Eisenhower, *Pret-a-Porter* (also known as *Ready to Wear* and *Pret-a-Porter: Ready to Wear*), Miramax, 1994.
Sabrina Peterson, *I Love Trouble,* Buena Vista, 1994.
Herself, *A Century of Cinema,* 1994.
Grace King Bichon, *Something to Talk About* (also known as *The Game of Love, Grace under Pressure, The King of Carolina,* and *Sisters*), Warner Bros., 1995.
Herself, *Elmo Says Boo,* 1996.
Kitty Kiernan, *Michael Collins,* Warner Bros., 1996.
Title role, *Mary Reilly,* TriStar, 1996.
Von, *Everyone Says I Love You,* Miramax, 1996.
Alice Sutton, *Conspiracy Theory,* Warner Bros., 1997.
Julianne Potter, *My Best Friend's Wedding* (also known as *Best Friend's Wedding*), Columbia/TriStar, 1997.
Isabel Kelly, *Stepmom* (also known as *Good Night Moon*), Columbia, 1998.
Anna Scott, *Notting Hill,* Universal, 1999.
Maggie Carpenter, *Runaway Bride* (also known as *Pretty Bride*), Paramount, 1999.
Title role, *Erin Brockovich,* Universal, 2000.
Herself, *Ljuset haaller mig saallskap* (documentary; also known as *Light Keeps Me Company* and *Sven Nykvist: Light Keeps Me Company*), First Run Features, 2000.
The Moviegoer, 2000.
Kathleen "Kiki" Harrison, *America's Sweethearts* (also known as *American Sweetheart*), Columbia, 2001.
Samantha Barzel, *The Mexican,* DreamWorks Distribution, 2001.
Tess Ocean, *Ocean's Eleven* (also known as *11* and *O11*), Warner Bros., 2001.
Herself, *Spotlight on Location: "Notting Hill,"* 2001.
Catherine/Francesca, *Full Frontal,* Miramax, 2002.
Patricia Watson, *Confessions of a Dangerous Mind* (also known as *Confession*), Artisan Entertainment, 2002.
Jolene, *Grand Champion,* 2002.
Herself, *"Ocean's Eleven": The Look of the Con,* 2002.
Katherine Ann Watson, *Mona Lisa Smile,* Sony Pictures Entertainment, 2003.
Anna, *Closer,* Columbia, 2004.
Tess Ocean, *Ocean's Twelve,* Warner Bros., 2004.
Herself, *Tell Them Who You Are* (documentary; also known as *My Cinematographer*), THINKFilm, 2004.

Voice of Charlotte the Spider, *Charlotte's Web* (animated), Paramount, 2006.

Voice of Hova, *The Ant Bully* (animated), Warner Bros., 2006.

Herself, *Who Needs Sleep?* (documentary), 2006.

Narrator, *Beslan: Three Days in September* (documentary), 2006.

Joanne Herring, *Charlie Wilson's War,* Universal, 2007.

Herself, *"Charlotte's Web": Some Voices* (short documentary), 2007.

Herself, *"Charlotte's Web": Making Some Movie* (short documentary), 2007.

Lisa Waechter, *Fireflies in the Garden,* 2008.

Herself, *Fields of Fuel* (documentary), 2008.

Herself, *Fuel* (documentary), Greenlight Theatrical, 2008.

Claire Stenwick, *Duplicity,* Universal, 2009.

Captain Kate Hazeltine, *Valentine's Day,* New Line Cinema, 2010.

Liz Gilbert, *Eat Pray Love,* Columbia, 2010.

Larry Crowne, Universal, 2011.

Film Work:

(With Susan Sarandon) Executive producer, *Stepmom* (also known as *Good Night Moon*), Columbia, 1998.

Producer, *Mona Lisa Smile,* Sony Pictures Entertainment, 2003.

Executive producer, *Kit Kittredge: An American Girl,* New Line Cinema, 2008.

Producer, *Jesus Christ Henry,* 2011.

Television Appearances; Movies:

Candy Hutchens, *Baja Oklahoma,* HBO, 1988.

Television Appearances; Specials:

Big Bird's Birthday, or Let Me Eat Cake, 1991.

Entertainers '91: The Top 20 of the Year, ABC, 1991.

The Barbara Walters Special, ABC, 1991, 1993, 2001.

Hollywood's Leading Ladies with David Sheehan (also known as *The Leading Ladies of the Movies*), NBC, 1993.

A Century of Cinema (documentary; also known as *Hollywood Stars: A Century of Cinema*), The Disney Channel, 1994.

Movie News Hot Summer Sneak Preview, CBS, 1994.

Hollywood Stars: A Century of Cinema, The Disney Channel, 1995.

Narrator, *Before Your Eyes: Angelie's Secret,* CBS, 1995.

Voice of herself, *Poetry, Passion, the Postman: The Poetic Return of Pablo Neruda,* 1996.

AFI's 100 Years ... 100 Movies: America's Greatest Movies, CBS, 1998.

Bravo Profiles: The Entertainment Business, Bravo, 1998.

AFI's 100 Years ... 100 Stars: America's Greatest Screen Legends, CBS, 1999.

Spotlight on Location: Erin Brockovich (documentary; also known as *The Making of "Erin Brockovich"*), 2000.

Host, *Silent Angels: The Rett Syndrome Story* (also known as *Silent Angels*), The Discovery Channel, 2000.

Hollywood Salutes Bruce Willis: An American Cinematheque Tribute, TNT, 2000.

America: A Tribute to Heroes, CBS, The WB, Fox, UPN, PBS, Telemundo, NBC, ABC, 2001.

Garry Marshall, Bravo, 2001.

Joan Rivers: The E! True Hollywood Story, E! Entertainment Television, 2001.

E!'s Live Countdown to the Golden Globes, E! Entertainment Television, 2001.

Live from the Red Carpet: The 2002 People's Choice Awards, 2002.

The Stars' First Time ... on Entertainment Tonight with Mary Hart, CBS, 2003.

Intimate Portrait: Erin Brockovich, Lifetime, 2003.

Comic Relief 2003: The Big Hair Do, 2003.

Shelter from the Storm: A Concert for the Gulf Coast, CBS, The WB, Fox, UPN, PBS, NBC, ABC, 2005.

Red Carpet Confidential, CBS, 2005.

Narrator, *Three Days in September* (documentary), Showtime, 2006.

CMT: The Greatest—Sexiest Southern Woman, Country Music Television, 2006.

George Clooney: An American Cinematheque Tribute, AMC, 2006.

Forbes 20 Richest Women in Entertainment, E! Entertainment Television, 2007.

The Oprah Winfrey Oscar Special, ABC, 2007.

AFI's 100 Years ... 100 Movies: 10th Anniversary Edition (also known as *AFI's 100 Years ... 100 Movies*), CBS, 2007.

Hope for Haiti Now: A Global Benefit for Earthquake Relief, CBS, Fox, PBS, NBC, The CW, ABC, 2010.

Premio Donostia a Julia Roberts, 2010.

Television Appearances; Awards Presentations:

The ... Annual Academy Awards Presentation, ABC, 1990, 1991, 2001, 2004.

The ... Blockbuster Entertainment Awards, UPN, 1998, Fox, 2000.

The ... Annual People's Choice Awards, CBS, 1998, 2000, 2002.

The ... Annual Golden Globe Awards, 1998, NBC, 2010.

Presenter, *The ... Annual Golden Globe Awards,* NBC, 2000, 2001.

Presenter, *GQ's 2000 Men of the Year Awards* (also known as *The 5th Annual GQ Men of the Year Awards*), Fox, 2000.

Presenter, *The ... Annual Academy Awards,* ABC, 2001, 2002, 2003, 2005.

The 7th Annual Screen Actors Guild Awards, TNT, 2001.

The 2001 MTV Movie Awards, MTV, 2001.

The 11th Annual Critics' Choice Awards, The WB, 2006.

The 60th Annual Tony Awards, CBS, 2006.

Julia Roberts: American Cinematheque Tribute, AMC, 2007.

AFI Life Achievement Award: A Tribute to Mike Nichols, TV Land, 2010.

Television Appearances; Episodic:

Tracy, "The Survivor," *Crime Story,* NBC, 1987.

Polly Wheeler, "Mirror Image," *Miami Vice,* NBC, 1988.

American Cinema, PBS, 1995.

Corazon, corazon, 1995.

Primer plano, 1996.

Susie Moss, "The One after the Super Bowl," *Friends,* NBC, 1996.

Film '96 (also known as *The Film Programme*), BBC, 1996.

"Cheetahs with Holly Hunter," *In the Wild,* 1997.

"On the Set: 'My Best Friend's Wedding,'" *HBO First Look,* HBO, 1997.

"Conspiracy Theory," *HBO First Look,* HBO, 1997.

"Orangutans with Julia Roberts," *In the Wild,* 1998.

Herself, "Never Can Say Goodbye: Parts 1 & 2," *Murphy Brown,* CBS, 1998.

Herself, "Telly and Rosita's Fix–It Shop," *Sesame Street* (also known as *Open Sesame, Sesame Street Unpaved,* and *The New Sesame Street*), PBS, 1998.

The Entertainment Business, 1998.

Katrina Ludlow, "Empire," *Law & Order,* NBC, 1999.

Mundo VIP, 1999.

Host and narrator, "In the Wild: Horsemen of Mongolia with Julia Roberts" (documentary; also known as "Wild Horses of Mongolia with Julia Roberts"), *Nature,* PBS, 2000.

Revealed with Jules Asner, E! Entertainment Television, 2001.

"The Making of 'The Mexican,'" *HBO First Look,* HBO, 2001.

"The Making of 'Ocean's Eleven,'" *HBO First Look,* HBO, 2001.

"The 25 Most Powerful People in Entertainment," *Rank,* E! Entertainment Television, 2002.

"TV & Movie Week," *Supermarket Sweep,* 2002.

"The Big Hair Do," *Comic Relief* (also known as *Comic Relief 2003: The Big Hair Do*), BBC, 2003.

"200 Greatest Pop Culture Icons," *The Greatest,* 2003.

Appleton's journal, "Yearning to Breathe Free," *Freedom: A History of Us,* 2003.

Virginia eyewitness, ""What Is Freedom?," *Freedom: A History of Us,* 2003.

Extra (also known as *Extra—The Entertainment Magazine*), syndicated, 2003, 2007.

Tinseltown TV, International Channel, 2004.

"Richard Gere," *Biography,* Arts and Entertainment, 2004.

"Brad Pitt," *Biography,* Arts and Entertainment, 2004.

"The Making of 'Ocean's Twelve,'" *HBO First Look,* HBO, 2004.

"From Orphan to King," *Nature,* PBS, 2005.

"Annie Leibovitz: Life Through a Lens," *American Masters,* PBS, 2006, then aired as an episode of *Imagine,* BBC, 2008.

"Special Edition: 'Charlotte's Web,'" *CMT Insider,* Country Music Television, 2006.

Host, *Soundstage,* PBS, 2006.

Film 2007 (also known as *The Film Programme*), BBC, 2007.

TMZ on TV, 2007.

E! News, E! Entertainment Television, 2007.

"Charlie Wilson's War," *HBO First Look,* HBO, 2007.

Entertainment Tonight (also known as *E.T.*), syndicated, 2007, 2008, 2009, 2010.

Made in Hollywood, 2010.

Le grand journal de Canal+, 2010.

Dias de cine, 2010.

Janela Indiscreta, 2010.

Also appeared as herself, *Telenoticias;* in *MovieReal,* Arts and Entertainment.

Television Talk Show Guest Appearances; Episodic:

Donahue (also known as *The Phil Donahue*), syndicated, 1989.

Late Night with David Letterman, NBC, 1989, 1992.

The Tonight Show with Jay Leno, NBC, 1993.

The Late Show with David Letterman (also known as *Letterman* and *The Late Show*), CBS, 1993, 1995, 1997, 2006, 2008, 2009, 2010.

Cinema 3, 1994, 2010.

Nyhetsmorgon, 1994, 1999, 2000, 2002, 2010.

Inside the Actors Studio (also known as *Inside the Actors Studio: The Craft of Theatre and Film* and *Actors Interview*), Bravo, 1996.

The Rosie O'Donnell Show, syndicated, 1997, 1998, 1999, 2000, 2002.

The Howard Stern Radio Show, 1999.

Howard Stern, 1999.

Charlie Rose (also known as *The Charlie Rose Show*), PBS, 2000, 2009.

The Oprah Winfrey Show (also known as *Oprah*), syndicated, 2003, 2004, 2005, 2006, 2008, 2010.

Today (also known as *NBC News Today* and *The Today Show*), NBC, 2007.

Live with Regis and Kelly, syndicated, 2009, 2010.

Loose Women, ITV, 2010.

Breakfast, ITV, 2010.

Television Work; Series:

Executive producer, *Queens Supreme,* CBS, 2003.

Television Work; Movies:

Producer, *The Pancho Gonzales Story,* HBO, 1999.

Executive producer, *Samantha: An American Girl Holiday,* The WB, 2004.

Executive producer, *Felicity: An American Girl Adventure,* The WB, 2005.

Executive producer, *Molly: An American Girl on the Home Front,* The Disney Channel, 2006.

Television Work; Pilots:
Executive producer, *Queens Supreme,* CBS, 2003.

Stage Appearances:
(Broadway debut) Nan and Lina, *Three Days of Rain,* Bernard B. Jacobs Theatre, 2006.

RECORDINGS

Albums:
(With others) Poetry reader, *The Postman (Il Postino): Music from the Miramax Motion Picture Soundtrack,* Hollywood Records, 1995.

Music Videos:
Appeared in "Dreamgirl" by Dave Matthews Band, 2005.

Taped Readings:
The Nanny Diaries: A Novel, Random House Audio, 2002.

OTHER SOURCES

Books:
Donnelley, Paul, *Julia Roberts Confidential,* Virgin Books, 2003.
International Dictionary of Films and Filmmakers, Volume 3: *Actors and Actresses,* St. James Press, 1996.
Ladowsky, Ellen, *Julia Roberts,* People Profiles, 1999.
Sanello, Frank, *Julia Roberts: Pretty Superstar,* Mainstream, 2000.
Spada, James, *Julia: Her Life,* St. Martin's Press, 2004.
St. James Encyclopedia of Popular Culture, St. James Press, 2000.

Periodicals:
American Film, July, 1990.
Daily Mail (London), January 21, 2005, p. 25.
Entertainment Weekly, June 24, 1994, p. 32; February 23, 1996, p. 22; August 6, 1999, p. 16.
Good Housekeeping, September, 1997, p. 90.
Harper's Bazaar, September, 1995.
In Style, December, 1998, p. 332.
Interview, January, 1995.
Ladies Home Journal, January, 1999, p. 102.
New York Times, March 18, 1990; May 2, 2010, p. 2.
Parade Magazine, December 6, 1998, p. 4.
People Weekly, July 7, 1997, p. 70; December 29, 1997, p. 109; May 14, 2001, pp. 122–23; July 16, 2001, p. 70; December 31, 2001, pp. 56–57;

March 11, 2002, pp. 94–95; May 13, 2002, pp. 178–79; May 27, 2002, p. 19; July 22, 2002, pp. 68–69; December 30, 2002, p. 95; May 12, 2003, p. 121; July 28, 2003, pp. 68–69.
Premiere, June, 1991; December, 1993; January, 2002, p. 84; October, 2002, p. 74.
Rolling Stone, July 14, 1994, p. 56.
Saturday Evening Post, May, 1999, p. 12.
Time, July 9, 2001, pp. 60, 62.
Times (London), March 13, 2003.
TV Guide, May 16, 1998.
Vogue, April, 1990.

ROBERTSON, Clive 1965–

PERSONAL

Full name, Clive Gladstone Robertson; born December 17, 1965, in Devizes, Wiltshire, England; father, an air force pilot; married Libby Purvis (an actress), May, 1999 (divorced October, 2003); children: Alexander, Amelia. *Education:* University of Oxford, B.A., business and management; attended Arts Educational School, London. *Avocational Interests:* Designing and building.

Addresses: *Agent*—The Chasin Agency, 8899 Beverly Blvd., Suite 716, Los Angeles, CA 90048. *Manager*—Larry Thompson, Larry A. Thompson Organization, 9663 Santa Monica Blvd., Suite 801, Beverly Hills, CA 90210.

Career: Actor. Former member of the band Jerk Me to Eternity. Worked in marketing.

Awards, Honors: *Soap Opera Digest* Award nominations, outstanding male newcomer, 1998, and (with Susan Ward) favorite couple, 1999, both for *Sunset Beach.*

CREDITS

Television Appearances; Series:
Ben Evans and Derek Evans, *Sunset Beach,* NBC, 1997–99.
Travis Montana, *Starhunter* (also known as *Starhunter 2300*), syndicated, 2003–2004.
Simon, *General Hospital* (also known as *Hopital central* and *Hospital general*), ABC, beginning 2004.
Theodore Crawford, *Wicked Wicked Games* (also known as *Art of Betrayal*), MyNetworkTV, 2006–2007.

Appeared in *London Bridge,* ITV.

Television Appearances; Movies:
Marine officer on leave, *Paparazzo,* ITV, 1995.
Damon Archer, *Las Vegas Crazy Girls Undercover* (also known as *Crazy Girls Undercover*), Showtime, 2008.

Television Appearances; Specials:
Cinderumplestiltskin (pantomime), Channel 4, 1993.
Rapist, *Before the Killing Starts,* [Great Britain], 1995.
71st Annual Macy's Thanksgiving Day Parade, NBC, 1997.
Member of the judging panel, *Miss World 2003 Pageant* (also known as *Miss World 2003*), Sky Television, 2003.

Television Appearances; Awards Presentations:
Presenter, *The 25th Daytime Emmy Awards,* NBC, 1998.
The 15th Annual Soap Opera Digest Awards, NBC, 1999.

Television Appearances; Episodic:
B Team police constable, "No Name, No Number," *The Bill,* ITV, 1994.
Himself, "Sunset Beach—Behind the Scenes," *Friday Night* (also known as *Friday Night Videos*), NBC, 1997.
Himself, *Leeza,* syndicated, 1998.
Himself, *Exclusive,* Channel 5, 1998, 2001.
Himself, "Actress Susan Ward's Cats," *Amazing Tails,* Animal Planet, 1999.
Himself, "Clive Robertson and Chance," *Amazing Tails,* Animal Planet, 2000.
Himself, "Goodbye to Sunset Beach," *Soap Fever,* ITV2, 2000.
Dr. Hank Jonas, "Diagnosis Val," *V.I.P.* (also known as *V.I.P.—Die Bodyguards*), syndicated, 2002.
Premiere episode, *The Buzz,* YTV, 2002.

Television Appearances; Pilots:
Theodore Crawford, *Wicked Wicked Games* (also known as *Art of Betrayal*), MyNetworkTV, 2006.

Film Appearances:
Topper, 1992.
Voice of Hova's wasp, *The Ant Bully* (animated), Warner Bros., 2006.

Some sources cite appearances in other films.

Stage Appearances:
Cinderumplestiltskin (pantomime), c. 1993.

Appeared as Alan Turing, *Breaking the Code,* Theatre Museum, London; also appeared in other productions, including *As You Like It,* Wimbledon Open Air Theatre, London; and *The Wild Ass's Skin,* Bridewell.

Video Games:
Voices, *Medal of Honor: European Assault,* Electronic Arts, 2005.
Voice of Captain John O'Neil, *Darkstar: The Interactive Movie,* Rush, 2006, some sources cite a release in 2010.

OTHER SOURCES

Periodicals:
Soap Opera Digest, July 20, 1999.

**ROBICHAUX, Richard
(Ricki Robichaux)**

PERSONAL

Born in Channelview, TX; married Natalie Griffith (an actress); children: Gus. *Education:* Rutgers University, M.F.A.; studied acting and improvisation; studied with different instructors in different programs.

Addresses: *Agent*—Collier Talent Agency, 2313 Lake Austin Blvd., Suite 103, Austin, TX 78703.

Career: Actor and teacher. Appeared in advertisements. The Robichaux Studio (acting studio), Austin, TX, founder and director; Elizabeth Mestnik Acting Studio, Hollywood, CA, instructor; The New York Conservatory for Dramatic Arts, New York City, member of the faculty; keynote speaker and instructor at institutions and educational conferences for performers.

Member: Screen Actors Guild, American Federation of Television and Radio Artists, Actors' Equity Association.

CREDITS

Stage Appearances:
Arthur, *Spring Storm,* Marin Theatre Company, Mill Valley, CA, 1999.
Moth, *Love's Labour's Lost,* Shakespeare Santa Cruz, University of California, Santa Cruz, Sinsheimer–Stanley Festival Glen, 2000.
Pisanio, *Cymbeline,* Shakespeare Santa Cruz, University of California, Santa Cruz, Sinsheimer–Stanley Festival Glen, 2000.
Zack, *The Legendary St. Vincent Design,* Wings Theatre, New York City, 2001.

(Sometimes known as Ricki Robichaux) Epicoene, *The Silent Woman,* Shakespeare Theatre Company, Lansburgh Theatre, Washington, DC, 2003.

Wolfgang Amadeus Mozart (title role), *Amadeus,* Syracuse Stage, Syracuse, NY, and Virginia Stage Company, Wells Theatre, Norfolk, VA, both 2003.

Ephraim, *The Salacious Uncle Baldrick,* The Salacious Company, New York International Fringe Festival (also known as FringeNYC), Players Theatre, New York City, 2005.

Parolles, *All's Well That Ends Well,* Yale Repertory Theatre, New Haven, CT, 2006.

Stanislas (steward) and member of the ensemble, *The School of Night,* Center Theatre Group, Mark Taper Forum, Los Angeles, 2008.

Appeared in other productions, including *The Complete Works of William Shakespeare, Abridged* (also known as *The Complete Works of William Shakespeare, (Abridged)),* Century Center for the Performing Arts, New York City; as Algernon Moncrieff, *The Importance of Being Earnest,* Indiana Repertory Theatre, Indianapolis, IN; as the narrator, *The Last Supper,* SoHo Playhouse; as Radu, *Mad Forest;* and as Sensible, *Right On, America!,* New York International Fringe Festival (also known as FringeNYC), New York City. Appeared in other productions, including productions of Colorado Shakespeare Festival.

Television Appearances; Series:
Charlie Dibble, *All My Children* (also known as *All My Children: The Summer of Seduction* and *La force du destin*), ABC, 2004.

Television Appearances; Movies:
Man in tights, *Porn 'n Chicken* (also known as *Chicken Club*), Comedy Central, 2002.

Television Appearances; Episodic:
Bellhop, "An American Deputy Mayor in Paris," *Spin City* (also known as *Spin*), ABC, 2000.

(Uncredited) Student, "The Pilgrim," *Law & Order: Criminal Intent* (also known as *Law & Order: CI*), NBC, 2002.

Coworker, "Sects," *Law & Order* (also known as *Law & Order Prime*), NBC, 2005.

Various characters, "Satan's Baby," *Scare Tactics,* Sci–Fi Channel, 2008.

Various characters, "The Screaming Room," *Scare Tactics,* Sci–Fi Channel, 2008.

Guess Who? segment, *Atom TV,* Comedy Central, 2008.

Mark, "The Impertence of Communicationizing," *Better Off Ted* (also known as *Untitled Victor Fresco Project*), ABC, 2010.

Appeared as Ritchie in "Swag the Dog," an unaired episode of *Better Off Ted* (also known as *Untitled Victor Fresco Project*), ABC.

Television Appearances; Pilots:
Brickman, *Hate,* Showtime, 2005.
Mike Gordan, *Taylor Made,* 2005.

Film Appearances:
Joey Vitale, *Tony n' Tina's Wedding* (also known as *Tony n' Tina's Wedding: The Movie*), 2004, Emerging Pictures, 2007.

Marc, *Flannel Pajamas,* 2006, Gigantic Pictures, 2007.

The boss, *Ready? OK!,* Wolfe Releasing, 2008.

John King, *Collecting Canada* (short film), 2008.

Mr. Mink, *Foreign Exchange,* Shoot Productions/Sycophant Films/Full Glass Films/StoneBrook Entertainment, 2008.

Bartender, *Mother's Little Helpers* (also known as *Mothers Little Helpers*), StoneBrook Entertainment/Lookout Films/Sycophant Films, 2010.

Internet Appearances:
Dr. Lane Jeffries and John "Jack" Worthing, *Live from Studio C Presents* (also known as *Live from Studio C Presents ...,* *Live from "Studio C Presents," Live from "Studio C Presents ...,"* and *Studio C Presents ... Don Ameche*), broadcast on *YouTube,* http://www.youtube.com, beginning c. 2007.

OTHER SOURCES

Electronic:
Richard Robichaux, http://www.richardrobichaux.com, September 30, 2010.

RONA, Andrew

PERSONAL

Education: Graduated from the School of Visual Arts, New York City.

Addresses: *Office*—Silver Pictures and Dark Castle Entertainment, 4000 Warner Blvd., Bldg. 90, Burbank, CA 91522.

Career: Producer, director, production executive, executive in charge of production, and studio executive. Began career as assistant to Harvey Weinstein at Miramax Films, 1993; moved through the ranks at Miramax Films, becoming a production executive and helping to launch the Dimension Films banner; became copresident of Dimension Films, 2000; Rogue Pictures, copresident, beginning 2005; Silver Pictures, Burbank, CA, president, 2009—; Dark Castle Entertainment, Burbank, CA, copresident.

Member: Academy of Motion Picture Arts and Sciences.

Awards, Honors: Hampton International Film Festival, best student film, c. 1994, for *Box Alley*.

CREDITS

Film Executive Producer:

Co–executive producer, *Scream 2* (also known as *Scream Again, Scream Louder,* and *Scream: The Sequel*), Miramax, 1997.

Co–executive producer, *Phantoms* (also known as *Dean Koontz's "Phantoms"* and *Phantom*), Miramax, 1998.

Allied Forces, Miramax, 1999.

Dracula 2000 (also known as *Dracula 2001, Dracula 2002, Wes Craven—Dracula 2000,* and *Wes Craven Presents "Dracula 2000"*), Miramax, 2000.

Reindeer Games (also known as *Deception* and *Wild Christmas*), Dimension Films, 2000.

Scream 3 (also known as *Ghostface* and *Scream 3: Ghostface Killer*), Miramax, 2000.

Takedown (also known as *Hackers 2, Hackers 2: Takedown, Operation Takedown, Takedown: The Pursuit and Capture of Kevin Mitnick, America's Most Wanted Computer Outlaw,* and *Track Down*), 2000.

Below (also known as *Proteus*), Miramax, 2002.

Equilibrium (also known as *Cubic, Equilibrium—Killer of Emotions, Librium,* and *Rebellion*), Miramax, 2002.

Mimic: Sentinel (also known as *Mimic 3, Mimic 3: Sentinel,* and *Mimic 3—sentinel*), Dimension Films, 2003.

My Boss's Daughter (also known as *Partyalarm*), Buena Vista, 2003.

Scary Movie 3 (also known as *Scary Movie III, Scary Movie 3.5,* and *Scary Movie 3: Episode I—Lord of the Brooms*), Miramax, 2003.

The Brothers Grimm (also known as *Brothers Grimm*), Miramax, 2005.

Curandero, Miramax, 2005.

Cursed (also known as *Wes Craven's "Cursed"*), Miramax/Dimension Films, 2005.

Dracula III: Legacy (also known as *Dracula: Resurrected* and *Dracula 3*), Dimension Films, 2005.

Venom (also known as *Backwater* and *The Reaper*), Dimension Films, 2005.

Doomsday, Rogue Pictures, 2008.

Fighting (also known as *Dito Montiel Project*), Rogue Pictures, 2009.

The Losers, Warner Bros., 2010.

My Soul to Take (also known as *Bug, 25/8,* and *Untitled Wes Craven Project*), Universal, 2010.

Project X, Warner Bros., 2011.

Also worked as an executive producer for *Deader* (also known as *Hellraiser: Deader*), Dimension Films.

Film Producer:

Coproducer, *Mimic* (also known as *Judus*), Dimension Films, 1997.

Coproducer, *Imposter* (also known as *Clone* and *Enemy of the Earth*), Dimension Films, 2001.

The Apparition, Warner Bros., 2011.

Unknown (also known as *Unknown White Male*), Warner Bros., 2011.

Film Production Executive:

Ging chat goo si 3: Chiu kup ging chat (also known as *Police Story 3, Police Story 3—Supercop, Police Story 3: Super Cop,* and *Supercop*), Golden Harvest Company, 1992, dubbed version, Dimension Films, 1996.

The Prophecy (also known as *God's Army, God's Secret Army,* and *Seraphim*), Miramax/Dimension Films, 1995.

Production executive: Miramax/Dimension Films, *The Crow: City of Angels* (also known as *The Crow II*), Miramax, 1996.

Sin City (also known as *Frank Miller's "Sin City"*), Dimension Films, 2005.

Film Executive in Charge of Production:

Halloween: The Curse of Michael Myers (also known as *Hall6ween, Halloween: The Origin of Michael Myers, Halloween 6: The Curse of Michael Myers, Halloween VI: The Curse of Michael Myers, Halloween 666: Curse of Michael Myers,* and *Halloween 666: The Origin of Michael Myers*), Dimension Films, 1995.

Hellraiser: Bloodline, (also known as *Hellraiser: Bloodline, Hellr4iser—bloodline, Hellraiser IV, Hellraiser IV: Bloodline,* and *Hellraiser IV: Bloodline Story,* Dimension Films, 1996.

Nightwatch, Dimension Films, 1997.

The Strangers (also known as *The Faces*), Rogue Pictures, 2008.

Coraline (animated; also known as *Coraline & the Secret Door*), Focus Features, 2009.

Fighting (also known as *Dito Montiel Project*), Rogue Pictures, 2009.

The Last House on the Left, Rogue Pictures, 2009.

(Uncredited) *The Unborn* (also known as *Born, Unborn, Undead,* and *Untitled David S. Goyer Project*), Rogue Pictures, 2009.

Film Studio Executive:

(Uncredited) *Below* (also known as *Proteus*), Miramax, 2002.

(Uncredited) *Equilibrium* (also known as *Cubic, Equilibrium—Killer of Emotions, Librium,* and *Rebellion*), Miramax, 2002.

(Uncredited) *Bad Santa* (director's cut also released as well as another version released as *Badder Santa*), Dimension Films, 2003.

(Uncredited) *My Boss's Daughter* (also known as *Partyalarm*), Buena Vista, 2003.

Mindhunters (also known as *Mind Hunters* and *Profession profiler*), 2004, Dimension Films, 2005.

(Uncredited) *The Adventures of Sharkboy and Lavagirl 3–D*, Dimension Films, 2005.

The Crow: Wicked Prayer (also known as *The Crow 4* and *Wicked Prayer*), Dimension Films, 2005.

Cursed (also known as *Wes Craven's "Cursed"*), Miramax/Dimension Films, 2005.

Feast, The Weinstein Company, 2006.

White Noise 2: The Light (also known as *Interferences 2, White Noise: The Light,* and *White Noise 2*), Rogue Pictures, 2007.

The Last House on the Left, Rogue Pictures, 2009.

Also worked as a studio executive for *Deader* (also known as *Hellraiser: Deader*), Dimension Films.

Film Director:

Box Alley (short student film), School of Visual Arts, c. 1994.

The Education of James Kaan, 1998.

Film Work; Other:

Dimension executive in charge (Los Angeles postproduction), *Twin Dragons* (also known as *Brother vs. Brother, Double Dragon, Duel of Dragons, The Twin Dragons,* and *When Dragons Collide;* dubbed and recut version of film originally known as *Shuang long hui* and released in Hong Kong in 1992, Dimension Films, 1999.

Copresident (Dark Castle Entertainment), *Splice,* Warner Bros., 2010.

Worked on other projects.

ROSE, Adam

PERSONAL

Mother, an opera singer. *Avocational Interests:* Tap, jazz, ballet, and martial arts.

Addresses: *Agent*—Agency for the Performing Arts, 405 South Beverly Dr., Beverly Hills, CA 90212. *Manager*—Lighthouse Entertainment, 409 North Camden Dr., Suite 202, Beverly Hills, CA 90210.

Career: Actor. Taught dance at the Broadway Dance Center, New York City.

CREDITS

Film Appearances:

Mel's son and Harry's character, *Deconstructing Harry,* Fine Line, 1997.

Brad's son, *Fare Well Miss Fortune,* 1999.

Addict Jewish child, *The Hebrew Hammer,* Strand Releasing, 2003.

Otto, *The Squid and the Whale,* Samuel Goldwyn Films, 2005.

Eddie, *Camouflage,* 2009.

Makeout Dave, *Up in the Air* (also known as *Mileage, My Life*), Paramount, 2009.

Jimmy, *The Bounty Hunter,* Columbia, 2010.

Louie, *The Back–Up Plan,* CBS Films, 2010.

Steven, *First Dates,* American Film Institute Conservatory, 2010.

Anthony, *Margaret,* Fox Searchlight, 2011.

Television Appearances; Series:

Max, *Veronica Mars,* UPN, 2006–2007.

Dooley, *Aliens in America,* The CW, 2007–2008.

Television Appearances; Miniseries:

HBO Voyeur Project, HBO, 2007.

Television Appearances; Pilots:

Dooley, *Aliens in America,* The CW, 2007.

Television Appearances; Episodic:

Russ, "Fun Night," *Casualty,* BBC1, 1987.

Ryan, "All Purpose Kablam!," *Kablam!,* Nickelodeon, 1996.

Peanut Otter, "Babbleberry Day," *PB&J Otter,* The Disney Channel, 1998.

Peanut Otter, "A Sledding We Will Go," *PB&J Otter,* The Disney Channel, 1998.

Isaac, "Hell Is What You Make of It," *Third Watch,* NBC, 1999.

Kid, *Ed,* NBC, 2001.

Todd, "All Happy Families," *The Sopranos,* HBO, 2004.

Ken, "Morp," *Malcolm in the Middle,* Fox, 2006.

Bradley Foster, "The Beginning," *Without a Trace* (also known as *W.A.T.*), CBS, 2007.

Bradley Foster, "Lost Boy," *Without a Trace* (also known as *W.A.T.*), CBS, 2007.

Dr. Andrew Hopp, "The Finger in the Nest," *Bones,* Fox, 2008.

Ronnie, "Got the Babysitter Pregnant," *My Name Is Earl,* NBC, 2009.

Assistant District Attorney Rob Kimball, "The Innocent Man," *Harry's Law,* NBC, 2010.

Joe Knock, "Bliss," *Weeds,* Showtime, 2010.

Joe Knock, "Boomerang," *Weeds,* Showtime, 2010.

Stage Appearances:

Eric, *Baby Anger,* Playwrights Horizons Theatre, New York City, 1997.

Angel, *Dead End,* Ahmanson Theatre, Los Angeles, 2005.

Major Tours:

Appeared in *The Gathering* (multiple tours).

RUEGSEGGER, Sean
See AFABLE, Sean Michael

RUNCORN, Elijah 1994–

PERSONAL

Born December 21, 1994, in Fort Belvoir, VA; son of James (an actor) and Tena (an actress and in casting) Runcorn.

Addresses: *Agent*—Diverse Talent Group, 9911 West Pico Blvd., Suite 350 West, Los Angeles, CA 90035. *Manager*—Williams Unlimited, 5010 Buffalo Ave., Sherman Oaks, CA 91423.

Career: Actor. Appeared in television and radio commercials.

Member: Screen Actors Guild, American Federation of Television and Radio Artists.

CREDITS

Film Appearances:
Bobby, *Crazylove* (also known as *Committed* and *crazylove*), PorchLight Entertainment, 2005.
Erin, *Fellowship* (short film), Wild Cub Productions, 2005.
(Uncredited) Young Ben, *Captivity,* After Dark Films, 2007.
Carl, *Belittled* (short film), Antic Pictures/Force Studios, 2008.

Television Appearances; Specials:
Ping Ting, *Sun Yat Sen: In the Mouth of the Dragon,* 2000.

Television Appearances; Episodic:
Himself, *Prime Time Country,* The Nashville Network, multiple episodes, 1999.
(In archive footage) Himself, *Talk Soup,* E! Entertainment Television, 1999.
Himself, *The Tonight Show with Jay Leno* (also known as *Jay Leno* and *Jay Leno Show*), NBC, 1999.
Himself, *The Rosie O'Donnell Show,* syndicated, 1999, 2002.
Himself, *The Maury Povich Show* (also known as *Maury, Maury Povich,* and *The Maury Show*), syndicated, 1999, 2004.

Jimmy, *MAD TV* (also known as *Mad TV* and *MADtv*), Fox, 2001.
First kid, "Monkey," *Malcolm in the Middle* (also known as *Fighting in Underpants*), Fox, 2002.
Himself, "Runcorn/Los Angeles," *Adoption Stories,* Discovery Health, 2004.
Boy, "The Cure," *The Shield* (also known as *The Barn* and *Rampart*), FX Network, 2005.
Young Tony, "Tony the Tiger," *Listen Up* (also known as *Shut Up and Listen*), CBS, 2005.
Young Tony, "Tony Whine–Man," *Listen Up* (also known as *Shut Up and Listen*), CBS, 2005.
Voice of Young Zuko, "Zuko Alone," *Avatar: The Last Airbender* (animated; also known as *Avatar, Avatar: The Legend of Aang,* and *Avatar—Der Herr der Elemente*), Nickelodeon, 2006.
Young Jim, "Jim's Birthday," *According to Jim* (also known as *The Dad, Immer wieder Jim, Jim hat immer recht, Jims vaerld, La vita secondo Jim,* and *Perheen kalleudet*), ABC, 2006.
Young Jim, "Sex Ed Fred," *According to Jim* (also known as *The Dad, Immer wieder Jim, Jim hat immer recht, Jims vaerld, La vita secondo Jim,* and *Perheen kalleudet*), ABC, 2006.
Voice of Ned, "Solomon FIX" segment, "Solomon FIX/MooBeard the Cow Pirate/Two Witch Sisters," *Random! Cartoons* (animated), Nickelodeon, 2008.

Television Work; Movies:
Provided automated dialogue replacement voices for television movies, including *A Grandpa for Christmas* (also known as *Bert & Becca*), Hallmark Channel, 2007.

RUPRECHT, David 1948–
(David Rupprecht, Dave Ruprecht)

PERSONAL

Full name, David Martin Ruprecht; born October 14, 1948, in St. Louis, MO; father, a Lutheran minister; married Patti Colombo (a director and choreographer), 1990. *Education:* Valparaiso University, B.A., theatre; studied acting with Milton Katselas, Gordon Hunt, and Glen Casale, and at the Brooklyn Academy, in Coventry, England; studied dance with Lou Conte and Roland Dupree; studied improvisation with The Groundlings, Viola Spolin, and Off the Wall; studied voice with Eric Vetro. *Politics:* Libertarian.

Addresses: *Office*—c/o Colony Theatre Company, Burbank Center Stage, 555 North Third St., Burbank, CA.

Career: Actor and writer. Colony Theatre Company, member of company, c. 2003; appeared in television commercials, including Amazon.com, 1999, and Brinks

Home Security, 2002. Libertarian Party of California, executive director, beginning 2004.

Member: Writers Guild of America.

CREDITS

Film Appearances:
(As David Rupprecht) *The Seniors* (also known as *The Senior*), Cinema Shares International, 1978.
(As David Rupprecht) Neighbor, *The Incredible Shrinking Woman,* Universal, 1981.
Radio voice, *Star Trek: The Wrath of Khan* (also known as *Star Trek II: The Wrath of Khan* and *Star Trek II: The Wrath of Khan—The Director's Edition*), Paramount, 1982.
Brigham, *Jekyll & Hyde … Together Again,* Paramount, 1982.
Dickens, *A Minor Miracle* (also known as *Young Giants*), Entertainment Enterprises, 1983.
Talking Walls (also known as *Motel Vacancy*), New World Pictures, 1987.
Yuppie dad, *Taking Care of Business* (also known as *Filofax*), Buena Vista, 1990.
Dealer, *I Lost My M in Vegas,* 1999.
Pastor, *Finding Home,* Castle Hill Productions, 2003.
Brandon Taylor, *The Daze Before Christmas,* 2004.
Brandon Taylor, *That's Easy for You to Say!,* 2005.

Television Appearances; Series:
Host, *Supermarket Sweep,* Lifetime, 1990–98, then PAX, 1999–2003.
Day Ryan, *Days of Our Lives* (also known as *DOOL* and *Days*), NBC, 1990–92.

Television Appearances; Miniseries:
Middle–aged man, *The '70s,* NBC, 2000.

Television Appearances; Movies:
Young Love, First Love, 1979.

Television Appearances; Pilots:
Thurston Howell IV, *The Harlem Globetrotters on Gilligan's Island,* NBC, 1981.

Also appeared in *What a Year; Who's On Call.*

Television Appearances; Specials:
Dan Ryan, *"Days of Our Lives": One Stormy Night,* NBC, 1992.
"Gilligan's Island": The E! True Hollywood Story, E! Entertainment Television, 2000.
Host, *Mrs. World 2001,* PAX, 2001.
Host, *PAX Presents Game Show Specials,* PAX, 2003.

Television Appearances; Episodic:
David, "The Mayor's Committee From Deer Lick Falls," *The Rockford Files,* 1977.
The Midnight Special, 1979.
(As David Rupprecht) Hal Hendricks, "Who's the Sexist Girl in the World," *Lobo* (also known as *The Misadventures of Sheriff Lobo*), 1980.
Sherman, "Chain of Command," *Benson,* ABC, 1980.
Dr. Wilkens, "The Flight of the Nightingale," *Quincy, M.E.* (also known as *Quincy*), 1982.
Himself, *The Shape of Things,* 1982.
Bernie, "Love Is the Question," *Fame,* 1983.
Gary, "Jonah Moves Out," *Foot in the Door,* 1984.
Match Game/Hollywood Squares Hour, 1984.
Philip Dawson, "The Heiress" (also known as "The Inheritance"), *Three's Company,* ABC, 1984.
Philip Dawson, "Cupid Works Overtime," *Three's Company,* ABC, 1984.
Philip Dawson, "Friends and Lovers: Parts 1 & 2," *Three's Company,* ABC, 1984.
Carlson, "The Truth about Holly," *Airwolf* (also known as *Lobo del aire*), CBS, 1984.
Dennis Coler, "Whistle, Wyler Works," *St. Elsewhere,* NBC, 1985.
Freddie Copperman, "Freddie Loves It, We Love It, You're Cancelled," *Too Close for Comfort,* 1985.
Randall Pierson, "The Play's the Thing," *Riptide,* NBC, 1986.
Chief Hansen, "A.W.O.L.," *Simon & Simon,* CBS, 1986.
Mr. Mallman, "You Better Watch Out," *Married … with Children* (also known as *Married with Children*), Fox, 1987.
Johnson, "Secrets," *Webster,* 1987.
Host of Dream Date, "The Matchmaker," *Punky Brewster,* 1987.
Zack Davis, "TV or Not TV," *Small Wonder,* 1987.
Mr. Bowen, "Radio Daze," *Punky Brewster,* NBC, 1988.
Minister, "Wedding Bells for Brandon," *Punky Brewster,* NBC, 1988.
Salesman, "The Mistress," *Matlock,* NBC, 1988.
"I'm Okay, You're All Crazy," *She's the Sheriff,* 1989.
"Perfetc," *Moonlighting,* ABC, 1989.
Television interviewer, "You've Come a Long Way, Baby Sitter," *Doogie Howser, M.D.,* ABC, 1993.
Host, "Different," *Sisters,* NBC, 1993.
Television announcer, "Making Out Is Hard to Do," *Full House,* ABC, 1994.
Lawyer, "The Things We Do for Love," *Beverly Hills, 90210* (also known as *The Class of Beverly Hills*), Fox, 1996.
Jasper Mullian, "The Iron Maiden," *Team Knight Rider,* 1997.
Lee, "What Do You Know?," *Family Matters,* 1997.
Dr. Anderson, Eddie's dad, "The Morgue," *Beyond Belief: Fact or Fiction,* 1998.
(As Dave Rupprecht) Announcer, "The Consultant," *Working,* NBC, 1998.
Foster Dad, "Metamorphosis," *Family Law,* CBS, 2000.
Inmate, "Bananas: Part 2," *The Drew Carey Show,* ABC, 2001.

Bill Cummins, "Vanity, Thy Name Is Human," *Joan of Arcadia*, CBS, 2004.
Radio broadcaster, "Colors," *Cold Case*, CBS, 2004.
Judge Bolan, *The Bold and the Beautiful* (also known as *Belleza y poder*), CBS, 2006.
Televangelist, "Mine," *True Blue*, HBO, 2008.

Also appeared in *Rosie O'Donnell Show*; *Oprah Winfrey*.

Stage Appearances:
(Broadway debut) *Perfectly Frank,* Helen Hayes Theatre, New York City, 1980.
Shadow of a Gunman, Colony Theatre Company, Burbank, CA, 1998.

Also appeared in *Sylvia,* Hermosa Beach Playhouse, Hermosa Beach, CA; *The Music Man,* Music Theatre of Wichita, Wichita, KS; *Honk!,* Music Theatre of Wichita; *Lend Me a Tenor,* La Mirada Theatre, La Mirada, CA; *Gypsy,* Austin Music Theatre, Austin, TX; *The Wonder Years,* Coronet Theatre, Los Angeles; *In Camera,* Mark Taper Forum, Los Angeles; *The Wizard of Oz,* La Mirada, CA; *Get Happy,* Westwood Playhouse, Los Angeles; *Rainbow Bar & Grill,* Victory Theatre, Burbank, CA; *Brigadoon,* San Bernardino, CA; *Hay Fever,* Drury Lane, Chicago, IL; *Barefoot in the Park,* Drury Lane; *Anything Goes,* Long Beach, CA; *Second Time Around,* Country Theatre, Columbus, OH; *Company,* La Mirada, CA; *Dandelion Wine,* Colony Theatre Company, Burbank, CA.

Major Tours:
Appeared in *How to Succeed in Business without Really Trying,* U.S. cities; *South Pacific.*

WRITINGS

Screenplay Stories:
Finding Home, Castle Hill Productions, 2003.

Also wrote *Charlie's Wake.*

Television Episodes:
Small Wonder, 1986–89.

Television Episode Stories:
"Haunted House," *Small Wonder,* 1987.

Books:
(With Ruth Ruprecht) *Radical Hospitality,* 1983.

OTHER SOURCES

Electronic:
David Ruprecht Official Site, http://www.davidruprecht. com, September 17, 2010.

RUSSELL, Jane 1921–2011
    (Ernestine Jane Geraldine Russell)

PERSONAL

Original name, Ernestine Jane Geraldine Russell; born June 21, 1921, in Bemidji, Minnesota; died of respiratory failure, February 28, 2011, in Santa Maria, California. Actress. Russell was one of the first bombshells to appear on American movie screens. Discovered by the legendary film producer Howard Hughes in the early 1940s, Russell was featured in the romantic Western *The Outlaw* in 1943. The film proved controversial because of Russell's revealing attire and Hughes' fixation on her 38-inch bust (he went so far as to design a special bra to accentuate her figure), and it was not cleared for wide release until 1946. In 1948 Russell starred alongside Bob Hope in the comedy Western *The Paleface,* and the two became lifelong friends, appearing together again in the 1952 sequel *Son of Paleface.* Russell also acted with Robert Mitchum in *His Kind of Woman* and *Macao,* as well as with Frank Sinatra and Groucho Marx in *Double Dynamite.* In perhaps her best-known film role, Russell starred with Marilyn Monroe in the 1953 musical *Gentlemen Prefer Blondes* and the sequel *Gentlemen Marry Brunettes.* A series of little-known Westerns, comedies, and adventure films followed throughout the 1950s and 60s, including *The Tall Men* with Clark Gable and *The Fuzzy Pink Nightgown,* in which she played a kidnapped movie star who eventually renounces her stardom. With her film career fading, Russell appeared in a Broadway production of *Company,* recorded a series of gospel songs, and became a spokeswoman for Playtex brassieres in the 1970s. Her autobiography, *Jane Russell: My Path and My Detours,* was published in 1985.

PERIODICALS

Guardian, March 1, 2011.
Los Angeles Times, February 28, 2011.
New York Times, March 1, 2011.
Telegraph, March 1, 2011.

S

St. JOHN, Trevor 1971–

PERSONAL

Full name, Trevor Marshall St. John; born September, 3, 1971, in Spokane, WA; married Sara, 2000; children: Aidan. *Education:* Whitworth College, theatre degree. *Avocational Interests:* Playing jazz percussion and Buddhist meditation.

Addresses: *Agent*—Innovative Artists, 235 Park Ave. South, 10th Floor, New York, NY 10003.

Career: Actor. Also a jazz percussionist, playing with Marshall Royal, Slide Hampton, Bill Berry, and Gene Harris. Bioconstructs (a fitness company), founder, 2001—. Previously worked as a personal trainer.

Awards, Honors: Special Fan Award nomination (with Kassie Wesley DePaiva), irresistible combination, Daytime Emmy Awards, 2005, for *One Life to Live.*

CREDITS

Film Appearances:
James, *Higher Learning,* Columbia, 1995.
Launcher, *Crimson Tide,* Buena Vista, 1995.
Eddie, *Nothing Man* (short film), 1995.
Parker, *Bio–Dome,* Metro–Goldwyn–Mayer, 1996.
Preston, *Back in Business* (also known as *Heart of Stone*), Columbia TriStar, 1997.
Philip Van Horn, *Dogtown,* 1997.
Johnny Bronson, *Payback,* Paramount, 1999.
Himself, *Karen Black: Actress at Work* (documentary), 1999.
Captain John Reynolds, *The King's Guard,* Shoreline Entertainment, 2000.

Tactical team leader, *The Bourne Ultimatum* (also known as *Bourne Ultimatum*), Universal, 2007.
Earl Ripon, *The Kingdom,* Universal, 2007.
The Art of Getting Over It (short film), 2008.
Luke, *My Soul to Take,* Rogue Pictures, 2010.

Film Work:
Stand–in, *Benny & Joon,* 1993.
Executive producer and codirector, *The Art of Getting Over It,* 2008.

Television Appearances; Series:
Todd Manning, *One Life to Live,* ABC, 2003—.
Walker Lawrence Flynn, *One Life to Live,* ABC, 2003.

Television Appearances; Movies:
College guy, *Sketch Artist II: Hands That See* (also known as *A Feel for Murder* and *Sketch Artist*), Showtime, 1995.
David, *Serving in Silence: The Margarethe Cammermeyer Story* (also known as *Serving in Silence*), NBC, 1995.
Jon Berry, *The Beach Boys: An American Family,* ABC, 2000.

Television Appearances; Specials:
The 31st Annual Daytime Emmy Awards, NBC, 2004.
The 37th Annual Daytime Emmy Awards, CBS, 2010.

Television Appearances; Pilots:
Eddie, *Spider,* The WB, 1996.
Devlin George, *Dirty Sexy Money,* ABC, 2007.

Television Appearances; Episodic:
Colin Forbes, "School for Murder," *Murder, She Wrote,* CBS, 1995.
"Spindrift," *SeaQuest DSV* (also known as *SeaQuest 2032*), NBC, 1995.
Jason, "Kill Switch," *Nash Bridges,* CBS, 1999.

Jason, "Skin Trade," *Nash Bridges,* CBS, 2000.
"A Thousand Words," *Pacific Blue,* syndicated, 2000.
Cameron, "A Beautiful Mind," *Just Shoot Me!,* NBC, 2002.
The View, ABC, 2003.
Kiley, "Now and Zen," *Hope & Faith,* NBC, 2006.

Also appeared in *Diagnosis Murder,* CBS.

Stage Appearances:
Appeared in *As You Like It; All My Sons; Judgment; Merry Wives of Windsor.*

WRITINGS

Screenplays:
(With others) *The Art of Getting Over It,* 2008.

Film Stories:
The Art of Getting Over It, 2008.

OTHER SOURCES

Electronic:
Trevor St. John Official Site, http://www.trevorstjohn.com, October 21, 2010.

SCHWARTZ, Ben

PERSONAL

Addresses: *Agent*—Brian DePersia, WME Entertainment, 9601 Wilshire Blvd., 3rd Floor, Beverly Hills, CA 90210. *Manager*—Tom Sawyer Entertainment, 315 South Beverly Dr., Suite 508, Beverly Hills, CA 90212.

Career: Actor, producer, director, and writer. Upright Citizens Brigade, member of improvisational theatre company, 2003—; RejectedJokes.com, Web site creator. Freelance writer of jokes and other comedy material for television talk show personalities; appeared at Montreal Just for Laughs Festival, 2007.

Awards, Honors: Two Webby Award nominations, best writing and best short film, International Academy of Digital Arts and Sciences, both 2007, for "Press Conference," *Bronx World Travelers;* Emmy Award nomination (with others), outstanding writing for a variety, music, or comedy special, 2009, for *81st Annual Academy Awards;* Emmy Award (with others), outstand-

ing original music and lyrics (with others), 2009, for "Hugh Jackman Opening Number," for *81st Annual Academy Awards.*

CREDITS

Television Appearances; Series:
Evan Mintz, *Mayne Street,* ESPN, 2008–2009.
Bill Hoyt, *Undercovers,* NBC, 2010.

Television Appearances; Pilots:
Voice of Glenn, *Starveillance,* E! Entertainment Television, 2007.
Jacky Hamburger, *Happiness Isn't Everything,* CBS, 2009.

Television Appearances; Episodic:
Late Night with Conan O'Brien, NBC, 2006.
Voice of Glenn, *Starveillance,* E! Entertainment Television, 2007.
Waiter, *Intercourse with a Vampire,* 2009.
Max, "Working Girl," *Accidentally on Purpose,* CBS, 2009.
Writer, "A Slip Slope," *The Sarah Silverman Program,* Comedy Central, 2010.
Jean–Ralphio, "The Set Up," *Parks and Recreation* (also known as *Parks and Rec*), NBC, 2010.
Jean–Ralphio, "Woman of the Year," *Parks and Recreation* (also known as *Parks and Rec*), NBC, 2010.
Jean–Ralphio, "The Master Plan," *Parks and Recreation* (also known as *Parks and Rec*), NBC, 2010.

Also appeared in one or more episodes of *Funny or Die Presents …,* HBO, 2009–10.

Film Appearances:
Russ, *New York City Serenade* (also known as *NYC Serenade*), 2007, Anchor Bay Entertainment, 2009.
Dougie's buddy, *Mystery Team,* Roadside Attractions, 2009.
Tammy's date, *I Hate Valentine's Day,* IFC Films, 2009.
Writer, *Everybody's Fine,* Miramax, 2009.
Beaman's assistant, *The Other Guys,* Columbia, 2010.
Nathan, *Peep World,* IFC Films, 2010.
Ira, *Manslaughter,* Hunga Rican Entertainment/IKM Productions, 2010.

Internet Appearances; Series:
Ben, *Bronx World Travelers,* RejectedJoked.com, 2007–2008.

Internet Work; Series:
Executive producer and director, *Bronx World Travelers,* RejectedJokes.com, 2007–2008.

WRITINGS

Television Series:
Robot Chicken (animated), Cartoon Network, 2007.

Television Specials:
Special material and song lyrics, "Hugh Jackman Opening Number," *81st Annual Academy Awards,* ABC, 2009.

Television Episodes:
Writer for one or more episodes of *Funny or Die Presents ...,* HBO, 2009–10.

Internet Series:
Bronx World Travelers, RejectedJoked.com, 2007–2008.

Books:
(With Amanda McCall) *Grandma's Dead: Breaking Bad News with Baby Animals,* HarperCollins, 2008.
(With McCall) *Why Is Daddy in a Dress: Asking Awkward Questions with Baby Animals,* HarperCollins, 2009.
(Editor) *The Best American Comics Criticism,* Fantagraphics Books, 2010.

SCHWEIG, Eric 1967–

PERSONAL

Original name, Ray Dean Thrasher; adoptive name, Eric Schweig; born June 19, 1967, in Inuvik, Northwest Territories, Canada; married; wife's name, Lean, September 9, 1999 (divorced, 2000).

Career: Actor. Also works as a woodcarver of Inuit masks and other items; public speaker on topics of interest to First Nations and other aboriginal people.

Awards, Honors: Grand Jury Prize, outstanding actor in a feature film, L.A. Outfest, 2000, for *Big Eden.*

CREDITS

Film Appearances:
Robert Crow, *The Shaman's Source* (also known as *Avenging Warriors*), 1990.
Uncas, *The Last of the Mohicans,* Twentieth Century–Fox, 1992.

Epenow, *Squanto: A Warrior's Tale* (also known as *The Last Great Warrior*), Buena Vista, 1994.
Ernest Ironplume, *Pontiac Moon,* Paramount, 1994.
Injun Joe, *Tom and Huck* (also known as *The Adventures of Tom and Huck* and *Tom Sawyer*), Buena Vista, 1995.
Metacomet, *The Scarlet Letter,* Buena Vista, 1995.
Pike Dexter, *Big Eden,* Joure de Fete Films, 2000.
Rudy Yellow Lodge, *Skins,* First Look Pictures, 2002.
Pesh–Chidin/El Brujo, *The Missing,* Columbia, 2003.
Joseph Riverwind, *It Waits,* New Arc Entertainment, 2005, Anchor Bay Entertainment, 2006.
Samuel, *Mr. Barrington,* Honey Tree Films/Pro–Active Entertainment Group, 2006.
Steve Lonethunder, *Mr. Soul,* Hollydan Works, 2007.
Chief Ponco, *Casino Jack,* ATO Pictures, 2010.
Mishomis, *A Flesh Offering,* High Definition Pictures, 2010.

Television Appearances; Series:
Assistant, *Arbor Live!,* 2009.
Mathew Tommy, *Cashing In,* 2009–10.

Television Appearances; Miniseries:
Black Thunder, *By the Way of the Stars,* The Disney Channel, 1994.
Voice, *500 Nations,* CBS, 1995.
Buffalo Hump, *Dead Man's Walk* (also known as *Larry McMurtry's "Dead Man's Walk"*), ABC, 1996.
Napoleon, *Les amants de riviere rouge* (also known as *Red River*), 1996.
Sitting Bull, *Into the West,* TNT, 2005.
Terry Doxtator, *Indian Summer: The Oka Crisis,* 2006.

Television Appearances; Movies:
Joseph Brandt/Theyendangea, *The Broken Chain,* TNT, 1993.
Moses Moon, *For Love and Glory,* CBS, 1993.
Wildcat, *Follow the River,* ABC, 1995.
Harry Wood, *Cowboys and Indians: The J. J. Harper Story* (also known as *Cowboys and Indians*), CBC, 2003.
Jerry Twain, *Shania: A Life in Eight Albums,* CBC, 2005.
Sam George, *One Dead Indian,* CTV, 2006.
Tim Blackbear, *Not Like Everyone Else* (also known as *Not Like Everyone Else: The True Story of Brandi Blackbear*), Lifetime, 2007.
Gall, *Bury My Heart at Wounded Knee,* HBO, 2007.

Television Appearances; Pilots:
Chief Andy Fraser, *Blackstone,* 2009.

Television Appearances; Specials:
Elysian Fields, CBS, 1993.

Television Appearances; Episodic:

Darrow Lonetree, "Dust to Dust," *War of the Worlds* (also known as *War of the Worlds: The Second Invasion*), syndicated, 1989.

Claw, "The Ally," *Hawkeye*, syndicated, 1995.

Eric, "Casino," *Hollywood Off–Ramp*, E! Entertainment Television, 2000.

Television Appearances; Pilots:

Inuit hunter, *Due South* (also known as *Direction: Sud*), CBS, 1994.

RECORDINGS

Videos:

New Frontiers: Making "The Missing," Columbia TriStar Home Entertainment, 2004.

Voices of Many Wounds and Fights–at–Dawn, *Gun* (video game), Activision, 2005.

OTHER SOURCES

Periodicals:

People Weekly, May 3, 1993, p. 70.

SCHWEIGER, Til 1963–

PERSONAL

Full name, Tilman Valentin Schweiger; born December 19 (some sources say December 10), 1963, in Cologne, West Germany (now Germany; some sources say Freiburg, West Germany, now Germany); father, a teacher; mother, a teacher; married Dana Carlsen (an actress and model), June 19, 1995 (separated); children: Valentin, Luna, Lilly, Emma Tiger. *Education:* Studied German for two years at a university to become a teacher; studied acting at a drama school in Cologne.

Addresses: *Office*—Barefoot Films GmbH, Saarbruckerstrasse 36, Berlin 10405, Germany. *Manager*—Anonymous Content, 3532 Hayden Ave., Culver City, CA 90232.

Career: Actor, director, writer, and producer. Mr. Brown Entertainment (production company), Berlin, Germany, cofounder and partner; Barefoot Films GmbH (a production company), Berlin, Germany, principal. appeared in German television commercials for Renault Clio supermini car, 1998, 1999, 2000; appeared in print advertisements for Renault Clio, 1999, 2000, Skiny bodywear, 2006, and Bally of Switzerland shoes and handbags, 2009.

Awards, Honors: Max Ophuels Award, best young actor, 1993, for *Ebbies Bluff;* Polish Film Festival Award, best actor, 1997, for *Bandyta;* Silver St. George, best actor, Moscow International Film Festival, 1997, *Knockin' on Heaven's Door;* German Comedy Award (with others), best feature film comedy, Special Bambi Award, 2004, both for *(T)Raumschiff Surprise—Periode 1;* Bambi Award, film—national, 2005, for *Barfuss;* Audience Award nomination, best film, Bambi Award (with Nora Tschirner), film—national, Ernst Lubitsch Award, German Comedy Award (with Nora Tschirner), best feature film, 2008, Audience Award, Bavarian Film Awards, all for *Rabbit without Ears;* Central Ohio Film Critics Association (with others), best ensemble, Screen Actors Guild Award (with others), outstanding performance by a cast in a motion picture, 2010, both for *Inglourious Basterds.*

CREDITS

Film Appearances:

Bertie, *Manta, Manta* (also known as *Racin' at the Streets*), 1991.

Rudy, *Ebbies Bluff*, 1993.

Axel Feldheim, *Der Bewegte mann* (also known as *Maybe, Maybe Not, Most Desired Man,* and *The Turbulent Man*), Orion Classics, 1994.

Man, *ABS serienmabig—Kondome schutzen,* 1994.

Pepe Brenner, *Bunte Hunde,* 1995.

Hajo Heiermann, *Das Superweib* (also known as *The Superwife*), 1996.

Nadler, *Das Maedchen Rosemarie* (also known as *A Girl Called Rosemary* and *The Girl Rosemarie*), Castle Hill Productions/Hawkeye Entertainment, 1996.

Ruediger Steinbock, *Maennerpension* (also known as *Jailbirds*), Ascot Video, 1996.

Brute, *Bandyta* (also known as *Bastard* and *Brute*), Delphi Filmverleih, 1997.

Martin Brest, *Knockin' on Heaven's Door,* Buena Vista, 1997.

Leo, *Der Eisbaer,* Constantin Film, 1998.

Mark, *S.L.C. Punk!,* Sony Pictures Classics, 1998.

Ryker, *The Replacement Killers,* Columbia, 1998.

Ruben Rubenbauer, *Judas Kiss,* 1998.

Max, *Magicians,* 1999.

Stanislaus Nagy, *Der Grosse Bagarozy* (also known as *The Devil and Ms. D*), Constantin Films, 1999.

Til, *Bang Boom Bang—Ein todsicheres ding* (also known as *Bang, Boom, Bang* and *Ein todsicheres ding*), Bavaria International, 1999.

Title role, *Brute,* 1999.

Kraemer "Die Spinne," *Jetzt oder nie—ziet ist geld* (also known as *Now or Never*), Senator Film, 2000.

Beau Brandenburg, *Driven* (also known as *A toute vitesse*), Warner Bros., 2001.

Monty, *Investigating Sex* (also known as *Intimate Affairs*), Janus Films/Kingsgate Films, 2001.

Tim, *Was tun, wenn's brennt?* (also known as *What to Do in Case of Fire?* and *Revolution 6*), Columbia, 2001.

Jonas Herdt, *U–Boat,* Artisan Entertainment, 2003.

Sean, *Lara Croft Tomb Raider: The Cradle of Life* (also known as *Lara Croft Tomb Raider: Die wiege des lebens*), Paramount, 2003.

Cynric, *King Arthur* (also known as *"King Arthur": Director's Cut*), Buena Vista, 2004.

Herdt, *In Enemy Hands* (also known as *U–Boat*), Artisan Entertainment, 2004.

Lucky Luke, *La vraie vie des Dalton* (also known as *The Daltons*), 2004.

Rock Fertig Aus, *(T)Raumschiff Surprise—Periode 1,* Constantin Film, 2004.

Freund in Bibliothek, *Agnes and His Brothers* (also known as *Agnes und seine bruder*), X Verlich AG, 2004.

Lucky Luke, *Les Dalton,* Falcom Media, 2004.

Nick Keller, *Barfuss* (also known as *Barefoot*), Buena Vista International, 2005.

Heinz Hummer, *Deuce Bigalow: European Gigolo,* Columbia, 2005.

Gantcho, *Bye Bye Harry!,* NFP Distribution, 2006.

Voice of Kleiner Tiger, *Oh, wie schon ist Panama* (animated), Warner Bros., 2006.

Eddie Shneider, *One Way* (also known as *The Fixer*), Universal, 2006.

Fred Kruppers, *Wo ist Fred?* (also known as *Where Is Fred?*), Senator Film, 2006.

Captain Red, *Video Kings,* Barnsteiner–Film, 2007.

John Ridley, *Body Armour,* Image Entertainment, 2007.

Ludo Dekker, *Rabbit without Ears* (also known as *Keinohrhasen*), Warner Bros., 2007.

The man, *Already Dead,* Arclight Films, 2007.

Werner Voss, *The Red Baron* (also known as *Der rote Baron*), Monterey Media, 2008.

Jack Carver, *Far Cry,* Touchstone Pictures, 2008.

Ritter Lanze, *1 1/2 Knights—In Search of the Ravishing Princess Herzelinde* (also known as *1 12 Ritter—Auf der suche nach der hinreiBenden Herzlinde*), Warner Bros., 2008.

Himself, *Inthierryview* (documentary), Paul Thiltges Distributions, 2008.

Marc Sumner, *Phantom Pain* (also known as *Pahtomschmerz*), Warner Bros., 2009.

Sergeant Hugo Stiglitz, *Inglourious Basterds,* Weinstein Company, 2009.

Jerome Ades, *Men in the City* (also known as *Mannerherzen*), Warner Bros., 2009.

Ludo Dekker, *Rabbit without Ears 2* (also known as *Zweiohrkuken*), Warner Bros., 2009.

Werner Voss, *The Red Baron,* Monterey Media, 2010.

Henry, *Kokowaah,* Warner Bros., 2011.

This Means War, Twentieth Century–Fox, 2011.

The Courier, VVS Films, 2011.

Jerome, *Mannerherzen ... und die ganz ganz grobe liebe,* Warner Bros. Home Entertainment, 2011.

Also appeared in *Zweiohrkuken.*

Film Work:

Producer, *Knockin' on Heaven's Door,* Buena Vista, 1997.

Director and co–producer, *Der Eisbaer,* Constantin Film, 1998.

Producer, *Jetzt oder nie—ziet ist geld* (also known as *Now or Never*), Senator Film, 2000.

Director, producer, and editor, *Auf Herz und nieren,* Warner Bros., 2001.

Director, producer, and editor, *Barfuss* (also known as *Barefoot*), Buena Vista International, 2005.

Producer, *One Way* (also known as *The Fixer*), Universal, 2006.

Director and producer, *Rabbit without Ears* (also known as *Keinohrhasen*), Warner Bros., 2007.

Director and producer, *1 1/2 Knights—In Search of the Ravishing Princess Herzelinde* (also known as *1 1/2 Ritter—Auf der suche nach der hinreibenden Herzelinde*), Warner Bros., 2008.

Coproducer, *Phantom Pain* (also known as *Phantomschmerz*), Warner Bros., 2009.

Coproducer, *Desert Flower,* National Geographic Entertainment, 2009.

Director and producer, *Rabbit without Ears 2* (also known as *Zweiohrkuken*), Warner Bros., 2009.

Director and producer, *Kokowaah,* Warner Bros., 2011.

Also worked as producer, *Zweiohrkuken;* coproducer, *The Drop;* producer, *Friendship!.*

Television Appearances; Series:

Jo Zenker, *Lindenstrasse,* 1990–92.

Nick Siegel, *Die Kommissarin,* 1994–96.

Himself, *POP 2000,* 1999.

Host, *Mission Hollywood,* 2009.

Television Appearances; Miniseries:

Uprising, NBC, 2001.

Television Appearances; Movies:

Jan Peters, *Lemgo,* 1994.

Martin Markward, *Polizeiruf 110—Schwelbrand,* 1995.

Freddy, *Die Halbstarken,* 1996.

Stefan Renner, *Adrenalin,* 1996.

Ruben Rubenbauer, *Judas Kiss,* Cinemax, 1998.

Max Schmeling, *Joe and Max,* Starz!, 2002.

Television Appearances; Specials:

The 2003 World Awards, 2003.

The Making of King Arthur, 2004.

Der grobe fuhrerscheintest 2005, 2005.

Der grobe tag der liebe, 2005.
Bambi Verleihung 2005, 2005.
Bambi Verleihung 2008, 2008.
Der groBe comedy adventskalender, 2008.
Deutschland gegen Holland—Das Duell, 2010.

Television Appearances; Episodic:
Wetten, dass ...?, 1994, 1997, 2000, 2007, 2008, 2009.
Martin Markward, "Schwelbrand," *Polizeiruf 110,* 1995.
Die Lotto–Show, 1998.
"Ein Herz fur Kinder 1998," *Ein Herz fur Kinder,* 1998.
"Driven," *HBO First Look,* HBO, 2001.
Millionar gesucht!—Die SKL Show, 2002.
"Ein Herz fur Kinder 2002," *Ein Herz fur Kinder,* 2002.
Die Johannes B. Kerner Show, 2002, 2003, 2005, 2006, 2007, 2008, 2009.
"Prominentenspecial #7," *Wer wird Millinar?,* 2003.
"25 Jahre 'Ein Herz fur Kinder,'" *Ein Herz fur Kinder,* 2003.
Der GroBe deutsche Prominenten–Buchstabiertest, 2004.
Beckmann, 2004, 2006, 2007.
Kellner, *Tramitz & Friends,* 2005.
"1999," *Die 90er show,* 2005.
Zimmer frei!, 2005.
" ... Deutschen 2005," *Die 100 nervigsten ...,* 2005.
"Prominentenspecial," *Das Quiz mit Jorg Pilawa,* 2005, 2007.
TV total, 2005, 2006, 2007, 2008.
Die Niels Ruf Show, 2006.
"Cuchillera," *Killer Women* (also known as *Mujeres asesinas*), 2006.
"Lieblingsschauspieler," *Unsere Besten,* 2006.
Extreme Activity, 2006.
NDR Talk Show, 2006, 2007, 2009.
"Der Wecker," *Pastewka,* 2007.
III nach neun, 2007.
Himself and private investigator 'Sperber,' "Highlights," *The Comedy–Trap* (also known as *Die Comedy Falle*), 2007.
Das unglaubliche quiz der Tiere, 2008.
Member of Team Weltenbummler, *Pilawas groBe Weltreise,* 2008.
Guinness World Records—Die groBten Weltrekorde, 2008.
"Der Deutsche Comedy–Preis 2008," *Der deutsche comedypreis,* 2008.
"Tomoya Nagase," *Premium 10,* 2008.
Marc, "Phantomschmerz," *Making Of ...,* 2009.
Markus Lanz, 2009.
Kerner, 2010.
Harald Schmidt, 2010.
Presenter, "The Dome 53," *The Dome,* 2010.
Prozhektorperiskhilton, 2010.
(Uncredited) Til Schweiger, "Fischvergiftung," *Wir mussen reden!,* 2010.

RECORDINGS

Music Videos:
Appeared in "Beyond Time" by Blank & Jones, 2000; "Try Again" by Keane, 2006.

WRITINGS

Screenplays:
Knockin' on Heaven's Door, Buena Vista, 1997.
Barfuss (also known as *Barefoot*), Buena Vista International, 2005.
Rabbit without Ears (also known as *Keinohrhasen*), Warner Bros., 2007.
Rabbit without Ears 2 (also known as *Zweiohrkuken*), Warner Bros., 2009.
Kokowaah, Warner Bros., 2011.

Film Stories:
Heaven's Door, Asmik Ace Entertainment, 2009.

OTHER SOURCES

Books:
Blum, Katharina, *Til Schweiger,* Heyne Filmbibliothek, 1997.
Kilzer, Annette, *Til Schweiger, vom Bewegten Mann zum Grossen Bagarozy,* Europa Verlag, 2001.

SCOTT, James 1979–

PERSONAL

Born January 14, 1979, in Newcastle–upon–Tyne, England.

Career: Actor.

Awards, Honors: Daytime Emmy Award nomination, outstanding lead actor in a drama series, 2010, for *Days of Our Lives.*

CREDITS

Film Appearances:
The man, *The Way We Weren't* (short film), 2009.

Television Appearances; Series:
EastEnders, BBC, 1999.
Ethan Cambias, *All My Children,* ABC, 2004–2006.

E. J. DiMera, *Days of Our Lives* (also known as *Days* and *DOOL*), NBC, 2006—.

Television Appearances; Specials:
The 37th Annual Daytime Emmy Awards, CBS, 2010.

Television Appearances; Episodic:
SoapTalk, SoapNet, 2004, 2006.
Himself, "Another Dying Day," *I Wanna Be a Soap Star,* SoapNet, 2007.
"Round 8," *Dancing with the Stars* (also known as *D.T.W.S.*), ABC, 2007.
The Bonnie Hunt Show, NBC, 2009.

SEACREST, Ryan 1974–

PERSONAL

Full name, Ryan John Seacrest; born December 24, 1974, in Atlanta, GA; son of Gary (an attorney) and Connie (a homemaker). *Education:* Attended the University of Georgia and Santa Monica College. *Avocational Interests:* Exercising, running, cooking, traveling.

Addresses: *Office*—Ryan Seacrest Productions, 5750 Wilshire Blvd., Los Angeles, CA 90036. *Agent*—Creative Artists Agency, 2000 Avenue of the Stars, Los Angeles, CA 90067. *Publicist*—42West, 11400 West Olympic Blvd., Suite 11400, Los Angeles, CA 90064.

Career: Host, television personality, radio personality, and producer. Ryan Seacrest Productions (a production company), principal. WSTR/Star 94 (radio station), Atlanta, GA, radio personality, 1990s. Appeared in television commercials, AT&T wireless, 2003, and Crest toothpaste, 2007. Katana (a sushi bar), Los Angeles, CA, co–owner.

Awards, Honors: Teen Choice Award nomination, favorite television personality, 2003; Family Television Award, choice television reality/variety host, Teen Choice Award nomination, 2003, Emmy Award nominations (with others), outstanding reality/competition program, 2003, 2004, 2005, 2006, 2007, Teen Choice Award nomination, television—choice personality, 2006, 2007, 2008, Emmy Award nominations, outstanding host for a reality or reality–competition program, 2008, 2009, 2010, Astra Award nomination, favourite international personality or actor, 2009, all for *American Idol;* Teen Choice Award nomination, choice television personality, 2004; Teen Choice Award nomination, choice television personality—male, 2005;

star on the Hollywood Walk of Fame, 2005; Daytime Emmy Award (with others), outstanding special class special, 2006, Daytime Emmy Award nominations (with others), outstanding special class special, 2007, 2008, 2009, all for *Walt Disney World Christmas Day Parade;* Teen Choice Award, choice movie—hissy fit, 2007, for *Knocked Up;* Teen Choice Award nomination, choice television personality, 2009, for *E! News Live;* Emmy Award (with others), outstanding reality program, 2010, for *Food Revolution.*

CREDITS

Film Appearances:
Himself, *Playboy: Hef's Halloween Spooktacular* (documentary), 2005.
Himself, *That Guy* (short film), 2006.
Himself, *Longtime Listener* (short film), 2006.
(Uncredited) Himself, *Knocked Up,* Universal, 2007.
Voice of himself, *Get Smart,* Warner Bros., 2008.
High–Five Hollywood! (short film), Funnyordie.com, 2008.
Himself, *The Chronicles of Holly–Weird* (short film), Under Dog Distribution, 2009.
Himself, *A Man's Story* (documentary), 2010.
Voice of Father Butter Pants, *Shrek Forever After* (animated; also known as *Forever After: The Final Chapter, Shrek Forever After: An IMAX 3D Experience, Shrek: The Final Chapter, The Final Chapter,* and *Shrek Forever*), Paramount, 2010.

Television Appearances; Series:
Host, *Radical Outdoor Challenge,* ESPN, c. 1993.
Correspondent, *Extra Weekends* (also known as *Extra: The Entertainment Magazine*), syndicated, beginning c. 1994.
Host, *Gladiators 2000,* syndicated, 1994.
Jack Craft, *Reality Check,* 1995.
Host, *Wild Animal Games,* The Family Channel, 1995–96.
Segment host, *CNet Central,* 1996.
Host, *The New Edge,* Sci–Fi Channel, 1996–99.
Host, *Click,* syndicated, 1997.
Announcer, *Life, Camera, Action,* Fox Family Channel, 1998.
Host, *NBC Saturday Night Movie,* NBC, 2000–2001.
Host, *Ultimate Revenge* (also known as *TNN's "Ultimate Revenge"*), The Nashville Network, 2002.
Host, *American Idol: The Search for a Superstar* (also known as *American Idol* and *American Idol 2*), Fox, 2002—.
Host, *American Juniors,* Fox, 2003.
Correspondent, *The Tonight Show with Jay Leno,* NBC, 2004.
Host, *On–Air with Ryan Seacrest,* syndicated, 2004.
Cohost, *E! News Live* (also known as *E! News Daily* and *E! New Live Weekend*), E! Entertainment Television, 2006–10.
Host, *American Idol Rewind,* 2007–2008.

Also appeared as host, *Total Rush.*

Television Appearances; Movies:

Himself, *The Fantasia Barrino Story: Life Is Not a Fairy Tale,* Lifetime, 2006.

Television Appearances; Specials:

Host, *Wild Animal Games,* The Family Channel, 1995.

Announcer, *The Crash of 2000: A CNET Special Report* (documentary), Sci–Fi Channel, 1997.

The WB Radio Music Awards, The WB, 1999.

Host, *Disneyland 2000: 45 Years of Magic,* 2000.

Presenter DJ, *The 2000 Radio Music Awards,* 2000.

Presenter, *The 30th Annual American Music Awards,* ABC, 2002.

Host, *America's Party: Live from Las Vegas* (also known as *America's Party: New Year's Live from Las Vegas*), Fox, 2002, 2003.

Host, *American Idol: Best of the Worst,* Fox, 2003.

Host, *American Idol: Halfway Home,* Fox, 2003.

Host, *American Idol: The Final Two,* Fox, 2003.

Host, *Jingle Ball Rock* (also known as *Jingleball Rock*), Fox, 2003.

The Disco Ball ... A 30–Year Celebration (also known as *The Disco Ball*), ABC, 2003.

Maxim Hot 100, NBC, 2003.

Playboy's 50th Anniversary Celebration, Arts and Entertainment, 2003.

American presenter, *World Idol,* 2003.

Host, *The 2003 Billboard Music Awards,* Fox, 2003.

Host, *The 2003 Radio Music Awards,* NBC, 2003.

Presenter, *The 55th Annual Primetime Emmy Awards,* Fox, 2003.

Presenter, *The 31st Annual American Music Awards,* ABC, 2003.

The 2003 Teen Choice Awards, Fox, 2003.

The Fifth Annual Family Television Awards, The WB, 2003.

Paula Abdul: The E! True Hollywood Story, E! Entertainment Television, 2003.

"American Idol": The E! True Hollywood Story, E! Entertainment Television, 2004.

2004 Radio Music Awards, 2004.

The 2004 Billboard Music Awards, Fox, 2004.

Host, *American Idol: The Road to Hollywood,* Fox, 2004.

Host, *American Idol: Uncut, Uncensored and Untalented,* Fox, 2004.

Host, *American Idol: The Phenomenon,* Fox, 2004.

Host, *American Idol: The Final Three,* Fox, 2004.

Host, *American Idol: Halfway Home,* Fox, 2004.

Britney Spears: E! Entertainment Special (documentary), E! Entertainment Television, 2004.

Host, *New Year's Eve Live with Times Square with Ryan Seacrest* (also known as *New Year's Eve: Live from Times Square*), Fox, 2004.

Tsunami Aid: A Concert of Hope, NBC, 2005.

What Did ITV Do for Me?, ITV, 2005.

"American Idol": Girls Rule: The E! True Hollywood Story, E! Entertainment Television, 2005.

The Teen Choice Awards 2005 (also known as *The Teen Choice Awards*), Fox, 2005.

Presenter, *The 2005 American Music Awards* (also known as *The 33rd Annual American Awards*), ABC, 2005.

Cohost, *New Year's Rockin' Eve* (also known as *Dick Clark's New Year's Rockin' Eve 2006*), ABC, 2005.

Unforgettable Moments in Television Entertainment: A Museum of Television & Radio Special, NBC, 2005.

Host, *American Top 40 Live,* Fox, 2005.

Host, *"American Idol" Presents The World's Worst Auditions,* Fox, 2005.

Host, *Walt Disney World Christmas Day Parade,* ABC, 2005, 2006, 2007, 2008.

Host, *Primetime New Year's Rockin' Eve 2007* (also known as *Dick Clark's "Primetime New Year's Rockin' Eve"*), ABC, 2006.

Host, *Dick Clark's "New Year's Rockin' Eve 2007,"* ABC, 2006.

E!'s Live Countdown to the Golden Globes, E! Entertainment Television, 2006.

Eva Longoria: The Interview with Ryan Seacrest, 2006.

Host, *Live from the Red Carpet: The 2006 Screen Actors Guild Awards,* E! Entertainment Television, 2006.

Host, *Live from the Red Carpet: The 2006 Grammy Awards,* E! Entertainment Television, 2006.

Host, *Live from the Red Carpet: The 2006 Academy Awards,* E! Entertainment Television, 2006.

Forbes Celebrity 100: Who Made Bank?, E! Entertainment Television, 2006.

Host, *Live from the Red Carpet: The 2006 Emmy Awards,* E! Entertainment Television, 2006.

E!'s Live Countdown to the Emmys, E! Entertainment Television, 2006.

The 2006 American Music Awards, ABC, 2006.

Nickelodeon's 19th Annual Kids' Choice Awards, Nickelodeon, 2006.

Cohost, *Nickelodeon Kids' Choice Awards '07* (also known as *Nickelodeon's 20th Annual Kids' Choice Awards*), Nickelodeon, 2007.

Host, *Live from the Red Carpet: The 2007 Golden Globe Awards,* E! Entertainment Television, 2007.

Host, *Live from the Red Carpet: The 2007 Screen Actors Guild Awards,* E! Entertainment Television, 2007.

Host, *E! Live from the Red Carpet: The 2007 Grammy Awards,* E! Entertainment Television, 2007.

E!'s Live Countdown to the Academy Awards, E! Entertainment Television, 2007.

Host, *Live from the Red Carpet: The 2007 Academy Awards,* E! Entertainment Television, 2007.

Presenter, *Concert with Diana,* NBC, 2007.

The Teen Choice Awards 2007 (also known as *The 2007 Teen Choice Awards*), Fox, 2007.

E!'s Live Countdown to the Emmys, E! Entertainment Television, 2007.

Host, *The 59th Primetime Emmy Awards,* Fox, 2007.

Host, *Live from the Red Carpet: The 2007 Emmy Awards,* E! Entertainment Television, 2007.

Presenter, *The 2007 American Music Awards,* ABC, 2007.

Cohost, *New Year's Rockin' Eve 2008,* 2007.

Host, *Idol Gives Back,* Fox, 2007.

What Perez Sez, VH1, 2007.

The 10th Annual Family Entertainment Awards, The CW, 2008.

Host, *Live from the Red Carpet: The 2008 Academy Awards,* E! Entertainment Television, 2008.

Nickelodeon Kids' Choice Awards (also known as *Nickelodeon's 2008 Kids' Choice Awards*), Nickelodeon, 2008.

(Uncredited) Himself, *The Philanthropist,* NBC, 2008.

Host, *The 60th Primetime Emmy Awards,* ABC, 2008.

Host, *Live from the Red Carpet: The 2008 Emmy Awards,* E! Entertainment Television, 2008.

Big Night of Stars (also known as *Jimmy Kimmel's "Big Night of Stars"*), ABC, 2008.

Host, *New Year's Rockin' Eve 2009* (also known as *Dick Clark's "New Year's Rockin' Eve 2008"* and *Dick Clark's "New Year's Rockin Eve with Ryan Seacrest 2009"*), ABC, 2008.

Host, *Dick Clark's Primetime New Year's Rockin' Eve 2009,* ABC, 2008.

Host, *Idol Gives Back 2,* Fox, 2008.

Host, *Live from the Red Carpet: The 2009 Golden Globe Awards,* E! Entertainment Television, 2009.

Host, *Live from the Red Carpet: The 2009 Grammy Awards,* E! Entertainment Television, 2009.

Host, *Live from the Red Carpet: The 2009 Academy Awards,* E! Entertainment Television, 2009.

Nickelodeon Kids' Choice Awards 2009, Nickelodeon, 2009.

Presenter, *The 2009 American Music Awards,* ABC, 2009.

Carrie Underwood: An All–Star Holiday Special, 2009.

Host, *Dick Clark's New Year's Rockin' Eve with Ryan Seacrest 2010,* ABC, 2009.

The 52nd Annual Grammy Awards, CBS, 2010.

Host, *The 37th Annual Daytime Emmy Awards,* CBS, 2010.

Countdown to the Red Carpet: The 2010 Primetime Emmy Awards, 2010.

Host, *Live from the Red Carpet: The 2010 Primetime Emmy Awards,* E! Entertainment Television, 2010.

Stand Up to Cancer, CBS, NBC, ABC, and Fox, 2010.

(Uncredited) Himself, *Teenage Paparazzo* (documentary), HBO, 2010.

Host, *Idol Gives Back 3,* Fox, 2010.

Host, *Dick Clark's "New Year's Rockin' Eve with Ryan Seacrest 2011,"* 2010.

Live from the Red Carpet: The 2011 Golden Globe Awards, 2011.

Countdown to the Red Carpet: The 2011 Grammy Awards, 2011.

Live from the Red Carpet: The 2011 Grammy Awards, 2011.

Live from the Red Carpet: The 2011 Academy Awards, 2011.

Countdown to the Red Carpet: The 2011 Academy Awards, 2011.

Also appeared as host of *An Evening at the Academy Awards.*

Television Appearances; Episodic:

Guest host, *Talk Soup,* E! Entertainment Television, 1999.

Voice of *Fighting Families* host, "Helga Sleepwalks/ Fighting Families," *Hey Arnold* (animated), Nickelodeon, 1999.

Melrose Place, Fox, c. 1999.

Host, "The Final Proof," *Beverly Hills, 90210* (also known as *Class of Beverly Hills*), Fox, 2000.

MADtv, Fox, 2002, 2005.

Hollywood Squares (also known as *H2* and *H2: Hollywood Squares*), syndicated, 2002.

"NFL Draftees," *Player$,* 2003.

Paula Abdul: The E! True Hollywood Story (documentary), E! Entertainment Television, 2003.

SoapTalk, SoapNet, 2003.

Extra (also known as *Extra: The Entertainment Magazine*), syndicated, 2003, 2008.

Himself, "Bad People: Corey Feldman," *High Chaparall,* Kanal 5, 2004.

"Idol–ization," *Live Like a Star,* syndicated, 2004.

Voice of himself, "Plastic Buffet," *Robot Chicken,* Cartoon Network, 2005.

Voice of himself, "The Deep End," *Robot Chicken,* Cartoon Network, 2005.

Himself, *Punk'd,* MTV, 2005.

Himself, "Is the Grass Greener?," *#1 Single,* 2006.

Himself, "The Season Finale," *There & Back: Ashley Parker Angel,* MTV, 2006.

Host, *American Idol Extra,* Fox Reality, 2006.

"Bowden Family," *The Simple Life,* Fox, 2006.

"Final Results," *Dancing with the Stars* (also known as *D.W.T.S.*), ABC, 2006.

Entertainment Tonight (also known as *E.T.*), syndicated, 2006, 2007, 2008, 2009, 2010.

(Uncredited) Voice of himself, "In with the New," *The Janice Dickinson Modeling Agency,* Oxygen, 2007.

"VMA's," *The Naked Brothers Band,* Nickelodeon, 2007.

"A Hollywood Ambush: Premier Impossible," *Dinner: Impossible,* Food Network, 2007.

Access Hollywood, syndicated, 2008.

"Our Friendship Is Over," *Paris Hilton Is My New BFF,* 2008.

"American Idol," *Infanity* (documentary), TV Guide Channel, 2009.

"Funbags or Die," *Denise Richards: It's Complicated,* 2009.

Voice of himself, "Judge Me Tender," *The Simpsons* (animated), Fox, 2010.

"Simon Cowell Says Goodbye," *ABC News Nightline,* ABC, 2010.

Also appeared in *Blind Date,* syndicated; *The Dating Game,* syndicated; *Leeza,* NBC and UPN.

Television Talk Show Guest Appearances; Episodic:

The Late Late Show with Craig Kilborn (also known as *The Late Late Show*), CBS, 2002.

The Tonight Show with Jay Leno, NBC, 2002, 2003, 2005, 2006, 2007, 2008, 2011.

Guest host, *Good Day Live,* Fox, 2003.

Guest host, *Larry King Live,* Cable News Network, 2003, 2004, 2005, 2006, 2007, 2008, 2009, 2010.

The New Tom Green Show, MTV, 2003.

Guest cohost, *Good Day Live,* 2003.

The View, ABC, 2003, 2005.

The Wayne Brady Show, syndicated, 2003.

Late Night with Conan O'Brien, NBC, 2003.

Today (also known as *NBC News Today* and *The Today Show*), NBC, 2003.

The Oprah Winfrey Show (also known as *Oprah*), 2003, 2008, 2010.

Jimmy Kimmel Live!, ABC, 2003, 2004, 2005, 2006, 2007, 2008.

The Late Show with David Letterman, CBS, 2004.

The Sharon Osbourne Show (also known as *Sharon*), syndicated, 2004.

Live with Regis and Kelly, syndicated, 2005, 2007.

Ellen: The Ellen DeGeneres Show, syndicated, 2005, 2006, 2007, 2008, 2009, 2010.

Talkshow with Spike Feresten, Fox, 2007.

The Paul O'Grady Show, ITV, 2007.

The Tonight Show with Conan O'Brien, NBC, 2009.

Television Work; Series:

Executive producer and creator, *On–Air with Ryan Seacrest,* syndicated, 2004.

Executive producer, *E! News Live* (also known as *E! News Daily* and *E! New Live Weekend*), E! Entertainment Television, 2006–10.

Executive producer, *Paradise City,* E! Entertainment Television, 2007.

Creator and executive producer, *Keeping Up with the Kardashians,* E! Entertainment Television, 2007–10.

Creator and executive producer, *Denise Richards: It's Complicated,* E! Entertainment Television, 2008–2009.

Creator, *Momma's Boys,* NBC, 2008–2009.

Creator and executive producer, *Bromance,* MTV, 2008–2009.

Executive producer, *Kourtney & Khloe Take Miami,* E! Entertainment Television, 2009—.

Executive producer, *Bank of Hollywood,* E! Entertainment Television, 2009–10.

Executive producer, *Food Revolution* (also known as *Jamie Oliver's "Food Revolution"*), ABC, 2010—.

Television Executive Producer; Specials:

New Year's Eve Live with Times Square with Ryan Seacrest, Fox, 2004.

American Top 40 Live, Fox, 2005.

New Year's Rockin' Eve (also known as *Dick Clark's "New Year's Rockin' Eve 2006"*), ABC, 2005.

Primetime New Year's Rockin' Eve 2007 (also known as *Dick Clark's "Primetime New Year's Rockin' Eve 2007"*), ABC, 2006.

Dick Clark's "New Year's Rockin' Eve 2007"), ABC, 2006.

Live from the Red Carpet: The 2006 Emmy Awards, E! Entertainment Television, 2006.

E!'s Live Countdown to the Emmys, E! Entertainment Television, 2006, 2007.

The Interview with Ryan Seacrest, E! Entertainment Television, 2007.

E!'s Live Countdown to the Academy Awards, E! Entertainment Television, 2007.

E!'s Live Countdown to the Golden Globe Awards, E! Entertainment Television, 2007.

E!'s Live Countdown to the SAG Awards, E! Entertainment Television, 2007.

E!'s Live Countdown to the Grammys, E! Entertainment Television, 2007.

Live from the Red Carpet: The 2007 Golden Globe Awards, E! Entertainment Television, 2007.

Live from the Red Carpet: The 2007 Screen Actors Guild Awards, E! Entertainment Television, 2007.

E! Live from the Red Carpet: The 2007 Grammy Awards, E! Entertainment Television, 2007.

Live from the Red Carpet: The 2007 Academy Awards, E! Entertainment Television, 2007.

Live from the Red Carpet: The 2007 Emmy Awards, E! Entertainment Television, 2007.

Crash My School, MTV, 2007.

New Year's Rockin' Eve 2008 (also known as *Dick Clark's "New Year's Rockin' Eve 2008"*), ABC, 2007.

Live from the Red Carpet: The 2008 Screen Actors Guild Awards, E! Entertainment Television, 2008.

Live from the Red Carpet: The 2008 Grammy Awards, E! Entertainment Television, 2008.

Live from the Red Carpet: The 2008 Academy Awards, E! Entertainment Television, 2008.

Live from the Red Carpet: The 2008 Golden Globe Awards, E! Entertainment Television, 2008.

Victoria's Secret: What Is Sexy?, E! Entertainment Television, 2008.

Dick Clark's "Primetime New Year's Rockin' Eve 2009," ABC, 2008.

Dick Clark's "New Year's Rockin' Eve with Ryan Seacrest 2009," ABC, 2008.

Dick Clark's "New Year's Rockin' Eve with Ryan Seacrest 2010," E! Entertainment Television, 2009.

Live from the Red Carpet: The 2009 Grammy Awards, E! Entertainment Television, 2009.

Live from the Red Carpet: The 2009 Academy Awards, E! Entertainment Television, 2009.

Dick Clark's "New Year's Rockin' Eve with Ryan Seacrest 2011," 2010.

Live from the Red Carpet: The 2011 Golden Globe Awards, 2011.

Countdown to the Red Carpet: The 2011 Golden Globe Awards, 2011.

Television Executive Producer; Pilots:
Tales from the Hoff, E! Entertainment Television, 2008.
The Incurables, Arts and Entertainment, 2010.
Kourtney and Kim Take New York, E! Entertainment Television, 2011.

Radio Appearances; Series:
Host, *Ryan Seacrest for the Ride Home,* KYSR/Star 98.7, c. 1995–2004.
Host, *Live from the Lounge,* syndicated, 2001–2002.
Host, *American Top 40,* 2004—.
Host, *American Top 40 (Hot AC Version),* 2004—.
Host, *On–Air with Ryan Seacrest,* KIIS–FM, 2004.
Host, *The Morning Show,* KIIS–FM, 2005.
Host, *The Entertainment Edge with Ryan Seacrest,* syndicated, 2007—.

Also appeared as cohost of drive–time radio program, KYSR–FM.

RECORDINGS

Music Videos:
Appeared in "A Public Affair" by Jessica Simpson, 2006.

Also appeared in a music video for Janet Jackson.

Video Games:
(Uncredited) Voice of host, *Karaoke Revolution Presents: "American Idol,"* Konami Digital Entertainment America, 2007.

OTHER SOURCES

Books:
Newsmakers, Gale, 2004.

Periodicals:
Entertainment Weekly, January 9, 2004, pp. 46–48.
Parade, January 4, 2004, p. 26.
People Weekly, May 1, 2003, pp. 26–27; January 19, 2004, p. 69.
Time, January 26, 2004, p. 62.
TV Guide, January 17, 2004, pp. 42–47.

SINGH, Sabine 1974–

PERSONAL

Full name, Sabine Erika Singh; born August 4, 1974, in New York, NY; mother, a pageant contestant; sister of Schandra Singh (an artist). *Education:* New York University, B.F.A.; attended the University of Michigan, Balliol College, Oxford, and the British American Drama Academy; trained with the Royal Shakespeare Company, Playwrights Horizons, and the Stella Adler Studio of Acting.

Career: Actress. The Flea Theatre, New York City, founding member of resident company, The Bats. Participated in various events.

Member: International Association for Human Values, Art of Living Foundation.

CREDITS

Television Appearances; Series:
Greenlee Smythe du Pres Lavery, *All My Children* (also known as *All My Children: The Summer of Seduction* and *La force du destin*), ABC, 2007–2008.

Television Appearances; Movies:
Alexis "Lexi" Stewart, *Martha behind Bars* (also known as *Martha Stewart: Behind Bars*), CBS, 2005.

Television Appearances; Episodic:
Allison, "Tabula Rasa," *Law & Order* (also known as *Law & Order Prime*), NBC, 1999.
Yasmine Sarong, "Jerri Is Only Skin Deep," *Strangers with Candy,* Comedy Central, 1999.
Tracy, "House Arrest," *The Sopranos* (also known as *Made in Jersey, Sopranos, Die Sopranos, Familia Soprano, Les Soprano, Los Soprano, Maffiozok,* and *Sopranod*), HBO, 2000.
Anna Evans, "Hopeless," *Dawson's Creek* (also known as *Dawson* and *Dawsons Creek*), The WB, 2001.
Anna Evans, "A Winter's Tale," *Dawson's Creek* (also known as *Dawson* and *Dawsons Creek*), The WB, 2001.
Jennie Slater, "Playing God," *Diagnosis Murder* (also known as *Dr. Mark Sloan*), CBS, 2001.
Missy Campbell, "Coyote Piper," *Charmed,* The WB, 2001.
Sydney, "Dangerous Liaisons," *The Random Years,* UPN, 2002.
Waitress, *One Life to Live* (also known as *Between Heaven and Hell, OLTL,* and *One Life to Live: The Summer of Seduction*), ABC, 2002.
Emmanuelle's friend, *Unscripted* (also known as *Untitled Section Eight Comedy*), HBO, 2005.
Erica Lancaster, "People with Money," *CSI: NY* (also known as *CSI: New York, CSI: New York 2, C.S.I. New York, C.S.I.: New York, C.S.I.: NY,* and *CSI: Weekends*), CBS, 2006.
Lissy, "Like a Virgin," *Las Vegas* (also known as *Casino Eye*), NBC, 2006.

Amy Townsend, "Alpha Dog," *Law & Order: Criminal Intent* (also known as *Law & Order: CI*), USA Network, 2009.

Wendy, *One Life to Live* (also known as *Between Heaven and Hell, OLTL,* and *One Life to Live: The Summer of Seduction*), ABC, multiple episodes in 2010.

Television Appearances; Pilots:

Jordan, *Student Affairs,* UPN, 1999.

Allison Price, *Nancy Drew,* broadcast as part of *The Wonderful World of Disney,* ABC, 2002.

Film Appearances:

Kelly Joseph, *Ricky 6* (also known as *Ricky Six* and *Say You Love Satan*), Shooting Gallery, 2000.

Girl in bar, *Someone Like You* (also known as *Animal Attraction, Animal Husbandry, Sex Guide,* and *Someone Like You ...*), Fox 2000, 2001.

Jill, *Maryam,* Streetlight Films, 2002.

Mary, *The Fine Line between Cute & Creepy* (short film; also known as *The Fine Line between Cute and Creepy*), Apollo Cinema, 2002.

Gin, *The Anarchist Cookbook* (also known as *The Anarchist*), Innovation Film Group, 2003.

Appeared in *Speak the Speech,* a documentary about approaches to Shakespeare.

Stage Appearances:

Olivia, *The Gold Standard,* Irish Arts Center, New York City, 2006.

LOVE: A Benefit Performance of Short Plays, WET (Women's Expressive Theatre), Angel Orensanz Foundation, New York City, 2008.

Appeared in other productions.

SKELTON, Stewart 1959–

PERSONAL

Born July 4, 1959, in St. Louis, MO.

Addresses: *Office*—c/o Theatre of NOTE, 1517 North Cahuenga Blvd., Los Angeles, 90028.

Career: Actor and producer. Participated in events for charity.

Awards, Honors: *LA Weekly* Award nomination (with others), best ensemble, 2007, for *Wreck of the Unfathomable.*

CREDITS

Film Appearances:

Aliens (fights), *Timesweep* (also known as *Killer–Beast*), The Shriek Company/Manley Films/Cori Films International, 1987.

(Uncredited) Secret service agent, *Hot Shots! Part Deux* (also known as *Hot shot 2, Hot Shots 2,* and *Hot Shot 2! The Exploitation*), Twentieth Century–Fox, 1993.

(Uncredited) Stunned museum guard, *Demolition Man,* Warner Bros., 1993.

Reverend, *The Last Attack of the Beast* (short film), 2002.

Father, *One Flight Stand* (short film), 2003.

Stranger, *Malachance,* Parthenon Films, 2004.

Dr. England, *The Five–Cent Curve* (short film), 2005.

Mr. Smythe, *Crazylove* (also known as *Committed* and *crazylove*), PorchLight Entertainment, 2005.

Barbecue guest, *Failure to Launch* (also known as *Mambo*), Paramount, 2006.

Doctor, *Danika,* Universal, 2006.

First financial newscaster, *I–See–You.Com* (also known as *Voyeurs.com*), VVS Films, 2006.

Ray Durley, *White Picket Fence* (short film), 2006.

Chairman of the Senate Arms Committee, *SEAL Team VI* (also known as *SEAL Team VI: Journey into Darkness*), Screen Media Ventures, 2008.

Bartender, *Act Like Men* (short film), 2009.

Man, *Volvo* (short film), Reel Kid Productions, 2009.

Senior agent, *Pawn* (short film), Dark Matter Films, 2009.

Karl Larsen, *The Lutefisk Wars,* Sojourner Pictures, 2010.

Doctor, *Zombie Holocaust & You!* (short film), c. 2010.

Television Appearances; Interstitial Series:

Pilgrim father, *Comedy Central Thanxgiveaway: Turkey vs. Pilgrims,* Comedy Central, 2002.

Father O'Shea, *Comedy Central Thanxgiveaway: Holiday Parade from Hell, MN,* Comedy Central, 2005.

Television Appearances; Movies:

Cousin Eb, *Across Five Aprils* (also known as *Civil War Diary*), Family Channel, 1990.

Television Appearances; Specials:

Dr. Scott Worthington, *Comedy Central Laughs for Life Telethon,* Comedy Central, 2004.

Television Appearances; Episodic:

Harold Jeakins, "Dear Boy," *Angel* (also known as *Angel: The Series, Angel—Jaeger der Finsternis,* and *Skoteinos angelos*), The WB, 2000.

FBI agent, "Gentle, Gentle," *CSI: Crime Scene Investigation* (also known as *C.S.I., CSI, CSI: Las Vegas, CSI: Weekends,* and *Les experts*), CBS, 2001.

Fundamentalist, "A Private Life," *Six Feet Under,* HBO, 2001.

John Spach, "The Beginning, the End and the Murky Middle," *Judging Amy,* CBS, 2001.

Detective Don Tremel, "Baby Killers," *Unsolved Mysteries,* Lifetime, 2002.

Dr. Patrick Webb, "Once Removed," *Family Law,* CBS, 2002.

John Taylor, "Secrets and Lies," *ER* (also known as *Emergency Room* and *E.R.*), NBC, 2002.

(Uncredited) Public defender, "Page 47," *Alias,* ABC, 2002.

Second man, "Suspicion," *7th Heaven* (also known as *Seventh Heaven* and *7th Heaven: Beginnings*), The WB, 2002.

William Roberts, "Due Process," *The Court,* ABC, 2002.

Federal agent, *General Hospital* (also known as *Hopital central* and *Hospital general*), ABC, 2002.

Prison technician, *Passions* (also known as *Harmony's Passions* and *The Passions Storm*), NBC, multiple episodes, 2002.

Agent, "Day Care," *Malcolm in the Middle* (also known as *Fighting in Underpants*), Fox, 2003.

First prosecutor, "Capitol Crimes," *The Practice,* ABC, 2003.

Dr. Neil Fisk, "Open Season," *The District* (also known as *Washington Police, The District—Einsatz in Washington, Mannions distrikt,* and *Poliisipaeael-likkkoe Mannion*), CBS, 2004.

Popcorn customer, "Movie Job," *Drake & Josh,* Nickelodeon, 2004.

David Stuart, "Blood Hungry," *Criminal Minds* (also known as *Quantico, Criminal Minds—FBI tutjijat, Esprits criminels, Gyilkos elmek, Kurjuse kannul,* and *Mentes criminales*), CBS, 2005.

Government agent, "Battle of the Hexes," *Charmed,* The WB, 2005.

Drunk driver, *Passions* (also known as *Harmony's Passions* and *The Passions Storm*), NBC, 2005.

Alumnus, "Mr. Monk and the Class Reunion," *Monk* (also known as *Detective Monk*), USA Network, 2006.

(Uncredited) Customer, "Flowers for Kim," *Lucky Louie* (also known as *American Dream*), HBO, 2006.

Pharmacist, "Affair," *Big Love,* HBO, 2006.

Church ghost, "Weight of What Was," *Ghost Whisperer,* CBS, 2007.

Colonel, "Nixon vs. Kennedy," *Mad Men,* AMC, 2007.

Dr. Fischer, "Desire," *Grey's Anatomy* (also known as *Complications, Procedure, Surgeons, Under the Knife,* and *Grey's Anatomy—Die jungen Aerzte*), ABC, 2007.

Dr. Flax, "Time Served," *General Hospital: Night Shift,* SOAPnet, 2007.

(Uncredited) Man, "Family Business," *Cane* (also known as *Los Duques*), CBS, 2007.

Minister, "Cold Ground," *True Blood,* HBO, 2008.

Judge Warner, *General Hospital* (also known as *Hopital central* and *Hospital general*), ABC, 2008.

Phil, "Boys' Club," *Parks and Recreation* (also known as *Parks and Rec, Public Service,* and *The Untitled Greg Daniels/Mike Schur/Amy Poehler Project*), NBC, 2009.

Minister, "It Hurts Me Too," *True Blood,* HBO, 2010.

Phil, "Leslie's House," *Parks and Recreation* (also known as *Parks and Rec, Public Service,* and *The Untitled Greg Daniels/Mike Schur/Amy Poehler Project*), NBC, 2010.

Television Appearances; Pilots:

ADCO, *Astronauts,* ABC, 2002.

Suit, *Skin,* Fox, 2003.

Doorman, *Good Behavior,* ABC, 2008.

Stage Appearances:

The governor, *Wreck of the Unfathomable,* Theatre of NOTE, Los Angeles, 2007.

Stadium Devildare, Theatre of NOTE, 2008.

Stage Producer:

Just Say No, Theatre of NOTE, Los Angeles, 2007.

Stadium Devildare, Theatre of NOTE, 2008.

SMART, Amy 1976–

PERSONAL

Full name, Amy Lysle Smart; born March 26, 1976, in Topanga Canyon, CA; daughter of John (a salesperson) and Judy (a museum worker) Smart; engaged to Carter Oosterhouse (a television host), 2011.

Addresses: *Agent*—Gersh, 9465 Wilshire Blvd., 6th Floor, Beverly Hills, CA 90212. *Manager*—Untitled Entertainment, 1801 Century Park East, Suite 700, Los Angeles, CA 90067.

Career: Actress. Also worked as a model; appeared in television commercials, including AT&T, 1998; appeared in print advertisements for Unionbay clothing, 1995, 1996, and J. Crew clothing, 1996. Heal the Bay (an organization that works on cleaning up the ocean), former spokesperson.

Awards, Honors: Teen Choice Award nomination (with Breckin Meyer), film—choice chemistry, 2000, for *Road Trip;* DVDX Award nomination, best supporting actress in a DVD premiere movie, 2003, for *Interstate 60: Episodes of the Road;* MTV Movie Award (with Owen

Wilson and Carmen Electra), best kiss, 2004, for *Starsky & Hutch;* Teen Choice Award nomination, choice movie actress—music/dance, 2009, for *Love N' Dancing.*

CREDITS

Film Appearances:

Jenny, "The Hook," *Campfire Tales,* New Line Cinema, 1996.

Queenie, *A & P,* 1996.

Pilot cadet Lumbreiser, *Starship Troopers,* TriStar, 1997.

Angela Stravelli, *Strangeland* (also known as *Dee Snider's "StrangeLand"* and *Rune*), Raucous Releasing/The Shooting Gallery, 1998.

Allison, *Circles* (also known as *Crossing Paths*), 1998.

Dot Bryant, *How to Make the Cruelest Month,* 1999.

Jane Weston, *Outside Providence,* Miramax, 1999.

Julie "Jules" Harbor, *Varsity Blues,* Paramount, 1999.

Beth, *Road Trip,* DreamWorks, 2000.

Stacy (first hippie), *Scotland, Pa.,* Lot 47 Films, 2001.

Tracy Faucet, *Rat Race* (also known as *Course folle*), Paramount, 2001.

Herself, *Making "Rat Race"* (short documentary), 2001.

Lynn Linden, *Interstate 60* (also known as *I–60* and *Interstate 60: Episodes of the Road*), Samuel Goldwyn, 2002.

Liz Culpepper, *Blind Horizon,* Nu Image, 2003.

Naomi Feldman, *After School Special* (also known as *National Lampooon's "Barely Legal"* and *Barely Legal*), Motion Picture Corporation of America, 2003.

Tabby Bowland, *The Battle of Shaker Heights,* Miramax, 2003.

Herself, *The Making of "Interstate 60"* (short documentary), Samuel Goldwyn Films, 2003.

Holly, *Starsky & Hutch,* Warner Bros., 2004.

Herself and Holly, *"Starsky & Hutch": A Last Look* (short film), 2004.

Kayleigh Miller, *The Butterfly Effect,* New Line Cinema, 2004.

Nurse Betty, *Win a Date with Tad Hamilton!,* DreamWorks, 2004.

Burglar, *Willowbee* (short film), 2004.

Girl, *A Love Story* (short film), 2005.

Grace Hargrove and Roxanne, *Bigger Than the Sky,* Metro–Goldwyn–Mayer, 2005.

Jamie Palamino, *Just Friends,* New Line Cinema, 2005.

Joy, *Peaceful Warrior,* DEJ Productions, 2006.

Ever, *Crank* (also known as *Adrenaline*), Lions Gate Films, 2006.

Catherine, *Life in Flight,* 2008.

Angela Carson, *Mirrors,* Twentieth Century–Fox, 2008.

Melissa, *Seventh Moon,* Ghosthouse Underground, 2008.

Jessica Donovan, *Love N' Dancing,* Screen Media Films, 2009.

Eve Lydon, *Crank: High Voltage* (also known as *Crank 2, High Voltage,* and *Adrenaline: High Voltage*), Lions Gate Films, 2009.

Herself, *Making "Crank 2"* (documentary), Lions Gate Films Home Entertainment, 2009.

Change Is Gonna Come (documentary), 2009.

Herself, *Sustainable America* (documentary), 2009.

Lillian Hart, *Columbus Circle,* 2010.

Herself, *Spill* (documentary), 2010.

Natalie, *Dead Awake,* New Line Cinema, 2011.

Television Appearances; Series:

Daly Roberts, *Brookfield,* ABC, 1999.

Ruby, *Felicity,* The WB, 1999–2001.

Herself, *Project Greenlight 2,* HBO, 2003.

Voice of Strawberry Shortcake and others, *Robot Chicken,* Cartoon Network, 2005–2009.

Annie, *Smith,* CBS, 2006–2007.

Television Appearances; Miniseries:

First girl, *Seduced by Madness* (also known as *Murderous Passion: The Diane Borchardt Story* and *Seduced by Madness: The Diane Borchardt Story*), NBC, 1996.

Christie Shales, *The '70s,* NBC, 2000.

Television Appearances; Movies:

Dee, *Her Costly Affair* (also known as *Consensual Relations*), NBC, 1996.

Jeananne, *The Last Time I Committed Suicide,* Cinemax, 1997.

Molly, *High Voltage,* HBO, 1997.

Tracey Beck, *Starstruck* (also known as *Dust and Stardust, Starfucker,* and *Starfuckers*), Starz!, 1998.

Sarah Marie Barker, *The Best Man* (also known as *Best Man, Worst Friend* and *Unhitched*), ABC Family, 2006.

Janine, *The Meant to Be's,* 2008.

Television Appearances; Specials:

Presenter, *The 2000 MTV Movie Awards,* MTV, 2000.

Reel Comedy: "Starsky & Hutch," Comedy Central, 2004.

Voice, *Robot Chicken: Star Wars Episode II,* Cartoon Network, 2008.

June Wandrey, *WWII in HD,* History Channel, 2009.

Also appeared in *Rock the Vote,* MTV.

Television Appearances; Pilots:

Daly Roberst, *Brookfield,* ABC, 1999.

Katherine Sullivan, *See Kate Run,* ABC, 2009.

Television Appearances; Episodic:

Hollywood Squares (also known as *H2* and *H2: Hollywood Squares*), syndicated, 2001.

Jamie Moyer, "My Drama Queen," *Scrubs,* NBC, 2003.
Jamie Moyer, "My Interpretation," *Scrubs,* NBC, 2003.
Jamie Moyer, "My T. C. W.," *Scrubs,* NBC, 2003.
"Impin' with a Pippin!," *Player$,* TechTV, 2004.
"Starsky & Hutch," *HBO First Look,* HBO, 2004.
"Ashton Kutcher," *Driven,* VH1, 2004.
(Uncredited) Jamie Moyer, "My Finale: Part 2," *Scrubs,* NBC, 2009.

Television Talk Show Guest Appearances; Episodic:
The Late Late Show with Craig Kilborn (also known as *The Late Late Show*), CBS, 1999.
The Wayne Brady Show, syndicated, 2003.
Jimmy Kimmel Live!, ABC, 2003, 2005.
The Sharon Osbourne Show (also known as *Sharon*), syndicated, 2004.
Ellen: The Ellen DeGeneres Show, syndicated, 2004.
The Showbiz Show with David Spade, Comedy Central, 2005.
Last Call with Carson Daly, NBC, 2005, 2006.
The Megan Mullally Show, syndicated, 2006.
The Late Late Show with Craig Ferguson, CBS, 2006, 2008, 2009.
Up Close with Carrie Keagan, 2008.
The Bonnie Hunt Show, NBC, 2009.

Also appeared as herself, *The Andy Dick Show,* MTV.

RECORDINGS

Music Videos:
Appeared in "Hanginaround" by Counting Crows; "It's about Time" by the Lemonheads; "Gel" by Collective Soul.

OTHER SOURCES

Periodicals:
Entertainment Weekly, April 21, 2000, p. 63.
Glamour, May, 2000, p. 96.
Harper's Bazaar, July, 2000.
TV Guide, April 29, 2000, pp. 34–36.

SOLOMON, David

PERSONAL

Full name, David F. Solomon; married Ali; children: two. *Education:* Studied biology in college.

Addresses: *Agent*—WME Entertainment, One William Morris Pl., Beverly Hills, CA 90212.

Career: Producer, editor, director, and writer. Previously worked at Hanna Barbera Studios and at Ruby–Spears Animation Studio as a tracker reader and quarter inch dialogue editor.

CREDITS

Film Work:
Assistant editor, *My Favorite Year,* 1982.
Second assistant film editor, *Risky Business,* Warner Bros., 1983.
Executive producer, *Paycheck,* Paramount, 2003.

Film Appearances:
Himself, *"Buffy": Season 5 Overview,* 2003.
Himself, *"Buffy": Season 6 Overview,* 2004.
Himself, *"Buffy": Season 7 Overview,* 2004.

Television Work; Series:
Coproducer, *Father Dowling Mysteries,* NBC, 1989, then ABC, 1990.
Coproducer, *Max Monroe: Loose Cannon,* 1990.
Coproducer, *Buffy the Vampire Slayer* (also known as *Buffy the Vampire Slayer: The Series* and *Buffy*), The WB, 1997–2000.
Producer, *Buffy the Vampire Slayer* (also known as *Buffy the Vampire Slayer: The Series* and *Buffy*), The WB, 2000–2001, then UPN, 2001–2002.
Co–executive producer, *Buffy the Vampire Slayer* (also known as *Buffy the Vampire Slayer: The Series* and *Buffy*), UPN, 2002–2003.
Co–executive producer, *Kevin Hill,* UPN, 2004.
Co–executive producer, *Las Vegas,* NBC, 2005–2007.
Co–executive producer, *Dollhouse,* Fox, 2009.
Executive producer, *Dollhouse,* Fox, 2009–10.

Also worked as a sound editor, *Miami Vice,* NBC.

Television Associate Producer; Movies:
Perry Mason: The Case of the Scandalous Scoundrel, NBC, 1987.
Perry Mason: The Case of the Murdered Madam, NBC, 1987.
Perry Mason: The Case of the Avenging Ace, NBC, 1988.
Perry Mason: The Case of the Lady in the Lake, NBC, 1988.

Television Coproducer; Movies:
Perry Mason: The Case of the Musical Murder, NBC, 1989.
Perry Mason: The Case of the Lethal Lesson, NBC, 1989.
Perry Mason: The Case of the All–Star Assassin, NBC, 1989.

Perry Mason: The Case of the Desperate Deception, NBC, 1990.

Perry Mason: The Case of the Silenced Singer, NBC, 1990.

Perry Mason: The Case of the Poisoned Pen, 1990.

Ray Alexander: A Taste for Justice, NBC, 1994.

Ray Alexander: A Menu for Murder, NBC, 1995.

Gramps, NBC, 1995.

Television Producer; Movies:

Perry Mason: The Case of the Defiant Daughter, NBC, 1990.

Perry Mason: The Case of the Ruthless Reporter, NBC, 1991.

Perry Mason: The Case of the Maligned Mobster (also known as *The Case of the Maligned Mobster*), NBC, 1991.

Perry Mason: The Case of the Glass Coffin, NBC, 1991.

Perry Mason: The Case of the Fatal Fashion, NBC, 1991.

Perry Mason: The Case of the Fatal Framing (also known as *Perry Mason: The Case of the Posthumous Painter*), NBC, 1992.

Television Post–Production Executive; Movies:

Brothers of the Frontier, ABC, 1996.

Television Editor; Movies:

Return to Mayberry, NBC, 1986.

Perry Mason: The Case of the Shooting Star, NBC, 1986.

Perry Mason: The Case of the Lost Love, NBC, 1987.

Perry Mason: The Case of the Sinister Spirit, NBC, 1987.

Perry Mason: The Case of the Scandalous Scoundrel, NBC, 1987.

Perry Mason: The Case of the Murdered Madam, NBC, 1987.

Perry Mason: The Case of the Avenging Ace, NBC, 1988.

Perry Mason: The Case of the Lady in the Lake, NBC, 1988.

A Whisper Kills (also known as *Whisperkill*), ABC, 1988.

Perry Mason: The Case of the All–Star Assassin, NBC, 1989.

Perry Mason: The Case of the Musical Murder, NBC, 1989.

Perry Mason: The Case of the Lethal Lesson, NBC, 1989.

Perry Mason: The Case of the Killer Kiss, NBC, 1993.

A Perry Mason Mystery: The Case of the Wicked Wives, NBC, 1993.

Ray Alexander: A Taste for Justice, NBC, 1994.

A Perry Mason Mystery: The Case of the Grimacing Governor, NBC, 1994.

Ray Alexander: A Menu for Murder, NBC, 1995.

A Perry Mason Mystery: The Case of the Jealous Jokester, NBC, 1995.

Gramps, NBC, 1995.

Television Work; Pilots:

Coproducer and editor, *Fast Company,* NBC, 1995.

Editor, *Melanie Darrow,* USA Network, 1997.

Television Work; Episodic:

Editor, "Brother's Keeper," *Miami Vice,* 1984.

Editor, "You're in Alice's," *Hill Street Blues,* 1985.

Director and editor, "The Vendetta," *Matlock,* 1989.

Director, *Buffy the Vampire Slayer* (also known as *Buffy the Vampire Slayer: The Series* and *Buffy*), The WB, 1997–2001, then UPN, 2001–2003.

Director, "Out of Gas," *Firefly* (also known as *Firefly: The Series*), Fox, 2002.

Director, "Wages of Sin," *Tarzan,* The WB, 2003.

(Uncredited) Second unit director, "Chosen," *Buffy the Vampire Slayer* (also known as *Buffy the Vampire Slayer: The Series* and *Buffy*), UPN, 2003.

Director, "Closure," *Tru Calling,* Fox, 2004.

Director, "Murder in the Morgue," *Tru Calling,* Fox, 2004.

Director, "Touched by an Idol," *Strong Medicine,* Lifetime, 2004.

Director, "The Good Life," *Kevin Hill,* UPN, 2004.

Director, "Man's Best Friend," *Kevin Hill,* UPN, 2004.

Director, *Las Vegas,* NBC, 2004–2007.

Director, "Only Sixteen," *Kevin Hill,* UPN, 2005.

Director, "Old Friends," *Burn Notice,* USA Network, 2007.

Director, "Chuck Versus the Sizzling Shrimp," *Chuck,* NBC, 2007.

Director, "Greatest Amerimart Hero," *Big Shots,* UPN, 2007.

Director, "In Which Charlotte Goes Down the Rabbit Hole," *Private Practice,* ABC, 2007.

Editor, *Made,* MTV, 2007.

Director, "The Fine Art of Surfacing," *October Road.,* ABC, 2008.

Director, "A Knight in Shining Armor," *Knight Rider,* NBC, 2008.

Director, *Dollhouse,* Fox, 2009–10.

Director, "Repercussions," *The Gates,* ABC, 2010.

Director, "Curse of the Rolling Stone," *Unnatural History* (documentary), BBC, 2010.

Director, *Nikita,* The CW, 2010.

WRITINGS

Screenplays:

Five Children and It, Capitol Films, 2004.

Television Movies:

Amazons, ABC, 1984.

The Hearst and Davies Affair, ABC, 1985.

Television Movie Stories:
Amazons, ABC, 1984.

Television Episodes:
(With Donald Ross) "Death in the Slow Lane," *Hart to Hart,* ABC, 1979.
"Cop Out," *Hart to Hart,* ABC, 1979.
(With Edward Martino) "Max in Love," *Hart to Hart,* ABC, 1979.
(With Edward Martino) "Color Jennifer Dead," *Hart to Hart,* ABC, 1979.
Paris, CBS, 1979.

OTHER SOURCES

Periodicals:
TV Zone, August, 2003.

SONG, Steph
(Li Ching Song, Stephanie Song)

PERSONAL

Born in Kuching, Malaysia; father, a plant genetics researcher; mother, a political scientist.

Addresses: *Agent*—Greene and Associates Talent Agency, 190 N. Canon Dr., Suite 202, Beverly Hills, CA 90210. *Manager*—Allman/Rea Management, 9255 Sunset Blvd., Suite #600, Los Angeles, CA 90049.

Career: Actress.

Awards, Honors: ATV Award, best drama series, 2004, for *The Singapore Short Story Project;* World Bronze Medal, situation comedy, New York TV Festival, 2005, for *Achar;* Vancouver Film Festival Award and Edmonton Film Festival Award, best Canadian film, 2006, Leo Award nomination, best lead performance by a female in a feature length drama, Motion Pictures Arts and Sciences Foundation of British Columbia, 2007, for *Everything's Gone Green;* Leo Award nomination, best lead performance by a female in a dramatic series, Gemini Award nomination, best performance by an actress in a leading role in a dramatic program or mini–series, Academy of Canadian Cinema and Television, 2007, both for *Dragon Boys;* Leo Award nomination, best supporting performance by a female in a dramatic series, 2008, for *jPod;* Leo Award nomination, best lead performance by a female in a feature length drama, 2009, for *Dim Sum Funeral.*

CREDITS

Television Appearances; Series:
Stephanie Chang, *Achar!,* 2004–2005.
Brianna "Bree" Jyang, *jPod,* CBC, 2008.

Television Appearances; Episodic:
Loretta, "The Butterfly Effect," *The Secret Life of Us,* Ten Network, 2001.
Loretta, "Piggy–in–the–Middle," *The Secret Life of Us,* Ten Network, 2001.
Michelle, "First Touch," *First Touch,* 2003.
Jane, "Champagne Kisses," *Godiva's,* Bravo, 2006.
Jane, "Inked," *Godiva's,* Bravo, 2006.
Jane, "Exit Strategies," *Godiva's,* Bravo, 2006.
Kim, "Foggy Notion," *The Listener,* NBC, 2009.
Victoria Sinclair/Roulette, "Roulette," *Smallville* (also known as *Smallville Beginnings*), The CW, 2009.

Television Appearances; Miniseries:
The Singapore Short Story Project, 2003.
Chavy, *Dragon Boys,* CBC, 2007.

Television Appearances; Movies:
Jane, *Love Poetry,* 2004.
Crossroads: A Story of Forgiveness, CBS, 2007.

Television Appearances; Specials:
The 10th Annual Leo Awards, 2008.
Presenter, *The 11th Annual Leo Awards,* 2009.
Presenter, *The 12th Annual Leo Awards,* 2010.

Film Appearances:
(As Stephanie Song) Production assistant, *Guru Wayne,* DVI, 2002.
Gracie, *The Long Lunch,* CDA Entertainment, 2003.
Jennifer, *Rice Rhapsody* (also known as *Hainan ji fan*), Arclight Films, 2004.
Ming, *Everything's Gone Green,* THINKFilm, 2006.
Diane Lone, *War* (also known as *Rogue Assassin*), Eagle Films, 2007.
(As Li Ching Song) Judy, *Waiting in Beijing,* 2008.
Meimei, *Dim Sum Funeral,* HBO Home Video, 2008.
Ling Chen, *The Thaw,* Paramount, 2009.
Lenore, *Paradox,* Bron Studios, 2010.
Chloe, *Stained,* E1 Entertainment, 2010.

SPEARS, Scott

PERSONAL

Born in Portsmouth, OH. *Education:* Ohio State University, B.F.A., M.F.A.

Career: Cinematographer, writer, producer, and film editor. Videographer for training and educational videos; cinematographer for commercials and music videos (also photographer). WBNS–TV, Columbus, OH, broadcast film editor, 1988–89; also worked as story editor, assistant director, foley artist, gaffer, grip, lighting director, and camera operator.

CREDITS

Film Cinematographer:
Womb at the Top (short film), 1986.
The Birthmark (short film), 1987.
(And producer) *Beyond Dream's Door,* VidAmerica, 1989.
Heartland of Darkness, 1989.
Where Shadows End (short film), 1990.
Blood Church, Donovan Productions, 1992.
The Greater Good (short film), 1992.
Cyber Seeker, Gigo Films, 1993.
Endangered Species (short film), 1993.
Nite Lite (short film), 1994.
With Criminal Intent, 1995.
Centrifuge, 1996.
Hell's Paradox (short film), 1996.
My F–ing Job (short film), 1996.
Evil Sister, 1996, Dead Alive Productions, 1998.
(And film editor) *Too Good to Be True,* Palmetto Film Productions/Vista Street Entertainment, 1997.
(Uncredited; additional cinematography) *Guns of El Chupacabra,* 1997.
Chekhov's Gun (short film), 1997.
Sammy the Screenplay (short film), 1997, Vanguard International Cinema, 2005.
Public Enemy, 1998, Maxim Media International, 2001.
Iron Thunder, Hollywood Pictures Home Video/Trinity, 1998.
A Letter from Death Row, Showcase Entertainment, 1998.
Unseen Evil (also known as *Unseen*), Monarch Home Video, 1999.
Films that Suck, Sightsound.com, 1999.
Battlestar Galactica: The Second Coming (short film), Su–Shan Productions, 1999.
Foreign Correspondents, Creative Light Entertainment, 1999.
Stuck in the Mudbugs (short film), 1999.
I/O Error (short film), 21st Century Pictures Group/ Archimedes Productions, 1999.
Witchcraft XI: Sisters in Blood, 2000.
Solve for X (short film), Quiet Please Productions, 2001.
Demon's Kiss, 2002.
Reflex Action, Bedford Entertainment/Castle Hill Productions/Shoreline Entertainment, 2002.
Green Card Fever, Net Effect Media, 2003.
The King of Iron Town, Leo's Pride Entertainment, 2004.

The Great War of Magellan, Su–Shan Productions, 2005.
Reunion, Treasure Films Entertainment, 2005.
The Atheist (short film), 15% Standard Productions, 2005.
Summer Nuts, Leo's Pride Entertainment, 2006.
Psychon Invaders, 2006.
(And film editor) *Blood Legend,* 2006.
Slaughterhouse Phi: Death Sisters, 2006.
Horrors of War (also known as *Dead Man Soldiers*), Maverick Entertainment, 2007.
Queen Cobra, 2007.
White Air, Monarch Home Video, 2007.
Cold Ones (also known as *Dead Letters*), Leo Films, 2008.
How to Deal with Telemarketers (short film), Sonnyboo Productions, 2008.
Uncle Pete's Play Time (short film), Sonnyboo Productions, 2008.
(Additional cinematography) *In the Trenches of an Indie Film,* Sonnyboo Productions, 2008.
Plaguers (also known as *Space Hazard*), Image Entertainment, 2009.
Relationship Card (short film), Sonnyboo Productions, 2009.
Live Evil, Rivercoast Films, 2010.

Film Work; Other:
Coproducer, *License Exam* (short film), Big Film Shorts, 2004.

Television Cinematographer:
The Storm, 1996.

RECORDINGS

Video Cinematographer:
The Basics of Filmmaking, Greenstem Productions, 2004.

WRITINGS

Screenplays:
Public Enemy, 1998, Maxim Media International, 2001.
Unseen Evil (also known as *Unseen;* also based on story by Spears), Monarch Home Video, 1999.

ADAPTATIONS

Screenplays based on stories by Spears include *Horrors of War* (also known as *Dead Man Soldiers*), released by Maverick Entertainment in 2007. The 2004 film *Unseen Evil* (also known as *Alien 3000*) was based on characters created by Spears.

OTHER SOURCES

Electronic:

Scott Spears Official Site, http://www.scottspears.net, October 14, 2010.

SPENCER, Abigail 1981–

PERSONAL

Full name, Abigail Leigh Spencer; born August 4, 1981, in Gulf Breeze, FL; married Andrew Pruett, 2004; children: Roman. *Avocational Interests:* Yoga, Pilates, dance classes, singing.

Addresses: *Agent*—International Creative Management, 10250 Constellation Blvd., 9th Floor, Los Angeles, CA 90067. *Manager*—Authentic Talent and Literary Management, 634 South Ridgeley Dr., Suite 2, Los Angeles, CA 90036.

Career: Actress. Appeared in television commercials, including Old Navy clothing stores, 2005, and Twix candy, 2008.

Awards, Honors: *Soap Opera Digest* Award, outstanding female newcomer, 2000, for *All My Children.*

CREDITS

Film Appearances:

Melissa, *Campfire Stories,* Velocity Home Entertainment, 2001.

Skye, *Graduation Night* (also known as *Truth and Dare* and *Party On*), 2003.

Sandy, *A Coat of Snow,* 2005.

Wendy, *Hooked* (short film), 2006.

Jessica, *Passing the Time* (short film), 2007.

Talia Carew, *Jekyll,* Lightyear Entertainment, 2007.

INST MSGS (Instant Messages) (short film), Revision3, 2009.

Gwen, *In My Sleep,* 2009.

Alice, *Cowboys & Aliens,* Universal, 2011.

Television Appearances; Series:

Rebecca "Becca" Tyree, *All My Children,* ABC, 1999–2001.

Angela Henson, *Angela's Eyes,* Lifetime, 2006.

Miss Farrell, *Mad Men,* AMC, 2009.

Dr. Erin Jameson, *Hawthorne* (also known as *HawthoRNe*), TNT, 2010.

Television Appearances; Movies:

Are We There Yet?, 2003.

Clarissa, *Fathers and Sons,* Showtime, 2005.

Lennie Rose, *Introducing Lennie Rose,* 2006.

Backyards & Bullets, NBC, 2007.

Television Appearances; Specials:

The 27th Daytime Emmy Awards, ABC, 2000.

Television Appearances; Pilots:

Angela Henson, *Angela's Eyes,* Lifetime, 2006.

Lindsey Steers, *Rex Is Not Your Lawyer,* NBC, 2010.

Television Appearances; Episodic:

Becky Lester, "Bite Me," *CSI: Crime Scene Investigation* (also known as *CSI: Las Vegas* and *C.S.I.*), CBS, 2005.

Violet Summers, "Love Hurts," *Killer Instinct,* Fox, 2006.

Megan, "Bridesmaid Revisited," *Gilmore Girls,* The WB, 2006.

Tricia Norwood, *The Wedding Bells,* Fox, 2006.

Cindy Brown, "Speed Demon," *Ghost Whisperer,* CBS, 2007.

Lyssa, "Douchebag in the City," *My Boys,* TBS, 2007.

Blahblah, "How I Met Everyone Else," *How I Met Your Mother* (also known as *H.I.M.Y.M.*), CBS, 2007.

Claire Tanner, "The Letter," *Welcome to the Captain,* CBS, 2008.

Phillipa Fitz, "The Man in the Mud," *Bones,* Fox, 2008.

Simone Walker, "Sonata," *Moonlight,* CBS, 2008.

Rachel, "Ex–Life," *Private Practice,* ABC, 2009.

Sarah Reed, "One Man's Treasure," *Castle,* ABC, 2009.

Ashley Carter, "The Girlfriend Experience," *The Glades,* Arts and Entertainment, 2010.

Young Chief, "The End of the Middle," *Childrens' Hospital,* 2010.

SPIER, Carol

PERSONAL

Born in Canada. *Education:* University of Manitoba, degree in interior design.

Addresses: *Agent*—Sandra Marsh Management, 9150 Wilshire Blvd., Suite 220, Beverly Hills, CA 90212.

Career: Production designer, art director, and costume designer. Canadian Broadcasting Corporation (CBC), Toronto, Ontario, Canada, worked as production designer; also worked as a designer for theatre groups in Winnipeg, Manitoba, Canada.

Awards, Honors: Genie Award nomination, best achievement in art direction, Academy of Canadian Cinema and Television, 1980, for *The Brood;* Genie Award nomination, best achievement in art direction, 1982, for *Scanners;* Genie Award nomination, best achievement in art direction, 1984, for *Videodrome;* Gemini Award, best achievement in production design or art direction, Academy of Canadian Cinema and Television, 1986, for *Anne of Green Gables;* Genie Award, best achievement in art direction/production design, 1989, for *Dead Ringers;* Genie Award, best achievement in art direction/production design, 1992, for *Naked Lunch;* Genie Award nomination, best achievement in art direction/production design, 1999, for *eXistenZ;* Directors Guild of Canada Craft Award nomination, outstanding production design—feature film, 2006, for *A History of Violence;* Directors Guild of Canada Craft Award nomination, outstanding production design—feature film, Directors Guild of Canada Team Award (with others), feature film, Genie Award nomination, best achievement in art direction/production design, 2008, all for *Eastern Promises;* Directors Guild of Canada Team Award (with others), feature film, Genie Award (with Janice Blackie–Goodine), best achievement in art direction/production design, 2009, both for *Paschendaele.*

CREDITS

Film Production Designer:
I Miss You Hugs and Kisses, 1976.
Hog Wild, Avco–Embassy, 1980.
Gas, Paramount, 1981.
The Funny Farm, New World/Mutual, 1982.
The Dead Zone, Paramount, 1983.
Running Brave, Buena Vista, 1983.
Sesame Street Presents: "Follow That Bird" (also known as *Follow That Bird*), Warner Bros., 1985.
The Fly, Twentieth Century–Fox, 1986.
Dead Ringers, Twentieth Century–Fox, 1988.
Dakota, Miramax, 1989.
Renegades, Universal, 1989.
Sing, TriStar, 1989.
Where the Heart Is, Buena Vista, 1990.
Naked Lunch, Twentieth Century–Fox, 1991.
Consenting Adults, Buena Vista, 1992.
M. Butterfly, Warner Bros., 1993.
Canadian Bacon, Gramercy Pictures, 1994.
The Santa Clause, Buena Vista, 1994.
Crash, Fine Line, 1996.
Joe's Apartment, Warner Bros., 1996.
Mimic, Miramax/Dimension Films, 1997.
eXistenZ, Miramax/Dimension Films, 1999.
Bless the Child (also known as *Die Prophezeiung*), Paramount, 2000.
Dracula 2000 (also known as *Dracula 2001* and *Wes Craven Presents: "Dracula 2000"*), Miramax, 2000.
Camera (short film), 2000.

Blade II, New Line Cinema, 2002.
The League of Extraordinary Gentlemen (also known as *LXG, The League, League of Legend, Extraordinary Gentlemen,* and *Die Liga der aussergewoehnlichen gentleman*), Twentieth Century–Fox, 2003.
Noel, Red Rose Productions, 2004.
A History of Violence, New Line Cinema, 2005.
The Man, New Line Cinema, 2005.
Silent Hill, TriStar, 2006.
Eastern Promises, Focus Features, 2007.
Passchendaele, 2008.
Dream House, Universal, 2011.

Film Art Director:
Fast Company, Topar Films, 1978.
I Miss You, Hugs and Kisses, 1978.
Search and Destroy (also known as *Striking Back*), 1979.
The Brood (also known as *La clinique de la terreur* and *David Cronenberg's "The Brood"*), New World, 1979.
Scanners (also known as *Telepathy 2000*), Avco–Embassy, 1980.
Humongous (also known as *Dog Island*), Embassy, 1981.
Videodrome, Universal, 1983.
Agnes of God, Columbia, 1985.
"Sesame Street" Presents: "Follow That Bird," 1985.
The Believers, Orion, 1987.

Film Assistant Art Director:
Find the Lady (also known as *Call the Cops!* and *Kopek and Broom*), 1976.
Equus, United Artists, 1977.
Why Shoot the Teacher?, 1977.

Film Costume Designer for Muppet Characters:
The Great Muppet Caper, Universal, 1981.
The Muppets Take Manhattan, TriStar, 1984.
The Muppet Christmas Carol, Buena Vista, 1992.
Muppet Treasure Island, Buena Vista, 1996.

Film Visual Consultant:
A Dangerous Method, 2011.

Film Appearances:
Herself, *The Blood Pact: The Making of "Blade II,"* 2002.
Herself, *Assembling the League,* 2003.
Herself, *Fear of the Flesh: The Making of "The Fly"* (documentary), Twentieth Century–Fox Home Entertainment, 2005.
Herself, *Path of Darkness: Making "Silent Hill"* (documentary), Sony Pictures Home Entertainment, 2006.
Herself, *Acts of Violence* (documentary), 2006.

Herself, *"Silent Hill": Entre Deux Mondes* (documentary), Metropolitan Filmexport, 2009.

Television Production Designer; Miniseries:
Anne of Green Gables, CBC and PBS, 1985.
Thanks of a Grateful Nation (also known as *The Gulf War*), Showtime, 1998.

Television Art Director; Miniseries:
Anne of Green Gables, CBC and PBS, 1985.

Television Production Designer; Movies:
Gotham (also known as *The Dead Can't Lie*), Showtime, 1988.
Dash and Lilly, Arts and Entertainment, 1999.
Gilda Radner: It's Always Something, ABC, 2002.
Ultra, 2006.

Television Art Director; Movies:
Escape from Iran: The Canadian Caper (also known as *Desert Blades*), CBS, 1981.

Television Set Decorator; Movies:
Horatio Hornblower: The Duel, Arts and Entertainment, 1999.

Television Production Designer; Specials:
Overdrawn at the Memory Bank, PBS, 1985.

Television Production Designer; Pilots:
Fringe, Fox, 2008.

Television Production Designer; Episodic:
"The Inheritance," *Friday the 13th: The Series* (also known as *Friday's Curse*), syndicated, 1987.
"The Poison Pen," *Friday the 13th: The Series* (also known as *Friday's Curse*), syndicated, 1987.
"Cupid's Quiver," *Friday the 13th: The Series* (also known as *Friday's Curse*), syndicated, 1987.
"The Same Old Story," *Fringe,* Fox, 2008.

Also worked as production designer, *Scales of Justice,* CBS.

Television Appearances; Specials:
Himself, *The Road to "Passchendaele"* (documentary), 2008.

Stage Work:
Costume designer, *Hothouse,* Chelsea Theatre Center of Brooklyn, Brooklyn Academy of Music, Brooklyn, New York City, 1974.

Costume designer, *Diamond Studs,* Ford's Theatre Society, Washington, DC, 1974–75.
Costume designer, *Polly,* Chelsea Theatre Center of Brooklyn, 1975.
Costume coordinator, *Lincoln,* Chelsea Theatre Center of Brooklyn, 1976, then Theatre Four, New York City, 1976–77.

SPILLER, Michael 1961–
(Michael A. Spiller, Mike Spiller)

PERSONAL

Full name, Michael A. Spiller; born August 1, 1961, in NJ; raised in Brooklyn, NY. *Education:* State University of New York College at Purchase, B.F.A., film, 1984.

Addresses: *Agent*—International Creative Management, 10250 Constellation Blvd., 9th Floor, Los Angeles, CA 90067.

Career: Cinematographer, director, and producer. Often worked in collaboration with Hal Hartley. Worked as director for television commercials, including Ross; worked as a cinematographer for television commercials and music videos; also worked as a photographer.

Member: International Cinematographers Guild.

Awards, Honors: Black Entertainment Television Comedy Award, outstanding directing for a comedy series, 2005, for *The Bernie Mac Show.*

CREDITS

Film Cinematographer:
Kid (short film), 1984.
Tommy's, 1985.
The Cartographer's Girlfriend (short film), 1987.
The Unbelievable Truth, Miramax, 1989.
Revolution, 1991.
Angry, 1991.
Trust, Fine Line, 1991.
Age Isn't Everything (also known as *Life in the Food Chain*), 1991.
Theory of Achievement, Alive from Off Center/Yo Productions #2, 1991.
Ambition (short film), Good Machine, 1991.
Simple Men (also known as *Uomini semplici*), Fine Line, 1992.
Wadeck's Mother's Friend's Son, 1992.

Opera No. 1 (short film), 1994.
Hand Gun, Shooting Gallery, 1994.
Amateur, Sony Pictures Classics, 1995.
Search and Destroy (also known as *The Four Rules*), October Films, 1995.
Flirt, Cinepix Film Properties, 1996.
Walking and Talking, Miramax, 1996.
Phinehas (short film), 1996.
Not Nude Though, a Portrait of Rudy Burckhardt, Two Boots, 1996.
The House of Yes, Miramax, 1997.
Niagara, Niagara (also known as *Niagra Niagra*), Artisan Entertainment, 1997.
Charles Mingus: Triumph of the Underdog, 1997.
Henry Fool, Sony Pictures Classics, 1998.
Hell's Kitchen (also known as *Hell's Kitchen N.Y.C.*), Cowboy Booking International, 1999.
Drop Dead Gorgeous (also known as *Gnadenlos schoen*), New Line Cinema, 1999.
No Such Thing, United Artists, 2002.
(As Mike Spiller) *No Direction Home: Bob Dylan* (documentary), Emerging Pictures, 2005.

Film Work; Other:
Grip, *Sudden Death,* 1985.
(As Mike Spiller) Electrician, *Streetwalkin',* 1985.
Best boy electric, New York and gaffer, New York second unit, *My Demon Lover,* 1987.
Camera operator: second unit, *Hangmen,* 1987.
Additional first assistant camera, *D.O.A.,* 1988.
Camera operator, *Trust,* 1990.
Camera operator, *Comrades in Arms,* 1992.
Additional camera operator and second unit cinematographer, *The Dark Half,* 1993.
Additional photographer, *Household Saints,* 1993.
Additional footage, *Instrument,* 1998.
(As Michael A. Spiller) Additional camera operator, *Chinese Coffee,* 2000.

Television Cinematographer; Series:
Fishing with John, Independent Film Channel, 1991.
The Adventures of Pete & Pete (also known as *Pete and Pete*), Nickelodeon, 1993–94.
Significant Others, Fox, 1997.
Sex and the City (also known as *S.A.T.C.* and *Sex and the Big City*), HBO, 1998–2002.

Television Work; Movies:
Cinematographer, "Surviving Desire," *American Playhouse,* PBS, 1991.
Director, *Mr. Ed,* Fox, 2004.

Television Camera Operator; Movies:
Framed, HBO, 1990.

Television Cinematographer; Specials:
Stood Up, ABC, 1990.

Punch and Judy Get Divorced (live puppet show), PBS, 1992.
Lincoln and the War Within, 1992.
"Jane Black," *The VH1 Fashion Awards,* VH1, 1996.
Dragtime, HBO, 1997.
Alexander Calder, PBS, 1998.

Television Work; Specials:
Camera assistant, "Tribe," *Imagining America,* PBS, 1989.
Photography, *Guns: A Day in the Death of America* (documentary), HBO, 1990.
Photography, *Real Sex 5,* HBO, 1993.
Photography, *The Telephone* (documentary), PBS, 1997.

Television Work; Pilots:
Director, *Septuplets,* Fox, 2002.
Supervising producer, *Big Day,* ABC, 2006.

Television Work; Episodic:
Focus puller, "The Cross of St. Ciricus," *Robin Hood* (also known as *Robin of Sherwood*), 1986.
Photography, *The Prize: The Epic Quest for Oil, Money & Power,* PBS, 1992.
Camera, "The Star," "The Hollywood Style," and "Film in the Television Age," *American Cinema,* PBS, 1994.
Cinematographer: additional photography, "The Telephone," *The American Experience,* PBS, 1997.
Director, *Sex and the City* (also known as *S.A.T.C.* and *Sex and the Big City*), HBO, 1999–2001.
Director, "Greg Gets Puppish," *Greg the Bunny,* Fox, 2002.
Director, "Whole in One," *Leap of Faith,* NBC, 2002.
Director, "Valentine's Day Dance," *Do Over,* 2002.
Director, *Scrubs* (also known as *Scrubs: Med School*), NBC, 2002–2003.
Director, *The Bernie Mac Show,* Fox, 2002–2004.
Director, "Savant," *Lucky,* FX Network, 2003.
Director, "It's in the Stars," *Lucky,* FX Network, 2003.
Director, "Mr. Monk Goes to the Ballgame," *Monk,* USA Network, 2003.
Director, "It's in the Stars," *Lucky,* FX Channel, 2003.
Director, *Oliver Beene,* Fox, 2003–2004.
Director, *Cracking Up,* 2004.
Director, "Kill Bill Volume 3," *Method & Red,* Fox, 2004.
Director, "Something About Brenda," *Method & Red,* Fox, 2004.
Director, "Partly Cloudy, Chance of Sex," *Life As We Know It,* ABC, 2004.
Director, "Secrets & Lies," *Life As We Know It,* ABC, 2004.
Director, "Dinner Date with Death," *Kitchen Confidential,* Fox, 2005.
Producer, "Jake or the Fat Man," *Jake in Progress,* ABC, 2005.

Director, *Jake in Progress,* ABC, 2005–2006.
Director, "Teddy Takes Off," *Kitchen Confidential,* Fox, 2006.
Supervising producer, "The Annie–dote," *Jake in Progress,* ABC, 2006.
Supervising producer, "Stolen Vows," *Big Day,* ABC, 2006.
Supervising producer, "Boobzilla," *Big Day,* ABC, 2006.
Director, "Eclipse," *Big Love,* HBO, 2006.
Director, "Eviction," *Big Love,* HBO, 2006.
Director, *Big Day,* ABC, 2006–2007.
Director, "The Good, the Bad, and the Really Ugly," *Big Shots,* ABC, 2007.
Director, "The Wedding," *Samantha Who?,* ABC, 2007.
Director, "The Hypnotherapist," *Samantha Who?,* ABC, 2007.
Supervising producer, "The Ceremony," *Big Day,* ABC, 2007.
Director, *Ugly Betty,* ABC, 2007–2008.
Director, "Mom's Coma," *Aliens in America,* The CW, 2008.
Director, *Scrubs* (also known as *Scrubs: Med School*), NBC, 2008, then ABC 2008–10.
Director, "Dead Calm," *The Riches,* FX Network, 2008.
Director, "The Ring," *Worst Week,* CBS, 2008.
Director, "The Puppy," *Worst Week,* CBS, 2008.
Director, "The Epidural," *Worst Week,* CBS, 2008.
Director, "The Front Door," *The Middle,* 2009.
Director, "Thanksgiving," *The Middle,* 2009.
Director, "I Won't Back Down," *Cougar Town,* ABC, 2009.
Director, "Goodbye, Mr. Chips," *Better Off Ted,* ABC, 2009.
Director, "Secrets and Lives," *Better Off Ted,* ABC, 2009.
Director, "The Long and Winding High Road," *Better Off Ted,* ABC, 2010.
Director, "It's a Party and I'll Lie if I Want To," *Better Off Ted,* ABC, 2010.
Director, "All the Wrong Reasons," *Cougar Town,* ABC, 2010.
Director, "The Search," *The Office,* NBC, 2011.
Director, *Modern Family,* ABC, 2010–11.

Also worked as camera operator, "Real Sex 16," *Real Sex.*

Television Appearances; Episodic:
Slick guy, "The Monogamists," *Sex and the City,* HBO, 1998.
(Uncredited) The balloon guy, "My Jerks," *Scrubs* (also known as *Scrubs: Medical School*), ABC, 2009.
Kathy's husband, "The Puppy," *Worst Week,* CBS, 2009.

RECORDINGS

Music Videos; Cinematographer:
"From a Motel 6" by Yo La Tengo, 1993.
"Iris" by the Breeders, 1993.

"The Only Living Boy in New York" by Everything But the Girl, 1993.
"Boom n' Bust" by Masatoshi Nagase, 1996.
"Walking Wounded" by Everything But the Girl, 1996.

Also worked as cinematographer on music videos by Arc Angels, Brand Nubian, Nitzer Ebb, Schooly D., Smashing Pumpkins, Sonic Youth, and Tecnotronic.

OTHER SOURCES

Periodicals:
American Cinematographer, Volume 8, number 76, 1995, pp. 70–74.
In Camera, spring, 1996.
International Photographer, Volume 3, number 67, 1996, pp. 44–47.
Lighting Dimensions, Volume 4, number 19, 1995, pp. 48–53; Volume 5, number 20, 1996, pp. 44–45, 69–76.

SPINOTTI, Dante 1943(?)–

PERSONAL

Born August 22, 1943 (some sources say 1941), in Tolmezzo, Italy; married; wife's name, Marcella.

Addresses: *Agent*—The Murtha Agency, 4240 Promenade Way, Suite 232, Marina Del Rey, CA 90292.

Career: Cinematographer. Worked at RAI (Italian television) and KENIA as a cinematographer; also worked as cinematographer on television commercials, including Diet Coke, 2003, and Kia Spectra automobiles, 2004.

Member: American Society of Cinematographers.

Awards, Honors: David di Donatello Award, best cinematography, 1989, for *La leggenda del santo bevitore;* Film Award nomination, best cinematography, British Academy of Film and Television Arts, American Society of Cinematographers Award nomination, outstanding achievement in cinematography in theatrical releases, Best Cinematography Award, British Society of Cinematographers, 1992, all for *The Last of the Mohicans;* David di Donatello Award, best cinematography, 1994, for *Il segreto del bosco vecchio;* David di Donatello Award nomination, best cinematography, Silver Ribbon, best cinematography, Italian National Syndicate of Film Journalists, 1996, both for *L'uomo delle stelle;* Los Angeles Film Critics Association Award, best cinematography, Golden Satellite Award nomination, best motion picture cinematography, International Press Academy, Film Award nomination, best cinematography, British Academy of Film and Television Arts, American Society of Cinematographers Award nomination, outstanding achievement in cinematography in theatrical releases, Academy Award nomination, best cinematography, 1997, Best Cinematography Award, British Society of Cinematographers, 1998, all for *L.A. Confidential*; Los Angeles Film Critics Association Award, best cinematography, 1999, American Society of Cinematographers Award nomination, outstanding achievement in cinematography in theatrical releases, Silver Ribbon, best cinematography, Italian National Syndicate of Film Journalists, 2000, all for *The Insider*; Outstanding Achievement Award, Los Angeles Italian Film Awards, 2000; David di Donatello Award nomination, best cinematography, 2003, for *Pinocchio*; Lifetime Achievement Award, Bearfest–Big Bear Lake International Film Festival, 2005; Satellite Award nomination, best cinematography, 2006, for *X–Men: The Last Stand*; Satellite Award nomination, best cinematography, 2009, for *Public Enemies*.

CREDITS

Film Cinematographer:

Il minestrone, 1980.

La disubbidienza (also known as *La desobeissance*), 1981.

Basileus Quartet (also known as *Il quartetto Basileus*), Libra, Cinema 5, Almi, 1982.

Cenerentola '80 (also known as *Cinderella '80* and *Cendrillon '80*), 1983.

Le armi e gli amori, 1983.

I paladini—Storia d'armi e d'amori (also known as *Hearts and Armour*), Warner Bros., 1983.

Sogno di una notte d'estate (also known as *Sogno di una notte di mezza estate*), 1983.

(First musical sequence) *Voyage of the Rock Aliens,* 1984.

Cosi parlo Bellavista (also known as *Il mistero di Bellavista*), 1984.

Fotografando Patrizia (also known as *The Dark Side of Love*), 1984.

Sotto, sotto (also known as *Softly, Softly* and *Sotto ... sotto ... strapazzato da anomala passione*), Triumph Releasing, 1984.

Interno Berlinese (also known as *The Berlin Affair* and *Leidenschaften*), Cannon Tuschinski Film Distribution, 1985.

Voyage of the Rock Aliens, (also known as *Voyage of the Rich Aliens* and *When the Rain Begins to Fall*), Prism Pictures, 1985.

Choke Canyon (also known as *On Dangerous Ground*), UFDC, 1986.

Crimes of the Heart, DD Entertainment, 1986.

Manhunter (also known as *Red Dragon: The Pursuit of Hannibal Lecter*), DEG, 1986.

"Die tote stadt," *Aria,* Miramax/Warner Bros., 1987.

From the Hip, DEG, 1987.

Beaches (also known as *Forever Friends*), Buena Vista, 1988.

Illegally Yours, Metro–Goldwyn–Mayer/United Artists, 1988.

La leggenda del Santo bevitore (also known as *The Legend of the Holy Drinker* and *La legende du saint buveur*), 1988.

Mamba (also known as *Fair Game*), Vidmark Entertainment, 1988.

Torrents of Spring, 1989.

Acque di primavera (also known as *Torrents of Spring* and *Les eaux printanieres*), Millimeter, 1990.

Una vita scellerata (also known as *Cellini, una vita violenta, Cellini, l'or et le sang, Cellini: A Violent Life,* and *A Violent Life*), 1990.

The Comfort of Strangers (also known as *Cortesie per gli ospiti*), Skouras, 1990.

True Colors, Paramount, 1991.

Hudson Hawk, TriStar, 1991.

Frankie & Johnny (also known as *Frankie and Johnnie*), Paramount, 1991.

The Last of the Mohicans, Twentieth Century–Fox, 1992.

Il segreto del boscho vecchio (also known as *The Secret of the Old Woods*), 1993.

La fine e nota (also known as *The End Is Known*), 1993.

Blink, New Line Cinema, 1994.

Nell, Twentieth Century–Fox, 1994.

The Quick and the Dead (also known as *Quick & Dead*), TriStar, 1995.

(With Andrey Barkowyak) *L'uomo delle stelle* (also known as *The Star Maker, The Star Man,* and *Starmaker*), Miramax, 1995.

Heat, Warner Bros., 1995.

The Mirror Has Two Faces, TriStar, 1996.

L.A. Confidential, Warner Bros., 1997.

Goodbye Lover (also known as *Patricia Arquette's "Goodbye Lover"*), Warner Bros., 1998.

The Other Sister, Buena Vista, 1999.

Man of the People, 1999.

The Insider, Buena Vista, 1999.

Wonder Boys (also known as *Die Wonder Boys*), Warner Bros., 2000.

The Family Man, Universal, 2000.

Bandits, Metro–Goldwyn–Mayer, 2001.

Red Dragon (also known as *Roter Drache*), Metro–Goldwyn–Mayer, 2002.

Pinocchio (also known as *Roberto Benigni's "Pinocchio"*), Miramax, 2002.

After the Sunset (also known as *Diamond in Paradise*), New Line Cinema, 2004.

X–Men: The Last Stand (also known as *X–Men 3, X3,* and *X–Men: Final Decision*), Twentieth Century–Fox, 2006.

The Contract, First Look International, 2006.

Slipstream (also known as *Slipstream Dream*), Strand Releasing, 2007.
Deception, Twentieth Century–Fox, 2008.
Visual Acoustics, 2008.
Flash of Genius, Universal, 2008.
Public Enemies, Universal, 2009.
(Additional photography) *State of Play,* Universal, 2009.
The Chronicles of Narnia: The Voyage of the Dawn Treader, Fox–Walden, 2010.

Film Work; Other:
Technical advisor, *A Director's Journey: The Making of "Red Dragon,"* Universal Home Video, 2003.
Creator, *ASC–DCI StEM* (also known as *ASC–DCI Standard Evaluation Material*), Digital Cinema Initiatives, 2004.
Additional camera operator, *Before, During and "After the Sunset,"* 2005.
Camera operator, *The Contract,* 2006.

Film Appearances:
(Uncredited) Man on bus, *Frankie and Johnny* (also known as *Frankie & Johnny*), 1991.
Dante Spinotti, 1993.
Himself, *The "Manhunter" Look: A Conversation with Dante Spinotti,* 2001.
Himself, *A Director's Journey: The Making of "Red Dragon"* (short documentary), Universal Home Video, 2003.
Himself, *Pacino and DeNiro: The Conversation* (short documentary), Warner Home Video, 2005.
Himself, *Before, During and "After the Sunset"* (documentary), New Line Home Video, 2005.
Himself, *The Making of "Heat"* (documentary), Warner Home Video, 2005.
Himself, *Cinematographer Style* (documentary), 2006.
Himself, *Visual Acoustics* (documentary; also known as *Visual Acoustics: The Modernism of Julius Shulman*), 2008.
Himself, *Dreaming "Slipstream Dream"* (short documentary), Sony Pictures Home Entertainment, 2008.
Himself, *Whatever You Desire: Making "L.A. Confidential"* (short documentary), Warner Home Video, 2008.
Himself, *Sunlight and Shadow: The Visual Style of "L.A. Confidential"* (short documentary), Warner Home Video, 2008.
Herr Kleiner/Mr. Moretti, *Deception,* 2008.
Himself, *On Dillinger's Trail* (short documentary), Universal Studios Home Entertainment, 2009.
Himself, *Michael Mann: Making "Public Enemies"* (short documentary), Universal Studios Home Entertainment, 2009.
Himself, *The Making of "Last of the Mohicans"* (documentary), Twentieth Century–Fox Home Entertainment, 2010.

Television Cinematographer; Miniseries:
(Second unit) *La donna di picche,* 1972.
I nicotera, 1972.

Television Cinematographer; Movies:
Tracce sulla neve, 1975.
Il quartetto Basileus, 1981.
Le ambizioni sbagliate, 1983.

Television Cinematographer; Pilots:
Prison Break, Fox, 2005.

Television Cinematographer; Episodic:
Women's Murder Club (also known as *wmc*), ABC, 2007.

Television Appearances; Specials:
The 70th Annual Academy Awards, ABC, 1998.

STANFORD, Aaron 1977–

PERSONAL

Full name, Aaron A. Stanford; born May 18, 1977, in Westford, MA; son of Don (a publishing executive) and Edith (a professor of English) Stanford. *Education:* Attended State University of New York College at Purchase, 2000; Rutgers University, graduated (magna cum laude), 2000; trained with London Academy of Theatre. *Avocational Interests:* Photography, playing cards.

Addresses: *Agent*—Daisy Wu, Gersh Agency, 9465 Wilshire Ave., 6th Floor, Beverly Hills, CA 90212. *Manager*—Lainie Sorkin–Becky, Management 360, 9111 Wilshire Blvd., Beverly Hills, CA 90210. *Publicist*—I/D Public Relations, 8409 Santa Monica Blvd., West Hollywood, CA 90069.

Career: Actor and producer. Began career as a stage actor in Westford, MA. Appeared in a commercial for Taco Bell restaurants, 2003.

Awards, Honors: Golden Satellite Award nomination, best actor in a motion picture comedy or musical, International Press Academy, 2003, for *Tadpole;* New York Emerging Talent Award, Big Apple Film Festival, 2009, for *How I Got Lost.*

CREDITS

Film Appearances:
Oscar Grubman, *Tadpole,* Miramax, 2002.
Actor, *Hollywood Ending,* DreamWorks, 2002.
Marcuse, *25th Hour,* Buena Vista, 2002.

John Allerdyce/Pyro, *X2* (also known as *X–Men 2, X–Men 2: X–Men United,* and *X2: X–Men United*), Twentieth Century–Fox, 2003.

Duke, *Rick,* ContentFilm International, 2003.

Gabe Winters, *Winter Solstice,* Paramount, 2004.

Michael Blake, *Spartan,* Warner Bros., 2004.

Michael Adler, *Runaway,* E1 Entertainment Distribution, 2005.

Rich, *Standing Still* (also known as *Amy Adams in "Night Before Wedding"*), Freestyle Releasing, 2006.

Doug Bukowski, *The Hills Have Eyes,* Fox Searchlight, 2006.

John Allerdyce/Pyro, *X–Men: The Last Stand* (also known as *X–Men: Final Decision, X–Men 3,* and *X3*), Twentieth Century–Fox, 2006.

John "Rugged" Rudgate, *Live Free or Die,* THINKFilm, 2007.

Neal Downs, *Flakes,* IFC First Take, 2007.

Dwight "Beagle" Kimbrough, *The Cake Eaters,* 2007, 7–57 Releasing, 2009.

Andrew Peterson, *How I Got Lost,* Osiris Entertainment, 2010.

Anthony Tregoni, *Holy Money,* Moviestream, 2010.

Film Producer:

Runaway, E1 Entertainment Distribution, 2005.

Television Appearances; Series:

Sergei, a recurring role, *Third Watch,* NBC, 2001–2002.

Will Traveler, *Traveler,* ABC, 2007.

Birkhoff, *Nikita,* The CW, 2010.

Television Appearances; Specials:

Narrator, *Breaking Vegas,* History Channel, 2004.

Television Appearances; Pilots:

Will Traveler, *Traveler,* ABC, 2007.

Birkhoff, *Nikita,* The CW, 2010.

Television Appearances; Episodic:

"Tadpole," *Anatomy of a Scene,* Sundance Channel, c. 2001.

Brett Chandler, "Hollywood Homicide," *Numb3rs* (also known as *Num3ers*), CBS, 2007.

Guest, "Waitress," *Secret's Out,* 2007.

Stephan, "Echoes," *Fear Itself,* NBC, 2009.

Josh Snow, "All In," *Law & Order: Criminal Intent* (also known as *Law & Order: CI*), NBC, 2009.

Horace Cook, Jr., "The Arrangements," *Mad Men,* AMC, 2009.

Stage Appearances:

Alan Strang, *Equus,* Towers Productions, 1995.

Biff, *Death of a Salesman,* New Ensemble Theatre, 1996.

Jack, *Sophistry,* Divine Intervention Productions, 1997.

Title role, *Sid Vicious Does the Dishes,* Love Creek Short Play Festival, New York City, 2000.

Tommy, *Life During Wartime,* Inertia Productions, New York City, 2000.

Dave the drug dealer, first young businessman, young white man, and other young white guy, *Where Do We Live?,* Vineyard Theatre, New York City, 2004.

RECORDINGS

Videos:

The Second Uncanny Issue of X–Men! Making "X2" (also known as *The Second Uncanny Issue of X–Men*), Twentieth Century–Fox Home Entertainment, 2003.

Surviving the Hills: Making of "The Hills Have Eyes," Twentieth Century–Fox, 2006.

Voice of Private Polonsky, *Call of Duty: World at War* (video game; also known as *Final Fronts*), Activision, 2008.

Cut, Good: The Making of "Runway," E1 Entertainment, 2009.

STATON, Aaron

PERSONAL

Married Connie Fletcher (an actress), December 18, 2006. *Education:* Graduated from Carnegie Mellon, 2004.

Addresses: *Agent*—International Creative Management, 10250 Constellation Blvd., 9th Floor, Los Angeles, CA 90067.

Career: Actor.

Awards, Honors: Screen Actors Guild Award nomination (with others), 2008, outstanding performance by an ensemble in a drama series, Screen Actors Guild Awards (with others), outstanding performance by an ensemble in a drama series, 2009, 2010, all for *Mad Men.*

CREDITS

Film Appearances:

Jared's friend, *Descent,* City Lights Pictures, 2007.

Rodney, *I Believe in America,* 2007.

John, *The Nanny Diaries,* Metro–Goldwyn–Mayer, 2007.

Leroy, *One Night,* GoDigital Media 2007.
Nick, *August Rush,* Warner Bros., 2007.
Journalist, *Che: Part Two,* IFC Films, 2008.
Boy, *Boy Meets Girl* (short film), 2010.

Television Appearances; Series:
Ken Cosgrove, *Mad Men,* AMC, 2007—.

Television Appearances; Specials:
The Making of "Mad Men," AMC, 2007.

Television Appearances; Episodic:
Andy Wall, "Hooked," *Law & Order: Special Victims Unit* (also known as *Law & Order: SVU* and *Special Victims Unit*), NBC, 2005.
Daniel, "Turn, Turn, Turn," *7th Heaven,* The WB, 2006.
Daniel, "The Replacements," *7th Heaven,* The WB, 2006.
Daniel, "Broken Hearts and Promises," *7th Heaven,* The WB, 2006.
Hugh Dolan, "Crash and Burn," *Without a Trace* (also known as *W.A.T.*), CBS, 2007.
The Soup, E! Entertainment Television, 2009.

Stage Appearances:
Sky, *Mamma Mia!,* Cadillac Winter Garden Theatre, New York City, 2004–2005.

Also appeared in *Jesus Christ Superstar; Oliver!*; as Claudio, *Measure for Measure*; Black, *The Wild Party.*

Internet Appearances; Episodic:
Bruce, "A New Leper in the Colony," *Imaginary Bitches,* imaginarybitches.com, 2008.

WRITINGS

Screenplays:
Boy Meets Girl (short film), 2010.

STAUNTON, Imelda 1956–

PERSONAL

Full name, Imelda Mary Philomena Bernadette Staunton; born January 9, 1956, in London, England; daughter of Joseph (a laborer) and Bridie (a hairdresser; maiden name, McNicholas) Staunton; married Jim Carter (an actor), October, 1983; children: Bessie (an actress). *Education:* Graduated from the Royal Academy of Dramatic Art, 1976; also attended the University of Cambridge.

Addresses: *Agent*—Artists Rights Group Ltd., 4 Great Portland St., London W1W 8 PA, England; Paradigm, 360 North Crescent Dr., North Bldg., Beverly Hills, CA 90210.

Career: Actress. Performed in repertory productions, 1976–81; Royal Academy of Dramatic Art, associate member. Also a comedienne and singer.

Member: Academy of Motion Picture Arts and Sciences.

Awards, Honors: Laurence Olivier Theatre Award, best supporting actress, Society of West End Theatre, 1985, for *A Chorus of Disapproval* and *The Corn Is Green;* London Critics Circle Award, best supporting actress, 1985, for *A Chorus of Disapproval* and *The Corn Is Green; Plays and Players* London Theatre Critics Award, best supporting actress, 1988, for *Uncle Vanya;* Laurence Olivier Theatre Award, best actress in a musical, Society of West End Theatre, 1990, for *Phoenix;* Laurence Olivier Theatre Award, best actress in a musical, Society of West End Theatre, 1991, for *Into the Woods;* Laurence Olivier Theatre Award, best actress in a musical, Society of West End Theatre, 1997, for *Guys and Dolls;* Screen Actors Guild Award nomination (with others), outstanding performance by a cast, 1999, for *Shakespeare in Love;* Irish Film and Television Award nomination, best actress, 2000, for *Rat;* British Independent Film Award, best actress, Chicago Film Critics Association Award, best actress, European Film Award, best actress, Los Angeles Film Critics Association Award, best actress, New York Film Critics Circle Award, best actress, San Diego Film Critics Society Award, best actress, Seattle Film Critics Award, best actress, Toronto Film Critics Association Award, best performance—female, Volpi Cup, best actress, Venice Film Festival, Washington DC Area Film Critics Association Award, best actress, 2004, Academy Award nomination, best performance by an actress in a leading role, ALFS Award, actress of the year, London Critics Circle, Film Award, best performance by an actress in a leading role, British Academy of Film and Television Arts, Chlotrudis Award, best actress, Critics Choice Award nomination, best actress, Broadcast Film Critics Association, Empire Award nomination, best British actress, *Evening Standard* British Film Award, best actress, Golden Globe Award nomination, best performance by an actress in a motion picture—drama, Golden Satellite Award nomination, best actress in a motion picture—drama, International Press Academy, National Society of Film Critics Award, best actress, Online Film Critics Society Award nomination, best actress, Screen Actors Guild Award nomination, outstanding performance by a female actor in a leading role, Vancouver Film Critics Circle, best actress, 2005, all for *Vera Drake;* decorated Officer of the Order of the British Empire, 2006; International Emmy Award nomination, best performance by an actress, 2006, for *My Family and Other Animals;* ALFS Award nomination, British supporting actress of the year, London Critics Circle, Saturn Award nomination, best supporting actress, Academy of Science Fiction, Fantasy, and Horror Films, 2008, both for *Harry Potter and the Order of the Phoenix;* Audience Award, best actress—comedy, California Independent Film Festival, 2009, for *A Deal Is a Deal.*

CREDITS

Film Appearances:
Betsy Loveless, *Comrades,* Curzon, 1987.
The producer, *They Never Slept,* 1990.
Jane Hartman, *Antonia and Jane,* Miramax, 1991.
Mary Charleston, *Peter's Friends,* Samuel Goldwyn, 1992.
Beth Greenwood, *Deadly Advice,* Castle Hill, 1993.
Margaret, *Much Ado About Nothing,* Samuel Goldwyn, 1993.
Charlotte Palmer, *Sense and Sensibility,* Columbia/TriStar, 1995.
Voice of Ivy and Angorra, *The Snow Queen,* 1995.
Maria, *Twelfth Night: Or What You Will* (also known as *Twelfth Night*), Fine Line, 1996.
Voice, *The Snow Queen's Revenge,* 1996.
Lorna, *Remember Me?,* Channel Four International, 1997.
Voice of Scruffy, *The Ugly Duckling* (animated), 1997.
Nurse, *Shakespeare in Love,* Miramax, 1998.
Conchita, *Rat,* Universal Focus, 2000.
Voice of Bunty, *Chicken Run* (also known as *C: R–1* and *Chicken Chicken Run Run*), DreamWorks Distribution, 2000.
Voice of Dilly, *Jack and the Beanstalk,* 2000.
Ethel Graydon, *Another Life,* Winchester Films, 2001.
Janine, *Crush* (also known as *Drei Freundinnen und ein liebhaber* and *Heiraten fuer fortgeschrittene*), Sony Pictures Classics, 2001.
Naomi, *Ready* (short film), 2002.
Bridget, *Blackball* (also known as *National Lampoon's "Blackball"*), Icon Film Distribution, 2003.
Dr. Bridget, *I'll Be There,* Warner Bros., 2003.
Lady Brown, *Bright Young Things,* Icon Film Distribution, 2003.
Sylvia, Conlon, *The Virgin of Liverpool,* Senator International, 2003.
Vera, *Vera Drake,* Fine Line, 2004.
Mrs. Blatherwick, *Nanny McPhee,* Universal, 2005.
Naomi, *Guilty Hearts,* 2006.
Ambassador Cochran, *Shadow Man,* Sony Pictures Home Entertainment, 2006.
Herself, *Bill Douglas: Intent on Getting the Image* (documentary), 400Blows Productions, 2006.
Margaret Campbell, *Freedom Writers,* Paramount, 2007.
Hazel Nightingale, *How About You ...,* Strand Releasing, 2007.
Dolores Umbridge, *Harry Potter and the Order of the Phoenix* (also known as *Harry Potter and the Order of the Phoenix: The IMAX Experience* and *The Order of the Phoenix*), Warner Bros., 2007.
Angela, *Where Have I Been All Your Life?* (short film), 2007.
Rosemary Cassidy, *A Deal Is a Deal* (also known as *Three and Out*), E1 Entertainment, 2008.
Mary, *A Bunch of Amateurs,* 2008.
Sonia Teichberg, *Taking Woodstock,* Focus Features, 2009.
Herself, *Lanterna Magicka: Bill Douglas and the Secret History of Cinema,* 891 Filmhouse, 2009.
Lynne McDermott, *White Other* (short film), 2010.
Voice of Tall Flower Faces, *Alice in Wonderland* (also known as *Alice in Wonderland: An IMAX 3D Experience*), Walt Disney Studios Motion Pictures, 2010.
Janet, *Another Year,* Sony Pictures Classics, 2010.
Dolores Umbridge, *Harry Potter and the Deathly Hallows: Part 1* (also known as *The Deathly Hallows*), Warner Bros., 2010.
Maud Hill, *The Awakening,* 2011.

Television Appearances; Series:
Various characters, *Thompson,* BBC and PBS, 1988.
Izzy, *Up the Garden Path,* Granada Television, 1990–93.
Muriel Spry, *If You See God, Tell Him,* BBC, 1993.
Stella Phelps, *Is It Legal?,* Carlton Television, 1995–96.
Mrs. Twit, *Let's Write a Story,* 2004.
Mrs. Mead, *Little Britain,* BBC America and BBC3, 2005.
Voice of Ruby and Twiba, *Big and Small,* 2008.

Television Appearances; Miniseries:
Nurse White, *The Singing Detective,* BBC, 1986, PBS, 1988.
Councillor Johnson, *Look at the State We're In!,* BBC, 1995.
Queen Elizabeth, *Cambridge Spies,* BBC2 and BBC America, 2003.
Mrs. Sucksby, *Fingersmith,* BBC, 2005.
Polly, "A Midsummer Night's Dream," *ShakespeaRe–Told,* BBC and BBC America, 2006.

Television Appearances; Movies:
Bridget Bennet, *A Masculine Ending,* BBC, 1992.
Roots, BBC, 1992.
Bridget Bennet, *Don't Leave Me This Way,* BBC, 1993.
Mrs. Burakova, *Citizen X,* HBO, 1995.
Mrs. Micawber, *David Copperfield,* BBC1, 1999, PBS, 2000.

Voice of Dilly, *Jack and the Beanstalk* (animated), HBO, 2000.

Detective chief inspector Billie Dory, *Murder*, 2002.

Mother, *My Family and Other Animals*, PBS, 2005.

Barge lady, *The Wind in the Willows*, PBS, 2006.

Miss Octavia Pole, *Cranford*, BBC1 and PBS, 2007.

Mary Doonan, *Clay*, 2008.

Miss Octavia Pole, *Return to Cranford*, PBS, 2009.

Television Appearances; Specials:

Louie, *The Heat of the Day*, PBS, 1989.

Edna, *Woodcock*, BBC, 1994.

Voice, *Mole's Christmas* (also known as *The Wind in the Willows Collection: Mole's Christmas*), The Disney Channel, 1994.

Voice, *The Adventures of Mole* (also known as *The Wind in the Willows Collection: The Adventures of Mole*), 1995.

Narrator (part two), *The Animal Family*, 1996.

Victoria Wood with All the Trimmings, BBC, 2000.

The 2004 European Film Awards, 2004.

The 62nd Annual Golden Globe Awards, NBC, 2005.

The 11th Annual Screen Actors Guild Awards, TNT, 2005.

The 77th Annual Academy Awards, ABC, 2005.

The Hidden Secrets of Harry Potter (also known as *Harry Potter: The Hidden Secrets*), 2007.

Achter de schermen bij "Harry Potter en de orde van de feniks," 2007.

Stephen Fry: 50 Not Out, BBC4, 2007.

Television Appearances; Episodic:

Mary Price, "Easy Money," *BBC2 Playhouse*, BBC, 1982.

Edith, "Double Act," *Ladies in Charge*, ITV, 1986.

Polly Flinders, "A Sleeping Life: Parts 1, 2 & 3," *The Ruth Rendell Mysteries*, PBS and Television South, 1989.

Jane Hartman, "Antonia and Jane," *Screenplay*, Granada Television, 1990.

Stephanie, "The Englishman's Wife," *Screenplay*, Granada Television, 1990.

Cheryl Newman, "Yellowbacks," *The Play on One*, 1990.

The producer, "They Never Slept," *Screen Two*, BBC, 1991.

Susan, "Charity," *Frank Stubbs Promotes*, ITV, 1993.

A Bit of Fry and Laurie, BBC, 1995.

Sarah, "About Face," *Tales from the Crypt* (also known as *HBO's "Tales from the Crypt"*), HBO, 1996.

Voice of the prioress, "Leaving London," *The Canterbury Tales* (animated), BBC and HBO, 1998.

Christine Cooper, "Dead Man's Eleven," *Midsomer Murders*, ITV and Arts and Entertainment, 1999.

Voice of the prioress, "The Journey Back," *The Canterbury Tales* (animated short), BBC and HBO, 2000.

Herself, *RI:SE*, Channel 4, 2002.

Reverend Mary Truegood, "Incubus," *Strange*, BBC, 2003.

Today with Des and Mel, ITV, 2004.

Richard & Judy, Channel 4, 2005.

The Late Late Show with Craig Ferguson, CBS, 2005.

"Imelda Staunton," *HARDtalk Extra*, BBC, 2005.

Shootout (also known as *Sunday Morning Shootout* and *Hollywood Shootout*), Bravo, 2005.

"The Singing Detective," *Drama Connections*, BBC, 2005.

"Little Britain," *The South Bank Show*, ITV, 2005.

This Morning, ITV, 2005, 2009.

Gwen Gregson, *Dogtown*, 2006.

"Harry Potter and the Order of the Phoenix: Fulfilling a Prophecy," *HBO First Look*, HBO, 2007.

Cartelera, 2007.

The Paul O'Grady Show, ITV, 2007.

Mother, "Lickle Bill Um," *Coming Up*, Channel 4, 2008.

Film 2008 (also known as *The Film Programme*), BBC, 2008.

Cinema 3, 2009.

"Imelda Staunton," *Mark Lawson Talks to ...*, 2009.

Breakfast, BBC, 2010.

The Michael Ball Show, 2010.

Stage Appearances:

Lucky, *Waiting for Godot*, Birmingham Repertory, England, 1976.

Travesties, Northcott Theatre, Exeter, England, 1978.

A Man for All Seasons, Northcott Theatre, 1978.

Elektra, Northcott Theatre, 1978.

Dear Daddy, Northcott Theatre, 1978.

Cinderella, Northcott Theatre, 1978.

'Tis a Pity She's a Whore, Northcott Theatre, 1978.

Macbeth, Northcott Theatre, 1978.

Cabaret, Northcott Theatre, 1978.

As You Like It, Northcott Theatre, 1978.

The Beggar's Opera, Northcott Theatre, 1979.

Title role, *Saint Joan*, Northcott Theatre, 1979.

Side by Side by Sondheim, Northcott Theatre, 1979.

Joseph and the Amazing Technicolor Dreamcoat, Northcott Theatre, 1979.

Anna, *Schweyk in the Second World War*, National Theatre, London, 1982.

Lucy Lockit, *The Beggar's Opera*, National Theatre, 1982.

Guys and Dolls, National Theatre, 1982.

Paulette, *Us Good Girls*, Soho Poly Theatre, London, 1984.

Janet, *It's a Mad World My Masters*, Theatre Royal, Stratford East, London, 1984.

Hannah, *A Chorus of Disapproval*, National Theatre, 1985.

Bessie, *The Corn Is Green*, Old Vic Theatre, London, 1985.

Performer, *Long Lankin*, Other Place Theatre, Stratford–upon–Avon, England, 1986.

The Fair Maid of the West, Swan Theatre, Royal Shakespeare Company, Stratford–upon–Avon, 1986.

Bess Bridges, *The Fair Maid of the West,* People's Theatre, Newcastle–upon–Tyne, England, 1987.

The Fair Maid of the West, Mermaid Theatre, London, 1987.

Dorothy Gale, *The Wizard of Oz,* Barbican Theatre, London, 1987.

Gloria Beatty, *They Shoot Horses, Don't They?,* Mermaid Theatre, 1987.

Venus, *Venus and Adonis,* Barbican Theatre, 1987.

Sonya, *Uncle Vanya,* Vaudeville Theatre, London, 1988.

Baker's wife, *Into the Woods,* Phoenix Theatre, London, 1990.

Phoenix, 1990.

Cassie, *Bold Girls,* Hampstead Theatre, London, 1991.

Bonfila, *Slavs!,* Hampstead Theatre, 1994.

Luba, *The Lady and the Clarinet,* Edinburgh Festival and King's Head Theatre, London, 1994.

Miss Adelaide, *Guys and Dolls,* National Theatre, 1996.

Mrs. Swabb, *Habeas Corpus,* Donmar Warehouse, 1997.

Ines, *Life x 3,* National Theatre, 2000–2001.

Nora, *Calico,* Duke of York's Theatre, London, 2004.

Margaret, *There Came a Gypsy Riding,* Almeida Theatre, London, 2007.

Also appeared in *Grease,* Theatre Royal, York, England; *Hay Fever,* Watermill Theatre, Newbury, England; *The Gingerbread Man,* Leeds Playhouse, England; *Henry V,* Leeds Playhouse; *Mrs. Warren's Profession,* Nottingham Playhouse, London; *A Little Night Music,* Nottingham Playhouse; as title role, *Piaf,* Nottingham Playhouse; Mabel, *Mack and Mabel,* Nottingham Playhouse.

Major Tours:

Appeared as Kate, *She Stoops to Conquer,* U.K. cities.

OTHER SOURCES

Periodicals:

The Daily Mail (London), November 20, 2009, p. 35.
USA Today, February 23, 2005, p. 8D.

STERLING, Rachel 1979–
    (Angel Veil)

PERSONAL

Born November 11, 1979, in Corpus Christi, TX. *Education:* Trained at Piero Dusa Conservatory; also trained as a dancer.

Addresses: *Manager*—Bleu, 5225 Wilshire Blvd., Suite 701, Los Angeles, CA 90036.

Career: Actress and dancer. Toured as a dancer with the Pussycat Dolls and with her own groups Purrfect Angelz, Rachel and the Dolls, and the Sugar Blush Beauties; also worked as a model.

CREDITS

Television Appearances; Series:

Dancer in Juggy Dance Squad, *The Man Show,* Comedy Central, 2002–2003.

Cohost, *The Red Carpet,* Showtime, 2003–2004.

Madam Caramel, a recurring role, *Reno 911!,* Comedy Central, 2005–2007.

Rachel, *VIP Passport,* 2006.

(Uncredited) Cheerleader for the series *X.F.L.,* NBC.

Television Appearances; Episodic:

Lucious, "Saving Private Irons," *V.I.P.,* syndicated, 2002.

Herself, *The Bronx Bunny Show,* Starz!, 2003.

Trashy lingerie model, *The Casino,* Fox, 2004.

Stacy, "The Count of Montecito," *Las Vegas,* NBC, 2004.

Summer, "Venice Boulevard of Broken Dreams," *One on One,* UPN, 2005.

Ana, "Fantasy Island," *Entourage,* HBO, 2008.

Samantha, "Chinatown," *NCIS: Los Angeles,* CBS, 2010.

(Uncredited) Bianca Jaguar, "The Carpet Brothers," *Funny or Die Presents ...,* HBO, 2010.

Television Appearances; Other:

Sherry, *Head Cases* (pilot), Fox, 2005.

Julia, *The Haunted Airman* (special), BBC, 2006.

April, *Glass Heels,* 2011.

Film Appearances:

Girl in bathtub, *Just Can't Get Enough,* 2001, Wolfe Video, 2003.

Cherry, *Tomcats,* Columbia, 2001.

Nurse Betty, *Destroying America,* Redline Entertainment, 2001.

Assia, *A Man Apart,* New Line Cinema, 2003.

Girl in car, *HellBent,* Regent Releasing, 2005.

Bernadette, *Wedding Crashers,* New Line Cinema, 2005.

Pretty girl at Mint, *Undiscovered,* Lions Gate Films, 2005.

Nicole, *Price to Pay,* Price Productions, 2006.

Zoe, *White Air,* Monarch Home Video, 2007.

Bridget, *Blink,* Two–Bit Films/Route 66 Pictures/Cinefugue, 2007.

Botanist, *All about Steve,* Twentieth Century–Fox, 2009.

Assistant, *Surrogates* (also known as *Vicarious*), Walt Disney, 2009.
Mimi, *Detention,* American World Pictures, 2010.
Stacy, *Crazy/Sexy/Awkward* (short film), FremantleMedia Enterprises, 2010.
Mercy, IFC Films, 2010.

Appeared in a few adult films, credited as Angel Veil.

RECORDINGS

Videos:
Appeared in several music videos, including "American Bad Ass" by Kid Rock; "Between Me and You" by Ja Rule; "Feel like Making Love"; "Freek" by George Michael; "Hey Baby" by No Doubt; "Hey, Sexy Lady" by Shaggy; "The Next Episode" by Dr. Dre; and "Slither and Dirty Little Thing" by Velvet Revolver; choreographer of the music video "Back in the Mud" by Bubba Sparxx.

OTHER SOURCES

Periodicals:
Stuff, August, 2005, pp. 76–86.

STEWART, Amy 1972–

PERSONAL

Full name, Amy Michelle Stewart; born July 13, 1972, in Palo Alto, CA; father, a politician; mother, a government teacher. *Education:* University of California, San Diego, degree (magna cum laude), psychology and political science; studied acting at La Jolla Playhouse Summer Conservatory.

Addresses: *Manager*—DiSante, Frank, and Company, 10061 Riverside Dr., Suite 377, Toluca Lake, CA 91602. *Agent*—Amsel, Eisenstadt, and Frazier, 5055 Wilshire Blvd., Ste. 865, Los Angeles, CA 90036; Reign Agency, 2216 Main St., Penthouse One, Santa Monica, CA 90405.

Career: Actress and producer. Appeared in television commercials.

CREDITS

Television Appearances; Series:
Sara Dolan, *Glory Days,* The WB, 2002.

Television Appearances; Episodic:
Helen, *Undressed* (also known as *MTV's "Undressed"*), MTV, 2000.
Linsey Cordova, "Family Matters," *ER,* NBC, 2000.
Linsey Cordova, "The Domino Heart," *ER,* NBC, 2000.
Leslie De Groot, "Gray Matters," *Chicago Hope,* CBS, 2000.
Maddie Werner, "The Thin Line," *The Practice,* ABC, 2001.
Nina Lombardi, "Second Chance," *Presidio Med,* CBS, 2002.
Nina Lombardi, "Do No Harm," *Presidio Med,* CBS, 2002.
Nina Lombardi, "When Approaching a Let–Go" *Presidio Med,* CBS, 2002.
Lindsay Beckman, "Flesh and Blood," *Strong Medicine,* Lifetime, 2002.
Katy Dyson, "Hell Week," *Wild Card* (also known as *Zoe Busiek: Wild Card*), Lifetime, 2003.
Lisa Zimmer, "Separation of Powers," *The West Wing* (also known as *The White House*), NBC, 2003.
Karen, "Year of the Tiger," *Las Vegas,* NBC, 2003.
Arlene Ross, "Crash," *JAG,* CBS, 2004.
Lois Hammond, "Dead in the Water," *Crossing Jordan,* NBC, 2004.
Brenda Dillard, "Summer in the City," *CSI: NY,* CBS, 2005.
"Double Take," *1–800–Missing* (also known as *Missing*), Lifetime, 2006.
Darla Johnson, "Escape," *Close to Home,* CBS, 2006.
Dr. Parsons, "Lost and Found," *Everwood,* The WB, 2006.
Tara Hathaway in 1987, "Offender," *Cold Case,* CBS, 2007.
Beth Burton, "In Which Addison Finds a Showerhead," *Private Practice,* ABC, 2007.
Sylvia Wicker, "Where and Why," *Without a Trace* (also known as *W.A.T*), CBS, 2007.
Catherine Cooper, "I Will, I'm Will," *Raising the Bar,* TNT, 2008.
Catherine Cooper, "Richie Richer," *Raising the Bar,* TNT, 2008.
Fiona, "The Forty–Year–Old Virgin Queen," *The Starter Wife,* USA Network, 2008.
Fiona, "The Diary of a Mad Ex–Housewife," *The Starter Wife,* USA Network, 2008.
Darcy, "There's Always a Woman," *Desperate Housewives,* ABC, 2008.
Janine Alexander, "The Organ Donor," *Dirty Sexy Money,* ABC, 2008.
Melissa Humphreys, "Miscarriage of Justice," *CSI: Crime Scene Investigation* (also known as *CSI: Las Vegas* and *C.S.I.*), CBS, 2009.
Juliet's mom, "The Incident," *Lost,* ABC, 2009.
Dania Stephens, "Manic at the Disco," *Mental,* Fox, 2009.
Brandy Rossi, "The Double Down," *Castle,* ABC, 2009.
Lucy the ex–wife, "Masquerade," *Trauma,* NBC, 2009.

Television Appearances; Movies:
Theresa, *Young at Heart,* CBS, 1995.
Rhondlyn Podubney, *Wild Iris,* Showtime, 2001.

Television Appearances; Miniseries:
Victoria Sheve, *And Never Let Her Go,* CBS, 2001.
Beth Hubbard, *Salem Witch Trials,* CBS, 2003.

Television Appearances; Specials:
Conquering Space, Showtime, 1990.
Rachel, *Life's Chronicles,* 2009.

Film Appearances:
Janet Hamilton, *Conquering Space,* Chanticleer Films, 1989.
Di, *Here Lies Lonely,* Brave Duck Films, 1999.
Tisha, *Maid of Honor,* Cinemax, 1999.
Amy Roe, *Monkey Love,* Ardustry Home Entertainment, 2002.
Susan Buckstead, *Church Ball,* KOAN, 2006.
Secret of the Black Cat (short film), 2010.

Film Executive Producer:
Secret of the Black Cat (short film), 2010.

Internet Appearances; Web Series:
Sondra, *The Lake,* www.thewb.com, 2009.

OTHER SOURCES

Electronic:
Amy Stewart Official Site, http://www.amystewart.net/, March 16, 2011.

STOFF, Erwin 1951–

PERSONAL

Born April 26, 1951, in Romania; married Deborah Aal (a producer); children: Rosanna.

Addresses: *Office*—3 Arts Entertainment, 9460 Wilshire Blvd., 7th Floor, Beverly Hills, CA 90212.

Career: Producer and talent manager. Began work as a personal manager, 1980; 3 Arts Entertainment, Beverly Hills, CA, founder, partner, and chairman; manager of film stars, including Matthew Broderick, Ethan Hawke, John Leguizamo, Richard Linklater, Mike Myers, Oliver Platt, Keanu Reeves, and Caroline Rhea.

CREDITS

Film Work:
Assistant director, *A Different Story,* Avco Embassy, 1978.
Production executive and producer (Elsboy), *Maxie,* 1985.
Coproducer, *Bill & Ted's Bogus Journey,* Orion, 1991.
Producer, *Excessive Force,* New Line Cinema, 1993.
Executive producer, *Loaded Weapon 1* (also known as *National Lampoon's "Loaded Weapon 1"*), New Line Cinema, 1993.
Executive producer, *Chain Reaction,* Twentieth Century–Fox, 1996.
Executive producer, *Feeling Minnesota,* Fine Line, 1996.
Executive producer, *The Devil's Advocate* (also known as *Diabolos, Devil's Advocate,* and *Im Auftrag des teufels*), Warner Bros., 1997.
Producer, *Picture Perfect,* Twentieth Century–Fox, 1997.
Executive producer, *The Matrix* (also known as *Matrix*), Warner Bros., 1999.
Executive producer, *Austin Powers: The Spy Who Shagged Me* (also known as *Austin Powers 2: The Spy Who Shagged Me* and *Austin Powers Deluxe*), New Line Cinema, 1999.
Executive producer, *The Replacements,* Warner Bros., 2000.
Executive producer, *Hard Ball* (also known as *Hardball*), Paramount, 2001.
Producer, *Sweet November,* Warner Bros., 2001.
Producer, *Biker Boyz,* DreamWorks, 2003.
Producer, *Constantine,* Warner Bros., 2005.
Producer, *Guess Who,* Columbia, 2005.
Producer, *A Scanner Darkly* (also known as *Scanner Darkly*), Warner Independent Pictures, 2006.
Executive producer, *The Lake House,* Warner Bros., 2006.
Executive producer, *I Am Legend* (also known as *I Am Legend: The IMAX Experience*), Warner Bros., 2007.
Producer, *Street Kings* (also known as *Fake City*), Fox Searchlight, 2008.
Producer, *The Day the Earth Stood Still* (also known as *D.T.E.S.S.* and *The Day the Earth Stood Still: The IMAX Experience*), Twentieth Century–Fox, 2008.
Executive producer, *The Blind Side,* Warner Bros., 2009.

Television Work; Series:
Executive producer, *Down the Shore,* Fox, 1991–93.
Co–executive producer, *Traps,* CBS, 1993.
Executive producer, *Queens Supreme,* CBS, 2003.
Executive producer, *The Orlando Jones Show,* FX Network, 2003.
Executive producer, *Kings,* NBC, 2009.

Television Work; Movies:
Executive producer, *Casebusters,* ABC, 1986.
Executive producer, *Save the Dog!,* The Disney Channel, 1988.
Co–executive producer, *Sophie and the Moonhanger,* Lifetime, 1996.

Television Executive Producer; Pilots:
These Guys, CBS, 1998.
$5.15/Hr., HBO, 2004.
Prime Suspect, NBC, 2010.

Television Executive Producer; Specials:
A Cool Like That Christmas, Fox, 1993.
John Leguizamo's Sexaholix ... A Love Story, HBO, 2002.

Television Appearances; Episodic:
Himself, "Constantine: Heaven, Hell and Beyond," *HBO First Look,* HBO, 2005.
Judge, *Mission Hollywood,* 2009.

STORM, Jim
(James Storm)

PERSONAL

Born August 12, in Highland Park, IL; brother of Michael Storm (an actor); children: Jeptha (an actor). *Avocational Interests:* Surfing, playing guitar, and singing.

Career: Actor.

CREDITS

Film Appearances:
The Trial of Billy Jack, Taylor–Laughlin, 1974.
Tommy, *Blue Sunshine,* Vestron Video, 1976.
Reporter, *Without a Trace,* Twentieth Century–Fox, 1983.
Himself, *"Dark Shadows": Behind the Scenes,* 1991.
Sheriff Jack Crowley, *Venomous,* New City Releasing, 2001.
Adam, *Breaking Adam* (short film), 2005.
Himself, *The Mistress of Collinwood: Miss Joan Bennett* (short film), MPI Media Group, 2006.
Frank, *Dark Mirror,* IFC Films, 2007.
Duncan, *Chain Link,* 2008.
Scott Farber, *Sex Drugs Guns,* Invincible Pictures, 2009.
Charlie, *Dispatch,* 2011.

Television Appearances; Series:
Dr. Larry Wolek, *One Life to Live,* ABC, 1968–69.
Gerard Styles, *Dark Shadows,* ABC, 1970–71.
Sean Childers, *The Secret Storm,* CBS, 1971.
Dr. Mike Powers, *The Doctors,* NBC, 1979–81.
Neil Fenmore, *The Young and the Restless* (also known as *Y&R*), CBS, 1983–86.
Mr. Kreiger, *Capitol,* CBS, 1986.
Bill Spencer, *The Bold and the Beautiful* (also known as *Belleza y poder*), CBS, 1987–94, 1997, 2000, 2003, 2009.
Charles Lakin, *Sunset Beach,* NBC, 1997–98.
Jim Storm, *When Actors Need Money,* 2009.

Television Appearances; Movies:
(As James Storm) Gerard Styles, *Night of Dark Shadows* (also known as *Curse of the Dark Shadows*), ABC, 1971.
(Uncredited) *The Invasion of Carol Enders,* 1973.
(As James Storm) Boy, *Scream of the Wolf,* ABC, 1974.
(As James Storm) Savage Hawk, *Murder in the First Person Singular,* 1974.
Eddie Nells, *Trilogy of Terror* (also known as *Tales of Terror* and *Terror of the Doll*), ABC, 1975.
Larry De Vol, *The Kansas City Massacre,* ABC, 1975.
Killer on Board, NBC, 1977.
Attendant, *It Happened at Lakewood Manor* (also known as *Ants, Ants!,* and *Panic at Lakewood Manor*), ABC, 1977.
Romar, *Farewell to the Planet of the Apes,* 1981.
Jack Galloway, *Firetrap,* HBO, 2001.
Dick Krantz, *Bone Eater* (also known as *Skeleton Rider*), Sci–Fi Channel, 2007.

Television Appearances; Pilots:
The Healers, NBC, 1974.
Change maker, *Dog and Cat,* ABC, 1977.
The Amazing Spider–Man (also known as *Spider–Man*), CBS, 1977.
David Barr, "Breathing Room," *Blacke's Magic,* NBC, 1986.

Television Appearances; Episodic:
(As James Storm) Joe Billy, "Empty Pages of a Dead Book," *Kung Fu,* ABC, 1974.
Romar, "Tomorrow's Tide," *Planet of the Apes,* CBS, 1974.
Resident, "The Fatal Dive," *Barnaby Jones,* CBS, 1976.
"The Lifeline Agency," *Police Woman,* 1976.
Officer, "Sticks and Stones May Break Your Bones but Waterbury Will Bury You," *The Rockford Files* (also known as *Jim Rockford, Private Investigator*), NBC, 1977.
Dr. Oliver George, "Qui Transtulit Sustinet," *St. Elsewhere,* NBC, 1983.
"Hotshoes," *Hardcastle and McCormick,* ABC, 1983.
Driver, "Staying Alive While Running a High Flashdance Fever," *Automan,* ABC, 1983.

Dr. Oliver George, "Family Feud," *St. Elsewhere,* NBC, 1986.

Dan Kates, "Unfinished Business," *Hotel,* ABC, 1987.

(As James Storm) Frank, "The Search for Grandpa Four," *Freddie,* ABC, 2006.

(As James Storm) Fitzpatrick, "Chapter Five 'Fight or Flight,'" *Heroes,* NBC, 2007.

Stage Appearances:

Slip, *The School for Scandal,* Lyceum Theatre, New York City, 1966.

94343 and understudy for the role of Unknown Solider, *The Unknown Soldier and His Wife,* Vivian Beaumont Theatre, then George Abbott Theatre, both New York City, 1967.

Alexander I, *War and Peace,* Lyceum Theatre, 1967.

G–man, *You Can't Take It With You,* Lyceum Theatre, 1967.

Jensen, *The Wild Duck,* Lyceum Theatre, 1967.

Rowdy Social Democrat, *Man and Superman,* Circle in the Square, New York City, 1978–79.

STRUCKMAN, Tino 1975–

PERSONAL

Full name, Tino Christian Nobel Von Struckmann; born May 27, 1975, in Denmark. *Education:* Aalborg (Denmark), bachelor's degree, 1990. *Avocational Interests:* Competed in bodybuilding competitions.

Addresses: *Publicist*—LA Media Consultants, 133510D Riverside Dr., Suite 621, Sherman Oaks, CA 91423. *Contact*—171 Pier Ave., Suite 488, Santa Monica, CA 90405.

Career: Actor, producer, and screenwriter. Almighty Dog Productions (a production company), Los Angeles, CA. Appeared in television commercial for U.S. Army recruitment. Also a technical consultant. International Special Service, Inc. (an international security firm), owner; worked as personal security for celebrities including Bill Gates, Robert DeNiro, Gloria Gaynor, Naomi Campbell, Sir Cliff Richard, Queen Margrethe of Denmark, and the Saudi royal family. *Military service:* Served in the army, 1994–2004; stationed at the Sergeant Academy, the United Nations, and with the North Atlantic Treaty Organization.

Awards, Honors: Slate Award (with Jerry Buteyn), best short film, California Independent Film Festival, 2006, for *The Doers of Coming Deeds.*

CREDITS

Film Appearances:

Blonde Heaven (also known as *Morgana* and *Morganna*), New City Releasing, 1995.

Fridas forste gang, Det Danske Filminstitut, 1996.

Schneider, Obersturmfuhrer, *The Doers of Coming Deeds,* Sacred Journey Films, 2006.

Southside Jiu–Jitsu academy fighter, *Redbelt,* Sony Pictures Classics, 2008.

Gunter, *Turning Point, Graf Zeppelin* (documentary), 2008.

Himself, *Coming to Light* (documentary), 2008.

(Uncredited) Black ops soldier, *Race to Witch Mountain* (also known as *Witch Mountain*), Walt Disney Studios Motion Picture, 2009.

Captain Klaus Mueller, *Brother's War* (also known as *End of War*), MTI Home Video, 2009.

Tony the doorman, *Groupie,* 2010.

Security guard J J, *Abandoned,* Anchor Bay Entertainment, 2010.

Film Work:

Executive producer and producer, *The Doers of Coming Deeds,* 2006.

Associate producer, *In the Name of the Son* (short film), Shorts International, 2007.

Executive producer, producer, and first assistant director, *Coming to Light* (documentary), 2008.

Associate producer, *Forever Plaid* (also known as *"Forever Plaid" 20th Anniversary Special*), National CineMedia, 2008.

Executive producer and producer, *Turning Point, Graf Zeppelin,* 2008.

Executive producer and producer, *Brother's War* (also known as *End of War*), 2009.

Executive producer, *Sisters* (short film), 2010.

Television Appearances; Movies:

Franz, *The Dog Who Saved Christmas,* ABC Family, 2009.

Television Appearances; Episodic:

(Uncredited) SWAT team leader, "With Honor," *Crossing Jordan,* NBC, 2002.

Geraldo at Large (also known as *At Large with Geraldo Rivera*), syndicated, 2004.

(Uncredited) DEA agent, "In Plain Sight," *Numb3rs* (also known as *Num3ers*), CBS, 2005.

(Uncredited) SWAT team officer, "Rampage," *Numb3rs* (also known as *Num3ers*), CBS, 2006.

Army officer, "Escape and Evade," *E–Ring,* NBC, 2006.

Serbian special forces officer, "War Crimes," *E–Ring,* NBC, 2006.

Terrorist, "Brothers in Arms," *E–Ring,* NBC, 2006.

E! News Live (also known as *E! News Daily* and *E! News Live Weekend*), E! Entertainment Television, 2006.

"Tino Struckmann," *Filmnut,* 2009.
Danske Hollywoodfruer, 2010.

Also appeared as guest, *Entertainment Tonight,* syndicated; *ABC News,* ABC; *CNN News,* Cable News Network; *Fox News; The Big Idea with Donny Deutsch,* CNBC.

WRITINGS

Film Stories:
Brother's Ware (also known as *End of War*), MTI Home Video, 2009.

Nonfiction:
Stalked, 2005.

Novels:
Children of Berlin, 2009.

OTHER SOURCES

Electronic:
Tino Struckmann Official Site, http://www.tinostruckman.com, September 7, 2010.

SURRATT, Ryan 1981–

PERSONAL

Born October 8, 1981, in Irvine, CA; son of a real estate agent and a public speaker. *Education:* University of Southern California, graduated; studied acting with various instructors.

Addresses: *Manager*—Christie Thomas, Commonwealth Talent Group, 5225 Wilshire Blvd., Suite 509, Los Angeles, CA 90036; Lara Rosenstock Management, 1314 North Hayworth Ave., Suite 503, West Hollywood, CA 90046.

Career: Actor.

CREDITS

Film Appearances:
Corey Williamson, *Hustler's Instinct* (short film), Latin Roc Star Films, 2005.
Bartender, *The Ugly Truth,* Columbia, 2009.

Eddie, *Fame,* Metro–Goldwyn–Mayer, 2009.
Arlington Heights (short film), 2009.
DJ, *Pizza with Bullets,* Radmks/D'Artagnan Entertainment/Mpire Films, 2010.
Mickey Rourke, *Gettin' through Life with Mickey Rourke* (short film), 2010.
The Algerian, Atlas Films, c. 2011.

Film Work:
Producer and (with Ryan Matthews) film editor, *Gettin' through Life with Mickey Rourke* (short film), 2010.

Television Appearances; Episodic:
Private Higgins, "Why We Fight," *The Color of War* (also known as *The War in Color: The American Story*), History Channel, 2001.
(Uncredited) Matt's friend, "Kurt Dempsey," *Nip/Tuck,* FX Network, 2003.
(Uncredited) Debate coach, "Forensics," *Cold Case* (also known as *Anexihniastes ypothesis, Caso abierto, Cold case—affaires classees, Cold Case—Kein Opfer ist je vergessen, Doegloett aktak, Kalla spaar, Todistettavasti syyllinen,* and *Victimes du passe*), CBS, 2009.

Appeared as Sean Garrett in episodes of *The Heartbreak Cafe,* cable stations in California.

Stage Appearances:
Appeared in various productions, including *The Apple Tree* (musical), *The Crucible, Dandelion Wine, Lost in Yonkers, Richard III, Romeo and Juliet,* and *West Side Story* (musical).

WRITINGS

Screenplays:
(And story) *Gettin' through Life with Mickey Rourke* (short film), 2010.

SUTTON, Linda Lee
(Linda Sutton, Linda L. Sutton, Linda Sutton–Doll)

PERSONAL

Career: Set decorator.

Awards, Honors: Excellence in Production Design Award nomination (with others), contemporary films, Art Directors Guild, 2010, for *Up in the Air.*

CREDITS

Film Set Decorator:
(Chicago) *Nothing in Common,* TriStar, 1986.
(As Linda Sutton) *Lucas,* Twentieth Century–Fox, 1986.
Poltergeist III, Metro–Goldwyn–Mayer, 1988.
Three of Hearts, New Line Cinema, 1993.
(As Linda Sutton; additional photography) *Albino Alligator,* Miramax, 1996.
(As Linda Sutton; Washington, DC) *Murder at 1600,* Warner Bros., 1997.
Kiss the Girls (also known as *Collector*), Paramount, 1997.
Living Out Loud, New Line Cinema, 1998.
(As Linda Sutton; additional) *Imposter* (also known as *Clone*), Dimension Films, 2001.
Tomcats, Columbia, 2001.
Frailty, Lions Gate Films, 2001.
(As Linda Sutton–Doll) *Crash,* 2004.
Freedom Writers, Paramount, 2007.
(As Linda Sutton–Doll) *In the Valley of Elah,* Warner Independent Pictures, 2007.
(As Linda Sutton–Doll) *The Great Buck Howard,* Magnolia Pictures, 2008.
(As Linda Sutton–Doll) *Appaloosa,* New Line Cinema, 2008.
Hotel for Dogs, Paramount, 2009.
Crossing Over, Weinstein Company, 2009.
(As Linda Sutton–Doll) *Up in the Air* (also known as *Mileage, My Life*), Paramount, 2009.
The Next Three Days, Lions Gate Films, 2010.
One for the Money, Lions Gate Films, 2011.

Film Art Director:
(As Linda Sutton; USA) *Frankie Starlight,* Fine Line, 1995.

Television Set Decorator; Series:
Crime Story, NBC, 1986–87.
Sable, ABC, 1987–88.
Brewster Place, ABC, 1990.
The Marshal, ABC, 1995–96.
The Pretender, NBC, 1998–2000.
The Bernie Mac Show, Fox, 2001–2006.
Miracles, ABC, 2003.

(As Linda Sutton–Doll) *Entourage,* HBO, 2004.
(As Linda Sutton–Doll) *Sleeper Cell* (also known as *Sleeper Cell: American Terror*), Showtime, 2005.
(As Linda Sutton–Doll) *Grey's Anatomy,* ABC, 2005.

Television Set Decorator; Miniseries:
(As Linda Sutton) *Trade Winds,* NBC, 1993.

Television Set Decorator; Movies:
The Toughest Man in the World, CBS, 1984.
(As Linda Sutton) *Lady Blue,* ABC, 1985.
Murderous Vision, USA Network, 1991.
(As Linda Sutton) *In the Shadow of a Killer,* NBC, 1992.
The Corpse Had a Familiar Face, CBS, 1994.
Take Me Home Again, NBC, 1994.
Down, Out & Dangerous, USA Network, 1995.
Marshal Law, Showtime, 1996.

Television Art Director and Set Dresser; Movies:
The Kid Who Loved Christmas, syndicated, 1990.

Television Property Master; Movies:
Two Fathers' Justice, NBC, 1985.

Television Set Designer; Specials:
On Trial, NBC, 1994.

Television Set Decorator; Pilots:
Crime Story (movie), NBC, 1986.
(As Linda L. Sutton) *Equal Justice,* ABC, 1990.

Television Set Decorator; Episodic:
"Time and Time Again," *Golden Years* (also known as *Stephen King's "Golden Years"*), CBS, 1991.
(As Linda Sutton–Doll) "Say Uncle," *CSI: Crime Scene Investigation* (also known as *CSI: Las Vegas* and *C.S.I.*), CBS, 2008.
(As Linda Sutton–Doll) "Epilogue," *CSI: NY* (also known as *CSI: New York*), CBS, 2009.
(As Linda Sutton–Doll) "Blacklist (Featuring Grave Digger)," *CSI: NY* (also known as *CSI: New York*), CBS, 2009.

T

TAMBLYN, Amber 1983–
   (Amber Rose Tamblyn)

PERSONAL

Full name, Amber Rose Tamblyn; born May 14, 1983, in Santa Monica, CA; daughter of Russ (an actor, dancer, and singer) and Bonnie (a singer, songwriter, artist, and teacher) Tamblyn; granddaughter of Eddie Tamblyn (a vaudeville performer). *Education:* Attended an alternative school in Santa Monica, CA. *Politics:* Liberal. *Religion:* Agnostic. *Avocational Interests:* Writing poetry, singing, dancing.

Addresses: *Agent*—WME Entertainment, One William Morris Pl., Beverly Hills, CA 90212. *Manager*—Hyler Management, 20 Ocean Park Blvd., Santa Monica, CA 90405.

Career: Actress. Appeared in stage productions. Traveled with the Junkyard Ghost Revival (a poetry/slam tour), 2008.

Awards, Honors: YoungStar Award nomination, best performance by a young actress in a daytime television series, 1999, YoungStar Award, 2000, best performance by a young actress in a daytime television series, *Hollywood Reporter, Soap Opera Digest* Award nomination, favorite teen star, 2000, *Soap Opera Digest* Award nomination, outstanding younger lead actress, 2001, all for *General Hospital;* Emmy Award nomination, outstanding lead actress in a drama series, Golden Globe Award nomination, best actress in a television drama series, Saturn Award, best actress in a television series, Academy of Science Fiction, Fantasy, and Horror Films, Teen Choice Award nomination, choice breakout television star—female, Teen Choice Award nomination, choice television actress—drama/action adventure, Young Artist Award nomination, best young adult performer in a teenage role, 2004, Golden Satellite Award nominations, best actress in a drama series, International Press Academy, 2004, 2005, Saturn Award nomination, best actress in a television series, Academy of Science Fiction, Fantasy, and Horror Films, 2005, all for *Joan of Arcadia;* Teen Choice Award nomination, choice movie actress: drama, 2005, for *The Sisterhood of the Traveling Pants;* Silver Leopard Award, best actress, Locarno International Film Festival, 2006, Independent Spirit Award nomination, best supporting female, Independent Features Project/West, 2007, both for *Stephanie Daley;* Teen Choice Award nomination, choice movie actress—horror/thriller, 2007, for *The Grudge 2.*

CREDITS

Film Appearances:
Deb, *Biker Poet,* 1994.
(As Amber Rose Tamblyn) Young Jill, *Live Nude Girls,* Republic, 1995.
Deb, *Rebellious,* 1995.
Kate, "Twelve Miles to Trona," *Ten Minutes Older: The Trumpet,* Blue Dolphin Film Distribution, 2002.
Katie Embry, *The Ring,* DreamWorks, 2002.
Tibby, *The Sisterhood of the Traveling Pants,* Warner Bros., 2005.
Title role, *Stephanie Daley* (also known as *What She Knew*), Regent Releasing, 2006.
Aubrey, *The Grudge 2,* Columbia, 2006.
Claudia, *Blackout,* Capitol Films, 2007.
Amber, *Spiral,* Anchor Bay Entertainment, 2007.
Wendy, *Normal Adolescent Behavior* (also known as *A Story of a Teenager* and *Havoc 2: Normal Adolescent Behavior*), New Line Cinema, 2007.
"The Grudge 2": Holding a Grudge (short documentary), 2007.
"The Grudge 2": Ready When You Are Mr Shimizu (short documentary), 2007.

Tibby Tomko–Rollins, *The Sisterhood of the Traveling Pants 2*, Warner Bros., 2008.

Herself, *The Making of "Spiral"* (short documentary), 2008.

Herself, *One Fast Move or I'm Gone: Kerouac's Big Sur* (documentary), 2008.

Ashley Hartmann, *Spring Breakdown*, Warner Bros., 2009.

Ella Crystal, *Beyond a Reasonable Doubt*, After Dark Films, 2009.

Herself, *The Drums Inside Your Chest* (documentary), 2009.

Megan, *127 Hours*, Fox Searchlight, 2010.

Mary Saunders, *Main Street*, Myriad Pictures, 2010.

Film Executive Producer:

The Drums Inside Your Chest, 2009.

Television Appearances; Series:

Emily Bowen Quartermaine, *General Hospital*, ABC, 1995–2001.

Emily Quartermaine, *Port Charles*, ABC, 1997–2001.

Joan Girardi (title role), *Joan of Arcadia*, CBS, 2003–2005.

Detective Casey Shraeger, *The Unusuals*, ABC, 2009.

Martha Masters, *House, M.D.*, Fox, 2010—.

Television Appearances; Movies:

Sprout, *Johnny Mysto: Boy Wizard*, HBO, 1996.

Sarah Russell, *The Russell Girl*, CBS, 2008.

Television Appearances; Specials:

Emily, *"General Hospital": Twist of Fate*, ABC, 1996.

The 30th Annual People's Choice Awards, 2004.

Presenter, *The 56th Annual Writers Guild Awards*, Starz!, 2004.

The 6th Annual Family Television Awards, The WB, 2004.

Presenter, *The 46th Annual Grammy Awards*, CBS, 2004.

A Tribute to Joe Mantegna, 2004.

Presenter, *The 5th Annual Latin Grammy Awards*, CBS, 2004.

Presenter, *The 10th Annual Screen Actors Guild Awards*, TNT, 2004.

VH1 Big in '04, VH1, 2004.

Presenter, *The 56th Annual Primetime Emmy Awards*, ABC, 2004.

Voice of Elizabeth Kaugmann and Miriam Korber, *I'm Still Here: Real Diaries of Young People Who Lived During the Holocaust*, MTV, 2005.

The Teen Choice Awards 2005, Fox, 2005.

Presenter, *Nickelodeon's 18th Annual Kids' Choice Awards*, Nickelodeon, 2005.

2007 Much Music Video Music Awards, MuchMusic, 2007.

Television Appearances; Pilots:

Paige, *No Ordinary Girl*, The WB, 2001.

Prep, The WB, 2002.

Miriam Quinn, *The Quinn–tuplets*, CBS, 2010.

Television Appearances; Episodic:

Janice, "All the Way," *Buffy the Vampire Slayer* (also known as *BtVS, Buffy, Buffy, the Vampire Slayer: The Series*, and *Nightfall*), UPN, 2001.

Melissa Campbell, "Chapter Thirty–two," *Boston Public*, Fox, 2002.

Jenna, "Evergreen," *The Twilight Zone*, UPN, 2002.

Senior Cadet Louise Ferraro, "Camp Fear," *CSI: Miami*, CBS, 2002.

Clare Metcalf, "Clare de Lune," *Without a Trace* (also known as *W.A.T.*), CBS, 2003.

Herself, *Punk'd*, MTV, 2003.

Herself, "White Socks Only," *Storyline Online*, 2003.

Herself, *Storyline Online 3*, 2004.

Life & Style, BBC, 2004.

CBS Cares, CBS, 2004, 2005.

Total Request Live (also known as *TRL* and *Total Request with Carson Daly*), MTV, 2004, 2005.

"Tournament 6, Game 4," *Celebrity Poker Showdown*, Bravo, 2005.

"Amber Tamblyn," *Fuse Celebrity Playlist*, Fuse, 2006.

HypaSpace (also known as *HypaSpace Daily* and *HypaSpace Weekly*), SPACE, 2006.

Entertainment Tonight (also known as *E.T.*), syndicated, 2006, 2008, 2009.

"Amber Tamblyn/James Cromwell/Todd McCarthy," *Shootout* (also known as *Sunday Morning Shootout* and *Hollywood Shootout*), Bravo, 2007.

Girl, "The Increasingly Poor Decisions of Todd Margaret," *Comedy Showcase*, NBC, 2009.

Girl, "In Which Claims Are Made and a Journey Ensues," *The Increasingly Poor Decisions of Todd Margaret*, Independent Film Channel, 2010.

Girl, "A Plan Is Hatched and a Date Is Not a Date," *The Increasingly Poor Decisions of Todd Margaret*, Independent Film Channel, 2010.

Television Talk Show Guest Appearances; Episodic:

Late Show with David Letterman (also known as *The Late Show*), CBS, 2004.

The Wayne Brady Show, syndicated, 2004.

The Sharon Osbourne Show (also known as *Sharon*), syndicated, 2004.

The View, ABC, 2004, 2005.

The Late Late Show with Craig Ferguson, CBS, 2005.

Late Night with Conan O'Brien, NBC, 2005.

Today (also known as *NBC News Today* and *The Today Show*), NBC, 2005.

The Tonight Show with Jay Leno, NBC, 2005.

The Tony Danza Show, syndicated, 2005.

Live with Regis and Kelly, syndicated, 2005, 2006, 2008, 2009.

Ellen: The Ellen DeGenres Show, syndicated, 2006.

Up Close with Carrie Keagan, 2007.
Good Morning America (also known as *G.M.A.*), ABC, 2008.
Late Night with Jimmy Fallon, NBC, 2009.

Stage Appearances:
Pippi Longstocking, 1993.
Amber, "And It Seems to Me a Very Good Sign," *The 24 Hour Plays 2009,* American Airlines Theatre, New York City, 2009.

RECORDINGS

Albums:
Recorded a single, "God and Me."

Music Videos:
Played a record executive in "French Made" by the Plasticines.

WRITINGS

Poetry Collections:
Free Stallion: Poems, Simon & Schuster, 2005.
Bang Ditto, Manic D. Press, 2009.

Author of the poetry collections *Of the Dawn* and *Plenty of Ships,* both privately printed; also contributor of poetry to magazines, including *Cups* and *Poetry USA.*

OTHER SOURCES

Periodicals:
Entertainment Weekly, December 12, 2002, p. 30.
Parade, January 11, 2004, p. 14.
People Weekly, October 27, 2003, p. 93.
Soap Opera Digest, January 20, 1998, pp. 28–30.

Electronic:
Amber Tamblyn Official Site, http://www.amtam.com, October 21, 2010.

TANAKA, Aiko 1979–

PERSONAL

Born December 13, 1979, in Tokyo, Japan; father, a sales and marketing manager; mother's name, Sue (a swimsuit model). *Education:* Attended college in the United States; studied theatre and dance. *Avocational Interests:* Cooking, reading.

Career: Actress. Began career as a child model; worked as a professional dancer; performed as a standup comedian.

CREDITS

Film Appearances:
Japan, *Miss Castaway and the Island Girls* (also known as *Miss Cast Away* and *Silly Movie 2*), Showcase Entertainment, 2004.
Second cowgirl at starting line, *The Fast and Furious: Tokyo Drift* (also known as *Fast and Furious 3: Tokyo Drift* and *Wild Speed X3: Tokyo Drift*), Universal, 2006.
"Nunchuck" girl, *Finishing the Game: The Search for a New Bruce Lee* (also known as *Finishing the Game*), IFC Films, 2007.
Japanese Iggy, *La revolucion de Iguodala!* (short film), Siho Media/Trailing Johnson Productions, 2007.
Snow bunny, *White Air,* Monarch Home Video, 2007.
Asian goddess, *TBS* (short film), 2007.
May, *China Dolls,* Don Barnhart Entertainment/ Chucklehut Entertainment, 2008.
Esther, *Cut the Fat* (short film), 2009.

Television Appearances; Specials:
Young, Beautiful, and Trying to Make It in Hollywood, 2005.

Television Appearances; Episodic:
Flower lady, "Table for Too Many: Part 1," *My Wife and Kids,* ABC, 2002.
Howard Stern, E! Entertainment Television, 2003.
Ajipon model, "More Mitsukan for Your Life," *Seikatsu! Hop, Step, Mitsuwa,* 2008.

Appeared as a dancer on *Soul Train,* syndicated; also appeared in episodes of *The Grind,* MTV; *Malcolm and Eddie;* and *The Man Show,* Comedy Central.

RECORDINGS

Videos:
Host, *Street Fury,* 2001.

Appeared in music videos recorded by Afroman, Destiny's Child, and the Offspring; voice for the video game *Street Racing Syndicate,* Namco.

OTHER SOURCES

Electronic:
Aiko Tanaka Official Site, http://www.aikotanaka.com, October 15, 2010.

TELLER, 1948–
(Raymond Joseph Teller)

PERSONAL

Full name, Raymond Joseph Teller; born February 14, 1948, in Philadelphia, PA; son of Joe (an advertising artist) and Irene Teller. *Education:* Amherst College. *Politics:* Libertarian. *Religion:* Atheist. *Avocational Interests:* Painting.

Addresses: *Office*—Buggs and Rudy A Discount Corporation/Star Rice Productions, 3555 West Reno Ave., Suite L, Las Vegas, NV 89118. *Agent*—Agency for the Performing Arts, 405 South Beverly Dr., Beverly Hills, CA 90212. *Manager*—Golden Entertainment West, 10921 Wilshire Blvd., Los Angeles, CA 90024.

Career: Actor, magician, and writer. Penn and Teller (comedy team), partner with Penn Jillette; appeared in nightly Penn and Teller show at Rio All–Suite Hotel and Casino, Las Vegas, NV, 2003; Buggs and Rudy A Discount Corporation, partner; Star Price Productions, Las Vegas, NV, partner. Appeared in television commercials for Powerstreet online trading, 1999, Pizza Hut restaurants, 2001, and HP Media Center, 2002. Massachusetts Institute of Technology, Cambridge, MA, visiting scholar; lectured at Oxford University and the Smithsonian Institution. Previously taught high school Latin in New Jersey.

Awards, Honors: Magician of the Year Award (with Penn Jillette), Academy of Magical Arts, 1996; Emmy Award nomination (with others), outstanding music and lyrics, 1999, for *Sin City Spectacular;* Hugh M. Hefner First Amendment Award, 2001; WGA Television nominations (with others), comedy/variety (including talk)—series, Writers Guild of America, 2004, 2005, 2006, 2007 Emmy Award nomination (with others), outstanding reality program, 2004, 2005, 2006, 2007, 2008, Emmy Award nominations (with others), outstanding writing for nonfiction programming, 2004, 2005, 2006, 2007, all for *Penn & Teller: Bullshit!*

CREDITS

Film Appearances:
Abdul, *My Chauffeur* (also known as *My Chauffeur: Licensed to Love*), Crown, 1986.

Himself, *Cruel Tricks for Dear Friends* (also known as *Penn & Teller's Cruel Tricks for Dear Friends*), 1987.
Voice of Octum, *Light Years* (animated; also known as *Gandahar*), Miramax, 1988.
Teller, *Penn & Teller Get Killed* (also known as *Dead Funny*), Warner Bros., 1989.
Luthers, *Car 54, Where Are You?*, Columbia/TriStar, 1994.
Mortimer, *The Fantasticks,* Metro–Goldwyn–Mayer, 1995.
Himself, *The Best of Ed's Night Party,* 1996.
Host, "The Sorcerer's Apprentice," *Fantasia/2000* (also known as *Fantasia 2000*), Buena Vista, 1999.
Mortimer, *The Fantasticks,* United Artists, 2000.
Himself, *The Aristocrats* (documentary; also known as *The @r!$t*(r@t$*), Lions Gate Films Home Entertainment, 2005.
Himself, *Magic: The Science of Illusion* (short film), 2005.
Narrator, *Spanking Lessons* (short film), 2007.
Himself, *Flow: For Love of Water* (documentary), Oscilloscope Pictures, 2008.
Himself, *Women in Boxes* (documentary), 2008.
Himself, *& Teller* (short film), Sony Pictures Home Entertainment, 2008.
Himself, *& Teller 2* (short film), Sony Pictures Home Entertainment, 2008.

Film Work:
Director, producer, and editor, *& Teller* (short film), Sony Pictures Home Entertainment, 2008.
Director, producer, and editor, *& Teller 2* (short film), Sony Pictures Home Entertainment, 2008.
Director, *Macbeth: Folger Shakespeare Library Edition,* 2009.
Executive producer, *The Growth,* 2009.
Executive producer, *Dracula's Daughters vs. the Space Brains* (short film), National Lampoon, 2010.

Television Appearances; Series:
The Unpleasant World of Penn & Teller, Channel 4, 1994.
Host, *Sin City Spectacular* (also known as *Penn & Teller's "Sin City Spectacular"*), FX Network, 1998–99.
Penn & Teller: Bullshit!, Showtime, 2003—.
Himself (geeks), *My Coolest Years,* VH1, 2004.

Television Appearances; Miniseries:
Himself, "Volume 4: Highway 93," *Great Drives,* PBS, 1996.

Television Appearances; Movies:
Hale Buchman, Jr., *Long Gone* (also known as *Stogies*), HBO, 1987.
Jake Clones, *Zoey's Zoo,* 1999.

Television Appearances; Specials:

Penn & Teller Go Public, PBS, 1985.

The Search for Houdini, syndicated, 1987.

Comic Relief II, HBO, 1987.

Penn & Teller's "Invisible Thread" (also known as *Invisible Thread*), Showtime, 1987.

Free to Be ... a Family, ABC, 1988.

Negligee and Underpants Party (also known as *Howard Stern's "Negligee and Underpants Party"*), 1988.

Host, *Showtime Comedy Club All–Stars III,* Showtime, 1989.

Comic Relief III, HBO, 1989.

Exploring Psychic Powers ... Live, syndicated, 1989.

Camera retriever number two, *The Magic of David Copperfield XII: The Niagara Falls, Challenge,* CBS, 1990.

Memory & Imagination: New Pathways to the Library of Congress, PBS, 1990.

Don't Try This at Home! (also known as *Penn & Teller's "Don't Try This at Home!"*), NBC, 1990.

Martin Mull: Talent Takes a Holiday, Showtime, 1991.

Host, *Fox New Year's Eve Live,* Fox, 1992, 1993.

The 10th Annual Montreal Comedy Festival, Showtime, 1992.

Behind the Scenes, 1992.

Aspen Comedy Festival, Comedy Central, 1994.

The World's Greatest Magic II, NBC, 1995.

Teller, *Phobophilia: The Love of Fear* (also known as *Penn & Teller "Phobophilia: The Love of Fear"*), 1995.

New Year's Eve in Vegas, Fox, 1995.

Caesars Palace 30th Anniversary Celebration, 1996.

The World's Wildest Magic, NBC, 1997.

Home Invasion (also known as *Penn & Teller's "Home Invasion"*), ABC, 1997.

The Secret World of Magicians and Mentalists, The Learning Channel, 1997.

The Mysteries of Magic, The Learning Channel, 1998.

NFL All–Star Comedy Blitz, CBS, 1999.

The Unpleasant World of Penn and Teller, Comedy Central, 2000.

The Great American History Quiz: America at War, History Channel, 2001.

The Great American History Quiz: 50 States, History Channel, 2001.

50 Greatest Magic Tricks, 2002.

Penn & Teller's Magic and Mystery Tour, The Learning Channel, 2002.

I Love the '70s, VH1, 2003.

Magic and Mystery Tour (also known as *Penn & Teller's "Magic and Mystery Tour"*), 2003.

Himself (illusionist), *Super Secret Movie Rules: Slashers* (also known as *SSMR: Slashers*), VH1, 2004.

Magic, 2004.

E! 101 Most Awesome Moments in Entertainment, E! Entertainment Television, 2004.

The 100 Most Memorable TV Moments, TV Land, 2004.

Evening at Pops: Keith Lockhart's 10th Anniversary Special, PBS, 2004.

Las Vegas Live!, Bravo, 2004.

50 Hottest Vegas Moments, E! Entertainment Television, 2005.

AFI's 100 Years ... 100 Movie Quotes: America's Greatest Quips, Comebacks and Catchphrases, CBS, 2005.

Houdini: Unlocking the Mystery, 2005.

Penn & Teller: Off the Deep End, NBC, 2005.

The 100 Most Unexpected TV Moments, TV Land, 2005.

History of the Joke, History Channel, 2008.

Cheech & Chong: Roasted, TBS, 2008.

Television Appearances; Awards Presentations:

The 1988 MTV Video Music Awards, MTV, 1988.

Presenter, *The 45th Annual Tony Awards,* CBS, 1991.

Discover Magazine's Technology Awards, 1992.

Host, *Discover Magazine's 5th Annual Technology Awards,* 1994.

Presenter, *The 12th Annual American Comedy Awards,* Fox, 1998.

The World of Magic Awards 2000, PAX, 2000.

Presenter, *The ... Annual Academy of Country Music Awards,* CBS, 2003, 2004.

Spike TV VGA Video Games Awards, Spike TV, 2003.

Presenter, *The 2004 Primetime Creative Arts Emmy Awards,* E! Entertainment Television, 2004.

The 2006 Primetime Creative Arts Emmy Awards, E! Entertainment Television, 2006.

Presenter, *The 2007 World Magic Awards,* MyNetworkTV, 2007.

Television Appearances; Pilots:

Skippy, *Sabrina, the Teenage Witch* (also known as *Sabrina* and *Sabrina Goes to College*), ABC, 1997.

Television Appearances; Episodic:

Saturday Night Live (also known as *SNL*), NBC, 1985, 1986.

(As Raymond Joseph Teller) Ralph Fisher, "Like a Hurricane," *Miami Vice,* 1987.

The Original Max Talking Headroom Show, Cinemax, 1987.

The Word, 1993.

"Houdini: The Great Escape," *Biography,* Arts and Entertainment, 1994.

Geller, "Drew Meets Lawyers," *The Drew Carey Show,* ABC, 1995.

Himself, "$20.01," *Space Ghost Coast to Coast* (also known as *SGC2C*), Cartoon Network, 1996.

Geller, "See Drew Run," *The Drew Carey Show,* ABC, 1997.

Skippy, "Jenny's Non–Dream," *Sabrina, the Teenage Witch* (also known as *Sabrina* and *Sabrina Goes to College*), ABC, 1997.

Himself, "The Gary Cahuenga Episode," *Muppets Tonight!,* 1997.

Himself, *Ed's Night Party* (also known as *Ed the Sock*), 1997.

Zooty, "Day of the Dead," *Babylon 5* (also known as *B5*), TNT, 1998.
Mr. Boots, "The Cat's Out of the Bag," *Dharma and Greg*, ABC, 1998.
Himself, "Val the Hard Way," *V.I.P.*, 1998.
Hollywood Squares (also known as *H2* and *H2: Hollywood Squares*), syndicated, 1998–2004.
Voice of himself, "Hello Gutter, Hello Fadder," *The Simpsons* (animated), Fox, 1999.
Himself, "Knee Deep," *Home Improvement*, ABC, 1999.
"Penn and Teller," *Bravo Profiles*, 2001.
Just for Laughs (also known as *Ed Byrne's "Just for Laughs,"* *Just for Laughs Comedy Festival*, and *Just for Laughs Montreal Comedy Festival*), 2002.
"Celebrity Fear Factor 3," *Fear Factor* (also known as *Factor miedo* and *Fear Factor: The Series*), 2002.
"Las Vegas: Live Reveal," *Trading Spaces*, The Learning Channel, 2003.
Himself, "Magic Jordan," *The Bernie Mac Show*, Fox, 2003.
"200 Greatest Pop Culture Icons," *The Greatest*, 2003.
Who Wants to Marry My Dad?, 2003.
Himself, "Luck Be a Lady," *Las Vegas*, NBC, 2003.
Super Secret Movie Rules, VH1, 2003.
"Keith Lockhart's 10th Anniversary Special," *Evening at Pops*, PBS, 2004.
Himself, "In the Room," *The West Wing* (also known as *The White House*), NBC, 2004.
Himself, "Las Vegas," *Listen Up*, CBS, 2005.
"C4 Crate," *Criss Angel Mindfreak* (also known as *The Five Lives of Criss Angel Mindfreak*), Arts and Entertainment, 2005.
Dirty Tricks, 2005.
"Steve Martin," *Biography*, Arts and Entertainment, 2006.
"Top 10 TV Weddings," *TV Land's Top Ten*, TV Land, 2006.
"Top Ten Musical Moments," *TV Land's Top Ten*, TV Land, 2006.
Free Radio, VH1, 2007.
Don't Forget the Lyrics, Fox, 2008.
Last Comic Standing (also known as *Last Comic Standing: The Search for the Funniest Person in America*), NBC, 2008.
"Round 1: Part 1," *Dancing with the Stars* (also known as *D.W.T.S.*), ABC, 2008.
"Round 1: Part 3," *Dancing with the Stars* (also known as *D.W.T.S.*), ABC, 2008.
"Round 1: Results," *Dancing with the Stars* (also known as *D.W.T.S.*), ABC, 2008.
Himself, "Lance's Birthday," *Free Radio*, Comedy Central, 2008.
"Wet and Wild," *Battleground Earth: Ludacris vs. Tommy Lee*, 2008.
"Vegas Baby," *Great American Road Trip*, 2009.
"Penn & Teller," *Top Chef*, Bravo, 2009.
Holly's World, E! Entertainment Television, 2009.
True Beauty, ABC, 2009.
Shaq vs ..., ABC, 2009.
The ONE Show, BBC, 2010.

WWF Raw (also known as *WWF Raw Is War, Raw Is War, WWE Monday Night RAW*, and *WWE Raw*), USA Network, 2010.

Also appeared in "Zoey's Zoo: Lots of Ocelots," *Oh Yeah! Cartoons* (animated); *Alan King: Inside the Comedy Mind*, Comedy Central; *The Pet Shop*, Animal Planet; as host, *Behind the Scenes*, PBS; guest, *Where in the World Is Carmen Sandiego?*, PBS.

Television Talk Show Guest Appearances; Episodic:
Late Night with David Letterman, NBC, 1986, 1987, 1988, 1989, 1990, 1991, 1992.
The Tonight Show Starring Johnny Carson, NBC, 1989.
The Howard Stern Interview (also known as *The Howard Stern "Interview"*), 1993.
Late Show with David Letterman, CBS, 1993, 1994, 1995, 1997, 1998, 2000, 2007, 2008.
Late Night with Conan O'Brien, NBC, 1997, 2003.
The Tonight Show with Jay Leno, 1998, 2002, 2004, 2008.
The Daily Show with Jon Stewart (also known as *The Daily Show, A Daily Show with Jon Stewart*, and *The Daily Show with Jon Stewart Global Edition*), Comedy Central, 1998, 2000.
Jimmy Kimmel Live!, ABC, 2003.
The Late Late Show with Craig Kilborn (also known as *The Late Late Show*), CBS, 2004.
The View, ABC, 2003, 2004, 2005, 2006.
Inside Dish with Rachael Ray, Food Network, 2005.
Last Call with Carson Daly, MTV, 2005, 2008, 2010.
Late Night with Jimmy Fallon, NBC, 2009.
Friday Night with Jonathan Ross, BBC1 and BBC America, 2010.

Television Work; Series:
(With Penn Jillette) Executive producer, *Sin City Spectacular* (also known as *Penn & Teller's Sin City Spectacular*), FX Network, 1998.
Co–executive producer, *Penn & Teller: Bullshit!*, Showtime, 2003–2006.
Executive producer, *Penn & Teller: Bullshit!*, Showtime, 2007—.

Television Work; Specials:
Creator, *Penn & Teller Go Public*, PBS, 1985.
Executive producer, *Phobophilia: The Love of Fear* (also known as *Penn & Teller Phobophilia: The Love of Fear*), 1995.
(With Penn Jillette) Executive producer, *Home Invasion* (also known as *Penn & Teller's Home Invasion* and *Penn & Teller's Home Invasion Magic*), ABC, 1997.

Stage Appearances:
Penn & Teller, off–Broadway production, 1985, then Ritz Theatre, New York City, 1987–88.
Penn & Teller: The Refrigerator Tour, Eugene O'Neill Theatre, New York City, 1991.

Comedy–Magic Revue (two–act), Wilshire Theatre, Los Angeles, 1998.
Guest narrator, *The Rocky Horror Picture Show,* Circle in the Square Theatre, New York City, 2001.

Also appeared in *The Secrets Revealed: Penn & Teller;* toured nationally in the 1990s.

Stage Work:
Codirector, *Comedy–Magic Revue* (two–act), Wilshire Theatre, Los Angeles, 1998.
Director, *Play Dead,* Players Theatre, New York City, 2010.

RECORDINGS

Video Games:
Teller, *Penn & Teller's Smoke and Mirrors,* Absolute, 1995.
Voice of Sigmund Terrore, *Steven Spielberg's Director's Chair,* 1996.

Music Videos:
Appeared in "It's Tricky" by Run DMC, 1986; also appeared in "Waking Up in Vegas" by Katy Perry.

WRITINGS

Screenplays:
Cruel Tricks for Dear Friends (also known as *Penn & Teller's Cruel Tricks for Dear Friends*), 1987.
Penn & Teller Get Killed (also known as *Dead Funny*), Warner Bros., 1989.
& Teller (short film), Sony Pictures Home Entertainment, 2008.
& Teller 2 (short film), Sony Pictures Home Entertainment, 2008.
Dracula's Daughters vs. the Space Brains (short film), National Lampoon, 2010.

Film Scores:
Cruel Tricks for Dear Friends (also known as *Penn & Teller's Cruel Tricks for Dear Friends*), 1987.

Television Specials:
Penn & Teller Go Public, PBS, 1985.
Penn & Teller's "Invisible Thread" (also known as *Invisible Thread*), Showtime, 1987.
Don't Try This at Home! (also known as *Penn & Teller's "Don't Try This at Home!"*), NBC, 1990.
(Host segments) *Behind the Scenes,* 1992.
Staired in Horror, HBO, 1994.
Phobophilia: The Love of Fear (also known as *Penn & Teller "Phobophilia: The Love of Fear"*), 1995.

Home Invasion (also known as *Penn & Teller's "Home Invasion"*), ABC, 1997.
Pen & Teller: Off the Deep End, NBC, 2005.

Television Episodes:
The Unpleasant World of Penn & Teller, 1994.
Penn & Teller: Bullshit!, Showtime, 2003—.

Also wrote "Staired in Horror," *Tales from the Crypt* (also known as *HBO's "Tales from the Crypt"*), HBO.

Stage Acts:
(Co–author) *Comedy–Magic Revue* (two–act), produced at Wilshire Theatre, Los Angeles, 1998.

Stage Plays:
(With Todd Robbins) *Play Dead,* Players Theatre, New York City, 2010.

Video Games:
Penn & Teller's Smoke and Mirrors, 1995.

Books:
(With Penn Jillette) *Penn & Teller's Cruel Tricks for Dear Friends,* Villard Books, 1989.
(With Jillette) *Penn & Teller's How to Play with Your Food,* Villard Books, 1992.
(With Jillette) *Penn & Teller's How to Play in Traffic,* Boulevard Books, 1997.
When I'm Dead All This Will Be Yours: Joe Teller—A Portrait by His Kid, Blast Books, 2000.

Periodicals:
Wrote "Rush to Judgment," *Atlantic Monthly,* 2001; also wrote articles for *Playboy, New York Times, New Yorker,* and other publications.

OTHER SOURCES

Periodicals:
Entertainment Weekly, November 21, 1997, p. 122.
Esquire, January, 2007, p. 100.
New York Times, August 16, 2010, p. C3.
Psychology Today, March/April, 2008, p. 39.
USA Today, November 16, 2007, p. 8D.
Variety, January 28, 2008, p. 66.

THACKER, Jossie 1970–
(Josie Harris, Josie B. Harris, Jossie Harris, Jossie B. Harris, Jossie Harris–Thacker, Jossie Harris Thacker)

PERSONAL

Born January 1, 1970, in Brooklyn, New York, NY.

Addresses: *Agent*—Hervey/Grimes Talent Agency, 10561 Missouri Ave., Suite 2, Los Angeles, CA 90025.

Career: Actress. Appeared in Janet Jackson's Janet tour. Worked as a dancer; worked as a model and appeared in fashion shows, print advertisements, and calendars. Also an acting instructor. Involved with charities. Also known as Josie B. Harris.

Member: Actors' Equity Association.

Awards, Honors: Gold Plaque, best supporting actress, Chicago International Film Festival, 2009, for *Mississippi Damned*.

CREDITS

Film Appearances:
(As Jossie Harris) Dancer, *Stay Tuned* (also known as *Tv–terror*), Warner Bros., 1992.
(As Jossie Harris) *The Results* (short film), 1997.
(As Jossie Harris) First stripper, *The Players Club*, New Line Cinema, 1998.
Nurse, *The Kiss*, 2003, MTI Home Video, 2004.
First reporter, *The Tao of Pong* (short film), Papa Wheelie Pictures, 2004.
Officer Hyland's wife, *A Day without a Mexican*, 2004.
Brooklyn Green, *Brooklyn's Bridge to Jordan* (short film), 2005.
Gina, *Ralph & Stanley* (short film), 2005.
Amanda, *Boxed* (short film), 2006.
Lupe, *Who Made the Potatoe Salad?*, Twentieth Century–Fox Home Entertainment, 2006.
Charlie, *Mississippi Damned*, Morgan's Mark, 2009.
Shirlee, *Boppin' at the Glue Factory* (also known as *Junkie Nurse*), Brooklyn Reptyle Productions/Giant Tarantula Productions, 2009.
Gwen Hines, *The Preacher's Family*, 3rd Day Productions/E and Jay Productions, 2011.

Appeared in other productions, including *The Halfway Diner* (short film); *No Man's Land*, Nubian Faith Entertainment; *Phone Heads* (documentary; also known as *PhoneHeads*); and *With or Without You*, Second–Line Entertainment.

Film Work:
(As Jossie Harris Thacker) Choreographer, *The Wood*, Paramount, 1999.

Provided automated dialogue replacement voices for films, including *Tyler Perry's "Madea Goes to Jail"* (also known as *Madea Goes to Jail*), Lionsgate, 2009.

Television Appearances; Series:
(As Jossie Harris) Fly girl, *In Living Color*, Fox, c. 1992–94.

Television Appearances; Movies:
Sunshine, *Walking on Sunshine* (short film), Black Entertainment Television, 2004.

Television Appearances; Specials:
Brooklyn Green, *Black Filmmakers Showcase*, Showtime, 2005.

Television Appearances; Episodic:
"Don't Be Afraid," *It's Showtime at the Apollo* (also known as *Showtime at the Apollo*), syndicated, 1991.
Fly girl, "There's a Fly Girl in My Soup," *Herman's Head* (also known as *4x Herman*), Fox, 1993.
Deputy Ryan, "The Song of Rome," *Picket Fences* (also known as *Smalltown USA, High Secret City—La ville du grand secret, La famiglia Brock, Picket Fences—Tatort Gartenzaun, Rome—Stadt im Zwielicht, Rooman sheriffi, Sheriffen, Smaastadsliv,* and *Un drole de sherif*), CBS, 1995.
(As Jossie B. Harris) Nurse Gottabody, "Why Can't We Be Friends: Part 2," *Martin*, Fox, 1996.
(As Jossie B. Harris) Catherine, "The Best Laid Plans," *Living Single* (also known as *My Girls*), Fox, 1997.
(As Jossie B. Harris) Kelly, "Prom Fright," *The Wayans Bros.*, The WB, 1997.
Morgan, "Me and Mrs. Robinson," *The Parent 'Hood*, The WB, 1997.
Caroline, "Baby Boom," *For Your Love* (also known as *You Send Me, Foer kaerleks skull,* and *Tris di cuori*), The WB, 1999.
(As Jossie Harris Thacker) Staffer, "The Fall's Gonna Kill You," *The West Wing* (also known as *West Wing, The White House,* and *El ala oeste de la Casablanca*), NBC, 2001.
(As Jossie Harris Thacker) Third staffer, "Bad Moon Rising," *The West Wing* (also known as *West Wing, The White House,* and *El ala oeste de la Casablanca*), NBC, 2001.
Judy, "Shift Happens," *Sabrina, the Teenage Witch* (also known as *Sabrina* and *Sabrina Goes to College*), The WB, 2002.
Female reporter, "Nymphs Just Wanna Have Fun (aka Naughty Nymphs)," *Charmed*, The WB, 2003.
Second reporter, "Sand Francisco Dreamin' (aka Dreamspell)," *Charmed*, The WB, 2003.
Chandra, "There Goes the Bride," *That's So Raven* (also known as *Absolutely Psychic, That's So Raven!, Es tan Raven, Phenomene Raven,* and *Raven blickt durch*), The Disney Channel, 2004.
Formidable woman, "Damaged," *ER* (also known as *Emergency Room* and *E.R.*), NBC, 2004.
Video technician sergeant, "It's Alright Ma, I'm Only Bleeding," *Over There* (also known as *Kaukana kotoa*), FX Network, 2005.

Meredith Burke, "Privilege," *Close to Home* (also known as *American Crime, Fiscal Chase, Juste cause,* and *Justicia cerrada*), CBS, 2006.
"Keeping Up Appearances," *Notes from the Underbelly,* ABC, 2007.
Anesthesiologist, "Playing God," *Private Practice* (also known as *Untitled "Grey's Anatomy" Spin–off*), ABC, 2010.
Commissioner Danielle Ross, "Off the Hook," *The Closer* (also known as *L.A.: Enquetes prioritaires* and *Se apostasi anapnois*), TNT, 2010.

Appeared in other programs, including *Gigantic,* Nickelodeon. While billed as Josie Harris, appeared in an episode of *Jenny Jones,* syndicated.

Television Appearances; Pilots:
(As Jossie Harris Thacker) Video technician sergeant, "Over There," *Over There* (also known as *Kaukana kotoa*), FX Network, 2005.

Stage Appearances:
Julia, *Becoming Cuban,* Hudson Guild Theatre, Los Angeles, 2002.
(As Jossie Harris–Thacker) Margo Mateo, *Havana Bourgeois,* Hayworth Theatre, Los Angeles, 2007, and Miracle Theatre, Actors' Playhouse, Coral Gables, FL, 2009.

Appeared in other productions, including an appearance as Desdemona, *Othello.*

Internet Appearances:
Appeared in footage posted on the Internet.

RECORDINGS

Videos:
(Performer in music videos, including "That's the Way Love Goes") Janet Jackson, *Janet Jackson: Design of a Decade 1986/1996,* A&M Video, 1996.

Music Videos:
Appeared in a number of music videos, including "Humpin' Around" by Bobby Brown, 1992; "Real Love" by Mary J. Blige, 1992; "Remember the Time" by Michael Jackson, 1992; and in Janet Jackson music videos, including "That's the Way Love Goes," 1993.

THOMAS, Emma

PERSONAL

Married Christopher Nolan (a director, producer, film editor, writer, and actor), 1997; some sources children's

names as Flora, Oliver, Rory, Magnus. *Education:* Attended University College, London.

Addresses: *Office*—Syncopy Films, 4000 Warner Blvd., Building 81, Suite 203, Burbank, CA 91522. *Agent*—Creative Artists Agency, 2000 Avenue of the Stars, Los Angeles, CA 90067.

Career: Producer and actress. Working Title Films, London, worked in physical production; Syncopy Films, Burbank, CA, principal; cofounder of a film society at University College, London.

Awards, Honors: Worked on a number of films that have garnered several awards; nomination for Motion Picture Producer of the Year Award (with others), Producers Guild of America, 2009, for *The Dark Knight.*

CREDITS

Film Producer:
Doodlebug (short film), 1997.
Following, Momentum Pictures, 1998, Zeitgeist Films, 1999.
Associate producer, *Memento* (also known as *Amnesia*), Newmarket Films, 2001.
Coproducer, *Insomnia,* Warner Bros., 2001.
Batman Begins (also known as *Batman 5, Batman: Intimidation,* and *The Intimidation Game;* IMAX version known as *Batman Begins: The IMAX Experience*), Warner Bros., 2005.
The Prestige (also known as *Prestige*), Buena Vista/Newmarket Films, 2006.
The Dark Knight (also known as *Batman Begins 2, Batman: The Dark Knight, The Dark Knight, Rory's First Kiss, Untitled Batman Begins Sequel,* and *Winter Green;* IMAX version known as *The Dark Knight: The IMAX Experience*), Warner Bros., 2008.
Executive producer, *Batman: Gotham Knight* (animated anthology; also known as *Batman Anime*), Warner Home Video, 2008.
Inception (also known as *Oliver's Arrow;* IMAX version known as *Inception: The IMAX Experience*), Warner Bros., 2010.

Worked on other projects.

Film Company Coordinator:
Bean (also known as *Bean: The Movie, Bean: The Ultimate Disaster Movie, Dr. Bean,* and *Mr. Bean: The Movie*), Gramercy, 1997.
The Borrowers, PolyGram Filmed Entertainment, 1997.
The Matchmaker (also known as *The MatchMaker*), Gramercy, 1997.

The Hi–Lo Country (also known as *Hi–Lo Country*), Gramercy, 1998.

Film Work; Other:
Production secretary, *Loch Ness,* Gramercy, 1996.
Los Angeles contact, *The Hi–Lo Country* (also known as *Hi–Lo Country*), Gramercy, 1998.
Assistant, *High Fidelity,* Buena Vista, 2000.

Film Appearances:
Following, Momentum Pictures, 1998, Zeitgeist Films, 1999.
Sophie, *Falling* (also known as *Vallen*), Cine–International Filmvertrieb, 2001.

Television Work; Series:
Associate producer, *Geo Genius,* National Geographic Channel, c. 2001.

Television Work; Specials:
Member of the production team, *Harry Potter at the Castle: Magic at Midnight,* ITV, 2005.

Television Appearances; as Herself; Episodic:
"Batman Begins: An Origin Story," *HBO First Look,* HBO, 2005.
"Batman Unmasked: The Psychology of the Dark Knight," *History Alive,* History, 2008.
"The Dark Knight: Escalation," *HBO First Look,* HBO, 2008.
"Inception," *HBO First Look,* HBO, 2010.

RECORDINGS

Videos; Short Documentaries; as Herself:
Batman Begins: Path to Discovery, Warner Home Video, 2005.
Batman: The Journey Begins, Warner Home Video, 2005.
Gotham City Rises, Warner Home Video, 2005.

Video Games:
Voice, *Batman Begins,* Electronic Arts, 2005.

THOMAS, Rob 1965–

PERSONAL

Born August 15, 1965, in Sunnyside, WA; married Katie Orr; children: Greta Mae. *Education:* University of Texas at Austin, B.A., history, 1987; also attended Texas Christian University, 1983.

Addresses: *Agent*—United Talent Agency, 9560 Wilshire Blvd., Suite 500, Beverly Hills, CA 90212.

Career: Writer, producer, creator, and developer. Previously worked an advisor for the University of Texas student magazine *Utmost,* 1991, as a journalism teacher at Reagan High School, Austin, TX, 1991–93, and at the Los Angeles–based Channel One, 1993–94; member of rock bands Public Bulletin, 1984–87, Hey Zeus, 1987–92, and Black Irish, 1992–93.

Member: Writers Guild, Society of Children's Book Writers and Illustrators, Austin Writer's League.

Awards, Honors: Violet Crown Award, best fiction, Austin Writer's League, 1996; WGA Television Award nomination, episodic drama, Writers Guild of America, 2006, for *Veronica Mars.*

CREDITS

Film Appearances:
Himself, *"Veronica Mars": Not Your Average Teen Detective* (short documentary), 2006.

Television Work; Series:
Co–executive producer, *Cupid,* ABC, 1998.
Supervising producer, *Cupid,* ABC, 1998.
Executive producer and creator, *Cupid,* ABC, 1998–99.
Consulting producer, *The Education of Max Bickford,* CBS, 2001.
Executive producer, *Playmakers,* ESPN, 2003.
Executive producer and creator, *Veronica Mars,* UPN then The CW, 2004–2007.
Consulting producer, *Big Shots,* ABC, 2007–2008.
Developer, *90210,* The CW, 2008—.
Executive producer and creator, *Cupid,* ABC, 2009.
Executive producer and creator, *Party Down,* Starz!, 2009–10.

Television Executive Producer; Episodic:
"We're Not in Kansas Anymore," *90210,* The CW, 2008.

Television Director; Episodic:
"Donut Run," *Veronica Mars,* UPN, 2006.
"Spit & Eggs," *Veronica Mars,* UPN, 2006.
Party Down, Starz!, 2009.

Television Appearances; Episodic:
(Uncredited) Johnny Scopes, "Debasement Tapes," *Veronica Mars,* The CW, 2007.

RECORDINGS

Albums:
(With Hey Zeus) *Call Your Mom,* 1989.
(With Hey Zeus) *Swimming Lessons,* 1991.
(with Black Irish) *Screen Door Kind,* 1993.

Also released (with Public Bulletin) *Broke from the Sound* and *First Station 87;* (with Hey Zeus) *With a Smiley Face.*

WRITINGS

Screenplays:
Fortune Cookie, KOAN, 1999.
Drive Me Crazy, Twentieth Century–Fox, 1999.

Television Pilots:
Cupid, ABC, 1998.
Veronica Mars, UPN, 2004.
Cupid, ABC, 2009.

Television Episodes:
"Explode," *Space Ghost Coast to Coast* (also known as *SGC2C*), Cartoon Network, 1996.
"Kiss," *Dawson's Creek,* The WB, 1998.
"Road Trip," *Dawson's Creek,* The WB, 1998.
"The Linguist," *Cupid,* ABC, 1998.
"Meat Market," *Cupid,* ABC, 1998.
"Pick–Up Schticks," *Cupid,* ABC, 1998.
"A Great Personality," *Cupid,* ABC, 1998.
The Education of Max Bickford, CBS, 2001.
Veronica Mars, UPN then The CW, 2004–2007.
"Greatest Amerimart Hero," *Big Shots,* ABC, 2007.
"Car Trouble," *Big Shots,* ABC, 2007.
"We're Not in Kansas Anymore," *90210,* The CW, 2008.
"The Better Man," *Big Shots,* 2008.
"My Fair Masseuse," *Cupid,* ABC, 2009.
"Willow Canyon Homeowners Annual Party," *Party Down,* Starz!, 2009.
"Investors Dinner," *Party Down,* Starz!, 2009.
"Cole Landry's Draft Day Party," *Party Down,* Starz!, 2010.
"Jackal Onassis Backstage Party," *Party Down,* Starz!, 2010.
"Precious Lights Pre–School Auction," *Party Down,* Starz!, 2010.

Also wrote "Botched Makeover," *Cupid,* ABC.

Television Episode Stories:
"Hung Jury," *Cupid,* ABC, 1998.
"California College Conservative Union Caucus," *Party Down,* Starz!, 2009.
"Investors Dinner," *Party Down,* Starz!, 2009.

"Jackal Onassis Backstage Party," *Party Down,* Starz!, 2010.
"Precious Lights Pre–School Auction," *Party Down,* Starz!, 2010.
"Nick Di Cintio's Orgy Night," *Party Down,* Starz!, 2010.

Young Adult Novels:
Rats Saw God, Simon & Schuster, 1996.
Slave Day, Simon & Schuster, 1997.
Satellite Down, Simon & Schuster, 1998.
Green Thumb, Simon & Schuster, 1999.

Short Story Collections:
Doing Time: Notes from the Undergrad, Simon & Schuster, 1997.

OTHER SOURCES

Books:
Authors and Artists for Young Adults, Gale, 1998.
Contemporary Authors Online, Gale, 2005.
St. James Guide to Young Adult Writers, St. James Press, 1999.

THOMPSON, Alys

PERSONAL

Raised in San Angelo, TX. *Education:* Earned a B.S. degree; graduate study at University of Texas at Austin; University of Bradford, doctoral study. *Avocational Interests:* Biking, boating, driving, fishing, geology, hiking, gardening, travel, beach walking.

Career: Production designer and art director. Also worked as set decorator and set dresser; art director for commercials, including work for Easy Life furniture stores, 2005. Anglo–American Project Pompeii, Pompeii, Italy, architecture specialist for eight years.

CREDITS

Film Art Director; Feature Films:
The Third Nail, Peacock Films, 2009.

Film Art Director; Short Films:
Three O'clock, American Film Institute, 2004.
Two Divorced Guys in a Bar, Macedon Media, 2005.
Girl with Gun, Russem Productions, 2006.
Curt's Brain, CocaCola Company, 2006.

Ablution, Baco Productions, 2007.
Fun on Earth, Lucky Eight Pictures, 2007.

Film Production Designer; Short Films:
Act Like You Mean It, 2005.
Dependency, American Film Institute, 2005.
Guilt, Flying Leap Productions, 2005.
Queen of Cactus Cove, Wild Card Productions, 2005.
2 Dogs Inside, Wild Card Productions, 2006.
Lost Brother, 2006.

Film Set Decorator:
Street 16 (short film), 2005.
Danny Roane: First Time Director, Lions Gate Films, 2006.
Entry Level, PorchLight Entertainment, 2008.
Plaguers (also known as *Space Hazard*), Image Entertainment, 2009.
Super Capers, Roadside Attractions, 2009.
Hurt, Monterey Media, 2009.
Road Rage (short film), 2010.

RECORDINGS

Videos:
Art director of music videos, including "Christmas in New York" by the Pointer Sisters, 2005, and "Caterpillar" by Disco Biscuits, 2006; production designer for Shawn Mullins music video, 2006.

OTHER SOURCES

Electronic:
Alys Thompson Official Site, http://www.alysthompson. com, October 15, 2010.

THOMPSON, Ernest 1949(?)–

PERSONAL

Full name, Richard Ernest Thompson; born November 6, 1949 (some sources cite 1950), in Bellows Falls, VT; son of Theson Barker (a college professor and administrator) and Esther (an educator) Thompson Brown–John. *Education:* Attended University of Maryland, 1967–68, Colorado College, 1969, and Catholic University of America, 1970; American University, B.A., 1971.

Addresses: *Agent*—Innovative Artists, 1505 Tenth St., Santa Monica, CA 90401.

Career: Actor, writer, and director. Owner of a theatre in Kittery, ME.

Member: American Federation of Television and Radio Artists, Actors' Equity Association, Screen Actors Guild, Writers Guild of America, Dramatists Guild.

Awards, Honors: Drama Desk Award nomination, outstanding new play, 1979, for *On Golden Pond;* Academy Award and WGA Screen Award (with Donald Stewart), both best screenplay adaptation, Writers Guild of America, and Golden Globe Award, best screenplay for a motion picture, all 1982, Film Award nomination, best screenplay, British Academy of Film and Television Arts, 1983, all for *On Golden Pond;* Daytime Emmy Award nomination, outstanding director of a children's special, 2001, for *Out of Time.*

CREDITS

Film Appearances:
Phil Wass, *Star 80,* Warner Bros., 1983.
Nathan, *Next Stop, Wonderland,* Miramax, 1998.
Terry Plant, *Friction,* Hyrax Films, 2010.
Jeremiah Ward, *Time and Charges,* Whitebridge Farm Productions, 2010.

Film Director:
1969, Atlantic Entertainment Group, 1988.
(And executive producer) *Time and Charges,* Whitebridge Farm Productions, 2010.

Television Appearances; Series:
Tony Cooper, *Somerset* (also known as *Another World: Somerset* and *Somerset: Bay City*), NBC, 1972–74.
Ranger Matt Harper, *Sierra,* NBC, 1974.
Dr. Philip Parker, *Westside Medical,* ABC, 1977.

Television Appearances; Movies:
Earl Shoen, *F. Scott Fitzgerald and "The Last of the Belles,"* ABC, 1974.
Cal, *Take Me Home Again* (also known as *The Lies Boys Tell*), NBC, 1994.
Manville, *The West Side Waltz,* CBS, 1995.

Television Appearances; Specials:
Waiter, "The Rimers of Eldritch," *Great Performances,* PBS, 1972.
The 54th Annual Academy Awards, ABC, 1982.

Television Director; Movies:
The West Side Waltz, CBS, 1995.
Out of Time, Showtime, 2000.
On Golden Pond, CBS, 2001.

Television Co–Executive Producer; Movies:
Take Me Home Again, NBC, 1994.

Stage Appearances:
Hal Carter, *Summer Brave,* American National Theatre and Academy Playhouse, New York City, 1975.

RECORDINGS

Videos:
Reflections on Golden Pond, Artisan Entertainment, 2003.
A Woman of Substance: Katharine Hepburn Remembered, Artisan Entertainment, 2003.

WRITINGS

Screenplays:
On Golden Pond (based on his 1979 stage play), Universal, 1981.
1969, Atlantic Entertainment Group, 1988.
Sweet Hearts Dance (also based on story by Thompson), TriStar, 1988.
Time and Charges, Whitebridge Farm Productions, 2010.

Television Movies:
A Good Time, CBS, 1982.
Take Me Home Again (also known as *The Lies Boys Tell*), NBC, 1994.
The West Side Waltz (based on his stage play), CBS, 1995.
Out of Time, Showtime, 2000.
On Golden Pond (based on his stage play), CBS, 2001.
The Lost Valentine, CBS, 2011.

Stage Plays:
On Golden Pond, Hudson Guild Theatre, New York City, 1978, then New Apollo Theatre, New York City, 1979, later Century Theatre, New York City, 1979–80; revived at Cort Theatre, New York City, 2005, published by Dodd, Mead, 1979.
The Kindness of Strangers (one–act), Odyssey Theatre, Los Angeles, 1980.
The West Side Waltz: A Play in Three Quarter Time (two–act), Ethel Barrymore Theatre, New York City, 1981–82, published (with introduction by Katharine Hepburn) by Dodd, Mead, 1982.
The Constituent (one–act), One–Act Theatre, San Francisco, CA, 1981.
Twinkle, Twinkle (one–act), Lunchtime Theatre, Old Place Theatre, Hartford, CT, 1981.
A Sense of Humor (two–act), Auditorium Theatre, Denver, CO, 1983, revised version, Los Angeles, 1983.

The One about the Guy in the Bar, Ensemble Studio Theatre, New York City, 1987.

ADAPTATIONS

The play *On Golden Pond* has been translated for production as television movies in French and Japanese. The collection *Answers* includes the three one–act plays "The Constituent," "Twinkle, Twinkle," and "A Good Time," which was produced as a television movie.

THORNE, Angela 1939–

PERSONAL

Full name, Angela Margaret Leslie Thorne; born January 25, 1939, in Karachi, Pakistan (then British India); daughter of William Herbert Alfred (a doctor) and Leslie Sylvia (a teacher; maiden name, May) Thorne; married Peter David Penry–Jones (an actor), September 22, 1967; children: Rupert William (an actor), Laurence David (an actor). *Education:* Trained for the stage at Guildhall Drama School.

Addresses: *Manager*—Shepherd Management Ltd., 13 Radnor Walk, London SW3 4BP, England.

Career: Actress. Appeared in television commercials, including Nescafe coffee, 1991. Chair of Actors' Charitable Trust and Theatrical Ladies Guild.

Awards, Honors: Nomination for Comedy Performance of the Year Award, 1981, for *Anyone for Denis.*

CREDITS

Stage Appearances:
Green goddess, *Mango Leaf Magic,* Mobile Theatre, England, 1961.
Gloria Clandon, *You Never Can Tell,* Haymarket Theatre, London, 1966.
Julia, *The Rivals,* Haymarket Theatre, 1966.
Lady Diana, *Ring 'round the Moon,* Haymarket Theatre, 1967.
Portia, *The Merchant of Venice,* Haymarket Theatre, 1969.
Io, *Prometheus Bound,* Mermaid Theatre, London, 1971.
Esther van Homrigh, *Yahoo,* Duke of York's Theatre, London, 1976.

Mrs. Thatcher, *Anyone for Denis,* Whitehall Theatre, London, 1981.

Lady Gay Spanker, *London Assurance,* Theatre Royal, London, 1989.

Body and Soul, Albery Theatre, London, 1992.

The Weekend, Strand Theatre, London, 1994.

Alice Berry, *New England,* Pit Theatre, London, 1994.

Communicating Doors, Savoy Theatre, London, 1996.

A Midsummer Night's Dream, Almeida Theatre, London, 1996.

Jean Horton, *Quartet,* Yvonne Arnaud Theatre, Albery Theatre, 1999.

Rosamond Lehmann, *The Reporter,* Cottesloe Theatre, London, 2007.

Major Tours:

Olivia, *Twelfth Night,* Prospect Theatre Company, Hong Kong Festival, then Soviet and Finnish cities, all 1972.

Film Appearances:

Betty Smith, *Oh! What a Lovely War!,* Paramount, 1969.

Jenny Alexander, *Yellow Dog,* Akari, 1973.

Sylvia Brown, *Ballet Shoes,* 1975.

Woman on train, *ffolkes* (also known as *Assault Force, Ffolkes,* and *North Sea Hijack*), Universal, 1979.

Lady Mary Hargreaves, *The Human Factor,* United Artists, 1979.

Madame Bertin, *Lady Oscar* (also known as *Berusaiyu no bara*), 1980.

Hotel manageress, *Bullshot* (also known as *Bullshot Crummond*), HandMade, 1983.

Voice of the Queen of England, *The BFG,* 1989.

Kitty, *Bright Young Things,* THINKFilm, 2003.

Dr. Gull, *Lassie,* Samuel Goldwyn Company, 2005.

Welcome to World War One, 2006.

Television Appearances; Series:

Charlotte Verney, *Emmerdale Farm,* YTV, 1978.

Marjorie Frobisher, *To the Manor Born,* BBC, 1979–81, 2007, then PBS, 1982.

Laura Bagthorpe, *The Bagthorpe Saga,* BBC, 1981.

Alice, *Paying Guests,* BBC, 1985.

Daphne Trenchard, *Three Up, Two Down,* BBC, 1985–89.

Harriet Farrington, *Farrington of the F.O.* (also known as *Farrington*), YTV, 1986–87.

Val Kirby, *Noah's Ark,* 1997–98.

Television Appearances; Miniseries:

Lettice, Lady Leicester, *Elizabeth R,* BBC, 1971, broadcast on *Masterpiece Theatre,* PBS, 1973.

Sylvia Brown, *Ballet Shoes,* BBC1, 1975.

The Glittering Prizes, BBC, 1976.

Nanny Butterfield, *Mistral's Daughter* (also known as *L'amour en heritage*), CBS, 1984.

Television Appearances; Movies:

Felice Charmon, *The Woodlanders,* 1970.

Louise Wilson, *Haunted: Poor Girl,* 1974.

Mother, *The Rocking Horse Winner,* 1977.

Margaret Thatcher, *Anyone for Denis?,* Thames Television, 1982.

Mary Dash, *The Demon Lover,* 1986.

Margaret Devize, *The Lady's Not for Burning,* ITV, 1987.

Television Appearances; Specials:

Comic Relief, BBC, 1988.

Voice of the queen of England, *The BFG* (also known as *The Big Friendly Giant*), 1989.

Margaret Thatcher, *Dunrulin,* BBC, 1990.

Mrs. Hawk–Monitor, *Cold Comfort Farm,* BBC, 1995.

RIP 2002, Channel 4, 2002.

Television Appearances; Episodic:

Receptionist, "Mission to Montreal," *The Avengers,* ITV, 1962.

Virginia, "The Canterville Ghost," *Mystery and Imagination,* ITY, 1965, ABC Weekend Television, 1966.

The Liars, Granada Television, 1966.

Sister Scholastika, "The Case of the Notorious Nun," *Sergeant Cork,* 1966.

Angela, "Pig Hoo–oo–ey!," *Blandings Castle,* 1967.

Nancy Chuff, *World in Ferment,* 1969.

Sybil, "Third Party," *Love Story,* ITV, 1972.

Eileen Rutherford, "Nobody's That Good," *Justice,* ITV, 1973.

Eileen Rutherford, "Covenant for Quiet Enjoyment," *Justice,* ITV, 1973.

Eileen Rutherford, "Trespass to the Person," *Justice,* ITV, 1973.

Portia, "The Conspirators," *Heil Caesear!,* 1973.

Portia, "Murder of a President," *Heil Caesear!,* 1973.

Portia, "Defeat," *Heil Caesear!,* 1973.

Eleanor, "Aunt Tatty," *Ten from the Twenties,* 1975.

Claire Rothwell, "The Animals Went in Two by Two," *Within These Walls,* ITV, 1975.

Mrs. Fairfax, "Coke," *Get Some In!,* Thames Television, 1976.

Mrs. Fairfax, "Crush," *Get Some In!,* Thames Television, 1976.

Sarah, "Up to a Point," *Well Anyway,* 1976.

Sarah, "To Change the Subject," *Well Anyway,* 1976.

Dr. Dorothy Conran, "Drunk, Who Cares," *Crown Court,* ITV, 1976.

Lady Georgette "George" Truscott, "Our Speaker Today," *The Good Life* (also known as *Good Neighbors*), BBC, 1977.

Mrs. Bunty Heseltine, "Burgle My Neighbour," *Mr. Big,* BBC, 1977.

Mrs. Bryan, "Association," *Crown Court,* ITV, 1978.

Lady Belinda Alvington, "Aristocracy in Decline," *House of Caradus,* 1979.

Mrs. Sinclair, "Black Day at Black Rock," *Cowboys,* 1980.

Panelist, *Call My Bluff,* BBC, 1982.

Lady Arabella Waterstone, "Accusations," *Drummonds,* 1985.

"Paying Guests," *Screenplay,* Granada Television, 1986.

Emma, "Easier for a Camel," *The Good Guys,* YTV, 1992.

Celia Hanson, "Chalk and Cheese," *Heartbeat,* ITV, 2000.

Herself, "Penelope Keith," *Funny Turns,* BBC, 2000.

Lady Lavinia Chetwood, "Market for Murder," *Midsomer Murders,* Arts and Entertainment and ITV, 2002.

Lady Anne Messinger, "The French Drop," *Foyle's War,* PBS, 2004.

Dorothy Bryant, "Dr Who?," *The Royal,* ITV, 2007.

Breakfast, BBC, 2008.

Loose Women, ITV, 2008.

Berta Duner, "The Man Who Smiled," *Wallander,* 2010.

TREMBLETT, Ken 1965–
(Ken Tremblet)

PERSONAL

Born November 22, 1965, in Pembroke, Ontario, Canada; son of Jim Tremblett (a police officer). *Education:* Studied criminal psychology in college; studied acting at University of British Columbia.

Addresses: *Agent*—Lucas Talent, Sun Tower, 100 West Pender St., 7th Floor, Vancouver, British Columbia V6B 1R8, Canada.

Career: Actor. Appeared in television commercials, including Dairyland (Armstrong Cheddar), 1995; online spokesperson for Stenner Investment Partners. Took a personal sabbatical and career break, 2008–10.

CREDITS

Film Appearances:
Deputy Davidson, *The Invader* (also known as *Star Child*), 1997.

Trevor, *Henry's Cafe* (short film), Greasy Spoon Films/Nexus Productions International, 1998.

Partygoer, *Shoes Off!* (short film), 1998.

Brent Frazer, *The Guilty,* Dogwood Pictures, 2000.

David, *Therapy* (short film), 2003.

Nick Stephens, *The Good Teacher,* PorchLight Entertainment, 2004.

(Uncredited) Brian Gibbs, *Pursued,* Artisan Entertainment, 2004.

Bob, *Firewall,* Warner Bros., 2006.

Brenda's husband, *Things We Lost in the Fire,* Paramount, 2007.

Hader, *The Betrayed,* Metro–Goldwyn–Mayer, 2008.

Keene Act anchor, *Watchmen* (also known as *Watchmen: The IMAX Experience*), Warner Bros., 2009.

Television Appearances; Series:
Detective Paul Schuhan, *Street Justice,* syndicated, 1991–92.

Community Centre director, *Northwood,* 1993–94.

Jim Lowe, *Caitlin's Way,* Nickelodeon, 2000–2002.

Television Appearances; Movies:
Moving man, *Burning Bridges,* ABC, 1990.

Jones, *The Comrades of Summer,* HBO, 1992.

Mountie, *Love on the Run,* NBC, 1994.

Stretch, *She Stood Alone: The Tailhook Scandal,* ABC, 1995.

Ric, *She Woke Up Pregnant* (also known as *Crimes of Silence*), ABC, 1996.

Scott, *Their Second Chance* (also known as *The Keller/Keller Story*), Lifetime, 1997.

Agent Barnes, *Murder in My Mind,* CBS, 1997.

Deputy Davidson, *The Invader,* HBO, 1997.

Steve Parker, *Convictions* (also known as *Zalinda's Story*), Lifetime, 1997.

Theme park sheriff, *Tourist Trap,* ABC, 1998.

Bret Milstead, *Don't Look Behind You* (also known as *Du Entkommst mir nicht*), Fox Family Channel, 1999.

SWAT Technician Dreesen, *Deadlocked* (also known as *Negotiator* and *Deadlocked—Die fuenfte gewalt*), TNT, 2000.

Dr. Morrisey, *First Shot* (also known as *Cross Line*), TBS, 2002.

Mark Landis, *Lightning: Bolts of Destruction* (also known as *Heaven's Fury*), PAX, 2003.

Peter, *The Ranch,* Showtime, 2004.

Nick Stephens, *Fatal Lessons: The Good Teacher,* Lifetime, 2004.

Rugby guy, *N.T.S.B.* (also known as *N.T.S.B.: The Crash of Flight 323* and *NTSB: The Crash of Flight 323*), ABC, 2004.

Jase Stratton, *Last Chance Cafe,* Lifetime, 2006.

Tim Powell, *My Neighbor's Keeper,* Lifetime, 2007.

Television Appearances; Pilots:
Charlie Ramsey, *Cupid,* ABC, 1998.

Police officer, *Killer Instinct,* Fox, 2005.

Television Appearances; Episodic:
(As Ken Tremblet) Large man, "The Worst Night of Your Life," *21 Jump Street,* Fox, 1987.

Steve Jackson, "Hell Week," *21 Jump Street,* Fox, 1988.

Barry Wells, "Number One with a Bullet," *21 Jump Street,* Fox, 1990.

"The Secret Life of Garret Tuggle," *Neon Rider,* syndicated, 1994.

Dyer, "Darkness Falls," *The X–Files,* Fox, 1994.

Tony, "Til Death Do Us Part," *University Hospital,* syndicated, 1995.

Businessman, "The Conversion," *The Outer Limits* (also known as *The New Outer Limits*), Showtime and syndicated, 1995.

Fireman Dan, "Trial Period," *Strange Luck,* Fox, 1995.

Bill Metcalfe, "Games People Play," *Two,* syndicated, 1996.

Agent Riley, "The Thin White Line," *Millennium,* Fox, 1997.

Uniformed officer, "Elegy," *The X–Files,* Fox, 1997.

Bill Lundy, "Wages of Sin," *Dead Man's Gun,* Showtime, 1998.

Mr. Wen, "Acute Triangle," *Welcome to Paradox,* Sci–Fi Channel, 1998.

Agent Samuel Hackford, "Pandora's Box," *The Net,* USA Network, 1998.

Miles Dean, "Four of a Kind," *Dead Man's Gun,* Showtime, 1999.

Sheriff Randy Smithers, "The Apostles," *First Wave,* Sci–Fi Channel, 1999.

Michael Dowd, "Decompression," *The Outer Limits* (also known as *The New Outer Limits*), Showtime and syndicated, 2000.

Open Mike with Mike Bullard (also known as *Open Mike* and *The Mike Bullard Show*), Global TV, 2000.

Tom, "Flower Child," *The Outer Limits* (also known as *The New Outer Limits*), Showtime and syndicated, 2001.

Governor McGrath, "The Siege" (also known as "Prison Riot"), *UC: Undercover,* NBC, 2001.

Pitchman, "Chosen," *The Twilight Zone,* UPN, 2002.

Jason, "Hurry," *Dead Like Me,* Showtime, 2004.

Jonah Darrega, "The Weight: Part 2," *Andromeda* (also known as *Gene Roddenberry's "Andromeda"*), Sci–Fi Channel, 2004.

David Peterson, "Overheard," *Kyle XY,* ABC Family, 2006.

David Peterson, "Endgame," *Kyle XY,* ABC Family, 2006.

Webster Ash, "Lez Girls," *The L Word,* Showtime, 2007.

Russell Camp, "Nothing to Fear But Fear Itself," *Painkiller Jane,* Sci–Fi Channel, 2007.

Ron, "Malleus Maleficarum," *Supernatural,* The CW, 2008.

Also appeared in *Bordertown.*

TUBMAN, Angela
    See LANDIS, Angela

V–W

VANDERBILT, James

PERSONAL

Grandson of Alfred G. Vanderbilt, a first cousin to Gloria Vanderbilt. *Education:* University of Southern California, School of Cinema–Television, degree, 1999.

Addresses: *Agent*—WME Entertainment, 1325 Avenue of the Americas, New York, NY 10019. *Manager*—Ufuse Management, 820 N. Ogden Dr., West Hollywood, CA 90046.

Career: Writer and producer.

Awards, Honors: Chicago Film Critics Association Award nomination, best screenplay—adapted, Satellite Award nomination, best screenplay—adapted, International Press Academy, 2007, Edgar Allen Poe Award nomination, best motion picture screen play, Mystery Writers of America, Online Film Critics Society Award nomination, best screenplay—adapted, USC Scripter Award nomination (with Robert Graysmith), WGA Screen Award nomination, best adapted screenplay, Writers Guild of America, 2008, for *Zodiac.*

CREDITS

Film Producer:
Basic, Sony, 2003.
Zodiac, Paramount, 2007.

RECORDINGS

Videos:
The Making of "Darkness Falls," Columbia TriStar, 2003.

Basic Ingredients: A Writer's Perspective, Columbia TriStar, 2003.
Basic: A Director's Design, Columbia TriStar, 2003.

WRITINGS

Screenplays:
Darkness Falls, Sony, 2003.
Basic, Sony, 2003.
The Rundown (also known as *Welcome to the Jungle*), Universal, 2003.
The Guardian, Walt Disney Studios, 2006.
Zodiac, Paramount, 2007.
X–Men Origins: Wolverine, Twentieth Century–Fox, 2009.
The Losers, Warner Bros., 2010.

VAN de VEN, Nadia 1979–

PERSONAL

Born May 15, 1979, in Copenhagen, Denmark; raised in the Netherlands, France, and Italy; father, Jos Van de Ven (an artist); niece of Monique Van de Ven (an actress). *Education:* Studied acting at Acting International, Paris; studied various disciplines with different instructors.

Career: Actress. Worked as a model and appeared in advertisements. World Wide Act association (international theatre association), France, founding member; Sogni Productions, president.

Member: Screen Actors Guild, American Federation of Television and Radio Artists.

CREDITS

Film Appearances:

Petite amie, *Le royaume des rapiats,* Tabb Productions/ E.D. Distribution, 2001.

Ghost, *Cortex,* Delight Films, 2004.

Kamermeisje, *Amazones,* A–Film Distribution, 2004.

(Uncredited) *Deuce Bigalow: European Gigolo* (also known as *Destination Amsterdam, Deuce Bigalow: Electric Gigolo,* and *Deuce Bigalow 2: Destination Amsterdam*), Columbia, 2005.

Dancer, *Ecstasy: The Real Story* (documentary; also known as *Ecstasy: The Real Story—Part 1, Ecstasy: The Real Story—Part 2, Xtasy: The Real Story—Part 1,* and *Xtasy: The Real Story—Part 2*), Friends of Narconon International, 2006.

Lilyana, *Miriam,* 2006, Seventh Art Releasing, 2007.

La llorona, *The Wailer II* (also known as *The Wailer 2* and *The Wailer II—La llorona 2*), Laguna Productions, 2007.

Side Bets (short film), Vine Entertainment, c. 2007.

Rebecca, *In a Different Key* (short film), 2008, Long-Tale, 2009.

Doctor, *Strawberries for the Homeless,* Colored Wind Productions/Stelly Entertainment, 2009.

Welcome Home, Amelie Pimont Productions, c. 2010.

Appeared in other films, including *Doggy Style* (short film; also known as *Doggie Style*); *Hurt Feelings Law Firm,* National Banana Productions; *Le saint,* Mairie Films; *A Little Lower,* Combined Production; *Night Movie,* SSM Films; and *Un mais pas un,* Otis Entertainment.

Film Work:

Dubbing, *Phileine zegt sorry* (also known as *Phileine Says Sorry*), A–Film Distribution, 2003.

Television Appearances; Series:

Aventure sur le net, TF6, c. 2001.

Karin, *Spangen,* Televisie Radio Omroep Stichting (TROS), c. 2003.

Assistant, *Onderweg naar morgen* (also known as *ONM*), Yorin and BNN TV, c. 2004.

English host, *Current TV* (also known as *Current US*), beginning c. 2005.

French host, *Current TV* (also known as *Current International*), beginning c. 2006.

Host, *YourLA* (also known as *Your L.A.*), KNBC, beginning c. 2006.

Served as the host for various television productions.

Television Appearances; Episodic:

Bandes a part (also known as *Bandes a part (with Michel Field)*), TF6, 2002.

Dutch flight attendant, "No Place to Hide," *ER* (also known as *Emergency Room* and *E.R.*), NBC, 2006.

Bar regular, *Days of Our Lives* (also known as *Cruise of Deception: Days of Our Lives, Days, DOOL, Tropical Temptation, Tropical Temptation: Days of Our Lives, Des jours et des vies, Horton–sagaen, I gode og onde dager, Los dias de nuestras vidas, Meres agapis, Paeivien viemaeae, Vaara baesta aar, Zeit der Sehnsucht,* and *Zile din viata noastra*), NBC, 2007.

Appeared in other programs, including *Meiden van de Wit,* NET 5.

Television Appearances; Pilots:

Sophie (an executive assistant), *Melting Pot,* 2007.

Appeared in other pilots, including an appearance as the host of *Eco.*

Television Work; Pilots:

Producer, *Melting Pot,* 2007.

Also the producer of the pilot *Eco.*

Stage Appearances:

Ira, *1953,* Bouffon Theatre, Paris, 1999–2000.

Lucy (the Devil), *A Perfect Life,* Write Act Repertory Theatre, Hollywood, CA, 2005.

Marisol, *The Devil's Bride,* Write Act Repertory Theatre, 2005.

Appeared as Ophelia, *Hamlet,* as a prostitute, *La mecanique des femmes,* as Beatrice, *Les amants malefiques,* and as an angel, *The War in Heaven* (solo show), all Acting International, Paris. Member of the Write Act Repertory Company.

Radio Appearances:

Host, *Nadia's moving the grass,* [France], 2001.

Appeared in other radio programs.

Internet Appearances and Work; Web Series:

Host and producer, *Jeudi C Permis,* posted on *YouTube,* http://www.youtube.com/jeudicpermis, beginning c. 2009.

Host and producer of *Love S.O.S.*

OTHER SOURCES

Periodicals:

Back Stage West, November 15, 2006, p. 1; December 7, 2006, p. 32.

Electronic:
Nadia Van de Ven, http://www.nadiavandeven.com, November 2, 2010.

VEIL, Angel
  See STERLING, Rachel

VELAZQUEZ, Nadine 1978–
  (Nadine E. Velazquez)

PERSONAL

Born November 20, 1978, in Chicago, IL; married Marc Provissiero. *Education:* Columbia College, Chicago, IL, B.A., marketing.

Addresses: *Agent*—Gersh, 9465 Wilshire Blvd., 6th Floor, Beverly Hills, CA 90212; Danis Panaro Nist, 9201 W. Olympic Blvd., Beverly Hills, CA 90212. *Manager*—Benderspink, 5870 W. Jefferson Blvd., Studio E, Los Angeles, CA 90016. *Publicist*—PMK*BNC, 8787 Melrose Avenue, 8th Floor, Los Angeles, CA 90069.

Career: Actress and producer.

Awards, Honors: Screen Actors Guild Award nomination, outstanding performance by an ensemble in a comedy series, 2006, ALMA Award nomination, outstanding supporting actress in a television series, American Latin Media Arts Awards, 2006, 2007, and 2008, for *My Name Is Earl.*

CREDITS

Television Appearances; Series:
Catalina, *My Name Is Earl,* NBC, 2005–2009.
Sofia, *The League,* FX Network, 2009–10.

Television Appearances; Movies:
J. J. Cruz, *The Last Ride,* USA Network, 2004.
Marla Flynt, *Hollywood Vice,* Fox, 2005.
Olivia Palacios, *Kings of South Beach* (also known as *Miami Gangstar*), Arts and Entertainment, 2007.
Lola, *Husband for Hire,* Oxygen, 2008.

Television Appearances; Episodic:
Latina girl, *Resurrection Blvd.,* Showtime, 2002.
Anna, *The Bold and the Beautiful* (also known as *Belleza y poder*), CBS, 2003.

Janeen, "New York," *Entourage,* HBO, 2004.
The Drop, 2005.
Myra Gonzalez, "Mothwoman," *Las Vegas,* NBC, 2005.
Catalina, "The Office vs. American Gladiators, Hickeys vs. Camden County," *Celebrity Family Feud,* NBC, 2008.
Attack of the Show!, G4, 2008.
Marcia Vasquez, "Dead Reckoning," *CSI: NY,* CBS, 2009.
Sophia, "Gary and Allison's Friend," *Gary Unmarried,* CBS, 2009.
Nicole, "Our True Lies," *Scrubs* (also known as *Scrubs: Med School*), ABC, 2010.
Sarah Walker, "Sudden Death," *CSI: Miami,* CBS, 2010.
Linda Leon, "Ko'olauloa," *Hawaii Five–O,* CBS, 2010.

Television Talk Show Guest Appearances; Episodic:
The Late Late Show with Craig Kilborn (also known as *The Late Late Show*), CBS, 2004.
Last Call with Carson Daly, NBC, 2006.
The Late Late Show with Craig Ferguson, CBS, 2006.
The Megan Mullally Show, syndicated, 2006.
Jimmy Kimmel Live!, ABC, 2007.
Today (also known as *NBC News Today* and *The Today Show*), NBC, 2008.
Chelsea Lately, E! Entertainment Television, 2009.

Television Appearances; Specials:
Arby's Action Sports Awards, 2006.
Backstage: Hollywood Fashion, Style, 2007.
2007 ALMA Awards, ABC, 2007.
Judge, *Miss Universe Pageant,* NBC, 2008.
Santa's helper/Candy Cans, *Larry the Cable Guy's Star–Studded Christmas Extravaganza,* Country Music Television, 2008.
Host, *Miss USA 2009,* NBC, 2009.

Film Appearances:
(As Nadine E. Velazquez) Allison, *Biker Boyz,* DreamWorks, 2003.
(As Nadine E. Velazquez) Attractive woman at conga club, *Chasing Papi,* Twentieth Century–Fox, 2003.
Luna, *Blast,* First Look International, 2004.
Claudia, *Sueno* (also known as *Dream*), Columbia TriStar, 2005.
Maria, *War* (also known as *Rogue Assassin*), Eagle, 2007.
Mathilda, *All's Faire in Love,* Metro–Goldwyn–Mayer, 2009.
Special Agent Natasha, *A Day in the Life,* Lions Gate Films, 2009.

VERNON, Conrad 1968–

PERSONAL

Full name, Conrad Vernon IV; born July 11, 1968, in Lubbock, TX.

Addresses: *Agent*—WME Entertainment, One William Morris Place, Beverly Hills, CA 90212. *Manager*—Mosaic, 9200 Sunset Blvd., 10th Floor, Los Angeles, CA 90069.

Career: Writer, director, voice performer, and actor. Appeared in television commercials.

Awards, Honors: Hollywood Film Award (with others), animation of the year, Golden Palm Award nomination (with others), Cannes Film Festival, 2004, Silver Ribbon Award nomination (with others), best director—foreign film, Italian National Syndicate of Film Journalists, Annie Award nominations, storyboarding in an animated feature production and directing in an animated feature production, International Animated Film Society, 2005, for *Shrek 2.*

CREDITS

Film Appearances:
Pesion, *Herd* (short film), 1999.
Voice of Gingerbread Man, *Shrek* (animated), DreamWorks, 2001.
Voice of Gingerbread Man, *Shrek in the Swamp of Karaoke Dance Party* (animated), DreamWorks, 2001.
Voice of Gingerbread Man, *Shrek 4–D* (also known as *Shrek 3–D* and *Shrek's Never Before Seen Adventure*), DreamWorks, 2003.
Voice of Jed, *Sinbad: Legend of the Seven Seas,* DreamWorks, 2003.
Voice of Gingerbread Man/Cedric/announcer/Muffin Man/Mongo, *Shrek 2* (animated), DreamWorks, 2004.
Voice of Gingy (Gingerbread Man), *Far Far Away Idol,* DreamWorks, 2004.
Voice of Mason, *Madagascar* (animated), Paramount, 2005.
Voice of Take Out, *Flushed Away* (animated), Paramount, 2006.
Voice of GingerBread Man/Rumplestiltskin/Headless Horseman, *Shrek the Third* (animated; also known as *Shrek 3* and *The Third*), Paramount, 2007.
Voice of Freddy, *Bee Movie* (animated), Paramount, 2007.
Voice of Mason, *Madagascar: Escape 2 Africa* (also known as *Madagascar 2* and *Madagascar: Escape 2 Africa–The IMAX Experience*), Paramount, 2008.
Voice of advisor Hawk/advisor Dither/minister/second Secret Service man/Mama Dietl, (animated; also known as *Monsters vs. Aliens: A Monstrous IMAX 3D Experience*), Paramount, 2009.
Voice of Gingerbread Man, *Shrek Forever After* (animated; also known as *Forever After: The Final Chapter, Shrek Forever After: An IMAX 3D Experience, Shrek: The Final Chapter, The Final Chapter,* and *Shrek Forever*), Paramount, 2010.

Film Director:
Morto the Magician, 2001.
Shrek 2 (animated) DreamWorks, 2004.
Monsters vs. Aliens (animated; also known as *Monsters vs. Aliens: A Monstrous IMAX 3D Experience*), Paramount, 2009.

Film Work:
Automated dialogue replacement (ADR) loop group, *Shrek 2,* DreamWorks, 2004.

Television Appearances; Series:
Voice of Mason, *The Penguins of Madagascar* (animated), 2009—.

Television Appearances; Movies:
Voice of Gingerbread Man, *Shrek the Halls* (animated), 2007.

Television Appearances; Episodic:
"Madagascar: Welcome to the Jungle," *HBO First Look,* HBO, 2005.
"Monsters on a Mission: The Making of Monsters vs. Aliens," *HBO First Look,* HBO, 2009.
The Movie Loft, 2009.

Television Director; Series:
The Itsy Bitsy Spider, USA Network, c. 1994.

RECORDINGS

Videos:
The Tech of Shrek 2, DreamWorks, 2004.
Meet the Cast of Shrek 2, DreamWorks, 2004.

Video Games:
Voice of Mason/captain/tour bus driver, *Madagascar,* Activision, 2005.
Voice of Gingerbread Man/evil knight/first jock, *Shrek the Third,* Activision, 2007.
Bee Movie Game, Activision, 2007.
Voice of Mason, *Madagascar Karz,* Activision, 2009.
Voice of Gingerbread Man, *Shrek Forever After: The Game,* Activision, 2010.

WRITINGS

Screenplays:
Monsters vs. Aliens (animated; also known as *Monsters vs. Aliens: A Monstrous IMAX 3D Experience*), Paramount, 2009.

Film Songs:
"Merry Men," *Shrek,* DreamWorks, 2001.

Television Specials:
Monsters vs. Aliens: Mutant Pumpkins from Outer Space, NBC, 2009.

WAGNER, Todd 1960(?)–

PERSONAL

Full name, Todd R. Wagner; born August 2, 1960 (some sources cite 1962), in Gary, IN. *Education:* Graduated from Indiana University, accounting degree, 1983; University of Virginia, law degree; also a CPA (certified public accountant).

Addresses: *Office*—Magnolia Pictures (also known as Magnolia Pictures International), 115 West 27th St., 7th Floor, New York, NY 10001; 2929 Entertainment and 2929 Productions, 1437 Seventh St., Suite 250, Santa Monica, CA 90401; HDNet Films (also known as HD-Net Films International), 122 Hudson St., Fifth Floor, New York, NY 10013; Truly Indie, 9100 Wilshire Blvd., Suite 500 West, Beverly Hills, CA 90212; Landmark Theatres, 2222 South Barrington Ave., Los Angeles, CA 90064; Dallas Mavericks, The Pavilion, 2909 Taylor St., Dallas, TX 75226; The Todd R. Wagner Foundation, 3008 Taylor St., Dallas, TX 75226.

Career: Producer and executive. Attorney for Akin Gump Strauss Hauer & Feld and partner at the law firm Hopkins & Sutter. Audionet (later known as Broadcast.com), cofounder and co–owner, 1995–99; Wagner/Cuban Companies, cofounder; frequent business partner of Mark Cuban; owned interest in Lions Gate Entertainment (later known as Lionsgate Entertainment), The Weinstein Company, and Peace Arch Entertainment; Content Partners, Los Angeles, founder and co-chairperson, 2929 Productions, co–owner and principal; Magnolia Pictures, New York City, partner; HDNet Films, New York City; Landmark Theatres, New York City, principal; co–owner of the Dallas Mavericks (professional basketball team); also a public speaker. The Todd R. Wagner Foundation, founder, 2000, chief executive, and philanthropist. Involved in the creation of neighborhood technology centers and the funding of initiatives for owners of technological businesses. American Film Institute, member of the board of trustees.

Member: Kappa Sigma (Beta Theta chapter).

Awards, Honors: Named one of the Texas Twenty, *Texas Monthly,* 1999; named Man of the Year, Inner–City Games Foundation, Los Angeles, 2000; Social Entrepreneur of the Year, Dallas Center for Nonprofit Manage-ment, 2002; Kappa Sigma Man of the Year, 2003; Trailblazer Award, Dallas International Film Festival, 2004; First Star Visionary Award, Dallas CASA Champion of Children, 2005; Tribute Award (with Mark Cuban), Gotham awards, Independent Feature Project, 2006; The Wagner–Cuban Pioneer in Entertainment and Media Award, given by the Savannah Film Festival, is named for Wagner and Cuban and Wagner.

CREDITS

Film Executive Producer:
Searching for Debra Winger (documentary), Lions Gate Films, 2002.
Criminal, Warner Independent Pictures, 2004.
Godsend (also known as *Adam*), Lions Gate Films, 2004.
Voices of Iraq (documentary), Magnolia Pictures, 2004.
Bubble, Magnolia Pictures, 2005.
Enron: The Smartest Guys in the Room (documentary), Magnolia Pictures, 2005.
Good Night, and Good Luck. (also known as *Good Night, and Good Luck*), Warner Independent Pictures, 2005.
The Jacket, Warner Independent Pictures, 2005.
One Last Thing ... (also known as *One Last Thing*), Magnolia Pictures, 2005.
The War Within (also known as *Over the Mountains*), Magnolia Pictures, 2005.
Akeelah and the Bee (also known as *Dreams Come True*), Lions Gate Films, 2006.
The Architect (also known as *All Fall Down*), Magnolia Pictures, 2006.
Black Christmas (also known as *Black X–Mas*), Metro–Goldwyn–Mayer, 2006.
Diggers, Magnolia Pictures, 2006.
Herbie Hancock: Possibilities (documentary), Magnolia Pictures, 2006.
Turistas (also known as *Blood Paradise, Paradise Lost,* and *Turistas: Holiday of Horror*), Fox Atomic, 2006.
Fay Grim, 2006, Magnolia Pictures, 2007.
Broken English, Magnolia Pictures, 2007.
The Life before Her Eyes (also known as *In Bloom*), Magnolia Pictures, 2007.
Redacted (also known as *Samarra*), Magnolia Pictures, 2007.
Surfwise (documentary), Magnolia Pictures, 2007.
We Own the Night (also known as *Undercover*), Columbia, 2007.
The Burning Plain, Magnolia Pictures, 2008.
Gonzo: The Life and Work of Dr. Hunter S. Thompson (documentary; also known as *Gonzo* and *Hunter*), 2008.
Quid Pro Quo, Magnolia Pictures, 2008.
Two Lovers, Magnolia Pictures, 2008.
What Just Happened (also known as *Inside Hollywood, Trouble in Hollywood,* and *What Just Happened?*), Magnolia Pictures, 2008.

American Swing (documentary), 2008, Magnolia Pictures, 2009.

The Road, The Weinstein Company, 2009.

Casino Jack and the United States of Money (documentary), Magnolia Pictures, 2010.

Film Producer:

The Girlfriend Experience (also known as *GfE* and *Girlfriend Experience*), Magnolia Pictures, 2009.

Film Appearances:

(Uncredited) Doctor, *Godsend* (also known as *Adam*), Lions Gate Films, 2004.

Assistant judge, *Akeelah and the Bee* (also known as *Dreams Come True*), Lions Gate Films, 2006.

Television Executive Producer; Series:

Co–executive producer, *Star Search,* CBS, 2002–2004.

The Benefactor, ABC, 2004.

Television Appearances; Awards Presentations:

The 16th Annual Gotham Awards, 2006.

Television Appearances; Episodic:

Himself, *Talking Movies,* BBC2, 2006.

OTHER SOURCES

Books:

Gale Encyclopedia of E–Commerce, Gale Group, 2002.

Periodicals:

Moving Pictures, March, 2007, pp. 18–19.

Texas Monthly, September, 1999, p. 122.

Variety, February 23, 2004, p. S13; May 7, 2007, pp. 12–13.

WAGONER, Bryce 1975–

PERSONAL

Full name, Bryce Ronald Wagoner III; born October 3, 1975, in Lynchburg, VA; brother of Zack Wagoner (an actor). *Education:* East Carolina University, graduated in 2002; studied with various instructors; certified personal trainer. *Avocational Interests:* Playing golf, cooking.

Career: Actor, stunt performer, producer, and director. Shield Pirate Productions (production company), founder. Appeared in advertisements. Also a personal trainer; was a bodybuilder and participated competitions. Worked in a bar.

Member: Phi Kappa Psi (North Carolina Beta chapter, served as philanthropy chairperson and in other positions).

Awards, Honors: Named 1992 Amateur Athletic Union (AAU) Mr. Teen USA.

CREDITS

Film Appearances:

Bert, *Jupiter Landing,* Newmark/Echelon Entertainment Group/Singa Home Entertainment, 2005.

Title role, *Marco Polo* (short film), West Wing Films, 2008.

Tim Nestle, *Gingerdead Man 2: The Passion of the Crust,* Full Moon Entertainment, 2008.

Sophia's uncle, *Shadowman,* High Vision Project/RockEngine Films, 2009.

Film Work:

Photo double: Larry Rippenkroeger, *Charlie's Angels: Full Throttle* (also known as *Charlie's Angels: Halo* and *Charlie's Angels 2*), Columbia, 2003.

Sword choreographer: Genovian Guard, *The Princess Diaries 2: Royal Engagement* (also known as *The Princess Diaries 2*), Buena Vista, 2004.

Stunt performer, *Marco Polo* (short film), West Wing Films, 2008.

Creator, director, and producer, *Exxxit: Life after Porn* (documentary; also known as *Life After* and *Triple Exxxit*), Oxymoron Entertainment/Mallick Media, 2010.

Worked on other projects.

Television Appearances; Movies:

Richard Guadagno, *The Flight That Fought Back* (also known as *Flight 93: The Flight That Fought Back* and *The Plane That Fought Back*), The Discovery Channel, 2005.

Television Appearances; Episodic:

Ron Logan, "Reality TV: No Survivors," *Crossballs: The Debate Show* (also known as *Crossballs*), Comedy Central, 2004.

Himself, *Access Hollywood,* syndicated, 2005.

Appeared as the handsome man in "Charity Begins in Cellblock D" and "Final Fantasy," both episodes of *Andy Richter Controls the Universe* (also known as *Anything Can Happen* and *ARCTU*), Fox.

Stage Appearances:

Appeared in various productions, including appearances as the first general, *Bury the Dead,* as Dutch, *Give Me Some Time to Think about It ...,* as Johnny, *Lovers and Other Strangers,* as Rudy, *Loyalties,* as Christian, *One Hundred Women,* and as Uncle Probst and a professor, *Spring Awakening* (also known as *Spring's Awakening*).

Stage Work:
Director, *One Flew over the Cuckoo's Nest,* East Carolina University, c. 2000.

RECORDINGS

Video Game Appearances:
Dictator and soldier, *SOCOM 3: U.S. Navy SEALs,* Sony Computer Entertainment America, 2005.

Triple H, *WWE SmackDown! vs. RAW 2006* (also known as *Exciting Pro Wrestling 7: SmackDown! vs. RAW 2006*), THQ, 2005.

Triple H, *WWE SmackDown vs. RAW 2007,* THQ, 2006.

Voice of Sarge, *Killzone: Liberation,* Sony Computer Entertainment America, 2006.

Triple H, *WWE SmackDown vs. RAW 2008* (also known as *WWE SmackDown vs. RAW 2008: ECW Invasion* and *WWE SmackDown vs. RAW Featuring ECW*), THQ, 2007.

Triple H, *WWE SmackDown vs. RAW 2009* (also known as *WWE 2009 SmackDown vs. Raw*), THQ, 2008.

Triple H, *WWE SmackDown vs. RAW 2010* (also known as *WWE 2010 SmackDown vs. Raw*), THQ, 2009.

Video Game Work:
Stunt performer and motion capture actor, *WWE SmackDown! vs. RAW 2006* (also known as *Exciting Pro Wrestling 7: SmackDown! vs. RAW 2006*), THQ, 2005.

Additional voices, *WWE SmackDown vs. RAW 2007,* THQ, 2006.

Stunt performer and additional voices, *WWE SmackDown vs. RAW 2008* (also known as *WWE SmackDown vs. RAW 2008: ECW Invasion* and *WWE SmackDown vs. RAW Featuring ECW*), THQ, 2007.

OTHER SOURCES

Periodicals:
Richmond Times–Dispatch, September 11, 2005, p. 1.

WALLACE, George 1952–
(George H. Wallace)

PERSONAL

Born July 21, 1952, in Atlanta, GA; son of George, Sr., and Mary Lou Wallace. *Education:* University of Akron, degrees in transportation and marketing.

Addresses: *Agent*—Paradigm, 360 North Crescent Dr., North Bldg., Beverly Hills, CA 90210. *Manager*—Elements Entertainment, 1635 North Cahuenga Blvd., 5th Floor, Los Angeles, CA 90028.

Career: Actor, comedian, and writer. Performer of standup comedy throughout the United States, including frequent appearances in Las Vegas, NV, and at clubs including Catch a Rising Star, The Comedy Store, and The Punchline. Previously worked in transit advertising; served as vice president of a transit advertising company.

Awards, Honors: American Comedy Award nominations, funniest male standup comic, 1991, 1992, 1993, 1994, and American Comedy Award, funniest male standup comic, 1995; man of the year award, West Angeles Church of God and West Angeles Community Development Corp., 2003.

CREDITS

Film Appearances:
The champ, *Things Are Tough All Over,* Columbia, 1982.

Man with his arm in a cast, *Punchline,* Sony Pictures Releasing, 1988.

Bartender, *Bert Rigby, You're a Fool,* 1989.

Gravedigger, *A Rage in Harlem,* Miramax, 1991.

Voice of card player number four, *Bebe's Kids,* 1992.

The mayor, *Batman Forever* (also known as *Forever*), Warner Bros., 1995.

Bartender, *Meet Wally Sparks,* 1997.

James, *Catfish in Black Bean Sauce,* Phaedra Cinema, 1999.

Pops, *3 Strikes,* Metro–Goldwyn–Mayer, 2000.

Mayor, *Little Nicky,* New Line Cinema, 2000.

Mr. Washington, *The Wash,* Lions Gate Films, 2001.

Host, *Living in the Spirit Revue,* 2001.

NAACP administrator, *Mr. Deeds,* Columbia/New Line Cinema, 2002.

Comedian, *Comedian* (documentary), Miramax, 2002.

Sheriff Wyner, *The Ladykillers,* Buena Vista, 2004.

Himself, *Before They Were Kings: Vol. 1,* 2004.

George Wallace, *George Wallace: Large and In Charge,* 2004.

Himself, *Mr. Warmth: The Don Rickles Project* (documentary), Vivendi Entertainment, 2007.

Himself, *Heckler* (documentary), Echo Bridge Home Entertainment, 2007.

Himself, *Why We Laugh: Black Comedians on Black Comedy* (documentary), Codeblack Entertainment, 2009.

Himself, *Funny People,* Universal, 2009.

Television Appearances; Series:
George Henry Wallace, *The Dom DeLuise Show,* syndicated, 1987–88.

George Harris, *Tall Hopes*, CBS, 1993.
Tough Crowd with Colin Quinn, Comedy Channel, 2002.

Television Appearances; Movies:
Big Dan, *Working Trash,* Fox, 1990.
Tommy Ammons, *In the Heat of the Night: Who Was Geli Bendl?,* CBS, 1994.
Norm Potter, *Santa, Jr.,* Hallmark Channel, 2002.

Television Appearances; Specials:
(As George H. Wallace) *Sally Field & Tom Hanks' Punchline Party,* HBO, 1988.
A Comedy Celebration: The Comedy & Magic Club's 10th Anniversary Special, Showtime, 1989.
The American Film Institute Presents: "TV or Not TV?," NBC, 1990.
The 19th Annual Black Filmmakers Hall of Fame, syndicated, 1992.
A Tribute to Sam Kinison, Fox, 1993.
But ... Seriously, Showtime, 1994.
The NFL at 75: An All–Star Celebration, ABC, 1994.
Uncle Rance, *The Last Days of Russell,* ABC, 1994.
"Space Traders," *Cosmic Slop,* HBO, 1994.
But Seriously '94, Showtime, 1995.
Comic Relief American Comedy Festival, ABC, 1995.
Comedy Club Superstars, ABC, 1995.
Comedy Club Superstars, ABC, 1996.
Comic Relief American Comedy Festival, ABC, 1996.
The 11th Annual Academy of Television Arts & Sciences' Hall of Fame, CBS, 1996.
Jerry Seinfeld: "I'm Telling You for the Last Time" (also known as *Jerry Seinfeld: "I'm Telling You for the Last Time"—Live on Broadway*), HBO, 1998.
The Comedy Central Presents the New York Friars Club Roast of Jerry Stiller, Comedy Channel, 1999.
The College of Comedy with Alan King, Part II, PBS, 2000.
The Joke's on Thee, Showtime, 2001.
Uncensored Comedy: That's Not Funny, TRIO, 2003.
Richard Pryor: I Ain't Dead Yet, #*%$#@!!* (also known as *Richard Pryor: I Ain't Dead Yet, #*%$#@!!—Uncensored), Comedy Channel, 2003.
"1976," *I Love the '70s,* VH1, 2003.
All Shades of Fine: 25 Hottest Women of the Past 25 Years, 2005.
Wiseman, *Larry the Cable Guy's Christmas Spectacular,* VH1, 2007.
Host, *Christmas at the Cathedral,* MyNetworkTV, 2007.
History of the Joke (documentary), History Channel, 2008.

Television Appearances; Awards Presentations:
Jim Thorpe Pro Sports Awards Presented by Footlocker, ABC, 1992, 1993.
Presenter, *The 8th Annual Soul Train Music Awards,* 1994.

The 10th Annual American Comedy Awards, ABC, 1996.
The 1996 ESPY Awards, 1996.
The 28th NAACP Image Awards, Fox, 1997.
Mark Twain Prize—Celebrating the Humor of Carl Reiner, PBS, 2001.
BET Comedy Awards, Black Entertainment Television, 2004.
The 2006 Trumpet Awards, 2006.

Television Appearances; Episodic:
The Alan Thicke Show (also known as *Fast Company* and *Prime Cuts*), 1980, 1981.
The New Hollywood Squares, 1987.
One Night Stand, HBO, 1991.
Vicki!, 1993.
Host, "Ralph Tresvant/Eric Gable/Justin Warfield," *Soul Train,* syndicated, 1994.
George, "The Script Formerly Known As ...," *The Fresh Prince of Bel–Air,* NBC, 1995.
Deacon Delbert Henry, "Negotiating: It's Never Personal," *Arli$$,* HBO, 1996.
Mr. Dawkins, *Dave's World,* CBS, 1996.
Doctor, "The Checks," *Seinfeld,* NBC, 1996.
"The College of Comedy with Alan King," *Great Performances,* PBS, 1997.
Game show host, "A Terrible Thing Happened on My Tour of College," *Moesha,* UPN, 1998.
Vet, "A Girl's Gotta Make Room for Daddy: Part 1," *Jenny,* NBC, 1998.
Hollywood Squares (also known as *H2* and *H2: Hollywood Squares*), syndicated, 1998–2004.
Father, "Cause and Effect," *Arli$$,* HBO, 1999.
Voice of Baba Mustafa, "Ali Baba and the Forth Thieves," *Happily Ever After: Fairy Tales for Every Child,* HBO, 1999.
Himself, "As Others See Us," *Arli$$,* HBO, 2001.
"Comedian's Edition #2," *The Weakest Link,* 2001.
Quincy DeJohn, "My Two Dads," *The Parkers,* UPN, 2002.
Tough Crowd with Colin Quinn, Comedy Central, 2002.
Ask Rita, syndicated, 2003.
Quincy DeJohn, "The Parent Trap," *The Parkers,* UPN, 2003.
Funny Money, Game Show Network, 2003.
Jimmy, "Back to the Club," *Wanda at Large,* Fox, 2003.
Funny Money (also known as *National Lampoon's "Funny Money"*), Game Show Network, 2003.
Judge, *Pet Star,* Animal Planet, 2003, 2005.
BET's Comicview, Black Entertainment Television, 2004.
Bill, Tanya's father, "Daddy Knows Best," *Like Family,* The WB, 2004.
Judge, *Coming to the Stage,* Black Entertainment Television, 2004.
Lingo, Game Show Network, 2005.
The Tom Joyner Show, 2005.
Guest cohost, *Street Smarts,* 2005.

"Turn a Poker Dud into a Five Card Stud: Ed M," *Queer Eye* (also known as *Queer Eye for the Straight Guy*), 2006.
"Top Ten Musical Moments," *TV Land's Top Ten*, TV Land, 2006.
Comics Unleashed, 2006.
Minister, "My Words of Wisdom," *Scrubs*, ABC, 2007.
Jimmy, "Crazy in Love," *House of Payne* (also known as *Tyler Perry's "Crazy in Love"*), TBS, 2007.
Just for Laughs (also known as *Just for Laughs Comedy Festival*), CBC, 2009.
"Your Mama," *Who's Got Jokes?*, 2009.
"Announcement Show: The Championship," *Who's Got Jokes?*, 2009.

Also appeared in *One–Night Stand*, HBO; *Russell Simmons' "Def Comedy Jam"* (also known as *Def Comedy Jam*), HBO; *London Underground*, Comedy Central; as celebrity judge, *MasterChef USA*, PBS; himself, "Jerry Seinfeld: Master of His Domain," *Biography*, Arts and Entertainment; himself, *The Big Laff Off;* guest, *The Test*, FX Network.

Television Talk Show Guest Appearances; Episodic:
Clive Anderson Talks Back, 1990.
The Tonight Show with Jay Leno, NBC, 1994, 1996, 2003, 2005, 2006.
The Rosie O'Donnell Show, syndicated, 1997.
The Daily Show with Jon Stewart (also known as *The Daily Show, A Daily Show with Jon Stewart*, and *The Daily Show with Jon Stewart Global Edition*), Comedy Central, 2000.
The Tonight Show with Jay Leno, NBC, 2003.
The Wayne Brady Show, syndicated, 2004.
The Sharon Osbourne Show (also known as *Sharon*), syndicated, 2004.
Tavis Smiley, PBS, 2004.
Dennis Miller, CNBC, 2004, 2005.
"George Wallace," *Talkshow with Spike Feresten*, Fox, 2008.
Chelsea Lately, E! Entertainment Television, 2008.
The Mo'Nique Show, Black Entertainment Television, 2009.
The Late, Late Show with Craig Ferguson, CBS, 2009, 2010.
The Bonnie Hunt Show, NBC, 2010.

Radio Appearances:
Appeared on *The Tom Joyner Morning Show;* also appeared in a series hosted by Isaac Hayes, WRKS.

WRITINGS

Screenplays:
Before They Were Kings: Vol. 1, 2004.

Television Episodes:
The Redd Foxx Show, ABC, 1986.
BET's Comicview, Black Entertainment Television, 2004.

OTHER SOURCES

Periodicals:
Jet, October 16, 2006, p. 46.

WATANABE, Ken 1959–
  (Watanabe Ken)

PERSONAL

Full name, Kensaku Watanabe; born October 21, 1959, in Koide (now Uonuma), Niigata, Japan; father, a teacher of calligraphy; mother, a teacher; married Yumiko (divorced April, 2005); married Kaho Minami (an actress), December, 2005; children: (first marriage) Anne (a model), Dai (an actor). *Education:* Studied acting in Tokyo, Japan; studied theatre in England. *Avocational Interests:* Baseball, rugby.

Addresses: *Office*—K DASH, 5F Okamoto LK Building, 2–7–10 Higashi, Shibuya–ku, Tokyo 150–0011, Japan. *Agent*—William Morris Endeavor Entertainment (WmEE2), One William Morris Place, Beverly Hills, CA 90212. *Manager*—Will Ward, ROAR, 9701 Wilshire Blvd., 8th Floor, Beverly Hills, CA 90212.

Career: Actor. En (theatre group; some sources cite name as Engeki–Syudan En), Tokyo, Japan, member until c. 2002; K DASH, Tokyo, Japan, actor, beginning 2002; appeared in advertisements. Also known as Watanabe Ken.

Member: Screen Actors Guild.

Awards, Honors: Ecran d'Or, best new actor, Japan Film and Television Producers Society, 1987, for *Umi to dokuyaku;* Japanese Academy Prize, best supporting actor, 1999, for *Kizuna;* Japanese Academy Prize, best supporting actor, 2002, for *Sennen no koi—Hikaru Genji monogatari;* nomination for Japanese Academy Prize, best supporting actor, 2003, for *Hi wa mata noboru;* Washington, DC Area Film Critics Association Award nomination, best supporting actor, 2003, Special Award, Blue Ribbon awards, Academy Award nomination, best actor in a supporting role, Golden Globe Award nomination, best performance by an actor in a supporting role in a motion picture, Screen Actors

Guild Award nomination, outstanding performance by a male actor in a supporting role, Saturn Award nomination, best supporting actor, Academy of Science Fiction, Fantasy & Horror Films, Golden Satellite Award nomination, best performance by an actor in a supporting role, drama, International Press Academy, Critics Choice Award nomination, best supporting actor, Broadcast Film Critics Association, Sierra Award nomination, best supporting actor, Las Vegas Film Critics Society, and Phoenix Film Critics Society Award nomination, best performance by an actor in a supporting role, all 2004, all for *The Last Samurai;* Hochi Film Award and Nikkan Sports Film Award, both best actor, 2006, and Japanese Academy Prize, Blue Ribbon Award, Kinema Junpo Award, and Asian Film Award nomination, all best actor, all 2007, for *Ashita no kioku;* Hochi Film Award, best actor, 2009, and Japanese Academy Prize, best actor, 2010, both for *Shizumanu taiyo.*

CREDITS

Film Appearances:

Tetsuo, *Setouchi shonen yakyu dan* (also known as *MacArthur's Children*), 1984, subtitled version, Orion, 1985.

Funayama Tetsuya and Masakazu Sekine, *Kekkon annai mystery,* Toei Company, 1985.

Gun, *Tampopo* (also known as *Dandelion*), 1985, subtitled version, New Yorker, 1987.

Toda, *Umi to dokuyaku* (also known as *The Sea and Poison*), 1986, subtitled version, Gades, 1987.

Ryouma Sakamoto, *Bakumatsu jyunjyoden,* Shochiku Eiga, 1991.

Raita Onuki, *Rajio no jikan* (also known as *Welcome Back, Mr. McDonald*), Toho Company, 1997, subtitled version, Tidepoint Pictures/Viz Films, 1997.

Wang, *Tenamonya syosha,* 1997.

Detective Sako Akio, *Kizuna* (also known as *Bonds*), Toho Company, 1998.

Ishida, *Zawa–zawa Shimokita–sawa,* 2000.

Sakamaki (Crusher), *Supesutoraberazu* (also known as *Space Travelers* and *Supaas Torabaraazu*), Toho Company, 2000.

Fujiwara no Michinaga and Fujiwara no Nobutaka, *Sennen no koi—Hikaru Genji monogatari* (also known as *Genji: A Thousand–Year Love* and *Sennen no koi*), Toei Company, 2001.

Miyota, *Oboreru sakana* (also known as *Drowning Fish*), 2001.

Osamu Okubo, *Hi wa mata noboru* (also known as *The Sun Will Rise Again*), Toei Company, 2002.

Hiroaki Fujimaki, *Shin jingi naki tatakai–bousatsu* (also known as *Fight without Loyalty/Murder*), 2003.

Katsumoto, *The Last Samurai* (also known as *Last Samurai, The Last Samurai: Bushido,* and *Samurai*), Warner Bros., 2003.

Masanobu Azuma, *T.R.Y.,* Toei Company, 2003.

The chairman, *Memoirs of a Geisha* (also known as *Geisha*), Columbia, 2005.

Hideaki Komatsubara, *Year One in the North* (also known as *Kita no zeronen*), Toei Company, 2005.

Ra's al Ghul, *Batman Begins* (also known as *Batman 5, Batman: Intimidation,* and *The Intimidation Game;* IMAX version known as *Batman Begins: The IMAX Experience*), Warner Bros., 2005.

Japanese voice, *Ashes and Snow* (documentary), Flying Elephants Productions, 2005, released in Japan, 2007.

General Tadamichi Kuribayashi, *Letters from Iwo Jima* (also known as *Red Sun, Black Sand*), Paramount, 2006.

Masayuki Saeki, *Ashita no kioku* (also known as *Memories of Tomorrow*), Toei Company, 2006, subtitled version, Eleven Arts, 2007.

Narrator of Japanese version, *Earth* (documentary; film version of documentary television series), different companies, including Lionsgate/Christal Films, 2007, Walt Disney Studios Motion Pictures, 2009.

Hajime Onchi, *Shizumanu taiyo* (also known as *The Sun That Doesn't Set, The Sun That Never Sets, The Unbroken,* and *Unsinking Sun*), Toho Company, 2009.

Mr. Hibernius Tall, *Cirque du Freak: The Vampire's Assistant* (also known as *Circus of the Freak, Cirque du Freak,* and *Darren Shan*), Universal, 2009.

Saito, *Inception* (also known as *Oliver's Arrow;* IMAX version known as *Inception: The IMAX Experience*), Warner Bros., 2010.

Security chief, *Shanghai,* The Weinstein Company, 2010.

Some sources cite appearances in other films.

Film Work:

Executive producer, *Ashita no kioku* (also known as *Memories of Tomorrow*), Toei Company, 2006, subtitled version, Eleven Arts, 2007.

Benefactor, *Half Kenneth* (short film), American Film Institute Conservatory, 2009.

Television Appearances; Series:

Samurai, *Mibu no koiuta,* NHK, 1983.

Nijitte monogatari, 1984.

Sanga moyu (also known as *The Burning Mountain River*), NHK, 1984.

Tenkou syojo Y, 1984.

Hanekonma, 1986.

Date Masamune, *Dokugan–ryu Masamune* (also known as *One–Eyed Dragon* and *Dokuganryu Masamune*), NHK, 1987.

Anata ga hoshii (also known as *I Want You*), 1989.

Harenochi Kaminari (also known as *Sunny and Then Thunder*), 1989, also broadcast in 2005.

Shikakenin Fujieda Baian, 1990–93.

Senjuro Fujiwara, *Kimitachi ga ite boku ga iru,* Fuji Television Network, 1992.

Senjuro Fujiwara, *Kimitachi ga ite boku ga iru II,* Fuji Television Network, 1992.

Homura tatsu, NHK, 1993–94.

Zankuro Matsudaira, *Gokenin zankuro,* Fuji Television Network, 1995–2002.

Yokoyama, *Ikebukuro Uesuto Geto Paku* (also known as *Ikebukuro West Gate Park*), Tokyo Broadcasting System (TBS), 2000.

Hojo Tokimune, NHK, 2001.

Kochira daisan syakaibu (also known as *The 3rd Society Department*), 2001.

Yoshimura, *Mibu gishi den* (also known as *When the Last Sword Is Drawn, Mbugishiden, Mibugishiden,* and *Mibu–Gishiden*), 2002.

Syuichiro Imanishi, *Suna no utsuwa,* Tokyo Broadcasting System (TBS), 2004.

Hachibei Hiratsuka, *Keiji ichidai: Hiratsuka Hachibei no Showa jiken shi,* TV Asahi, 2009.

Narrator, *Saka no ue no kumo* (title means *A Cloud upon a Slope*), NHK, beginning 2009.

Television Appearances; Miniseries:

Narrator, *Takeda Shingen,* Tokyo Broadcasting System (TBS), 1990.

Musuko no gokikan, 1990.

Wagamachi, 1992.

Kagishi, 1993.

Shuzo, *Sushi kuine 3: Nigire!! Tokyo natsu no aji,* Kansai Telecasting Corporation (KTV), 1996.

Shimei tehai, 1998.

Television Appearances; Movies:

(As Watanabe Ken) Title role, *Oda Nobunaga,* 1989.

Detective, *Ningen no shomei* (also known as *Ningen no shomei 2001*), BS Japan and TV Tokyo, 2001.

Chushingura 1/47, Fuji Television Network, 2001.

Television Appearances; Specials:

Bakayaro special "humor tte nanda," 1999.

Guest, *Tetsuko no heya 30nen special,* TV Asahi, 2005.

Himself and the chairman, *On the Set: Memoirs of a Geisha,* Starz!, 2005.

Narrator, *Sekai ga moshi hyaku nin no mura dattara 3,* Fuji Television Network, 2005.

(Uncredited; in archive footage) The chairman, *Alberto Iglesias, el musico fiel,* Canal+ Espana, 2006.

Himself, *Live Earth* (also known as *Live Earth: The Concerts for a Climate in Crisis, Live Earth 7.7.07,* and *SOS: The Movement for a Climate in Crisis*), NBC, 2007.

Sohei Fukumoto, *Tomawari no ame,* Nippon Television Network Corporation (NTV), 2010.

Student, *Hei no naka no chugakko,* Tokyo Broadcasting System (TBS), 2010.

Television Appearances; Awards Presentations:

Presenter, *The 79th Annual Academy Awards,* ABC, 2007.

The 33rd Annual Japan Academy Awards, Nippon Television Network Corporation (NTV), 2010.

Television Appearances; Episodic:

Master of ceremonies, *Tetsuko no heya* (also known as *Tetsuko's Room*), TV Asahi, 1996.

Himself, "Batman Begins: An Origin Story," *HBO First Look,* HBO, 2005.

Himself, *Current TV,* 2006.

Himself, "Kumai Kei: Sengo Nihon no yami ni idomu," *ETV tokushu* (also known as *ETV Special*), NHK Educational, 2007.

(As Watanabe Ken) Himself, "Watanabe Ken," *100 nen intabyu* (also known as *100 Nen Interview*), NHK, 2007.

Himself, "Ken Watanabe," *Tetsuko no heya* (also known as *Tetsuko's Room*), TV Asahi, 2009.

Himself, *Waratte iitomo!* (also known as *Waratte iitomo!: Morita Kazuyoshi awa*), Fuji Television Network, 2009.

Himself, *Janela indiscreta,* Radiotelevisao Portuguesa (RTP), 2010.

Television Appearances; Other:

Michinaru Hanran (also known as *Unknown Rebellion*), 1982.

Kazoku no onna, 1983.

Taiyo ni joeri "Bouken no umi," 1983.

Umi akeru toki, 1984.

Orecchi no noshizora yakyu, 1985.

Ose ni iki Ose ni shisu, 1986.

Tabidachi, 1988.

Aniki, 1992.

Ganryujima–Kojiro to Musashi (also known as *Ganryujima: Kojiro and Musashi*), 1992.

Izakaya Choji, 1992.

Machibugyo nikki, 1992.

Shiawase kazoku, 1992.

Daisainan, 1993.

Goyokiba, 1994.

Chushingura, 1996.

Tatakai sunde higa kurete, 1997.

Chokusen no shikaku, 1998.

Jikan no nai machi, 1999.

Yonimo kimyona monogatari, 1999.

Asakusa Hanaoka syashinkan, 2000.

Hatsuru sokonaki, Fuji Television Network, 2000.

Chinmoku no ariibai, 2002.

Kyokohan sousa dainanagakari, 2002.

To–san no natsumatsuri (also known as *Tou–san no Natsu Matsuri*), Nippon Television Network Corporation (NTV), 2002.

Tatsumi, *Itan no natsu,* BS Japan and TV Tokyo, 2003.

Joshi keimusho higashi 3 go to 4, 2003.

Hoshi hitotsu no yoru, Fuji Television Network, 2007.

Television Work; Episodic:
Director, *Gokenin zankuro,* Fuji Television Network, final episode, 2002.

Stage Appearances:
Britannicus hendo, 1980.
Fuyu no raion (Japanese version of *The Lion in Winter*), 1981.
Pajaze, 1981.
Shitaya mannencho monogatari (also known as *Shimandi mannencho monogatari* and *Shitaya mannen–cho monogatari;* title means *The Story of Shitaya Mannen Street*), Madok (theatre company), Tokyo, 1981.
Platonof, 1982.
Kafun netsu, 1985.
Pizarro, 1985.
Hamlet, 1988.
Voice, *Eien part1—kanojo to kare,* 2000.
Hamlet no gakuya–anten, 2000.
Eien part2—kanojo to kare, 2001.

RECORDINGS

Videos:
Himself, *Making of "Tampopo"* (documentary), Toho Video, 1986, Geneon Entertainment, 2005.

Video Games:
Voice of Ra's al Ghul, *Batman Begins,* Electronic Arts, 2005.

WRITINGS

Nonfiction:
Dare? Who Am I? (autobiography; also published in Japanese), 2006.

OTHER SOURCES

Periodicals:
Entertainment Weekly, December 10, 2003, pp. 38–39; February 6, 2004, pp. 60–61; January 12, 2007, p. 23.
Parade, December 11, 2005, p. 22.
USA Today, December 11, 2003; June 15, 2007, p. 12E.

WEAVER, Lee 1930–
    (Lee W. Weaver)

PERSONAL

Born April 10, 1930, in Fort Lauderdale, FL; son of Primus Jest (a chef) and Josephine Weaver; married Ta–Tanisha (an actress), July 10, 1971; children: Leis La–Te

(a daughter). *Education:* Florida A & M University, B.A.

Addresses: *Agent*—Contemporary Artists Agency, 1888 Century Park E., Suite 1400, Los Angeles, CA, 90067.

Career: Actor. Appeared in numerous television commercials, including Kool–Aid beverages, 1993, Burger King restaurants, 2001, Target department stores, 2002, FedEx delivery services, 2002, and Cingular wireless, 2004. *Military service:* U.S. Army.

Member: Screen Actors Guild, American Federation of Television and Radio Artists.

CREDITS

Film Appearances:
(Uncredited) Reporter, *Al Capone,* Warner Bros., 1959.
Willie, *The Lost Man,* Universal, 1969.
Jake, Denver drug dealer, *Vanishing Point,* Twentieth Century–Fox, 1971.
Voice, *Heavy Traffic* (animated), American International, 1973.
Friend, *Cleopatra Jones,* Warner Bros., 1973.
Airport '75, Universal, 1974.
Anesthesiologist, *House Calls,* Universal, 1978.
Way station attendant, *Heaven Can Wait,* Paramount, 1978.
Cheatem, *Mean Dog Blues,* 1978.
Billy, *The Onion Field,* AVCO–Embassy, 1979.
Mr. King, *Kiss Me Goodbye,* Twentieth Century–Fox, 1982.
The Escape Artist, Warner Bros., 1982.
Ray, *The Buddy System,* Twentieth Century–Fox, 1984.
Maurice, *Wildcats* (also known as *First and Goal*), Warner Bros., 1986.
Voice of Alpine, *G.I. Joe: The Movie,* 1987.
First caddy, *The Two Jakes,* Paramount, 1990.
Ben, *The Scout,* Twentieth Century–Fox, 1994.
Wino, *Just Your Luck* (also known as *Whiskey Down*), PolyGram, 1996.
Airline passenger, *Fathers' Day,* Warner Bros., 1997.
Man in church number two, *Bulworth,* Twentieth Century–Fox, 1998.
Homeless man, *Godzilla,* TriStar, 1998.
Nate, *How Stella Got Her Groove Back,* Twentieth Century–Fox, 1998.
Porter, *Music from Another Room,* Orion, 1998.
Wino, *Brown's Requiem,* Avalanche, 1998.
30's limo driver, *The Thirteenth Floor* (also known as *Abwaerts in die Zukunft*), Columbia, 1999.
Old Codger, *Goodbye Lover* (also known as *Patricia Arquette's "Goodbye Lover"*), Warner Bros., 1999.
Blind seer on handcar, *O Brother, Where Art Thou?* (also known as *Oh, Brother!*), Buena Vista, 2000.
Leroy, *Donnie Darko* (also known as *Donnie Darko: The Director's Cut*), Pandora, 2001.

Military policeman, *Evolution*, 2001.
Mr. Fishbau, *The Failures*, Yankee Films, 2003.
Joe, *The Box*, 2003.
Joe, *The 40 Year Old Virgin* (also known as *The 40 Year–old Virgin* and *The 40–Year–Old Virgin*), Universal, 2005.
Leroy, *Swedish Auto*, IFC Films, 2006.
Ralph, *Mr. Fix It*, First Look International, 2006.
Barney, *Little Fish, Strange Pond* (also known as *Frenemy*), Grindstone Entertainment Group, 2009.

Television Appearances; Series:
Various, *Sheena: Queen of the Jungle*, 1955–56.
Brian Kincaid, *The Bill Cosby Show*, NBC, 1969–71.
Ralph Prentiss, *Guess Who's Coming to Dinner?*, ABC, 1975.
Mose, *The Blue Knight*, CBS, 1976.
Voice of Alpine/E4 Albert M. Pine, *G.I. Joe* (animated), syndicated, 1985–86.
Ricardo Williams, *Easy Street*, NBC, 1986–87.
Gideon Oliver (also known as *By the Rivers of Babylon*), ABC, 1989.

Television Appearances; Miniseries:
The Blue Knight, NBC, 1973.

Television Appearances; Movies:
Bartender, *In Name Only*, ABC, 1969.
Bob, *Daddy, I Don't Like It Like This*, CBS, 1978.
Flamingo Road, NBC, 1979.
Our Family Honor, ABC, 1985.
Voice of Alpine, *G.I. Joe: Arise, Serpentor, Arise!* (animated), 1986.
Biloxi Slim, *A Hobo's Christmas*, CBS, 1987.
Frank Monroe, "Meet the Munceys," *Disney Sunday Movie*, ABC, 1988.
Ollie, *My Brother's Wife*, ABC, 1989.
The Edge, 1989.
Harry, *Lush Life*, Showtime, 1993.
Elmer, *A Season of Hope* (also known as *The Lemon Grove*), CBS, 1995.
Odelle, "Homecoming Day," *Riot*, Showtime, 1995.

Television Appearances; Pilots:
Ralph Prentiss, *Guess Who's Coming to Dinner*, ABC, 1975.
Flamingo Road, NBC, 1980.
Our Family Honor, 1985.
Supervisor, *Lois & Clark: The New Adventures of Superman*, ABC, 1993.
Mr. Bibbs, *Sparks*, UPN, 1996.
Third passenger, *Temporarily Yours* (also known as *Temp Yours, Temp Mine*), CBS, 1997.
Alfred Montgomery, *A.U.S.A.*, NBC, 2003.

Television Appearances; Episodic:
Cab driver, "Don't Call Us and We Won't Call You," *Good Morning, World*, 1967.

Senator's valet, "Suitable for Framing," *I Spy*, 1968.
Desk clerk number two, "The Night of the Sedgewick Curse," *The Wild Wild West*, CBS, 1968.
Charlie Willis, "Death in a Minor Key," *Mannix*, CBS, 1969.
Ace, "Love and the Hustler," *Love, American Style*, ABC, 1969.
Second truck driver, "The Prodigy," *Nanny and the Professor*, ABC, 1971.
Ringwald, "Delegate at Large," *Cade's County*, CBS, 1971.
Neighbor, "Pressure Point," *Adam–12*, NBC, 1975.
"Earl's Dad and Mama's Glad," *That's My Mama*, ABC, 1975.
Ozzie Turnball, "Out of the Frying Pan ...," *Kojak*, CBS, 1975.
"Greatest Show in Watts," *Sanford and Son*, NBC, 1976.
Second man, "The Big Move: Part 2," *Good Times*, CBS, 1976.
Scooter, "Danger Zone," *Serpico*, NBC, 1976.
Willie, "George's Guilt," *The Jeffersons*, CBS, 1977.
Chambers, "The Hot Dog Murder," *Quincy, M.E.* (also known as *Quincy*), NBC, 1977.
Sergeant, "Episode 17," *Soap*, ABC, 1978.
Bogeman, "Huggy Can't Go Home," *Starsky and Hutch*, ABC, 1979.
"The Hostages: Part 1," *Flamingo Road*, NBC, 1981.
"A Mother's Revenge," *Flamingo Road*, NBC, 1981.
"The Fish Fry," *Flamingo Road*, NBC, 1981.
"The Election," *Flamingo Road*, NBC, 1981.
Gus, "My Dad Can't Beat Up Anybody," *Mork and Mindy*, ABC, 1981.
"Neither a Borrower," *Shannon*, CBS, 1981.
Bartender, "The Shooter," *Hill Street Blues*, NBC, 1982.
Buck Naked, "Santaclaustrophobia," *Hill Street Blues*, NBC, 1982.
Dave, "All Fall Down," *Voyagers!*, NBC, 1983.
Buck Naked, "Here's Adventure, Here's Romance," *Hill Street Blues*, NBC, 1983.
William "Buck Naked" Tully, "Midway to What?," *Hill Street Blues*, NBC, 1983.
William "Buck Naked" Tully, "Parting Is Such Sweep Sorrow," *Hill Street Blues*, NBC, 1984.
Joe, "Blue Collar Drummond," *Diff'rent Strokes*, NBC, 1985.
Ticket clerk, "Aunt Shirley," *What's Happening Now?*, syndicated, 1985.
Frank, "Pick Six," *227*, NBC, 1986.
Frank, "The Handwriting on the Wall," *227*, NBC, 1987.
Waiter, "Planning Parenthood," *The Cosby Show*, NBC, 1987.
The New Hollywood Squares, syndicated, 1987.
Mort, "Dear Sam: Part 1," *Mr. President*, 1987.
Henry, "San Francisco: Parts 1, 2 & 3," *Webster*, 1987.
Man who stole the money, "To Catch a Thief," *Amen*, NBC, 1988.
Snookie Reams, "John's New Job: Part 1," *Dear John*, NBC, 1990.
Ray Nay, "Love Thy Neighbor," *A Different World*, NBC, 1990.

Mr. Fields, "Home Remedies," *The Cosby Show,* NBC, 1991.

Mr. Mitchell, "Real News," *The Man in the Family,* ABC, 1991.

Ed, "Granny Gets Busy," *The Fresh Prince of Bel–Air,* NBC, 1991.

Cody, "Justice—May 11, 1965," *Quantum Leap,* NBC, 1991.

Reverend Harrington, "Patriots," *Homefront,* ABC, 1991.

Stubblefield, "Pure Gold," *Reasonable Doubts,* NBC, 1991.

Stumpy, "Gunz 'n Boyz," *MacGyver,* ABC, 1991.

Augustus Murphy, "The Vandals," *Dragnet* (also known as *The New Dragnet*), 1991.

Reverend Curtis, "Eat Something," *Nurses,* NBC, 1992.

Mr. Burke, "Opportunity Knock Knocks: Part 2," *Night Court,* NBC, 1992.

Bus boy, "Boyz'r Us," *Martin,* Fox, 1992.

Leonard, "If I Were a Rich Man," *Step by Step,* ABC, 1993.

Bartender, "Living Kringle," *Living Single,* Fox, 1993.

Buck Naked, "Up on the Roof," *NYPD Blue* (also known as *N.Y.P.D.*), ABC, 1994.

Ollie, "No Place Live Home," *Roc,* Fox, 1994.

Buck Naked, "Serge the Concierge," *NYPD Blue* (also known as *N.Y.P.D.*), ABC, 1994.

Buck Naked, "Dead and Gone," *NYPD Blue* (also known as *N.Y.P.D.*), ABC, 1994.

Priest, "Free Billy," *Sister, Sister,* ABC, 1994.

Old man, "High Noon," *Martin,* Fox, 1995.

Stan, "Fortunate Son," *Beverly Hills, 90210* (also known as *Class of Beverly Hills*), Fox, 1995.

(As Lee W. Weaver) Hilton Brown, "Invasion," *Sliders,* Fox, 1996.

Mr. Bibbs, "No Sweat," *Sparks,* UPN, 1996.

"Seems Like Old Times," *The Jamie Foxx Show,* The WB, 1996.

Earlee, "On Golden Pons," *Chicago Hope,* CBS, 1997.

Beans, "Back in the Day: Parts 1 and 2," *The Good News,* UPN, 1998.

Clyde, "A Day in the Life," *Suddenly Susan,* NBC, 1999.

Church member, "The Trouble with Angels," *For Your Love,* The WB, 1999.

Mr. Brody, "Prototype," *City of Angels,* CBS, 2000.

Isaiah, "A Resting Place," *Diagnosis Murder* (also known as *Dr. Mark Sloan*), CBS, 2000.

Mr. Horton, "The Jackal," *The District,* CBS, 2000.

Harold, "Roots," *One World,* NBC, 2000.

Buster, "The Magic Three–Legged Sex Dog," *Men, Women & Dogs,* The WB, 2001.

Harry Rosemont, "Tracy," *Kate Brasher,* CBS, 2001.

Candy McCloud, "The Perfect Game," *Touched by an Angel,* CBS, 2001.

Louis Nolman, "Call Him Macaroni," *Any Day Now,* Lifetime, 2002.

Attendant, "Table for Too Many: Part 2," *My Wife and Kids,* ABC, 2002.

"The Sound of Music," *Providence,* NBC, 2002.

Photo shop owner, "Ockham's Razor," *Crossing Jordan,* NBC, 2003.

Tebo, "Dead Clown Walking," *The Parkers,* UPN, 2003.

Danny, *The Tracy Morgan Show,* NBC, 2003.

Schooney, "Hair Jordan," *The Bernie Mac Show,* Fox, 2004.

James Dubois Marshall, "Coming and Going," *Six Feet Under,* HBO, 2004.

Mr. Jenkins, "The Four Acres," *That's So Raven* (also known as *That's So Raven!*), The Disney Channel, 2006.

Burt, "Cursed," *Love, Inc.,* UPN, 2006.

Walter, "Charlie Don't Surf," *Veronica Mars,* UPN, 2006.

Junkyard owner, "Bums: Making a Mess All Over the City," *It's Always Sunny in Philadelphia* (also known as *It's Always Sunny*), FX Network, 2007.

Kerwinkle Lord, "For Gedda," *CSI: Crime Scene Investigation* (also known as *CSI: Las Vegas* and *C.S.I.*), CBS, 2008.

Wrinkles, "Stole a Motorcycle," *My Name Is Earl,* NBC, 2008.

Homeless guy, "Joy in a Bubble," *My Name Is Earl,* NBC, 2008.

William, "James Ellison Funeral," *Party Down,* Starz!, 2010.

Also appeared in *Who's the Boss?,* ABC; *Family Honor,* NBC; *Palmerstown, U.S.A.,* CBS; as Albert Jones, "This Land Is Your Land," *Line of Fire,* ABC.

Television Appearances; Specials:
"Black Pudding," *The Edge,* HBO, 1989.

Television Work; Series:
Stunt man and stand–in for Bill Cosby, *I Spy,* NBC, 1965–68.

WERNER, Peter 1947–

PERSONAL

Born January 17, 1947, in New York, NY; brother of Tom Werner (a television producer). *Education:* Attended Dartmouth College. *Religion:* Buddhist.

Addresses: *Agent*—Paradigm, 360 North Crescent Dr. North Building, Beverly Hills, CA 90210.

Career: Director and producer.

Awards, Honors: Academy Award (with Andre R. Guttfreund), best short film—live action, 1977, for *In the Region of Ice;* Emmy Award nomination, outstanding directing in a drama series, Directors Guild of American Award nomination, 1986, both for *Moonlighting;* Emmy Award nomination, outstanding directing in a miniseries or a special, 1987, for *LBJ: The Early Years;* Directors Guild of America Award nomination, outstanding directorial achievement in dramatic specials, 1991, for *Hiroshima: Out of the Ashes;* Emmy Award nomination, outstanding individual achievement in directing for a miniseries or a special, Directors Guild of America Award nomination, outstanding directorial achievement in dramatic specials, 1996, both for *Almost Golden: The Jessica Savitch Story;* Emmy Award nomination (with others), outstanding made for television movie, 2007, for *Why I Wore Lipstick to My Mastectomy;* CableAce Award, *The '70s: The Image.*

CREDITS

Film Director:
Hidden and Seeking, 1971.
In the Region of Ice (short film), 1976.
Prisoners, Twentieth Century–Fox, 1981.
Don't Cry, It's Only Thunder (also known as *Vietnam: Hell or Glory*), Samuel Goldwyn Company, 1982.
No Man's Land, Orion, 1987.
The Good Policeman, 1991.
Lone Justice, 1994.

Also directed *Findhorn and Frances* (documentary); *Flaherty: Hidden & Seeking* (documentary).

Film Appearances:
(Uncredited) Dr. Werner, *Don't Cry, It's Only Thunder,* 1982.

Television Work; Series:
Executive producer, *Men,* ABC, 1989.
Visual consultant, *DEA,* Fox, 1990.
Co–executive producer, *Middle Ages,* CBS, 1992.

Television Director; Miniseries:
House of Frankenstein 1997, NBC, 1997.
Mama Flora's Family, CBS, 1998.
The '70s, NBC, 2000.

Television Director; Movies:
Battered, NBC, 1978.
"Aunt Mary," *Hallmark Hall of Fame,* CBS, 1979.
Barn Burning (also known as *The American Short Story Collection: "Barn Burning"*), 1980.
Hard Knox, NBC, 1984.
I Married a Centerfold, NBC, 1984.
Sins of the Father, NBC, 1985.
LBJ: The Early Years, NBC, 1987.
The Image, HBO, 1990.

Hiroshima: Out of the Ashes, NBC, 1990.
Ned Blessing: The True Story of My Life (also known as *Lone Justice* and *Ned Blessing*), CBS, 1992.
The Substitute Wife, NBC, 1994.
The Four Diamonds, The Disney Channel, 1995.
Almost Golden: The Jessica Savitch Story (also known as *Almost Golden*), Lifetime, 1995.
The Unspoken Truth (also known as *Living the Lie*), Lifetime, 1995.
Inflammable, CBS, 1995.
Two Mothers for Zachary, ABC, 1996.
Blue Rodeo, CBS, 1996.
On the Edge of Innocence, NBC, 1997.
Tempting Fate, ABC, 1998.
Hefner: Unauthorized (also known as *Hugh Hefner: The True Story*), USA Network, 1999.
After Amy (also known as *No Ordinary Baby*), Lifetime, 2001.
Ruby's Bucket of Blood, Showtime, 2001.
Call Me Claus, TNT, 2001.
No Ordinary Baby, Lifetime, 2001.
We Were the Mulvaneys, Lifetime, 2002.
The Pact, Lifetime, 2002.
Killer Instinct: From the Files of Agent Candice DeLong, Lifetime, 2003.
Gracie's Choice, Lifetime, 2003.
Mom at Sixteen, Lifetime, 2005.
Amber Frey: Witness for the Prosecution, CBS, 2005.
Snow Wonder, CBS, 2005.
Why I Wore Lipstick to My Mastectomy (also known as *Why I Wore Lipstick*), Lifetime, 2005.
Girl, Positive (also known as *Girl Posi+I've*), Lifetime, 2007.
The Circuit, ABC Family, 2008.
Vinegar Hill, CBS, 2008.
"Front of the Class," *Hallmark Hall of Fame,* CBS, 2008.
"A Dog Named Christmas," *Hallmark Hall of Fame,* CBS, 2009.
Front of the Class, CBS, 2009.
Bond of Silence, Lifetime, 2010.

Television Work; Movies:
Producer, *We Were the Mulvaneys,* Lifetime, 2002.
Producer, *The Pact,* Lifetime, 2002.
Co–executive producer, *Killer Instinct: From the Files of Agent Candice DeLong,* Lifetime, 2003.
Co–executive producer, *Gracie's Choice,* Lifetime, 2003.
Co–executive producer, *Mom at Sixteen,* Lifetime, 2005.
Co–executive producer, *Amber Frey: Witness for the Prosecution,* CBS, 2005.
Co–executive producer, *Why I Wore Lipstick to My Mastectomy* (also known as *Why I Wore Lipstick*), Lifetime, 2006.
Co–executive producer, *Girl, Positive,* Lifetime, 2007.
Co–executive producer, *The Circuit,* ABC Family, 2008.
Co–executive producer, *Vinegar Hill,* CBS, 2008.

Television Work; Pilots:
Director, *Outlaws,* CBS, 1986.
Director, "DEA," *DEA,* Fox, 1990.
Director and co–executive producer, *Doorways,* 1993.
Director, *Soul Mates,* Fox, 1997.
Director, *Ghost Cop,* Fox, 1998.
Director, *The Expert,* HBO, 1999.
Director, *For the People,* Lifetime, 2002.
Producer and director, *Follow the Leeds,* Lifetime, 2003.

Television Director; Episodic:
"An Endangered Species," *Family,* ABC, 1977.
"The Move," *Call to Glory,* ABC, 1984.
"A Nation Divided," *Call to Glory,* ABC, 1984.
"Joey's Ex–Wife," *Hometown,* CBS, 1985.
Moonlighting, 1985–86.
"Deck the Cell with Bars of Folly," *Hooperman,* ABC, 1987.
Men, ABC, 1989.
"The Journey," *The Wonder Years,* ABC, 1990.
"War and Peace," *A Different World,* NBC, 1991.
"Cats in the Cradle," *A Different World,* NBC, 1992.
"Night Moves," *Middle Ages,* 1992.
"Forever Young," *Middle Ages,* 1992.
Winnetka Road, NBC, 1993.
"Genesis," *Nash Bridges,* CBS, 1996.
"Light My Fire," *Philly,* ABC, 2001.
"Rubber Sold," *Grounded for Life,* Fox, 2001.
"The Mini–Jerry Episode," *Maybe It's Me,* The WB, 2001.
"The Rick's in Love Episode," *Maybe It's Me,* The WB, 2002.
"Insured by Smith & Wesson," *Boomtown,* NBC, 2002.
"The David McNorris Show," *Boomtown,* NBC, 2002.
For the People (also known as *Para la gente*), Lifetime, 2002.
Medium, CBS then NBC, 2005–11.
Raines, NBC, 2006.
The Ghost Whisperer, CBS, 2006–2009.
"Reconstructing Alice," *Raines,* 2007.
"Do Unto Others," *Kidnapped* (also known as *Kidnap*), NBC, 2007.
"Vanishing Act," *Law & Order: Criminal Intent* (also known as *Law Order: CI*), NBC, 2008.
"Great Expectations," *Army Wives,* Lifetime, 2008.
"Disengagement," *Army Wives,* Lifetime, 2009.
"Hatless," *Justified,* FX Network, 2010.
"The I of the Storm," *Justified,* FX Network, 2011.
"No Ordinary Love," *No Ordinary Family,* ABC, 2011.

WICHERLEY, Don
    See WYCHERLEY, Don

WILLIAMS, Chuck

PERSONAL

Born August 19 in Helena, AR. *Education:* Attended Point Loma Nazarene University.

Addresses: *Contact*—c/o Chuck Williams Fan Club, PO Box 950477, Mission Hills, CA 91395.

Career: Producer, director, actor, and writer. Chuck Williams Productions, Mission Hills, CA, owner, 1997—. Participated in various events.

Awards, Honors: Multiple high school Emmy awards and other awards, including the Fred Smith Award for outstanding achievement.

CREDITS

Film Producer:
Eddie Presley, Raven Pictures International, 1992.
Double Blast, 1994.
High Tomb (also known as *Ghost Gunfighter* and *Last Chance*), Sea Dog Productions, 1995.
Halloween ... The Happy Haunting of America! (documentary; also known as *Chuck Williams Presents: "Halloween ... The Happy Haunting of America"* and *Halloween: The Happy Haunting of America*), Whiz Bang Entertainment, 1997, anniversary collector's edition with new footage released by Chuck Williams Productions, 2007.
Up against Amanda (also known as *Malicious*), New Concorde Home Entertainment, 2000.
The Vault, 2000, Full Moon Entertainment, 2001.
Stitches, Full Moon Entertainment, 2001.
Coproducer, *Horrorvision,* Full Moon Entertainment, 2001.
Groom Lake (also known as *Visitor* and *The Visitor*), Full Moon Entertainment, 2002.
Dark Walker, Shadow Entertainment, 2003.
The Low Budget Time Machine (also known as *Spacebabes Meet the Monsters*), Doodle Barnett Productions/Irena Belle Films, 2003.
Straight into Darkness (also known as *Platoon of Children*), Screen Media Ventures, 2004.
Mil Mascaras vs. the Aztec Mummy (also known as *Mil Mascaras: Resurrection*), Osmium Entertainment/Rain Moon Productions, 2007.
The Telling, Breakout Entertainment, 2009.

Film Associate Producer:
Terror Eyes, Victory Pictures, 1989.
Dark Rider, 1991.

Witchouse II: Blood Coven (also known as *Witchouse 2*), Full Moon Entertainment, 2000.

Killer Pad, Grindstone Entertainment Group, 2008.

Film Director:
Assistant director, *Dudes,* New Century Vista Film Company, 1987.

Third assistant director, *Near Dark,* Anchor Bay Entertainment, 1987.

Third assistant director, *Disorganized Crime* (also known as *Disorganised Crime*), Buena Vista, 1989.

Assistant director, *Killer Tomatoes Eat France!,* New World, 1992.

(With Daniel Roebuck) *Halloween ... The Happy Haunting of America!* (documentary; also known as *Chuck Williams Presents: "Halloween ... The Happy Haunting of America"* and *Halloween: The Happy Haunting of America*), Whiz Bang Entertainment, 1997, anniversary collector's edition with new footage released by Chuck Williams Productions, 2007.

Film Work; Other:
Editor and stunt performer, *High Tomb* (also known as *Ghost Gunfighter* and *Last Chance*), Sea Dog Productions, 1995.

Cinematographer, *Halloween ... The Happy Haunting of America!* (documentary; also known as *Chuck Williams Presents: "Halloween ... The Happy Haunting of America"* and *Halloween: The Happy Haunting of America*), Whiz Bang Entertainment, 1997, anniversary collector's edition with new footage released by Chuck Williams Productions, 2007.

Creator of idea and still photographer, *Dark Walker,* Shadow Entertainment, 2003.

EPK camera operator, *Carbon Copy* (also known as *The Carbon Copy*), Carbon Copy Productions, c. 2008.

Film Appearances:
(Uncredited) Demon, *Demon Wind,* United Filmmakers, 1990.

Tommy Marcetto, *Soultaker,* Park–Schilling Productions/Victory Pictures Production/Pacific West Entertainment Group, 1990.

Bobby, *Dark Rider,* 1991.

President Nixon robber, *Project Eliminator* (also known as *The Eliminator* and *Stroker*), Victory Pictures Production, 1991.

Kevin in the booth, *Eddie Presley,* Raven Pictures International, 1992.

Boggus, *Double Blast,* 1994.

Police officer, *Puppet Master 5: The Final Chapter* (also known as *The Final Chapter: Puppet Master 5, Puppet Master 5,* and *Puppet Master V*), Full Moon Entertainment, 1994.

Joe the police officer, *Scot–free* (also known as *Smoke & Mirrors*), 1995.

Shane, *High Tomb* (also known as *Ghost Gunfighter* and *Last Chance*), Sea Dog Productions, 1995.

With Criminal Intent, 1995.

Igor, *Halloween ... The Happy Haunting of America!* (documentary; also known as *Chuck Williams Presents: "Halloween ... The Happy Haunting of America"* and *Halloween: The Happy Haunting of America*), Whiz Bang Entertainment, 1997, anniversary collector's edition with new footage released by Chuck Williams Productions, 2007.

Buzz, *Up against Amanda* (also known as *Malicious*), New Concorde Home Entertainment, 2000.

Kendall, *Twice the Fun* (short film), 2000.

Security guard, *Witchouse II: Blood Coven* (also known as *Witchouse 2*), Full Moon Entertainment, 2000.

Mongo, *The Vampire Hunters Club* (short film), Doodle Barnett Productions/Irena Belle Films, 2001.

Schizo the hotel clerk, *Horrorvision,* Full Moon Entertainment, 2001.

Alien, *Groom Lake* (also known as *Visitor* and *The Visitor*), Full Moon Entertainment, 2002.

Title role and radio deejay, *Dark Walker,* Shadow Entertainment, 2003.

Elvis's boy, *Bubba Ho–tep,* Vitagraph Films, 2003.

Ramboona, *The Low Budget Time Machine* (also known as *Spacebabes Meet the Monsters*), Doodle Barnett Productions/Irena Belle Films, 2003.

Zuckermire, *Up against the 8 Ball,* Mee Productions, 2004.

(Uncredited) Half–naked unshaven towel man, *Trail of the Screaming Forehead,* Chanceuse Productions, 2007.

Mark, *Night Visit* (short film), BV Entertainment, 2007.

Voices of elf and selves, *Christmas Is Here Again* (animated musical; also known as *Who Stole Santa's Sack?*), Universal Studios Home Entertainment, 2007.

Gus, *Loved Ones* (also known as *Loved Ones a Vampire Tale*), R–Squared Films, 2008.

Sheridan, *Bryan Loves You,* Anchor Bay Entertainment, 2008.

Jimmy, *Carbon Copy* (also known as *The Carbon Copy*), Carbon Copy Productions, c. 2008.

The boss, "The Exterminator" segment, *Slices,* 2008, Brain Damage Films, 2009.

Amos, *Fistful of Brains,* c. 2008, Brain Damage Films, 2010.

Arnie Smith, *Allure,* R–Squared Films, 2009.

Himself, *Ultimate Death Match,* R–Squared Films, 2009.

Desert bartender, *Live Evil,* LEM Enterprises, 2009.

First mystery man, *The Co$t of Living* (also known as *The Cost of Living*), Designers Warehouse Pictures/Erebus Media/Galloping Films/Raging Gopher Films/TPR Production, 2010.

Killer, *Horrorween* (3D version known as *Horrorween 3D*), 2010.

Queen Anne's pirate, *Pirates of the Caribbean: On Stranger Tides* (also known as *Pirates 4* and *P.O.T.C. 4*), Walt Disney Pictures, 2011.

Television Work; Movies:
First assistant director, *Fugitive X: Innocent Target,* HBO, 1996.

Television Appearances; Specials:
Igor, *Monsterama: A Tribute to Horror Hosts,* 2004.

Television Appearances; Episodic:
Himself (horror film producer), "Scream Test," *The Girls Next Door* (also known as *The Girls of the Playboy Mansion*), E! Entertainment Television, 2008.
Himself (horror film producer), "Fangs for the Mammaries," *The Girls Next Door* (also known as *The Girls of the Playboy Mansion*), E! Entertainment Television, 2009.
Himself (horror film producer), "Transitions: Parts 1 & 2," *The Girls Next Door* (also known as *The Girls of the Playboy Mansion*), E! Entertainment Television, 2009.
Nakelski security guard, "The Power of Three," *Kamen Ride: Dragon Knight,* The CW, 2009.
Detective, *Californication* (also known as *Untitled David Duchovny Series* and *Untitled Tom Kapinos Project*), Showtime, 2011.

WRITINGS

Screenplays:
(With Bob Ivy) *Dark Rider,* 1991.
(With Judy Mathai) *High Tomb* (also known as *Ghost Gunfighter* and *Last Chance*), Sea Dog Productions, 1995.
(With Buddy Barnett and Kathe Duba–Barnett) *The Low Budget Time Machine* (story by Brad Linaweaver; also known as *Spacebabes Meet the Monsters*), Doodle Barnett Productions/Irena Belle Films, 2003.

WILSON, Brian Anthony 1960–

    (Brian Wilson, Brian A. Wilson, Brian A. D. Wilson)

PERSONAL

Born February 22, 1960, in Philadelphia, PA; married Greer M. Richardson, September 30, 2005. *Education:* Studied acting at TVI Actors Studio and at various theatres.

Career: Actor. Appeared in promotional clip for Comedy Central.

Member: Screen Actors Guild, Actors' Equity Association.

Awards, Honors: Barrymore Award nomination, outstanding supporting actor in a play, 1995, for *Fences.*

CREDITS

Film Appearances:
Woody, *The Postman,* Warner Bros., 1997.
(As Brian A. Wilson) Casino security guard number two, *Snake Eyes,* Paramount, 1998.
Derald, *Rounders,* Miramax, 1998.
Spear, *Cold Hearts,* Raven Releasing, 1999.
T–Bone, *Keeping the Faith,* Touchstone Pictures, 2000.
Fourteenth audience member, *Let's Talk,* The Asylum, 2000.
(As Brian Wilson) Carl, *Killer Instinct,* Trimark Video, 2000.
Loc, *Diary of a City Priest,* Heartland Film Festival, 2001.
Twin's father, *Proximity,* Warner Bros., 2001.
Prison commanding officer, *Prison Song,* New Line Cinema, 2001.
Barney (first policeman), *Down* (also known as *The Shaft*), Buena Vista International, 2001.
Phil, *The Perfect You* (also known as *Crazy Little Thing*), Thompson Street Entertainment, 2002.
Kelvin, *For da Love of Money,* Urbanworld Films, 2002.
Damon J, *Ice Grill,* York Entertainment, 2002.
Louis, *The Good Thief* (also known as *Saint Christopher*), Twentieth Century–Fox, 2002.
Narrator, *A Matter of National Security* (short film), 2003.
Detective McCue, *Motive* (short film), 2003.
(Uncredited) Tapia muscle crew, *Bad Boys II* (also known as *Good Cops: Bad Boys II* and *Bad Boys: 2 Bad*), Columbia, 2003.
Jerome, *Dirty Laundry (Air It Out),* Repnet, 2003.
Cox, *X, Y,* 2004.
Willy, *The Amazing Floydini,* Sterling Films, 2004.
Number man, *Forget Tomorrow* (short film), 2004.
Chris, *Destiny* (short film), 2004.
Buck, *White Men Can't Rap,* 2005.
Sheriff, *Eventide* (short film), 2005.
Detective Dick Moon, *The Good Student* (also known as *Mr. Gibb*), Screen Media Ventures, 2006.
Male guard, *Shadow: Dead Riot,* Media Blasters, 2006.
Quade, *The Father, Unblinking* (short film), 2006.
Simon, *El otro lado* (short film), Shorts International, 2007.
K. C.'s attorney, *Eye See Me,* 2007.
Coach Michael Bailey, *A Diamond in the Sky,* Diamond Entertainment Productions, 2007.
Metaphys–Ed Coach, *Holy Sapien* (short film), 2008.
Mr. Joel, *Leaf,* 2008.
Demetri's dad, *Explicit Ills,* Peace Arch Releasing, 2008.

Arguing man in crowd, *The Happening,* Twentieth Century–Fox, 2008.

Jules, *Jersey Justice,* 2008.

Morgenthau, *After You're Gone,* 2009.

Big Daddy, *The Mind,* 2009.

Guard Jones, *Oral Fixation,* 2009.

Homeland Security supervisor, *Law Abiding Citizen,* Overture Films, 2009.

Johnny X, *Bamboo Shark,* 2009.

Rufus, *99 Perfect Sure,* 2009.

Frank, *A Turn of the Blinds* (short film), 2010.

(As Brian A. Wilson) Virgil, *Shelter,* Weinstein Company, 2010.

Lew Burns, *Watching the Detectives,* 2010.

Cop, *See You in September,* 2010.

Shareef, *The Best and the Brightest,* 2010.

Charlie, *The Fields,* 2010.

Television Appearances; Series:

Detective Vernon Holley, *The Wire,* HBO, 2002–2008.

Television Appearances; Miniseries:

Lanny, *The Corner,* HBO, 2000.

Television Appearances; Movies:

Ponchie, *Animal Factory,* Cinemax, 2000.

Television Appearances; Pilots:

Pit boss, *Outlaw,* NBC, 2010.

Television Appearances; Episodic:

First diner, "Identity Crisis," *Homicide: Life on the Street* (also known as *Homicide* and *H: LOTS*), NBC, 1999.

Warren Dupree, "Fortunate Son," *The Sopranos,* HBO, 2001.

Raymond Henley, "Bad Choices," *Hack,* CBS, 2002.

Crater, Rose's bodyguard, *As the World Turns,* CBS, 2003.

Milton Sarlove, "Pretend," *Law & Order: Special Victims Unit* (also known as *Law & Order: SVU* and *Special Victims Unit*), NBC, 2007.

Detective Jawarski, "Swing," *Law & Order: Special Victims Unit* (also known as *Law & Order: SVU* and *Special Victims Unit*), NBC, 2008.

Detective Gardner, "Necessities," *Bleeder,* 2009.

Detective Gardner, "Common Bonds," *Bleeder,* 2009.

Stage Appearances:

(As Brian A. D. Wilson) Gabriel, "Fences," Herald Loomis, "Joe Turner's Come and Gone," and Boy Willie, "The Piano Lesson," *Bushfire Trilogy,* Bushfire Theatre of Performing Arts, 1995.

Amiens, *As You Like It,* Pennsylvania Shakespeare Festival, Allentown College of St. Frances de Sales Theatre, Center Valley, PA, 1996.

Ezra Johnson Brown, *Dog Days: The Legend of O. V. Catto,* Venture Theatre, Philadelphia, PA, c. 1998.

Daniel Freeman, *Deep Down,* Venture Theatre, 1999.

Alexandre Dumas, the father, *Les trois Dumas,* People's Light and Theatre Company, Malvern, PA, 2001.

(As Brian A. D. Wilson) *Before It Hits Home,* First World Theatre Ensemble, Willow Theatre, Philadelphia, 2002.

Johnson Family Saga (staged reading), Philadelphia, 2002.

The Tempest, Lantern Theatre Company, St. Stephen's Theatre, Philadelphia, 2003.

Johnny–Boy, *Twilight Time,* First World Theatre Ensemble, Hedgerow Theatre, Media, PA, 2003.

Title role, *Othello,* Philadelphia Shakespeare Festival, Philadelphia, 2003 and 2007.

Title role, *King Hedley II,* Philadelphia Theatre Company, Philadelphia, 2003.

Lyons, *Fences,* Arden Theatre Company, F. Otto Haas Stage, Philadelphia, 2005.

George, *Intimate Apparel,* Indiana Repertory Theatre, Indianapolis, IN, 2006.

Becker, *Jitney,* Kansas City Repertory Theatre, Kansas City, MO, 2006.

Avery Brown, *The Piano Lesson,* Ardern Theatre Company, F. Otto Haas Stage, 2008.

Alonzo Fields, *Looking Over the President's Shoulder,* Hedgerow Theatre, Media, PA, 2009.

Also appeared as grand inquisitor and member of ensemble, *Candide,* Prince Music Theatre; Ghost of Christmas Present, *A Christmas Carol,* Actors Theatre of Louisville, Louisville, KY; Reverend Jamison, *The Contract,* National Black Artists' Festival, Atlanta, GA; Oscar McKinley Charleston, *Cobb,* Act II Playhouse; Senator Charles Lincoln, *Fraternity,* Bushfire Theatre of Performing Arts; Duane Wilson, *Harvey,* Cleveland Playhouse, Cleveland, OH; Mayor R. Franklin Brown III, *The Mayor's Wife;* as Lucio, *Measure for Measure,* Vasey Theatre, Villanova, PA; Malcolm X, *The Meeting,* Bushfire Theatre of Performing Arts; Sergeant Bert Hopkins, *The Ninth Wave,* Vasey Theatre; Dr. Terry Allen and the marshal, *Notes on 6finity,* National Black Theatre Festival, North Carolina; Biglow Brown, *St. Louis Woman,* Prince Music Theatre; Alonzo Maldonado, *A Salt Water Oasis,* Fringe Festival; Brighella Caviccio, *Servant of Two Masters,* Venture Theatre, Plays and Players Theatre; Ali Baba and policeman, *Simply Heavenly,* Freedom Theatre; Matthew and beggar, *The Threepenny Opera,* Merriam Theatre; sixth juror, *12 Angry Men,* Cleveland Playhouse; Hambone, *Two Trains Running,* Cleveland Playhouse; W. E. B. Du Bois, *The Winter of Our Discontent,* Bushfire Theatre of Performing Arts; in *Rosa,* Venture Theatre.

Radio Appearances:

The Howard Stern Show, Sirius Satellite Radio, 2009.

WILSON, Vaughn 1976–
(Vaughan Wilson)

PERSONAL

Born December 24, 1976, in Wilmington, NC. *Education:* Pomona College, B.A., psychology, 1999.

Addresses: *Contact*—c/o 310 North Front St., #372, Suite 4, Wilmington, NC 28401.

Career: Actor.

Member: Screen Actors Guild.

CREDITS

Film Appearances:

McCord slave, *The Last Confederate: The Story of Robert Adams* (also known as *Strike the Tent*), THINKFilm, 2005.

Kareem's pal, *Two Tickets to Paradise* (also known as *Dirt Nap* and *Life's a Trip*), First Look International, 2006.

The man, *Wait ...* (short film), 2007, Kissin' Cousins Productions, 2008.

Tobias (third nabber), *Whispers* (short film), HighFall Films, 2008.

Bobby, *Cabin Fever 2: Spring Fever* (also known as *Cabin Fever 2, Cabin Fever II,* and *Unrated—Cabin Fever 2: Spring Fever*), Lionsgate, 2009.

Duckett, *Mississippi Damned,* Morgan's Mark, 2009.

Clarinet player, *Bolden!,* King Bolden, 2011.

Television Appearances; Series:

Ferguson "Fergie" Thompson, *One Tree Hill* (also known as *Ravens, Filoi gia panta, Les freres Scott, Tunteet pelissae,* and *Tuti gimi*), The WB, 2003–2006, The CW, beginning 2006.

Television Appearances; Episodic:

Pizza man, *Surface* (also known as *Fathom, A Melyseg fantomja,* and *Surface—Unheimliche Tiefe*), NBC, 2005.

Television Appearances; Pilots:

(As Vaughan Wilson) Second janitor, "Chapter 1: Career Errors" (also known as "Chapter 1"), *Eastbound & Down* (also known as *P.E.* and *Untitled Will Ferrell/ Adam McKay Project*), HBO, 2009.

Internet and Television Appearances; Episodic:

Willie T, "Closed Mouths," *Port City PD* (also known as *Port City P.D.*), PortCityPD.com, 2006, broadcast by various outlets, including American Unleashed Satellite TV network, 2009.

Willie T, "Triple Threat," *Port City PD* (also known as *Port City P.D.*), PortCityPD.com, 2006, broadcast by various outlets, including American Unleashed Satellite TV network, 2009.

WINGER, Debra 1955(?)–

PERSONAL

Full name, Mary Debra Winger; born May 16, 1955 (some sources cite May 1 or 1953), in Cleveland, OH; daughter of Robert (a meat packer) and Ruth (an office manager; maiden name, Felder) Winger; married Timothy Hutton (an actor, producer, and director), March 16, 1986 (divorced, 1990); married Arliss Howard (an actor and director), November, 1996; children: (first marriage) Emmanuel Noah; (second marriage) Gideon Babe. *Education:* Attended California State University, Northridge.

Addresses: *Agent*—WME Entertainment, 9601 Wilshire Blvd, 3rd Floor, Beverly Hills, CA 90210; IFA Talent Agency, 8730 Sunset Blvd., Suite 490, Los Angeles, CA 90069; Emma Sweeney Agency, LLC, 245 East 80th St. Suite 7E, New York, NY 10075–0506. *Manager*— Johnnie Planco, Parseghian and Planco, 23 East 22nd St., 3rd Floor, New York, NY 10010.

Career: Actress and producer. Worked on a collective farm in Israel as a teenager; worked at Magic Mountain Amusement Park, 1973. Appeared in commercials. *Military service:* Israel Defense Forces, 1972–73.

Awards, Honors: Golden Globe Award nominations, best supporting actress in a motion picture and female new star of the year in a motion picture, and Film Award nomination, best newcomer, British Academy of Film and Television Arts, all 1981, for *Urban Cowboy;* Academy Award nomination, best actress, and Golden Globe Award nomination, best actress in a motion picture drama, both 1983, for *An Officer and a Gentleman;* ShoWest Award, female star of the year, National Association of Theatre Owners, 1983; Academy Award nomination, best actress, Golden Globe Award nomination, best performance by an actress in a motion picture drama, and National Society of Film Critics Award, best actress, all 1984, for *Terms of Endearment;* Academy Award nomination, best actress, and Film Award nomination, best actress, British Academy of Film and Television Arts, both 1994, for *Shadowlands;* Golden Globe Award nomination, best performance by an actress in a motion picture drama, and Best Actress Award, Tokyo International Film Festival, both 1994, for *A Dangerous Woman;* Mast Screen Artist Tribute, USA Film Festival, 2002; Emmy Award nomination, outstanding lead actress in a miniseries or a movie, 2005, for *Dawn Anna;* Best Ensemble Cast nomination (with others), Gotham Awards, 2008, Critics Choice Award nomination (with others), best acting ensemble, Broadcast Film Critics Association, Independent Spirit Award nomination, best supporting female, both 2009, for *Rachel Getting Married.*

CREDITS

Film Appearances:
Debbie, *Slumber Party '57* (also known as *Teenage Slumber Party*), Cannon, 1977.
Jennifer, *Thank God It's Friday,* Columbia, 1978.
Melanie, *French Postcards,* Paramount, 1979.
Sissy Davis, *Urban Cowboy,* Paramount, 1980.
Suzy DeSoto, *Cannery Row* (also known as *John Steinbeck's "Cannery Row"*), Metro–Goldwyn–Mayer/United Artists, 1982.
Paula Pokrifki, *An Officer and a Gentleman,* Paramount, 1982.
One of the voices of E. T., *E. T. the Extra–Terrestrial* (also known as *A Boy's Life, E. T., E. T. and Me,* and *Night Skies*), Universal, 1982, longer version released as *E. T. the Extra–Terrestrial: The 20th Anniversary,* 2002.
Emma Greenway Horton, *Terms of Endearment,* Paramount, 1983.
Betty Parrish, *Mike's Murder,* Warner Bros., 1984.
Laura Kelly, *Legal Eagles,* Universal, 1986.
Alexandra "Alex" Barnes, *Black Widow,* Twentieth Century–Fox, 1987.
(Uncredited) Emmett Humbird, *Made in Heaven,* Lorimar, 1987.
Katie Phillips/Cathy Weaver, *Betrayed,* United Artists, 1988.
Angela Crispini, *Everybody Wins,* Orion, 1990.
Kit Moresby, *The Sheltering Sky* (also known as *Il te nel deserto*), Warner Bros., 1990.
Jane, *Leap of Faith,* Paramount, 1992.
Vida Foudroyant, *Wilder Napalm,* TriStar, 1993.
Martha Horgan, *A Dangerous Woman* (also known as *Dangerous Women*), Gramercy, 1993.
Joy Gresham, *Shadowlands,* Savoy Pictures, 1993.
Guest, *George Balanchine's "The Nutcracker,"* Warner Bros., 1993.
Narrator, *In Search of Angels,* 1994.
Ellen Andrews, *Forget Paris,* Columbia, 1995.
Narrator, *Rumi: Poet of the Heart,* 1998.
Marilyn Barlow, *Big Bad Love,* IFC Films, 2002.

Searching for Debra Winger (documentary), 2002.
Linda Jones, *Radio,* Columbia, 2003.
Alice Collins, *Eulogy,* Artisan Entertainment, 2004.
Chaos and Order: Making American Theater (documentary), Films for the Humanities, 2005.
Narrator, *Can You Hear Me? Israeli and Palestinian Women Fight for Peace* (documentary), Parallel Lines, 2006.
Abby, *Rachel Getting Married,* Sony Pictures Classics, 2008.
In the Woods (documentary), The Development Productions, 2010.

Film Work:
Executive producer and producer, *Big Bad Love,* IFC Films, 2002.

Television Appearances; Series:
Frances, *In Treatment,* HBO, 2010.

Television Appearances; Movies:
Sherrie Hensley, *Special Olympics* (also known as *A Special Kind of Love*), CBS, 1978.
The Wicked Witch of the West, *The Wizard of Oz in Concert: Dreams Come True* (also known as *The Wizard of Oz in Concert*), TNT, 1995.
Herself, *Searching for Debra Winger,* Showtime, 2003.
Dawn Anna Townsend, *Dawn Anna,* Lifetime, 2005.
Prudence Bushnell, *Sometimes in April,* HBO, 2005.

Television Appearances; Episodic:
Drusilla Prince/Wonder Girl, "The Feminum Mystique: Parts 1 & 2," *The New, Original Wonder Woman* (also known as *Wonder Woman*), ABC, 1976.
Drusilla Prince/Wonder Girl, "Wonder Woman in Hollywood," *The New, Original Wonder Woman* (also known as *Wonder Woman*), ABC, 1977.
"The Runaway," *Szysznyk,* CBS, 1977.
James at 16, NBC, 1978.
"Battered Teachers," *Police Woman,* NBC, 1978.
The Alan Thicke Show (also known as *Fast Company* and *Prime Cuts*), 1980.
De pelicula, 1987–2008.
Host, *Saturday Night Live* (also known as *SNL*), NBC, 1990.
Late Night with David Letterman, NBC, 1990.
Late Show with David Letterman (also known as *Late Night* and *Letterman*), CBS, 1993.
The View, 2002.
Richard & Judy, Channel 4, 2004.
The Late Late Show, CBS, 2005.
This Morning, ITV, 2006.
"Debra Winger," *Shootout* (also known as *Sunday Morning Shootout* and *Hollywood Shootout*), AMC, 2008.

Entertainment Tonight (also known as *E.T.* and *This Week in Entertainment*), syndicated, 2008, 2009.
Access Hollywood, syndicated, 2009.
Principal Woodside, "Boy on Fire," *Law & Order,* NBC, 2010.

Also interviewee in an episode of *Inside the Actors Studio,* Bravo.

Television Appearances; Specials:

The Best of Farm Aid: An American Event, HBO, 1986.
The Barbara Walters Special, ABC, 1987.
What Is This Thing Called Love? The Barbara Walters Special, ABC, 1993.
Narrator, *In Search of Angels,* PBS, 1994.
The Wicked Witch of the West, The Wizard of Oz in Concert: Dreams Come True (also known as *The Wizard of Oz in Concert*), TNT, 1995.
In the Wild: Pandas, PBS, 1995.
50 Years of Funny Females, 1995.
The Making of "Forget Paris," 1995.
Narrator, *Rumi: Poet of the Heart,* PBS, 1998.
Paula Pokrifki, *Premio Donostia a Richard Gere,* 2007.

Television Appearances; Awards Presentations:

The 38th Annual Golden Globe Awards, 1981.
Presenter, *The 54th Annual Academy Awards,* 1982.
The 56th Annual Academy Awards, 1984.
Presenter, *The 63rd Annual Academy Awards Presentation,* ABC, 1991.
The 66th Annual Academy Awards, 1994.

Television Executive Producer; Movies:

Gas Land, HBO, 2010.

Stage Appearances:

Li'l Bit, *How I Learned to Drive,* American Repertory Theatre, Loeb Drama Center, Cambridge, MA, 1998.
Anna, *Ivanov,* American Repertory Theatre, Loeb Drama Center, 1999–2000.
The Exonerated, Bleecker Street Theatre, New York City, 2002–2004.

RECORDINGS

Albums:

The Boy Who Made Dragonfly, 1992.
The Brothers Karamazov, 1993.

OTHER SOURCES

Books:

Cahill, M. J., *Debra Winger: Hollywood's Wild Child,* 1984.

International Dictionary of Films and Filmmakers, Volume 3: *Actors and Actresses,* St. James Press, 1996.

Periodicals:

American Film, July/August, 1988, pp. 20–25.
Esquire, February, 1993, p. 70.
People Weekly, March 18, 2002, p. 132.
Premiere, February, 2002, pp. 54–57, 95.

WINICK, Gary 1961–2011

PERSONAL

Original name, Gary Scott Winick; born March 31, 1961, in New York City; died of complications from brain cancer, February 27, 2011, in New York City. Producer and director. Winick created both personal, inexpensive films and large-scale Hollywood productions. He began in 1986, editing the Carl Franklin short *Punk* before directing the violent 1989 action film *Curfew.* He gained a small amount of recognition with the release of *The Tic Code* and formed InDigEnt, a small-budget production company dedicated to the use of digital equipment, in 1999. InDigEnt's first production was the Richard Linklater film *Tape,* followed by *Final* and *Chelsea Walls* in 2001. In 2002 Winick screened *Tadpole,* his directorial debut under InDigEnt, at the Sundance Film Festival. The film was acquired for distribution by Miramax and earned Winick the best director prize, launching his career in mainstream film. His big-budget features include *13 Going on 30, Charlotte's Web, Bride Wars,* and *Letters to Juliet,* which Winick directed just a year after he underwent surgery from brain cancer. Winick also directed episodes of the television series *Ugly Betty* and *Lipstick Jungle.* InDigEnt continued to produce films such as the Peter Hedges comedy *Pieces of April* and the Steve Buscemi project *Lonesome Jim* throughout the 2000s.

PERIODICALS

Guardian, March 2, 2011.
Los Angeles times, March 1, 2011.
New York Times, March 21, 2009.
Variety, March 2, 2011.

WISDOM, Tom 1973–

PERSONAL

Born February 18, 1973, in Swindon, England; father in Royal Air Force. *Education:* Attended Academy Drama School. *Avocational Interests:* Spectator sports, playing soccer.

Addresses: *Agent*—International Creative Management, 10250 Constellation Way, 9th Floor, Los Angeles, CA 90067; Emptage Hallet, 14 Rathbone Pl., London W1T 1HT, England.

Career: Actor.

CREDITS

Film Appearances:
Ryan, *Hey Mr. DJ,* Ardustry Home Entertainment, 2003.
Astinos, *300* (also released as *300: The IMAX Experience*), Warner Bros., 2006.
Ian, *The Sisterhood of the Traveling Pants,* Warner Bros., 2008.
Midnight Mark, *Pirate Radio* (also known as *The Boat that Rocked*), Focus Features, 2009.
John Brown, *The Lightkeepers,* New Films International, 2009.

Television Appearances; Series:
Brand Spanking New Show (also known as *Harry Enfield's Brand Spanking New Show*), Sky Television, 2000.
Marco Bailey, *Mile High,* BBC America, 2003–2004.

Television Appearances; Miniseries:
Fothers, *Blackhearts in Battersea,* BBC, 1996.
Edward Beverly, *Children of the New Forest,* BBC, 1998.
Ivor Claire, *Sword of Honour,* Channel 4, 2001.
Stephen Clarke, *Suspicion,* ITV, 2003.

Television Appearances; Movies:
Jan Turek, *Good King Wenceslas,* The Family Channel, 1994.
Gabriel, *Fire & Ice* (also known as *Fire & Ice: The Dragon Chronicles*), Sci–Fi Channel, 2008.

Television Appearances; Episodic:
Neil Pender, "Last Judgement," *Wycliffe,* ITV, 1996.
Tom Ferguson, *Coronation Street,* ITV, 1999.
Oliver Manders, "Three Act Tragedy," *Agatha Christie: Poirot,* PBS, 2010.

Stage Appearances:
Steven Carter, *What's Wrong with Angry?,* 1994.
Guy Bennett, *Another Country,* Arts Theatre, London, 2000.
Journey's End, West End production, c. 2005.

Also appeared in productions of *Borders of Paradise; Escape to Somerset; The Importance of Being Earnest; The Rose and the Ring; Sleeping Beauty;* and *Twelfth Night.*

Major Tours:
Journey's End, British cities, 2005.

WYCHERLEY, Don 1967–
   (Don Wicherley)

PERSONAL

Born September 15, 1967, in Skibbereen, County Cork, Ireland.

Addresses: *Agent*—Derick Mulvey, MacFarlane Chard Associates, 7 Adelaide St., Dun Laoghaire, County Dublin, Ireland; (voice work) Voicebank, The Barracks, 76 Irishtown Rd. 4, Dublin, Ireland.

Career: Actor.

Awards, Honors: Irish Film and Television Award nomination, best supporting actor in a feature film, 2008, for *Speed Dating;* Irish Film and Television Award nomination, best lead actor in a television role, 2008, for *The Running Mate.*

CREDITS

Film Appearances:
Rural lout, *Widows' Peak,* Fine Line, 1994.
Second Republican, *Michael Collins,* Geffen/Warner Bros., 1996.
Peter Colcannon, *The Last of the High Kings* (also known as *Summer Fling*), Miramax, 1996.
Joe McEvoy, *A Soldier's Song* (short film), 1997.
Young Frank, *I Went Down,* Artisan Entertainment, 1998.
(As Don Wicherley) Henry Mackie, *The General,* Sony Pictures Classics, 1998.
Brian Athlone, *One Man's Hero,* Orion, 1999.
Zonad, 2000.
Niall, *When Brendan Met Trudy,* Shooting Gallery, 2001.
Dave, *Selfish Minds* (short film), 2003.
Chris Mulligan, *Veronica Gherin,* Buena Vista, 2003.
The Silent City (short film), Image Now Films, 2006.
Detective Noel Long, *Speed Dating,* Buena Vista International, 2007.
Breffini, *Garage,* Element Pictures Distribution, 2007.
Simon, *Poker Nights* (short film), Long Shong Entertainment Multimedia, 2007.
Ernie, *Shrooms,* Magnolia Pictures, 2008.
Dulally, *Wide Open Spaces,* Grand Pictures, 2009.

(Uncredited) Orlando, *Perrier's Bounty,* IFC Films, 2010.
Kettle, *Ondine,* Magnolia Pictures, 2010.
Da, *My Brothers,* Rubicon Films, 2010.

Television Appearances; Series:
Father Aidan O'Connell, a recurring role, *Ballykissangel,* BBC1 (later broadcast by PBS), 1998–99.
Raymond, *Bachelors Walk,* 2001–2003.
Donncha, *An Crisis,* 2010.

Television Appearances; Miniseries:
Young man, *Scarlett,* CBS, 1994.
Rory, *Kidnapped,* The Family Channel, 1995.
Willie Costello, *The Running Mate,* 2007.
Minister Ultan Keane, *Rasai na Gaillimhe,* 2009.

Television Appearances; Movies:
Drunken sailor, *The Tale of Sweeney Todd,* Showtime, 1998.
Paul, *Double Carpet,* 1999.
Sean, *Filleann an Feall* (also known as *The Treachery Returns*), TG4, 2000.
Harry, *Life in the Fast Lane,* RTE, 2001.
Eugene, *Black Day at Black Rock,* 2001.

Television Appearances; Specials:
Porter, *Before I Sleep,* Network Ireland, 1997.
Happy Birthday Oscar Wilde, BBC, 2004.
Frank, *Showbands,* RTE, 2005.
Frank, *Showbands II,* RTE, 2006.
Raymond, *Bachelors Walk Christmas Special,* 2006.
The 7th Annual Irish Film and Television Awards, 2010.

Television Appearances; Episodic:
Father Cyril MacDuff, "Competition Time," *Father Ted,* Channel 4 (later broadcast by BBC America), 1995.
Father Cyril MacDuff, "A Song for Europe," *Father Ted,* Channel 4 (later broadcast by BBC America), 1996.
Father Cyril MacDuff, "Cigarettes and Alcohol and Rollerblading," *Father Ted,* Channel 4 (later broadcast by BBC America), 1996.
"Den Tod im Nacken," *Der Kapitaen,* 1997.
Embassy receptionist, "A Cluster of Betrayals," *The Ambassador,* BBC, 1998.
Father Cyril MacDuff, "Escape from Victory," *Father Ted,* Channel 4 (later broadcast by BBC America), 1998.
The Late Late Show (Irish version), 2003.
Wild Trials, RTE, 2004.
Xpose, TV3, 2007, 2009.
The Podge and Rodge Show, 2008.

Stage Appearances:
Away Alone, Abbey Theatre, Dublin Ireland, 1992.
The Honey Spike, Abbey Theatre, c. 1992.
The Shaughraun, Albery Theatre, London, 2005.

Also appeared in other production at Abbey Theatre, c. 1992–93.

WRITINGS

Television Movies:
Filleann an Feall (also known as *The Treachery Returns*), TG4, 2000.

OTHER SOURCES

Electronic:
Don Wycherley Official Site, http://www.donwycherley.com, October 15, 2010.

Y–Z

YATES, Reggie 1983–
(No–Bizzi)

PERSONAL

Full name, Reginald Yates; born May 31, 1983, in Archway, London, England. *Education:* Studied drama. *Avocational Interests:* Soccer.

Addresses: *Agent*—Creative Artists Management, 55–59 Shaftesbury Ave., First Floor, London W1D 6LD, England. *Manager*—Karen Forrest, James Grant Media, Ltd., 94 Strand on the Green, Chiswick, London W4 3NN, England.

Career: Actor and television host. Performed voices for albums and singles and for commercials. Founder of a musical group and performer at venues, sometimes using the name No–Bizzi.

Awards, Honors: Children's Award nomination, best presenter, British Academy of Film and Television Arts, 2003, for *Smile.*

CREDITS

Television Appearances; Series:
Jenks, *Agent "Z" and the Penguin from Mars* (also known as *Agent Zed*), Children's BBC, 1996.
Cohost, *Diggit* (also known as *Diggin' It* and *Diggit Extra*), GMTV in ITV, beginning 1998.
Presenter and host, *Kids Passport to the World*, beginning 2000.
Carl Fenton, *Grange Hill*, BBC, 2002.
Presenter, *Smile* (also known as *Smile on Sunday*), BBC2, 2002–2004.

Calvin, *UgetMe* (also known as *Ugetme*), BBC2 and CBBC, 2003.
Presenter, *Top of the Pops* (also known as *All New Top of the Pops* and *TOTP*), BBC, episodes and affiliated specials, beginning 2003.
Host, *Beckham's "Hotshots"* (also known as *David Beckham Hotshots* and *Hotshots*), CBBC, 2004.
Archie, *The Crust,* CBBC, 2005.
Presenter, *Dance Factory,* CBBC, 2005.
Himself, *Comic Relief Does Fame Academy* (also known as *Celebrity Fame Academy*), BBC, 2005.
Himself, *Only in America,* CBBC, 2005.
Presenter, *Celebrity Scissorhands: Keep Your Hair On* (also known as *Keep Your Hair On*), BBC, 2006.
Presenter, *Mighty Truck of Stuff* (also known as *MTOS*), BBC2 and CBBC, 2006.
Host, *Get 100,* CBBC, 2007.
Presenter, *Escape from Scorpion Island,* CBBC, 2007.
Himself, *DJ Takeover,* MTV Base, 2007.
Himself, *Bring It On* (also known as *Bring It On, Series 3*), BBC2, 2008.
Presenter, *The Lick* (also known as *The Lick with Trevor Nelson*), MTV UK, beginning c. 2008.
Host, *Move Like Michael Jackson,* BBC3, 2009.
Presenter, *The Almost Perfect Guide to Life,* BBC, 2009.
Presenter, *Radio 1's "Big Weekend"* (also known as *One Big Weekend*), BBC, 2009.
Presenter, *Reading and Leeds 2009,* BBC3, 2009.
Theo Mackenzie, *Trinity,* ITV2, 2009.
Presenter, *Radio 1's "Big Weekend"* (also known as *One Big Weekend*), BBC, 2010.
Presenter, *T in the Park 2010,* BBC3, 2010.
Voice of title role, *Rastamouse* (animated), CBeebies, beginning 2011.

Television Appearances; Miniseries:
Presenter, *Autistic Superstars,* BBC3, 2010.

Television Appearances; Movies:
Priest, broadcast as part of *Screen Two* (also known as *Screen 2*), BBC2, 1995, released as a film, Miramax, 1995.

Television Appearances; Specials:

Celebrity participant, *Test the Nation: The 2004 Test,* BBC, 2004.

Cohost, *The Big C—Fundraising Concert* (also known as *The Big C Concert*), BBC, 2004.

Himself, *Comic Relief: Red Nose Night Live 05* (also known as *Red Nose Night Live 05*), BBC, 2005.

Himself, *Sport Relief* (also known as *Sport Relief— Guatemala, Sports Relief,* and *Sports Relief— Guatemala*), BBC, 2006.

Himself, *MTV Base Backstage EMA 2007,* MTV Base, 2007.

Cohost, *Brit Awards Launch Party* (also known as *Brits Launch Show*), ITV2, 2008.

Presenter, *Barclaycard World Freerun Championships* (also known as *WFC, World Freerun Champion- ships,* and *World Free Run Championships*), BBC3, 2009.

Presenter, *Glastonbury 2009,* BBC, 2009.

Presenter, *Glastonbury 2010,* BBC3, 2010.

Himself, *Family Guy: The Top 20 Characters,* BBC3, 2010.

Himself, *50 Greatest Pop Videos,* Channel 4, 2010.

Presenter of other programs, including *Blue Peter Jubilee Special,* BBC; *MOBO Awards Back Stage,* BBC3; and *MTV Europe Music Awards Back Stage,* MTV. Also affiliated with other programs.

Television Appearances; Awards Presentations:

Cohost, *The MOBO Awards,* BBC, 2009.

Cohost, *The MOBO Awards,* 2010.

Television Appearances; Episodic:

Little brother, "Lollipop Man," *Desmond's,* Channel 4, 1993.

Marcus Banthorpe, "Jumping the Lights," *Between the Lines* (also known as *Inside the Line*), BBC, 1993.

Ghostbusters of East Finchley, BBC2, 1995.

Sunshine as a teenager, "I Bring You Frankincense," *Crucial Tales,* BBC2, 1996.

Jimmy, "A Gathering Storm," *The Bill,* ITV1, 2000.

Himself, *Xchange,* BBC2, 2003.

Himself, *Stars in Fast Cars,* BBC, 2005.

Himself, *Top of the Pops Saturday* (originally part of *The Saturday Show*), BBC, 2005.

Himself, *Departure Lounge,* BBC, c. 2005.

Himself, "Celebrity Reality TV Special" (also known as "Reality TV Contestants"), *The Weakest Link* (also known as *Weakest Link Champions' League*), BBC, 2006.

Leo Jones, "Last of the Time Lords," *Doctor Who* (also known as *Dr. Who*), BBC, Sci–Fi Channel, and other channels, 2007.

Leo Jones, "The Lazarus Experiment," *Doctor Who* (also known as *Dr. Who*), BBC, Sci–Fi Channel, and other channels, 2007.

Leo Jones, "Smith and Jones," *Doctor Who* (also known as *Dr. Who*), BBC, Sci–Fi Channel, and other chan- nels, 2007.

Leo Jones, "The Sound of Drums," *Doctor Who* (also known as *Dr. Who*), BBC, Sci–Fi Channel, and other channels, 2007.

Himself, "Meet Martha Jones," *Doctor Who Confiden- tial,* BBC, 2007.

Himself, "Monsters Inc.," *Doctor Who Confidential,* BBC, 2007.

Himself, "Saturday—Zoe Expelled.," *Comic Relief Does Fame Academy* (also known as *Celebrity Fame Academy*), BBC, 2007.

Himself, "The Story So Far," *Heroes Unmasked,* BBC, 2007.

Himself, *Loose Women,* ITV, 2007.

Himself, *Totally Doctor Who,* BBC, 2007.

Himself, "Elijah Wood," *The Sunday Night Project,* Channel 4, 2008.

Himself, "Episode 28—Sound Goes to Radio 1's 'Big Weekend,'" *Sound,* BBC2, 2008.

Himself, *The Friday Night Project,* Channel 4, 2008.

Himself, "Episode 3," *Jack Osborne: Celebrity Adrena- line Junkie 2* (also known as *Jack Osborne: Celeb- rity Adrenaline Junkie, Jack Osborne's "Celebrity Adrenaline Junkie,"* and *Jack Osborne's "Celebrity Adrenaline Junkie 2*), ITV2, Travel Channel, and MuchMusic, 2009.

Himself, "Episode 4," *Jack Osborne: Celebrity Adrena- line Junkie 2* (also known as *Jack Osborne: Celeb- rity Adrenaline Junkie, Jack Osborne's "Celebrity Adrenaline Junkie,"* and *Jack Osborne's "Celebrity Adrenaline Junkie 2*), ITV2, Travel Channel, and MuchMusic, 2009.

Himself, *Live from Studio Five* (also known as *Studio Five*), Five, multiple episodes, 2009.

Himself, *The Paul O'Grady Show,* ITV, multiple episodes, 2009.

Music presenter, *Breakfast* (also known as *BBC Break- fast*), BBC, 2010.

Appeared as Harrison, *Focus,* BBC Schools. Appeared in other programs, including *A Bit of Fry & Laurie* (also known as *A Bit of Fry and Laurie*), BBC and BBC2; *Fam- ily Affairs,* Channel 5 (Five); *Spanking New Music Ses- sion* (also known as *Spanking New Music Sessions*), MTV Base; and *Trevor Nelson's "Lowdown,"* BBC3. Some sources cite other television appearances.

Television Appearances; Other:

Appeared in other programs, including *Pirates;* also presented other programs, including *Road.*

Film Appearances:

Priest, Miramax, 1995, broadcast on television as part of *Screen Two* (also known as *Screen 2*), BBC2, 1995.

Radio Appearances; Series:

Presenter, *Weekend Breakfast Show* (also known as *Fearne & Reggie* and *Fearne & Reggie Weekend Breakfast*), BBC Radio 1, c. 2006–2007.

Cohost, *The Chart Show and The Request Show* (also known as *Fearne & Reggie, The Fearne & Reggie Saturday Request Show,* and *Request & Chart Show*), BBC Radio 1, c. 2007–2009.
Presenter, *Radio 1's "Big Weekend"* (also known as *One Big Weekend*), BBC Radio 1, 2009.
Host, *BBC Radio 1's "Chart Show"* (also known as *BBC Radio One's "Chart Show," The Chart Show, The Official Chart, The Official Chart with Reggie Yates, Radio 1's "Chart Show,"* and *The UK Top 40*), BBC Radio 1, beginning c. 2009.
Host, *The Request Show with Reggie Yates* (also known as *Reggie Yates*), BBC Radio 1, beginning c. 2009.
Presenter, *Radio 1's "Big Weekend"* (also known as *One Big Weekend*), BBC Radio 1, 2010.

While cited as No–Bizzi, hosted a program on BBC 1Xtra, c. 2002–04. Also presenter of *Ras Kwame UK HomeGrown* (also known as *100% HomeGrown* and *100% HomeGrown with Ras Kwame*) and *The Trevor Nelson Show,* both BBC Radio 1; and *Reg & Dev,* BBC Radio 1Xtra.

Internet Appearances:
Appeared in footage on the Internet. Some sources cite appearances in *Smile Radio* on the *Smile* website.

Stage Appearances:
Musical performer at venues, sometimes using the name No–Bizzi.

RECORDINGS

Audiobooks:
Stephen Cole, *Sting of the Zygons,* BBC Audiobooks, 2007.

Music Videos:
Appeared in the music video "Flex" by Dizzee Rascal, c. 2007.

OTHER SOURCES

Periodicals:
Independent, April 19, 2008, p. 16.

Electronic:
Reggie Yates, http://www.officialreggieyates.com, July 17, 2010.

YOUNG, Sita 1984–

PERSONAL

Born June 17, 1984, in New York, NY. *Education:* Graduated from Hunter College High School, 2002.

Career: Actress.

CREDITS

Film Appearances:
Hash, *Desperate Hippies* (short film), Peacetrain Productions, 2005.
Lucy, *Bad Blood,* Conmar Productions, 2006.
Tasha, *KwameWorld* (short film), Citric Sentiments Cinema/IRE Productions, 2006.
Val Espinoza, *Drive Thru* (also known as *Burger Kill, Death Burger, Drive–Thru,* and *HellaBurger*), Lions Gate Films, 2006.
Colder, *The Go–Getter,* 2007, Peach Arch Releasing, 2008.
Beth, *The Last Resort,* Grindstone Entertainment Group, 2009.
Girl, *Prey for the Island,* Last Escape Productions, 2009.
Lisa, *Moonlight Sonata,* Fog City Pictures, 2009.
Lola, *B–Girl,* Screen Media Films, 2009.
Lucy, *Bad Blood ... the Hunger,* Miracon Pictures, 2009.
Molly, *Penance* (also known as *The Devil's Dungeon*), Clever Worm Entertainment, 2009.
The Rotation (short film), 2009.
Tina, *A Lure* (also known as *Lure* and *Lure: Teen Fight Club*), A Plus Entertainment, 2010.
Greek chorus, *The Humdrummer,* c. 2010.
Girl, *Black Velvet,* Last Escape Productions, c. 2011.
Sue, *City of Jerks,* Burgundy Films, c. 2012.

Television Appearances; Episodic:
Hailey, *Days of Our Lives* (also known as *Cruise of Deception: Days of Our Lives, Days, DOOL, Tropical Temptation, Tropical Temptation: Days of Our Lives, Des jours et des vies, Horton–sagaen, I gode og onde dager, Los dias de nuestras vidas, Meres agapis, Paeivien viemaeae, Vaara baesta aar, Zeit der Sehnsucht,* and *Zile din viata noastra*), NBC, 2007.
Nurse, "I Am Not Afraid of Any Ghost," *Children's Hospital,* Cartoon Network, 2010.
Student, "Dead to Me," *Ghost Whisperer,* CBS, 2010.

YOUNG, Warren Alan 1965–
(Warren Young, Warren A. Young)

PERSONAL

Born March 15, 1965, in Los Angeles, CA. *Education:* Graduated from the American College for the Applied Arts.

Addresses: *Agent*—Grant, Savic, Kopaloff and Associates, 6399 Wilshire Blvd., Suite 414, Los Angeles, CA 90048.

Career: Production designer, art director, and property master. Also worked as a furniture designer, interior designer, and photographer, and worked in production development.

CREDITS

Film Production Designer:
No Time (short film), Big Boy Pictures, 1994.
Twin Falls Idaho (also known as *Twin Falls, Idaho*), Sony Pictures Classics, 1999.
Fast Sofa, 2001.
Sacred Is the Flesh (also known as *Sacred*), Strange Fruit Films, 2001.
Tara (also known as *Hoodrat, Hood Rat,* and *Hoodratz*), Universal Studios Home Video, 2001.
Staring at the Sun (short film), 2002.
Ride or Die (also known as *Hustle and Heat* and *RAP Connection*), Destination Films, 2003.
Mind Games (also known as *Something Borrowed*), Showcase Entertainment, 2003, Ventura Distribution, 2005.
The Eavesdropper (also known as *Experiment 14* and *Patient 14*), Showcase Entertainment/Freestyle Home Entertainment, 2004.
Full Clip (also known as *Blood Money*), Lions Gate Films, 2004.
The Seat Filler, 2004, The Momentum Experience, 2005.
Akeelah and the Bee (also known as *Dreams Come True*), Lions Gate Films, 2006.
Home of the Brave, Metro–Goldwyn–Mayer, 2006.
Phat Girlz, Fox Searchlight, 2006.
(As Warren A. Young) *Waist Deep,* Focus Features/Rogue Pictures, 2006.
Talk to Me (also known as *Petey Greene's Washington*), Focus Features, 2007.
The Secret Lives of Bees, Fox Searchlight, 2008.

Film Art Director:
Watch Me, Triboro Entertainment Group, 1995.
(As Warren Young) *Street Corner Justice,* New City Releasing, 1996.
Tara (also known as *Hoodrat, Hood Rat,* and *Hoodratz*), Universal Studios Home Video, 2001.

Film Property Master:
One Last Flight (also known as *Fly Boy*), A–Pix Entertainment/Promark Entertainment Group, 1999.
Treehouse Hostage, Trimark Pictures, 1999.

Film On–Set Dresser:
The Glass Shield, 1994, Miramax, 1995.
(As Warren Young) *A Thin Line between Love and Hate* (also known as *Mister Bombastic* and *A Thin Line between Love & Hate*), New Line Cinema, 1996.

Film Work; Other:
(As Warren Young) Assistant director, *A Thin Line between Love and Hate* (also known as *Mister Bombastic* and *A Thin Line between Love & Hate*), New Line Cinema, 1996.
Interior designer, *The Young Unknowns,* 2000, Indican Pictures, 2003.

Film Appearances:
Bartender, *Talk to Me* (also known as *Petey Greene's Washington*), Focus Features, 2007.

Television Production Designer; Series:
Comicview (also known as *BET's "Comicview"*), Black Entertainment Television, 2000–2001.
Doggy Fizzle Televizzle, MTV, c. 2002–2003.
Hawthorne (also known as *HawthoRNe* and *Time Heals*), TNT, beginning 2010.

Television Work; Other; Series:
Art director, *Pacific Blue,* USA Network, beginning c. 1995.
Set designer, *Foody Call* (also known as *Foodie Call*), Style Network, 2005.

Television Production Designer; Movies:
(As Warren Young) *Hidden Blessings,* Black Entertainment Television, 2000.
Midnight Blue, Black Entertainment Television, 2000.
Playing with Fire, Black Entertainment Television, 2000.
A Private Affair, Black Entertainment Television, 2000.
Commitments, Black Entertainment Television, 2001.
Fire & Ice, Black Entertainment Television, 2001.
One Special Moment, Black Entertainment Television, 2001.
America, Lifetime, 2009.
Gifted Hands: The Ben Carson Story (also known as *Gifted Hands*), TNT, 2009.
Pregnancy Pact, Lifetime, 2009.

Television Property Master; Movies:
Finding Kelly (also known as *Mystery Kids*), Showtime, 1999.

Television Production Designer; Specials:
Cedric the Entertainer: Starting Lineup (also known as *Cedric the Entertainer's Starting Lineup* and *Platinum Comedy Series: Cedric the Entertainer: Starting Lineup*), c. 2002.
Dense (short), part of the Soul Decisions trilogy, Showtime, 2004.

Worked on other programs.

Television Production Designer; Pilots:
Skip Tracer, CBS, 2008.

Stage Work:
Worked on productions, including *This Poetry Thing.*

RECORDINGS

Music Video Work:
Worked as an art designer for music videos by Dru Hill, Joe, Mic Geronimo, and Queen Pen.

ZIRILLI, Daniel 1965(?)–

PERSONAL

Born c. 1965; son of Richard Buchta and Diane Zirilli. *Education:* Pepperdine University, B.A., 1989. *Avocational Interests:* Nautical activities, collecting nautical antiques.

Addresses: *Office*—PopArt Film Factory, 23679 Calabasas Rd., Suite 696, Calabasas, CA 91302.

Career: Director, producer, writer, actor, and executive. PopArt Film Factory, Calabasas, CA, founder, c. 1989, chief executive officer, and director. Producer and director of more than 250 music videos for recording artists ranging from Bobby Womack to Bokeem Woodbine, including Redman, Cypress Hill, Master P, Freddie Jackson, and Scarface; director and producer of documentaries for Michael Jackson and Moonwalker Entertainment; producer and director of public service announcements for Earth Communication Office, Earth Summit, Save Our Skies, Garden Project L.A., and other clients. Lecturer at University of California, Los Angeles, and at seminars and film festivals.

Awards, Honors: Visionaries in Film Award, Bahamas One World Film Festival, c. 2007, for *The Stonecutter;* Garland of Honor, best sports movie of the year, Federation Internationale Cinema Television Sportifs, Milan, Italy, 2008, for *Fast Girl;* winner of several Telly Awards, nominations for *Billboard* Music Video Awards and Music Video Producers Association Awards.

CREDITS

Film Producer and Director:
Black Spring Break 2: The Sequel, 2001.
Voodoo Tailz (also known as *Voodoo Mardi Gras*), Spartan Home Entertainment, 2002.
Latin Kingz, Spartan/El Matador, 2003.
Vengeance, Force Entertainment, 2004.
CrossBones, Lions Gate Films, 2005.
Clash, Polychrome Pictures, 2006.

The Champagne Gang, Maverick Entertainment Group, 2006.
Aces, Polychrome Pictures, 2006.
The Stonecutter, Maverick Entertainment Group, 2007.
Curse of Alcatraz, Lions Gate Films/Grindstone Entertainment Group, 2007.
Locked Down, Lions Gate Films/Grindstone Entertainment Group, 2010.
The Lazarus Papers, Lunaflux Productions, 2010.
Alcatraz Prison Escape: Deathbed Confession, PopArt Film Factory, 2010.

Film Executive Producer:
Black Spring Break: The Movie, Xenon Entertainment Group, 1998.
Co–executive producer, *Guilty by Association,* 2003.
Tha Crib, Trinity Home Entertainment, 2004.
The Legend of Diablo, Silver Nitrate, 2004.
Border Warz, Third Millennium, 2004.
(And director) *Circle of Pain,* Lions Gate Films/Grindstone Entertainment Group, 2010.
Beatdown, Grindstone Entertainment Group, 2010.
Dead Man's Gold, StoneBrook Entertainment, 2011.

Film Producer:
15 to Life, Spartan Entertainment/Urban Domain, 2002.
The Sweep (also known as *What Up?*), Lions Gate Films, 2008.

Film Director:
Choices 2, 2004.
Fast Girl, Allumination Filmworks, 2008.

Film Work; Other:
Associate producer, *Devil's Knight,* MTI Home Video, 2003.

Film Appearances:
Interviewee, *Rap Soul of the Streets* (documentary), 1996.
Black Spring Break: The Movie, Xenon Entertainment Group, 1998.
Laundry guard, *Tha Eastsidaz,* 2000.
Black Spring Break 2: The Sequel, 2001.
Officer French, *15 to Life,* Spartan Entertainment/Urban Domain, 2002.
Nicolas, *Voodoo Tailz* (also known as *Voodoo Mardi Gras*), Spartan Home Entertainment, 2002.
Movie producer, *Tha Crib,* Trinity Home Entertainment, 2004.
Danny the Shark, *Aces,* Polychrome Pictures, 2006.
Tiny's best man, *The Lazarus Papers,* Lunaflux Productions, 2010.

Television Work; Movies:
Producer, director, and film editor, *Winner Takes All,* Black Entertainment Television, 1998.

Television Appearances; Movies:
Winner Takes All, Black Entertainment Television, 1998.

RECORDINGS

Videos:
Producer of film and video segments, *Rolling Stones: Voodoo Lounge* (video game; also known as *Rolling Stones Voodoo Lounge CD–ROM*), GTE Entertainment, 1995.

Director, "Homies and Thuggs," *Scarface: Greatest Hits on DVD,* PopArt Film Factory/5th Gear Entertainment/Big Dog Films, 2003.

Director, *Legendz of Tap,* Entertainment Worldwide, 2005.

Other work includes *Cypress Hill Live* and *Vocal Secrets of the Stars.* Recent music videos include "Do It to Me," and "Get on the Dance Floor," and *Private Dancer* by Cushh, and "Ghetto Chick" for Three 6 Mafia, all 2007.

Albums:
Co–executive producer of the compilation album *Memories of Amnesia.*

WRITINGS

Screenplays:
Voodoo Tailz (also known as *Voodoo Mardi Gras*), Spartan Home Entertainment, 2002.

Latin Kingz (also based on story by Zirilli), Spartan/El Matador, 2003.

Vengeance (also based on story by Zirilli), Force Entertainment, 2004.

CrossBones, Lions Gate Films, 2005.

Clash, Polychrome Pictures, 2006.

The Champagne Gang, Maverick Entertainment Group, 2006.

Locked Down, Lions Gate Films/Grindstone Entertainment Group, 2010.

Alcatraz Prison Escape: Deathbed Confession, PopArt Film Factory, 2010.

Television Movies:
Winner Takes All, Black Entertainment Television, 1998.

ADAPTATIONS

Films based on stories by Zirilli include *Hot Parts,* released be Megastar Pictures in 2003; *Tha Crib,* released by Trinity Home Entertainment in 2004; *Aces,* released by Polychrome Pictures in 2006; *Curse of Alcatraz,* released by Lions Gate Films/Grindstone Entertainment Group in 2007; *Fast Girl,* released by Allumination Filmworks in 2008; and *Circle of Pain,* released by Lions Gate Films/Grindstone Entertainment Group in 2010.

OTHER SOURCES

Electronic:
PopArt Film Factory Web Site, http://www.popart filmfactory.com, October 15, 2010.

Cumulative Index

To provide continuity with *Who's Who in the Theatre*, this index interfiles references to *Who's Who in the Theatre*, 1st–17th Editions, and *Who Was Who in the Theatre* (Gale, 1978) with references to *Contemporary Theatre, Film and Television*, Volumes 1–112.

References in the index are identified as follows:

CTFT and volume number—*Contemporary Theatre, Film and Television*, Volumes 1–112
WWT and edition number—*Who's Who in the Theatre*, 1st–17th Editions
WWasWT—*Who Was Who in the Theatre*

C

E

J

L

N

Cumulative Index

Cumulative Index

X

Y